Dictionary of
Human Resources
and Personnel
Management

Specialist dictionaries

Dictionary of Accounting	0 7475 6991 6
Dictionary of Aviation	0 7475 7219 4
Dictionary of Banking and Finance	0 7136 7739 2
Dictionary of Business	0 7136 7913 2
Dictionary of Computing	0 7475 6622 4
Dictionary of Economics	0 7475 6632 1
Dictionary of Environment and Ecology	0 7475 7201 1
Dictionary of ICT	0 7475 6990 8
Dictionary of Information and Library Management	0 7136 7591 8
Dictionary of Law	0 7475 6636 4
Dictionary of Leisure, Travel and Tourism	0 7475 7222 4
Dictionary of Marketing	0 7475 6621 6
Dictionary of Media Studies	0 7136 7593 4
Dictionary of Medical Terms	0 7136 7603 5
Dictionary of Nursing	0 7475 6634 8
Dictionary of Politics and Government	0 7475 7220 8
Dictionary of Publishing and Printing	0 7136 7589 6
Dictionary of Science and Technology	0 7475 6620 8

Easier English™ titles

Easier English Basic Dictionary	0 7475 6644 5
Easier English Basic Synonyms	0 7475 6979 7
Easier English Dictionary: Handy Pocket Edition	0 7475 6625 9
Easier English Intermediate Dictionary	0 7475 6989 4
Easier English Student Dictionary	0 7475 6624 0
English Thesaurus for Students	1 9016 5931 3

Check Your English Vocabulary workbooks

Academic English	0 7475 6691 7
Business	0 7475 6626 7
Computing	1 9016 5928 3
Human Resources	0 7475 6997 5
Law	0 7136 7592 6
Leisure, Travel and Tourism	0 7475 6996 7
FCE +	0 7475 6981 9
IELTS	0 7136 7604 3
PET	0 7475 6627 5
TOEFL®	0 7475 6984 3
TOEIC	0 7136 7508 X

Visit our website for full details of all our books: **www.acblack.com**

Dictionary of
Human Resources
and Personnel
Management

third edition

A & C Black • London

www.acblack.com

Third edition published 2003, reprinted 2006
Second edition 1997, reprinted 1998
First edition published in 1988 as *Dictionary of Personnel Management*

A & C Black Publishers Ltd
38 Soho Square, London W1D 3HB

© A. Ivanovic MBA & P. H. Collin 1988, 1997
© A & C Black Publishers Ltd 2006

A CIP record for this book is available from the British Library

ISBN-10: 0 7136 8142 X
ISBN-13: 978 0 7136 8142 0

Text Production and Proofreading
Heather Bateman, Katy McAdam

A & C Black uses paper produced with elemental chlorine-free pulp,
harvested from managed sustainable forests.

Text typeset by A & C Black
Printed in Italy by Legoprint

Preface

This dictionary provides the user with a comprehensive vocabulary of terms used in human resource management. It covers all aspects of the subject including recruitment and selection, appraisals, payment systems, dismissals and other aspects of industrial relations.

The main words are explained in simple English, and pronunciations are given in the International Phonetic Alphabet. Where appropriate, examples are included to show how the words are used in context. Quotations are also given from various magazines and newspapers, which give an idea of how the terms are used in real life. The supplement at the back of the book gives various documents which provide useful guidelines as to how a company's own documents can be constructed.

We are grateful to the following for their valuable comments on the text: Dena Michelli, Michael Furlong, Yvonne Quinn, Stephen Curtis, Margaret Jull Costa, Georgia Hole, Dinah Jackson and Sandra Anderson.

Pronunciation Guide

The following symbols have been used to show the pronunciation of the main words in the dictionary.

Stress is indicated by a main stress mark (') and a secondary stress mark (ˌ). Note that these are only guides, as the stress of the word changes according to its position in the sentence.

Vowels		*Consonants*	
æ	back	b	buck
ɑː	harm	d	dead
ɒ	stop	ð	other
aɪ	type	dʒ	jump
aʊ	how	f	fare
aɪə	hire	g	gold
aʊə	hour	h	head
ɔː	course	j	yellow
ɔɪ	annoy	k	cab
e	head	l	leave
eə	fair	m	mix
eɪ	make	n	nil
eʊ	go	ŋ	sing
ɜː	word	p	print
iː	keep	r	rest
i	happy	s	save
ə	about	ʃ	shop
ɪ	fit	t	take
ɪə	near	tʃ	change
u	annual	θ	theft
uː	pool	v	value
ʊ	book	w	work
ʊə	tour	x	loch
ʌ	shut	ʒ	measure
		z	zone

A

AA /'eɪ 'eɪ/ same as **attendance allowance**

ability /ə'bɪlɪti/ *noun* the capacity or power to do something ○ *Ability to sell is essential for the job.*

ability test /ə'bɪlɪti test/ *noun* same as **aptitude test**

able /'eɪb(ə)l/ *adjective* capable or working well ○ *She's a very able manager.*

able-bodied /ˌeɪb(ə)l 'bɒdid/ *adjective* with no physical handicap ○ *The work is strenuous and only suitable for the young and able-bodied.*

abroad /ə'brɔːd/ *adverb* to or in another country ○ *The consignment of cars was shipped abroad last week.* ○ *The chairman is abroad on business.* ○ *He worked abroad for ten years.* ○ *Half of our profit comes from sales abroad.*

absence /'æbsəns/ *noun* the fact of not being at work or at a meeting □ **in the absence of** when someone is not there ○ *In the absence of the chairman, his deputy took the chair.* □ **unauthorised absence from work, absence without leave** being away from work without permission and without a good reason

absent /'æbsənt/ *adjective* not at work or not at a meeting ○ *He was absent owing to illness.* ○ *Ten of the workers are absent with flu.* ○ *The chairman is absent in Holland on business.*

absentee /ˌæbsən'tiː/ *noun* a person who is absent or an employee who stays away from work for no good reason

absenteeism /ˌæbs(ə)n'tiːɪz(ə)m/ *noun* the practice of staying away from work for no good reason ○ *Low productivity is largely due to the high level of*

absenteeism. ○ *Absenteeism is high in the week before Christmas.*

'…but the reforms still hadn't fundamentally changed conditions on the shop floor: absenteeism was as high as 20% on some days' [*Business Week*]

absenteeism rate /ˌæbsən-'tiːɪz(ə)m reɪt/ *noun* the percentage of the workforce which is away from work with no good excuse ○ *The rate of absenteeism or the absenteeism rate always increases in fine weather.*

ACAS /'eɪkæs/ *abbr* Advisory, Conciliation and Arbitration Service

accept /ək'sept/ *verb* **1.** to take something which is being offered □ **to accept delivery of a shipment** to take goods into the warehouse officially when they are delivered **2.** to say 'yes' or to agree to something ○ *She accepted the offer of a job in Australia.* ○ *He accepted £2000 in lieu of notice.*

acceptable /ək'septəb(ə)l/ *adjective* which can be accepted ○ *Both parties found the offer acceptable.* ○ *The terms of the contract of employment are not acceptable to the candidate.*

acceptance /ək'septəns/ *noun* □ **acceptance of an offer** the act of agreeing to an offer □ **to give an offer a conditional acceptance** to accept an offer provided that specific things happen or that specific terms apply □ **we have their letter of acceptance** we have received a letter from them accepting the offer

acceptance bonus /ək,septəns 'bəʊnəs/ *noun* a bonus paid to a new employee when they agree to join an organisation (NOTE: an acceptance bonus can be a feature of a **golden hello** and is designed both to attract and to retain staff)

acceptance sampling /ək'septəns ˌsɑːmplɪŋ/ *noun* the process of testing a small sample of a batch to see if the whole batch is good enough to be accepted

access /'ækses/ *noun* □ **to have access to something** to be able to obtain or reach something ○ *She has access to large amounts of venture capital.* ■ *verb* to call up data which is stored in a computer ○ *She accessed the address file on the computer.*

accession /ək'seʃ(ə)n/ *noun* the act of joining an organisation

accession rate /ək'seʃ(ə)n reɪt/ *noun* **1.** the percentage of employees in an organisation who have joined it during a particular period of time **2.** a rate of pay for employees when first hired ○ *After the first year, pay went up considerably despite the low accession rate.* ○ *The accession rate depends on whether the entrants are skilled or unskilled.*

access time /'ækses taɪm/ *noun* the time taken by a computer to find data stored in it

accident /'æksɪd(ə)nt/ *noun* something unpleasant which can be caused by carelessness or which happens by chance such as a plane crash

COMMENT: Fatal accidents and accidents which cause major injuries or which prevent an employee from working for more than three days must be reported to the Health and Safety Executive.

accidental /ˌæksɪ'dent(ə)l/ *adjective* happening by chance, not done intentionally ○ *accidental destruction of the computer files*

accident book /'æksɪd(ə)nt bʊk/ *noun* a book in which details of accidents at work are noted down

accident frequency rate /ˌæksɪd(ə)nt 'friːkwənsi reɪt/ *noun* the number of accidents involving injury or death during a specified number of man-hours ○ *The accident frequency rate has risen since the new machinery was installed.*

accident prevention /ˌæksɪd(ə)nt prɪ'venʃən/ *noun* measures taken to prevent accidents

accident-prone worker /ˌæksɪd(ə)nt prəʊn 'wɜːkə/ *noun* a worker who is more likely to have accidents than other workers

accident report /'æksɪd(ə)nt rɪˌpɔːt/ *noun* a report of an accident which has taken place at work

accommodate /ə'kɒmədeɪt/ *verb* to provide someone with a place to live in ○ *The company accommodates its employees near their workplace.*

accommodation /əˌkɒmə'deɪʃ(ə)n/ *noun* **1.** money lent for a short time **2.** a place to stay temporarily or live in ○ *Visitors have difficulty in finding hotel accommodation during the summer.*

'…any non-resident private landlord can let furnished or unfurnished accommodation to a tenant' [*Times*]

'…the airline providing roomy accommodations at below-average fares' [*Dun's Business Month*]

accommodation address /əˌkɒmə'deɪʃ(ə)n əˌdres/ *noun* an address used for receiving messages but which is not the real address of the company

accordance /ə'kɔːdns/ *noun* □ **in accordance with** in agreement with, according to, as someone says or writes ○ *In accordance with your instructions we have deposited the money in your current account.* ○ *I am submitting the claim for damages in accordance with the advice of our legal advisers.*

accordingly /ə'kɔːdɪŋli/ *adverb* in agreement with what has been decided ○ *We have received your letter and have altered the contract accordingly.*

according to /ə'kɔːdɪŋ tuː/ *preposition* as stated or shown by someone ○ *The computer was installed according to the manufacturer's instructions.*

'…the budget targets for employment and growth are within reach according to the latest figures' [*Australian Financial Review*]

account /ə'kaʊnt/ *noun* **1.** a record of financial transactions over a period of time, such as money paid, received, borrowed or owed ○ *Please send me your account or a detailed or an itemized account.* **2.** □ **accounts of a business, a company's accounts** a detailed record of a company's financial affairs **3.** a customer who does a large amount of business with a firm and has an account with it ○ *Smith Brothers is one of our largest accounts.* ○ *Our sales people call on their best accounts twice a month.* **4.** □ **to keep the accounts** to write each sum of money in the account book ○ *The bookkeeper's job is to enter all the money received in the accounts.* **5.** notice □ **to take account of inflation, to take inflation into account** to assume that there will be a specific percentage of inflation when making calculations ■ *verb* □ **to account for** to explain and record a money transaction ○ *to account for a loss* or *a discrepancy* ○ *The reps have to account for all their expenses to the sales manager.*

accountability /ə,kaʊntə'bɪlɪti/ *noun* the fact of being responsible to someone for something (such as the accountability of directors to the shareholders)

accountable /ə'kaʊntəb(ə)l/ *adjective* referring to a person who has to explain what has taken place or who is responsible for something (NOTE: you are accountable **to** someone **for** something)

accountancy /ə'kaʊntənsi/ *noun* the work of an accountant ○ *They are studying accountancy* or *They are accountancy students.* (NOTE: American English is **accounting** in this meaning)

accountant /ə'kaʊntənt/ *noun* a person who keeps a company's accounts ○ *The chief accountant of a manufacturing group.* ○ *The accountant has shown a sharp variance in our labour costs.*

account director /ə'kaʊnt daɪ,rektə/ *noun* a person who works in an advertising agency and who oversees various account managers who are each responsible for specific clients

account executive /ə'kaʊnt ɪg,zekjʊtɪv/ *noun* an employee of an organisation such as a bank, public relations firm, or advertising agency who is responsible for looking after particular clients and handling their business with the organisation

accounting /ə'kaʊntɪŋ/ *noun* the work of recording money paid, received, borrowed or owed ○ *accounting methods* ○ *accounting procedures* ○ *an*

accounting system ○ *an accounting machine*

'...applicants will be professionally qualified and have a degree in Commerce or Accounting' [*Australian Financial Review*]

accounting period /ə'kaʊntɪŋ ,pɪəriəd/ *noun* a period of time at the end of which the firm's accounts are made up

accounts department /ə'kaʊnts dɪ,pɑːtmənt/ *noun* a department in a company which deals with money paid, received, borrowed or owed

accounts manager /ə'kaʊnts ,mænɪdʒə/ *noun* the manager of an accounts department

accounts payable /ə,kaʊnts 'peɪəb(ə)l/ *noun* money owed by a company

accounts receivable /ə,kaʊnts rɪ'siːvəb(ə)l/ *noun* money owed to a company

accreditation /ə,kredɪ'teɪʃ(ə)n/ *noun* the process of certifying the competence of a person in a certain area □ **accreditation of union officials** official recognition by a company that certain employees are representatives of a trade union and are treated as such by the company

accreditation of prior learning /əkredɪ,teɪʃ(ə)n əv ,praɪə 'lɜːnɪŋ/ *noun* a process that enables people to obtain formal recognition of qualifications and experience that they have gained before joining an organisation (NOTE: accreditation of prior learning may be used to support the award of a vocational qualification)

accredited /ə'kredɪtɪd/ *adjective* referring to an agent who is appointed by a company to act on its behalf

accrual /ə'kruːəl/ *noun* a gradual increase by addition □ **accrual of interest** automatic addition of interest to capital

accrual rate /ə'kruːəl reɪt/ *noun* the rate at which an employee's pension increases as each year of service is completed, so forming the basis for calculating their pension

accrue /ə'kruː/ *verb* **1.** to record a financial transaction in accounts when it takes place, and not when payment is made or received **2.** to increase and be due for payment at a later date ○ *Interest accrues from the beginning of the month.*

accurate /'ækjʊrət/ *adjective* correct ○ *The sales department made an accurate forecast of sales.* ○ *The designers produced an accurate copy of the plan.*

accurately /'ækjʊrətli/ *adverb* correctly ○ *The second quarter's drop in sales was accurately forecast by the computer.*

accuse /ə'kjuːz/ *verb* to say that someone has committed a crime ○ *She was accused of stealing from the petty cash box.* ○ *He was accused of industrial espionage.* (NOTE: you accuse someone **of** a crime or **of** doing something)

achieve /ə'tʃiːv/ *verb* to succeed in doing something, to do something successfully ○ *He has achieved his long-term training objectives.* ○ *The company has achieved great success in the Far East.* ○ *We achieved all our objectives in 2001.*

'...the company expects to move to profits of FFr 2m next year and achieve equally rapid growth in following years' [*Financial Times*]

achievement /ə'tʃiːvmənt/ *noun* success or something that has been achieved

achievement test /ə'tʃiːvmənt test/ *noun* a test designed to measure the skills which someone is currently using (as opposed to an aptitude test, which measures the skills a person could use in the future) (NOTE: also called **attainment test**)

achiever /ə'tʃiːvə/ *noun* a person who is successful or who tends to achieve his or her objectives ○ *It was her reputation as a high achiever that made us think of headhunting her.*

across-the-board /ə,krɒs ðə 'bɔːd/ *adjective* applying to everything or everyone ○ *an across-the-board price increase* ○ *an across-the-board wage increase*

act /ækt/ *noun* a law passed by parliament which must be obeyed by the people ■ *verb* **1.** to work ○ *He has agreed to act as an agent for an American company.* ○ *The solicitor is acting for us* or

on our behalf. □ **to act as someone** to do someone's job while he is away ○ *She will act as marketing manager while Mr Smith is on holiday.* **2.** to do something ○ *The board will have to act quickly if the company's losses are going to be reduced.* ○ *The lawyers are acting on our instructions.* □ **to act on a letter** to do what a letter asks to be done

acting /'æktɪŋ/ *adjective* working in place of someone for a short time ○ *acting manager* ○ *the Acting Chairman*

action /'ækʃən/ *noun* **1.** a thing which has been done □ **actions short of dismissal** ways of disciplining an employee who has committed an offence, which stop short of dismissing them (such as demotion, removal of privileges, etc.) **2.** □ **to take industrial action** to do something (usually to go on strike) to show that you are not happy with conditions at work **3.** a case in a law court where a person or company sues another person or company □ **to take legal action** to sue someone ○ *an action for libel* or *a libel action* ○ *an action for damages* ○ *She brought an action for wrongful dismissal against her former employer.*

actionable /'ækʃənəb(ə)l/ *adjective* referring to writing, speech or an act which could provide the grounds for bringing an action against someone ○ *Was the employer's treatment of the employee actionable?*

action-centred leadership /,ækʃən sentəd 'liːdəʃɪp/ *noun* a theory of leadership which focuses on what leaders actually have to do in order to be effective, rather than on the personal qualities that they need to be good leaders, and which believes that leadership can be taught (NOTE: action-centred leadership is usually illustrated by three overlapping circles, which represent the three key activities undertaken by leaders: achieving the task, building and maintaining the team and developing the individual)

action learning /'ækʃən ,lɜːnɪŋ/ *noun* the process of learning by doing or participating in an activity

Action Programme /'ækʃən ,prəʊɡræm/ *noun* an EU initiative containing various draft directives to implement the Social Charter

active /'æktɪv/ *adjective* involving many transactions or activities ○ *an active demand for oil shares* ○ *Computer shares are very active.* ○ *an active day on the Stock Exchange*

active interview /ˌæktɪv 'ɪntəvjuː/ *noun* an interview where the interviewee is encouraged to answer fully the questions asked (as in an open-end interview)

active listening /ˌæktɪv 'lɪs(ə)nɪŋ/ *noun* a technique which involves not only listening to the words someone uses, but also taking into account their tone of voice, their body language and other non-verbal signs in order to gain a fuller understanding of what they are actually communicating

actively /'æktɪvli/ *adverb* in a busy way ○ *The company is actively recruiting new personnel.*

active partner /ˌæktɪv 'pɑːtnə/ *noun* a partner who works in a company that is a partnership

activity /æk'tɪvɪti/ *noun* **1.** the fact of being active or busy ○ *a low level of business activity* ○ *There was a lot of activity on the Stock Exchange.* □ **monthly activity report** a report by a department on what has been done during the past month **2.** something which is done ○ *out-of-work activities*

'…preliminary indications of the level of business investment and activity during the March quarter will provide a good picture of economic activity in the year' [*Australian Financial Review*]

activity chart /æk'tɪvɪti tʃɑːt/ *noun* a plan showing work which has been done so that it can be compared to the plan of work to be done

activity sampling /æk'tɪvɪti ˌsɑːmplɪŋ/ *noun* an observation of tasks and their performances, carried out at random intervals ○ *Activity sampling was carried out to see how fast the machinists worked.*

actuarial analysis /æktʃuˌeəriəl ə-'næləsɪs/ *noun* a calculation carried out by an actuary to assess somebody's life expectancy or the degree of risk involved in an insurance proposal

actuary /'æktʃuəri/ *noun* a person employed by an insurance company or other organisation to calculate the risk involved in an insurance, and therefore the premiums payable by people taking out insurance

acute shortage /əˌkjuːt 'ʃɔːtɪdʒ/ *noun* a very severe shortage for a period of time

ad /æd/ *noun* same as **advertisement** (*informal*) ○ *We put an ad in the paper.* ○ *She answered an ad in the paper.* ○ *He found his job through an ad in the paper.*

adaptable /ə'dæptəb(ə)l/ *adjective* **1.** being able to change working practices **2.** being able to change from job to job

adaptation /ˌædæp'teɪʃ(ə)n/ *noun* something which has been adapted ○ *This machine is an adaptation of our original model.*

add /æd/ *verb* **1.** to put figures together to make a total ○ *If you add the interest to the capital you will get quite a large sum.* ○ *Interest is added monthly.* **2.** to put things together to make a large group ○ *We are adding to the sales force.* ○ *They have added two new products to their range.* □ **this all adds to the company's costs** this makes the company's costs higher

adding machine /'ædɪŋ məˌʃiːn/ *noun* a machine which adds numbers

addition /ə'dɪʃ(ə)n/ *noun* **1.** a thing or person added ○ *The management has stopped all additions to the staff.* ○ *We are exhibiting several additions to our product line.* ○ *The marketing director is the latest addition to the board.* **2.** □ **in addition to** added to, as well as ○ *There are twelve registered letters to be sent in addition to this packet.* **3.** an act of putting numbers together ○ *You don't need a calculator to do simple addition.*

additional /ə'dɪʃ(ə)nəl/ *adjective* extra which is added ○ *additional costs* ○ *They sent us a list of additional charges.* ○ *Some additional clauses were added to the contract.* ○ *Additional duty will have to be paid.*

additional award /əˌdɪʃ(ə)nəl ə-'wɔːd/ *noun* an extra payment ordered by an industrial tribunal to a dismissed employee if the company refuses to reinstate them. ♦ **special award**

additional voluntary contributions /ə,dɪʃ(ə)nəl ,vɒlənt(ə)ri kɒntrɪ'bjuːʃ(ə)nz/ *plural noun* extra payments made voluntarily by an employee to a pension scheme (on top of the normal contributions, up to a maximum of 15% of gross earnings). Abbr **AVCs**

address /ə'dres/ *noun* the details of number, street and town where an office is or a person lives ○ *My business address and phone number are printed on the card.* ■ *verb* **1.** to write the details of an address on an envelope or package ○ *a letter addressed to the managing director* ○ *an incorrectly addressed package* ○ *Please address your enquiries to the manager.* **2.** to speak ○ *The chairman addressed the meeting.*

addressee /,ædre'siː/ *noun* a person to whom a letter or package is addressed

addressing machine /ə'dresɪŋ mə,ʃiːn/ *noun* a machine which puts addresses on envelopes automatically

add up /,æd 'ʌp/ *verb* **1.** to put several figures together to make a total ○ *He made a mistake in adding up the column of figures.* □ **the figures do not add up** the total given is not correct **2.** to make sense ○ *The complaints in the letter just do not add up.*

add up to /,æd 'ʌp tʊ/ *verb* to make a total of ○ *The total expenditure adds up to more than £1,000.*

adequate /'ædɪkwət/ *adjective* large enough □ **to operate without adequate cover** to act without being completely protected by insurance

ad hoc /æd 'hɒk/ *adjective* for this particular purpose ○ *They run ad hoc surveys to test customer reaction when products are launched.* ○ *Shipping by airfreight was an ad hoc arrangement initially.*

ad hoc decision /,æd hɒk dɪ'sɪʒ(ə)n/ *noun* a decision taken to solve a particular problem

adhocracy /æd'hɒkrəsi/ *noun* management which works by taking short-term decisions, but fails to make long-term plans

adjourn /ə'dʒɜːn/ *verb* to stop a meeting for a period ○ *The chairman adjourned the meeting until three o'clock.* ○ *The meeting adjourned at midday.*

adjournment /ə'dʒɜːnmənt/ *noun* an act of adjourning ○ *He proposed the adjournment of the meeting.*

adjudicate /ə'dʒuːdɪkeɪt/ *verb* to give a judgement between two parties in law or to decide a legal problem ○ *to adjudicate a claim* ○ *to adjudicate in a dispute* □ **he was adjudicated bankrupt** he was declared legally bankrupt

adjudication /ə,dʒuːdɪ'keɪʃ(ə)n/ *noun* the act of giving a judgement or of deciding a legal problem

adjudication officer /ə,dʒuːdɪ'keɪʃ(ə)n ,ɒfɪsə/ *noun* an official who decides whether someone is qualified to receive benefit

adjudication tribunal /ə,dʒuːdɪ'keɪʃ(ə)n traɪ,bjuːn(ə)l/ *noun* a group which adjudicates in industrial disputes

adjudicator /ə'dʒuːdɪkeɪtə/ *noun* a person who gives a decision on a problem ○ *an adjudicator in an industrial dispute*

adjust /ə'dʒʌst/ *verb* to change something to fit new conditions ○ *Prices are adjusted for inflation.*

'…inflation-adjusted GNP moved up at a 1.3% annual rate' [*Fortune*]

'Saudi Arabia will no longer adjust its production to match short-term supply with demand' [*Economist*]

'…on a seasonally-adjusted basis, output of trucks, electric power, steel and paper decreased' [*Business Week*]

adjuster /ə'dʒʌstə/ *noun* a person who calculates losses for an insurance company

adjustment /ə'dʒʌstmənt/ *noun* the act of adjusting ○ *to make an adjustment to salaries* ○ *adjustment of prices to take account of rising costs* ○ *Details of tax adjustments are set out in the enclosed document.* ○ *an adjustment of prices to take account of rising costs*

adjustor /ə'dʒʌstə/ *noun* same as **adjuster**

admin /'ædmɪn/ *noun* **1.** the work of administration, especially paperwork (*informal*) ○ *All this admin work takes a lot of my time.* ○ *There is too much* *admin in this job.* ○ *Admin costs seem to be rising each quarter.* ○ *The admin people have sent the report back.* **2.** administration staff or the administration department ○ *Admin say they need the report immediately.* ○ *She did not answer my note but sent it on to admin.* (NOTE: no plural; as a group of people it can have a plural verb)

administer /əd'mɪnɪstə/ *verb* to organise, manage or direct the whole of an organisation or part of one ○ *She administers a large pension fund.* ○ *It will be the HR manager's job to administer the induction programme.*

administration /əd,mɪnɪ'streɪʃ(ə)n/ *noun* **1.** the action of organising, controlling or managing a company ○ *He has a qualification in business administration.* **2.** a person or group of people who manage or direct an organisation ○ *It is up to the administration to solve the problem, not the government.* **3.** the running of a company in receivership by an administrator appointed by the courts

administration costs /əd,mɪnɪ'streɪʃ(ə)n ,kɒsts/, **administration expenses** /əd,mɪnɪ'streɪʃ(ə)n ɪk,spensɪz/ *plural noun* the costs of management, not including production, marketing or distribution costs

administrative /əd'mɪnɪstrətɪv/ *adjective* referring to administration ○ *administrative details* ○ *administrative expenses*

administrator /əd'mɪnɪstreɪtə/ *noun* **1.** a person who directs the work of other employees in a business ○ *After several years as a college teacher, she hopes to become an administrator.* **2.** a person appointed by a court to manage the affairs of someone who dies without leaving a will **3.** a person appointed by a court to administer a company which is insolvent

admonish /əd'mɒnɪʃ/ *verb* to give a warning or reprimand (*formal*) ○ *The workers were admonished by the manager for careless work.*

adoption leave /ə'dɒpʃən liːv/ *noun* time away from work allowed to an employee for dealing with matters relating to the adoption of a child

adult education /,ædʌlt edjʊ-'keɪʃ(ə)n/ *noun* education provided for adults

ad valorem tax /,æd və'lɔːrem tæks/ *noun* tax calculated according to the value of the goods taxed

advance /əd'vɑːns/ *noun* **1.** money paid as a loan or as a part of a payment to be made later ○ *She asked if she could have a cash advance.* ○ *We paid her an advance on account.* ○ *Can I have an advance of £100 against next month's salary?* **2.** an increase **3.** □ **in advance** early, before something happens ○ *freight payable in advance* ○ *prices fixed in advance* ■ *adjective* early ○ *advance booking* ○ *advance payment* ○ *Advance holiday bookings are up on last year.* ○ *You must give seven days' advance notice of withdrawals from the account.* ■ *verb* **1.** to lend ○ *The bank advanced him £100,000 against the security of his house.* **2.** to increase ○ *Prices generally advanced on the stock market.* **3.** to make something happen earlier ○ *The date of the AGM has been advanced to May 10th.* ○ *The meeting with the German distributors has been advanced from 11.00 to 09.30.*

advanced course /əd,vɑːnst 'kɔːs/ *noun* a course for students who are not beginners

advancement /əd'vɑːnsmənt/ *noun* promotion ○ *The only way to get advancement in this company is through further training.* ○ *The job is attractive because of the potential for advancement.*

advantage /əd'vɑːntɪdʒ/ *noun* something useful which may help you to be successful ○ *Knowledge of two foreign languages is an advantage.* ○ *There is no advantage in arriving at the exhibition before it opens.* ○ *Fast typing is an advantage in a secretary.* □ **to take advantage of something** to use something which helps you

adventure training /əd'ventʃə ,treɪnɪŋ/, **adventure learning** /əd-'ventʃə ,lɜːnɪŋ/ *noun* a type of training in which employees engage in group games and physically demanding outdoor activities such as climbing and abseiling away from their usual work environment (NOTE: the aim of adventure training is to develop skills in leadership, problem-solving, decision-making and to build team spirit)

adverse /'ædvɜːs/ *adjective* unfavourable □ **adverse balance of trade** a situation in which a country imports more than it exports

adverse action /ˌædvɜːs 'ækʃən/ *noun* a decision which has unfavourable consequences for employees ○ *The new bonus system was considered adverse action by underachievers in the organisation.*

adverse impact /ˌædvɜːs 'ɪmpækt/ *noun* an undesirable and unexpected result of an action ○ *Offering bonuses only for very high productivity rates had an adverse impact, discouraging rather than motivating workers.*

advert /'ædvɜːt/ *noun* same as **advertisement** (*informal*) ○ *to put an advert in the paper* ○ *to answer an advert in the paper* ○ *classified adverts* ○ *display adverts*

advertise /'ædvətaɪz/ *verb* **1.** to arrange and pay for publicity designed to help sell products or services or to find new employees ○ *to advertise a vacancy* ○ *to advertise for a secretary* **2.** to announce that something is for sale or that a job is vacant or that a service is offered ○ *to advertise a new product*

advertisement /əd'vɜːtɪsmənt/ *noun* a notice which shows that something is for sale, that a service is offered, that someone wants something or that a job is vacant

advertisement manager /əd-'vɜːtɪsmənt ˌmænɪdʒə/ *noun* the manager in charge of the advertisement section of a newspaper

advertiser /'ædvətaɪzə/ *noun* a person or company that advertises ○ *The catalogue gives a list of advertisers.*

advertising /'ædvətaɪzɪŋ/ *noun* the business of announcing that something is for sale or of trying to persuade customers to buy a product or service ○ *She works in advertising* or *She has a job in*

advertising. ○ *Their new advertising campaign is being launched next week.* ○ *The company has asked an advertising agent to prepare a presentation.* □ **to take advertising space in a paper** to book space for an advertisement in a newspaper

advertising manager /'ædvətaɪzɪŋ ˌmænɪdʒə/ *noun* the manager in charge of advertising a company's products

advertising space /'ædvətaɪzɪŋ speɪs/ *noun* a space in a newspaper set aside for advertisements

advice /əd'vaɪs/ *noun* **1.** a notification telling someone what has happened **2.** an opinion as to what action to take □ **to take legal advice** to ask a lawyer to say what should be done ○ *The accountant's advice was to send the documents to the police.* ○ *We sent the documents to the police on the advice of the accountant.* ○ *We took the accountant's advice and sent the documents to the police.* ◇ **as per advice** according to what is written on the advice note

advise /əd'vaɪz/ *verb* **1.** to tell someone what has happened ○ *We have been advised that the shipment will arrive next week.* **2.** to suggest to someone what should be done ○ *The lawyer advised us to send the documents to the police.*

advise against /əd,vaɪz ə'genst/ *verb* to suggest that something should not be done ○ *The HR manager advised against dismissing the staff without notice.*

adviser /əd'vaɪzə/, **advisor** *noun* a person who suggests what should be done ○ *He is consulting the company's legal adviser.*

advisory /əd'vaɪz(ə)ri/ *adjective* as an adviser ○ *He is acting in an advisory capacity.*

Advisory, Conciliation and Arbitration Service /əd,vaɪz(ə)ri kən,sɪli,eɪʃ(ə)n ənd ,ɑːbɪ'treɪʃ(ə)n ,sɜːvɪs/ *noun* a British government service which arbitrates in disputes between management and employees. Abbr **ACAS**

COMMENT: ACAS has three roles: it will conciliate in a dispute if asked; it advises employers, trade unions and employees on matters concerning industrial relations; it arbitrates in cases where industrial disputes cannot be settled inside the company's own grievance structure.

advisory arbitration /ədˌvaɪz(ə)ri ɑːbɪˈtreɪʃ(ə)n/ *noun* arbitration which recommends a solution to a dispute, but is not binding on either party ○ *The two parties resorted to advisory arbitration to avoid the legal process.* ○ *Though the two parties had agreed to advisory arbitration, neither of them agreed with the recommendation.*

advisory board /ədˈvaɪz(ə)ri bɔːd/ *noun* a group of advisors

affect /əˈfekt/ *verb* to cause some change in or to have a bad effect on something ○ *The new government regulations do not affect us.*

affiliated /əˈfɪlieɪtɪd/ *adjective* connected with or owned by another company ○ *Smiths Ltd is one of our affiliated companies.*

affiliated societies /əˌfɪlieɪtɪd səˈsaɪətiz/ *plural noun* non-profit-making organisations which exist to provide financial support to members and their families in sickness and old age

affiliated trade union /əˌfɪlieɪtɪd treɪd ˈjuːnjən/ *noun* trade unions which a member of a larger organisation, such as a national association

affirmative /əˈfɜːmətɪv/ *adjective* meaning 'yes' □ **the answer was in the affirmative** the answer was yes

affirmative action /əˌfɜːmətɪv ˈækʃən/ *noun US* the practice of providing opportunities for disadvantaged groups such as ethnic minorities, women or people with disabilities

COMMENT: Affirmative recruitment is usually carried out by central or local government organisations.

affirmative action group /əˌfɜːmətɪv ˈækʃən gruːp/ *noun* a group of people who are eligible for or need affirmative action ○ *People in affirmative action groups get special consideration when applying for local government jobs.*

affirmative action program /əˌfɜːmətɪv ˈækʃən ˌprəʊgræm/ *noun US* a programme to avoid discrimina-

tion in employment (NOTE: the British equivalent is **equal opportunities**)

affirmative recruitment /əˌfɜːmətɪv rɪˈkruːtmənt/ *noun* recruitment which gives special consideration to applicants from affirmative action groups (NOTE: the British equivalent is **equal opportunities**)

afford /əˈfɔːd/ *verb* to be able to pay for or buy something ○ *We could not afford the cost of two telephones.* ○ *The company cannot afford the time to train new staff.* (NOTE: only used after **can, cannot, could, could not, able to**)

AFL-CIO *noun* an organisation linking US trade unions. Abbr of **American Federation of Labor – Congress of Industrial Organisations**

after-tax profit /ˌɑːftə ˈtæks ˌprɒfɪt/ *noun* profit after tax has been deducted

against /əˈgenst/ *preposition* relating to or part of ○ *Can I have an advance against next month's salary?* ○ *The bank advanced him £10,000 against the security of his house.*

'…investment can be written off against the marginal rate of tax' [*Investors Chronicle*]

age /eɪdʒ/ *noun* the number of years someone has lived

age bracket /ˈeɪdʒ ˌbrækɪt/, **age group** /ˈeɪdʒ gruːp/ *noun* a group of people of about the same age ○ *the 25–30 age group*

age discrimination /ˈeɪdʒ dɪskrɪmɪˌneɪʃ(ə)n/ *noun* unfair treatment resulting from prejudice against a person on the grounds of their age (NOTE: countries such as Australia and the United States have passed laws to make age discrimination illegal)

ageism /ˈeɪdʒɪz(ə)m/ *noun* unfair discrimination against older people

age limit /ˈeɪdʒ ˌlɪmɪt/ *noun* the top age at which you are allowed to do a job ○ *There is an age limit of thirty-five on the post of buyer.*

agency /ˈeɪdʒənsi/ *noun* **1.** an office or job of representing another company in an area ○ *They signed an agency agreement* or *an agency contract.* **2.** an office or business which arranges things for other companies

agency labour /'eɪdʒənsi ˌleɪbə/ noun staff supplied by an employment agency

agency shop /'eɪdʒənsi ʃɒp/ noun US a provision that requires non-union employees to pay union dues if they are part of a bargaining unit

agenda /ə'dʒendə/ noun a list of things to be discussed at a meeting ○ The conference agenda or the agenda of ○ After two hours we were still discussing the first item on the agenda. ○ We usually put put finance at the top of the agenda. ○ The chair wants two items removed from or taken off the agenda.

agent /'eɪdʒənt/ noun **1.** a person who represents a company or another person in an area ○ to be the agent for BMW cars ○ to be the agent for IBM **2.** a person in charge of an agency ○ an advertising agent ○ The estate agent sent me a list of properties for sale. ○ Our trip was organised through our local travel agent. ○ Management would only discuss the new payment scheme with agents officially representing the workers. **3.** a person who is formally acting on behalf of employees or a union ○ Management would only discuss the new payment scheme with agents officially representing the workers. ○ Certain workers were selected as agents to voice the grievances of the men and women on the shop floor. □ **(business) agent** US the chief local official of a trade union

agent's commission /ˌeɪdʒənts kə'mɪʃ(ə)n/ noun money, often a percentage of sales, paid to an agent

age pension /'eɪdʒ ˌpenʃən/ noun a sum of money paid regularly by a government to people who have reached the official age of retirement

aggrieved /ə'griːvd/ adjective upset and annoyed

aggrieved party /əˌgriːvd 'pɑːti/ noun the person who has a grievance

AGM abbr Annual General Meeting

agree /ə'griː/ verb **1.** to approve ○ The figures were agreed between the two parties. ○ We have agreed the budgets for next year. ○ The terms of the contract are still to be agreed. **2.** to say yes to something that is suggested ○ We all agreed on the plan. **3.** □ **to agree to** or **on something** to approve something ○ After some discussion she agreed to our plan. ○ The bank will never agree to lend the company £250,000. ○ We all agreed on the need for action. □ **to agree to do something** to say that you will do something ○ She agreed to be chairman. ○ Will the finance director agree to resign?

agreed /ə'griːd/ adjective which has been accepted by everyone ○ We pay an agreed amount each month. ○ The shop is leased on agreed terms. ○ The agreed terms of employment are laid down in the contract.

agreement /ə'griːmənt/ noun **1.** a spoken or written contract between people or groups which explains how they will act ○ a written agreement ○ an unwritten or verbal agreement ○ to draw up or to draft an agreement ○ to break an agreement ○ to sign an agreement ○ to reach an agreement or to come to an agreement on something ○ a collective wage agreement **2.** a contract between two parties which explains how they will act ○ a written agreement ○ an unwritten or verbal agreement ○ to draw up or to draft an agreement ○ to break an agreement ○ to sign an agreement ○ to reach an agreement or to come to an agreement on something ○ a collective wage agreement

'...after three days of tough negotiations the company has reached agreement with its 1,200 unionized workers' [Toronto Star]

agree with /ə'griː wɪð/ verb **1.** to say that your opinions are the same as someone else's ○ I agree with the chairman that the figures are lower than normal. **2.** to be the same as ○ The auditors' figures do not agree with those of the accounts department.

agricultural labourer /ˌægrɪkʌltʃərəl 'leɪb(ə)rə/ noun a person who does heavy work on a farm

aim /eɪm/ noun something which you try to do ○ One of our aims is to increase the quality of our products. □ **the company has achieved all its aims** the company has done all the things it had hoped to do ■ verb to try to do something ○ Each member of the sales team *must aim to double their previous year's sales. ○ We aim to be No. 1 in the market within two years.*

air /eə/ *verb* □ **to air a grievance** to talk about or discuss a grievance ○ *The management committee is useful because it allows the workers' representatives to air their grievances.*

AIRC *abbr* Australian Industrial Relations Commission

airmail letter /'eəmeɪl ˌletə/ *noun* a letter sent by air

alarm /ə'lɑːm/ *noun* a device which gives a loud warning

alcoholism /'ælkəhɒlɪz(ə)m/ *noun* the excessive drinking of alcohol which becomes addictive

alien /'eɪliən/ *noun* **1.** a person who is not a citizen of a country **2.** (*in the UK*) a person who is not a citizen of the United Kingdom, a Commonwealth country or the Irish Republic

alienation /ˌeɪliə'neɪʃ(ə)n/ *noun* a lack of a sense of fulfilment when an employee cannot see the result of their work ○ *The monotony of the job created a sense of alienation.* ○ *The management wanted to combat any sense of alienation by involving the employees in company decisions.*

allegation /ˌælə'geɪʃ(ə)n/ *noun* the suggestion that something has happened, without being able to prove it

allege /ə'ledʒ/ *verb* to suggest something, without being able to prove it ○ *The management alleged that the union had broken the agreement.*

all-in /ˌɔːl 'ɪn/ *adjective* including everything ○ *The fee payable is £150 all-in.*

all-in policy /ˌɔːl ɪn 'pɒlɪsi/ *noun* insurance which covers all risks

all-in rate /ˌɔːl ɪn 'reɪt/, **all-in price** /ˌɔːl ɪn 'praɪs/ *noun* **1.** a price which covers all items in a purchase such as delivery, tax and insurance, as well as the goods themselves **2.** a wage which includes all extra payments such as bonuses and merit pay

all-out /ˌɔːl 'aut/ *adjective* complete or very serious ○ *The firm has launched an*

all-out campaign to improve productivity on Friday afternoons.

all-out strike /ˌɔːl aut 'straɪk/ *noun* a complete strike by all employees

allow /ə'lau/ *verb* **1.** to say that someone can do something ○ *Junior members of staff are not allowed to use the chairman's lift.* ○ *The company allows all members of staff to take six days' holiday at Christmas.* **2.** to give ○ *to allow 5% discount to members of staff* ○ *We allow her a discount because she's the manager's sister.* **3.** to agree to or accept legally ○ *to allow a claim* or *an appeal*

allowable /ə'lauəb(ə)l/ *adjective* legally accepted

allowance /ə'lauəns/ *noun* **1.** money which is given for a special reason ○ *a travel allowance* or *a travelling allowance* **2.** part of an income which is not taxed ○ *allowances against tax* or *tax allowances* ○ *personal allowances* **3.** money removed in the form of a discount ○ *an allowance for depreciation* ○ *an allowance for exchange loss*

'…the compensation plan includes base, incentive and car allowance totalling $50,000+' [*Globe and Mail (Toronto)*]

allowed time /ə,laud 'taɪm/ *noun* paid time which the management agrees an employee can spend on rest, cleaning or meals, not working

allow for /ə'lau fɔː/ *verb* to give a discount for or to add an extra sum to cover something ○ *to allow for money paid in advance* ○ *Allow an extra 10% for postage and packing.* □ **delivery is not allowed for** delivery charges are not included □ **allow 28 days for delivery** calculate that delivery will take up to 28 days

all-risks policy /ˌɔːl 'rɪsks ˌpɒlɪsi/ *noun* an insurance policy which covers risks of any kind, with no exclusions

alphabetical order /ˌælfəbetɪk(ə)l 'ɔːdə/ *noun* the arrangement of records (such as files and index cards) in the order of the letters of the alphabet (A,B,C,D, etc.)

alter /'ɔːltə/ *verb* to change ○ *to alter the terms of a contract*

alteration /ˌɔːltəˈreɪʃ(ə)n/ *noun* a change which has been made ○ *He made some alterations to the terms of a contract.* ○ *The agreement was signed without any alterations.*

alternate /ˈɔːltəneɪt/ *verb* to do something by turns or in rotation ○ *Two workers alternate on the machine.*

alternating shift system /ˌɔːltəneɪtɪŋ ˈʃɪft ˌsɪstəm/ *noun* a system where two groups of employees work day or night shifts, and after a certain period, change round

alternation ranking /ˌɔːltəˈneɪʃ(ə)n ˌræŋkɪŋ/ *noun* a method of ranking, beginning with the highest and lowest, then the second highest and lowest, and so on

alternative /ɔːlˈtɜːnətɪv/ *noun* a thing which can be done instead of another ○ *What is the alternative to firing half the staff?* □ **we have no alternative** there is nothing else we can do ■ *adjective* other, which can take the place of something □ **to find someone alternative employment** to find someone another job

amalgamate /əˈmælɡəmeɪt/ *verb* to join together with another group ○ *The amalgamated union has a total membership of 250,000.*

amalgamation /əˌmælɡəˈmeɪʃ(ə)n/ *noun* the joining together of several trade unions to increase their strength

ambition /æmˈbɪʃ(ə)n/ *noun* what someone wants to do or achieve in their life ○ *We insist that our sales representatives have plenty of ambition.* ○ *Her ambition is to become the senior partner in the firm.*

ambitious /æmˈbɪʃəs/ *adjective* full of ambition, wanting to do or achieve something ○ *He is ambitious, but not very competent.*

amend /əˈmend/ *verb* to change and make more correct or acceptable ○ *Please amend your copy of the contract accordingly.*

amendment /əˈmendmənt/ *noun* a change to a document ○ *to propose an amendment to the constitution* ○ *to make amendments to a contract*

amenities /əˈmiːnɪtiz/ *plural noun* services provided by an organisation for the people who work in it ○ *The staff amenities included a subsidised canteen and sports facilities.*

amount /əˈmaʊnt/ *noun* a quantity of money ○ *a small amount invested in gilt-edged stock* ○ *A small amount has been deducted to cover our costs.* ○ *A large amount is still owing.* ○ *What is the amount to be written off?* ○ *What is the amount outstanding?* ■ *verb* □ **to amount to** to make a total of ○ *Their debts amount to over £1m.*

analogue /ˈæn(ə)lɒɡ/ *noun* a person's opposite in another organisation ○ *The conference of production managers gave those attending the opportunity to meet their analogues in other industries.* (NOTE: US spelling is also **analog**)

analyse /ˈænəlaɪz/, **analyze** *verb* to examine someone or something in detail ○ *to analyse a statement of account* ○ *to analyse the market potential*

analysis /əˈnæləsɪs/ *noun* a detailed examination and report ○ *a job analysis* ○ *market analysis* ○ *Her job is to produce a regular sales analysis.* (NOTE: plural is analyses)

analyst /ˈænəlɪst/ *noun* a person who analyses ○ *a market analyst* ○ *a systems analyst*

analytical /ˌænəˈlɪtɪk(ə)l/ *adjective* using analysis

analytical estimating /ˌænəlɪtɪk(ə)l ˈestɪmeɪtɪŋ/ *noun* a work measurement technique where the time taken to perform a job is estimated on the basis of prior experience ○ *Analytical estimating was not considered a satisfactory work measurement technique because the union complained that previously established time period* ○ *Analytical estimating was used on those jobs that hadn't changed since the original work measurement.*

analytical job evaluation /ˌænəlɪtɪk(ə)l ˈdʒɒb ɪvæljuˌeɪʃ(ə)n/ *noun* a method of evaluating a job using a points system to compare one job with another (as opposed to non-analytical evaluation)

ancillary staff /ˌænˈsɪləri stɑːf/ *noun* staff who are not administrators, production staff or sales staff (such as cleaners, porters, canteen staff, etc.)

andragogy /ˈændrəgɒgi/ *noun* the science of adult learning, that is of teaching adults in an adult way, as opposed to teaching them as if they were children ○ *Andragogy has developed in response to the increasing number of adults with the time and money to spend on further education.* ○ *The training manager was aware of the latest theories in andragogy of importance in the training of machinists.*

Anglo-Saxon work ethic /ˌæŋgləʊ sæksən ˈwɜːk ˌeθɪk/ *noun* a feeling in Britain and the USA that work is the most important task for an adult

anniversary /ˌænɪˈvɜːs(ə)ri/, **anniversary date** /ˌænɪˈvɜːs(ə)ri deɪt/ *noun* a date in a following year which is the same as a particular occasion, e.g. the date of joining a pension scheme

announce /əˈnaʊns/ *verb* to tell something to the public ○ *to announce the first year's trading results* ○ *to announce the results for 2002* ○ *The director has announced a programme of investment.*

announcement /əˈnaʊnsmənt/ *noun* an act of telling something in public ○ *the announcement of a cutback in expenditure* ○ *the announcement of the appointment of a new managing director* ○ *The managing director made an announcement to the staff.*

annual /ˈænjuəl/ *adjective* for one year ○ *an annual statement of income* ○ *They have six weeks' annual leave.* ○ *The company has an annual growth of 5%.* ○ *We get an annual bonus.* □ **on an annual basis** each year ○ *The figures are revised on an annual basis.*

'...real wages have risen at an annual rate of only 1% in the last two years' [*Sunday Times*]

'...the remuneration package will include an attractive salary, profit sharing and a company car together with four weeks' annual holiday' [*Times*]

Annual General Meeting /ˌænjuəl ˌdʒen(ə)rəl ˈmiːtɪŋ/ *noun* an annual meeting of all shareholders of a company, when the company's financial sit-

uation is presented by and discussed with the directors, when the accounts for the past year are approved and when dividends are declared and audited. Abbr **AGM** (NOTE: the American equivalent is **annual meeting** or **annual stockholders' meeting**)

annual holiday /ˌænjuəl ˈhɒlɪdeɪ/ *noun* a holiday which is taken once a year

annual hours /ˌænjuəl ˈaʊəz/ *plural noun* the total of all the hours worked in a year (e.g. 1720 hours per annum), laid out in a contract of employment, so allowing an employee more flexibility than a weekly hour system

annual income /ˌænjuəl ˈɪnkʌm/ *noun* money received during a calendar year

annualised /ˈænjuəlaɪzd/, **annualized** *adjective* shown on an annual basis

'...he believes this may have caused the economy to grow at an annualized rate of almost 5 per cent in the final quarter of last year' [*Investors Chronicle*]

annualised percentage rate /ˌænjuəlaɪzd pəˈsentɪdʒ reɪt/ *noun* a yearly percentage rate, calculated by multiplying the monthly rate by twelve (not as accurate as the APR, which includes fees and other charges)

annually /ˈænjuəli/ *adverb* each year ○ *The figures are updated annually.*

Annual Percentage Rate /ˌænjuəl pəˈsentɪdʒ reɪt/ *noun* a rate of interest (such as on a hire-purchase agreement) shown on an annual compound basis, including fees and charges. Abbr **APR**

annual report /ˌænjuəl rɪˈpɔːt/ *noun* a report of a company's financial situation at the end of a year, sent to all the shareholders

annual salary /ˌænjuəl ˈsæləri/ *noun* a salary for one year's work

annuitant /əˈnjuːɪtənt/ *noun* a person who receives an annuity

annuity /əˈnjuːɪti/ *noun* money paid each year to a retired person, usually in return for a lump-sum payment; the value of the annuity depends on how long the person lives, as it usually cannot be passed on to another person; annuities are fixed payments, and lose their value with inflation, whereas a pension can be index-linked ○ *to buy* or *to take out an annuity* ○ *He has a government annuity* or *an annuity from the government.* □ **contingent annuity** an annuity paid to someone on the death of another person

COMMENT: When a person retires, he or she is required by law to purchase a 'compulsory purchase annuity' with the funds accumulated in his or her pension fund. This gives them a taxable income for the rest of their life, but usually it is a fixed income which does not change with inflation.

annuity for life /əˌnjuːɪti fə ˈlaɪf/ *noun* annual payments made to someone as long as they are alive

annul /əˈnʌl/ *verb* to cancel or to stop something being legal ○ *The contract was annulled by the court.* (NOTE: **annulling – annulled**)

annullable /əˈnʌləb(ə)l/ *adjective* which can be cancelled

annulling /əˈnʌlɪŋ/ *adjective* which cancels ○ *an annulling clause in a contract* ■ *noun* the act of cancelling ○ *the annulling of a contract*

annulment /əˈnʌlmənt/ *noun* the act of cancelling ○ *the annulment of a contract*

answer /ˈɑːnsə/ *verb* to speak or write after someone has spoken or written to you □ **to answer a letter** to write a letter in reply to a letter which you have received □ **to answer the telephone** to lift the telephone when it rings and listen to what the caller is saying

answerphone /ˈɑːnsəfəʊn/ *noun* a machine which answers the telephone automatically when a person is not in the office and allows messages to be recorded ○ *He wasn't in when I called so I left a message on his answerphone.*

antedate /ˌænti'deɪt/ *verb* to put an earlier date on a document ○ *The invoice was antedated to January 1st.* ○ *The contract was antedated to January 1st.*

anticipation /ænˌtɪsɪˈpeɪʃ(ə)n/ *noun* the act of doing something before it is due to be done

anticipatory /ænˈtɪsɪpət(ə)ri/ *adjective* done before it is due

anticipatory breach /ænˌtɪsɪpət(ə)ri ˈbriːtʃ/ *noun* the refusal by a party to a contract to perform their obligations under the contract at a time before they were due to be performed

anti-inflationary measure /ˌænti ɪnˈfleɪʃ(ə)n(ə)ri ˌmeʒə/ *noun* a measure taken to reduce inflation

any other business /ˌeni ʌðə ˈbɪznɪs/ *noun* an item at the end of an agenda, where any matter can be raised. Abbr **AOB**

appeal /əˈpiːl/ *noun* **1.** the fact of being attractive **2.** the act of asking a law court or a government department to change its decision ○ *He lost his appeal for damages against the company.* □ **she won her case on appeal** her case was lost in the first court, but the appeal court said that she was right ■ *verb* **1.** to attract ○ *The idea of working in Australia for six months appealed to her.* **2.** to ask a law court or a government department or to alter its decision ○ *The union appealed against the decision of the tribunal.* (NOTE: you appeal **to** a court or a person **against** a decision)

appeal proceedings /əˈpiːl prəˌsiːdɪŋz/ *plural noun* the formal hearing of an appeal by a tribunal

appeals procedure /əˈpiːlz prəˌsiːdʒə/ *noun* the way in which an employee can appeal against a decision

appendix /əˈpendɪks/ *noun* **1.** additional sheets at the back of a contract **2.** additional pages at the back of a book

applicant /ˈæplɪkənt/ *noun* a person who applies for something ○ *an applicant for a job* or *a job applicant* ○ *an applicant to an industrial tribunal* ○ *There were thousands of applicants for shares in the new company.*

application /ˌæplɪˈkeɪʃ(ə)n/ *noun* **1.** the act of asking for something, usually in writing ○ *shares payable on application* ○ *She sent off six applications for job* or *six job applications.* **2.** effort or diligence ○ *She has shown great application in her work on the project.*

application blank /ˌæplɪˈkeɪʃ(ə)n blæŋk/ *noun US* a form for recording an applicant's qualifications for a job

application form /ˌæplɪˈkeɪʃ(ə)n fɔːm/ *noun* a form to be filled in when applying for a new issue of shares or for a job

apply /əˈplaɪ/ *verb* **1.** to ask for something, usually in writing ○ *to apply in writing* ○ *to apply in person* ○ *About fifty people have applied so far.* ○ *The more ambitious of the office workers will apply for the management trainee programme.* (NOTE: applies- applying- applied) **2.** to affect or to relate to ○ *This clause applies only to deals outside the EU.*

appoint /əˈpɔɪnt/ *verb* to choose someone for a job ○ *We have appointed a new distribution manager.* ○ *They've appointed Janet Smith (to the post of) manager.* (NOTE: you appoint a person **to** a job)

appointee /əpɔɪnˈtiː/ *noun* a person who is appointed to a job

appointment /əˈpɔɪntmənt/ *noun* **1.** an arrangement to meet ○ *to make* or *to fix an appointment with someone for two o'clock* ○ *He was late for his appointment.* ○ *She had to cancel her appointment.* **2.** the act of being appointed to a job □ **on his appointment as manager** when he was made manager **3.** a job

appointments book /əˈpɔɪntmənts bʊk/ *noun* a desk diary in which appointments are noted

appointments vacant /əˌpɔɪntmənts ˈveɪkənt/ *noun* a list (in a newspaper) of jobs which are available

apportion /əˈpɔːʃ(ə)n/ *verb* to share out costs, blame, etc. ○ *Costs are apportioned according to projected revenue.*

apportionment /əˈpɔːʃ(ə)nmənt/ *noun* the sharing out of costs

apportionment of wages /əˌpɔːʃ(ə)nmənt əv ˈweɪdʒɪz/ *noun* a decision as to what payment is made to an employee who leaves before pay day ○ *A generous apportionment of wages was favoured by the human resources department so that employees would not lea* ○ *The union objected to the company's apportionment of wages, claiming that employees were not receiving amounts corresponding to days worked.*

appraisal /əˈpreɪz(ə)l/ *noun* a calculation of the value of someone or something

'...we are now reaching a stage in industry and commerce where appraisals are becoming part of the management culture. Most managers now take it for granted that they will appraise and be appraised' [*Personnel Management*]

appraisal interview /əˈpreɪz(ə)l ˌɪntəvjuː/ *noun* an interview where the manager (the appraiser) discusses with the employee (the appraisee) his or her performance

appraise /əˈpreɪz/ *verb* to assess or to calculate the value of something or someone

appraisee /əˌpreɪˈziː/ *noun* an employee who is being appraised by their manager in an appraisal interview

appraiser /əˈpreɪzə/ *noun* a person who conducts an appraisal inteview

appreciate /əˈpriːʃieɪt/ *verb* **1.** to notice how good something is **2.** (*of currency, shares, etc.*) to increase in value

appreciation /əˌpriːʃiˈeɪʃ(ə)n/ *noun* **1.** an increase in value **2.** the act of valuing something highly ○ *He was given a rise in appreciation of his excellent work.*

apprentice /əˈprentɪs/ *noun* a young person who works under contract for a period in order to be trained in a skill ■ *verb* □ **to be apprenticed to someone** to work with a skilled worker to learn from them

apprenticeship /əˈprentɪsʃɪp/ *noun* the time spent learning a skilled trade ○ *He served a six-year apprenticeship in the steel works.*

approach /əˈprəʊtʃ/ *noun* an act of getting in touch with someone with a proposal ○ *She has had an approach from a firm of headhunters.* ■ *verb* to get in touch with someone with a proposal ○ *She was approached by a headhunter with the offer of a job.*

appropriate *adjective* /əˈprəʊpriət/ suitable ○ *I leave it to you to take appropriate action.*

approval /əˈpruːv(ə)l/ *noun* **1.** agreement ○ *to submit a budget for approval* □ **to give something your approval** to approve something **2.** □ **on approval** a sale where the buyer only pays for goods if they are satisfactory ○ *to buy a photocopier on approval*

approve /əˈpruːv/ *verb* **1.** □ **to approve of something** to think something is good ○ *The chairman approves of the new company letter heading.* ○ *The sales staff do not approve of interference from the accounts division.* **2.** to agree to something officially ○ *to approve the terms of a contract* ○ *The proposal was approved by the board.*

approximate /əˈprɒksɪmət/ *adjective* not exact, but almost correct ○ *The sales division has made an approximate forecast of expenditure.*

approximately /əˈprɒksɪmətli/ *adverb* almost correctly ○ *Expenditure on marketing is approximately 10% down on the previous quarter.*

approximation /əˌprɒksɪˈmeɪʃ(ə)n/ *noun* a rough calculation ○ *Each department has been asked to provide an approximation of expenditure for next year.* ○ *The final figure is only an approximation.*

APR *abbr* Annual Percentage Rate

aptitude /ˈæptɪtjuːd/ *noun* the ability to do something

aptitude test /ˈæptɪˌtjuːd test/ *noun* test to see if a candidate is suitable for a certain type of work. Compare **attainment test**

arbitrate /ˈɑːbɪtreɪt/ *verb* (*of an outside party*) to try to settle an industrial dispute by talking to representatives of both sides, who agree in advance to abide by the arbitrator's decision

arbitration /ˌɑːbɪˈtreɪʃ(ə)n/ *noun* the settling of a dispute by an outside party, agreed on by both sides ○ *to take a dispute to arbitration* or *to go to arbitration* ○ *arbitration in an industrial dispute* ○ *The two sides decided to submit the dispute to arbitration* or *to refer the question to arbitration.*

arbitration agreement /ˌɑːbɪˈtreɪʃ(ə)n əˌɡriːmənt/ *noun* an agreement between two parties that any dif-

ferences between them shall be settled by arbitration

arbitration award /ˌɑːbɪˈtreɪʃ(ə)n əˌwɔːd/ *noun* a decision by an arbitration tribunal

arbitration board /ˌɑːbɪˈtreɪʃ(ə)n bɔːd/ *noun* a group which arbitrates

arbitration clause /ˌɑːbɪˈtreɪʃ(ə)n klɔːz/ *noun* a clause in a contract stating how differences between the parties can be settled by arbitration

arbitration tribunal /ˌɑːbɪˈtreɪʃ(ə)n traɪˌbjuːn(ə)l/ *noun* a group which adjudicates in industrial disputes

arbitrator /ˈɑːbɪtreɪtə/ *noun* a person not concerned with a dispute who is chosen by both sides to try to settle it ○ *an industrial arbitrator* ○ *They refused to accept* or *they rejected the arbitrator's ruling.*

area /ˈeəriə/ *noun* **1.** a measurement of the space taken up by something (calculated by multiplying the length by the width) ○ *a no-smoking area* ○ *The area of this office is 3,400 square feet.* ○ *We are looking for a shop with a sales area of about 100 square metres.* **2.** a region of the world **3.** a subject ○ *a problem area* or *an area for concern* **4.** a district or part of a town ○ *The office is in the commercial area of the town.* ○ *Their factory is in a very good area for getting to the motorways and airports.* **5.** a part of a country, a division for commercial purposes ○ *Her sales area is the North-West.* ○ *He finds it difficult to cover all his area in a week.* **6.** part of a room, factory, restaurant, etc. ○ *a no-smoking area*

area code /ˈeəriə kəʊd/ *noun* a special telephone number which is given to a particular area ○ *The area code for central London is 0207.*

area manager /ˌeəriə ˈmænɪdʒə/ *noun* a manager who is responsible for a company's work in a specific part of the country

argue /ˈɑːɡjuː/ *verb* to discuss something about which you do not agree ○ *The union officials argued among themselves over the best way to deal with the ultimatum from the management.* ○ *We spent hours arguing with the managing* director about the site for the new factory. □ **to argue against something** to give reasons why you think something should not be done

argument /'ɑːgjʊmənt/ *noun* **1.** an act of discussing something without agreeing ○ *She was sacked after an argument with the managing director.* **2.** a reason for supporting or rejecting something ○ *The document gives the management's arguments in favour of flexible working hours.*

arising /əˈraɪzɪŋ/ *adjective* which comes from ○ *differences arising from the contract*

around /əˈraʊnd/ *preposition* approximately ○ *His salary is around $85,000.*

arrange /əˈreɪndʒ/ *verb* **1.** to put into a suitable or pleasing order ○ *The office is arranged as an open-plan area with small separate rooms for meetings.* ○ *The files are arranged in alphabetical order.* **2.** to organise ○ *We arranged to have the meeting in their offices.* (NOTE: you arrange **for** someone to do something; you arrange **for** something to be done; or you arrange **to do** something)

arrangement /əˈreɪndʒmənt/ *noun* **1.** the way in which something is organised ○ *The company secretary is making all the arrangements for the meeting.* **2.** the settling of a financial dispute ○ *He came to an arrangement with his creditors.*

arrears /əˈrɪəz/ *plural noun* **1.** money which is owed, but which has not been paid at the right time ○ *We are pressing the company to pay arrears of interest.* **2.** □ **in arrears** owing money which should have been paid earlier ○ *The payments are six months in arrears.* ○ *He is six weeks in arrears with his rent.*

article /'ɑːtɪk(ə)l/ *noun* **1.** a product or thing for sale ○ *to launch a new article on the market* **2.** a section of a legal agreement such as a contract or treaty ○ *See article 8 of the contract.* □ **Article 117 of the Treaty of Rome** an article which requires member states to improve working conditions and workers' living conditions □ **Article 118(a) of the Treaty of Rome** an article which requires member states to improve health and safety in the working environment □

Article 119 of the Treaty of Rome an article which requires all member states to apply equal pay to men and women doing equal jobs

articled clerk /ˌɑːtɪk(ə)ld ˈklɑːk/ *noun* a clerk who is bound by contract to work in a solicitor's office for some years to learn the law (NOTE: officially now called a **trainee solicitor,** though the old term is still used)

articles /'ɑːtɪk(ə)lz/ *plural noun* a time when a clerk is working in a solicitor's office learning the law (NOTE: officially now called a **training contract,** though the old term is still used) □ **to serve articles** to work in a solicitor's office to learn the law

articles of association /ˌɑːtɪk(ə)lz əv əsəʊsiˈeɪʃ(ə)n/ *plural noun* a document which lays down the rules for a company regarding such matters as the issue of shares, the conduct of meetings and the appointment of directors ○ *He is a director appointed under the articles of association of the company.* ○ *This procedure is not allowed under the articles of association of the company.*

articles of incorporation /ˌɑːtɪk(ə)lz əv ɪnkɔːpəˈreɪʃ(ə)n/ *plural noun US* a document which sets up a company and lays down the relationship between the shareholders and the company (NOTE: the British equivalent is **Memorandum of Association**)

articles of indenture /ˌɑːtɪk(ə)lz əv ɪnˈdentʃə/ *plural noun* a contract by which an apprentice works for a master for some years to learn a trade

articles of partnership /ˌɑːtɪk(ə)lz əv ˈpɑːtnəʃɪp/ *plural noun* a document which sets up the legal conditions of a partnership

artisan /ˌɑːtɪˈzæn/ *noun* a worker who has special training in a manual skill

asap /ˌeɪ es eɪ ˈpiː, ˈeɪsæp/, **ASAP** as soon as possible

ascribed status /əˌskraɪbd ˈsteɪtəs/ *noun* status which someone has in an organisation by right (as opposed to status achieved by merit)

aspirations /ˌæspɪˈreɪʃ(ə)nz/ *plural noun* ambitions or hopes of advancement in your job

aspire /əˈspaɪə/ *verb* □ **to aspire to** to have a strong ambition to

assembly line /əˈsembli laɪn/ *noun* a production system where a product such as a car moves slowly through the factory with new sections added to it as it goes along ○ *She works on an assembly line* or *She is an assembly line worker.*

assembly point /əˈsembli pɔɪnt/, **meeting point** /ˈmiːtɪŋ pɔɪnt/ *noun* a place where people can meet (such as at a railway station or for checking during fire drill)

assert /əˈsɜːt/ *verb* □ **to assert yourself** to show that you have control or can make decisions ○ *She doesn't assert herself much in public meetings, but her sales figures are impressive.*

assertiveness /əˈsɜːtɪvnəs/ *noun* the ability to state opinions or show that you can make decisions

assertiveness training /əˈsɜːtɪvnəs ˌtreɪnɪŋ/ *noun* the process of training employees to have more confidence in themselves

assess /əˈses/ *verb* to calculate the value of something or someone ○ *to assess damages at £1,000* ○ *to assess a property for the purposes of insurance*

assessment /əˈsesmənt/ *noun* a calculation of value ○ *a property assessment* ○ *a tax assessment* ○ *They made a complete assessment of each employee's contribution to the organisation.*

assessment centre /əˈsesmənt ˌsentə/ *noun* a special place which assesses the abilities of a group of employees sent by their organisations ○ *The three days at the assessment centre consisted of in-basket tests and personal interviews.* ○ *The assessment centre aims to spot those individuals with management potential.*

assessment of competence /əˌsesmənt əv ˈkɒmpɪt(ə)ns/ *noun* an assessment of an employee's ability to do a job properly as measured by an agreed set of standards

assessor /əˈsesə/ *noun* **1.** a person who assesses someone **2.** a person who advises a tribunal

assign /əˈsaɪn/ *verb* **1.** to give legally ○ *to assign a right to someone* ○ *to assign shares to someone* **2.** to give someone something to use or a job of work to do, and be responsible for ○ *He was assigned the job of checking the sales figures.*

assignee /ˌæsaɪˈniː/ *noun* a person who receives something which has been assigned to him or her

assignment /əˈsaɪnmənt/ *noun* **1.** the legal transfer of a property or right ○ *the assignment of a patent* or *of a copyright* ○ *to sign a deed of assignment* **2.** a particular task given to someone ○ *Her first assignment was to improve the company's image.* ○ *The oil team is on an assignment in the North Sea.*

assignment of wages /əˌsaɪnmənt əv ˈweɪdʒɪz/ *noun* a procedure in which a deduction is made from an employee's wages and is paid to a third party ○ *An assignment of wages was arranged to pay a worker who had filled in while the regular employee was ill.*

assignor /ˌæsaɪˈnɔː/ *noun* a person who assigns something to someone

assist /əˈsɪst/ *verb* to help ○ *Can you assist the stock controller in counting the stock?* ○ *She assists me with my income tax returns.* (NOTE: you assist someone **in** doing something or **with** something)

assistance /əˈsɪst(ə)ns/ *noun* help ○ *Some candidates need assistance in filling in the form.*

assistant /əˈsɪst(ə)nt/ *noun* a person who helps or a clerical employee

assistant manager /əˌsɪst(ə)nt ˈmænɪdʒə/ *noun* a person who helps a manager

associate /əˈsəʊsiət/ *adjective* linked ■ *noun* a person who works in the same business as someone ○ *She is a business associate of mine.*

associate company /əˌsəʊsiət ˈkʌmp(ə)ni/ *noun* a company which is partly owned by another company

associated /əˈsəʊsieɪtɪd/ *adjective* linked

associated company /ə,səʊsieɪtɪd ˈkʌmp(ə)ni/ *noun* a company which is partly owned by another (though less than 50%), and where the share-owning company exerts some management control or has a close trading relationship with the associate ○ *Smith Ltd and its associated company, Jones Brothers*

associate director /ə,səʊsiət daɪˈrektə/ *noun* a director who attends board meetings, but has not been elected by the shareholders

association /ə,səʊsiˈeɪʃ(ə)n/ *noun* a group of people or companies with the same interest ○ *an employers' association* ○ *Our company has applied to join the trade association.*

assume /əˈsjuːm/ *verb* **1.** to suppose, to believe something to be true ○ *I assume you have enough money to pay these expenses?* **2.** to take for yourself ○ *He has assumed responsibility for marketing.* ○ *The company will assume all risks.*

assumption /əˈsʌmpʃən/ *noun* **1.** a general belief ○ *We are working on the assumption that the exchange rate will stay the same.* **2.** the act of taking for yourself ○ *assumption of risks*

assurance /əˈʃʊərəns/ *noun* **1.** insurance, an agreement that in return for regular payments a company will pay compensation for loss of life **2.** a firm statement that something will happen ○ *He received an assurance from the HR director that he would not be demoted.*

assure /əˈʃʊə/ *verb* **1.** to insure or to have a contract with a company where if regular payments are made, the company will pay compensation if you die ○ *He has paid the premiums to have his wife's life assured.* **2.** □ **to assure someone that** to state something firmly so that someone is sure that it is true

assurer /əˈʃʊərə/, **assuror** *noun* an insurer or a company which insures (NOTE: **assure, assurer,** and **assurance** are used in Britain for insurance policies relating to something which will certainly happen (such as death); for other types of policy (i.e. those against something which may or may not happen, such as an accident) use

the terms **insure, insurer,** and **insurance**)

attach /əˈtætʃ/ *verb* to fasten or to link ○ *I am attaching a copy of my previous letter.* ○ *Please find attached a copy of my letter of June 24th.* ○ *The company attaches great importance to good timekeeping.*

attachment /əˈtætʃmənt/ *noun* the act of holding a debtor's property to prevent it being sold until debts are paid

attachment of earnings order /ə,tætʃmənt əv ˈɜːnɪŋz ,ɔːdə/ *noun* a court order to make an employer pay part of an employee's salary to the court to pay off debts

attainment /əˈteɪnmənt/ *noun* the act of reaching a certain standard or goal

attainment test /əˈteɪnmənt test/ *noun* a test designed to measure the skills which someone is currently using. Compare **aptitude test**

attend /əˈtend/ *verb* to be present at ○ *The chairman has asked all managers to attend the meeting.* ○ *None of the shareholders attended the AGM.*

attendance /əˈtendəns/ *noun* the fact of being present at a meeting or at work ○ *Attendance at the staff meeting is not compulsory.* ○ *Some of the employees were reprimanded for poor attendance.* ○ *The supervisor kept a strict record of the workers' attendance.* ○ *Promotion to the post of supervisor depends to a certain extent on a person's attendance record.*

attendance allowance /əˈtendəns ə,laʊəns/ *noun* a benefit paid to a disabled person over 65 to cover the costs of having someone to care for them. Abbr **AA**

attendance bonus /əˈtendəns ,bəʊnəs/ *noun* a bonus given to employees for good attendance ○ *You may find that payment of an attendance bonus will motivate workers.* ○ *An attendance bonus is awarded for a 95% attendance record.*

attendance money /əˈtendəns ,mʌni/ *noun* payment made to workers who turn up even when there is no work for them to do

attendance time /ə'tendəns taɪm/ *noun* hours spent at work that are paid for

attendant /ə'tendənt/ *noun* a lower-level employee who is given a measure of responsibility

attend to /ə'tend tuː/ *verb* to give careful thought to something and deal with it ○ *The managing director will attend to your complaint personally.* ○ *We have brought in experts to attend to the problem of installing the new computer.*

attention /ə'tenʃən/ *noun* careful thought or consideration □ **to pay attention to** to study carefully and follow instructions, rules, etc.

attitude /'ætɪtjuːd/ *noun* the way in which a person behaves or thinks

attract /ə'trækt/ *verb* to make something or someone join or come in ○ *We have difficulty in attracting skilled staff to this part of the country.*

attractive /ə'træktɪv/ *adjective* which attracts □ **attractive salary** a good salary to make high-quality applicants apply for the job

attribution theory of leadership /ˌætrɪ'bjuːʃ(ə)n θɪəri əv ˌliːdəʃɪp/ *noun* the theory that leaders observe the behaviour of the people they lead, decide what it is that is causing them to behave in that particular way, e.g. what is causing them to perform well or perform badly, and base their own actions on what they believe those causes to be

attrition /ə'trɪʃ(ə)n/ *noun* **1.** a decrease in the loyalty of consumers to a product, due to factors such as boredom or desire for a change **2.** loss of labour through natural wastage

at will /ət 'wɪl/ *adverb* ◊ **employment-at-will**

audio-typing /'ɔːdiəʊ ˌtaɪpɪŋ/ *noun* typing to dictation from a recording on a dictating machine

audio-typist /'ɔːdiəʊ ˌtaɪpɪst/ *noun* a typist who types to dictation from a recording on a dictating machine

audit /'ɔːdɪt/ *noun* **1.** the examination of the books and accounts of a company ○ *to carry out the annual audit* ○ *A thorough job audit was needed for job*

evaluation. **2.** a detailed examination of something in order to assess it ○ *A thorough job audit was needed for job evaluation.* ○ *A manpower audit showed up a desperate lack of talent.* ■ *verb* to examine the books and accounts of a company ○ *Messrs Smith have been asked to audit the accounts.* ○ *The books have not yet been audited.*

auditing /'ɔːdɪtɪŋ/ *noun* the act of examining the books and accounts of a company

auditor /'ɔːdɪtə/ *noun* a person who audits

COMMENT: Auditors are appointed by the company's directors and voted by the AGM. In the USA, audited accounts are only required by corporations which are registered with the SEC, but in the UK all limited companies with a turnover over a certain limit must provide audited annual accounts.

audit trail /'ɔːdɪt treɪl/ *noun* the records that show all the stages of a transaction, e.g. a purchase, a sale or a customer complaint, in the order in which they happened (NOTE: an audit trail can be a useful tool for problem-solving and, in financial markets, may be used to ensure that the dealers have been fair and accurate in their proceedings.)

Aufsichtsrat /'aʊfzɪkts,rɑːt/ *German noun* a supervisory board

Australian Industrial Relations Commission /ɒˌstreɪliən ɪnˌdʌstriəl rɪ'leɪʃ(ə)nz kəˌmɪʃ(ə)n/ *noun* an administrative body in Australia, established in 1988, that is responsible for settling industrial disputes by conciliation and for setting the standards that companies must meet to qualify for industrial awards

authorisation /ˌɔːθəraɪ'zeɪʃ(ə)n/, **authorization** *noun* permission or power to do something ○ *Do you have authorisation for this expenditure?* ○ *He has no authorisation to act on our behalf.*

authorise /'ɔːθəraɪz/, **authorize** *verb* **1.** to give permission for something to be done ○ *to authorise payment of £10,000* **2.** to give someone the authority to do something ○ *to authorise someone to act on the company's behalf*

authoritarian /ɔːˌθɒrɪˈteəriən/ *adjective* demanding a high level of discipline or obedience ○ *The employees disliked the authoritarian management style.* ○ *The managing director is very authoritarian and expects immediate obedience.*

authority /ɔːˈθɒrɪti/ *noun* the power to do something ○ *a manager with authority to sign cheques* ○ *He has no authority to act on our behalf.* ○ *Without the necessary authority, the manager could not command respect.* ○ *Only senior managers have the authority to initiate these changes.*

authority chart /ɔːˈθɒrɪti tʃɑːt/ *noun* a diagram that shows who has authority over whom and who is accountable to whom within an organisation (NOTE: an authority chart is similar to an organisation chart.)

autocratic management style /ˌɔːtəkrætɪk ˈmænɪdʒmənt ˌstaɪl/ *noun* a style of management where the managers tell the employees what to do, without involving them in the decision-making processes (NOTE: the opposite is **democratic management style**)

automated /ˈɔːtəmeɪtɪd/ *adjective* worked automatically by machines ○ *a fully automated car assembly plant*

automatic /ˌɔːtəˈmætɪk/ *adjective* which works or takes place without any person making it happen ○ *There is an automatic increase in salaries on January 1st.*

automatically /ˌɔːtəˈmætɪkli/ *adverb* working without a person giving instructions ○ *Addresses are typed in automatically.* □ **automatically unfair dismissals** dismissals which are always unfair, whatever the circumstances (such as when a woman employee is dismissed for being pregnant or someone is dismissed for belonging to a trade union)

automatic data processing /ˌɔːtəmætɪk ˈdeɪtə ˌprəʊsesɪŋ/ *noun* data processing done by a computer

automatic sanction /ˌɔːtəmætɪk ˈsæŋkʃən/ *noun* a penalty which is applied automatically, outside the legal process, to an employee taking part in industrial action ○ *The fear of automatic sanction stopped many employees going on strike for better working conditions.*

automatic telling machine /ˌɔːtəmætɪk ˈtelɪŋ məˌʃiːn/ *noun* a machine which gives out money when a special card is inserted and special instructions given

automatic wage progression /ˌɔːtəmætɪk ˈweɪdʒ prəˌgreʃ(ə)n/ *noun* an automatic increase in wages according to the time a person has worked in the organisation ○ *Automatic wage progression was seen as a way of motivating employees to stay in the company.*

automation /ˌɔːtəˈmeɪʃ(ə)n/ *noun* the use of machines to do work with very little supervision by people

autonomous /ɔːˈtɒnəməs/ *adjective* which rules itself ○ *The workforce in the factory is made up of several autonomous work groups.*

autonomous bargaining /ɔːˌtɒnəməs ˈbɑːgɪnɪŋ/ *noun* direct bargaining between management and employees, without involving trade unions

autonomous learning /ɔːˌtɒnəməs ˈlɜːnɪŋ/ *noun* learning by yourself, without teachers

autonomous teamworking /ɔːˌtɒnəməs ˈtiːmwɜːkɪŋ/, **autonomous working group** /ɔːˌtɒnəməs ˈwɜːkɪŋ gruːp/ *noun* a group of employees who can work independently, taking decisions together as a group (NOTE: also called **self-managing team**)

autonomy /ɔːˈtɒnəmi/ *noun* working by yourself, without being managed

available capital /əˌveɪləb(ə)l ˈkæpɪt(ə)l/ *noun* capital which is ready to be used

AVCs *abbr* additional voluntary contributions

average /ˈæv(ə)rɪdʒ/ *noun* **1.** a number calculated by adding several figures together and dividing by the number of figures added ○ *the average for the last three months* or *the last three months'* *average* ○ *sales average* or *average of sales* **2.** □ **on average**, **on an average** in general ○ *On average, £15 worth of goods are stolen every day.* **3.** the sharing of the cost of damage or loss of a ship between the insurers and the owners ■ *adjective* **1.** the middle of a set of figures ○ *the average figures for the last three months* ○ *the average increase in salaries* **2.** not very good ○ *The company's performance has been only average.* ○ *He's only an average worker.* ■ *verb* to produce as an average figure ○ *Price increases have averaged 10% per annum.* ○ *Days lost through sickness have averaged twenty-two over the last four years.*

'...a share with an average rating might yield 5 per cent and have a PER of about 10' [*Investors Chronicle*]

'...the average price per kilogram for this season to the end of April has been 300 cents' [*Australian Financial Review*]

average adjustment /ˌæv(ə)rɪdʒ ə-ˈdʒʌstmənt/ *noun* a calculation of the share of cost of damage or loss of a ship

average age /ˌæv(ə)rɪdʒ ˈeɪdʒ/ *noun* the age of a group of people, calculated by adding all the ages and dividing by the number of people in the group ○ *The average age of our managers is 32.*

average earnings scheme /ˌæv(ə)rɪdʒ ˈɜːnɪŋz skiːm/ *noun* a pension scheme where the benefit is calculated annually on the earnings in each year

average out /ˌæv(ə)rɪdʒ ˈaʊt/ *verb* to come to a figure as an average ○ *It averages out at 10% per annum.* ○ *Sales increases have averaged out at 15%.*

average-sized /ˌævərɪdʒ ˈsaɪzd/ *adjective* not large or small ○ *They are an* average-sized company. ○ *He has an average-sized office.*

avert /əˈvɜːt/ *verb* to stop something happening ○ *The management made an increased offer in the hope of averting the strike.*

avoid /əˈvɔɪd/ *verb* to try not to do something ○ *My aim is to avoid paying too much tax.* ○ *We want to avoid direct competition with Smith Ltd.* ○ *The company is struggling to avoid bankruptcy.* (NOTE: you avoid something or avoid **doing** something)

avoidance /əˈvɔɪdns/ *noun* trying not to do something ○ *avoidance of an agreement* or *of a contract*

await /əˈweɪt/ *verb* to wait for ○ *We are awaiting the decision of the planning department.* ○ *They are awaiting a decision of the court.* ○ *The agent is awaiting our instructions.*

award /əˈwɔːd/ *noun* a decision which settles a dispute or claim ○ *an award by an industrial tribunal* ○ *The arbitrator's award was set aside on appeal.* ○ *The latest pay award has been announced.* ■ *verb* to decide the amount of money to be given to someone ○ *to award someone a salary increase* □ **to award a contract to someone** to decide that someone will have the contract to do work

award wage /əˈwɔːd weɪdʒ/ *noun* a rate of pay set by an industrial court or tribunal in Australia or New Zealand for a particular occupation

axe /æks/ *noun* □ **the project got the axe** the project was stopped ■ *verb* to cut or to stop ○ *to axe expenditure* ○ *Several thousand jobs are to be axed.* (NOTE: the usual US spelling is **ax**)

B

back /bæk/ *noun* the opposite side to the front ○ *Write your address on the back of the envelope.* ■ *adjective* referring to the past ○ *a back payment* ■ *adverb* as things were before ○ *He will pay back the money in monthly instalments.* ○ *The store sent back the cheque because the date was wrong.* ○ *The company went back on its agreement to supply at £1.50 a unit.* ■ *verb* □ **to back someone** to help someone financially ○ *The bank is backing us to the tune of £10,000.* ○ *She is looking for someone to back her project.*

'...the businesses we back range from start-up ventures to established companies in need of further capital for expansion' [*Times*]

backdate /bæk'deɪt/ *verb* to put an earlier date on a document such as a cheque or an invoice ○ *The pay increase is backdated to January 1st.*

back down /ˌbæk 'daʊn/ *verb* to give up something which you claimed

background /'bækgraʊnd/ *noun* **1.** past work or experience ○ *My background is in the steel industry.* ○ *The company is looking for someone with a background of success in the electronics industry.* ○ *She has a publishing background.* ○ *What is his background?* ○ *Do you know anything about his background?* **2.** past details ○ *He explained the background of the claim.* ○ *I know the contractual situation as it stands now, but can you fill in the background details?*

backhander /'bæk,hændə/ *noun* a bribe or money given to persuade someone to do something for you (*informal*) ○ *He was accused of taking backhanders from the company's suppliers.*

backing /'bækɪŋ/ *noun* **1.** support ○ *He gave his backing to the proposal.* ○ *The proposal has the backing of the*

board. **2.** financial support ○ *She has the backing of an Australian bank.* ○ *The company will succeed only if it has sufficient backing.* ○ *Who is providing the backing for the project?* ○ *Where does the backing for the project come from?* ○ *She gave her backing to the proposal.*

'...the company has received the backing of a number of oil companies who are willing to pay for the results of the survey' [*Lloyd's List*]

backlog /'bæklɒg/ *noun* work which has piled up waiting to be done, e.g. orders or letters ○ *The warehouse is trying to cope with a backlog of orders.* ○ *We're finding it hard to cope with the backlog of paperwork.*

back orders /'bæk ˌɔːdəz/ *plural noun* orders received and not yet fulfilled, usually because the item is out of stock ○ *It took the factory six weeks to clear all the accumulated back orders.*

back out /ˌbæk 'aʊt/ *verb* to stop being part of a deal or an agreement ○ *The bank backed out of the contract.* ○ *We had to cancel the project when our German partners backed out.*

back pay /'bæk peɪ/ *noun* a salary which has not been paid ○ *I am owed £500 in back pay.*

back payments /'bæk ˌpeɪmənts/ *plural noun* payments which are due

backpedal /'bæk,ped(ə)l/ *verb* to go back on something which was stated earlier ○ *When questioned by reporters about the redundancies, the MD backpedalled fast.* (NOTE: backpedalling- backpedalled)

backshift /'bækʃɪft/ *noun* the afternoon shift in a three-shift system, working from late afternoon until late evening (after the morning shift and before the night shift)

back tax /'bæk tæks/ *noun* a tax which is owed

back to work /ˌbæk tə 'wɜːk/ *noun* the act of returning to work after being unemployed

backtrack /'bæktræk/ *verb* to go back on what has been said before

back up /ˌbæk 'ʌp/ *verb* to support or help ○ *He brought along a file of documents to back up his claim.* ○ *The employee said his union had refused to back him up in his argument with management.*

backup /'bækʌp/ *adjective* supporting or helping ○ *We offer a free backup service to customers.* ○ *After a series of sales tours by representatives, the sales director sends backup letters to all the contacts.*

backup copy /'bækʌp ˌkɒpi/ *noun* a copy of a computer disk to be kept in case the original disk is damaged

back-up facility /'bæk ʌp fəˌsɪlɪti/ *noun* something that performs the same task or contains the same information as something else and can replace it if it fails

back wages /'bæk weɪdʒɪz/ *plural noun* same as **back pay**

bad /bæd/ *adjective* not good

bad buy /bæd 'baɪ/ *noun* a thing bought which was not worth the money paid for it

badge /bædʒ/ *noun* a piece of plastic or card which can be clipped to a person's shirt or coat and on which a name can be written ○ *All the staff at the exhibition must wear badges.* ○ *Visitors have to sign in at reception, and will be given visitors' badges.*

balance /'bæləns/ *noun* **1.** the amount to be put in one of the columns of an account to make the total debits and credits equal □ **balance in hand** cash held to pay small debts □ **balance brought down** *or* **forward** the closing balance of the previous period used as the opening balance of the current period □ **balance carried down** *or* **forward** the closing balance of the current period **2.** the rest of an amount owed ○ *You can pay £100 deposit and the balance within 60 days.* □ **balance due to us** the amount owed to

us which is due to be paid ■ *verb* **1.** (*of two sides in a balance sheet*) to be equal (i.e. the assets owned must always equal the total liabilities plus capital) □ **the February accounts do not balance** the two sides are not equal **2.** to calculate the amount needed to make the two sides of an account equal ○ *I have finished balancing the accounts for March.* **3.** to plan a budget so that expenditure and income are equal ○ *The president is planning for a balanced budget.*

balance sheet /'bæləns ʃiːt/ *noun* a statement of the financial position of a company at a particular time such as the end of the financial year or the end of a quarter showing the company's assets and liabilities ○ *Our accountant has prepared the balance sheet for the first half-year.* ○ *The company balance sheet for the last financial year shows a worse position than for the previous year.* ○ *The company balance sheet for 1984 shows a substantial loss.*

COMMENT: The balance sheet shows the state of a company's finances at a certain date; the profit and loss account shows the movements which have taken place since the end of the previous accounting period. A balance sheet must balance, with the basic equation that assets (i.e. what the company owns, including money owed to the company) must equal liabilities (i.e. what the company owes to its creditors) plus capital (i.e. what it owes to its shareholders). A balance sheet can be drawn up either in the horizontal form, with (in the UK) liabilities and capital on the left-hand side of the page (in the USA, it is the reverse) or in the vertical form, with assets at the top of the page, followed by liabilities, and capital at the bottom. Most are usually drawn up in the vertical format, as opposed to the more old-fashioned horizontal style.

ball /bɔːl/ *noun* □ **the ball is in the management's court** the management has to make the next move

ballot /'bælət/ *noun* **1.** an election where people vote for someone by marking a cross on a paper with a list of names ○ *Six names were put forward for three vacancies on the committee so a ballot was held.* **2.** a vote where voters decide on an issue by marking a piece of paper **3.** a selection made by taking papers at random out of a box ○ *The share issue was oversubscribed, so there was a ballot for the shares.* ■ *verb* to take a vote by ballot ○ *The union is balloting for the post of president.*

ballot box /'bælət bɒks/ *noun* a sealed box into which ballot papers are put

ballot paper /'bælət ˌpeɪpə/ *noun* a paper on which the voter marks a cross to show who they want to vote for

ballot-rigging /'bælət ˌrɪgɪŋ/ *noun* the illegal arranging of the votes in a ballot, so that a particular candidate or party wins

ban /bæn/ *noun* an order which forbids someone from doing something □ **to impose a ban on smoking** to make an order which forbids smoking □ **to lift the ban on smoking** to allow people to smoke ■ *verb* to forbid something ○ *The council has banned the sale of alcohol at the sports ground.* ○ *The company has banned drinking on company premises.* (NOTE: **banning – banned**)

band /bænd/ *noun* **1.** a strip of paper or plastic or a rubber ring put round articles to attach them together **2.** a range of figures between low and high, within which a figure can move ○ *a salary band* **3.** a grade or level ■ *verb* to divide into bands

bandwidth /'bændwɪdθ/ *noun* limits such as upper and lower performance levels or work hours that define a range

bank /bæŋk/ *noun* a business which holds money for its clients, lends money at interest, and trades generally in money ○ *Lloyds Bank* ○ *the First National Bank* ○ *the Royal Bank of Scotland* ○ *She put all her earnings into her bank.* ○ *I have had a letter from my bank telling me my account is overdrawn.*

bank account /'bæŋk əˌkaʊnt/ *noun* an account which a customer has with a bank, where the customer can deposit and withdraw money ○ *to open a bank account* ○ *to close a bank account* ○ *How much money do you have in your bank account?* ○ *If you let the balance in your bank account fall below £100, you have to pay bank charges.*

bank giro /'bæŋk ˌdʒaɪrəʊ/ *noun* a method used by clearing banks to transfer money rapidly from one account to another

bank holiday /bæŋk 'hɒlɪdeɪ/ *noun* a weekday which is a public holiday when the banks are closed ○ *New Year's Day is a bank holiday.* ○ *Are we paid for bank holidays in this job?*

banking /'bæŋkɪŋ/ *noun* the business of banks ○ *He is studying banking.* ○ *She has gone into banking.* □ **a banking crisis** a crisis affecting the banks

bank manager /'bæŋk ˌmænɪdʒə/ *noun* the person in charge of a branch of a bank ○ *They asked their bank manager for a loan.*

bankrupt /'bæŋkrʌpt/ *adjective*, *noun* a person who has been declared by a court not to be capable of paying their debts and whose affairs are put into the hands of a receiver ○ *a bankrupt property developer* ○ *She was adjudicated* or *declared bankrupt.* ○ *He went bankrupt after two years in business.* □ **undischarged bankrupt** a person who has been declared bankrupt and has not been released from that state ■ *verb* to make someone become bankrupt ○ *The recession bankrupted my father.*

bankruptcy /'bæŋkrʌptsi/ *noun* the state of being bankrupt ○ *The recession has caused thousands of bankruptcies.* (NOTE: plural is **bankruptcies**)

COMMENT: In the UK, 'bankruptcy' is applied only to individual persons, but in the USA the term is also applied to corporations. In the UK, a bankrupt cannot hold public office (for example, they cannot be elected an MP) and cannot be the director of a company. They also cannot borrow money. In the USA, there are two types of bankruptcy: 'involuntary', where the creditors ask for a person or corporation to be made bankrupt; and 'voluntary', where a person or corporation applies to be made bankrupt (in the UK, this is called 'voluntary liquidation').

bank transfer /'bæŋk ˌtrænsfɜː/ *noun* an act of moving money from a bank account to another account

bar chart /'bɑː tʃɑːt/ *noun* a chart where values or quantities are shown as columns of different heights set on a base line, the different lengths expressing the quantity of the item or unit

bargain /'bɑːgɪn/ *noun* **1.** an agreement on the price of something ○ *to strike a bargain* or *to make a bargain* **2.** something which is cheaper than usual ○ *That car is a (real) bargain at £500.* ■ *verb* to discuss a price for something ○ *You will have to bargain with the dealer if you want a discount.* (NOTE: you bargain **with** someone **over** or **about** or for something)

bargaining /'bɑːgɪnɪŋ/ *noun* the act of discussing between two people or groups, to achieve a settlement, usually wage increases for workers □ **to come to, to sit round the bargaining table** to meet for negotiations

bargaining level /'bɑːgɪnɪŋ ˌlev(ə)l/ *noun* the level at which bargaining takes place (i.e. at department level, whole company level, industry level, etc.)

bargaining position /'bɑːgɪnɪŋ pəˌzɪʃ(ə)n/ *noun* the statement of position by one group during negotiations

bargaining structure /'bɑːgɪnɪŋ ˌstrʌktʃə/ *noun* a structure of collective bargaining negotiations, comprising the subjects dealt with, the number of employees covered, whether the negotiations apply to a single factory or to the whole industry, etc.

bargaining table /'bɑːgɪnɪŋ ˌteɪb(ə)l/ *noun* a table where negotiators sit ○ *The arbitrators are trying to get the parties to return to the bargaining table.*

bargaining theory of wages /'bɑːgɪnɪŋ θɪəri əv ˌweɪdʒɪz/ *noun* a theory which states that the relative bargaining power of the employers and employees will decide wage levels

bargaining unit /'bɑːgɪnɪŋ ˌjuːnɪt/ *noun* a group of employees who negotiate with their employer to reach a collective agreement ○ *The bargaining unit had a meeting with top management in order to thrash out their differences.* ○ *The bargaining unit was supported by the union in its attempt to improve conditions.*

BARS *abbr* behaviourally anchored rating scales

base /beɪs/ *noun* **1.** the lowest or first position ○ *Turnover increased by 200%, but started from a low base.* **2.** a place where a company has its main office or factory, or a place where a businessperson's office is located ○ *The company has its base in London and branches in all the European countries.* ○ *He has an office in Madrid which he uses as a base while travelling in Southern Europe.* □ **to touch base** to get in touch with someone to see how things are going ■ *verb* **1.** to start to calculate or to negotiate from a position ○ *We based our calculations on the forecast turnover.* □ **based on** calculating from ○ *based on last year's figures* ○ *based on population forecasts* **2.** to set up a company or a person in a place ○ *The European manager is based in our London office.* ○ *Our overseas branch is based in the Bahamas.*

'…the base lending rate, or prime rate, is the rate at which banks lend to their top corporate borrowers' [*Wall Street Journal*]

'…other investments include a large stake in the Chicago-based insurance company' [*Lloyd's List*]

base pay /'beɪs peɪ/ *noun US* pay for a job which does not include extras such as overtime pay or bonuses

base period /'beɪs ˌpɪəriəd/ *US* **1.** a period against which comparisons are made **2.** the time that an employee must work before becoming eligible for state unemployment insurance benefits ○ *Because he had not worked for the base period, he had to rely on the support of his family when he lost his job.* ○ *The new government shortened the base period, in order to increase social service spending.*

basic /'beɪsɪk/ *adjective* **1.** normal **2.** most important **3.** simple, or from which everything starts ○ *She has a basic knowledge of the market.* ○ *To work at the cash desk, you need a basic qualification in maths.*

BASIC /'beɪsɪk/ *noun* a simple language for writing computer programs. Full form **beginner's all-purpose symbolic instruction code**

basically /'beɪsɪkli/ *adverb* seen from the point from which everything starts

basic award /ˈbeɪsɪk əˌwɔːd/ *noun* an award by an industrial tribunal based on the employee's age, length of service and current salary and equal to what the employee would have received if they had been made redundant (used in cases of unfair dismissal)

basic education /ˌbeɪsɪk edjʊˈkeɪʃ(ə)n/ *noun* a first level education, giving basic skills and information

basic industry /ˌbeɪsɪk ˈɪndəstri/ *noun* the most important industry of a country, e.g. coal, steel or agriculture

basic pay /ˌbeɪsɪk ˈpeɪ/ *noun* a normal salary without extra payments

basic rate tax /ˈbeɪsɪk reɪt ˌtæks/ *noun* the lowest rate of income tax

basics /ˈbeɪsɪks/ *plural noun* simple and important facts ○ *She has studied the basics of foreign exchange dealing.* □ **to get back to basics** to consider the main facts again

basic salary /ˌbeɪsɪk ˈsæləri/ *noun* same as **basic pay**

basic time /ˈbeɪsɪk taɪm/ *noun* the normal time taken to do a job, established by work study ○ *The basic time for the job was not accepted by the employees who found it too demanding.*

basic wage /ˌbeɪsɪk ˈweɪdʒ/ *noun* same as **basic pay** ○ *The basic wage is £110 a week, but you can expect to earn more than that with overtime.*

basis /ˈbeɪsɪs/ *noun* **1.** a point or number from which calculations are made ○ *We have calculated the turnover on the basis of a 6% price increase.* **2.** general terms of agreement or general principles on which something is decided □ **on a short-term, long-term basis** for a short or long period ○ *He has been appointed on a short-term basis.* ○ *We have three people working on a freelance basis.*

batch /bætʃ/ *noun* **1.** a group of items which are made at one time ○ *This batch of shoes has the serial number 25–02.* **2.** a group of documents which are processed at the same time ○ *Today's batch of invoices is ready to be mailed.* ○ *The factory is working on yesterday's batch of orders.* ○ *The accountant signed a batch of cheques.* ○ *We deal with the orders in batches of fifty at*

a time. ■ *verb* to put items together in groups ○ *to batch invoices* or *cheques*

batch processing /ˈbætʃ ˌprəʊsesɪŋ/ *noun* a system of data processing where information is collected into batches before being loaded into the computer

battery /ˈbæt(ə)ri/ *noun* **1.** a small object for storing electric power ○ *a battery-powered calculator* ○ *My phone battery needs charging.* **2.** a series of similar things ○ *Candidates have to pass a battery of tests.*

beat /biːt/ *verb* to win in a fight against someone ○ *They have beaten their rivals into second place in the computer market.*

beginner /bɪˈɡɪnə/ *noun* a person who is starting in a job

beginners' course /bɪˈɡɪnəz kɔːs/ *noun* a course for students who know nothing about the subject

behalf /bɪˈhɑːf/ *noun* □ **on behalf of** acting for someone or a company ○ *solicitors acting on behalf of the American company* ○ *I am writing on behalf of the minority shareholders.* ○ *She is acting on my behalf.*

behaviour /bɪˈheɪvjə/ *noun* the way in which someone behaves ○ *The manager had to talk to him about his disruptive behaviour.* (NOTE: the usual US spelling is **behavior**)

behavioural /bɪˈheɪvjərəl/ *adjective* referring to behaviour (NOTE: the usual US spelling is **behavioral**)

behavioural interview /bɪˈheɪvjərəl ˌɪntəvjuː/ *noun* a type of interview that aims to find out how applicants have behaved in the past when faced with the kind of situations they might meet in the job they are being interviewed for

behaviourally anchored rating scales /bɪˌheɪvjərəli ˌæŋkəd ˈreɪtɪŋ ˌskeɪlz/ *plural noun* a method of appraising performance based on typical performance criteria set for each individual member of staff. Abbr **BARS**

behavioural modelling /bɪˌheɪvjərəl ˈmɒd(ə)lɪŋ/ *noun* **1.** a process that tries to capture skills that people possess or use unconsciously in a form that makes it possible to teach those skills to others **2.** a technique used in skills training that involves encouraging somebody to imitate what another person does and then to retain the skill or type of behaviour they have learned from that other person

behavioural sciences /bɪ-ˌheɪvjərəl 'saɪənsɪz/ *plural noun* sciences which study human behaviour, such as sociology and psychology

behaviour expectation rate /bɪ-ˌheɪvjə ekspek'teɪʃ(ə)n reɪt/ *noun* same as **behaviourally anchored rating scales**

behind /bɪ'haɪnd/ *preposition* at the back or after ○ *The company is No. 2 in the market, about £4m behind their rivals.* ■ *adverb* □ **she has fallen behind with her loan repayments** she is late with her payments

belong /bɪ'lɒŋ/ *verb* □ **to belong to** to be the property of ○ *The company belongs to an old American banking family.*

belongings /bɪ'lɒŋɪŋz/ *plural noun* things which belong to someone ○ *The company is not responsible for personal belongings left in the cloakrooms.* ○ *When I was sacked I had five minutes to collect my personal belongings.*

below /bɪ'ləʊ/ *preposition* lower down than or less than ○ *We sold the property at below the market price.* ○ *You can get a ticket for New York at below £150 on the Internet.* ○ *The company has a policy of paying staff below the market rates.*

benchmark /'bentʃmɑːk/ *noun* **1.** a point or level which is important, and can be used as a reference when making evaluations or assessments **2.** a standard used to measure performance (NOTE: a benchmark was originally a set of computer programs that was used to measure how well a particular computer performed in comparison with similar models)

benchmarking /'bentʃmɑːkɪŋ/ *noun* the practice of measuring the performance of a company against the performance of other companies in the same sector

benchmark job /'bentʃmɑːk dʒɒbz/ *noun* a job used as a measure of performance

beneficiary /ˌbenɪ'fɪʃəri/ *noun* a person who gains money from something ○ *the beneficiaries of a will*

benefit /'benɪfɪt/ *noun* **1.** payments which are made to someone under a national or private insurance scheme ○ *She receives £75 a week as unemployment benefit.* ○ *Sickness benefit is paid monthly.* ○ *The insurance office sends out benefit cheques each week.* **2.** something of value given to an employee in addition to their salary ■ *verb* **1.** to make better or to improve ○ *A fall in inflation benefits the exchange rate.* **2.** □ **to benefit from** *or* **by something** to be improved by something, to gain more money because of something ○ *Exports have benefited from the fall in the exchange rate.* ○ *The employees have benefited from the profit-sharing scheme.*

'…the retail sector will also benefit from the expected influx of tourists' [*Australian Financial Review*]

'…what benefits does the executive derive from his directorship? Compensation has increased sharply in recent years and fringe benefits for directors have proliferated' [*Duns Business Month*]

'…salary is negotiable to £30,000, plus car and a benefits package appropriate to this senior post' [*Financial Times*]

'California is the latest state to enact a program forcing welfare recipients to work for their benefits' [*Fortune*]

'…salary range is $54,957 – $81,189, with a competitive benefits package' [*Washington Post*]

benefit in kind /ˌbenɪfɪt ɪn 'kaɪnd/ *noun* a benefit other than money received by an employee as part of their total compensation package, e.g. company cars or private health insurance. Such benefits are usually subject to tax.

benefits entitlement /'benɪfɪts ɪn-ˌtaɪt(ə)lmənt/ *noun* the type of social security benefit to which someone has the right

benefits plan /'benɪfɪts plæn/ *noun* a Canadian government programme intended to promote the employment of Canadian citizens and to provide Canadian manufacturers, consultants, contractors and service companies with opportunities to compete for projects

benevolent /bə'nev(ə)lənt/ *adjective* which does good to other people

benevolent fund /bə'nev(ə)lənt fʌnd/ *noun* a fund contributed to by employers and employees to provide employees and their families with financial help in case of sickness, injury or death ○ *Benevolent funds are set up to provide employees with more security.* ○ *The employer's contribution to the staff benevolent fund was the most attractive of the fringe benefits offered with the job.*

best practice /ˌbest 'præktɪs/ *noun* the most effective and efficient way to do something or to achieve a particular aim (NOTE: in business, best practice is often determined by benchmarking, that is by comparing the method one organisation uses to carry out a task with the methods used by other similar organisations and determining which method is most efficient and effective)

bi- /baɪ/ *prefix* twice □ **bi-monthly** twice a month □ **bi-annually** twice a year

bias /'baɪəs/ *noun* the practice of favouring of one group or person rather than another ○ *A postal survey will do away with bias.* ○ *The trainee interviewers were taught how to control bias and its effects.* ○ *Management has shown bias in favour of graduates in its recent appointments.*

biased /'baɪəst/ *adjective* referring to a person who favours one group rather than another ○ *She is biased towards younger staff.*

bid /bɪd/ *noun* **1.** an offer to buy something at a specific price □ **to make a cash bid** to offer to pay cash for something □ **to put in** *or* **enter a bid for something** to offer to buy something, usually in writing **2.** an offer to sell something or do a piece of work at a specific price ○ *She made the lowest bid for the job.* ■ *verb* to offer to buy □ **to bid for something** (*at an auction*) to offer to buy something □ **he bid £1,000 for the jewels** he offered to pay £1,000 for the jewels

bidding /'bɪdɪŋ/ *noun* **1.** the act of making offers to buy, usually at an auction □ **the bidding started at £1,000** the first and lowest bid was £1,000 □ **the bidding stopped at £250,000** the last bid, i.e. the successful bid, was for £250,000 **2.** an attempt by an employee to be considered for a vacant post in the same organisation ○ *When the vacancy was pinned up on the notice board there was much bidding for the job among the staff in the department.*

big business /bɪg 'bɪznɪs/ *noun* very large commercial firms

big picture /bɪg 'pɪktʃə/ *noun* a broad view of a subject that takes into account all the factors that are relevant to it and considers the future consequences of action taken now (*informal*)

bilateral /baɪ'læt(ə)rəl/ *adjective* between two parties or countries ○ *The minister signed a bilateral trade agreement.*

bilingual /baɪ'lɪŋgwəl/ *adjective* referring to a person who is able to speak and write two languages fluently ○ *a bilingual secretary* ○ *Secretaries working overseas are required to be bilingual.* ○ *Having worked for a French company for some years, he is now completely bilingual.* (NOTE: in the USA, the word **bilingual** normally means speaking English and Spanish)

bind /baɪnd/ *verb* to tie or to attach ○ *The company is bound by its articles of association.* ○ *He does not consider himself bound by the agreement which was signed by his predecessor.* (NOTE: **binding – bound**)

binder /'baɪndə/ *noun* **1.** a stiff cardboard cover for papers **2.** *US* a temporary agreement for insurance sent before the insurance policy is issued (NOTE: the British equivalent is **cover note**)

binding /'baɪndɪŋ/ *adjective* which legally forces someone to do something ○ *a binding contract* ○ *This document is not legally binding.* □ **the agreement is binding on all parties** all parties signing it must do what is agreed

biodata /'baɪəʊdeɪtə/ *noun* biographical information about an employee and their employment history

biological clock /ˌbaɪəlɒdʒɪk(ə)l 'klɒk/ *noun* the system inside a person's body which regulates cyclical activities such as biorhythms and has an effect on night-shift working

biorhythms /ˈbaɪəʊˌrɪðəmz/ *plural noun* recurring cycles of different lengths which some people believe affect a person's behaviour, sensitivity and intelligence

birth certificate /ˈbɜːθ səˌtɪfɪkət/ *noun* a paper giving details of a person's parents and date and place of birth

black /blæk/ *adjective* □ **in the black, into the black** in or into credit ○ *The company has moved into the black.* ○ *My bank account is still in the black.* ■ *verb* to forbid trading in specific goods or with specific suppliers ○ *Three firms were blacked by the government.* ○ *The union has blacked a trucking firm.*

black-coated worker /blæk ˈkəʊtɪd ˌwɜːkə/ *noun* a white-collar worker, a worker in an administrative job, not a manual worker

blacking /ˈblækɪŋ/ *noun* the refusal by employees to work with materials normally supplied by employees of another organisation who are engaged in industrial action ○ *Blacking of the rubber already delivered to the factory held up tyre production for days.* ○ *Blacking of materials was carried out by workers in another factory who were sympathetic to the strikers' cause.*

blackleg /ˈblækleg/ *noun* an employee who continues working when there is a strike

black list /ˈblæk lɪst/ *noun* **1.** a list of goods, people or companies which have been blacked **2.** a list of people considered by an employer to be too dangerous or disruptive to employ

blacklist /ˈblæklɪst/ *verb* to put goods, people or a company on a black list ○ *Their firm was blacklisted by the government.*

blame /bleɪm/ *noun* the act of saying that someone has done something wrong or that someone is responsible ○ *The sales staff got the blame for the poor sales figures.* ■ *verb* to say that someone has done something wrong or is responsible for a mistake ○ *The managing director blamed the chief accoun-*

tant for not warning her of the loss. ○ *The union is blaming the management for poor industrial relations.*

blamestorming /ˈbleɪmstɔːmɪŋ/ *noun* group discussion of the reasons why a project has failed or is late and who is to blame for it (*slang*) (NOTE: the term is modelled on the word 'brainstorming')

blame-time /ˈbleɪm taɪm/ *noun* the moment when an organisation announces publicly who or what is to blame for the failure of a project or task (*informal*)

blank /blæŋk/ *adjective* with nothing written ■ *noun* a space on a form which has to be completed ○ *Fill in the blanks and return the form to your local office.*

blank cheque /blæŋk ˈtʃek/ *noun* a cheque with the amount of money and the payee left blank, but signed by the drawer

blanket agreement /ˌblæŋkɪt əˈɡriːmənt/ *noun* an agreement which covers many different items

blanket dismissal /ˌblæŋkɪt dɪsˈmɪs(ə)l/ *noun* the dismissal of a group of employees because one unidentified employee is suspected of having committed an offence, and the others refuse to reveal the identity of the culprit

blank vote /blæŋk ˈvəʊt/ *noun* a voting paper which has not been marked

block /blɒk/ *noun* **1.** a series of items grouped together ○ *I bought a block of 6,000 shares.* **2.** a series of buildings forming a square with streets on all sides ○ *They want to redevelop a block in the centre of the town.* □ **a block of offices, an office block** a large building which only contains offices ■ *verb* to stop something taking place ○ *He used his casting vote to block the motion.*

block capitals /ˌblɒk ˈkæpɪt(ə)lz/, **block letters** /ˌblɒk ˈletəz/ *plural noun* capital letters such as A,B,C ○ *Write your name and address in block letters.*

blocked mobility /blɒkt məʊˈbɪlɪti/ *noun* limited potential for promotion that is not dependent on the educational background of the employee

block release /blɒk rɪˈliːs/ *noun* permission for an employee to attend a series of courses outside their place of work

blue circle rate /bluː 'sɜːk(ə)l reɪt/ *noun US* a pay rate which is below the minimum rate of an employee's evaluated pay level

blue-collar union /bluː 'kɒlə ˌjuːnjən/ *noun* a trade union formed mainly of blue-collar workers

blue-collar worker /bluː 'kɒlə ˌwɜːkə/ *noun* a manual worker in a factory

Blue Laws /'bluː lɔːz/ *plural noun US* regulations governing business activities on Sundays

blueprint /'bluːprɪnt/ *noun* a plan or model of something ○ *The agreement will be the blueprint for other agreements in the industry.*

blueshirt /'bluːʃɜːt/ *noun* an employee of the computer company IBM

bluetooth /'bluːtuːθ/ *trademark* a type of technology allowing for communication between mobile phones, computers and the Internet

board /bɔːd/ *noun* **1.** ◊ **board of directors 2.** a group of people who run an organisation, trust or society **3.** an official group of people **4.** an official body **5.** a large flat piece of wood or card

'CEOs, with their wealth of practical experience, are in great demand and can pick and choose the boards they want to serve on' [*Duns Business Month*]

board interview /'bɔːd ˌɪntəvjuː/ *noun* an interview in which a candidate is asked questions by several representatives of an organisation

board meeting /'bɔːd ˌmiːtɪŋ/ *noun* a meeting of the directors of a company

board member /'bɔːd ˌmembə/ *noun* one of the directors of a company

board of directors /'bɔːd əv daɪ'rektəz/ *noun* **1.** *GB* a group of directors elected by the shareholders to run a company ○ *The bank has two representatives on the board.* ○ *He sits on the board as a representative of the bank.* ○ *Two directors were removed from the board at the AGM.* **2.** *US* a group of people elected by the shareholders to draw up company policy and to appoint the president and other executive offi-

cers who are responsible for managing the company. See also the comment at **director**

'...a proxy is the written authorization an investor sends to a stockholder meeting conveying his vote on a corporate resolution or the election of a company's board of directors' [*Barrons*]

boardroom /'bɔːdruːm/ *noun* a room where the directors of a company meet

board seat /'bɔːd siːt/ *noun* a position as a member of a board, especially a board of directors

board secretary /'bɔːd ˌsekrɪt(ə)ri/ *noun* a person who acts as secretary to a board of directors or governors

body language /'bɒdɪ ˌlæŋgwɪdʒ/ *noun* gestures, expressions and movements which show what somebody's response is to a situation ○ *Trainee salespeople learn how to interpret a customer's body language.* ○ *The interviewer of prospective marketing managers observed the body language of the candidates very carefully.* ○ *The candidate claimed to be very confident about taking the job, but her body language was saying the opposite.*

bogus degree /ˌbəʊgəs dɪ'griː/ *noun* a university degree or similar qualification that has little or no value because it is awarded by an organisation that is not recognised as a genuinely educational institution by the country in which it operates (NOTE: bogus degrees are usually awarded by organisations with names that are similar to those of respected universities, which take advantage of the naivety of foreign students)

bona fide /ˌbəʊnə 'faɪdi/ *adjective* trustworthy, which can be trusted □ **a bona fide offer** an offer which is made honestly

bona fide union /ˌbəʊnə ˌfaɪdi 'juːnjən/ *noun* a union which is freely chosen by employees without any influence from the employer ○ *Most of the workers in the industry are members of bona fide unions.*

bonus /'bəʊnəs/ *noun* an extra payment in addition to a normal payment

bonus scheme /'bəʊnəs skiːm/, **bonus system** /'bəʊnəs ˌsɪstəm/ *noun* a scheme by which workers can earn bonuses (such as for exceeding targets or completing a task within the deadline)

bonus share /ˈbəʊnəs ʃeə/ *noun* an extra share given to an existing shareholder

book /bʊk/ *noun* a set of sheets of paper attached together □ **a company's books** the financial records of a company ■ *verb* to order or to reserve something ○ *to book a room in a hotel* or *a table at a restaurant* or *a ticket on a plane* ○ *I booked a table for 7.45.* ○ *He booked a ticket through to Cairo.* □ **to book someone into a hotel** *or* **on/onto a flight** to order a room or a plane ticket for someone else ○ *He was booked on the 09.00 flight to Zurich.* □ **the hotel, flight is fully booked** *or* **is booked up** all the rooms *or* seats are reserved ○ *The restaurant is booked up over the Christmas period.*

booking /ˈbʊkɪŋ/ *noun* the act of reserving something such as a room or a seat ○ *Hotel bookings have fallen since the end of the tourist season.* □ **to confirm a booking** to say that a booking is certain

booking clerk /ˈbʊkɪŋ klɑːk/ *noun* a person who sells tickets in a booking office

bookkeeper /ˈbʊkkiːpə/ *noun* a person who keeps the financial records of a company or an organisation

bookkeeping /ˈbʊkkiːpɪŋ/ *noun* the keeping of the financial records of a company or an organisation

booklet /ˈbʊklət/ *noun* a small book with a paper cover

book sales /ˈbʊk seɪlz/ *plural noun* sales as recorded in the sales book

bookwork /ˈbʊkwɜːk/ *noun* the keeping of financial records

boomerang worker /ˈbuːməræŋ ˌwɜːkə/ *noun* an employee who returns to work for a previous employer (*slang*)

boom industry /ˈbuːm ˌɪndəstri/ *noun* an industry which is expanding rapidly

boost /buːst/ *noun* help given to increase something ○ *This publicity will give sales a boost.* ○ *The government hopes to give a boost to industrial development.* ■ *verb* to make something increase ○ *We expect our publicity campaign to boost sales by 25%.* ○ *The company hopes to boost its market share.* ○ *Incentive schemes are boosting production.*

'…the company expects to boost turnover this year to FFr 16bn from FFr 13.6bn last year' [*Financial Times*]

boot /buːt/ *noun* □ **to get the boot** to be sacked (*informal*)

boot camp /ˈbuːt kæmp/ *noun US* a demanding programme for new employees, designed to teach them technical skills and introduce them to the corporate culture of the organisation they are joining (NOTE: boot camps are modelled on the basic training of the US Marine Corps)

border crosser /ˈbɔːdə krɒsə/ *noun* an employee who has a variety of skills and is able to move from job to job within a company (*slang*)

borderline case /ˈbɔːdəlaɪn keɪs/ *noun* **1.** a situation which is not easy to resolve, being either one way or the other **2.** a worker who may or may not be recommended some action such as for promotion or dismissal

borrowings /ˈbɒrəʊɪŋz/ *plural noun* money borrowed ○ *The company's borrowings have doubled.*

boss /bɒs/ *noun* an employer or person in charge of a company or an office (*informal*) ○ *If you want a pay rise, go and talk to your boss.* ○ *He became a director when he married the boss's daughter.*

bottom /ˈbɒtəm/ *noun* the lowest part or point □ **the bottom has fallen out of the market** sales have fallen below what previously seemed to be the lowest point □ **rock-bottom price** the lowest price of all ■ *verb* to reach the lowest point □ **the market has bottomed out** the market has reached the lowest point and does not seem likely to fall further

bottom line /ˌbɒtəm ˈlaɪn/ *noun* **1.** the last line on a balance sheet indicating profit or loss **2.** the final decision on a matter ○ *The bottom line was that any workers showing dissatisfaction with conditions would be fired.*

bottom price /'bɒtəm praɪs/ *noun* the lowest price

boycott /'bɔɪkɒt/ *noun* a refusal to buy or to deal in certain products ○ *The union organised a boycott against* or *of imported cars.* ■ *verb* to refuse to buy or deal in a product ○ *We are boycotting all imports from that country.* □ **the management has boycotted the meeting** the management has refused to attend the meeting

bracket /'brækɪt/ *noun* a group of items or people taken together □ **people in the middle-income bracket** people with average incomes, not high or low □ **she is in the top tax bracket** she pays the highest level of tax

brain /breɪn/ *noun* a part of the body in which decisions are taken □ **she is the brains behind the organisation** she is the clever person who is running the organisation

brain drain /'breɪn dreɪn/ *noun* the movement of clever people away from a country to find better jobs in other countries

brainiac /'breɪniæk/ *noun* a very intelligent and creative employee who is also unpredictable and eccentric (slang)

brainstorming /'breɪnˌstɔːmɪŋ/ *noun* an intensive discussion by a small group of people as a method of producing new ideas or solving problems

brainstorming session /'breɪnˌstɔːmɪŋ ˌseʃ(ə)n/ *noun* a meeting to thrash out problems, where everyone puts forward different ideas

branch /brɑːntʃ/ *noun* **1.** the local office of a bank or large business, or a local shop which is part of a large chain **2.** the local office of a union, based in a factory

branch committee /brɑːntʃ kəˈmɪti/ *noun* an elected committee of union members which deals with general day-to-day problems

branch manager /brɑːntʃ ˈmænɪdʒə/ *noun* a person in charge of a branch of a company

'...a leading manufacturer of business, industrial and commercial products requires a branch manager to head up its mid-western Canada operations based in Winnipeg' [*Globe and Mail (Toronto)*]

branch office /brɑːntʃ ˈɒfɪs/ *noun* a less important office, usually in a different town or country from the main office

breach /briːtʃ/ *noun* a failure to carry out the terms of an agreement

breach of contract /ˌbriːtʃ əv ˈkɒntrækt/ *noun* the failure to do something which has been agreed in a contract □ **the company is in breach of contract** the company has failed to do what was agreed in the contract

breach of discipline /ˌbriːtʃ əv ˈdɪsɪplɪn/ *noun* an action which goes against the company rules or against instructions

breadwinner /'bredwɪnə/ *noun* a person who earns the main income in a family, and so provides food for the others

break /breɪk/ *verb* **1.** to fail to carry out the duties of a contract ○ *The company has broken the contract* or *the agreement by selling at a lower price.* □ **to break an engagement to do something** not to do what has been agreed **2.** to cancel a contract ○ *The company is hoping to be able to break the contract.* (NOTE: **breaking – broke – broken**)

break down /ˌbreɪk ˈdaʊn/ *verb* **1.** to stop working because of mechanical failure ○ *The fax machine has broken down.* **2.** to stop ○ *Negotiations broke down after six hours.* **3.** to show all the items in a total list of costs or expenditure ○ *We broke the expenditure down into fixed and variable costs.*

breakdown /'breɪkdaʊn/ *noun* **1.** an act of stopping working because of mechanical failure **2.** an act of stopping talking ○ *a breakdown in wage negotiations* **3.** an act of showing details item by item ○ *Give me a breakdown of investment costs.*

break off /ˌbreɪk ˈɒf/ *verb* to stop ○ *We broke off the discussion at midnight.* ○ *Management broke off negotiations with the union.*

break point /'breɪk pɔɪnt/ *noun* the dividing point between one job or element and the next, or between one level established on a job evaluation and the next ○ *A break point was established* *between unskilled and semi-skilled jobs, separating the two categories, with different rates of pay.*

break up /ˌbreɪk ˈʌp/ *verb* **1.** to split something large into small sections ○ *The company was broken up and separate divisions sold off.* **2.** to come to an end ○ *The meeting broke up at 12.30.*

bribe /braɪb/ *noun* money given to someone in authority to get them to help ○ *The minister was dismissed for taking bribes.* ■ *verb* to pay someone money to get them to do something illegal or dishonest for you

bribery /ˈbraɪb(ə)ri/ *noun* the illegal or dishonest act of offering somebody cash or a gift in order to persuade them to give you an unfair advantage

bridge job /ˈbrɪdʒ dʒɒb/ *noun* a position designed to help the movement of employees from one job category to another ○ *She was given a bridge job while being considered for real promotion.* ○ *The bridge job between machinist and supervisor consisted of some tasks from each of these posts.*

brief /briːf/ *noun* instructions given to someone ○ *He went into the negotiations with the brief to get a deal at any price.* ■ *verb* to explain something to someone in detail ○ *The salespeople were briefed on the new product.* ○ *The managing director briefed the board on the progress of the negotiations.*

briefing /ˈbriːfɪŋ/ *noun* an act of telling someone details ○ *All sales staff have to attend a sales briefing on the new product.*

briefing group /ˈbriːfɪŋ gruːp/ *noun* a group of people who are briefed, especially a group who take part in team briefings

briefing session /ˈbriːfɪŋ ˌseʃ(ə)n/ *noun* a meeting between managers and staff where the staff are informed of matters such as decisions or plans

brightsizing /ˈbraɪtsaɪzɪŋ/ *noun* the practice of reducing the size of the workforce by making the most capable or intelligent employees redundant (NOTE: this usually happens accidentally when a company has a policy of laying off its most re-

cently recruited employees first, since these are often the best trained and best educated members of its staff)

bring /brɪŋ/ *verb* to come to a place with someone or something ○ *He brought his documents with him.* ○ *The finance director brought her assistant to take notes of the meeting.* (NOTE: **bringing- brought**)

bring down /ˌbrɪŋ ˈdaʊn/ *verb* **1.** to reduce ○ *Petrol companies have brought down the price of oil.* **2.** to add a figure to an account at the end of a period to balance expenditure and income ○ *balance brought down: £365.15*

bring forward /ˌbrɪŋ ˈfɔːwəd/ *verb* **1.** to make earlier ○ *to bring forward the date of repayment* ○ *The date of the next meeting has been brought forward to March.* **2.** to take an account balance from the end of the previous period as the starting point for the current period ○ *balance brought forward: £365.15*

bring in /ˌbrɪŋ ˈɪn/ *verb* to earn an amount of interest ○ *The shares bring in a small amount.*

bring out /ˌbrɪŋ ˈaʊt/ *verb* to produce something new ○ *They are bringing out a new model of the car for the Motor Show.*

bring up /ˌbrɪŋ ˈʌp/ *verb* to refer to something for the first time ○ *The chairman brought up the question of redundancy payments.*

broadbanding /ˈbrɔːdbændɪŋ/ *noun* the reorganisation of the ranges of pay that an organisation offers for various types of jobs, so that its pay scale has fewer, but wider bands (NOTE: broadbanding makes the pay structure more flexible and is especially suited to flat organisations)

broke /brəʊk/ *adjective* having no money (*informal*) ○ *The company is broke.* ○ *She cannot pay for the new car because she is broke.*

BR tax code /ˌbiː ɑː ˈtæks kəʊd/ *noun* a number given to an employee and sent to the employer, which allows the employer to deduct tax from the employee's pay at the correct rate

BS *plural noun* quality standards which apply to various products or services. Full form **British Standards**

B share /'biː ʃeə/ *noun* an ordinary share with special voting rights (often owned by the founder of the company and their family)

buddy system /'bʌdi ˌsɪstəm/ *noun* US an on-the-job training system, where a trainee works with an experienced employee ○ *The buddy system teaches the trainee the practical realities of the job.* ○ *The company operates both a buddy system and some off-the-job classroom instruction for its trainees.*

budget /'bʌdʒɪt/ *noun* a plan of expected spending and income for a period of time ○ *to draw up a budget for salaries for the coming year* ○ *We have agreed the budgets for next year.* ■ *verb* to plan probable income and expenditure ○ *We are budgeting for £10,000 of sales next year.*

'...he budgeted for further growth of 150,000 jobs (or 2.5 per cent) in the current financial year' [*Sydney Morning Herald*]

'...the Federal government's budget targets for employment and growth are within reach according to the latest figures' [*Australian Financial Review*]

budgetary /'bʌdʒɪt(ə)ri/ *adjective* referring to a budget

budgetary policy /ˌbʌdʒɪt(ə)ri 'pɒlɪsi/ *noun* the policy of planning income and expenditure

budget variance /ˌbʌdʒɪt 'veəriəns/ *noun* the difference between the cost as estimated for a budget and the actual cost

build /bɪld/ *verb* to make by putting pieces together ○ *The new director's job is to build a sales structure.* ○ *They want to demolish the old factory and build an office block on the site.* □ **to build on past experience** to use experience as a base on which to act in the future

building /'bɪldɪŋ/ *noun* a structure such as a house, factory or office block ○ *They have redeveloped the site of the old office building.*

building site /'bɪldɪŋ saɪt/ *noun* a place where a building is being constructed ○ *All visitors to the site must wear safety helmets.*

build into /'bɪld ɪntuː/ *verb* to add something to something being set up ○ *You must build all the forecasts into the budget.* □ **we have built 10% for contingencies into our cost forecast** we have added 10% to our basic forecast to allow for items which may appear suddenly

build up /ˌbɪld 'ʌp/ *verb* **1.** to create something by adding pieces together ○ *She bought several shoe shops and gradually built up a chain.* **2.** to expand something gradually ○ *to build up a profitable business* ○ *to build up a team of sales representatives*

buildup /'bɪldʌp/ *noun* a gradual increase ○ *a buildup in sales* or *a sales buildup* ○ *There will be a big publicity buildup before the launch of the new model.* ○ *There has been a buildup of complaints about customer service.*

built-in /'bɪlt ɪn/ *adjective* forming part of the system or of a machine ○ *The PC has a built-in modem.* ○ *The accounting system has a series of built-in checks.* ○ *The microwave has a built-in clock.*

bulletin board /'bʊlɪtɪn bɔːd/ *noun* a board fixed to a wall where notices can be put up

bully /'bʊli/ *noun* a person who is in a powerful position and continually harasses others ■ *verb* to threaten and intimidate other members of staff ○ *She complained that she was being bullied by the assistant manager.* (NOTE: **bullies- bullying- bullied**)

bullying /'bʊliɪŋ/ *noun* intimidation and harassment of someone by another member of staff in a more powerful position

bumping /'bʌmpɪŋ/ *noun* **1.** US a lay-off procedure that allows an employee with greater seniority to displace a more junior employee ○ *The economic recession led to extensive bumping in companies where only the most qualified were retained for some jobs.* ○ *The trade unions strongly objected to bumping practices since they considered that many employees were being laid off unfairly.* **2.** the situation where a senior employee takes the place of a junior (in a restaurant)

Bundy /'bʌndi/ *noun* a timing system in Australia and New Zealand that records the time at which employees arrive at and leave their place of work

Bundy off /ˌbʌndi 'ɒf/ *verb* (*in Australia and New Zealand*) to clock off from work

Bundy on /ˌbʌndi 'ɒn/ *verb* (*in Australia and New Zealand*) to clock on for work

burden /'bɜːdn/ *noun* a heavy load which you have to carry

bureau /'bjʊərəʊ/ *noun* an office which specialises in a specific service

bureaucracy /bjʊə'rɒkrəsi/ *noun* a system of administration where an individual person's responsibilities and powers are strictly defined and processes are strictly followed

bureaucratic /ˌbjʊərə'krætɪk/ *adjective* following strict administrative principles

burn out /ˌbɜːn 'aʊt/ *verb* to become tired and incapable for further work because of stress (NOTE: **burning- burnt or burned**)

burnout /'bɜːnaʊt/, **burnt out case** /'bɜːnt aʊt keɪs/ *noun* a case where an employee is tired and incapable of doing any more work as a result of overwork ○ *He's a burnt-out case and had to give up his job.*

business /'bɪznɪs/ *noun* **1.** work in buying or selling ○ *We do a lot of business with Japan.* ○ *Business is expanding.* ○ *Business is slow.* ○ *Repairing cars is 90% of our business.* ○ *We did more business in the week before Christmas than we usually do in a month.* ○ *Strikes are very bad for business.* ○ *What's your line of business?* □ **to be in business** to run a commercial firm □ **on business** doing commercial work ○ *She had to go abroad on business.* ○ *The chairman is in Holland on business.* **2.** a commercial company ○ *He owns a small car repair business.* ○ *She runs a business from her home.* ○ *I set up in business as an insurance broker.* **3.** affairs discussed ○ *The main*

business of the meeting was finished by 3 p.m.

business address /'bɪznɪs əˌdres/ *noun* the details of number, street and town where a company is located

business agent /'bɪznɪs ˌeɪdʒənt/ *noun* US the chief local official of a trade union

business card /'bɪznɪs kɑːd/ *noun* a card showing a businessperson's name and the name and address of the company they work for

business centre /'bɪznɪs ˌsentə/ *noun* the part of a town where the main banks, shops and offices are located

business class /'bɪznɪs klɑːs/ *noun* a type of airline travel which is less expensive than first class and more comfortable than economy class

business college /'bɪznɪs ˌkɒlɪdʒ/ *noun* same as **business school**

business correspondence /'bɪznɪs kɒrɪˌspɒndəns/ *noun* letters concerned with a business

business correspondent /'bɪznɪs kɒrɪˌspɒndənt/ *noun* a journalist who writes articles on business news for newspapers

business cycle /'bɪznɪs ˌsaɪk(ə)l/ *noun* the period during which trade expands, slows down and then expands again

business equipment /'bɪznɪs ɪˌkwɪpmənt/ *noun* the machines used in an office

business expenses /'bɪznɪs ɪkˌspensɪz/ *plural noun* money spent on running a business, not on stock or assets

business letter /'bɪznɪs ˌletə/ *noun* a letter which deals with business matters

businessman /'bɪznɪsmæn/, **businesswoman** /'bɪznɪsˌwʊmən/ *noun* a man or woman engaged in business

business plan /'bɪznɪs plæn/ *noun* a document drawn up to show how a business is planned to work, with cash flow forecasts, sales forecasts, etc., often used when trying to raise a loan, or when setting up a new business

business school /'bɪznɪs skuːl/ *noun* an educational institution at university level that offers courses in subjects related to business such as management, technology, finance, and interpersonal skills (NOTE: business schools provide courses of varying length and level, up to Master of Business Administration, and besides catering for full-time students, also offer part-time courses and distance learning to people already in employment)

busy /'bɪzi/ *adjective* occupied in doing something or in working ○ *He is busy preparing the annual accounts.* ○ *The manager is busy at the moment, but she will be free in about fifteen minutes.* ○ *The busiest time of year for stores is the week before Christmas.* ○ *Summer is the busy season for hotels.* □ **the line is busy** the telephone line is being used

busy season /'bɪzi ˌsiːz(ə)n/ *noun* the period when a company is busy

buyout /'baɪaʊt/ *noun* the purchase of a controlling interest in a company

'…we also invest in companies whose growth and profitability could be improved by a management buyout' [*Times*]

'…in a normal leveraged buyout, the acquirer raises money by borrowing against the assets or cash flow of the target company' [*Fortune*]

C

CAC *abbr* Central Arbitration Committee

cafeteria /ˌkæfəˈtɪəriə/ *noun* a self-service restaurant which belongs to a factory or office, where the staff can eat ○ *Most people have lunch in the staff cafeteria.*

cafeteria-style benefits plan /kæfəˌtɪəriə staɪl ˈbenɪfɪts plæn/ *noun* a scheme for benefits for employees, where the employee can choose from a range of benefits on offer, depending on different levels of contribution

calculate /ˈkælkjʊlcɪt/ *verb* **1.** to find the answer to a problem using numbers ○ *The bank clerk calculated the rate of exchange for the dollar.* **2.** to estimate ○ *I calculate that we have six months' stock left.*

calculating machine /ˈkælkjʊleɪtɪŋ məˌʃiːn/ *noun* same as **calculator**

calculation /ˌkælkjʊˈleɪʃ(ə)n/ *noun* the answer to a problem in mathematics ○ *According to my calculations, we have six months' stock left.* □ **we are £20,000 out in our calculations** we have £20,000 too much or too little

calculator /ˈkælkjʊleɪtə/ *noun* an electronic machine which does calculations such as adding, subtracting and multiplying ○ *He worked out the discount on his calculator.*

calendar /ˈkælɪndə/ *noun* a book or set of sheets of paper showing the days and months in a year, often attached to pictures ○ *For the New Year, the garage sent me a calendar with photographs of old cars.*

calendar month /ˈkælɪndə mʌnθ/ *noun* a whole month as on a calendar, from the 1st to the 30th or 31st ○ *Ninety*

days' credit is almost three calendar months.

calendar year /ˈkælɪndə jɪə/ *noun* a year from the 1st January to 31st December

call /kɔːl/ *noun* **1.** a conversation on the telephone □ **to make a call** to dial and speak to someone on the telephone □ **to log calls** to note all details of telephone calls made **2.** a demand for repayment of a loan by a lender **3.** an official request for something **4.** a visit ○ *The salespeople make six calls a day.* ■ *verb* **1.** to telephone someone ○ *I'll call you at your office tomorrow.* **2.** □ **to call on someone** to visit someone ○ *Our salespeople call on their best accounts twice a month.* **3.** to ask someone to do something □ **the union called a strike** the union told its members to go on strike

call-back pay /ˈkɔːl bæk peɪ/ *noun* pay given to an employee who has been called back to work after their normal working hours

call centre /ˈkɔːl ˈsentə/ *noun* a department or business that operates a large number of telephones and specialises in making calls to sell products or in receiving calls from customers to helplines or information or after-sales services (NOTE: a call centre often acts as the central point of contact between an organisation and its customers)

caller /ˈkɔːlə/ *noun* **1.** a person who telephones **2.** a person who visits

call in /ˌkɔːl ˈɪn/ *verb* **1.** to visit ○ *Their sales representative called in twice last week.* **2.** to telephone to make contact ○ *We ask the reps to call in every Friday to report the weeks' sales.* **3.** to ask for a debt to be paid

call-in pay /ˈkɔːl ɪn peɪ/ *noun* payment guaranteed to employees who report for work even if there is no work for them to do ○ *Call-in pay is often necessary to ensure the attendance of workers where there is at least the possibility of work needing to be done.*

call off /ˌkɔːl 'ɒf/ *verb* to ask for something not to take place ○ *The union has called off the strike.* ○ *The deal was called off at the last moment.*

can /kæn/ *verb* to dismiss somebody from employment (*informal*) (NOTE: **canning- canned**)

cancel /'kænsəl/ *verb* to stop something which has been agreed or planned ○ *The manager is still ill, so the interviews planned for this week have been cancelled.* (NOTE: **cancelling-cancelled**)

cancellation /ˌkænsə'leɪʃ(ə)n/ *noun* the act of stopping something which has been agreed or planned ○ *the cancellation of an appointment* ○ *the cancellation of an agreement*

cancellation clause /ˌkænsə-'leɪʃ(ə)n klɔːz/ *noun* a clause in a contract which states the terms on which the contract may be cancelled

cancel out /ˌkænsəl 'aʊt/ *verb* (*of two things*) to balance or act against each other and so make each other invalid ○ *The two clauses cancel each other out.* ○ *Higher costs have cancelled out the increased sales revenue.*

candidate /'kændɪdeɪt/ *noun* a person who applies for or is considered suitable for a job or for a training course ○ *I don't consider him as suitable candidate for management training.* ○ *Ten out of fifty candidates were shortlisted.* ○ *The candidates for department manager were each given a personality test and an intelligence test.*

can-do /'kæn duː/ *adjective* go-ahead, liking to cope with new challenges ○ *She's a can-do individual.*

canteen /kæn'tiːn/ *noun* a restaurant which belongs to a factory or office, where the staff can eat ○ *Most people have lunch in the canteen.*

cap /kæp/ *noun* an upper limit placed on something, such as an interest rate (the opposite, i.e. a lower limit, is a 'floor') ■ *verb* to place an upper limit

on something ○ *to cap a local authority's budget* ○ *to cap a department's budget* (NOTE: **capping – capped**)

capability /ˌkeɪpə'bɪlɪti/ *noun* a skill which an employee has learnt and which can be applied to their work

capable /'keɪpəb(ə)l/ *adjective* efficient ○ *She is a very capable departmental manager.* (NOTE: you are **capable of** something or **of doing** something)

capacity /kə'pæsɪti/ *noun* **1.** the amount which can be produced, or the amount of work which can be done ○ *industrial* or *manufacturing* or *production capacity* □ **to work at full capacity** to do as much work as possible **2.** the amount of space □ **to use up spare** or **excess capacity** to make use of time or space which is not fully used **3.** ability ○ *She has a particular capacity for detailed business deals with overseas companies.* **4.** □ **in one's capacity** as acting as ○ *I signed the document in my capacity as chairman.*

'…analysts are increasingly convinced that the industry simply has too much capacity' [*Fortune*]

capacity planning /kə'pæsɪti ˌplænɪŋ/ *noun* forward planning to relate production needs to anticipated demand

capital bonus /ˌkæpɪt(ə)l 'bəʊnəs/ *noun* an extra payment by an insurance company which is produced by a capital gain

capital goods /'kæpɪt(ə)l gʊdz/ *plural noun* machinery, buildings and raw materials which are used to make other goods

captain of industry /ˌkæptɪnz əv 'ɪndəstri/ *noun* a head of a major industrial company

car /kɑː/ *noun* a small motor vehicle for carrying people

carbon copy /ˌkɑːbən 'kɒpi/ *noun* a copy made with carbon paper ○ *Give me the original, and file the carbon copy.*

carbonless /'kɑːbənləs/ *adjective* which makes a copy without using carbon paper ○ *Our reps use carbonless order pads.*

card /kɑːd/ *noun* **1.** stiff paper ○ *We have printed the instructions on thick white card.* **2.** a small piece of cardboard or plastic, usually with information printed on it ○ *He showed his staff card to get a discount in the store.* **3.** a postcard □ **to get one's cards** to be dismissed

card-carrying /'kɑːd ˌkæriɪŋ/ *adjective* referring to a person who has a membership card of an organisation such as a union ○ *The union had many sympathisers, but few actual card-carrying members.*

card vote /'kɑːd vəʊt/ *noun* a vote at a Trades Union Congress where the representatives of unions vote according to the numbers of union members

career /kə'rɪə/ *noun* a job which you are trained for and which you expect to do all your life ○ *He made his career in electronics.* ○ *She has had a varied career, having worked in education and industry.* ○ *The company offered its employees no advice on their future careers.* □ **to embark on a career** to start a career □ **to pursue a career as** to follow a career as

career anchor /kə'rɪər ˌæŋkə/ *noun* a basic, sometimes subconscious factor that strongly influences all the choices and decisions that people make when shaping their careers (NOTE: a career anchor may be a special skill that somebody wants to use, an ambition somebody wants to achieve, or an ethical principle that is particularly important to somebody, but it always something that is very important to that person's sense of who they are)

career break /kə'rɪə breɪk/ *noun* a period when an employee leaves a career job for several years to undertake another activity such as studying for a degree or having a baby and then returns at the same level

career change /kə'rɪə tʃeɪndʒ/ *noun* a change in a person's profession or in the type of job they do, that often involves going to work for a different employer (NOTE: career changes may be planned as part of somebody's CPD or career development, or may be forced on somebody as a result of

redundancy, ill-health, or a change in their personal circumstances.)

career development /kə'rɪə dɪˌveləpmənt/ *noun* the planning of an employee's future career in an organisation ○ *a career development programme* ○ *If the company does not spend more time on career development, many employees will leave.* ○ *Career development involves a very comprehensive training programme.*

career expectations /kə'rɪər ekspekˌteɪʃ(ə)nz/ *plural noun* hopes which an employee has of how their career will develop in terms of matters such as promotion or salary

career ladder /kə'rɪə ˌlædə/ *noun* a sequence of jobs within an organisation or department, starting with the most junior and ending with most senior, through which an employee can advance in the course of their working life

career-limiting move /kə'rɪə ˌlɪmɪtɪŋ muːv/ *noun* full form of **CLM**

career opportunities /kə'rɪər ɒpəˌtjuːnɪtiz/, **career prospects** /kə'rɪə ˌprɒspekts/ *plural noun* possibilities of advancement in a career

career path /kə'rɪə pɑːθ/ *noun* a planned logical sequence of jobs within one or more professions through which a person can progress in the course of their working life (NOTE: it is much easier to plan a career path when the market is stable and there is little change in business conditions; in uncertain times people need to be more adaptable and the idea of a planned career path has much less value, according to some experts)

career pattern /kə'rɪə ˌpætn/ *noun* the way in which a person has spent their employed life (such as years employed in each firm, promotions or salary)

career planning /kə'rɪə ˌplænɪŋ/ *noun* the examination of the way in which career opportunities are available, leading to advice on which careers to pursue or how to further an employee's existing career

careers guidance /kəˌrɪəz 'gaɪdns/ *noun* professional help given to people in choosing their career ○ *Many employees are in the wrong jobs due to poor careers guidance at school.*

careers officer /kə'rɪəz ˌɒfɪsə/ *noun* a person who gives advice to students or new employees on their career prospects

career structure /kə'rɪə ˌstrʌktʃə/ *noun* the way in which jobs in a company are planned to lead on to other posts at a higher level ○ *I left the company because of its poor career structure.*

career woman /kə'rɪə ˌwʊmən/ *noun* a woman who is working in business and does not plan to stop working to look after the house or children

careline /'keəlaɪn/ *noun* a telephone number which links people to services which can help them such as social services departments, hospitals, or a similar service offered by shops to their customers

caretaker /'keəteɪkə/ *noun* a person who looks after a building, making sure it is clean and that the rubbish is cleared away (a caretaker often lives on the premises) ○ *Go and ask the caretaker to replace the light bulb.* (NOTE: American English is **janitor**)

car expenses /'kɑːr ɪkˌspensɪz/ *plural noun* money spent on a private car used during work for a company

car-hire /'kɑː haɪə/ *noun* the business of lending cars to people for a payment ○ *He runs a car-hire business.*

car hire firm /'kɑː haɪə ˌfɜːm/ *noun* a company which owns cars or equipment and lends them to customers for a payment

car insurance /'kɑːr ɪnˌʃʊərəns/ *noun* the insuring of a car, the driver and passengers in case of accident

carousel training /ˌkærə'sel ˌtreɪnɪŋ/ *noun* training which involves moving from job to job or from department to department in an organisation ○ *Carousel training was instituted in order to provide trainees with a wide range of practical experience.* ○ *During their carousel training, trainee managers spend time in the marketing, HR and finance departments.*

carry /'kæri/ *verb* **1.** to take from one place to another ○ *a tanker carrying oil from the Gulf* ○ *The truck was carrying goods to the supermarket.* ○ *The train was carrying a consignment of cars for export.* **2.** to vote to approve □ **the motion was carried** the motion was accepted after a vote **3.** to produce ○ *The bonds carry interest at 10%.* **4.** to keep in stock ○ *to carry a line of goods* ○ *We do not carry pens.* (NOTE: **carries – carrying – carried**)

carry on /ˌkæri 'ɒn/ *verb* to continue or to go on doing something ○ *The staff carried on working in spite of the fire.* □ **to carry on a business** to be active in running a business

carry out /ˌkæri 'aʊt/ *verb* □ **to carry out one's duties** to do what one has to do in one's job

case /keɪs/ *noun* **1.** a cardboard or wooden box for packing and carrying goods □ **to state one's case** to put forward arguments which support your position **2.** a typical example of something ○ *The company has had several cases of petty theft in the post room.* **3.** reasons for doing something ○ *The negotiations put the union's case for a pay rise.* **4.** □ **the case is being heard next week** the case is coming to court next week

cash /kæʃ/ *verb* □ **to cash a cheque** to exchange a cheque for cash

cash-flow life /'kæʃ fləʊ laɪf/ *noun* a working life in which a person works for fees paid for individual projects rather than for a regular salary

cashless pay /ˌkæʃləs 'peɪ/ *noun* a weekly or monthly wage paid directly into an employee's bank account through an electronic transfer of funds

casual /'kæʒuəl/ *adjective* **1.** informal or not serious **2.** not permanent or not regular

casual job /'kæʒuəl dʒɒb/ *noun* a job which exists for a short period only

casual labour /ˌkæʒuəl 'leɪbə/ *noun* workers who are hired for a short period

casual labourer /ˌkæʒuəl 'leɪbərə/ *noun* a worker who can be hired for a short period

casual leave /'kæʒuəl liːv/ *noun* paid time off from work given to an employee to deal with personal affairs ○ *He was granted casual leave to settle his family affairs.*

casual vacancy /ˌkæʒuəl 'veɪkənsi/ *noun* a job which has become vacant because the previous employee left unexpectedly

casual work /'kæʒuəl wɜːk/ *noun* work where the workers are hired for a short period

casual worker /ˌkæʒuəl 'wɜːkə/ *noun* a worker who can be hired for a short period

catastrophe /kə'tæstrəfi/ *noun* a sudden disaster

catastrophic /ˌkætə'strɒfɪk/ *adjective* disastrous

catastrophic health insurance /ˌkætəstrɒfɪk 'helθ ɪnˌʃʊərəns/ *noun* health insurance which provides for the high cost of treating severe or lengthy illnesses ○ *Miners are advised to take out catastrophic health insurance since lung diseases are expensive to treat.*

categorical /ˌkætə'gɒrɪk(ə)l/ *adjective* straightforward or definite

category /'kætɪg(ə)ri/ *noun* a type or sort of item ○ *We deal only in the most expensive categories of watches.* ○ *The company has vacancies for most categories of office staff.*

caution /'kɔːʃ(ə)n/ *noun* **1.** a warning from someone in authority, telling someone not to repeat a minor crime ○ *The boys were let off with a caution.* **2.** a warning by a police officer, that someone will be charged with a crime, and that what he says will be used in evidence ■ *verb* **1.** to warn someone that what they have done is wrong and should not be repeated ○ *The manager cautioned the clerks after she caught them drinking beer in the office.* **2.** to warn someone that they will be charged with a crime, and that what they say will be used as evidence at their trial ○ *The accused was arrested by the detectives and cautioned.*

COMMENT: The person who is cautioned has the right not to answer any question put to them.

CBI *abbr* Confederation of British Industry

ceiling /'siːlɪŋ/ *noun* the highest point that something can reach, e.g. the highest rate of a pay increase ○ *What ceiling has the government put on wage increases this year?*

cell work system /'sel wɜːk ˌsɪstəm/ *noun* a system of working where an item is produced within a separate production unit, and does not move round an assembly line

central /'sentrəl/ *adjective* organised by one main point

Central Arbitration Committee /ˌsentrəl ɑːbɪ'treɪʃ(ə)n kəˌmɪti/ *noun* an independent arbitration body dealing mainly with union claims for disclosure of information by management. Abbr **CAC**

centralisation /ˌsentrəlaɪ'zeɪʃ(ə)n/, **centralization** *noun* the organisation of everything from a central point

centralise /'sentrəlaɪz/, **centralize** *verb* to organise from a central point ○ *All purchasing has been centralised in our main office.* ○ *The group benefits from a highly centralised organisational structure.* ○ *The company has become very centralised, and far more staff work at headquarters.*

central office /ˌsentrəl 'ɒfɪs/ *noun* the main office which controls all smaller offices

Central Provident Fund /ˌsentrəl 'prɒvɪd(ə)nt fʌnd/ *noun* (*in Singapore*) a retirement benefit scheme to which all employees and employers must make contributions each month

central purchasing /ˌsentrəl 'pɜːtʃɪsɪŋ/ *noun* purchasing organised by a central office for all branches of a company

centre /'sentə/ *noun* **1.** an important town ○ *Sheffield is a major industrial centre.* ○ *Nottingham is the centre for the shoe industry.* (NOTE: the usual US spelling is **center**) **2.** a group of items in an account (NOTE: the usual US spelling is **center**)

centre of excellence /ˌsentər əv 'eksələns/ *noun* an organisation which is recognised as being successful and having a world-wide reputation in its field, and so receives special funding

CEO *abbr* chief executive officer

certificate /sə'tɪfɪkət/ *noun* an official document carrying an official declaration by someone, and signed by that person

certificate of approval /sə,tɪfɪkət əv ə'pruːv(ə)l/ *noun* a document showing that an item has been approved officially

certification /sə,tɪfɪ'keɪʃ(ə)n/ *noun* the act of giving an official certificate of approval

certification officer /,sɜːtɪfɪ-'keɪʃ(ə)n ,ɒfɪsə/ *noun* the official responsible for trade unions, ensuring that they are properly registered, well conducted and that trade union legislation is adhered to

certified public accountant /,sɜːtɪfaɪd ,pʌblɪk ə'kaʊntənt/ *noun* US an accountant who has passed professional examinations

certify /'sɜːtɪfaɪ/ *verb* to make an official declaration in writing ○ *I certify that this is a true copy.* ○ *The document is certified as a true copy.* (NOTE: **certifies – certifying – certified**)

CGI Joe /,siː dʒiː aɪ 'dʒəʊ/ *noun* a computer programmer who lacks personal charm and is not very good at communicating with other people (*slang*) (NOTE: the term is modelled on 'GI Joe', a word for a US soldier in the Second World War; its first part is an abbreviation of 'computer generated imagery')

chain /tʃeɪn/ *noun* **1.** a series of stores or other businesses belonging to the same company ○ *a chain of hotels* or *a hotel chain* ○ *the chairman of a large do-it-yourself chain* ○ *He runs a chain of shoe shops.* ○ *She bought several garden centres and gradually built up a chain.* **2.** a series of things linked together ○ *an unfortunate chain of events*

'...the giant US group is better known for its chain of cinemas and hotels rather than its involvement in shipping' [*Lloyd's List*]

chain of command /,tʃeɪn əv kə-'mɑːnd/ *noun* a series of links between directors, management and employees, by which instructions and information are passed up or down

chainsaw consultant /'tʃeɪnsɔː kən,sʌltənt/ *noun* an outside expert brought into a company to reduce the number of its employees drastically (*slang*)

chair /tʃeə/ *noun* the position of the chairman, presiding over a meeting ○ *to be in the chair* ○ *Mr Smith was in the chair.* ○ *Mrs Brown was voted into the chair.* □ **Mr Jones took the chair** Mr Jones presided over the meeting □ **to address the chair** to speak to the chairman and not to the rest of the people at the meeting ○ *Please address your remarks to the chair.* ■ *verb* to preside over a meeting ○ *The meeting was chaired by Mrs Smith.*

chairman /'tʃeəmən/ *noun* **1.** a person who is in charge of a meeting ○ *Mr Howard was chairman* or *acted as chairman* **2.** a person who presides over the board meetings of a company ○ *the chairman of the board* or *the company chairman* □ **the chairman's report, the chairman's statement** an annual report from the chairman of a company to the shareholders

'...the corporation's entrepreneurial chairman seeks a dedicated but part-time president. The new president will work a three-day week' [*Globe and Mail (Toronto)*]

chairman and managing director /,tʃeəmən ən ,mænɪdʒɪŋ daɪ-'rektə/ *noun* a managing director who is also chairman of the board of directors

chairmanship /'tʃeəmənʃɪp/ *noun* the fact of being a chairman ○ *The committee met under the chairmanship of Mr Jones.*

chairperson /'tʃeəpɜːs(ə)n/ *noun* a person who is in charge of a meeting (NOTE: plural is **chairpersons**)

chairwoman /'tʃeəwʊmən/ *noun* a woman who is in charge of a meeting (NOTE: plural is **chairwomen**)

chance /tʃɑːns/ *noun* **1.** the fact of being possible ○ *The company has a good chance of winning the contract.* ○ *His promotion chances are small.* **2.** the opportunity to do something ○ *She is waiting for a chance to see the managing director.* ○ *He had his chance of promotion when the finance director's* *assistant resigned.* (NOTE: you have a chance **of doing** something or **to do** something)

change /tʃeɪndʒ/ *noun* **1.** money in coins or small notes □ **to give someone change for £10** to give someone coins or notes in exchange for a ten pound note **2.** money given back by the seller, when the buyer can pay only with a larger note or coin than the amount asked ○ *She gave me the wrong change.* ○ *You paid the £5.75 bill with a £10 note, so you should have £4.25 change.* □ **keep the change** keep it as a tip (said to waiters, taxi-drivers, etc.) **3.** an alteration of the way something is done or of the way work is carried out ■ *verb* **1.** □ **to change a £20 note** to give change in smaller notes or coins for a £20 note **2.** to give one type of currency for another ○ *to change £1,000 into dollars* ○ *We want to change some traveller's cheques.* **3.** □ **to change hands** (*of a business, property, etc.*) to be sold to a new owner ○ *The shop changed hands for £100,000.*

change of use /ˌtʃeɪndʒ əv ˈjuːs/ *noun* permission given by a local authority for premises to be used for a different purpose (such as house to become a shop or a shop to become a restaurant)

channel /ˈtʃæn(ə)l/ *noun* a means by which information or goods pass from one place to another □ **to go through the official channels** to deal with government officials, especially when making a request ■ *verb* to send in a certain direction ○ *They are channelling their research funds into developing European communication systems.* (NOTE: **channelling – channelled**)

channels of communication /ˌtʃæn(ə)lz əv kəmjuːnɪˈkeɪʃ(ə)n/ *noun* ways in which information can be passed (post, telephone, fax, the Internet, newspapers, TV, etc.) □ **to open up new channels of communication** to find new ways of communicating with someone

character /ˈkærɪktə/ *noun* **1.** the general nature or qualities of a person, which make that person different from others ○ *You need an easy-going character to work in this office.* **2.** strong

will or decisiveness ○ *a post needing character and a willingness to work hard*

character analysis /ˈkærɪktə əˌnæləsɪs/ *noun* the analysis of a job applicant's general nature and qualities ○ *All candidates for the job underwent a character analysis.*

character assessment /ˈkærɪktə əˌsesmənt/ *noun* the process of judging the personality of an employee

character reference /ˈkærɪktə ˌref(ə)rəns/ *noun* a report showing the strength of someone's character

charge /tʃɑːdʒ/ *noun* **1.** money which must be paid, or the price of a service ○ *to make no charge for delivery* ○ *to make a small charge for rental* ○ *There is no charge for this service* or *No charge is made for this service.* □ **bank charges**, **service charge** US charges made by a bank for carrying out work for a customer **2.** management or control □ **to be in charge of something** to be the manager or to deal with something ○ *She is in charge of all our HR documentation.* □ **to take charge of something** to start to deal with something or to become responsible for something ○ *When the manager was ill, his deputy took charge of the department.* **3.** an official statement in a court accusing someone of having committed a crime ○ *He appeared in court on a charge of embezzling* or *on an embezzlement charge.* □ **to take charge of something** to start to deal with something or to become responsible for something ○ *When the manager was ill, her deputy took charge of the department.* □ **to be in charge of something** to be the manager or to deal with something ○ *She is in charge of all our personnel documentation.* ■ *verb* **1.** to ask someone to pay for services later **2.** to ask for money to be paid ○ *to charge £5 for delivery* ○ *How much does he charge?* □ **he charges £16 an hour** he asks to be paid £16 for an hour's work **3.** to pay for something by putting it on a charge account ○ *Can you charge the meal to my room?* ○ *I want to charge these purchases to the company account.* ○ *They were charged with murder.* **4.** (*in a court*) to accuse someone formally of having committed a crime ○ *He was charged with embezzling his clients' money.* ○ *Reps charge their hotel expenses to the company's account.*

chargehand /'tʃɑːdʒhænd/ *noun* a senior operator in a group of workers under a foreman who has responsibility for seeing that day-to-day problems are solved

chart /tʃɑːt/ *noun* a diagram displaying information as a series of lines, blocks, etc.

chartered accountant /ˌtʃɑːtəd ə-'kaʊntənt/ *noun* an accountant who has passed the professional examinations and is a member of the Institute of Chartered Accountants. Abbr **CA**

cheap /tʃiːp/ *adjective, adverb* not costing a lot of money or not expensive

cheap labour /tʃiːp 'leɪbə/ *noun* workers who do not earn much money

cheaply /'tʃiːpli/ *adverb* without paying much money ○ *The salesman was living cheaply at home and claiming an enormous hotel bill on expenses.*

cheapness /'tʃiːpnəs/ *noun* the fact of being cheap ○ *The cheapness of the pound means that many more tourists will come to London.*

check /tʃek/ *noun* **1.** a sudden stop □ **to put a check on imports** to stop some imports coming into a country **2.** investigation or examination ○ *a routine check of the fire equipment* ○ *The auditors carried out checks on the petty cash book.* ■ *verb* **1.** to stop or to delay ○ *to check the entry of contraband into the country* ○ *to check the flow of money out of a country* **2.** to examine or to investigate ○ *to check that an invoice is correct* ○ *to check and sign for goods* □ **she checked the computer printout against the invoices** she examined the printout and the invoices to see if the figures were the same

checking /'tʃekɪŋ/ *noun* an examination or investigation ○ *The inspectors found some defects during their checking of the building.*

checklist /'tʃeklɪst/ *noun* a list of points which have to be checked before something can be regarded as finished,

or as part of a procedure for evaluating something

checkoff /'tʃekɒf/ *noun US* a system where union dues are automatically deducted by the employer from a worker's paycheck ○ *Checkoffs are seen by most employees as worthwhile as long as their interests are well represented by the union.* ○ *After checkoffs and tax deductions the workers' pay had been reduced by one third.*

check time /'tʃek taɪm/ *noun* the time recorded between the start of a work study and the start of the first element observed, plus the time recorded between the last element observed and the end of the study

checkup /'tʃekʌp/ *noun* a medical examination ○ *All staff have to have regular checkups.*

cherry-picking /'tʃeri ˌpɪkɪŋ/ *noun* the practice of choosing only the best or most valuable items from among a group

chief /tʃiːf/ *adjective* most important ○ *He is the chief accountant of an industrial group.* ○ *She is the chief buyer for a department store.*

chief clerk /tʃiːf 'klɑːk/ *noun* the most important clerk

chief executive /tʃiːf ɪɡ'zekjʊtɪv/, **chief executive officer (CEO)** /tʃiːf ɪɡ'zekjʊtɪv ˌɒfɪsə/ *noun US* the most important director in charge of a company

childcare provision /'tʃaɪldkeə prəˌvɪʒ(ə)n/ *noun* a human relations policy designed to help employees with the cost of paying somebody to care for their children during working hours (NOTE: Childcare provision is intended to enable people who have children to look after to return to work. Equal opportunities laws stipulate that it must be available to both male and female employees.)

chilling effect /'tʃɪlɪŋ ɪˌfekt/ *noun* a negative effect on employees of regulations or practices that limit their freedom and opportunities ○ *the chilling effect of punctuality checks* ○ *Too many restrictions have a chilling effect which is counterproductive.*

Chinese walls /ˌtʃaɪniːz 'wɔːlz/ *plural noun* imaginary barriers between departments in the same organisation, set up to avoid insider dealing or conflict of interest (as when a merchant bank is advising on a planned takeover bid, its investment department should not know that the bid is taking place, or they would advise their clients to invest in the company being taken over)

choice /tʃɔɪs/ *noun* **1.** a thing which is chosen ○ *You must give the customer time to make their choice.* **2.** a range of items to choose from ○ *We have only a limited choice of suppliers.* □ **the shop carries a good choice of paper** the shop carries many types of paper to choose from ■ *adjective* (*of food*) specially selected ○ *choice meat* ○ *choice wines* ○ *choice foodstuffs*

choose /tʃuːz/ *verb* to decide to do a particular thing or to buy a particular item (as opposed to something else) ○ *There were several good candidates to choose from.* ○ *They chose the only woman applicant as sales director.* ○ *You must give the customers plenty of time to choose.* (NOTE: **choosing – chose – has chosen**)

Christmas /'krɪsməs/ *noun* a Christian holiday celebrated on 25th December ○ *The office closes for ten days at Christmas.* ○ *We have allocated £50 for organising the office Christmas party.*

Christmas bonus /ˌkrɪsməs 'bəʊnəs/ *noun* an extra payment made to staff at Christmas

chronic illness /ˌkrɒnɪk 'ɪlnəs/ *noun* an illness or condition which lasts for a long time

chronic shortage /ˌkrɒnɪk 'ʃɔːtɪdʒ/ *noun* a shortage which continues for a period of time ○ *a chronic shortage of skilled staff*

chronological order /ˌkrɒnəlɒdʒɪk(ə)l 'ɔːdə/ *noun* the arrangement of records such as files and invoices in order of their dates

circadian rhythm /sɜːˌkeɪdiən 'rɪðəmz/ *plural noun* **1.** the rhythms of daily activities and bodily processes such as eating, defecating or sleeping which are frequently controlled by hormones and which repeat every twenty-four hours **2.** biorhythms, recurring cycles of different lengths which some people believe affect a person's behaviour, sensitivity and intelligence

circular /'sɜːkjʊlə/ *adjective* sent to many people ■ *noun* a leaflet or letter sent to many people ○ *They sent out a circular offering a 10% discount.* ○ *Senior management sent out a circular to all the employees explaining the changes in the payment scheme.*

circularise /'sɜːkjʊləraɪz/, **circularize** *verb* to send a circular to ○ *The committee has agreed to circularise the members of the society.* ○ *They circularised all their customers with a new list of prices.* ○ *The committee has agreed to circularise the members.*

circulate /'sɜːkjʊleɪt/ *verb* to send information to ○ *They circulated information about job vacancies to all colleges in the area.*

circulation /ˌsɜːkjʊ'leɪʃ(ə)n/ *noun* **1.** the act of sending information ○ *The company is trying to improve the circulation of information between departments.* **2.** movement **3.** the number of readers of a newspaper or magazine. It is audited and is not the same as 'readership'.

Ciro method *noun* a method of assessing the value of a training programme under the four headings of context, input, reaction and outcome

civil /'sɪv(ə)l/ *adjective* referring to ordinary people

civil rights /ˌsɪv(ə)l 'raɪts/ *plural noun* the rights and privileges of each individual according to the law

civil servant /ˌsɪv(ə)l 'sɜːvənt/ *noun* a person who works in the civil service

civil service /ˌsɪv(ə)l 'sɜːvɪs/ *noun* the organisation and personnel which administer a country ○ *You have to pass an examination to get a job in the civil service* or *to get a civil service job.*

claim /kleɪm/ *noun* **1.** an act of asking for money □ **the union put in a 6% wage claim** the union asked for a 6% increase in wages for its members **2.** □ **to file** *or* **lodge a claim against someone** to make an official claim against someone ■ *verb* **1.** to ask for money ○ *She* *claimed for repairs to the car against her insurance policy.* **2.** to say that something is your property ○ *No one claimed the umbrella found in my office.* **3.** to state that something is a fact ○ *She claims that the shares are her property.*

claimant /'kleɪmənt/ *noun* a person who claims a state benefit such as unemployment benefit

claim back /ˌkleɪm 'bæk/ *verb* to ask for money to be paid back

claimer /'kleɪmə/ *noun* same as **claimant**

claiming /'kleɪmɪŋ/ *noun* the act of making a claim

claims department /'kleɪmz dɪˌpɑːtmənt/ *noun* a department of an insurance company which deals with claims

claims manager /'kleɪmz ˌmænɪdʒə/ *noun* the manager of a claims department

class /klɑːs/ *noun* **1.** a category or group into which things are classified **2.** a group of students

Class 1 NI contributions /klɑːs ˌwʌn en 'aɪ kɒntrɪˌbjuːʃ(ə)nz/ *plural noun* National Insurance contributions paid by an employee

Class 2 NI contributions /klɑːs ˌtuː en 'aɪ kɒntrɪˌbjuːʃ(ə)nz/ *plural noun* National Insurance contributions paid by a self-employed person at a flat rate

Class 3 NI contributions /klɑːs ˌθriː en 'aɪ kɒntrɪˌbjuːʃ(ə)nz/ *plural noun* voluntary National Insurance contributions paid by someone who is not earning enough to pay Class 1 contributions and is not self-employed

Class 4 NI contributions /klɑːs ˌfɔːr en 'aɪ kɒntrɪˌbjuːʃ(ə)nz/ *plural noun* National Insurance contributions paid by a self-employed person whose earnings are higher than for Class 2 contributions (Class 4 contributions are a percentage of profits, not a flat fee)

class action /klɑːs 'ækʃən/, **class suit** /klɑːs 'suːt/ *noun US* a legal action brought on behalf of a group of people

classification /ˌklæsɪfɪ'keɪʃ(ə)n/ *noun* arrangement into classes or categories according to specific characteristics ○ *the classification of employees by ages or skills* ○ *Jobs in this organisation fall into several classifications.*

classified advertisements /ˌklæsɪfaɪd əd'vɜːtɪsmənts/, **classified ads** /ˌklæsɪfaɪd 'ædz/ *plural noun* advertisements listed in a newspaper under special headings such as 'property for sale' or 'jobs wanted' ○ *Look in the small ads to see if anyone has a filing cabinet for sale.*

classify /'klæsɪfaɪ/ *verb* to put into classes or categories according to specific characteristics (NOTE: **classifies – classifying – classified**)

clause /klɔːz/ *noun* a section of a contract ○ *There are ten clauses in the contract of employment.* ○ *There is a clause in this contract concerning the employer's right to dismiss an employee.*

clear /klɪə/ *adjective* (*of a period of time*) free, total □ **three clear days** three whole working days ○ *Allow three clear days for the cheque to be paid into your account.* ■ *verb* □ **to clear one's desk** to remove personal belongings from one's desk when leaving a job ○ *He was given five minutes to clear his desk.*

clerical /'klerɪk(ə)l/ *adjective* (*of work*) done in an office or done by a clerk

clerical work /'klerɪk(ə)l wɜːk/ *noun* work done in an office

clerical worker /'klerɪk(ə)l ˌwɜːkə/ *noun* a person who works in an office

clerical work improvement programme /ˌklerɪk(ə)l wɜːk ɪm'pruːvmənt ˌprəʊɡræm/ *noun* a programme based on data obtained by clerical work measurement that aims to improve the productivity and efficiency of staff engaged in administrative and clerical work

clerical work measurement /'klerɪk(ə)l wɜːk ˌmeʒəmənt/ *noun* a form of work measurement that focuses on the administrative and clerical tasks such as filing and keyboarding done by employees in order to set standard times for these activities

clerk /klɑːk/ *noun* a person who works in an office ■ *verb US* to work as a clerk

clerkess /klɑːˈkes/ *noun* (*in Scotland*) a woman clerk

clicks-and-mortar /ˌklɪks ən ˈmɔːtə/ *adjective* conducting business both through e-commerce and also in the traditional way in buildings such as shops and warehouses (NOTE: Compare this term with bricks-and-mortar.)

'…there may be a silver lining for 'clicks-and-mortar' stores that have both an online and a high street presence. Many of these are accepting returns of goods purchased online at their traditional stores. This is a service that may make them more popular as consumers become more experienced online shoppers' [*Financial Times*]

clipboard /ˈklɪpbɔːd/ *noun* a stiff board with a clip at the top so that a piece of paper can be clipped to the board to allow you to write on it easily

CLM *noun* an action that could endanger your career prospects, e.g. criticising your boss publicly. Full form **career-limiting nerve**

clock /klɒk/ *noun* a machine which shows the time ○ *The office clock is fast.* ○ *All computers have built-in clocks.* ○ *The micro has a built-in clock.*

clock card /ˈklɒk kɑːd/ *noun* a special card which a worker puts into the time clock when clocking on or off

clock in /ˌklɒk ˈɪn/, **clock on** /ˌklɒk ˈɒn/ *verb* (*of a worker*) to record the time of arriving for work by putting a card into a special timing machine ○ *If workers do not clock in on arrival at the factory, they may be sent a written warning.*

clocking in /ˌklɒkɪŋ ˈɪn/, **clocking on** /ˌklɒkɪŋ ˈɒn/ *noun* the act of arriving for work and recording the time on a time-card

clocking out /ˌklɒkɪŋ ˈaʊt/, **clocking off** /ˌklɒkɪŋ ˈɒf/ *noun* the act of leaving work and recording the time on a time-card

clock out /ˌklɒk ˈaʊt/, **clock off** /ˌklɒk ˈɒf/ *verb* (*of a worker*) to record the time of leaving work by putting a card into a special timing machine

close /kləʊs/ *noun* the end of a day's trading on the Stock Exchange ○ *At the close of the day's trading the shares had fallen 20%.* ■ *adjective* □ **close to** very near, almost ○ *The company was close to bankruptcy.* ○ *We are close to meeting our sales targets.* ■ *verb* **1.** □ **to close the accounts** to come to the end of an accounting period and make up the profit and loss account **2.** to bring to an end **3.** to stop doing business for the day ○ *The office closes at 5.30.* ○ *We close early on Saturdays.* **4.** □ **the shares closed at $15** at the end of the day's trading the price of the shares was $15

close company /ˌkləʊs ˈkʌmp(ə)ni/ *noun* a privately owned company controlled by a few shareholders (in the UK, less than five) where the public may own a small number of the shares (NOTE: the American equivalent is **close corporation** or **closed corporation**)

closed /kləʊzd/ *adjective* **1.** not open for business, or not doing business ○ *The office is closed on Mondays.* ○ *These warehouses are usually closed to the public.* ○ *All the banks are closed on Christmas Day.* **2.** restricted

closed interview /ˌkləʊzd ˈɪntəvjuː/ *noun* an interview where the interviewer asks only fixed questions with 'yes' or 'no' answers

close down /ˌkləʊz ˈdaʊn/ *verb* to shut a shop, factory or service for a long period or for ever ○ *The company is closing down its London office.* ○ *The accident closed down the station for a period.*

'…the best thing would be to have a few more plants close down and bring supply more in line with current demand' [*Fortune*]

closed shop /kləʊzd ˈʃɒp/ *noun* a system where a company agrees to employ only union members for specific jobs ○ *The union is asking the management to agree to a closed shop.*

COMMENT: Closed shops are illegal in many countries.

closed system /kləʊzd ˈsɪstəm/ *noun* a work system which is inflexible and does not allow the employees much freedom to work in their own way (NOTE: the opposite is **open system**)

closing /'kləʊzɪŋ/ *adjective* **1.** final or coming at the end **2.** at the end of an accounting period ○ *At the end of the quarter the bookkeeper has to calculate the closing balance.* ■ *noun* the shutting of a shop or being shut

closing date /'kləʊzɪŋ deɪt/ *noun* the last date ○ *The closing date for tenders to be received is May 1st.*

closing session /'kləʊzɪŋ ˌseʃ(ə)n/ *noun* the last part of a meeting or conference

closing time /'kləʊzɪŋ taɪm/ *noun* the time when a shop or office stops work

closure /'kləʊʒə/ *noun* the act of closing

clothing /'kləʊðɪŋ/ *noun* the clothes which a person wears ○ *The company provides special clothing for its employees.*

clothing allowance /'kləʊðɪŋ əˌlaʊəns/ *noun* an addition to normal salary to cover the cost of buying special clothing to wear when on duty

club /klʌb/ *noun* a group of people who have the same interest, or the place where these people meet ○ *If you want the managing director, you can phone him at his club.* ○ *She has applied to join the sports club.* □ **club membership** all the members of a club □ **club subscription** money paid to belong to a club ■ *verb* □ **to club together** to give money each for a special purpose ○ *They clubbed together to buy the manager a wedding present.*

co- /kəʊ/ *prefix* working or acting together

coaching /'kəʊtʃɪŋ/ *noun* a face-to-face instruction where a subordinate is shown how to change their behaviour ○ *The HR manager found coaching useful in dealing with employers needing a more tactful approach when attempting to change their attitude.* ○ *In our company coaching has made management more aware of workers' attitudes.*

code /kəʊd/ *noun* **1.** a system of signs, numbers or letters which mean something **2.** a set of rules

code of conduct /ˌkəʊd əv 'kɒndʌkt/ *noun* the guideline showing how someone (such as shop assistants or railway station staff) should behave towards customers

code of ethics /ˌkəʊd əv 'eθɪks/ *noun* a code of working which shows how a professional group should work, and in particular what type of relationship they should have with their clients

code of practice /ˌkəʊd əv 'præktɪs/ *noun* rules drawn up by an association which the members must follow when doing business

co-determination /ˌkəʊ dɪtɜːmɪ'neɪʃ(ə)n/ *noun* (*in Germany and some other countries*) a system where a certain percentage of representatives of the workers must be part of the supervisory board of a company

coding /'kəʊdɪŋ/ *noun* the act of putting a code on something ○ *the coding of invoices*

co-director /'kəʊ daɪˌrektə/ *noun* a person who is a director of the same company as you

coercion /kəʊ'ɜːʃ(ə)n/ *noun* the act of forcing someone to do something

coffee break /'kɒfi breɪk/ *noun* a rest time during work when the employees can drink coffee or tea

cognition /kɒg'nɪʃ(ə)n/ *noun* thinking processes

cognitive /'kɒgnɪtɪv/ *adjective* relating to thinking processes

cohort /'kəʊhɔːt/ *noun* a group of people who do the same thing at the same time (such as a group of managers who joined a company as trainees together)

cohort study /'kəʊhɔːt ˌstʌdi/ *noun* a study in which a group of individuals who have something in common with each other, e.g. children with the same birth date, are observed over several years

cold /kəʊld/ *adjective* **1.** not hot ○ *The machines work badly in cold weather.* ○ *The office was so cold that the staff started complaining.* ○ *The coffee machine also sells cold drinks.* **2.** without being prepared

'…the board is considering the introduction of a set of common provisions on unsolicited calls to investors. The board is aiming to permit the cold calling of customer agreements for the provision of services relating to listed securities. Cold calling would be allowed when the investor is not a private investor' [*Accountancy*]

cold storage training /kəʊld ˈstɔːrɪdʒ ˌtreɪnɪŋ/ *noun* the training of employees for jobs that will be created in the future ○ *Cold storage training was set up in the company based on forecasts of future increases in productivity.* ○ *Start your cold storage training in good time so that you have the skilled manpower available when you need it.*

collaborate /kəˈlæbəreɪt/ *verb* to work together ○ *We collaborated with a French firm on a building project.* ○ *They collaborated on the new aircraft.* (NOTE: you collaborate **with** someone **on** something)

collaboration /kəˌlæbəˈreɪʃ(ə)n/ *noun* the act of working together ○ *Their collaboration on the project was very profitable.*

collaborative working /kəˌlæb(ə)rətɪv ˈwɜːkɪŋ/ *noun* a method of working in which people at different locations or from different organisations work together, usually using videoconferencing, email, networks and other electronic communications tools

collaborator /kəˈlæbəreɪtə/ *noun* a person who works together with someone on a project

collapse /kəˈlæps/ *noun* **1.** a sudden fall in price ○ *the collapse of the market in silver* ○ *The collapse of the dollar on the foreign exchange markets.* **2.** a sudden failure ○ *the collapse of the pay negotiations* ○ *Investors lost thousands of pounds in the collapse of the company.* ■ *verb* **1.** to fall suddenly ○ *The market in silver collapsed.* ○ *The yen collapsed on the foreign exchange markets.* **2.** to fail suddenly ○ *The company collapsed with £250,000 in debts.* ○ *Talks between management and unions collapsed last night.*

collar /ˈkɒlə/ *noun* a part of a coat or shirt which goes round the neck

colleague /ˈkɒliːɡ/ *noun* **1.** a person who does the same type of work as another ○ *His colleagues gave him a pres-*

ent when he got married. ○ *I know Jane Gray – she was a colleague of mine at my last job.* ○ *She was unpopular with her colleagues in the machine room.* **2.** a person who works in the same organisation as another

collect /kəˈlekt/ *verb* **1.** to make someone pay money which is owed □ **to collect a debt** to go and make someone pay a debt **2.** to take things away from a place ○ *We have to collect the stock from the warehouse.* ■ *adverb, adjective* referring to a phone call which the person receiving the call agrees to pay for

collecting agency /kəˈlektɪŋ ˌeɪdʒənsi/ *noun* an agency which collects money owed to other companies for a commission

collection /kəˈlekʃən/ *noun* **1.** the act of getting money together, or of making someone pay money which is owed ○ *tax collection* or *collection of tax* □ **bills for collection** bills where payment is due **2.** the fetching of goods ○ *The stock is in the warehouse awaiting collection.* □ **to hand something in for collection** to leave something for someone to come and collect **3.** the act of taking letters from a letter box or mail room to the post office for dispatch ○ *There are four collections a day from the letter box at the corner of the street.*

collections /kəˈlekʃənz/ *plural noun* money which has been collected

collective /kəˈlektɪv/ *adjective* referring to a group of people together

collective agreement /kəˌlektɪv əˈɡriːmənt/ *noun* an agreement on salaries, working conditions, etc., negotiated through collective bargaining

collective bargaining /kəˌlektɪv ˈbɑːɡənɪŋ/ *noun* negotiations between employers and workers' representatives over wage increases and conditions ○ *The sudden wave of strikes shows that collective bargaining is not working.* ○ *The government has put through legislation to make collective bargaining easier.*

collective ownership /kəˌlektɪv ˈəʊnəʃɪp/ *noun* ownership of a business by the employees who work in it

collective relations /kə,lektɪv rɪ-'leɪʃ(ə)nz/ *plural noun* relations between employers associations and trade unions

collective wage agreement /kə-,lektɪv 'weɪdʒ ə,griːmənt/ *noun* an agreement signed between management and the trade union about wages

collectivism /kə'lektɪvɪz(ə)m/ *noun* the belief that society flourishes if the individual gives up some rights to the group of which they are a member, in return for support and protection from the group (NOTE: the opposite is **individualism**)

college /'kɒlɪdʒ/ *noun* a place where people can study after they have left school

command /kə'mɑːnd/ *noun* □ **she has a good command of German** she speaks and writes German well

commercial college /kə'mɜːʃ(ə)l ,kɒlɪdʒ/ *noun* a college which teaches business studies

commercial law /kə,mɜːʃ(ə)l 'lɔː/ *noun* the laws regarding business

commercial lawyer /kə,mɜːʃ(ə)l 'lɔːjə/ *noun* a person who specialises in company law or who advises companies on legal problems

commission /kə'mɪʃ(ə)n/ *noun* **1.** money paid to a salesperson or agent, usually a percentage of the sales made ○ *She gets 10% commission on everything she sells.* ○ *He is paid on a commission basis.* □ **he charges 10% commission** he asks for 10% of sales as his payment **2.** a group of people officially appointed to examine some problem ○ *He is the chairman of the government commission on export subsidies.*

commission agent /kə'mɪʃ(ə)n ,eɪdʒənt/ *noun* an agent who is paid a percentage of sales

commissioner /kə'mɪʃ(ə)nə/ *noun* an ombudsman

Commission for Racial Equality /kə,mɪʃ(ə)n fə ,reɪʃ(ə)l ɪ'kwɒlɪti/ *noun* a statutory body set up to monitor racial matters in companies, and to issue guidelines on best practice. Abbr **CRE**

commission of inquiry /kə-,mɪʃ(ə)n əv ɪn'kwaɪəri/ *noun* a group of people appointed to investigate something officially ○ *The government has appointed a commission of inquiry to look into the problems of small exporters.*

commission sale /kə'mɪʃ(ə)n seɪl/ *noun* a sale where the salesperson is paid a commission

commit /kə'mɪt/ *verb* **1.** to carry out a crime ○ *She was accused of committing several thefts from the storeroom.* **2.** to agree to do something (NOTE: **committing- committed**) □ **to commit funds to a project** to agree to spend money on a project □ **to commit yourself** to state publicly that you will do something ○ *The MD refused to commit herself on the question of redundancies.*

commitment /kə'mɪtmənt/ *noun* **1.** something which you have agreed to do ○ *to make a commitment* or *to enter into a commitment to do something* ○ *The company has a commitment to provide a cheap service.* **2.** money which you have agreed to spend

commitments /kə'mɪtmənts/ *plural noun* things which you have agreed to do, especially money which you have agreed to spend □ **to meet your commitments** to pay money which you had agreed to pay

committee /kə'mɪti/ *noun* an official group of people who organise or plan for a larger group ○ *to be a member of a committee* or *to sit on a committee* ○ *He was elected to the committee of the staff club.* ○ *The new plans have to be approved by the committee members.* ○ *He is the secretary of the finance committee.* □ **to chair a committee** to be the chairman of a committee

common /'kɒmən/ *adjective* **1.** which happens frequently ○ *Unrealistic salary expectations in younger staff was a common problem they had to deal with.* ○ *Being caught by the customs is very common these days.* **2.** belonging to several different people or to everyone

common carrier /,kɒmən 'kæriə/ *noun* a firm which carries goods or passengers, and which anyone can use

common law /,kɒmən 'lɔː/ *noun* **1.** a law as laid down in decisions of courts, rather than by statute **2.** a general system of laws which formerly were the only laws existing in England, and which in some cases have been superseded by statute (NOTE: you say **at common law** when referring to something happening according to the principles of common law)

common ownership /ˌkɒmən ˈəʊnəʃɪp/ *noun* a situation where a business is owned by the employees who work in it

communicate /kəˈmjuːnɪkeɪt/ *verb* to exchange views or information with someone ○ *We need to find better ways of communicating with staff* ○ *In her presentation she communicated her knowledge of details and her enthusiasm for the project well.*

communication /kəˌmjuːnɪˈkeɪʃ(ə)n/ *noun* **1.** the passing on of views or information ○ *A house journal was started to improve communication between management and staff.* ○ *Customers complained about the lack of communication about the unexpected delay.* □ **to enter into communication with someone** to start discussing something with someone, usually in writing ○ *We have entered into communication with the relevant government department.* **2.** an official message ○ *We have had a communication from the local tax inspector.*

communications /kəˌmjuːnɪˈkeɪʃ(ə)nz/ *plural noun* the fact of being able to contact people or to pass messages ○ *After the flood all communications with the outside world were broken.* □ **a breakdown of communications** a time when people do not communicate with each other ○ *There has been a breakdown of communications between management and shopfloor workers.*

communicative /kəˈmjuːnɪkətɪv/ *adjective* referring to a person who can communicate easily with others

'…that kind of approach will require a new style of communication, both upwards and downwards, throughout the organisation it has a forward-looking and communicative management team' [*Personnel Management*]

commutation /ˌkɒmjʊˈteɪʃ(ə)n/ *noun* the act of exchanging something for money in another form

commutation of pension rights /ˌkɒmjʊteɪʃ(ə)n əv ˈpenʃən raɪts/ *noun* the act of taking a lump sum instead of a pension

commute /kəˈmjuːt/ *verb* **1.** to travel to work from home each day ○ *He commutes from the country to his office in the centre of town.* ○ *She spends two hours a day commuting to and from work.* ○ *We have bought a house within commuting distance of London.* **2.** to exchange one form of payment for another ○ *I decided to commute part of my pension rights into a lump sum payment.*

'Commuting is never business use. A trip to work is personal and not deductible. And making a business phone call or holding a business meeting in your car while you drive will not change that fact' [*Nation's Business*]

commuter /kəˈmjuːtə/ *noun* a person who commutes to work

commuter belt /kəˈmjuːtə belt/ *noun* an area of country where the commuters live round a town

commuter train /kəˈmjuːtə treɪn/ *noun* a train which commuters take in the morning and evening

Companies Act /ˈkʌmp(ə)niz ækt/ *noun* an Act of Parliament which regulates the workings of companies, stating the legal limits within which companies may do their business

Companies Registration Office /ˌkʌmp(ə)niz redʒɪˈstreɪʃ(ə)n ˌɒfɪs/ *noun* an office of the Registrar of Companies, the official organisation where the records of companies must be deposited, so that they can be inspected by the public. Abbr **CRO** (NOTE: also called **Companies' House**)

company /ˈkʌmp(ə)ni/ *noun* **1.** a business, a group of people organised to buy, sell or provide a service **2.** □ **to put a company into liquidation** to close a company by selling its assets for cash

COMMENT: A company can be incorporated (with memorandum and articles of association) as a private limited company, and adds the initials 'Ltd' after its name, or as a public limited company, when its name must end in 'Plc'. Unincorporated companies are partnerships such as firms of solicitors, architects, accountants, etc., and they add the initials 'Co.' after their name.

company car /ˌkʌmp(ə)ni ˈkɑː/ *noun* a car which belongs to a company and is lent to an employee to use for business or other purposes

company director /ˌkʌmp(ə)ni daɪˈrektə/ *noun* a person appointed by the shareholders to help run a company

company doctor /ˌkʌmp(ə)ni ˈdɒktə/ *noun* **1.** a doctor who works for a company and looks after sick workers ○ *The staff are all sent to see the company doctor once a year.* **2.** a specialist businessperson who rescues businesses which are in difficulties

company executive /ˌkʌmp(ə)ni ɪgˈzekjʊtɪv/ *noun* a person in a business who takes decisions or top or senior manager or director

company handbook /ˌkʌmp(ə)ni ˈhændbʊk/ *noun* a booklet containing information about the company's structure, employees' rights, grievance procedure, etc.

company law /ˌkʌmp(ə)ni ˈlɔː/ *noun* laws which refer to the way companies work

company lawyer /ˌkʌmp(ə)ni ˈlɔːjə/ *noun* a person who specialises in company law or who advises companies on legal problems

company loyalty /ˌkʌmp(ə)ni ˈlɔɪəlti/ *noun* the dedication of staff to the company and its objectives

company newspaper /ˌkʌmp(ə)ni ˈnjuːspeɪpə/ *noun* a regular news bulletin, published by a company, to keep the workforce informed about recent developments within the company

company pension scheme /ˌkʌmp(ə)ni ˈpenʃən skiːm/ *noun* same as **occupational pension scheme** ○ *He decided to join the company's pension scheme.*

company secretary /ˌkʌmp(ə)ni ˈsekrɪt(ə)ri/ *noun* a person who is responsible for a company's legal and financial affairs

company town /ˈkʌmp(ə)ni taʊn/ *noun* a town in which most of the property and shops are owned by a large company which employs most of the population

company union /ˌkʌmp(ə)ni ˈjuːnjən/ *noun* an association of employees in a single business company

company-wide /ˈkʌmp(ə)ni waɪd/ *adjective* affecting all the employees in a company ○ *We are introducing a company-wide bonus system.*

comparability /ˌkɒmp(ə)rəˈbɪlɪti/ *noun* the fact of being able to be compared

comparability claim /ˌkɒmp(ə)rəˈbɪlɪti kleɪm/ *noun* a claim by employees to bring their wages and fringe benefits into line with those in other industries

comparable /ˈkɒmp(ə)rəb(ə)l/ *adjective* which can be compared ○ *The two sets of figures are not comparable.* □ **which is the nearest company comparable to this one in size?** which company is of a similar size and can be compared with this one?

comparable worth /ˌkɒmp(ə)rəb(ə)l ˈwɜːθ/ *noun* the principle of paying the same rate for jobs which are worth the same ○ *Comparable worth is difficult to apply to jobs of very diverse character.* ○ *The salary scale is drawn up on the principle of comparable worth.*

compare /kəmˈpeə/ *verb* to look at several things to see how they differ ○ *The finance director compared the figures for the first and second quarters.*

compare with /kəmˈpeə wɪð/ *verb* to put two things together to see how they differ ○ *How do the sales this year compare with last year's?* ○ *Compared with the previous month, last month was terrific.*

comparison /kəmˈpærɪs(ə)n/ *noun* the act of comparing one thing with another ○ *Sales are down in comparison with last year.* □ **there is no comparison between overseas and home sales** overseas and home sales are so different they cannot be compared

compassionate leave /kəmˌpæʃ(ə)nət ˈliːv/ *noun* time off work granted to an employee to deal with personal or family problems

compatibility /kəmˌpætɪˈbɪlɪti/ *noun* the ability of people to work together ○ *the compatibility of employees sharing an office*

compatible /kəm'pætɪb(ə)l/ *adjective* which can exist or function together ○ *It soon became clear that the new member of staff was not compatible with his colleagues.* ○ *Are the objectives of senior management and the interests of the employees compatible?*

compensate /'kɒmpənseɪt/ *verb* to give someone money to make up for a loss or injury ○ *In this case we will compensate a manager for loss of commission.* ○ *The company will compensate the employee for the burns suffered in the accident.* (NOTE: you compensate someone **for** something)

compensation /ˌkɒmpən'seɪʃ(ə)n/ *noun* **1.** □ **compensation for damage** payment for damage done □ **compensation for loss of office** payment to a director who is asked to leave a company before their contract ends □ **compensation for loss of earnings** payment to someone who has stopped earning money or who is not able to earn money **2.** *US* a salary

'...compensation can also be via the magistrates courts for relatively minor injuries' [*Personnel Management*]

compensation package /ˌkɒmpən'seɪʃ(ə)n ˌpækɪdʒ/ *noun* a salary, pension and other benefits offered with a job

'...golden parachutes are liberal compensation packages given to executives leaving a company' [*Publishers Weekly*]

compensatory /ˌkɒmpən'seɪt(ə)ri/ *adjective* which compensates for something

compensatory award /kɒmpən-'seɪt(ə)ri əˌwɔːd/ *noun* an award by an industrial tribunal based on what the tribunal considers is just compensation for the employee's loss of pension rights, etc., when dismissed

compete /kəm'piːt/ *verb* □ **to compete with someone, with a company** to try to do better than another person or another company ○ *We have to compete with cheap imports from the Far East.* ○ *They were competing unsuccessfully with local companies on their home territory.* □ **two companies are competing for a market share** *or* **for a contract**

each company is trying to win a larger part of the market or to win the contract

competence /'kɒmpɪt(ə)ns/ *noun* the ability to do the tasks required in a job ○ *The training sessions are intended to increase staff competence.*

competence framework /'kɒmpɪt(ə)ns ˌfreɪmwɜːk/ *noun* the set of duties or tasks performed as part of a job with the standards which should be achieved in these duties

competency /'kɒmpɪt(ə)nsi/ *noun* same as **competence**

competency statement /'kɒmpɪt(ə)nsi ˌsteɪtmənt/ *noun* a list of qualities which an employee needs to do their work

competent /'kɒmpɪt(ə)nt/ *adjective* able to do the tasks required in a job

competing /kəm'piːtɪŋ/ *adjective* which competes □ **competing firms** firms which compete with each other □ **competing products** products from different companies which have the same use and are sold in the same markets at similar prices

competition /ˌkɒmpə'tɪʃ(ə)n/ *noun* the action of companies or individuals who are trying to do better than others, to win a larger share of the market, to control the use of resources, etc.

'...profit margins in the industries most exposed to foreign competition are worse than usual' [*Sunday Times*]

'...competition is steadily increasing and could affect profit margins as the company tries to retain its market share' [*Citizen (Ottawa)*]

competitive /kəm'petɪtɪv/ *adjective* which competes fairly □ **competitive price** a low price aimed to compete with a rival product □ **competitive product** a product made to compete with existing products

'...the company blamed fiercely competitive market conditions in Europe for a £14m operating loss last year' [*Financial Times*]

competitive edge /kəmˌpetɪtɪv 'edʒ/, **competitive advantage** /kəmˌpetɪtɪv ədˈvɑːntɪdʒ/ *noun* an advantage that one company or product has over its rivals in the market ○ *Any competitive edge we have in this market is due to our good after-sales service.* ○

Why does this product have the competitive edge over its rivals?

competitive exam /kəm,petɪtɪv ɪg-ˈzæm/ *noun* an examination (such as for entry to the civil service) where only the best candidates are offered jobs

competitively /kəmˈpetɪtɪvli/ *adverb* □ **competitively priced** sold at a low price which competes with the price of similar products from other companies

competitiveness /kəmˈpetɪtɪvnəs/ *noun* the fact of being competitive

'…farmers are increasingly worried by the growing lack of competitiveness for their products on world markets' [*Australian Financial Review*]

competitive pricing /kəm,petɪtɪv ˈpraɪsɪŋ/ *noun* the practice of putting low prices on goods so as to compete with other products

competitive tender /kəm,petɪtɪv ˈtendə/ *noun* a form of tender where different organisations are asked to tender for a contract, especially for government or local government work

competitor /kəmˈpetɪtə/ *noun* a person or company that competes ○ *Two German firms are our main competitors.*

'…sterling labour costs continue to rise between 3% and 5% a year faster than in most of our competitor countries' [*Sunday Times*]

complain /kəmˈpleɪn/ *verb* to say that something is no good or does not work properly ○ *The office is so cold the staff have started complaining.* ○ *She complained about the service.* ○ *They are complaining that our prices are too high.* ○ *If you want to complain, write to the manager.*

complaint /kəmˈpleɪnt/ *noun* a statement that you feel something is wrong ○ *complaints from the workforce about conditions in the factory* ○ *She sent her letter of complaint to the managing director.* □ **to make** *or* **to lodge a complaint against someone** to write and send an official complaint to someone's superior □ **to uphold a complaint** to agree that a complaint is well founded

complaints management /kəmˈpleɪnts ˌmænɪdʒmənt/ *noun* the management of complaints from customers

complaints procedure /kəmˈpleɪnts prəˌsiːdʒə/ *noun* a way of presenting complaints formally from a trade union to a management ○ *The trade union has followed the correct complaints procedure.*

complete /kəmˈpliːt/ *adjective* whole, with nothing missing ○ *The order is complete and ready for sending.* ○ *The shipment will be delivered only if it is complete.* ■ *verb* to finish ○ *The factory completed the order in two weeks.* ○ *How long will it take you to complete the job?* ○ *He has completed his probationary period.*

completion /kəmˈpliːʃ(ə)n/ *noun* the act of finishing something

completion date /kəmˈpliːʃ(ə)n deɪt/ *noun* a date when something will be finished

compliance /kəmˈplaɪəns/ *noun* agreement to do what is ordered □ **in compliance with** doing what has been ordered ○ *in compliance with EU directives on workers' pension rights* □ **compliance with company rules** obeying the rules set out by the company for good behaviour of employees

comply /kəmˈplaɪ/ *verb* to agree to do what is ordered (NOTE: complies – complying – complied)

comprehensive /ˌkɒmprɪˈhensɪv/ *adjective* which includes everything

compressed (working) time /ˌkɒmprest ˈwɜːkɪŋ taɪm/ *noun* a normal number of hours of work spread over fewer days (such as four 10-hour days instead of five 8-hour days) ○ *Compressed time is popular because it enables more people to enjoy long weekend breaks.* ○ *Compressed time will become more common when flexible work hours are accepted by more organisations.*

compromise /ˈkɒmprəmaɪz/ *noun* an agreement between two sides, where each side gives way a little ○ *Management offered £5 an hour, the union asked for £9, and a compromise of £7.50 was reached.* ■ *verb* to reach an agreement by giving way a little ○ *He asked £15 for it, I offered £7 and we compromised on £10.*

compulsory /kəm'pʌlsəri/ *adjective* which is forced or ordered

compulsory liquidation /kəm-ˌpʌlsəri lɪkwɪ'deɪʃ(ə)n/ *noun* liquidation which is ordered by a court

compulsory redundancy /kəm-ˌpʌlsəri rɪ'dʌndənsi/ *noun* a situation where an employee is made redundant by the company

computer /kəm'pjuːtə/ *noun* an electronic machine which calculates or stores information and processes it automatically

computer-based training /kəm-ˌpjuːtə beɪst 'treɪnɪŋ/ *noun* training that is carried out on computer, using programs that are usually interactive so that the trainees can select from multiple-choice options or key in their own answers

computer bureau /kəm'pjuːtə ˌbjʊərəʊ/ *noun* an office which offers to do work on its computers for companies which do not own their own computers

computer department /kəm-'pjuːtə dɪˌpɑːtmənt/ *noun* a department in a company which manages the company's computers

computer error /kəmˌpjuːtər 'erə/ *noun* a mistake made by a computer

computer file /kəm'pjuːtə faɪl/ *noun* a section of information on a computer, e.g. the payroll, list of addresses or customer accounts

computer fraud /kəm'pjuːtə frɔːd/ *noun* a fraud committed by using computer files (as in a bank)

computerise /kəm'pjuːtəraɪz/, **computerize** *verb* to change from a manual system to one using computers ○ *We have computerised all our records.* ○ *Stock control is now completely computerised.* ○ *We should computerise the personnel records to save time.*

computerised /kəm'pjuːtəraɪzd/, **computerized** *adjective* worked by computers ○ *a computerised invoicing system* ○ *a computerised filing system*

computer language /kəm'pjuːtə ˌlæŋgwɪdʒ/ *noun* a system of signs, letters and words used to instruct a computer

computer listing /kəmˌpjuːtə 'lɪstɪŋ/ *noun* a printout of a list of items taken from data stored in a computer

computer-literate /kəmˌpjuːtə 'lɪt(ə)rət/ *adjective* referring to a person who knows how to use more or less any type of computer

computer manager /kəm'pjuːtə ˌmænɪdʒə/ *noun* a person in charge of a computer department

computer operating system /kəmˌpjuːtər 'ɒpəreɪtɪŋ ˌsɪstəm/ *noun* the main program which operates a computer

computer programmer /kəm-ˌpjuːtə 'prəʊgræmə/ *noun* a person who writes computer programs

computer-readable /kəmˌpjuːtə 'riːdəb(ə)l/ *adjective* which can be read and understood by a computer ○ *computer-readable codes*

computer services /kəmˌpjuːtə 'sɜːvɪsɪz/ *plural noun* work using a computer, done by a computer bureau

computer system /kəm'pjuːtə ˌsɪstəm/ *noun* a set of programs, commands, etc., which run a computer

computer time /kəm'pjuːtə taɪm/ *noun* the time when a computer is being used, paid for at an hourly rate

comrade /'kɒmreɪd/ *noun* a friend or fellow employee or fellow member of a union

comradeship /'kɒmreɪdʃɪp/ *noun* a feeling of friendship and solidarity with other employees

concentration /ˌkɒnsən'treɪʃ(ə)n/ *noun* **1.** the degree to which a small number of businesses control a large section of the market ○ *Too much concentration created resentment among small businesses trying to enter the market.* ○ *Concentration has meant too little competition and therefore higher prices to the consumer.* **2.** a situation in which members of a specific social group are overrepresented ○ *The high percentage of nursery nurses who are women is an example of concentration.*

concern /kən'sɜːn/ *noun* **1.** a business or company **2.** the fact of being worried about a problem ○ *The management showed no concern at all for the workers' safety.* ■ *verb* to deal with or be connected with ○ *The sales staff are not concerned with the cleaning of the store.* ○ *She filled in a questionnaire concerning computer utilisation.* □ **to whom it may concern** words used at the heading of a letter of recommendation, etc., addressed to anyone who may be interested (such as a potential employer)

concession /kən'seʃ(ə)n/ *noun* **1.** the right to use someone else's property for business purposes **2.** an allowance such as a reduction of tax or price **3.** the act of allowing something to be done, which is not normally done ○ *The union obtained some important concessions from management during negotiations.*

concession bargaining /kən-'seʃ(ə)n ˌbɑːɡɪnɪŋ/ *noun* a situation where a union sees that it cannot negotiate large pay increases for its members, and so negotiates improvements in areas such as working conditions instead

conciliation /kən,sɪli'eɪʃ(ə)n/ *noun* the practice of bringing together the parties in a dispute with an independent third party, so that the dispute can be settled through a series of negotiations.

conciliation officer /kən,sɪli-'eɪʃ(ə)n ,ɒfɪsə/ *noun* an official of ACAS who tries to get the parties in an industrial dispute to settle their differences

Conciliation Service /kən,sɪli-'eɪʃ(ə)n ,sɜːvɪs/ *noun* same as **Advisory, Conciliation and Arbitration Service**

condition /kən'dɪʃ(ə)n/ *noun* **1.** something which has to be carried out as part of a contract or which has to be agreed before a contract becomes valid □ **on condition that** provided that ○ *They were granted the lease on condition that they paid the legal costs.* **2.** a general state or the general way of life in a certain place ○ *The union has complained of the bad working conditions in the factory.* ○ *Adverse trading conditions affected our*

profits. ○ *Working in unhealthy conditions is responsible for various illnesses after retirement.*

conditional /kən'dɪʃ(ə)nəl/ *adjective* provided that specific conditions are taken into account □ **to give a conditional acceptance** to accept, provided that specific things happen or that specific terms apply □ **offer is conditional on board's acceptance** the offer is made provided the board accepts

conditional offer /kən,dɪʃ(ə)nəl 'ɒfə/ *noun* an offer to buy provided that specific terms apply

conditions of employment /kən-,dɪʃ(ə)nz əv ɪm'plɔɪmənt/ *plural noun* the terms of a contract of employment

conduct *verb* /kən'dʌkt/ to carry on ○ *to conduct negotiations* ○ *The chairman conducted the negotiations very negligently.* ○ *She conducted the training session very efficiently.* ■ *noun* /'kɒndʌkt/ a way of behaving ○ *He was sacked for bad conduct at the staff Christmas party.*

Confederation of British Industry /kɒnfedə,reɪʃ(ə)n əv ,brɪtɪʃ 'ɪndəstri/ *noun* an organisation which represents British employers in commerce and industry. Abbr **CBI**

confer /kən'fɜː/ *verb* to discuss a problem with another person or within a group ○ *The interview board conferred in the next room before announcing the names of the successful candidates.* (NOTE: **conferring – conferred**)

conference /'kɒnf(ə)rəns/ *noun* **1.** a meeting of people to discuss problems ○ *Many useful tips can be picked up at a sales conference.* ○ *The conference of HR managers included talks on payment and recruitment policies.* □ **to be in conference** to be in a meeting **2.** a meeting of an organisation such as an association, society or union

conference call /'kɒnf(ə)rəns kɔːl/ *noun* a telephone call that connects three or more lines so that people in different places can talk to one another (NOTE: conference calls reduce the cost of meetings by making it unnecessary for the participants to spend time and money on getting together in one place)

conference delegate /'kɒnf(ə)rəns ˌdelɪgət/ *noun* a person who attends a conference as the representative of a group

conference method /'kɒnf(ə)rəns ˌmeθəd/ *noun* a method of teaching using discussion or exchange of ideas amongst students

conference phone /'kɒnf(ə)rəns fəʊn/ *noun* a telephone arranged in such a way that several people can speak into it from around a table

confidence /'kɒnfɪd(ə)ns/ *noun* **1.** the state of feeling sure or being certain ○ *The sales teams do not have much confidence in their manager.* ○ *The board has total confidence in the managing director.* **2.** □ **in confidence** in secret ○ *I will show you the report in confidence.*

confident /'kɒnfɪd(ə)nt/ *adjective* certain or sure ○ *I am confident the turnover will increase rapidly.* ○ *Are you confident the sales team can handle this product?*

confidential /ˌkɒnfɪ'denʃəl/ *adjective* not to be told or shown to other people ○ *The references sent by the applicant's last employer were in an envelope marked 'Private and Confidential'.* ○ *Whatever an employee says in an appraisal interview should be treated as confidential.* ○ *The consultants sent a confidential report to the chairman.*

confidential information /ˌkɒnfɪdenʃəl ˌɪnfə'meɪʃ(ə)n/ *noun* information which has to be kept secret

confidentiality /ˌkɒnfɪdenʃi'ælɪti/ *noun* the fact of being secret □ **she broke the confidentiality of the discussions** she told someone about the secret discussions

confidentiality agreement /ˌkɒnfɪdenʃi'ælɪti əˌgriːmənt/ *noun* an agreement in which an organisation that has important information about the plans and activities of another organisation promises not to pass that information on to outsiders (NOTE: confidentiality agreements are often used when someone is planning to buy a company and is given access to confidential information and in partnerships and benchmarking programmes.)

confidential report /ˌkɒnfɪdenʃəl rɪ'pɔːt/ *noun* a secret document which must not be shown to other people

confirm /kən'fɜːm/ *verb* to say that something is certain ○ *to confirm a hotel reservation* or *a ticket* or *an agreement* or *a booking* □ **to confirm someone in a job** to say that someone is now permanently in the job

confirmation /ˌkɒnfə'meɪʃ(ə)n/ *noun* **1.** the act of making certain **2.** a document which confirms something

conflict /'kɒnflɪkt/ *noun* antagonism between people, e.g. between management and workers ○ *There was conflict between the two groups of workers.*

conflict management /'kɒnflɪkt ˌmænɪdʒmənt/ *noun* a system of work that involves identifying possible sources of conflict within an organisation and dealing with and settling conflicts when they occur

conflict of interest /ˌkɒnflɪkt əv 'ɪntrəst/ *noun* a situation where a person or firm may profit personally from decisions taken in an official capacity

conflict of interest(s) /ˌkɒnflɪkt əv 'ɪntrəsts/ *noun* a situation in which a person or institution has difficulty in making a fair and impartial decision on some issue through having divided loyalties or being likely to benefit if the issue is decided in one way rather than another, as, e.g., when someone is connected with two or more companies who are competing with each other (NOTE: the correct thing to do in such cases is for the person concerned to declare any interests, to make known the way in which those interests conflict and to abstain from participating in the decision-making process)

conflict of rights /ˌkɒnflɪkt əv 'raɪts/ *noun* a situation where it is claimed that the terms of the employees contracts of employment or a negotiated agreement have not been met

conformance /kən'fɔːməns/ *noun* the process of acting in accordance with a rule ○ *The machine used is not in conformance with safety regulations.*

conformance quality /kən-ˈfɔːməns ˌkwɒlɪti/ *noun* (*in total quality management*) the way in which the product is made to fit the desired specifications

congratulate /kənˈɡrætʃʊleɪt/ *verb* to give someone your good wishes for having done something well ○ *The sales director congratulated the sales staff on doubling sales.* ○ *I want to congratulate you on your promotion.*

congratulations /kənˌɡrætʃʊ-ˈleɪʃ(ə)nz/ *plural noun* good wishes ○ *The staff sent her their congratulations on her promotion.*

conjunctive bargaining /kən-ˌdʒʌŋktɪv ˈbɑːɡɪnɪŋ/ *noun* collective bargaining where the union has to settle on the management's terms

conscientious /ˌkɒnʃiˈenʃəs/ *adjective* referring to a person who works carefully and well ○ *She's a very conscientious worker.*

consensual /kənˈsensjʊəl/ *adjective* by means of a consensus

consensual validation /kən-ˌsensjʊəl vælɪˈdeɪʃ(ə)n/ *noun* the process of validating an action by agreeing with other people's attitudes

consensus /kənˈsensəs/ *noun* an opinion which most people agree on ○ *management by consensus*

consent /kənˈsent/ *noun* agreement that something should be done ○ *Change of use requires the consent of the local planning authorities.* □ **by mutual consent** by agreement between the parties concerned ■ *verb* to agree that something should be done ○ *The management consented to the union's proposals.*

consider /kənˈsɪdə/ *verb* to think seriously about something □ **to consider the terms of a contract** to examine a contract and discuss whether the terms are acceptable

consideration /kənˌsɪdəˈreɪʃ(ə)n/ *noun* **1.** serious thought ○ *We are giving consideration to moving the head office to Scotland.* □ **the proposal under consideration** the proposal which is being considered at the moment **2.** something valuable exchanged as part of a contract

consist of /kənˈsɪst ɒv/ *verb* to be formed of ○ *The trade mission consists of the sales directors of ten major companies.*

conspiracy /kənˈspɪrəsi/ *noun* a legal term used to describe the intention of employees to break the law when resorting to industrial action ○ *Sanctions were laid down to discourage conspiracy.* ○ *The dockers resorted to conspiracy since they felt they could only oppose the bad working conditions through an illegal strike.*

constitutional strike /ˌkɒnstɪtjuːʃ(ə)n(ə)l ˈstraɪk/ *noun* US a strike that takes place when all the procedures agreed between a trade union and an employer for the avoidance of strikes have been gone through and the dispute has still not been resolved

construct /kənˈstrʌkt/ *verb* to build ○ *The company has tendered for the contract to construct the new bridge.*

construction site /kənˈstrʌkʃən saɪt/ *noun* a place where a building is being constructed ○ *All visitors to the construction site must wear safety helmets.*

constructive /kənˈstrʌktɪv/ *adjective* which helps in the making of something ○ *She made some constructive suggestions for improving management-worker relations.* ○ *We had a constructive proposal from a distribution company in Italy.*

consult /kənˈsʌlt/ *verb* to ask an expert for advice ○ *We consulted our accountant about our tax.*

consultancy /kənˈsʌltənsi/ *noun* the act of giving specialist advice ○ *a consultancy firm* ○ *She offers a consultancy service.*

consultant /kənˈsʌltənt/ *noun* a specialist who gives advice ○ *an engineering consultant* ○ *a management consultant* ○ *a tax consultant*

consultant's fee /kənˈsʌltənts fiː/ *noun* money paid to a consultant

consultation /ˌkɒnsəlˈteɪʃ(ə)n/ *noun* the process of asking other people for advice before coming to a decision

consultation agreement /ˌkɒnsəl-ˈteɪʃ(ə)n əˌɡriːmənt/ *noun* an agreement which lays down the areas where management commits itself to consult the opinion of the employees

consultative /kən'sʌltətɪv/ *adjective* which advises □ **to play a consultative role in** to act as consultant in

consultative committee /kən-'sʌltətɪv kə,mɪti/ *noun* a committee of representatives of the employees which meets regularly with top management ○ *The consultative committee was able to keep senior management in touch with feelings in the organisation.* ○ *Two workers and a foreman form the workers' part of the consultative committee.*

consulting /kən'sʌltɪŋ/ *adjective* giving specialist advice ○ *a consulting engineer*

consumer /kən'sjuːmə/ *noun* a person or company that buys and uses goods and services ○ *Gas consumers are protesting at the increase in prices.* ○ *The factory is a heavy consumer of water.*

'...forecasting consumer response is one problem which will never be finally solved' [*Marketing Week*]

'...consumer tastes in the UK are becoming much more varied' [*Marketing*]

'...the marketing director's brief will be to develop the holiday villages as a consumer brand, aimed at the upper end of the tourist market' [*Marketing Week*]

contact /'kɒntækt/ *noun* **1.** a person you know or a person you can ask for help or advice ○ *He has many contacts in the city.* ○ *Who is your contact in the ministry?* **2.** the act of getting in touch with someone □ **I have lost contact with them** I do not communicate with them any longer □ **he put me in contact with a good lawyer** he told me how to get in touch with a good lawyer ■ *verb* /'kɒntækt, kən'tækt/ to get in touch with someone, to communicate with someone ○ *He tried to contact his office by phone.* ○ *Can you contact the managing director at his club?*

contact effect /'kɒntækt ɪ,fekt/ *noun* the impression received when comparing the various performances of candidates in interviews

contention /kən'tenʃən/ *noun* **1.** an opinion or belief ○ *It is our contention that the decision of the tribunal is*

wrong. **2.** a dispute ○ *an area of contention between management and workers*

contentious /kən'tenʃəs/ *adjective* which is a source of dispute ○ *Management made a series of contentious proposals.*

contingency /kən'tɪndʒənsi/ *noun* a possible state of emergency when decisions will have to be taken quickly □ **to add on 10% to provide for contingencies** to provide for further expenditure which may be incurred

contingency allowance /kən-'tɪndʒənsi ə,laʊəns/ *noun* time added to the basic time established for a job to allow for irregularities in the job content ○ *A contingency allowance was necessary since the machinery used was not wholly reliable.* ○ *The unions protested that no contingency allowances were established in those jobs where delays were not the fault of the workers.*

contingency fund /kən'tɪndʒənsi fʌnd/ *noun* money set aside in case it is needed urgently

contingency plan /kən'tɪndʒənsi plæn/ *noun* a plan which will be put into action if something unexpected happens

contingency reserve /kən-'tɪndʒənsi rɪ,zɜːv/ *noun* money set aside in case it is needed urgently

contingent expenses /kən-,tɪndʒənt ɪk'spensɪz/ *plural noun* expenses which will be incurred only if something happens

continual /kən'tɪnjuəl/ *adjective* which happens again and again ○ *Production was slow because of continual breakdowns.*

continually /kən'tɪnjuəli/ *adverb* again and again ○ *The photocopier is continually breaking down.*

continuation /kən,tɪnju'eɪʃ(ə)n/ *noun* the act of continuing

continue /kən'tɪnjuː/ *verb* to go on doing something or to do again something which you were doing earlier ○ *The meeting started at 10 a.m. and continued until 6 p.m.* ○ *Negotiations will continue next Monday.*

continuing education /kən-,tɪnjuɪŋ edjʊ'keɪʃ(ə)n/ *noun* education which continues after school and university or college

continuing professional development /kən,tɪnjuɪŋ prə,feʃ(ə)n(ə)l dɪ'veləpmənt/ *noun* full form of **CPD**

continuous /kən'tɪnjuəs/ *adjective* with no end or with no breaks ○ *a continuous production line* □ **in continuous employment** employed for a period of time, without more than a week's gap (holidays, sickness, etc., are not counted as gaps) ○ *She was in continuous employment for the period 1998 to 2002.*

continuous assessment /kən,tɪnjuəs ə'sesmənt/ *noun* an assessment of a trainee's work carried out through the course (as opposed to terminal assessment at the end of the course)

continuous development /kən,tɪnjuəs dɪ'veləpmənt/ *noun* a system of continuous training for employees

continuous feed /kən,tɪnjuəs 'fiːd/ *noun* a device which feeds continuous stationery into a printer

continuous improvement /kən,tɪnjuəs ɪm'pruːvmənt/ *noun* a procedure and management philosophy that focuses on looking all the time for ways in which small improvements can be made to processes and products, with the aim of increasing quality and reducing waste and cost (NOTE: Continuous improvement is one of the tools that underpin the philosophies of total quality management and lean production; in Japan it is known as kaizen.)

continuous learning /kən,tɪnjuəs 'lɜːnɪŋ/ *noun* a system of training which continues during an employee's career with a company

continuous service /kən,tɪnjuəs 'sɜːvɪs/ *noun* a period of employment with one employer, which begins on the day on which the employee starts work and ends on the day which they resign or are dismissed

continuous shift system /kən,tɪnjuəs 'ʃɪft ,sɪstəm/ *noun* a system where groups of employees work shifts throughout the week, including weekends

continuous shiftwork /kən,tɪnjuəs 'ʃɪftwɜːk/ *noun* a system of working designed to ensure that an organisation can operate seven days a week, 24 hours a day, e.g. in order to make full use of expensive equipment or to provide round-the-clock customer service (NOTE: Continuous shiftwork usually comprises three eight-hour or two twelve-hour shifts, or a mix of the two.)

contract *noun* /'kɒntrækt/ **1.** a legal agreement between two parties ○ *to draw up a contract* ○ *to draft a contract* ○ *to sign a contract* □ **the contract is binding on both parties** both parties signing the contract must do what is agreed □ **under contract** bound by the terms of a contract ○ *The firm is under contract to deliver the goods by November.* □ **to void a contract** to make a contract invalid **2.** □ **by private contract** by private legal agreement **3.** an agreement for the supply of a service or goods ○ *to enter into a contract to supply spare parts* ○ *to sign a contract for £10,000 worth of spare parts* □ **to put work out to contract** to decide that work should be done by another company on a contract, rather than by employing members of staff to do it □ **to award a contract to a company**, **to place a contract with a company** to decide that a company shall have the contract to do work for you □ **to tender for a contract** to put forward an estimate of cost for work under contract ■ *verb* /kən'trækt/ to agree to do some work on the basis of a legally binding contract ○ *to contract to supply spare parts* or *to contract for the supply of spare parts* □ **to contract out of an agreement** to withdraw from an agreement with the written permission of the other party

COMMENT: A contract is an agreement between two or more parties to create legal obligations between them. Some contracts are made 'under seal', i.e. they are signed and sealed by the parties; most contracts are made orally or in writing. The essential elements of a contract are: (a) that an offer made by one party should be accepted by the other; (b) consideration (i.e. payment of money); (c) the intention to create legal relations. The terms of a contract may be express or implied. A breach of contract by one party entitles the other party to sue for damages or to ask for something to be done.

contracted-out pension scheme /kən,træktɪd aʊt 'penʃən skiːm/ *noun* a private pension scheme which gives benefits at least as high as the state scheme

contract for services /ˌkɒntrækt fə 'sɜːvɪsɪz/ *noun* an agreement between employer and employee where the employee is hired as an independent party for a limited time and is not under the control of the employer

contracting out /ˌkɒntræktɪŋ 'aʊt/ *noun* **1.** the process, on the part of an employee, of withdrawing from the UK State Earnings-Related Pension Scheme and buying an appropriate personal pension **2.** the process, on the part of an employer, of withdrawing employees from the UK's State Earnings-Related Pension Scheme and enrolling them in an occupational pension scheme that meets specified standards

contracting party /kən,træktɪŋ 'pɑːti/ *noun* a person or company that signs a contract

contract law /'kɒntrækt lɔː/ *noun* laws relating to private agreements

contract of employment /ˌkɒntrækt əv ɪm'plɔɪmənt/ *noun* a contract between employer and an employee stating all the conditions of work

contract of service /ˌkɒntrækt əv 'sɜːvɪs/ *noun* a legal agreement between an employer and an employee whereby the employee will work for the employer and be directed by them, in return for payment

contractor /kən'træktə/ *noun* a person or company that does work according to a written agreement

contract out /ˌkɒntrækt 'aʊt/ *verb* to hire another organisation or person to carry out part or all of a certain piece of work ○ *The catering firm has contracted out the distribution of its products to a delivery firm.* ○ *We shall contract out any work we are not specialised in.* ○ *The supply of spare parts was contracted out to Smith Ltd.*

contractual /kən'træktʃuəl/ *adjective* according to a contract □ **to fulfil your contractual obligations** to do what you have agreed to do in a contract

contractual liability /kən,træktʃuəl ,laɪə'bɪlɪti/ *noun* a legal responsibility for something as stated in a contract

contractually /kən'træktʃuəli/ *adverb* according to a contract ○ *The company is contractually bound to pay our expenses.*

contract work /'kɒntrækt wɜːk/ *noun* work done according to a written agreement

contrary /'kɒntrəri/ *noun* the opposite □ **failing instructions to the contrary** unless different instructions are given

contribute /kən'trɪbjuːt/ *verb* to give money or add to money ○ *We agreed to contribute 10% of the profits.* ○ *They had contributed to the pension fund for 10 years.*

contribution /ˌkɒntrɪ'bjuːʃ(ə)n/ *noun* money paid to add to a sum

contributor /kən'trɪbjʊtə/ *noun* a person who gives money

contributory /kən'trɪbjʊt(ə)ri/ *adjective* which helps to cause ○ *Falling exchange rates have been a contributory factor in the company's loss of profits.*

contributory fault /kən,trɪbjʊt(ə)ri 'fɔːlt/ *noun* a situation in an unfair dismissal where the employee was to a certain extent at fault

contributory negligence /kən,trɪbjʊt(ə)ri 'neglɪdʒəns/ *noun* negligence partly caused by the plaintiff and partly by the defendant, resulting in harm done to the plaintiff

contributory pension plan /kən,trɪbjʊt(ə)ri 'penʃən plæn/**, contributory pension scheme** /kən,trɪbjʊt(ə)ri 'penʃən skiːm/ *noun* a pension plan where the employee has to contribute a percentage of salary

control /kən'trəʊl/ *noun* **1.** the power or ability to direct something ○ *The company is under the control of three shareholders.* ○ *Top management exercises tight control over spending.* □ **to lose control of a business** to find that you have less than 50% of the shares in a company, and so are no longer able to direct it ○ *The family lost control of its business.* **2.** the act of restricting or checking something or making sure that something is kept in check □ **under control** kept in check ○ *Expenses are kept under tight control.* ○ *The company is trying to bring its overheads back under control.* □ **out of control** not kept in check ○ *Costs have got out of control.* ■ *verb* **1.** □ **to control a business** to direct a business ○ *The business is controlled by a company based in Luxembourg.* ○ *The company is controlled by the majority shareholder.* **2.** to make sure that something is kept in check or is not allowed to develop ○ *The government is fighting to control inflation* or *to control the rise in the cost of living.* (NOTE: **controlling – controlled**)

control group /kən'trəʊl gruːp/ *noun* a small group which is used to check a sample group

controlled /kən'trəʊld/ *adjective* ruled or kept in check

controller /kən'trəʊlə/ *noun* **1.** a person who controls something (especially the finances of a company) **2.** *US* the chief accountant in a company

controlling /kən'trəʊlɪŋ/ *adjective* □ **to have a controlling interest in a company** to own more than 50% of the shares so that you can direct how the company is run

convene /kən'viːn/ *verb* to ask people to come together ○ *to convene a meeting of shareholders* ○ *to convene a meeting of union members*

convenience /kən'viːniəns/ *noun* □ **at your earliest convenience** as soon as you find it possible

convenor /kən'viːnə/ *noun* a trade unionist who organises union meetings

convention /kən'venʃən/ *noun* an international agreement ○ *the Geneva Convention on Human Rights*

conversion of funds /kən,vɜːʃ(ə)n əv 'fʌndz/ *noun* the act of using money which does not belong to you for a purpose for which it is not supposed to be used

convict /kən'vɪkt/ *verb* □ **to convict someone of a crime** to find that someone is guilty of a crime

conviction /kən'vɪkʃən/ *noun* an act of finding that someone accused of a crime is guilty ○ *He has had ten convictions for burglary.*

cooling-off period /,kuːlɪŋ 'ɒf ,pɪəriəd/ *noun* (*during an industrial dispute*) a period when negotiations have to be carried on and no action can be taken by either side

co-op /'kəʊ ɒp/ *noun* same as **cooperative**

co-operate /kəʊ'ɒpəreɪt/ *verb* to work together ○ *The regional governments are co-operating in the fight against piracy.* ○ *The two firms have co-operated on the computer project.*

co-operation /kəʊ,ɒpə'reɪʃ(ə)n/ *noun* the act of working together ○ *The project was completed ahead of schedule with the co-operation of the workforce.*

cooperative /kəʊ'ɒp(ə)rətɪv/ *adjective* willing to work together ○ *The workforce has not been cooperative over the management's productivity plan.* ■ *noun* a business run by a group of employees who are also the owners and who share the profits ○ *an industrial cooperative* ○ *The product is marketed by an agricultural cooperative.* ○ *They set up a workers' cooperative to run the factory.*

co-opt /kəʊ'ɒpt/ *verb* □ **to co-opt someone onto a committee** to ask someone to join a committee without being elected

co-owner /kəʊ'əʊnə/ *noun* a person who owns something with another person ○ *The two sisters are co-owners of the property.*

co-ownership /kəʊ'əʊnəʃɪp/ *noun* an arrangement where two people own a property or where partners or employees have shares in a company

copartner /kəʊ'pɑːtnə/ *noun* a person who is a partner in a business with another person

copartnership /kəʊ'pɑːtnəʃɪp/ *noun* an arrangement where partners or employees have shares in the company

cope /kəʊp/ *verb* to manage to do something ○ *The new assistant manager coped very well when the manager was on holiday.* ○ *The warehouse is trying to cope with the backlog of orders.*

core /kɔː/ *noun* the central or main part

core skills /'kɔː skɪlz/ *noun* basic skills, which are needed by everyone

core time /'kɔː taɪm/ *noun* a period when people working under a flexitime system must be present at work

core values /kɔː 'væljuːz/ *plural noun* a set of concepts and ideals that guide someone's life and help them to make important decisions

core workers /'kɔː ˌwɜːkəz/ *plural noun* workers who are in full-time employment (as opposed to part-timers or casual workers who are called 'peripheral workers')

corporate /'kɔːp(ə)rət/ *adjective* **1.** referring to a whole company **2.** referring to a large organisation

'...the prime rate is the rate at which banks lend to their top corporate borrowers' [*Wall Street Journal*]

'...if corporate forecasts are met, sales will exceed $50 million next year' [*Citizen (Ottawa)*]

corporate climate /ˌkɔːp(ə)rət 'klaɪmət/ *noun* the general feeling and atmosphere within an organisation that is mainly created by the attitudes of its managers towards their work, their staff and their customers and that can affect such things as productivity, creativity, and customer focus

corporate communication /ˌkɔːp(ə)rət kəmjuːnɪ'keɪʃ(ə)n/ *noun* the activities undertaken by an organisation to pass on information both to its own employees and to its existing and prospective customers and the general public

corporate culture /ˌkɔːp(ə)rət 'kʌltʃə/ *noun* the way of managing a corporation, by increasing the importance of the corporation itself, and therefore the loyalty of the workforce to the corporation

corporate ethos /ˌkɔːp(ə)rət 'iːθɒs/ *noun* a company's special way of working and thinking

corporate hospitality /ˌkɔːp(ə)rət hɒspɪ'tælɪti/ *noun* entertainment provided by an organisation, originally intended to help salespeople build relationships with customers, but now increasingly used as an incentive for staff and in team-building and training exercises for employees

corporate image /ˌkɔːp(ə)rət 'ɪmɪdʒ/ *noun* an idea which a company would like the public to have of it

corporate planning /ˌkɔːp(ə)rət 'plænɪŋ/ *noun* the process of planning the future work of a whole company

corporate restructuring /ˌkɔːp(ə)rət riː'strʌktʃərɪŋ/ *noun* a fundamental change in the way in which an organisation is structured that may involve increasing or decreasing the various layers of staff between the top and the bottom of the hierarchy or re-assigning roles and responsibilities within it (NOTE: Corporate restructuring has generally come to mean reorganising after a period of unsatisfactory performance, and often involves the closure of parts of the business and the laying-off of personnel.)

corporate strategy /ˌkɔːp(ə)rət 'strætədʒi/ *noun* the plans for future action by a corporation

corporate university /ˌkɔːp(ə)rət juːnɪ'vɜːsɪti/ *noun* an educational centre run by an organisation that offers opportunities for training and development only to its own employees, especially in skills that the organisation needs to fulfil its own needs

corporate vision /ˌkɔːp(ə)rət 'vɪʒ(ə)n/ *noun* the overall aim or purpose of an organisation that all its business activities are designed to help it achieve (NOTE: An organisation's corporate vision is usually summed up in its vision statement.)

corporation /ˌkɔːpə'reɪʃ(ə)n/ *noun* a large company

COMMENT: A corporation is formed by registration with the Registrar of Companies under the Companies Act (in the case of public and private companies) or other Acts of Parliament (in the case of building societies and charities).

correct /kə'rekt/ *adjective* accurate or right ○ *The published accounts do not give a correct picture of the company's financial position.* ■ *verb* to remove mistakes from something ○ *The accounts department have corrected the invoice.* ○ *You will have to correct all these typing errors before you send the letter.*

correction /kə'rekʃən/ *noun* an act of making something correct ○ *She made some corrections to the text of the speech.*

'…there were fears in October that shares were overvalued and bears were ready to enter the market. This only proved to be a small correction' [*Investors Chronicle*]

correspondence /ˌkɒrɪ'spɒndəns/ *noun* letters, emails or other messages exchanged

correspondence course /ˌkɒrɪ-'spɒndəns kɔːs/ *noun* a course done by mail ○ *She learnt accountancy through a correspondence course.* ○ *He is taking a correspondence course in company law.*

cost /kɒst/ *noun* the amount of money which has to be paid for something ○ *Computer costs are falling each year.* ○ *We cannot afford the cost of two cars.* □ **to cover costs** to produce enough money in sales to pay for the costs of production ○ *The sales revenue barely covers the costs of advertising or the advertising costs.* □ **to sell at cost** to sell at a price which is the same as the cost of manufacture or the wholesale cost ■ *verb* **1.** to have a price ○ *How much does the machine cost?* ○ *This cloth costs £10 a metre.* **2.** □ **to cost a product** to calculate how much money will be needed to make a product, and so work out its selling price

cost accountant /'kɒst əˌkaʊntənt/ *noun* an accountant who gives managers information about their business costs

cost accounting /'kɒst əˌkaʊntɪŋ/ *noun* the process of preparing special accounts of manufacturing and sales costs

cost analysis /'kɒst əˌnæləsɪs/ *noun* the process of calculating in advance what a new product will cost

cost-benefit analysis /kɒst 'benɪfɪt əˌnæləsɪs/ *noun* the process of comparing the costs and benefits of different possible ways of using available resources

cost centre /'kɒst ˌsentə/ *noun* a person or group whose costs can be itemised and to which costs can be allocated in accounts

cost-cutting /'kɒst ˌkʌtɪŋ/ *noun* the process of reducing costs ○ *We have made three secretaries redundant as part of our cost-cutting programme.*

cost-effective /ˌkɒstɪ 'fektɪv/ *adjective* which gives good value when compared with the original cost ○ *We find advertising in the Sunday newspapers very cost-effective.*

cost-effectiveness /ˌkɒst ɪ-'fektɪvnəs/, **cost efficiency** /ˌkɒst ɪ-'fɪʃənsi/ *noun* the quality of being cost-effective ○ *Can we calculate the cost-effectiveness of air freight against shipping by sea?*

cost factor /'kɒst ˌfæktə/ *noun* the problem of cost

costing /'kɒstɪŋ/ *noun* a calculation of the manufacturing costs, and so the selling price of a product ○ *The costings give us a retail price of $2.95.* ○ *We cannot do the costing until we have details of all the production expenditure.*

costly /'kɒstli/ *adjective* costing a lot of money, or costing too much money ○ *Defending the court case was a costly process.* ○ *The mistakes were time-consuming and costly.*

cost of living /ˌkɒst əv 'lɪvɪŋ/ *noun* money which has to be paid for basic items such as food, heating or rent ○ *to allow for the cost of living in the salary adjustments*

cost-of-living allowance /ˌkɒst əv 'lɪvɪŋ əˌlaʊəns/ *noun* an addition to normal salary to cover increases in the cost of living (NOTE: the American equivalent is **COLA**)

cost-of-living bonus /ˌkɒst əv 'lɪvɪŋ ˌbəʊnəs/ *noun* money paid to meet the increase in the cost of living

cost-of-living increase /ˌkɒst əv 'lɪvɪŋ ˌɪnkriːs/ *noun* an increase in salary to allow it to keep up with the increased cost of living

cost of sales /ˌkɒst əv 'seɪlz/ *noun* all the costs of a product sold, including manufacturing costs and the staff costs of the production department, before general overheads are calculated

costs /kɒsts/ *plural noun* the expenses involved in a court case ○ *The judge awarded costs to the defendant.* ○ *Costs of the case will be borne by the prosecution.* □ **to pay costs** to pay the expenses of a court case

cottage industry /ˌkɒtɪdʒ 'ɪndəstri/ *noun* the production of goods or some other type of work, carried out by people working in their own homes

council /'kaʊnsəl/ *noun* an official group chosen to run something or to advise on a problem

counselling /'kaʊnsəlɪŋ/ *noun* the act of giving professional advice to others on personal matters ○ *An office is being set up for counselling employees who have professional or social problems.* ○ *Counselling helps employees get accustomed to their new environment, by offering advice and guidance.* (NOTE: the usual US spelling is **counseling**)

counsellor /'kaʊnsələ/ *noun* a person who gives professional advice to others on personal matters (NOTE: the usual US spelling is **counselor**)

counter- /kaʊntə/ *prefix* against

counterbid /'kaʊntəbɪd/ *noun* a higher bid in reply to a previous bid ○ *When I bid £20 she put in a counterbid of £25.*

counter-claim /'kaʊntə kleɪm/ *noun* a claim for damages made in reply to a previous claim ○ *Jones claimed £25,000 in damages against Smith, and Smith entered a counter-claim of £50,000 for loss of office.* ○ *The union negotiators entered a counter-claim for a reduction in work hours.* ■ *verb* to put in a counter-claim ○ *Jones claimed £25,000 in damages and Smith counter-claimed £50,000 for loss of office.*

countermand /ˌkaʊntə'mɑːnd/ *verb* to say that an order must not be carried out □ **to countermand an order**

counter-offer /'kaʊntər ˌɒfə/ *noun* a higher or lower offer made in reply to another offer ○ *Smith Ltd made an offer of £1m for the property, and Blacks replied with a counter-offer of £1.4m.*

'...the company set about paring costs and improving the design of its product. It came up with a price cut of 14%, but its counter-offer – for an order that was to have provided 8% of its workload next year – was too late and too expensive' [*Wall Street Journal*]

counterpart /'kaʊntəpɑːt/ *noun* a person who has a similar job in another company □ **John is my counterpart in Smith's** John has the same post as I have here

counter-productive /ˌkaʊntə prə'dʌktɪv/ *adjective* which has the opposite effect to what you expect ○ *Increasing overtime pay was counter-productive, the workers simply worked more slowly.* ○ *The MD's talk about profitability was quite counter-productive, as it encouraged the employees to ask for higher wages.*

countersign /'kaʊntəsaɪn/ *verb* to sign a document which has already been signed by someone else ○ *All our cheques have to be countersigned by the finance director.* ○ *The sales director countersigns all my orders.*

couple /'kʌp(ə)l/ *noun* two things or people taken together ○ *We only have enough stock for a couple of weeks.* ○ *A couple of the directors were ill, so the board meeting was cancelled.*

course /kɔːs/ *noun* **1.** □ **in the course of** during or while something is happening ○ *In the course of the discussion, the managing director explained the company's expansion plans.* ○ *Sales have risen sharply in the course of the last few months.* **2.** a series of lessons or a programme of instruction ○ *She has finished her secretarial course.* ○ *The company has paid for her to attend a course for trainee sales managers.* ○ *Management trainees all took a six-month course in business studies.* ○ *The training officer was constantly on the lookout for new courses in management studies.* ○ *The company sent her on a management course.* □ **she went on a course** she attended a course of study

court /kɔːt/ *noun* a place where a judge listens to a case and decides legally which of the parties in the argument is right □ **to take someone to court** to tell someone to appear in court to settle an argument □ **settlement was reached out of court, the two parties reached an out-of-court settlement** the dispute was settled between the two parties privately without continuing the court case

court case /ˈkɔːt keɪs/ *noun* a legal action or trial

court hearing /kɔːt ˈhɪərɪŋ/ *noun* a court case

covenant /ˈkʌvənənt/ *noun* a legal contract ■ *verb* to agree to pay a sum of money each year by contract ○ *to covenant to pay £10 per annum*

cover *noun* /ˈkʌvə/ something put over a machine, etc., to keep it clean ○ *Put a cover over your PC when the office is being redecorated.* ■ **1.** protection guaranteed by insurance □ **to operate without adequate cover** to operate without being protected by insurance □ **to ask for additional cover** to ask the insurance company to increase the amount for which you are insured **2.** □ **to provide cover for someone** to work in place of someone who is ill or on holiday ■ *noun* /ˈkʌvə/ □ **to send something under separate cover** in a separate envelope □ **to send a magazine under plain cover** in an ordinary envelope with no company name printed on it ■ *verb* /ˈkʌvə/ **1.** to put something over a machine, etc., to keep it clean ○ *Don't forget to cover your PC when they are repainting the office.* **2.** to protect □ **to be fully covered** to have insurance against all risks ○ *The insurance covers fire, theft and loss of work.*

'…three export credit agencies have agreed to provide cover for large projects in Nigeria' [*Business Times (Lagos)*]

Coverdale training /ˈkʌvədeɪl ˌtreɪnɪŋ/ *noun* a system of training that concentrates on improving teamwork and methods of getting a job done (NOTE: Coverdale training often involves asking groups of people to act out everyday situations and experiment until they find the best way of dealing with them)

covering letter /ˌkʌvərɪŋ ˈletə/, **covering note** /ˌkʌvərɪŋ ˈnəʊt/ *noun* a letter or note sent with documents to say why you are sending them ○ *He sent a covering letter with his curriculum vitae, explaining why he wanted the job.* ○ *The job advertisement asked for a CV and a covering letter.*

CPD *noun* training and education that continues throughout a person's career in order to improve the skills and knowledge they use to do a job or succession of jobs. Full form **continuing personal development**

CPF *abbr* Central Provident Fund

CPM *abbr* cost per mille

craft /krɑːft/ *noun* traditional manufacture done by hand

craftsman /ˈkrɑːftsmən/, **craftswoman** /ˈkrɑːftsˌwʊmən/ *noun* a man or woman who works in a craft

craftsmanship /ˈkrɑːftsmənʃɪp/ *noun* skill in doing craft work

craft union /ˈkrɑːft ˌjuːnjən/ *noun* the oldest type of trade union, for skilled workers in a particular craft or trade

craft worker /ˈkrɑːft ˌwɜːkə/ *noun* a skilled manual worker, especially one who has been through an apprenticeship

CRE *abbr* Commission for Racial Equality

create /kriˈeɪt/ *verb* to make something new ○ *By acquiring small unprofitable companies he soon created a large manufacturing group.* ○ *The government scheme aims at creating new jobs for young people.*

'…he insisted that the tax advantages he directed towards small businesses will help create jobs and reduce the unemployment rate' [*Toronto Star*]

creation /kriˈeɪʃ(ə)n/ *noun* the process of making something

creative director /kriˌeɪtɪv daɪˈrektə/ *noun* an employee of an advertising agency who is in overall charge of finding the right words and images to promote the product during an advertising campaign

creativity /ˌkriːeɪˈtɪvɪti/, **creative thinking** /kriˌeɪtɪv ˈθɪŋkɪŋ/ *noun* the ability to use the imagination to produce new ideas or things

creativity test /ˌkriːeɪˈtɪvɪti test/ *noun* a test designed to assess the originality or imagination which someone can apply to solving problems ○ *Creativity tests will be given to those applying for jobs in our company where new approaches are needed to solve old problems.* ○ *The HR manager favours creativity tests instead of the more traditional IQ tests.*

crèche /kreʃ/ *noun* a special room or building on a company's premises where babies and small children can be looked after ○ *The company provides crèche facilities for its staff.* Compare **nursery**

credentials /krɪˈdenʃəlz/ *plural noun* letters or documents which describe a person's qualities and skills ○ *The new production manager has very impressive credentials.*

crème de la crème /ˌkrem də læ ˈkrem/ *noun* the elite or the very best of a profession ○ *It is a very exclusive recruitment agency and only looks for the crème de la crème.*

criminal record /ˌkrɪmɪn(ə)l ˈrekɔːd/ *noun* same as **police record**

crisis /ˈkraɪsɪs/ *noun* a serious economic situation where decisions have to be taken rapidly ○ *a banking crisis* ○ *The government stepped in to try to resolve the international crisis.* ○ *Withdrawals from the bank have reached crisis level.* ○ *The crisis in the mortgage banks has caused problems for the central bank.* □ **to take crisis measures** to take severe measures rapidly to stop a crisis developing

crisis bargaining /ˈkraɪsɪs ˌbɑːɡɪnɪŋ/ *noun* collective bargaining under the threat of a strike deadline ○ *If crisis bargaining doesn't produce agreement on the 12% pay increase, a strike will be called.*

crisis management /ˈkraɪsɪs ˌmænɪdʒmənt/ *noun* actions taken by an organisation to protect itself when unexpected events or situations occur that could threaten its success or continued operation (NOTE: Crisis situations may result from external factors such as the development of a new product by a competitor or changes in legislation, or from internal factors such as a product failure or faulty decision-making, and often involve the need to make quick decisions on the basis of uncertain or incomplete information.)

criterion /kraɪˈtɪəriən/ *noun* the standard by which something can be judged ○ *Using the criterion of the ratio of cases solved to cases reported, the police force is becoming more efficient.* (NOTE: plural is **criteria**)

critical path analysis /ˌkrɪtɪk(ə)l ˈpɑːθ əˌnæləsɪs/ *noun* the analysis of the way a project is organised in terms of the minimum time it will take to complete, calculating which parts can be delayed without holding up the rest of the project. Abbr **CPM**

critical success factors /ˌkrɪtɪk(ə)l səkˈses ˌfæktəz/ *plural noun* the aspects of a business that are considered to be most necessary for it to be able to achieve its aims and continue to operate successfully over time

criticise /ˈkrɪtɪsaɪz/, **criticize** *verb* to say that something or someone is wrong or is working badly ○ *The MD criticised the sales manager for not improving the volume of sales.* ○ *The design of the new catalogue has been criticised.*

criticism /ˈkrɪtɪsɪz(ə)m/ *noun* words showing that you consider that someone or something is wrong ○ *The tribunal made some criticisms of the way in which the company had presented its case.*

cross-functional /krɒs ˈfʌŋkʃən(ə)l/ *adjective* referring to an employee who can work at different and varied tasks

cross-picketing /krɒs ˈpɪkɪtɪŋ/ *noun* picketing by more than one trade union, when each claims to represent the workforce ○ *Cross-picketing damaged the workers' case by showing up the divisions in their ranks.* ○ *Cross-picketing was due to the rivalry between the two unions rather than any real attempt to represent the workers' interests.*

cultural creative /ˌkʌltʃərəl kriˈeɪtɪv/ *noun* someone who values personal and spiritual development, enjoys change, likes learning about new cultures and, usually, wants a simpler way of life

culture /'kʌltʃə/ *noun* a way of living in a society or a country

culture shock /'kʌltʃə ʃɒk/ *noun* the shock when a person moves from one type of society to another (as for emigrants from European countries to the USA)

current /'kʌrənt/ *adjective* referring to the present time ○ *the current round of wage negotiations*

'...crude oil output plunged during the past month and is likely to remain at its current level for the near future' [*Wall Street Journal*]

currently /'kʌrəntli/ *adverb* at the present time ○ *We are currently negotiating with the bank for a loan.*

curriculum vitae /kə,rɪkjʊləm 'viːtaɪ/ *noun* a summary of a person's work experience and qualifications sent to a prospective employer by someone applying for a job ○ *Candidates should send a letter of application with a curriculum vitae to the HR manager.* ○ *The curriculum vitae listed all the candidate's previous jobs and her reasons for leaving them.* Abbr **CV** (NOTE: the plural is **curriculums** or **curricula vitae.** American English is **résumé**)

cushy /'kʊʃi/ *adjective* which does not involve any effort (*informal*)

cushy number /,kʊʃi 'nʌmbə/ *noun* work that offers the same money for less effort than another similar job ○ *He spends all his time looking for a cushy number.* (NOTE: American English is **gravy job**)

customer focus /,kʌstəmə 'fəʊkəs/ *noun* the aiming of all marketing operations towards the customer

cut /kʌt/ *noun* **1.** the sudden lowering of a price, salary or the number of jobs ○ *price cuts* or *cuts in prices* □ **he took a cut in salary**, **he took a salary cut** he

accepted a lower salary **2.** a share in a payment ○ *She introduces new customers and gets a cut of the sales rep's commission.* ■ *verb* **1.** to lower suddenly ○ *We are cutting prices on all our models.* □ **to cut (back) production** to reduce the quantity of products made ○ *The company has cut back its sales force.* ○ *We have taken out the second telephone line in order to try to cut costs.* **2.** to reduce the number of something □ **to cut jobs** to reduce the number of jobs by making people redundant □ **he cut his losses** he stopped doing something which was creating a loss **3.** □ **to be cut out for** to be very suitable for ○ *She was not cut out for a post as a personal secretary.*

'...state-owned banks cut their prime rates a percentage point to 11%' [*Wall Street Journal*]

'...the US bank announced a cut in its prime from 10½ per cent to 10 per cent' [*Financial Times*]

'Opec has on average cut production by one third since 1979' [*Economist*]

cutback /'kʌtbæk/ *noun* a reduction ○ *cutbacks in government spending*

cut down (on) /,kʌt 'daʊn ɒn/ *verb* to reduce suddenly the amount of something used ○ *The government is cutting down on welfare expenditure.* ○ *The office is trying to cut down on electricity consumption.* ○ *We have installed networked computers to cut down on paperwork.*

CV *abbr* curriculum vitae ○ *Please apply in writing, enclosing a current CV.*

cybernetics /,saɪbə'netɪks/ *plural noun* the study of information communication systems and how they can be improved (NOTE: takes a singular verb)

cycle /'saɪk(ə)l/ *noun* a set of events which happen in a regularly repeated sequence

cycle time /'saɪk(ə)l taɪm/ *noun* the time taken to complete a job ○ *The cycle time for the job will decrease with the introduction of new machinery.*

D

daily rate /ˌdeɪli 'reɪt/ *noun* money paid for one day's work

damaged /'dæmɪdʒd/ *adjective* which has suffered damage or which has been harmed ○ *goods damaged in transit*

damages /'dæmɪdʒɪz/ *plural noun* money claimed as compensation for harm done ○ *to claim £1000 in damages* ○ *to be liable for damages* ○ *to pay £25,000 in damages* □ **to bring an action for damages against someone** to take someone to court and claim damages

danger /'deɪndʒə/ *noun* **1.** the possibility of being harmed or killed ○ *The old machinery poses a danger to the workforce.* ○ *The red light means danger.* **2.** the likelihood or possibility of something □ **there is no danger of the sales force leaving** it is not likely that the sales force will leave □ **in danger of** which may easily happen ○ *The company is in danger of being taken over.* ○ *She is in danger of being made redundant.*

danger money /'deɪndʒə ˌmʌni/ *noun* extra money paid to employees in dangerous jobs ○ *The workforce has stopped work and asked for danger money.* ○ *He decided to go to work on an oil rig because of the danger money offered as an incentive.*

dangerous /'deɪndʒərəs/ *adjective* which can be harmful □ **dangerous job** a job where the workers may be hurt or killed

danger zone bonus /'deɪndʒə zəʊn ˌbəʊnəs/ *noun* a bonus for working in a particularly dangerous area ○ *Danger-zone bonuses are awarded to workers employed in countries experiencing civil unrest or war.*

data /'deɪtə/ *noun* information available on computer, e.g. letters or figures ○ *All important data on employees was fed into the computer.* ○ *To calculate the weekly wages, you need data on hours worked and rates of pay.* (NOTE: takes singular or plural verb)

data bank /'deɪtə bæŋk/ *noun* a store of information in a computer

database /'deɪtəbeɪs/ *noun* a set of data stored in an organised way in a computer system ○ *We can extract the lists of potential customers from our database.*

data protection /'deɪtə prəˌtekʃən/ *noun* the safeguards that protect people whose personal details are held on computers or in paper-based filing systems against improper use or storage of the data that relates to them (NOTE: The growing use of computers to store information about individuals has led many countries to pass laws designed to protect the privacy of individuals and prevent the disclosure of information to unauthorised people.)

Data Protection Act (1984) /ˌdeɪtə prəˈtekʃən ækt/ *noun* an Act of Parliament which prevents the use of details of a person which are stored in a database for other uses than that for which the record was originally made

date /deɪt/ *noun* **1.** the number of a day, month and year ○ *I have received your letter of yesterday's date.* □ **date of receipt** the date when something is received **2.** □ **to date** up to now □ **interest to date** interest up to the present time ■ *verb* to put a date on a document ○ *The cheque was dated March 24th.* ○ *You forgot to date the cheque.*

dated /'deɪtɪd/ *adjective* **1.** with a date written on it ○ *Thank you for your letter* *dated June 15th.* **2.** out-of-date ○ *The unions have criticised management for its dated ideas.*

date of birth /ˌdeɪt əv ˈbɜːθ/ *noun* the day, month and year when someone was born

date of departure /ˌdeɪt əv dɪˈpɑːtʃə/, **departure date** /dɪˈpɑːtʃə deɪt/ *noun* the date on which an employee leaves the company

day /deɪ/ *noun* **1.** a period of 24 hours ○ *There are thirty days in June.* ○ *The first day of the month is a public holiday.* **2.** a period of work from morning to night □ **she works three days on, two days off** she works for three days, then has two days' holiday □ **to work an eight-hour day** to spend eight hours at work each day **3.** one of the days of the week

day care /ˈdeɪ keə/ *noun* a provision of care for small children while their parents are at work ○ *One of the fringe benefits of the job was a free day care centre.* ○ *The excellent day care facilities in the area have increased the availability of staff.*

day of action /ˌdeɪ əv ˈækʃən/ *noun* a day when workers do not work, but take part in strikes or protests

day rate /ˈdeɪ reɪt/ *noun* a payment system where employees are paid per day worked ○ *Temporary workers are paid on a day rate.* ○ *They receive a flat day rate of £100.*

day shift /ˈdeɪ ʃɪft/ *noun* a shift worked during the daylight hours (from early morning to late afternoon)

day-to-day /ˌdeɪ tə ˈdeɪ/ *adjective* ordinary or going on all the time ○ *He organises the day-to-day running of the company.* ○ *Sales only just cover the day-to-day expenses.*

day work /ˈdeɪ wɜːk/ *noun* **1.** work done on the day shift **2.** work done during a day

day worker /ˈdeɪ ˌwɜːkə/ *noun* a person who works the day shift

dead /ded/ *adjective* **1.** not alive ○ *Six people were dead as a result of the accident.* ○ *The founders of the company are all dead.* **2.** not working □ **the line went**

dead the telephone line suddenly stopped working

dead end /ded ˈend/ *noun* a point where you cannot go any further forward ○ *Negotiations have reached a dead end.*

dead end job /ˌded end ˈdʒɒb/ *noun* a job where there are no chances of promotion

deadline /ˈdedlaɪn/ *noun* the date by which something has to be done □ **to meet a deadline** to finish something in time □ **to miss a deadline** to finish something later than it was planned ○ *We've missed our October 1st deadline.*

deadlock /ˈdedlɒk/ *noun* a point where two sides in a dispute cannot agree ○ *The negotiations have reached deadlock or a deadlock.* □ **to break a deadlock** to find a way to start discussions again after being at a point where no agreement was possible ■ *verb* to be unable to agree to continue negotiations □ **talks have been deadlocked for ten days** after ten days the talks have not produced any agreement

dead loss /ded ˈlɒs/ *noun* a total loss ○ *The car was written off as a dead loss.*

dead season /ˈded ˌsiːz(ə)n/ *noun* the time of year when there are few tourists about

dead wood /ded ˈwʊd/ *noun* employees who are old or who do not work well ○ *The new management team is weeding out the dead wood from the sales department.*

deal /diːl/ *noun* a business agreement, affair or contract ○ *The sales director set up a deal with a Russian bank.* ○ *The deal will be signed tomorrow.* ○ *They did a deal with an American airline.* □ **to call off a deal** to stop an agreement ○ *When the chairman heard about the deal he called it off.* □ **to reach a deal**, **to strike a deal** to come to an agreement ■ *verb* □ **to deal with** to organise something ○ *Leave it to the filing clerk – he'll deal with it.* □ **to deal with a problem** to decide how to solve a problem

death /deθ/ *noun* the act of dying

death duty /ˈdeθ ˌdjuːti/, **death tax** /ˈdeθ tæks/ *noun US* a tax paid on the property left by a dead person (NOTE: the British equivalent is **inheritance tax**)

death in service /ˌdeθ ɪn ˈsɜːvɪs/ *noun* an insurance benefit or pension paid when someone dies while employed by a company

deauthorisation /diːˌɔːθəraɪˈzeɪʃ(ə)n/, **deauthorization** *noun US* a way in which unionised employees can vote to determine whether or not they want an open shop

debt collection /ˈdet kəˌlekʃ(ə)n/ *noun* the act of collecting money which is owed

debt collection agency /ˈdet kəˌlekʃən ˌeɪdʒənsi/ *noun* a company which collects debts for other companies for a commission

debt collector /ˈdet kəˌlektə/ *noun* a person who collects debts

decentralisation /diːˌsentrəlaɪˈzeɪʃ(ə)n/, **decentralization** *noun* organisation from various points, with little power concentrated at the centre ○ *the decentralisation of the buying departments*

decentralise /diːˈsentrəlaɪz/, **decentralize** *verb* to organise from various points, with little power concentrated at the centre ○ *Formerly, the bank was decentralised, with many decisions being taken by branch managers.* ○ *Since the company was decentralised, its headquarters have moved to a tiny office.* ○ *The group has a policy of decentralised purchasing where each division has its own buying department.*

decentralised bargaining /diːˌsentrəlaɪzd ˈbɑːɡɪnɪŋ/ *noun* separate bargaining between management and unions in different areas, not at national or industry-wide level

decertification /diːˌsɜːtɪfɪˈkeɪʃ(ə)n/ *noun US* a vote by a group of unionised employees to take away a union's right to represent them in bargaining

decide /dɪˈsaɪd/ *verb* to make up your mind to do something ○ *to decide on a course of action* ○ *to decide to appoint a new managing director*

deciding factor /dɪˌsaɪdɪŋ ˈfæktə/ *noun* the most important factor which

influences a decision ○ *A deciding factor in marketing our range of sports goods in the country was the rising standard of living there.*

deciding vote /dɪˈsaɪdɪŋ vəʊt/ *noun* a vote which decides an issue

decision /dɪˈsɪʒ(ə)n/ *noun* a choice made after thinking about what to do ○ *It took the committee some time to come to a decision* or *to reach a decision.* □ **to put off a decision** to delay deciding something

decision-maker /dɪˈsɪʒ(ə)n ˌmeɪkə/ *noun* a person who takes decisions

decision-making /dɪˈsɪʒ(ə)n ˌmeɪkɪŋ/ *noun* the act of coming to a decision

decisive /dɪˈsaɪsɪv/ *adjective* referring to a person who makes up their mind or who comes to a decision (NOTE: the opposite is **indecisive**)

decisiveness /dɪˈsaɪsɪvnəs/ *noun* the ability to come to a decision quickly (NOTE: opposites are **indecision, indecisiveness**)

declaration /ˌdekləˈreɪʃ(ə)n/ *noun* an official statement

decline /dɪˈklaɪn/ *noun* **1.** a gradual fall ○ *the decline in the value of the dollar* ○ *a decline in buying power* ○ *The last year has seen a decline in real wages.* **2.** the final stage in the life cycle of a product when the sales and profitability are falling off and the product is no longer worth investing in ■ *verb* to fall slowly or decrease ○ *New job applications have declined over the last year.* ○ *The purchasing power of the currency declined over the decade.*

'Saudi oil production has declined by three quarters to around 2.5m barrels a day' [*Economist*]

'…this gives an average monthly decline of 2.15 per cent during the period' [*Business Times (Lagos)*]

'…share prices disclosed a weak tendency right from the onset of business and declined further, showing losses over a broad front' [*The Hindu*]

decrease *noun* /ˈdiːkriːs/ a fall or reduction ○ *The decrease in the prices of consumer goods is reflected in the fall in the cost of living.* ○ *Exports have registered a decrease.* ○ *Sales show a 10% decrease on last year.* ■ *verb* /dɪˈkriːs/

to fall or to become less ○ *Imports are decreasing.* ○ *The value of the currency has decreased by 5%.*

decruiting /diːˈkruːtɪŋ/ *noun* the policy of replacing permanent employees with temporary ones ○ *Decruiting is an important factor in running a young industry.*

deduct /dɪˈdʌkt/ *verb* to take money away from a total ○ *to deduct £3 from the price* ○ *to deduct a sum for expenses* ○ *After deducting costs the gross margin is only 23%.* ○ *Expenses are still to be deducted.*

deductible /dɪˈdʌktɪb(ə)l/ *adjective* which can be deducted

deductible expenses /dɪˌdʌktɪb(ə)l ɪkˈspensɪz/ *plural noun* expenses which can be deducted against tax

deduction /dɪˈdʌkʃən/ *noun* the removing of money from a total, or the money removed from a total ○ *Net salary is salary after deduction of tax and social security.* ○ *The deduction from his wages represented the cost of repairing the damage he had caused to the machinery.* □ **deductions from salary**, **salary deductions**, **deductions at source** money which a company removes from salaries to give to the government as tax, national insurance contributions, etc.

deduction at source /dɪˌdʌkʃən ət ˈsɔːs/ *noun* (*in the UK*) a system of collecting taxes in which the organisation or individual that pays somebody an income, e.g. an employer paying wages, a bank paying interest or a company paying dividends, is responsible for deducting and paying tax, not the person who receives the income

deed /diːd/ *noun* a legal document or written agreement

defence /dɪˈfens/ *noun* **1.** protecting someone or something against attack ○ *The merchant bank is organising the company's defence against the takeover bid.* (NOTE: the usual US spelling is **defense**) **2.** the act of fighting a lawsuit on behalf of a defendant (NOTE: the usual US spelling is **defense**) **3.** the explanation of actions ○ *His defence was that the expenditure had been authorised*

verbally by his manager. (NOTE: the usual US spelling is **defense**)

defend /dɪˈfend/ *verb* to fight to protect someone or something which is being attacked ○ *The company is defending itself against the takeover bid.* ○ *They hired the best lawyers to defend them against the tax authorities.* □ **to defend a lawsuit** to appear in court to state your case when accused of something

defendant /dɪˈfendənt/ *noun* a person against whom a legal action is taken or who is accused of doing something to harm someone (NOTE: the other side in a case is the **claimant**)

defer /dɪˈfɜː/ *verb* to put back to a later date, or to postpone ○ *We will have to defer payment until January.* ○ *The decision has been deferred until the next meeting.* (NOTE: **deferring – deferred**)

deferred /dɪˈfɜːd/ *adjective* put back to a later date

deferred pension /dɪˌfɜːd ˈpenʃən/ *noun* a pension plan where the pension is taken late, so as to allow benefits to accrue

deferred retirement /dɪˌfɜːd rɪˈtaɪəmənt/ *noun* retirement which starts later than the statutory age

degree /dɪˈɡriː/ *noun* **1.** a qualification awarded to someone who has passed a course of study at a university or polytechnic ○ *He has a degree in business studies.* ○ *She has a degree in social work.* **2.** an amount or level ○ *Being promoted to a management position means a greater degree of responsibility.* ○ *The HR director is trying to assess the degree of discontent among the workforce.*

degree mill /dɪˈɡriː mɪl/ *noun* an establishment that claims to be an educational institution and offers to award a qualification for little or no work, often on payment of a large sum of money (*informal*) (NOTE: The qualifications offered by degree mills are mostly considered worthless and are not accepted by employers.)

delay /dɪˈleɪ/ *noun* the time when someone or something is later than planned ○ *We are sorry for the delay in* *supplying your order* or *in replying to your letter.* ■ *verb* to make someone or something late ○ *The company has delayed payment of all invoices.* ○ *She was delayed because her taxi was involved in an accident.*

delegate *noun* /'delɪgət/ a person who represents others at a meeting ○ *The management refused to meet the trade union delegates.* ■ *verb* /'delɪgeɪt/ to pass authority or responsibility to someone else ○ *to delegate authority* □ **she cannot delegate** she wants to control everything herself and refuses to give up any of her responsibilities to her subordinates

delegate conference /'delɪgət ˌkɒnf(ə)rəns/ *noun* a meeting of representatives from each of the main branches of a trade union

delegation /delɪ'geɪʃ(ə)n/ *noun* **1.** a group of delegates ○ *A Chinese trade delegation is visiting the UK.* ○ *The management met a union delegation.* **2.** an act of passing authority or responsibility to someone else

demand /dɪ'mɑːnd/ *noun* **1.** the act of asking for payment **2.** asking for something and insisting on getting it ○ *the union's list of demands* ○ *The management refused to give in to union demands for a meeting.* □ **to meet the union's demands** to agree to what the union is asking for **3.** the requirement by a prospective purchaser for a commodity ○ *There was an active demand for oil shares on the stock market.* ○ *The factory had to cut production when demand slackened.* □ **there is not much demand for this item** not many people want to buy it □ **this book is in great demand, there is a great demand for this book** many people want to buy it □ **to meet** *or* **fill a demand** to supply what is needed ○ *The factory had to increase production to meet the extra demand.* ○ *The factory had to cut production when demand slackened.* ■ *verb* to ask for something and expect to get it ○ *She demanded a refund.* ○ *The suppliers are demanding immediate payment of their outstanding invoices.* ○ *The shop stewards demanded an urgent meeting with the managing director.*

'…spot prices are now relatively stable in the run-up to the winter's peak demand' [*Economist*]

'…the demand for the company's products remained strong throughout the first six months of the year with production and sales showing significant increases' [*Business Times (Lagos)*]

'…growth in demand is still coming from the private rather than the public sector' [*Lloyd's List*]

demarcation /ˌdiːmɑː'keɪʃ(ə)n/ *noun* a clear definition of the responsibilities of each employee or category of employment ○ *The union insisted on clear demarcation when tasks were assigned to different workers.* ○ *Demarcation ensures that no one does work which is not defined in their job description.*

demerge /diː'mɜːdʒ/ *verb* to separate a company into several separate parts

demerger /diː'mɜːdʒə/ *noun* the separation of a company into several separate parts (especially used of companies which have grown by acquisition)

democracy /dɪ'mɒkrəsi/ *noun* a system of government by freely elected representatives

democratic management style /ˌdeməˌkrætɪk 'mænɪdʒmənt staɪl/ *noun* a management style in which the managers involve the employees in decision-making processes (NOTE: the opposite is **autocratic management style**)

demographic /ˌdemə'græfɪk/ *adjective* referring to demography ○ *A full demographic study of the country must be done before we decide how to export there.*

demographic change /ˌdeməgræfɪk 'tʃeɪndʒ/ *noun* a change in the population which may affect the working population in the future (e.g. a fall in the birth rate means fewer potential workers, a rise in life expectancy means more people drawing pensions)

demographics /ˌdemə'græfɪks/ *plural noun* the details of the population of a country, in particular its age and gender, which affect marketing (NOTE: takes a singular verb)

demographic time-bomb /ˌdeməgræfɪk 'taɪm bɒm/ *noun* a catastrophic population trend, e.g. a sharp increase in the number of people of pensionable age and a decrease in the number of younger people of working age

demography /dɪˈmɒɡrəfi/ *noun* the study of populations and population statistics such as age, sex, income and education

demote /dɪˈməʊt/ *verb* to give someone a less important job or to reduce an employee to a lower rank or grade ○ *He was demoted from manager to salesman.* ○ *Her salary was reduced when she was demoted.*

demotion /dɪˈməʊʃən/ *noun* the act of reducing an employee to a lower rank or giving someone a less important job ○ *Demotion would mean a considerable drop in income.* ○ *Demotion ended his dreams of becoming managing director.*

department /dɪˈpɑːtmənt/ *noun* **1.** a specialised section of a large organisation ○ *Trainee managers work for a while in each department to get an idea of the organisation as a whole.* **2.** a section of the British government containing several ministries

departmental /ˌdiːpɑːtˈment(ə)l/ *adjective* referring to a department

departmental manager /ˌdiːpɑːtment(ə)l ˈmænɪdʒə/ *noun* the manager of a department

Department for Education and Skills /dɪˌpɑːtmənt fər edjʊˌkeɪʃ(ə)n ənd ˈskɪlz/ *noun* a British government department responsible for education and training. Abbr **DFES**

Department for Work and Pensions /dɪˌpɑːtmənt fə wɜːk ən ˈpenʃ(ə)nz/ *noun* a British government department responsible for services to people of working age, pensioners and families. Abbr **DWP**

Department of Trade and Industry /dɪˌpɑːtmənt əv treɪd ənd ˈɪndəstri/ *noun* a British government department which deals with areas such as commerce, international trade and the stock exchange. Abbr **DTI**

departure /dɪˈpɑːtʃə/ *noun* **1.** going away ○ *The plane's departure was delayed by two hours.* **2.** a new venture or new type of business ○ *Selling records will be a departure for the local book-*shop. **3.** □ **departure from normal practice** an act of doing something in a different way from the usual one

depend /dɪˈpend/ *verb* **1.** □ **to depend on** to need someone or something to exist ○ *The company depends on efficient service from its suppliers.* ○ *We depend on government grants to pay the salary bill.* **2.** to happen because of something ○ *The success of the launch will depend on the publicity campaign.* □ **depending on** which varies according to something ○ *Depending on the circumstances, she may be reprimanded or have the money docked from her pay.*

dependant /dɪˈpendənt/ *noun* a person who depends financially on someone else ○ *He has to provide for his family and dependants out of a very small salary.*

dependence /dɪˈpendəns/, **dependency** /dɪˈpendənsi/ *noun* the fact of being dependent on someone or something ○ *dependence on drugs*

dependent /dɪˈpendənt/ *adjective* supported financially by someone else ○ *Employees may be granted leave to care for dependent relatives.* ○ *Tax relief is allowed for dependent relatives.*

deploy /dɪˈplɔɪ/ *verb* to send staff to a certain place to carry out a certain job

deployment of personnel /dɪˌplɔɪmənt əv pɜːsəˈnel/ *noun* the sending of staff to certain places to carry out certain jobs

depreciation /dɪˌpriːʃiˈeɪʃ(ə)n/ *noun* a reduction in value of an asset

depressed /dɪˈprest/ *adjective* feeling miserable and hopeless ○ *She was depressed when she was not promoted.*

depression /dɪˈpreʃ(ə)n/ *noun* **1.** a period of economic crisis with high unemployment and loss of trade ○ *an economic depression* ○ *The country entered a period of economic depression.* **2.** a mental state in which someone feels miserable and hopeless ○ *He suffers from bouts of depression.*

dept *abbr* department

deputise /ˈdepjʊtaɪz/, **deputize** *verb* □ **to deputise for someone** to take the place of someone who is absent ○ *He deputised for the chairman who was ill.*

deputy /'depjʊti/ *noun* a person who takes the place of another ○ *to act as deputy for someone* or *to act as someone's deputy* ○ *He is deputy manager of the accounts department.* ○ *Her title is deputy managing director.*

derecognise /diː'rekəgnaɪz/ *verb* to cease to recognise a union as the representative of the workers

derecognition /ˌdiːrekəg'nɪʃ(ə)n/ *noun* the act of ceasing to recognise a union as able to represent the employees (typical reasons are: few of the workforce actually belong to the union, or the company has changed owner)

describe /dɪ'skraɪb/ *verb* to say what someone or something is like ○ *The leaflet describes the services the company can offer.* ○ *The managing director described the difficulties the company was having with cash flow.*

description /dɪ'skrɪpʃən/ *noun* a detailed account of what something is like

designate *adjective* /'dezɪgnət/ appointed to a job but not yet working ○ *the chairman designate* (NOTE: always follows a noun) ■ *verb* /'dezɪgneɪt/ to appoint someone to a post

designer /dɪ'zaɪnə/ *adjective* expensive and fashionable ○ *designer jeans*

desk /desk/ *noun* a writing table in an office, usually with drawers for stationery ○ *a desk diary* ○ *a desk drawer* ○ *a desk light*

deskilling /diː'skɪlɪŋ/ *noun* the process of reducing the number of skilled jobs and replacing them with unskilled jobs

desk pad /'desk pæd/ *noun* a pad of paper kept on a desk for writing notes

detail /'diːteɪl/ *noun* 1. a small part of a description ○ *The catalogue gives all the details of our product range.* ○ *We are worried by some of the details in the contract.* □ **in detail** giving many particulars ○ *The catalogue lists all the products in detail.* 2. the temporary assignment of an employee to a different position for a specified time ○ *The union is complaining that employees are being given details that were never mentioned at the time of their recruitment.* ○ *The manager was sent to another*

branch *on a two-week detail.* ■ *verb* 1. to list in detail ○ *The terms of the licence are detailed in the contract.* 2. to give someone a temporary assignment ○ *Two men were detailed to deal with the urgent order.*

detailed /'diːteɪld/ *adjective* in detail □ **detailed account** an account which lists every item

determination of salaries /dɪˌtɜːmɪneɪʃ(ə)n əv 'sæləriz/ *noun* the process of fixing the amount of salaries to be paid to different categories of employees

determine /dɪ'tɜːmɪn/ *verb* to fix, arrange or decide ○ *to determine prices* or *quantities* ○ *conditions still to be determined*

develop /dɪ'veləp/ *verb* 1. to plan and produce ○ *to develop a new product* 2. to plan and build an area ○ *to develop an industrial estate*

DFEE *abbr* Department for Education and Employment

DFES *abbr* Department for Education and Skills

diagram /'daɪəgræm/ *noun* a drawing which presents information visually ○ *a diagram showing sales locations* ○ *a diagram of the company's organisational structure* ○ *The first diagram shows how our decision-making processes work.*

diagrammatic /ˌdaɪəgrə'mætɪk/ *adjective* □ **in diagrammatic form** in the form of a diagram ○ *The chart showed the work flow in diagrammatic form.*

diagrammatically /ˌdaɪəgrə'mætɪkli/ *adverb* using a diagram ○ *The chart shows the sales pattern diagrammatically.*

dialogue /'daɪəlɒg/ *noun* a discussion between two people or groups, in which views are exchanged ○ *The management refused to enter into a dialogue with the strikers.*

diarise /'daɪəraɪz/, **diarize** *verb* to enter a date you have to remember in a diary

differ /'dɪfə/ *verb* not to be the same as something else ○ *The two managerial vacancies differ considerably – one* *deals with product design and the other with customer services.*

difference /'dɪf(ə)rəns/ *noun* a way in which two things are not the same ○ *What is the difference between a junior manager and a managerial assistant?*

different /'dɪf(ə)rənt/ *adjective* not the same ○ *Our product range is quite different in design from that of our rivals.* ○ *We offer ten models each in six different colours.*

differential /ˌdɪfə'renʃəl/ *adjective* which shows a difference ■ *noun* □ **to erode wage differentials** to reduce differences in salary gradually

differential piecework /ˌdɪfərenʃəl 'piːswɜːk/ *noun* payment for each piece of work completed, determined by the total number of pieces produced over a period, with extra bonus payments for work completed more quickly ○ *The management decided that differential piecework provided the best balance between incentives and wage security.*

digerati /ˌdɪdʒə'rɑːti/ *plural noun* people who claim to have a sophisticated understanding of Internet or computer technology (*slang*)

digithead /'dɪdʒɪt,hed/ *noun* a person who is very knowledgeable about technology and mathematics but who is not very good at talking or relating to people (*slang*)

dilberted /'dɪlbɜːtɪd/ *adjective US* badly treated by your employer, like the cartoon character Dilbert (*slang*) (NOTE: see **Dilbert Principle**)

Dilbert principle /'dɪlbɜːt ˌprɪnsɪp(ə)l/ *noun* the principle that the most inefficient employees are moved to the place where they can do the least damage (NOTE: Dilbert is the main character in a comic strip and cartoon series by Scott Adams which satirises office and corporate life.)

dilutee /ˌdaɪluː'tiː/ *noun* an unskilled or semi-skilled worker who has taken a short training course, instead of a longer full course, and is seen as someone who is diluting the pool of skilled labour (*informal*)

dilution agreement /daɪ'luːʃ(ə)n əˌgriːmənt/ *noun* agreement by which unskilled labour can be employed when skilled workers are not available ○ *The dilution agreement allowed for untrained administrative workers until more qualified manpower came to the area.*

dilution of labour /daɪˌluːʃ(ə)n əv 'leɪbə/ *noun* the process of deskilling, reducing the number of skilled jobs and replacing them with unskilled jobs

diploma /dɪ'pləʊmə/ *noun* a document which shows that a person has reached a certain level of skill in a subject ○ *He is studying for a diploma in engineering.* ○ *The new assistant HR manager has a diploma in human resources management.* ○ *A diploma is awarded at the end of the two-year course in accountancy.*

direct /daɪ'rekt/ *verb* to manage or organise ○ *He directs our South-East Asian operations.* ○ *She was directing the development unit until last year.* ■ *adjective* straight or without interference ■ *adverb* with no third party involved ○ *We pay income tax direct to the government.*

direct action /daɪˌrekt 'ækʃən/ *noun* a strike or go-slow by a workforce

directed interview /daɪˌrektɪd 'ɪntəvjuː/ *noun* an interview built round specific questions instead of an open discussion ○ *Directed interviews are easier to conduct, but may fail to extract as much as less formal methods of interviewing.*

direction /daɪ'rekʃən/ *noun* **1.** the process of organising or managing ○ *He took over the direction of a multinational group.* **2.** □ **directions for use** instructions showing how to use something

directive /daɪ'rektɪv/ *noun* an order or command to someone to do something (especially an order from the Council of Ministers or Commission of the European Community referring to a particular problem in certain countries)

directive interview /daɪ'rektɪv 'ɪntəvjuː/ *noun* an interview using preset questions and following a fixed pattern

direct line /daɪˌrekt ˈlaɪn/ *noun* a telephone number which goes direct to someone, without passing through an operator

directly /daɪˈrektlɪ/ *adverb* **1.** immediately ○ *She left for the airport directly after receiving the telephone message.* **2.** with no third party involved ○ *We deal directly with the manufacturer, without using a wholesaler.*

director /daɪˈrektə/ *noun* the person who is in charge of a project, an official institute or other organisation ○ *the director of the government research institute* ○ *She was appointed director of the trade association.*

'…the research director will manage and direct a team of business analysts reporting on the latest developments in retail distribution throughout the UK' [*Times*]

COMMENT: Directors are elected by shareholders at the AGM, though they are usually chosen by the chairman or chief executive. A board will consist of a chairman (who may be non-executive), a chief executive or managing director and a series of specialist directors in charge of various activities of the company (such as a finance director, production director or sales director). The company secretary will attend board meetings, but need not be a director. Apart from the executive directors, who are in fact employees of the company, there may be several non-executive directors, appointed either for their expertise and contacts, or as representatives of important shareholders such as banks. The board of an American company may be made up of a large number of non-executive directors and only one or two executive officers; a British board has more executive directors.

directorate /daɪˈrekt(ə)rət/ *noun* a group of directors

director's fees /daɪˈrektəz fiːz/ *plural noun* money paid to a director for attendance at board meetings

directorship /daɪˈrektəʃɪp/ *noun* the post of director ○ *She was offered a directorship with Smith Ltd.*

'…what benefits does the executive derive from his directorship? In the first place compensation has increased sharply in recent years' [*Duns Business Month*]

direct taxation /daɪˌrekt tækˈseɪʃ(ə)n/ *noun* a tax such as income tax which is paid direct to the government ○ *The government raises more money by direct taxation than by indirect.*

disability /ˌdɪsəˈbɪlɪti/ *noun* a condition of being unable to use your body properly (because you are blind or cannot walk) ○ *The government awards special disability allowances for handicapped people who cannot find work.*

disability working allowance /ˌdɪsəbɪliti ˈwɜːkɪŋ əˌlaʊəns/ *noun* a benefit paid to people working more than 16 hours a week who have an illness or disability. Abbr **DWA**

disabled /dɪsˈeɪb(ə)ld/ *adjective* having a physical disability ○ *Each company is required by law to employ a certain percentage of disabled staff.* ○ *There are special facilities for disabled employees.* ○ *One of our managers is disabled and cannot travel far.*

disabled person /dɪsˌeɪb(ə)ld ˈpɜːs(ə)n/ *noun* a person who has a physical disability

disablement benefit /dɪsˈeɪb(ə)lmənt ˌbenɪfɪt/ *noun* a government payment to a person who is disabled

disadvantage /ˌdɪsədˈvɑːntɪdʒ/ *noun* something which makes you less successful ○ *It is a disadvantage for an HR manager to have had no experience of industry.* □ **to be at a disadvantage** to be in a more awkward position than another person ○ *Not having taken a management course puts him at a disadvantage.*

discharge *noun* /ˈdɪstʃɑːdʒ/ **1.** a payment of debt □ **in full discharge of a debt** payment of a debt completely **2.** carrying out of a job □ **in discharge of her duties as director** carrying out her duties as director **3.** dismissal from a job ■ *verb* /dɪsˈtʃɑːdʒ/ **1.** □ **to discharge a bankrupt** to release someone from bankruptcy because they have has paid their debts **2.** to dismiss or to sack ○ *to discharge an employee for negligence*

disciplinary /ˈdɪsɪˌplɪnəri/ *adjective* referring to punishment

'…disciplinary action is often regarded as synonymous with dismissal, but the new ACAS handbook takes a more positive view' [*Employment Gazette*]

disciplinary action /ˌdɪsɪ'plɪnəri ˌækʃən/ *noun* an action taken to control or punish bad behaviour by employees ○ *Disciplinary action had to be taken to prevent further disputes between workers and managers.* ○ *The union complained that the disciplinary action was too harsh.*

disciplinary board /ˌdɪsɪ'plɪnəri bɔːd/ *noun* a group of people who conduct a disciplinary interview

disciplinary interview /ˌdɪsɪplɪnəri 'ɪntəvjuː/ *noun* an interview between a manager and an employee to discuss a breach of discipline (the worker may be accompanied by a union representative)

disciplinary lay-off /ˌdɪsɪplɪnəri 'leɪ ɒf/ *noun* temporary dismissal of an employee as a punishment

disciplinary measures /ˌdɪsɪ'plɪnəri ˌmeʒəz/ *plural noun* same as **disciplinary action**

discipline /'dɪsɪplɪn/ *noun* the self-control needed to do a job ○ *Working his way up the company ladder gave him the discipline to take on further management responsibilities.* ○ *Lack of discipline is responsible for poor attendance figures.* □ **to keep discipline** to make sure that everyone obeys the rules ■ *verb* to punish an employee for misconduct ○ *Three members of staff were disciplined by the manager.*

disclosure /dɪs'kləʊʒə/ *noun* the act of telling details ○ *The disclosure of the takeover bid raised the price of the shares.*

disclosure of information /dɪsˌkləʊʒər əv ˌɪnfə'meɪʃ(ə)n/ *noun* the giving of information to someone, such as the union representatives in collective bargaining, so that they know all the relevant facts about a case before presenting the defence

discontinuous shift system /dɪskən,tɪnjuəs 'ʃɪft ˌsɪstəm/ *noun* a working system where three groups of employees work morning, noon and night shifts, but do not work at weekends

discounted cash flow /ˌdɪskaʊntɪd 'kæʃ fləʊ/ *noun* a calculation of forecast sales of a product in current terms with reductions for current interest rates

discretion /dɪ'skreʃ(ə)n/ *noun* the ability to decide correctly what should be done □ **I leave it to your discretion** I leave it for you to decide what to do □ **at the discretion of someone** according to what someone decides ○ *Membership is at the discretion of the committee.*

discretionary /dɪ'skreʃ(ə)n(ə)ri/ *adjective* which can be done if someone wants □ **the minister's discretionary powers** powers which the minister could use if they thought it necessary

discriminate /dɪ'skrɪmɪneɪt/ *verb* to treat people in different ways because of class, religion, race, language, colour, sex, or physical or mental ability ○ *The management appeared to discriminate against handicapped applicants.*

discrimination /dɪˌskrɪmɪ'neɪʃ(ə)n/ *noun* the practice of treating people in different ways because of class, religion, race, language, colour or sex

discriminatory /dɪ'skrɪmɪnət(ə)ri/ *adjective* which shows discrimination ○ *The appointment of only males to the three posts was clearly discriminatory.*

'EEC legislation should formally recognize that sexual harassment is discrimination on grounds of sex' [*Personnel Management*]

'...she claimed she was a victim of sex discrimination but this was rejected by the industrial tribunal and the Court of Appeal' [*Personnel Today*]

'...discrimination in pensions is set to continue' [*Personnel Management*]

discuss /dɪ'skʌs/ *verb* to talk about a problem ○ *They spent two hours discussing the details of the contract.* ○ *The committee discussed the question of import duties on cars.* ○ *The board will discuss wage rises at its next meeting.* ○ *We discussed delivery schedules with our suppliers.*

discussion /dɪ'skʌʃ(ə)n/ *noun* the act of talking about a problem ○ *After ten minutes' discussion the board agreed the salary increases.* ○ *We spent the whole day in discussions with our suppliers.* □ **to hold discussions** to discuss formally ○ *Management is holding discussions with representatives of the union.*

disease /dɪˈziːz/ *noun* an illness in which the body functions abnormally

disincentive /ˌdɪsɪnˈsentɪv/ *noun* something which discourages, especially something which discourages people from working ○ *The low salary offered was a disincentive to work.*

disk /dɪsk/ *noun* a round flat object, used to store information in computers

disk drive /ˈdɪsk draɪv/ *noun* a part of a computer which makes a disk spin round in order to read it or store information on it

diskette /dɪˈsket/ *noun* a small floppy disk ○ *He sent a diskette of the accounts to his accountant.*

dismiss /dɪsˈmɪs/ *verb* **1.** □ **to dismiss an employee** to remove an employee from a job ○ *She was dismissed for being late.* **2.** to refuse to accept ○ *The court dismissed the claim.*

dismissal /dɪsˈmɪs(ə)l/ *noun* the removal of an employee from a job, either by sacking or by not renewing a contract

dismissal procedures /dɪsˈmɪs(ə)l prəˌsiːdʒəz/ *plural noun* the correct actions to take in order to dismiss someone, following the rules in the contract of employment

disobedience /ˌdɪsəˈbiːdiəns/ *noun* the act of not doing what you are told to do

disobey /ˌdɪsəˈbeɪ/ *verb* not to do what someone tells you to do ○ *The workers disobeyed their union's instructions and held a 24-hour strike.*

disparity /dɪˈspærɪti/ *noun* a difference (NOTE: plural is disparities) □ **disparities between salary levels** differences between salaries paid to different employees at the same level of responsibility

disposable /dɪˈspəʊzəb(ə)l/ *adjective* which can be used and then thrown away ○ *The machine serves soup in disposable paper cups.*

disposable income /dɪˌspəʊzəb(ə)l ˈɪnkʌm/, **disposable personal income** /dɪˌspəʊzəb(ə)l ˌpɜːs(ə)nəl ˈɪnkʌm/ *noun* the income left after tax and national insurance have been deducted

disposal /dɪˈspəʊz(ə)l/ *noun* a sale ○ *a disposal of securities* ○ *The company has started a systematic disposal of its property portfolio.* □ **lease** *or* **business for disposal** a lease or business for sale

dispose /dɪˈspəʊz/ *verb* □ **to dispose of** to get rid of or to sell cheaply ○ *to dispose of excess stock* ○ *to dispose of excess equipment* ○ *He is planning to dispose of his business in the new year.* □ **to dispose of day-to-day matters** to deal with routine matters

dispute /dɪˈspjuːt, ˈdɪspjuːt/ *noun* disagreement ○ *dispute between two departments in an organisation* □ **to adjudicate** *or* **mediate in a dispute** to try to settle a dispute between other parties

dispute benefit /dɪˈspjuːt ˌbenɪfɪt/ *noun* same as **strike pay**

disputes procedures /dɪˈspjuːts prəˌsiːdʒəz/ *plural noun* the correct actions to take to deal with disputes, following the rules agreed between management and unions

disregard /ˌdɪsrɪˈɡɑːd/ *noun* the act of not paying any attention to something □ **in complete disregard of regulations** without paying any attention to the regulations ■ *verb* to take no notice of or not to obey ○ *The workers disregarded the instructions of the shop stewards.*

dissatisfaction /dɪsˌsætɪsˈfækʃən/ *noun* the state of being discontented or not being satisfied ○ *dissatisfaction with bad working conditions* ○ *Although the work itself was interesting, there was a lot of dissatisfaction with the organisation and its rules.*

dissociate /dɪˈsəʊsieɪt/ *verb* □ **to dissociate oneself from a statement** not to agree with what someone has said

distance learning /ˈdɪstəns ˌlɜːnɪŋ/ *noun* learning in one's own time away from the centre producing the course, by mail, radio, television or by occasional visits to centres

distribute /dɪˈstrɪbjuːt/ *verb* **1.** to share out dividends ○ *Profits were distributed among the shareholders.* **2.** to send out goods from a manufacturer's warehouse to retail shops ○ *Smith Ltd distributes for several smaller compa-*

nies. ○ *All orders are distributed from our warehouse near Oxford.*

distribution /ˌdɪstrɪˈbjuːʃ(ə)n/ *noun*
1. the act of sending goods from the manufacturer to the wholesaler and then to retailers ○ *Stock is held in a distribution centre which deals with all order processing.* ○ *Distribution costs have risen sharply over the last 18 months.* ○ *She has several years' experience as distribution manager.* **2.** sharing something among several people □ **distribution of the workload** sharing in a fair way the work which has to be done

'British distribution companies are poised to capture a major share of the European market' [*Management News*]

distribution channels /ˌdɪstrɪˈbjuːʃ(ə)n ˌtʃæn(ə)lz/ *plural noun* ways of sending goods from the manufacturer for sale by retailers

distribution of profits /dɪstrɪˌbjuːʃ(ə)n əv ˈprɒfɪts/ *noun* the sharing of profits between shareholders, staff and other parties

distributive bargaining /dɪˌstrɪbjʊtɪv ˈbɑːɡɪnɪŋ/ *noun* collective bargaining where the workers try to obtain as good a share of limited resources as possible

division /dɪˈvɪʒ(ə)n/ *noun* **1.** the main section of a large company ○ *the marketing division* ○ *the production division* ○ *the retail division* ○ *the hotel division of the leisure group* **2.** a company which is part of a large group ○ *Smith's is now a division of the Brown group of companies.* **3.** the act of separating a whole into parts ○ *the division of responsibility between managers*

divisional /dɪˈvɪʒ(ə)n(ə)l/ *adjective* referring to a division ○ *a divisional director* ○ *the divisional headquarters*

divisional headquarters /dɪˌvɪʒ(ə)nəl ˌhedˈkwɔːtez/ *plural noun* the main office of a division of a company

division of labour /dɪˌvɪʒ(ə)n əv ˈleɪbə/ *noun* a production system where work is split up into clearly defined tasks and areas of responsibility

dock /dɒk/ *verb* to remove money from someone's wages ○ *We will have to dock your pay if you are late for work*

again. ○ *He had £20 docked from his pay for being late.*

doctor /ˈdɒktə/ *noun* a specialist who examines people when they are sick to see how they can be made well

doctor's certificate /ˈdɒktəz səˌtɪfɪkət/ *noun* a document written by a doctor to say that a worker is ill and cannot work ○ *He has been off sick for ten days and still has not sent in a doctor's certificate.*

documentary evidence /ˌdɒkjumənt(ə)ri ˈevɪd(ə)ns/ *noun* evidence in the form of documents

dogsbody /ˈdɒɡzbɒdi/ *noun* a person who does all types of work in an office for very low wages (*informal*)

dole /dəʊl/ *noun* money given by the government to unemployed people □ **he is receiving dole payments, he is on the dole** he is receiving unemployment benefits

dole bludger /ˈdəʊl ˌblʌdʒə/ *noun* (*in Australia and New Zealand*) someone who lives off social security payments and makes no attempt to find work

dole queue /ˈdəʊl kjuː/ *noun* a line of people waiting to collect their unemployment money (NOTE: the American term is **dole line**)

domicile /ˈdɒmɪsaɪl/ *verb* □ **she is domiciled in Denmark** she lives in Denmark officially □ **bills domiciled in France** bills of exchange which have to be paid in France

dotted-line relationships /ˌdɒtɪd ˈlaɪn rɪˌleɪʃ(ə)nʃɪps/ *plural noun* relationships between managers and staff whom they supervise indirectly rather than on a day-to-day basis (NOTE: The name comes from the fact that these links are shown as dotted lines on organisational charts.)

double /ˈdʌb(ə)l/ *adjective* twice as large or two times the size ○ *Their turnover is double ours.* □ **to be on double time** to earn twice the usual wages for working on Sundays or other holidays □ **to work double shifts** to work with two shifts of workers on duty □ **in double figures** with two figures, from 10 to 99 ○ *Inflation is in double figures.* ○ *We* have had double-figure inflation for some years. ■ *verb* to become twice as big, or make something twice as big ○ *We have doubled our profits this year* or *our profits have doubled this year.* ○ *The company's borrowings have doubled.*

double day shift /ˌdʌb(ə)l 'deɪ ʃɪft/ *noun* a system of working two shifts during the day time (as from 8.00 a.m. to 2.00 p.m, and then 2.00 p.m. to 8.00 p.m.)

double dipping /ˌdʌb(ə)l 'dɪpɪŋ/ *noun US* the practice of receiving two incomes from a government, one in the form of a pension, the other in social security benefits

double-jobbing /ˌdʌb(ə)l 'dʒɒbɪŋ/ *noun* the practice of doing a second job, usually without paying tax ○ *Double-jobbing has become more important since inflation made it difficult for workers to make ends meet.* ○ *She makes thousands a year from double-jobbing.* ○ *Double-jobbing meant that he spent almost no time with his family.* ♦ **moonlighting**

double taxation /ˌdʌb(ə)l tæk-'seɪʃ(ə)n/ *noun* the act of taxing the same income twice

double taxation agreement /ˌdʌb(ə)l tæk'seɪʃ(ə)n əˌgriːmənt/, **double taxation treaty** /ˌdʌb(ə)l tæk-'seɪʃ(ə)n ˌtriːti/ *noun* an agreement between two countries that a person living in one country shall not be taxed in both countries on the income earned in the other country

double time /ˌdʌb(ə)l 'taɪm/ *noun* a time for which work is paid at twice the normal rate ○ *She is on double time on Sundays.*

down /daʊn/ *adverb, preposition* in a lower position or to a lower position ○ *The inflation rate is gradually coming down.* ○ *Shares are slightly down on the day.* ○ *The price of petrol has gone down.* □ **to pay money down**, **to make a down payment** to make a deposit ○ *He paid £50 down and the rest in monthly instalments.*

downgrade /'daʊngreɪd/ *verb* to reduce the importance of someone or of a job ○ *The post was downgraded in the company reorganisation.*

downgrading /'daʊngreɪdɪŋ/ *noun* the act of moving an employee to a lower grade of job ○ *The reassessment of staff has led to some downgrading, which is never popular.* ○ *We never resort to downgrading because it causes too much resentment.*

downloading /'daʊnləʊdɪŋ/ *noun* reducing the amount of work done in a department, factory or other place of work

down payment /ˌdaʊn 'peɪmənt/ *noun* a part of a total payment made in advance ○ *We made a down payment of $100.*

downshifting /'daʊnʃɪftɪŋ/ *noun* the process of giving up all or part of your work and income in exchange for an improved quality of life (NOTE: Downshifting has increased in popularity because of rising stress in the workplace and is integral to the idea of portfolio working, in which people opt out of a formal employment to sell their services to companies as freelances.)

downsize /'daʊnsaɪz/ *verb* to reduce the number of people employed in order to make a company more profitable

downsizing /'daʊnsaɪzɪŋ/ *noun* the process of reducing the size of something, especially reducing the number of people employed in a company to make it more profitable

down time /'daʊn taɪm/ *noun* **1.** the time when a machine is not working or not available because it is broken or being mended **2.** the time when a worker cannot work because machines have broken down or because components are not available

down tools /ˌdaʊn 'tuːlz/ *verb* to stop working ○ *The entire workforce downed tools in protest.*

downward /'daʊnwəd/ *adjective* towards a lower position ○ *The downward movement of shares continued during the day.*

downward communication /ˌdaʊnwəd kəmjuːnɪ'keɪʃ(ə)n/ *noun* communication from the top management to the lower levels of employee in an organisation ○ *More effective downward communication will be helped by starting a house journal and by more informal talks between directors and employees.*

downwards /'daʊnwədz/ *adverb* towards a lower position ○ *The company's profits have moved downwards over the last few years.*

drag on /ˌdræg 'ɒn/ *verb* to continue slowly without ending ○ *Negotiations dragged on into the night.* (NOTE: dragging-dragged)

draw up /ˌdrɔː 'ʌp/ *verb* to write a legal document ○ *to draw up a contract* or *an agreement* ○ *to draw up a company's articles of association* (NOTE: drawing-drew)

dress code /'dres kəʊd/ *noun* a policy on which type of clothes are considered suitable for a specific activity, especially the clothes worn at work ○ *The dress code is suit and tie for men or smart casual clothes on Fridays.* ○ *The company has a strict dress code for members of staff who meet the public.*

dress-down day /dres 'daʊn deɪ/ *noun* a day on which employees are allowed to wear informal clothes to work

drift /drɪft/ *noun* gradual movement without any control ■ *verb* to move gradually in a particular direction ○ *Shares drifted lower in a dull market.* ○ *Strikers are drifting back to work.*

drive /draɪv/ *noun* 1. an energetic way of doing things □ **She has a lot of drive** she is very energetic in business 2. a part of a machine which makes other parts work ■ *verb* 1. to make a motor vehicle go in a specific direction ○ *He was driving to work when he heard the news on the car radio.* ○ *She drives a company car.* 2. □ **She drives a hard bargain** she is a difficult person to negotiate with

driver /'draɪvə/ *noun* something or someone that provides an impetus for something to happen

driving licence /'draɪvɪŋ ˌlaɪs(ə)ns/ *noun* the official document which shows someone is legally allowed to drive a car, truck or other vehicle ○ *Applicants for the job should hold a valid*

driving licence. (NOTE: the American English is **driver's license**)

DTI *abbr* Department of Trade and Industry

dual /'djuːəl/ *adjective* 1. referring to two things at the same time 2. operated by two people

dual career couple /ˌdjuːəl kəˈrɪə ˌkʌp(ə)l/ *noun* a married couple where both husband and wife have different careers

dual ladder /ˌdjuːəl 'lædə/ *noun* two career paths in an organisation leading to positions of equal importance and open to the same type of employee ○ *Dual ladders attract employees who want to keep their career options open.*

dual unionism /ˌdjuːəl 'juːnjənɪz(ə)m/ *noun* the fact of being a member of two trade unions ○ *Dual unionism is common in industries where the workers want to be as well represented as possible.*

due /djuː/ *adjective* 1. owed ○ *a sum due from a debtor* □ **to fall** *or* **become due** to be ready for payment □ **bill due on May 1st** a bill which has to be paid on May 1st □ **balance due to us** the amount owed to us which should be paid 2. expected to arrive ○ *She is due to come for interview at 10.30.* 3. □ **in due form** written in the correct legal form ○ *a receipt in due form* ○ *a contract drawn up in due form* □ **after due consideration of the problem** after thinking seriously about the problem □ **due to** caused by ○ *The company pays the wages of staff who are absent due to illness.*

'…many expect the US economic indicators for April, due out this Thursday, to show faster economic growth' [*Australian Financial Review*]

dues /djuːz/ *plural noun* regular subscription payments made by a union member to the union

duly /'djuːli/ *adverb* 1. properly ○ *duly authorised representative* 2. as was expected ○ *We duly received his letter of 21st October.* ○ *We duly met the union representatives to discuss the takeover.*

dumbsizing /'dʌmsaɪzɪŋ/ *noun* the process of reducing the size of a company to such an extent that it is no longer profitable or efficient (*slang*)

duration /djʊˈreɪʃ(ə)n/ *noun* the length of time that something lasts ○ *the duration of a contract of employment* ○ *The clause is binding during the duration of the contract.*

duties /ˈdjuːtiz/ *plural noun* specified tasks which have to be done ○ *The job description lists the duties of a director's secretary.* ○ *His duties are onerous but he's very well-paid.*

duty /ˈdjuːti/ *noun* **1.** work which has to be done □ **on duty** doing official work which is part of your job ○ *She has been on duty all day.* ○ *Two security guards were on duty at the time of the theft.* **2.** moral or legal obligation ○ *the employee's duty to his employer* ○ *He felt he had a duty to show his successor how the job was done.*

'...the Department of Customs and Excise collected a total of N79m under the new advance duty payment scheme' [*Business Times (Lagos)*]

duty of reasonable care /ˌdjuːti əv ˌriːz(ə)nəb(ə)l ˈkeə/ the duty of employers to look after the safety of their employees and not act negligently

duty receptionist /ˈdjuːti rɪˌsepʃənɪst/ *noun* the receptionist who is working at the time

duty roster /ˈdjuːti ˌrɒstə/ *noun* a list of times showing when each person is on duty at those times

duvet day /ˈduːveɪ deɪ/ *noun* a day on which an employer allows an employee to call in and say that they do not feel like coming to work and will be absent (NOTE: Duvet days are more popular in the United States – where they are called 'personal days' – than in the United Kingdom. Organisations that allow them do not usually make them part of written policy, limit them to two or three per year and sometimes only offer them to key employees.)

DWA *abbr* disability working allowance

DWP *abbr* Department for Work and Pensions

E

e. & o.e. *abbr* errors and omissions excepted

ear candy /'ɪə kændi/ *noun* pleasant but meaningless noise or talk

early /'ɜːli/ *adjective, adverb* before the usual time ○ *The mail arrived early.* ○ *We retired early and bought a house in Cornwall.* □ **at an early date** very soon ■ *adjective* at the beginning of a period of time ○ *He took an early flight to Paris.* □ **we hope for an early resumption of negotiations** we hope negotiations will start again soon

early adopter /ˌɜːli ə'dɒptə/ *noun* an individual or organisation that is one of the first to make use of a new technology

early retirement /ˌɜːli rɪ'taɪəmənt/ *noun* a scheme where a company encourages employees to retire earlier than usual, and receive financial compensation for this ○ *early retirement at fifty-five* ○ *He took early retirement.* ○ *The management offered some of the senior staff early retirement.*

earn /ɜːn/ *verb* **1.** to be paid money for working ○ *to earn £100 a week* ○ *Our agent in Paris certainly does not earn his commission.* ○ *Her new job is more of a transfer than a promotion, since she doesn't earn any more.* ○ *How much do you earn in your new job?* **2.** to produce interest or dividends ○ *a building society account which earns interest at 10%* ○ *What level of dividend do these shares earn?*

earning capacity /'ɜːnɪŋ kəˌpæsɪti/ *noun* the amount of money someone should be able to earn

earning power /'ɜːnɪŋ ˌpaʊə/ *noun* the amount of money someone should be able to earn ○ *She is such a fine de-*

signer that her earning power is very large.

earnings /'ɜːnɪŋz/ *plural noun* **1.** salary, wages, dividends or interest received ○ *High earnings in top management reflect the heavy responsibilities involved.* ○ *The calculation is based on average earnings over three years.* **2.** profit made by a company

'…the US now accounts for more than half of our world-wide sales. It has made a huge contribution to our earnings turnaround' [*Duns Business Month*]

'…last fiscal year the chain reported a 116% jump in earnings, to $6.4 million or $1.10 a share' [*Barrons*]

earnings drift /'ɜːnɪŋz drɪft/ *noun* a situation where an increase in pay is greater than that of officially negotiated rates ○ *The earnings drift is caused by a sudden increased demand for a certain class of employee.* (NOTE: also called **salary drift** or **wage drift**)

earnings rule /'ɜːnɪŋz ruːl/ *noun* a system where retirement pensions are reduced for those who earn more than a specified amount when working ○ *The earnings rule can be considered as a way of compensating for salary differentials.*

EAT *abbr* employment appeal tribunal

echelon /'eʃəlɒn/ *noun* a group of people of a certain grade in an organisation ○ *the upper echelons of industry* ○ *Communications have improved between the higher and lower echelons in the company.*

economic cycle /ˌiːkənɒmɪk 'saɪk(ə)l/ *noun* a period during which trade expands, then slows down and then expands again

economic model /ˌiːkənɒmɪk 'mɒd(ə)l/ *noun* a computerised plan of a country's economic system, used for forecasting economic trends

economics /ˌiːkə'nɒmɪks/ *noun* the study of the production, distribution, selling and use of goods and services (NOTE: takes a singular verb) ■ *plural noun* the study of financial structures to show how a product or service is costed and what returns it produces ○ *I do not understand the economics of the coal industry.* (NOTE: takes a plural verb)

'...believers in free-market economics often find it hard to sort out their views on the issue' [*Economist*]

economic tort /ˌiːkənɒmɪk 'tɔːt/ *noun* economic harm done to one of the parties in an industrial dispute (such as when shops stewards induce workers to take industrial action and so harm the company's finances)

economy /ɪ'kɒnəmi/ *noun* the quality of being careful not to waste money or materials

'...the European economies are being held back by rigid labor markets and wage structures, huge expenditures on social welfare programs and restrictions on the free movement of goods' [*Duns Business Month*]

economy class /ɪ'kɒnəmi klɑːs/ *noun* a lower quality, less expensive way of travelling ○ *I travel economy class because it is cheaper.* ○ *I always travels first class because tourist class is too uncomfortable.*

economy drive /ɪ'kɒnəmi draɪv/ *noun* a vigorous effort to save money or materials

economy measure /ɪ'kɒnəmi ˌmeʒə/ *noun* an action to save money or materials

education /ˌedjʊ'keɪʃ(ə)n/ *noun* training of the mind, especially through instruction at school or college ○ *Jobs in management require a good basic education.* ○ *People with no more than a basic education can be considered for manual positions.*

educational leave /ˌedjʊkeɪʃ(ə)n(ə)l 'liːv/ *noun* special leave given to employees who want to undertake a course of study

effect /ɪ'fekt/ *noun* 1. a result ○ *The effect of the pay increase was to raise productivity levels.* 2. □ **terms of a con-**

tract which take effect, come into effect from January 1st terms which start to operate on January 1st □ **to remain in effect** to continue to be applied □ **salaries are increased 10% with effect from January 1st** a salary increase of 10% will apply from January 1st

effective /ɪ'fektɪv/ *adjective* 1. actual, as opposed to theoretical 2. which works or produces results ○ *Advertising in the Sunday papers is the most effective way of selling.* ○ *She is an effective marketing manager.* ♦ **cost-effective**

effective date of termination /ɪˌfektɪv deɪt əv ˌtɜːmɪ'neɪʃ(ə)n/ *noun* on the date at which an employee's employment ends (i.e. the date after notice, on which they leave the company)

effective demand /ɪˌfektɪv dɪ'mɑːnd/ *noun* the actual demand for a product which can be paid for

effective labour market /ɪˌfektɪv 'leɪbə ˌmɑːkɪt/ *noun* a labour market from which an employer actually draws applicants for posts, as opposed to the labour market from which the employer actually gets applicants

effectiveness /ɪ'fektɪvnəs/ *noun* the quality of working or producing results ○ *I doubt the effectiveness of television advertising.* ○ *His effectiveness as a manager was due to his quick grasp of detail.* ♦ **cost-effectiveness**

efficiency /ɪ'fɪʃ(ə)nsi/ *noun* the ability to work well or to produce the right result or the right work quickly ○ *a business efficiency exhibition* ○ *The bus system is run with a high degree of efficiency.* ○ *We called in an efficiency expert to report on ways of increasing profitability.*

'...increased control means improved efficiency in purchasing, shipping, sales and delivery' [*Duns Business Month*]

efficiency bonus /ɪ'fɪʃ(ə)nsi ˌbəʊnəs/ *noun* an extra payment for efficiency in a job

efficiency rating /ɪ'fɪʃ(ə)nsi ˌreɪtɪŋ/ *noun* an evaluation of an employee's efficiency in performing a job ○ *Her efficiency rating is so high she will soon be promoted.*

efficient /ɪ'fɪʃ(ə)nt/ *adjective* able to work well or to produce the right result quickly ○ *the efficient working of a system* ○ *An efficient assistant is invaluable.* ○ *An efficient new machine would save time.*

efficiently /ɪˈfɪʃ(ə)ntli/ *adverb* in an efficient way ○ *She organised the sales conference very efficiently.*

effort /ˈefət/ *noun* an act of using the mind or body to do something ○ *The sales staff made great efforts to increase sales.* ○ *Thanks to the efforts of the finance department, overheads have been reduced.* ○ *If we make one more effort, we should clear the backlog of orders.*

e.g. /ˈiːˈdʒiː/ for example or such as ○ *The contract is valid in some countries (e.g. France and Belgium) but not in others.*

ego drive /ˈiːɡəʊ draɪv/ *noun* a person's ambition or motivation to succeed ○ *Ego drive is highly valued in sales representatives*

eighty per cent rule /ˌeɪti pə ˈsent ruːl/ *noun US* the principle which states that if selection of a particular ethnic, age or sex group is less than 80% of another group, then the selection system is defective ○ *According to the eighty per cent rule our recruitment practices used to be highly discriminatory.*

elasticity /ˌɪlæˈstɪsəti/ *noun* the ability to change easily in response to a change in circumstances □ **elasticity of supply and demand** changes in supply and demand of an item depending on its market price

e-learning /ˈiː ˌlɜːnɪŋ/ *noun* learning by means of courses or aids to study provided on the Internet or an intranet (NOTE: E-learning is a development from **computer-based training** and, because it is Internet based, it is very flexible: it allows the learner to proceed at their own pace and can be adapted to suit the changing needs of the company. Full form is **electronic learning**)

elect /ɪˈlekt/ *verb* **1.** to choose someone by a vote ○ *She was elected president of the staff club.* **2.** to choose to do something ○ *He elected to take early retirement.*

-elect /ɪˈlekt/ *suffix* referring to a person who has been elected but has not yet started the term of office

elected officer /ɪˌlektɪd ˈɒfɪsə/ *noun* an official with decision-making powers, e.g. a director or union representative, who is chosen by a vote of the members or shareholders of an organisation

election /ɪˈlekʃən/ *noun* the act of electing someone ○ *the election of officers of an association* ○ *the election of directors by the shareholders* □ **to stand for election** to be a candidate in an election

electronic cottage /ˌelɪktrɒnɪk ˈkɒtɪdʒ/ *noun* somone's home from which they work for a company on a computer, usually linked to the office via a modem

electronic learning /ˌelɪktrɒnɪk ˈlɜːnɪŋ/ *noun* same as **e-learning**

electronic mail /ˌelɪktrɒnɪk ˈmeɪl/ *noun* same as **email 1**

element /ˈelɪmənt/ *noun* a basic part or the smallest unit into which something can be divided ○ *the elements of a settlement* ○ *Work study resulted in a standard time for each job element.*

eligibility /ˌelɪdʒɪˈbɪlɪti/ *noun* the fact of being eligible ○ *The chairman questioned her eligibility to stand for re-election.*

eligible /ˈelɪdʒɪb(ə)l/ *adjective* which can be chosen ○ *She is eligible for re-election.*

eligible list /ˈelɪdʒɪb(ə)l lɪst/ *noun* a list of qualified applicants in an order based on the results of tests ○ *After marking the candidates' tests, they drew up an eligible list.*

eliminate /ɪˈlɪmɪneɪt/ *verb* to remove ○ *to eliminate defects in the system* ○ *Using a computer should eliminate all possibility of error.* ○ *We have decided to eliminate this series of old products from our range.*

email /ˈiːmeɪl/ *noun* **1.** a system of sending messages from one computer terminal to another, using a modem and telephone lines ○ *You can contact me by phone or email if you want.* **2.** a message sent electronically ○ *I had six*

emails from him today. ■ *verb* to send a
message from one computer to another,
using a modem and telephone lines ○
She emailed her order to the warehouse.
○ *I emailed him about the meeting.*

embezzle /ɪmˈbez(ə)l/ *verb* to use illegally money which is not yours, or
which you are looking after for someone
○ *He was sent to prison for six months
for embezzling his clients' money.*

embezzlement /ɪmˈbez(ə)lmənt/
noun the act of embezzling ○ *He was
sent to prison for six months for
embezzlement.*

embezzler /ɪmˈbez(ə)lə/ *noun* a person who embezzles

emergency exit /ɪˈmɜːdʒ(ə)nsi
ˈegzɪt/ *noun* the special way out of a
building, used if there is a fire or other
emergency

emigrant /ˈemɪgrənt/ *noun* a person
who emigrates. ♦ **immigrant**

emigrate /ˈemɪgreɪt/ *verb* to go to another country to live permanently

emigration /ˌemɪˈgreɪʃ(ə)n/ *noun* the
act of leaving a country to go to live permanently in another country. ♦
immigration

emoluments /ɪˈmɒljʊmənts/ *plural
noun* pay, salary or fees, or the earnings
of directors who are not employees
(NOTE: American English uses the singular **emolument**)

emotional intelligence /ɪ-
ˌməʊʃ(ə)n(ə)l ɪnˈtelɪdʒəns/ *noun* the
ability to understand your own personal feelings and those of other people,
to take other people's feelings into
account when reaching decisions and
to respond to people's feelings in a
restrained and thoughtful way (NOTE:
Emotional intelligence can greatly improve people's interpersonal communication and people skills.)

empathy /ˈempəθi/ *noun* the ability to
appreciate the feelings of a subordinate
in a particular situation ○ *the need for
empathy to understand the frustration of
an employee in the wrong job* ○ *She had
little empathy with less ambitious
colleagues.*

employ /ɪmˈplɔɪ/ *verb* to give someone regular paid work □ **to employ**

twenty staff to have twenty people
working for you □ **to employ twenty
new staff** to give work to twenty new
people

'70 per cent of Australia's labour force was
employed in service activity'
[*Australian Financial Review*]

employability /ɪmˌplɔɪəˈbɪlɪti/ *noun*
the quality of having skills that will enable you to find and keep work (NOTE:
Employability is also affected by market demand for particular skills and by
personal circumstances.)

employed /ɪmˈplɔɪd/ *adjective* in regular paid work □ **he is not gainfully employed** he has no regular paid work □ **to
be employed** to be in regular paid work
■ *plural noun* people who are working
○ *the employers and the employed*

employee /ɪmˈplɔɪiː/ *noun* a person
employed by another ○ *Employees of
the firm are eligible to join a
profit-sharing scheme.* ○ *Relations between management and employees are
good.* ○ *The company has decided to
take on new employees.*

'…companies introducing robotics think it
important to involve individual employees in
planning their introduction' [*Economist*]

**employee assistance
programme** /ɪmˌplɔɪiː əˈsɪst(ə)ns
ˌprəʊgræm/ *noun* a programme set up
to help employees with personal problems. Abbr **EAP**

employee association /ɪmˈplɔɪiː
əsəʊsiˌeɪʃ(ə)n/ *noun* an association of
employees who work for the same organisation, formed to promote professional solidarity or to arrange social
activities

employee attitude survey /ɪm-
ˌplɔɪiː ˈætɪtjuːd ˌsɜːveɪ/ *noun* a survey
carried out among the employees of an
organisation to discover what they think
and feel generally about the work of the
organisation and their role within it, or
about some particular issue such as a
new company policy

employee commitment /ɪmˌplɔɪiː
kəˈmɪtmənt/ *noun* the feeling of loyalty that employees have towards the organisation that they work for, which
largely depends on the extent to which
they believe in the values and aims of
the organisation and feel personally in-

volved in the task of making the organisation successful

employee communication(s) /ɪmˌplɔɪiː kəˌmjuːnɪˈkeɪʃ(ə)nz/, **communication with employees** /kəmjuːnɪˌkeɪʃ(ə)n wɪð ɪmˈplɔɪiːz/ *noun* the process of passing information to employees and receiving information from employees

employee development /ɪmˌplɔɪiː dɪˈveləpmənt/ *noun* additional training dedicated to increasing the skills, knowledge and experience of employees in order to improve their performance

employee discount /ɪmˌplɔɪiː ˈdɪskaʊnt/ *noun* a reduction in the price that employees have to pay for the goods or services produced by their company, offered as one of their fringe benefits

employee handbook /ɪmˌplɔɪiː ˈhændbʊk/ *noun* a book that gives employees the information they need on the organisation that they work for and the job that they do (NOTE: Employee handbooks typically describe terms and conditions of employment, the policies and procedures of the organisation and fringe benefits.)

employee involvement /ɪmˌplɔɪiː ɪnˈvɒlvmənt/ *noun* a management policy that aims to increase employee commitment by giving employees greater individual responsibility for the work they do and a greater share in decision-making

employee ownership /ɪmˌplɔɪiː ˈəʊnəʃɪp/ *noun* ownership of all or some of the shares in a company by the people who work for it (NOTE: Forms of employee ownership include employee share schemes, employee buy-outs, co-operatives and employee trusts.)

employee participation /ɪmˌplɔɪiː pɑːtɪsɪˈpeɪʃ(ə)n/ *noun* the practice of employees sharing in the company's planning and decision-making (such as in works councils and quality circles) (NOTE: also called **worker participation**)

employee profile /ɪmˌplɔɪiː ˈprəʊfaɪl/ *noun* a person specification or form of job description which gives the ideal personal qualities needed for

the job and a description of the ideal candidate for the job

employee referral programme /ɪmˌplɔɪiː rɪˈfɜːrəl ˌprəʊgræm/ *noun* a policy popular in the US that encourages employees, usually through cash incentives, to nominate potential candidates for various jobs as part of the recruiting process

employee representation /ɪmˌplɔɪiː reprɪzenˈteɪʃ(ə)n/ *noun* the fact of having representatives of the employees on committees or boards

employee retention /ɪmˌplɔɪiː rɪˈtenʃən/ *noun* the process of keeping employees on the staff, and not losing them to rival firms

employee share ownership plan /ɪmˈplɔɪiː ʃeə ˈəʊnəʃɪp plæn/, **employee share ownership programme** /ɪmˈplɔɪiː ʃeə ˈəʊnəʃɪp ˌprəʊgræm/, **employee share scheme** /ɪmˌplɔɪiː ˈʃeə skiːm/ *noun* a plan which allows employees to obtain shares in the company for which they work. Abbr **ESOP**

employee stock fund /ɪmˌplɔɪiː ˈstɒk fʌnd/ *noun* (*in the US*) a fund from which money is taken to buy shares of a company's stock for its employees

employer /ɪmˈplɔɪə/ *noun* a person or company that has regular employees and pays them

employer's liability /ɪmˌplɔɪəz laɪəˈbɪlɪti/ *noun* the legal responsibility of an employer when employees suffer accidents due to negligence on the part of the employer

employers' liability insurance /ɪmˌplɔɪəz ˌlaɪəˈbɪlɪti ɪnˌʃʊərəns/ *noun* insurance to cover accidents which may happen at work, and for which the company may be responsible

employers' organisation /ɪmˈplɔɪəz ɔːgənaɪˌzeɪʃ(ə)n/, **employers' association** /ɪmˈplɔɪəz əsəʊsiˌeɪʃ(ə)n/ *noun* a group of employers with similar interests

employment /ɪmˈplɔɪmənt/ *noun* regular paid work □ **to be without employment** to have no work □ **to be in continuous employment** to be employed for a period of time, without more than a week's gap (holidays, sickness are not counted as gaps) ○ *She was in continuous employment for the period 1993 to 1996.*

'...the blue-collar unions are the people who stand to lose most in terms of employment growth' [*Sydney Morning Herald*]

employment agency /ɪmˈplɔɪmənt ˌeɪdʒənsi/ *noun* an office which finds jobs for staff

employment appeal tribunal /ɪmˌplɔɪmənt əˈpiːl traɪˌbjuːn(ə)l/ *noun* a tribunal which deals with appeals against the decisions of industrial tribunals. Abbr **EAT**

employment-at-will /ɪmˌplɔɪmənt ət ˈwɪl/ *noun* a term in common law that a contract of employment with no specified period of service may be terminated by either side without notice or reason

COMMENT: This is a basic principle of US employment law, where employers have the right to hire workers as they feel necessary and sack them for any reason and at any time, provided this is under the terms of the contract of employment agreed between the employer and the employee.

employment benefits /ɪmˈplɔɪmənt ˌbenɪfɪts/ *plural noun* extra items given by a company to workers in addition to their salaries (such as company cars or private health insurance) (NOTE: also called **fringe benefits**)

employment bureau /ɪmˈplɔɪmənt ˌbjʊərəʊ/ *noun* an office which finds jobs for people

Employment Court /ɪmˈplɔɪmənt kɔːt/ *noun* a higher court in New Zealand that is responsible for settling industrial relations disputes, e.g. between employers and employees or unions, and for deciding on appeals referred to it by employment tribunals

employment equity /ɪmˌplɔɪmənt ˈekwɪti/ *noun* the policy of giving preference in employment opportunities to qualified people from sectors of society that were previously discriminated against, e.g., black people, women and people with disabilities

employment law /ɪmˈplɔɪmənt lɔː/ *noun* the law as referring to workers, employers and their rights

employment office /ɪmˈplɔɪmənt ˌɒfɪs/ *noun* an office which finds jobs for people

employment opportunities /ɪmˈplɔɪmənt ɒpəˌtjuːnɪtiz/ *plural noun* new jobs being available (NOTE: also called **job opportunities**)

employment pass /ɪmˈplɔɪmənt pɑːs/ *noun* (*in South Africa*) a visa issued to a citizen of a foreign country who is a professional earning more than R1,500 per month

empower /ɪmˈpaʊə/ *verb* to give someone the power to do something ○ *She was empowered by the company to sign the contract.* ○ *Her new position empowers her to hire and fire at will.*

empowerment /ɪmˈpaʊəmənt/ *noun* the act of giving someone (such as an employee) the power to take decisions

'...a district-level empowerment programme run in one of the government's executive agencies failed because middle managers blocked it. Empowerment was officially defined by the agency as involving delegation of responsibility and the encouragement of innovation' [*People Management*]

empty suit /ˌempti ˈsuːt/ *noun* a company executive who dresses very smartly and follows all the procedures exactly without actually contributing anything important to the company (*slang*)

enc, encl *abbr* enclosure

enclose /ɪnˈkləʊz/ *verb* to put something inside an envelope with a letter ○ *to enclose an invoice with a letter* ○ *I am enclosing a copy of the contract.* ○ *Please find the cheque enclosed herewith.* ○ *Please enclose a recent photograph with your CV.*

enclosure /ɪnˈkləʊʒə/ *noun* a document enclosed with a letter or package ○ *a letter with enclosures* ○ *The enclosure turned out to be a free sample of perfume.* ○ *Sales material on other products was sent out as an enclosure.*

encounter group /ɪnˈkaʊntə gruːp/ *noun* a form of group psychotherapy which encourages people with personal problems to express their emotions ○

Encounter groups are used to accustom management trainees to criticism. ○ *The use of encounter groups to develop assertiveness in salesmen.*

encourage /ɪnˈkʌrɪdʒ/ *verb* **1.** to make it easier for something to happen ○ *The general rise in wages encourages consumer spending.* ○ *Leaving your credit cards on your desk encourages people to steal* or *encourages stealing.* ○ *The company is trying to encourage sales by giving large discounts.* **2.** to help someone to do something by giving advice ○ *He encouraged me to apply for the job.*

encouragement /ɪnˈkʌrɪdʒmənt/ *noun* the act of giving advice to someone to help them to succeed ○ *The designers produced a very marketable product, thanks to the encouragement of the sales director.* ○ *My family has been a source of great encouragement to me.*

energetic /ˌenəˈdʒetɪk/ *adjective* with a lot of energy ○ *The sales staff have made energetic attempts to sell the product.*

energy /ˈenədʒi/ *noun* a force or strength ○ *He hasn't the energy to be a good salesman.* ○ *They wasted their energies on trying to sell cars in the German market.* (NOTE: plural is **energies**)

enforce /ɪnˈfɔːs/ *verb* to make sure something is done or that a rule is obeyed ○ *to enforce the terms of a contract*

enforcement /ɪnˈfɔːsmənt/ *noun* the act of making sure that something is obeyed ○ *enforcement of the terms of a contract*

engage /ɪnˈgeɪdʒ/ *verb* to arrange to employ workers or advisors ○ *If we increase production we will need to engage more machinists.* ○ *He was engaged as a temporary replacement for the marketing manager who was ill.* ○ *The company has engaged twenty new sales representatives.*

engagement /ɪnˈgeɪdʒmənt/ *noun* **1.** an agreement to do something **2.** an arrangement to employ workers, or to re-employ them in the same job but not necessarily under the same conditions ○ *The engagement of two new secretaries*

will relieve management of some of the administrative duties.

English disease /ˈɪŋglɪʃ dɪˌziːz/ *noun* industrial and economic problems caused by workers continually going on strike (NOTE: The term originated from the fact that in the UK in the 1960s and 1970s workers commonly used strikes as a way of resolving disputes with management. Government legislation in the 1980s, however, made striking more difficult.)

enhance /ɪnˈhɑːns/ *verb* to make better or more attractive ○ *Working for a German company enhances the value of her work experience.*

enquire, enquiry /ɪnˈkwaɪə, ɪnˈkwaɪəri/ same as **inquire, inquiry**

enter /ˈentə/ *verb* **1.** to go in ○ *They all stood up when the chairman entered the room.* ○ *The company has spent millions trying to enter the do-it-yourself market.* **2.** to write ○ *to enter a name on a list* ○ *The clerk entered the interest in my bank book.*

enter into /ˌentə ˈɪntuː/ *verb* to begin ○ *to enter into relations with someone* ○ *to enter into negotiations with a foreign government* ○ *to enter into a partnership with a friend* ○ *The company does not want to enter into any long-term agreement.*

enterprise /ˈentəpraɪz/ *noun* **1.** initiative or willingness to take risks or to take responsibility ○ *We are looking for enterprise and ambition in our top managers.* **2.** a system of carrying on a business **3.** a business

enterprise culture /ˈentəpraɪz ˌkʌltʃə/ *noun* a general feeling that the commercial system works better with free enterprise, increased share ownership, property ownership, etc.

enterprise union /ˈentəpraɪz ˌjuːnjən/ *noun* a single union which represents all the workers in a company

enterprise zone /ˈentəpraɪz zəʊn/ *noun* an area of the country where businesses are encouraged to develop by offering special conditions such as easy planning permission for buildings or a reduction in the business rate

enterprising /ˈentəpraɪzɪŋ/ *adjective* having initiative ○ *An enterprising sales rep can always find new sales outlets.*

entertainment /ˌentəˈteɪnmənt/ *noun* the practice of offering meals or other recreation to business visitors

entertainment allowance /ˌentəˈteɪnmənt əˌlaʊəns/ *noun* money which managers are allowed by their company to spend on meals with visitors

entertainment expenses /ˌentəˈteɪnmənt ɪkˌspensɪz/ *plural noun* money spent on giving meals to business visitors

entice /ɪnˈtaɪs/ *verb* to try to persuade someone to do something ○ *The company was accused of enticing staff from other companies by offering them higher salaries.*

enticement /ɪnˈtaɪsmənt/ *noun* the act of attracting someone away from their job to another job which is better paid

entitle /ɪnˈtaɪt(ə)l/ *verb* to give the right to someone to have something ○ *After one year's service the employee is entitled to four weeks' holiday.*

entitlement /ɪnˈtaɪt(ə)lmənt/ *noun* a person's right to something

entrance /ˈentrəns/ *noun* 1. a way in ○ *The taxi will drop you at the main entrance.* 2. going into a new job ○ *Entrance to the grade is by qualifications and several years' experience.*

entrance rate /ˈentrəns reɪt/ *noun* a rate of pay for employees when first hired ○ *Though the entrance rate is very low, the salary goes up considerably after the first year.* ○ *The entrance rate depends on whether the entrants are skilled or not.*

entrant /ˈentrənt/ *noun* a person who is going into a new job ○ *There are several highly qualified people in this month's batch of entrants.*

entrepreneur /ˌɒntrəprəˈnɜː/ *noun* a person who directs a company and takes commercial risks

entrepreneurial /ˌɒntrəprəˈnɜːriəl/ *adjective* taking commercial risks ○ *an entrepreneurial decision*

entrust /ɪnˈtrʌst/ *verb* □ **to entrust someone with something, to entrust something to someone** to give someone the responsibility for looking after something ○ *He was entrusted with the keys to the office safe.*

entry /ˈentri/ *noun* 1. an item of written information put in an accounts ledger (NOTE: plural is **entries**) □ **to make an entry in a ledger** to write in details of a transaction 2. the act of going into a new job ○ *entry of recruits from school*

entry level job /ˈentri ˌlev(ə)l dʒɒb/ *noun* a job for which no previous experience is needed ○ *It is only an entry level job, but you can expect promotion within six months.*

entry level pay /ˈentri ˌlev(ə)l peɪ/ *noun* pay for an entry level job

entry requirement /ˈentri rɪˌkwaɪəmənt/ *noun* the qualifications which a beginner needs to start a job

environment /ɪnˈvaɪrənmənt/ *noun* 1. the area in which an organisation works 2. internal or external surroundings ○ *Trade unions demand a good working environment for employees.*

environmental /ɪnˌvaɪrənˈment(ə)l/ *adjective* referring to the environment

environmental audit /ɪnˌvaɪrənment(ə)l ˈɔːdɪt/ *noun* an assessment made by a company or organisation of the financial benefits and disadvantages to be derived from adopting a more environmentally sound policy

Environmental Health Officer /ɪnˌvaɪrənment(ə)l ˈhelθ ˌɒfɪsə/ *noun* an official of a local authority who examines the environment and tests for air pollution, bad sanitation or noise pollution etc. Abbr **EHO** (NOTE: also called **Public Health Inspector**)

EOC *abbr* Equal Opportunities Commission

equal /ˈiːkwəl/ *adjective* exactly the same ○ *Male and female employees have equal pay.*

equality /ɪˈkwɒlɪti/ *noun* the state of being equal

equality bargaining /ɪˈkwɒliti ˌbaːɡɪnɪŋ/ *noun* collective bargaining where the conditions and advantages agreed apply to both male and female employees equally

equality of opportunity /ɪˌkwɒlɪti əv ɒpəˈtjuːnɪti/ *noun* a situation where everyone, regardless of sex, race, class, etc., has the same opportunity to get a job

equality of treatment /ɪˌkwɒlɪti əv ˈtriːtmənt/ *noun* the practice of treating male and female employees equally

equal opportunities /ˌiːkwəl ɒpəˈtjuːnɪtiz/ *plural noun* the practice of avoiding discrimination in employment ○ *Does the political party support equal opportunities for women?*

equal opportunities programme /ˌiːkwəl ɒpəˈtjuːnɪtiz ˌprəʊɡræm/ *noun* a programme to avoid discrimination in employment (NOTE: the American equivalent is **affirmative action**)

equal treatment /ˌiːkwəl ˈtriːtmənt/ *noun* a principle of the European Union that requires member states to ensure that there is no discrimination with regard to employment, vocational training and working conditions

equity /ˈekwɪti/ *noun* **1.** a right to receive dividends as part of the profit of a company in which you own shares **2.** fairness of treatment, e.g. equality of pay for the same type of job ○ *Equity was the most important factor taken into account in drawing up the new pay structure.*

equivalence /ɪˈkwɪvələns/ *noun* the condition of having the same value or of being the same

equivalent /ɪˈkwɪvələnt/ *adjective* □ **to be equivalent to** to have the same value as or to be the same as ○ *Our managing director's salary is equivalent to that of far less experienced employees in other organisations.* ■ *noun* a person who is the equal of someone else

equivalent pension benefit /ɪˌkwɪvələnt ˈpenʃən ˌbenɪfɪt/ *noun* the right of opted-out pensioners to receive the same pension as they would have done under the state graduated pension scheme

ergonometrics /ˌɜːɡənəˈmetrɪks/ *noun* a measurement of the quantity of

work done (NOTE: takes a singular verb)

ergonomics /ˌɜːɡəˈnɒmɪks/ *noun* the study of the relationship between people at work and their working conditions, especially the machines they use (NOTE: takes a singular verb)

ergonomist /ɜːˈɡɒnəmɪst/ *noun* a scientist who studies people at work and tries to improve their working conditions

erode /ɪˈrəʊd/ *verb* to wear away gradually □ **to erode wage differentials** to reduce gradually differences in salary between different grades

erosion /ɪˈrəʊʒ(ə)n/ *noun* the gradual wearing away ○ *erosion of differentials*

error /ˈerə/ *noun* a mistake ○ *He made an error in calculating the total.* ○ *I must have made a typing error.* ○ *They made an error in calculating the tax deductions.* □ **in error, by error** by mistake ○ *The letter was sent to the London office in error.*

escalate /ˈeskəleɪt/ *verb* to increase steadily

escalation /ˌeskəˈleɪʃ(ə)n/ *noun* a steady increase ○ *an escalation of wage demands* ○ *The union has threatened an escalation in strike action.*

escalator clause /ˈeskəleɪtə klɔːz/ *noun* a clause in a contract allowing for regular price increases because of increased costs, or regular wage increases because of the increased cost of living

escape /ɪˈskeɪp/ *noun* an act of getting away from a difficult situation

ESOP *abbr* employee share ownership plan

essay method /ˈeseɪ ˌmeθəd/ *noun* an evaluation method in performance appraisal where the evaluator writes a short description of the employee's performance

establish /ɪˈstæblɪʃ/ *verb* to set up or to open ○ *The company has established a branch in Australia.* ○ *The business was established in Scotland in 1823.* ○ *It is still a young company, having been established for only four years.* □ **to establish oneself in business** to become successful in a new business

establishment /ɪˈstæblɪʃmənt/ *noun* the number of people working in a company □ **to be on the establishment** to be a full-time employee □ **office with an establishment of fifteen** an office with a budgeted staff of fifteen

establishment charges /ɪˈstæblɪʃmənt ˌtʃɑːdʒɪz/ *plural noun* the costs of people and property in a company's accounts

ethic /ˈeθɪk/ *noun* the general rules of conduct in society

ethnic /ˈeθnɪk/ *adjective* belonging to a certain racial group

COMMENT: In a recent British survey, the main ethnic groups were defined as: White, Black-Caribbean, Black-African, Black-Other, Indian, Pakistani, Bangladeshi, Chinese and Other.

ethnic minority /ˌeθnɪk maɪˈnɒrɪti/ *noun* a section of the population from a certain racial group, which does not make up the majority of the population

ethnic monitoring /ˌeθnɪk ˈmɒnɪt(ə)rɪŋ/ *noun* the recording of the racial origins of employees or customers in order to ensure that all parts of the population are represented

ethos /ˈiːθɒs/ *noun* a characteristic way of working and thinking

EU *abbr* European Union ○ *EU ministers met today in Brussels.* ○ *The USA is increasing its trade with the EU.*

EU national /ˌiː juː ˈnæʃ(ə)n(ə)l/ *noun* a person who is a citizen of a country which is a member of the EU

European Commission /ˌjʊərəpiːən kəˈmɪʃ(ə)n/ *noun* the main executive body of the EU, made up of members nominated by each member state (NOTE: also called the **Commission of the European Community**)

European Social Charter /ˌjʊərəpiːən ˌsəʊʃ(ə)l ˈtʃɑːtə/ *noun* a charter for employees, drawn up by the EU in 1989, by which employees have the right to a fair wage, to equal treatment for men and women, a safe work environment, training, freedom of association and collective bargaining, provision for disabled workers, freedom of movement from country to country, guaranteed standards of living both for the working population as well as for retired people, etc. (There is no machinery for enforcing the Social Charter.)

European Union /ˌjʊərəpiːən ˈjuːnjən/ *noun* (formerly, the European Economic Community (EEC), the Common Market) a group of European countries linked together by the Treaty of Rome in such a way that trade is more free, people can move from one country to another more freely and people can work more freely in other countries of the group

COMMENT: The European Community was set up in 1957 and changed its name to the European Union when it adopted the Single Market. It has now grown to include fifteen member states. These are: Austria, Belgium, Denmark, Finland, France, Germany, Greece, Ireland, Italy, Luxembourg, the Netherlands, Portugal, Spain, Sweden and the United Kingdom; other countries are negotiating to join. The member states of the EU are linked together by the Treaty of Rome in such a way that trade is more free, money can be moved from one country to another freely, people can move from one country to another more freely and people can work more freely in other countries of the group.

evacuate /ɪˈvækjueɪt/ *verb* to get people to leave a dangerous building, an aircraft on fire etc. ○ *They evacuated the premises when fire broke out in the basement.*

evacuation /ɪˌvækjuˈeɪʃ(ə)n/ *noun* the action of getting people out of a dangerous building or aircraft, etc.

evaluate /ɪˈvæljueɪt/ *verb* to calculate a value ○ *to evaluate costs* ○ *We will evaluate jobs on the basis of their contribution to the organisation as a whole.* ○ *We need to evaluate the experience and qualifications of all the candidates.*

evaluation /ɪˌvæljuˈeɪʃ(ə)n/ *noun* the calculation of value

evaluation of training /ɪvælju-ˌeɪʃ(ə)n əv ˈtreɪnɪŋ/ *noun* a continuous process of analysis that evaluates the training carried out by an organisation, defining its aims, assessing the need for it, finding out how people react to it and measuring its effects of the organisation's financial performance

evaluator /ɪ'væljueɪtə/ *noun* a person who carries out an evaluation

evening class /'iːvnɪŋ ˌklɑːs/ *noun* a course of study, usually for adults, organised in the evening

evening shift /'iːvnɪŋ ʃɪft/ *noun* a shift which works from 6.00 p.m. to 10.00 or 11.00 p.m. (usually manned by part-timers)

evict /ɪ'vɪkt/ *verb* to force someone to leave premises which they are occupying ○ *They had to call in the police to evict the squatters.* ○ *The company obtained an injunction to evict the striking workers from the factory.*

eviction /ɪ'vɪkʃən/ *noun* the act of forcing someone to leave premises which they are occupying

evidence /'evɪd(ə)ns/ *noun* **1.** written or spoken information ○ *What evidence is there that the new employee is causing all the trouble?* **2.** a written or spoken report produced in a court of law to prove a fact □ **the secretary gave evidence against her former employer** the secretary was a witness, and her report suggested that her former employer was guilty □ **the secretary gave evidence for her former employer** the secretary was a witness, and her report suggested that her former employer was not guilty

ex- /eks/ *prefix* former ○ *an ex-director of the company*

examination /ɪgˌzæmɪ'neɪʃ(ə)n/ *noun* **1.** looking at something very carefully to see if it is acceptable **2.** a written or oral test to see if someone has passed a course ○ *He passed his accountancy examinations.* ○ *She came first in the final examination for the course.* ○ *He failed his proficiency examination.* ○ *Examinations are given to candidates to test their mathematical ability.* □ **to sit** *or* **to take an examination** to write the answers to an examination test

examine /ɪg'zæmɪn/ *verb* to look at someone or something very carefully ○ *Customs officials asked to examine the inside of the car.* ○ *The police are examining the papers from the managing director's safe.*

example /ɪg'zɑːmpəl/ *noun* something chosen to show how things should be done ○ *Her sales success in Europe is an example of what can be achieved by determination.* □ **to follow someone's example** to do what someone else has done earlier □ **to set a good** *or* **bad example to someone** to work well or badly, and show others how the work should or should not be done ○ *The foreman worked hard to set a good example to the others.*

exceed /ɪk'siːd/ *verb* to be more than ○ *a discount not exceeding 15%* ○ *Last year costs exceeded 20% of income for the first time.* □ **she exceeded his target** she did more than she aimed to do □ **he exceeded his powers** he acted in a way which was not allowed

excellent /'eksələnt/ *adjective* very good ○ *The quality of the firm's products is excellent, but its sales force is not large enough.*

except /ɪk'sept/ *preposition, conjunction* not including ○ *VAT is levied on all goods and services except books, newspapers and children's clothes.* ○ *Sales are rising in all markets except the Far East.*

excepted /ɪk'septɪd/ *adverb* not including

excess /ɪk'ses, 'ekses/ *noun, adjective* (an amount) which is more than what is allowed ○ *an excess of expenditure over revenue* ○ *Excess costs have caused us considerable problems.* □ **in excess of** above, more than ○ *quantities in excess of twenty-five kilos*

'…most airlines give business class the same baggage allowance as first class, which can save large sums in excess baggage' [*Business Traveller*]

'…control of materials provides manufacturers with an opportunity to reduce the amount of money tied up in excess materials' [*Duns Business Month*]

excess plan /'ekses plæn/ *noun* a pension plan providing higher pensions for higher wages

exclude /ɪk'skluːd/ *verb* to keep out or not to include ○ *The interest charges have been excluded from the document.*

○ *Damage by fire is excluded from the policy.*

excluding /ɪkˈskluːdɪŋ/ *preposition* not including ○ *All sales staff, excluding those living in London, can claim expenses for attending the sales conference.*

exclusion /ɪkˈskluːʒ(ə)n/ *noun* **1.** the act of not including something **2.** cutting people off from being full members of society, because of lack of education, alcoholism or drug abuse, unemployment, etc.

exclusive /ɪkˈskluːsɪv/ *adjective* □ **exclusive of** not including ○ *All payments are exclusive of tax.* ○ *The invoice is exclusive of VAT.*

exclusive of tax /ɪkˌskluːsɪv əv ˈtæks/ *noun* not including tax

excuse *noun* /ɪkˈskjuːs/ a reason for doing something wrong ○ *His excuse for not coming to the meeting was that he had been told about it only the day before.* □ **the managing director refused to accept the sales manager's excuses for the poor sales** she refused to believe that there was a good reason for the poor sales ■ *verb* /ɪkˈskjuːz/ to forgive a small mistake ○ *She can be excused for not knowing the French for 'photocopier'.*

execute /ˈeksɪkjuːt/ *verb* to carry out an order ○ *Failure to execute orders may lead to dismissal.* ○ *There were many practical difficulties in executing the managing director's instructions.*

execution /ˌeksɪˈkjuːʃ(ə)n/ *noun* the carrying out of a commercial order or contract

executive /ɪɡˈzekjʊtɪv/ *adjective* which puts decisions into action ■ *noun* a person in a business who takes decisions, a manager or director ○ *a sales executive* ○ *a senior or junior executive*

'…one in ten students commented on the long hours which executives worked' [*Employment Gazette*]

'…our executives are motivated by a desire to carry out a project to the best of their ability' [*British Business*]

executive board /ɪɡˈzekjʊtɪv bɔːd/ *noun* a board of directors which deals with the day-to-day running of the company (as opposed to a supervisory

board, which deals with policy and planning)

executive chairman /ɪɡˌzekjʊtɪv ˈtʃeəmən/ *noun* a title sometimes given to the most senior executive in an organisation

executive coaching /ɪɡˌzekjʊtɪv ˈkəʊtʃɪŋ/ *noun* regular one-to-one teaching or feedback sessions, designed to provide managers with knowledge and skills in a particular area as part of a management development programme

executive director /ɪɡˌzekjʊtɪv daɪˈrektə/ *noun* a senior employee of an organisation who is usually in charge of one or other of its main functions, e.g. sales or human relations, and is usually, but not always, a member of the board of directors

executive officer /ɪɡˈzekjʊtɪv ˌɒfɪsə/ *noun* same as **executive**

executive pension plan /ɪɡˌzekjʊtɪv ˈpenʃən plæn/ *noun* a special pension plan for managers and directors of a company

executive search /ɪɡˈzekjʊtɪv sɜːtʃ/ *noun* the process of looking for new managers for organisations, often by approaching managers in their existing jobs and asking them if they want to work for different companies (NOTE: a more polite term for **headhunting**)

executive share option scheme /ɪɡˌzekjʊtɪv ˈʃeər ɒpʃən ˌskiːm/ *noun* a special scheme for senior managers, by which they can buy shares in the company they work for at a fixed price at a later date

exemplary /ɪɡˈzempləri/ *adjective* excellent, so good it can be used as an example ○ *Her behaviour has been exemplary.*

exempt /ɪɡˈzempt/ *adjective* not covered by a law, or not forced to obey a law ○ *Anyone over 65 is exempt from charges* ○ *He was exempt from military service in his country.* □ **exempt from tax** not required to pay tax ○ *As a non-profit-making organisation we are exempt from tax.* ■ *verb* **1.** to free something from having tax paid on it ○ *Non-profit-making organisations are exempted from tax.* **2.** to free someone from having to pay tax ○ *Food is exempted from sales tax.* **3.** to free someone from having to do a task ○ *I hope to be exempted from taking these tests.* ○ *She was exempted from fire duty.*

'Companies with sales under $500,000 a year will be exempt from the minimum-wage requirements' [*Nation's Business*]

exemption /ɪgˈzempʃ(ə)n/ *noun* the act of exempting something from a contract or from a tax □ **exemption from tax, tax exemption** the fact of being free from having to pay tax ○ *As a non-profit-making organisation you can claim tax exemption.*

exempt personnel /ɪgˌzempt pɜːsəˈnel/ *noun* personnel who do not receive payment for overtime or whose wages are not affected by minimum wage legislation

exercise /ˈeksəsaɪz/ *noun* a use of something □ **exercise of a right** the using of a right ■ *verb* to use ○ *The chairwoman exercised her veto to block the motion.* □ **to exercise a right** to put a right into action ○ *He exercised his right to refuse to do tasks not listed on his employment contract.*

ex gratia /eks ˈgreɪʃə/ *adjective* done as a favour

ex gratia payment /eks ˌgreɪʃə ˈpeɪmənt/ *noun* a payment made as a gift, with no other obligations

exhaust /ɪgˈzɔːst/ *verb* to use up totally ○ *We will go on negotiating until all possible solutions have been exhausted.*

exit /ˈegzɪt/ *noun* **1.** the way out of a building ○ *The customers all rushed towards the exits.* **2.** leaving a job

exit interview /ˈegzɪt ˌɪntəvjuː/ *noun* an interview with an employee when they are leaving an organisation to find out their views on how the organisation is run and reasons for leaving ○ *Only at his exit interview did he admit how much he had disliked working for the company.*

ex officio /eks əˈfɪʃiəʊ/ *adjective, adverb* because of an office held ○ *The treasurer is ex officio a member* or *an ex officio member of the finance committee.*

ex parte /eks ˈpɑːti/ *Latin phrase meaning* 'on behalf of' □ **an ex parte application** application made to a court where only one side is represented and no notice is given to the other side (often where the application is for an injunction). ♦ **inter partes**

expatriate /eksˈpætriət/ *noun, adjective* a person, who lives and works in a country which is not their own ○ *Expatriate staff are paid higher rates than locally recruited staff.* ○ *All expatriates in the organisation have two months' leave a year.*

expect /ɪkˈspekt/ *verb* to hope that something is going to happen ○ *We are expecting him to arrive at 10.45.* ○ *They are expecting a cheque from their agent next week.* ○ *The house was sold for more than the expected price.*

'…he observed that he expected exports to grow faster than imports in the coming year' [*Sydney Morning Herald*]

'American business as a whole has seen profits well above the levels normally expected at this stage of the cycle' [*Sunday Times*]

expectancy theory /ɪkˈspektənsi ˌθɪəri/ *noun* a theory that employees will only be motivated to produce if they expect that higher performance will lead to greater personal satisfaction

expectations /ˌekspekˈteɪʃ(ə)nz/ *plural noun* hopes of what is to come ○ *She has great expectations of her new job, and I hope she won't be disappointed.*

expel /ɪkˈspel/ *verb* to throw someone out of an organisation ○ *The worker was expelled from the union for embezzlement.* (NOTE: expelling-expelled)

expense account /ɪkˈspens əˌkaʊnt/ *noun* an allowance of money which a business pays for an employee to spend on travelling and entertaining clients in connection with that business ○ *I'll put this lunch on my expense account.*

expenses /ɪkˈspensɪz/ *plural noun* money paid to cover the costs incurred by someone when doing something ○ *The salary offered is £10,000 plus expenses.* ○ *He has a high salary and all his travel expenses are paid by the company.* □ **all expenses paid** with all costs paid by the company ○ *The company sent him to San Francisco all expenses paid.*

experience /ɪkˈspɪəriəns/ *noun* knowledge or skill that comes from having had to deal with many different situations ○ *She has a lot of experience of dealing with German companies.* ○ *I gained most of my experience abroad.* ○ *Considerable experience is required for this job.* ○ *The applicant was pleasant, but did not have any relevant experience.*

experienced /ɪkˈspɪəriənst/ *adjective* referring to a person who has lived through many situations and has learnt from them ○ *You are the most experienced negotiator I know.* ○ *We have appointed a very experienced candidate as sales director.* ○ *Our more experienced staff will have dealt with a crisis like this before.*

experience rating /ɪkˈspɪəriəns ˌreɪtɪŋ/ *noun* the evaluation of a person to decide on their eligibility for insurance coverage

experiential learning /ɪk-ˌspɪərienʃəl ˈlɜːnɪŋ/ *noun* the process of learning skills through practice

expert /ˈekspɜːt/ *noun* a person who knows a lot about something ○ *an expert in the field of electronics* or *an electronics expert* ○ *The company asked a financial expert for advice* or *asked for expert financial advice.* □ **expert's report** a report written by an expert

expertise /ˌekspəˈtiːz/ *noun* specialist knowledge or skill in a particular field ○ *We hired Mr Smith because of his financial expertise* or *because of his expertise in finance.* ○ *With years of experience in the industry, we have plenty of expertise to draw on.* ○ *Lack of marketing expertise led to low sales figures.*

expert system /ˈekspɜːt ˌsɪstəm/ *noun* software that applies the knowledge, advice and rules defined by experts in a particular field to a user's data to help solve a problem

expiration /ˌekspəˈreɪʃ(ə)n/ *noun* the act of coming to an end ○ *the expiration of an insurance policy* ○ *to repay before the expiration of the stated period* □ **on** **expiration of the lease** when the lease comes to an end

expire /ɪkˈspaɪə/ *verb* to come to an end ○ *The lease expires in 2010.*

expiry /ɪkˈspaɪəri/ *noun* the act of coming to an end ○ *the expiry of an insurance policy*

explain /ɪkˈspleɪn/ *verb* to give reasons for something ○ *The sales director tried to explain the sudden drop in unit sales.*

explanation /ˌekspləˈneɪʃ(ə)n/ *noun* a reason for something ○ *The human resources department did not accept her explanation for being late.*

exploding bonus /ɪkˌspləʊdɪŋ ˈbəʊnəs/ *noun* a bonus, offered to recent graduates who take a job with an organisation, that encourages them to make a decision as quickly as possible because it reduces in value with every day of delay (*informal*)

exploit /ɪkˈsplɔɪt/ *verb* to use something to make a profit ○ *The directors exploit their employees, who have to work hard for very little pay.*

exploitation /ˌeksplɔɪˈteɪʃ(ə)n/ *noun* the unfair use of cheap labour to get work done ○ *The exploitation of migrant farm workers was only stopped when they became unionised.*

express letter /ɪkˌspres ˈletə/ *noun* a letter sent very fast

expulsion /ɪkˈspʌlʃən/ *noun* the act of being thrown out of an organisation ○ *What is the chance of expulsion for breaking house rules?*

extend /ɪkˈstend/ *verb* **1.** to offer ○ *to extend credit to a customer* **2.** to make longer ○ *Her contract of employment was extended for two years.* ○ *We have extended the deadline for making the appointment by two weeks.*

extension /ɪkˈstenʃən/ *noun* **1.** allowing a longer time for something than was originally agreed □ **extension of a contract of employment** the act of continuing a contract for a further period **2.** (*in an office*) an individual telephone linked to the main switchboard ○ *The sales manager is on extension 53.* ○ *Can you get me extension 21? Extension 21 is engaged.*

'...the White House refusal to ask for an extension of the auto import quotas' [*Duns Business Month*]

extensive /ɪkˈstensɪv/ *adjective* very large or covering a wide area ○ *an extensive network of sales outlets* ○ *an extensive recruitment drive*

external /ɪkˈstɜːn(ə)l/ *adjective* outside a company

external audit /ɪk̩stɜːn(ə)l ˈɔːdɪt/ *noun* an audit carried out by an independent auditor (who is not employed by the company)

external auditor /ɪk̩stɜːn(ə)l ˈɔːdɪtə/ *noun* an independent person who audits the company's accounts

externally /ɪkˈstɜːn(ə)li/ *adverb* from outside an organisation ○ *The new sales director was recruited externally.* (NOTE: the opposite is **internally**)

external recruitment /ɪk̩stɜːn(ə)l rɪˈkruːtmənt/ *noun* the recruitment of employees from outside an organisation ○ *Internal recruitment is normally attempted before resorting to external recruitment.*

external workers /ɪk̩stɜːn(ə)l ̩wɜːkəz/ *plural noun* workers who are outside the company such as casual workers, freelancers or contract workers

extra /ˈekstrə/ *adjective* which is added or which is more than usual ○ *to charge 10% extra for postage* ○ *There is no extra charge for heating.* ○ *Service is extra.* ○ *We get £25 extra pay for working on Sunday.*

extra hours /̩ekstrə ˈaʊəz/ *noun* working more hours than are normal ○ *She worked three hours extra.* ○ *He claimed for extra hours.*

extraordinary /ɪkˈstrɔːdn(ə)ri/ *adjective* different from normal

extremely /ɪkˈstriːmli/ *adverb* very much ○ *It is extremely difficult to break into the US market.* ○ *Their management team is extremely efficient.*

extrinsic reward /ekˈstrɪnsɪk rɪˌwɔːd/ *noun* a financial or material reward for work ○ *Extrinsic rewards can be measured, whereas intrinsic rewards cannot.* Compare **intrinsic reward**

eye service /ˈaɪ ̩sɜːvɪs/ *noun* the practice of working only when a supervisor is present and able to see you (*slang*)

F

F2F *abbr* face-to-face (*slang*)

face time /ˈfeɪs taɪm/ *noun* time spent communicating with other people face-to-face as opposed to time spent communicating with them electronically (*informal*)

face validity /ˈfeɪs vəˌlɪdɪti/ *noun* the degree to which a test seems to be valid

face value /ˌfeɪs ˈvæljuː/ *noun* the value written on a coin, banknote or share certificate □ **to take something at face value** to believe something to be true or genuine

'…travellers cheques cost 1% of their face value – some banks charge more for small amounts' [*Sunday Times*]

facilitation /fəˌsɪlɪˈteɪʃ(ə)n/ *noun* the process of helping people to do something, e.g. to learn or to find a solution to a problem, without dictating how they do it

facilitator /fəˈsɪlɪteɪtə/ *noun* a person who actively encourages discussion, new initiatives, etc.

facilities /fəˈsɪlɪtiz/ *plural noun* services, equipment or buildings which make it possible to do something ○ *There are no facilities for disabled visitors.* ○ *There are very good sports facilities on the company premises.*

fact /fækt/ *noun* **1.** a piece of information ○ *The chairman asked to see all the facts on the income tax claim.* ○ *The sales director can give you the facts and figures about the African operation.* **2.** □ **the fact of the matter is** what is true is that

fact-finding /ˈfækt ˌfaɪndɪŋ/ *noun* the process of looking for information

fact-finding commission /ˈfækt faɪndɪŋ kəˌmɪʃ(ə)n/ *noun* a committee set up by a third party to carry out an impartial review of issues in a labour dispute ○ *A fact-finding commission was set up to look into the reasons for the pay dispute.*

factor /ˈfæktə/ *noun* something which is important or which is taken into account when making a decision ○ *The drop in sales is an important factor in the company's lower profits.* ○ *Motivation was an important factor in drawing up the new pay scheme.*

factor comparison /ˈfæktə kəmˌpærɪs(ə)n/ *noun* a method of comparing jobs in relation to factors such as training or effort

factor evaluation /ˈfæktər ɪvæljuˌeɪʃ(ə)n/ *noun* a method of evaluating or assessing jobs in relation to factors such as training or effort

Factories Act /ˈfækt(ə)riz ækt/ *noun* an Act of Parliament which governs the conditions in which employees work (such as heating, lighting or toilet facilities)

factor ranking /ˈfæktə ˌræŋkɪŋ/ *noun* a method of grading jobs in relation to factors such as training or effort

factory /ˈfækt(ə)ri/ *noun* a building where products are manufactured ○ *a car factory* ○ *a shoe factory* ○ *The company is proposing to close three of its factories with the loss of 200 jobs.*

factory floor /ˌfækt(ə)ri ˈflɔː/ *noun* the main works of a factory

factory hand /ˈfækt(ə)ri hænd/ *noun* a person who works in a factory

factory inspector /ˈfækt(ə)ri ɪnˌspektə/ *noun* a government official who inspects factories to see if they are well run

factory inspectorate /ˈfækt(ə)ri ɪnˌspekt(ə)rət/ *noun* all inspectors of factories

factory work /ˈfækt(ə)ri wɜːk/ *noun* work on the production line in a factory

factory worker /ˈfækt(ə)ri ˌwɜːkə/ *noun* a person who works in a factory

fail /feɪl/ *verb* not to do something which you were trying to do ○ *They failed to agree on an agenda for the meeting.* ○ *Negotiations continued until midnight but the two sides failed to come to an agreement.*

failure /ˈfeɪljə/ *noun* **1.** an act of breaking down or stopping ○ *the failure of the negotiations* **2.** not doing something which you promised to do

fair /feə/ *noun* same as **trade fair** ○ *The computer fair runs from April 1st to 6th.*

fair deal /feə ˈdiːl/ *noun* an arrangement where both parties are treated equally ○ *The employees feel they did not get a fair deal from the management.*

fair dismissal /feə dɪsˈmɪs(ə)l/ *noun* the dismissal of an employee for reasons such as the employee's bad conduct, e.g. theft or drunkenness, failure of the employee to work capably, or redundancy, which are regarded as valid causes

fair employment /feər ɪmˈplɔɪmənt/ *noun* employment where no racial, religious or sex discrimination takes place ○ *The company has a strong policy of fair employment.* ○ *The recruitment of twice as many men as women was a denial of the principle of fair employment.*

fairly /ˈfeəli/ *adverb* **1.** quite ○ *She is a fairly fast keyboarder.* ○ *The company is fairly close to breaking even.* **2.** reasonably or equally ○ *The union representatives put the employees' side of the case fairly and without argument.*

fair representation /feə reprɪzenˈteɪʃ(ə)n/ *noun* representation of all members of a bargaining unit fairly and without discrimination

fair share agreement /feə ˈʃeər əˌɡriːmənt/ *noun* an arrangement where both management and unions agree that employees are not obliged to join a un-

ion, but that all employees pay the union a share of bargaining costs as a condition of employment ○ *A fair share agreement was reached, since even employees who were not union members benefited from bargains struck between union and management.*

fair trading /feə ˈtreɪdɪŋ/ *noun* a way of doing business which is reasonable and does not harm the consumer

fair wear and tear /ˌfeə weər ən ˈteə/ *noun* acceptable damage caused by normal use ○ *The insurance policy covers most damage but not fair wear and tear to the machine.*

faith /feɪθ/ *noun* □ **to have faith in something** *or* **someone** to believe that something or a person is good or will work well ○ *The sales teams do not have much faith in their manager.* ○ *The board has faith in the managing director's judgement.* □ **to buy something in good faith** to buy something thinking that is of good quality, that it has not been stolen or that it is not an imitation

faith validity /ˈfeɪθ vəˌlɪdɪti/ *noun* same as **face validity**

fall behind /ˌfɔːl bɪˈhaɪnd/ *verb* to be in a worse position than □ **we have fallen behind our rivals** we have fewer sales or make less profit than our rivals

falling unemployment /ˌfɔːlɪŋ ʌnɪmˈplɔɪmənt/ *noun* unemployment rates which are falling because more people are finding jobs

false /fɔːls/ *adjective* not true or not correct ○ *to make a false claim for a product*

false negative /fɔːls ˈneɡətɪv/ *noun* the exclusion of a suitable candidate by a screening process

false positive /fɔːls ˈpɒzɪtɪv/ *noun* the inclusion of an unsuitable candidate by a screening process ○ *False positive results from recruitment tests can end in the selection of very unsuitable candidates.*

falsification of accounts /fɔːlsɪfɪˌkeɪʃ(ə)n əv əˈkaʊnts/ *noun* the act of making false entries in a record or of destroying a record

falsify /ˈfɔːlsɪfaɪ/ *verb* to change something to make it wrong ○ *They* *were accused of falsifying the accounts.* □ **to falsify accounts** to change or destroy a record

family allowance /ˌfæm(ə)li ə-ˈlaʊəns/ *noun* a payment to a mother, in addition to regular wages, based on the number of dependent children in the family ○ *Family allowances were increased since the government had put a limit on basic wage increases.*

family company /ˈfæm(ə)li ˌkʌmp(ə)ni/ *noun* a company where most of the shares are owned by members of a family

family-friendly policy /ˌfæm(ə)li ˈfrendli ˌpɒlɪsi/ *noun* a policy that is designed to help employees to combine their work with their family responsibilities in a satisfactory way, e.g. by enabling them to work flexible hours or by helping them with childcare

farm out /ˌfɑːm ˈaʊt/ *verb* □ **to farm out work** to hand over work for another person or company to do for you ○ *She farms out the office typing to various local bureaux.*

fast track /ˈfɑːst træk/, **fast tracking** /ˈfɑːst ˌtrækɪŋ/ *noun* rapid promotion for able employees ○ *He entered the company at 21, and by 25 he was on the fast track.*

fatigue /fəˈtiːg/ *noun* great tiredness

fatigue curve /fəˈtiːg kɜːv/ *noun* a curve on a chart showing how output varies depending on how long an employer has been working ○ *The fatigue curve helps to determine when rest periods should be allowed.* ○ *The fatigue curve shows a sharp slump in output after three hours' work.*

fat work /ˈfæt wɜːk/ *noun* (*in the printing industry*) a job that offers the same money for less effort than another similar job ○ *Workers were moving to more prosperous areas of the country in search of fat work.*

fault /fɔːlt/ *noun* **1.** the fact of being to blame for something which is wrong ○ *It is the stock controller's fault if the warehouse runs out of stock.* ○ *The chairman said the lower sales figures were the fault of a badly motivated sales force.* **2.** an act of not working properly

○ *The technicians are trying to correct a programming fault.* ○ *We think there is a basic fault in the product design.*

faulty /ˈfɔːlti/ *adjective* which does not work properly ○ *Faulty equipment was to blame for the defective products.* ○ *They installed faulty computer programs.*

favour /ˈfeɪvə/ *noun* □ **as a favour** to help or to be kind to someone ○ *He asked me for a loan as a favour.* ■ *verb* to agree that something is right or suitable ○ *The board members all favour Smith Ltd as partners in the project.* (NOTE: the usual US spelling is **favor**)

favourable /ˈfeɪv(ə)rəb(ə)l/ *adjective* which gives an advantage □ **on favourable terms** on specially good terms ○ *The shop is let on very favourable terms.* (NOTE: the usual US spelling is **favorable**)

favourable balance of trade /ˌfeɪv(ə)rəb(ə)l ˌbæləns əv ˈtreɪd/, **favourable trade balance** /ˌfeɪv(ə)rəb(ə)l ˈtreɪd ˌbæləns/ *noun* a situation where a country's exports are larger than its imports

favourite /ˈfeɪv(ə)rət/ *noun, adjective* (something) which is liked best ○ *This brand of chocolate is a favourite with the children's market.* (NOTE: the usual US spelling is **favorite**)

favouritism /ˈfeɪv(ə)rətɪz(ə)m/ *noun* the practice of treating one subordinate better than the others ○ *The promotion of an inexperienced keyboarder to supervisor was seen as favouritism by the rest of the workforce.* (NOTE: the usual US spelling is **favoritism**)

feasibility /ˌfiːzəˈbɪlɪti/ *noun* the ability to be done ○ *to report on the feasibility of a project*

feasibility study /ˌfiːzəˈbɪlɪti ˌstʌdi/ *noun* the careful investigation of a project to see whether it is worth undertaking ○ *We will carry out a feasibility study to decide whether it is worth setting up an agency in North America.*

feather-bedding /ˌfeðə ˈbedɪŋ/ *noun* **1.** the heavy subsidising of unprofitable industry by government **2.** the practice of employing more staff than necessary, usually as a result of union pressure ○ *Feather-bedding has raised the cost of labour.* ○ *Management complained that feather-bedding was holding up the introduction of new technology.*

fee /fiː/ *noun* **1.** money paid for work carried out by a professional person (such as an accountant, a doctor or a lawyer) ○ *We charge a small fee for our services.* ○ *The consultant's fee was much higher than we expected.* **2.** money paid for something ○ *an entrance fee* or *admission fee* ○ *a registration fee*

feedback /ˈfiːdbæk/ *noun* information, especially about the result of an activity which allows adjustments to be made to the way it is done in future ○ *The management received a lot of feedback on how popular the new pay scheme was proving.*

feeling /ˈfiːlɪŋ/ *noun* the way in which someone reacts to something ○ *The board's insensitive attitude has created bad feelings* or *ill-feeling between the managers and the junior staff.* □ **feelings are running high** people are getting angry

fellow- /feləʊ/ *prefix* meaning 'person working with'

fellow-director /ˌfeləʊ daɪˈrektə/ *noun* one of the other directors

fellow-servant doctrine /ˌfeləʊ ˈsɜːvənt/ *noun* a common law concept that removes responsibility from an employee for an accident to another employee, if the accident was caused by negligence

fellow-worker /ˌfeləʊ ˈwɜːkə/ *noun* one of the other workers

fiddle /ˈfɪdl/ (*informal*) *noun* an act of cheating ○ *It's all a fiddle.* □ **he's on the fiddle** he is trying to cheat ■ *verb* to cheat ○ *He tried to fiddle his tax returns.* ○ *The salesman was caught fiddling his expense account.*

field /fiːld/ *noun* **1.** an area of study or interest **2.** □ **in the field** outside the office, among the customers ○ *We have sixteen reps in the field.* ■ *verb* □ **field a call** to answer a telephone call from someone who is likely to cause problems or make a complaint (*informal*)

field of research /ˌfiːld əv rɪˈsɜːtʃ/ *noun* an area of research interest

field of work /ˌfiːld əv ˈwɜːk/ *noun* the type of work a person does ○ *What's his field?*

field research /ˈfiːld rɪˌsɜːtʃ/, **field work** /ˈfiːld wɜːk/ *noun* looking for information that is not yet published and must be obtained in surveys ○ *They had to do a lot of fieldwork before they found the right market for the product.* ○ *Field research is carried out to gauge potential demand.*

field review /ˈfiːld rɪˌvjuː/ *noun* a form of employee appraisal whereby the employee's work performance is assessed at the place of work (and not in the manager's office)

field sales manager /fiːld ˈseɪlz ˌmænɪdʒə/ *noun* the manager in charge of a group of salespeople

field staff /ˈfiːld stɑːf/ *noun* employees who work outside the organisation's offices

field work /ˈfiːld wɜːk/ *noun* ◊ **field research** ○ *They had to do a lot of field work to find the right market for the product.*

FIFO /ˈfaɪfəʊ/ *abbr* first in first out

fight /faɪt/ *verb* □ **to fight against something** to struggle to try to overcome something ○ *The unions are fighting (against) the proposed redundancies.*

file /faɪl/ *noun* **1.** a cardboard holder for documents, which can fit in the drawer of a filing cabinet ○ *Put these letters in the customer file.* ○ *Look in the file marked 'Scottish sales'.* **2.** documents kept for reference □ **to place something on file** to keep a record of something □ **to keep someone's name on file** to keep someone's name on a list for reference **3.** a section of data on a computer (such as payroll, address list, customer accounts) ○ *How can we protect our computer files?* ■ *verb* to store information so that it can be found easily ○ *You will find the salary scales filed by department.* ○ *The correspondence is filed under 'complaints'.* ◊ **to file a petition in bankruptcy, to file for bankruptcy 1.** to ask officially to be made bankrupt **2.** to ask officially for someone else to be made bankrupt

file copy /'faɪl ˌkɒpi/ *noun* a copy of a document which is kept for reference in an office

filing /'faɪlɪŋ/ *noun* documents which have to be put in order ○ *There is a lot of filing to do at the end of the week.* ○ *The manager looked through the week's filing to see what letters had been sent.*

filing basket /'faɪlɪŋ ˌbɑːskɪt/ *noun* same as **filing tray**

filing card /'faɪlɪŋ kɑːd/ *noun* a card with information written on it, used to classify information into the correct order

filing system /'faɪlɪŋ ˌsɪstəm/ *noun* a way of putting documents in order for easy reference

filing tray /'faɪlɪŋ treɪ/ *noun* a container kept on a desk for documents which have to be filed

fill /fɪl/ *verb* **1.** to make something full ○ *We have filled our order book with orders for Africa.* ○ *The production department has filled the warehouse with unsellable products.* **2.** □ **to fill a gap** to provide a product or service which is needed, but which no one has provided before ○ *The new range of small cars fills a gap in the market.*

fill in /ˌfɪl 'ɪn/ *verb* **1.** to write the required information in the blank spaces on a form ○ *Fill in your name and address in block capitals.* **2.** □ **to fill in for someone** to do someone else's job temporarily ○ *I'll fill in for him while he is away at his brother's wedding.*

fill out /ˌfɪl 'aʊt/ *verb* to write the required information in the blank spaces on a form ○ *To get customs clearance you must fill out three forms.*

fill up /ˌfɪl 'ʌp/ *verb* **1.** to make something completely full ○ *He filled up the car with petrol.* ○ *My appointments book is completely filled up.* **2.** to finish writing on a form ○ *He filled up the form and sent it to the bank.*

final /'faɪn(ə)l/ *adjective* last, coming at the end of a period ○ *to pay the final instalment* ○ *to make the final payment* ○ *to put the final details on a document*

final average monthly salary /ˌfaɪn(ə)l ˌæv(ə)rɪdʒ ˌmʌnθli 'sæləri/ *noun US* the earnings on which most defined benefit pensions are based

final demand /ˌfaɪn(ə)l dɪ'mɑːnd/ *noun* the last reminder from a supplier, after which they will sue for payment

final salary /ˌfaɪn(ə)l 'sæləri/ *noun* the salary earned by an employee on the date of leaving or retiring

finance company /'faɪnæns ˌkʌmp(ə)ni/, **finance corporation** /ˌfaɪnæns ˌkɔːpə'reɪʃ(ə)n/, **finance house** *noun* a company, usually part of a commercial bank, which provides money for hire-purchase

financial assistance /faɪˌnænʃəl ə'sɪstəns/ *noun* help in the form of money

financial incentive scheme /faɪˌnænʃəl ɪn'sentɪv skiːm/ *noun* a scheme that offers share options or a cash bonus as a reward if employees improve their performance

financial participation /faɪˌnænʃəl pɑːtɪsɪ'peɪʃ(ə)n/ *noun* the holding by employees of shares in the company they work for

financial penalty /faɪˌnænʃəl 'pen(ə)lti/ *noun* a penalty in the form of a fine or money deducted from wages

fine-tune /faɪn 'tjuːn/ *verb* to make small adjustments to a plan or the economy so that it works better

fine-tuning /faɪn 'tjuːnɪŋ/ *noun* **1.** the making of small adjustments in areas such as interest rates, tax bands or the money supply, to improve a nation's economy **2.** the making of small adjustments so that something works better

finished goods /ˌfɪnɪʃt 'ɡʊdz/ *noun* manufactured goods which are ready to be sold

fink /fɪŋk/ *noun US* a worker hired to replace a worker who is on strike (*informal*)

fire /faɪə/ *noun* something which burns □ **to catch fire** to start to burn ○ *The papers in the waste paper basket caught fire.*

fire alarm /'faɪər əˌlɑːm/ *noun* a bell which rings if there is a fire

fire certificate /'faɪə sə,tɪfɪkət/ *noun* a document from the local fire brigade stating that a building meets official requirements as regards fire safety

fire door /'faɪə dɔː/ *noun* a special door to prevent fire going from one part of a building to another

fire drill /'faɪə drɪl/ *noun* a procedure to be carried out to help people to escape from a burning building

fire exit /'faɪər ,egzɪt/ *noun* a door which leads to a way out of a building if there is a fire

fire extinguisher /'faɪər ɪk-,stɪŋgwɪʃə/ *noun* a portable device, usually painted red, for putting out fires

fire hazard /'faɪə ,hæzəd/, **fire risk** /'faɪə rɪsk/ *noun* a situation or goods which could start a fire ○ *That warehouse full of paper is a fire hazard.*

fire insurance /'faɪər ɪn,ʃʊərəns/ *noun* insurance against damage by fire

fire precautions /'faɪə prɪ-,kɔːʃ(ə)nz/ *plural noun* care taken to avoid damage or casualties by fire

fire risk /'faɪə rɪsk/ *noun* ◊ **fire hazard**

fire safety officer /faɪə 'seɪfti ,ɒfɪsə/ *noun* a person responsible for fire safety in a building

firm /fɜːm/ *noun* a company, business or partnership ○ *a manufacturing firm* ○ *an important publishing firm* ○ *She is a partner in a law firm.*

firm up /'fɜːm 'ʌp/ *verb* to agree on final details ○ *We expect to firm up the deal at the next trade fair.*

first /fɜːst/ *noun* a person or thing that is there at the beginning or earlier than others ○ *Our company was one of the first to sell into the European market.*

first aid /fɜːst 'eɪd/ *noun* help given by an ordinary person to someone who is suddenly ill or injured, given until full-scale medical treatment can be given

first aid kit /fɜːst 'eɪd kɪt/, **first aid box** /fɜːst 'eɪd bɒks/ *noun* a box with bandages and dressings kept ready to be used in an emergency

first aid post /fɜːst 'eɪd pəʊst/ *noun* a special place where injured people can be taken for immediate attention

first-class /,fɜːst 'klɑːs/ *adjective, noun* **1.** top quality or most expensive ○ *he is a first-class accountant* **2.** (a type of travel or type of hotel which is) most expensive and comfortable ○ *I always travel first-class.* ○ *First-class travel provides the best service.* ○ *A first-class ticket to New York costs more than I can afford.* ○ *The MD prefers to stay in first-class hotels.*

first-class mail /,fɜːst klɑːs 'meɪl/ *noun* a more expensive mail service, designed to be faster ○ *A first-class letter should get to Scotland in a day.*

first half /fɜːst 'hɑːf/ *noun* a period of six months from January to the end of June

first half-year /,fɜːst hɑːf 'jɪə/ *noun* the first six months or the second six months of a company's accounting year

first-line supervisor /,fɜːst laɪn 'suːpəvaɪzə/ *noun* a supervisor who is in direct control of production workers ○ *The HR department will liaise with first-line supervisors with regard to individual workers.*

first quarter /fɜːst 'kwɔːtə/ *noun* the period of three months from January to the end of March ○ *The first quarter's rent is payable in advance.*

five-fold system /'faɪv fəʊld ,sɪstəm/, **five-point system** /'faɪv pɔɪnt ,sɪstəm/ *noun* a system of grading an employee or a candidate for a job

fix /fɪks/ *verb* **1.** to arrange or to agree ○ *to fix a budget* ○ *to fix a meeting for 3 p.m.* ○ *The date has still to be fixed.* **2.** to mend ○ *The technicians are coming to fix the phone system.* ○ *Can you fix the photocopier?*

fixed /fɪkst/ *adjective* unable to be changed or removed

fixed automation /,fɪkst ɔːtə-'meɪʃ(ə)n/ *noun* the practice of using machines in a way which does not allow any change in their operation

fixed benefit retirement plan /fɪkst ,benɪfɪt rɪ'taɪəmənt plæn/ *noun* a pension plan where the benefits are not related to earnings

fixed(-term) contract worker /ˌfɪkst tɜːm ˈkɒntrækt ˌwɜːkə/ *noun* a worker who has a fixed-term contract for a period of time (e.g. one year)

fixed day rate /fɪkst ˈdeɪ reɪt/, **fixed day work** a pay scheme where pay for the day's work does not vary with the amount of output

fixed shift /fɪkst ˈʃɪft/ *noun* a period of work assigned to an employee for an indefinite length of time ○ *Some workers complain that fixed shifts make for monotony.*

fixed shift system /fɪkst ˈʃɪft ˌsɪstəm/ *noun* a system where employees are given fixed hours of work under a shift system

fixed-term contract /ˌfɪkst tɜːm ˈkɒntrækt/ *noun* a contract of employment valid for a fixed period of time ○ *I have a fixed-term contract with the company, and no guarantee of an extension when it ends in May.*

flag /flæg/ *noun* **1.** a piece of cloth with a design on it which shows which country it belongs to ○ *a ship flying a British flag* □ **ship sailing under a flag of convenience** a ship flying the flag of a country which may have no ships of its own, but allows ships from other countries to be registered in its ports **2.** a mark which is attached to information in a computer so that the information can be found easily ■ *verb* to insert marks on information in a computer so that the information can be found easily (NOTE: **flagging – flagged**)

flagged rate /flægd ˈreɪt/ *noun* a special pay rate paid to employees whose positions warrant lower rates of pay ○ *Flagged rates helped to reduce the pay differentials in the organisation.*

flat /flæt/ *adjective* not changing in response to different conditions

flat organisation /ˈflæt ɔːgənaɪˌzeɪʃ(ə)n/ *noun* an organisation with few grades in the hierarchical structure ○ *A flat organisation does not appeal to those who like traditional bureaucratic organisations.*

flat out /flæt ˈaʊt/ *adverb* working hard or at full speed ○ *The factory worked flat out to complete the order on time.*

flat rate /flæt ˈreɪt/ *noun* a charge which always stays the same ○ *a flat-rate increase of 10% ○ We pay a flat rate for electricity each quarter. ○ He is paid a flat rate of £2 per thousand.*

flexecutive /flekˈsekjʊtɪv/ *noun* an executive with many different skills who is able to switch jobs or tasks easily (*slang*)

flexibility /ˌfleksɪˈbɪlɪti/ *noun* the ability to be easily changed ○ *There is no flexibility in the company's pricing policy.*

flexible /ˈfleksɪb(ə)l/ *adjective* which can be altered or changed ○ *We try to be flexible where the advertising budget is concerned. ○ The company has adopted a flexible pricing policy.*

flexible automation /ˌfleksɪb(ə)l ɔːtəˈmeɪʃ(ə)n/ *noun* the practice of using machines in a way which allows the operator to change the operation of the machine and so improve productivity

flexible manufacturing system /ˌfleksɪb(ə)l mænjʊˈfæktʃərɪŋ ˌsɪstəm/ *noun* a way of manufacturing using computerised systems to allow certain quantities of the product to be made to a specific order. Abbr **FMS**

flexible retirement scheme /ˌfleksɪb(ə)l rɪˈtaɪəmənt skiːm/ *noun* a scheme where employees can choose the age at which they retire (between certain age limits, e.g. 55 and 65)

flexible working hours /ˌfleksɪb(ə)l ˈwɜːkɪŋ aʊəz/, **flexible work** /ˌfleksɪb(ə)l ˈwɜːk/ *plural noun* a system where employees can start or stop work at different hours of the morning or evening provided that they work a certain number of hours per day or week

Flexible Work Regulations /ˌfleksɪb(ə)l ˈwɜːk regjʊˌleɪʃ(ə)nz/ *plural noun* (*in the UK*) the legal right for a parent with a child under the age of 6, or with a disabled child under the age of 18, to ask that their working hours should be arranged to help them with their responsibilities

flexilagger /'fleksi,lægə/ *noun* a company or organisation that puts too little emphasis on flexibility in its employment practices (*slang*)

flexileader /'fleksi,liːdə/ *noun* a company or organisation that puts a great deal of emphasis on flexibility in its employment practices (*slang*)

flexitime /'fleksitaɪm/ *noun* a system where employees can start or stop work at different hours of the morning or evening, provided that they work a certain number of hours per day or week ○ *We work flexitime.* ○ *The company introduced flexitime working two years ago.* ○ *Flexitime should mean that employees work when they feel most productive.* Same as **flexible working hours** (NOTE: American English also uses **flextime**)

flight risk /'flaɪt rɪsk/ *noun* an employee who may be planning to leave a company in the near future (*slang*)

flipchart /'flɪptʃɑːt/ *noun* a way of showing information to a group of people by writing on large sheets of paper which can then be turned over to show the next sheet

floor /flɔː/ *noun* **1.** the part of the room which you walk on **2.** all the rooms on one level in a building ○ *Her office is on the 26th floor.* (NOTE: In Britain the floor at street level is the **ground floor**, but in the USA it is the **first floor**. Each floor in the USA is one number higher than the same floor in Britain.) **3.** a bottom limit ○ *The government will impose a floor on wages to protect the low-paid.* (NOTE: the opposite is **ceiling**)

floorwalker /'flɔːwɔːkə/ *noun* an employee of a department store who advises customers, and supervises the shop assistants in a department

floppy disk /,flɒpi 'dɪsk/ *noun* a small disk for storing information through a computer

flow /fləʊ/ *noun* a movement ○ *the flow of capital into a country* ○ *the flow of investments into Japan* ■ *verb* to move smoothly ○ *Production is now flowing normally after the strike.*

flow chart /'fləʊtʃɑːt/, **flow diagram** /'fləʊ ,daɪəgræm/ *noun* a chart which shows the arrangement of work processes in a series

flowcharting /'fləʊ,tʃɑːtɪŋ/ *noun* setting out the arrangement of work processes in the form of a chart

flow diagram /'fləʊ ,daɪəgræm/ *noun* same as **flow chart**

fluidity /fluːˈɪdɪti/ *noun* ease of movement or change

flying picket /,flaɪɪŋ 'pɪkɪt/ *noun* a picket who travels round the country to try to stop workers going to work

FMS *abbr* flexible manufacturing system

follow up /'fɒləʊ ʌp/ *verb* to examine something further ○ *I'll follow up your idea of targeting our address list with a special mailing.* □ **to follow up an initiative** to take action once someone else has decided to do something

forbid /fəˈbɪd/ *verb* to tell someone not to do something or to say that something must not be done ○ *Smoking is forbidden in our offices.* ○ *The contract forbids resale of the goods to the USA.* ○ *Staff are forbidden to speak directly to the press.* (NOTE: **forbidding – forbade – forbidden**)

force /fɔːs/ *noun* **1.** strength □ **to be in force** to be operating or working ○ *The rules have been in force since 1986.* □ **to come into force** to start to operate or work ○ *The new regulations will come into force on January 1st.* **2.** a group of people ■ *verb* to make someone do something ○ *Competition has forced the company to lower its prices.* ○ *After the takeover several of the managers were forced to take early retirement.*

forced distribution method /,fɔːst dɪstrɪˈbjuːʃ(ə)n ,meθəd/ *noun* a performance appraisal technique where certain percentages of workers are put in various categories in advance

forecast /'fɔːkɑːst/ *noun* a description or calculation of what will probably happen in the future ○ *The chairman did not believe the sales director's forecast of higher turnover.* ■ *verb* to calculate or to say what will probably happen in the future ○ *She is forecasting sales of £2m.* ○ *Economists have forecast a fall* *in the exchange rate.* (NOTE: **forecasting – forecast**)

forecasting /'fɔːkɑːstɪŋ/ *noun* the process of calculating what will probably happen in the future ○ *Manpower planning will depend on forecasting the future levels of production.*

foreign national /ˌfɒrɪn 'næʃ(ə)n(ə)l/ *noun* a person who is a citizen of another country, not this one

foreign worker /ˌfɒrɪn 'wɜːkə/ *noun* a worker who comes from another country

foreman /'fɔːmən/, **forewoman** /'fɔːwʊmən/ *noun* a skilled worker in charge of several other workers (NOTE: plural is **foremen** or **forewomen**)

for hire contract /fə 'haɪə ˌkɒntrækt/ *noun* US a freelance contract

form /fɔːm/ *noun* **1.** □ **form of words** words correctly laid out for a legal document **2.** an official printed paper with blank spaces which have to be filled in with information ○ *a pad of order forms* ○ *The reps carry pads of order forms.* ■ *verb* to start to organise ○ *The brothers have formed a new company.*

formal /'fɔːm(ə)l/ *adjective* clearly and legally written ○ *to make a formal application* ○ *to send a formal order* ○ *Is this a formal job offer?* ○ *The factory is prepared for the formal inspection by the government inspector.*

formality /fɔː'mælɪti/ *noun* something which has to be done to obey the law

formally /'fɔːməli/ *adverb* in a formal way ○ *We have formally applied for planning permission for the new shopping precinct.*

formal procedures /ˌfɔːm(ə)l prə'siːdʒəz/ *plural noun* agreed written rules for dealing with matters such as grievances and dismissals

formal warning /ˌfɔːm(ə)l 'wɔːnɪŋ/ *noun* a warning to an employee according to formal procedures. ♦ **informal warning**

formation /fɔː'meɪʃ(ə)n/, **forming** /'fɔːmɪŋ/ *noun* the act of organising ○ *the formation of a new company*

formative assessment /ˌfɔːmətɪv ə'sesmənt/ *noun* the appraisal of an employee, where the employee is given notes on what is wrong and what they should do to improve their performance

former /'fɔːmə/ *adjective* before or at an earlier time ○ *The former chairman has taken a job with a rival company.* ○ *She got a reference from her former employer.*

formerly /'fɔːməli/ *adverb* at an earlier time ○ *He is currently managing director of Smith Ltd, but formerly he worked for Jones Brothers.*

formica parachute /fɔːˌmaɪkə 'pærəʃuːt/ *noun* unemployment insurance (*slang*)

forward /'fɔːwəd/ *adverb* □ **to date a cheque forward** to put a later date than the present one on a cheque

forwarding instructions /'fɔːwədɪŋ ɪnˌstrʌkʃənz/ *plural noun* instructions showing how the goods are to be shipped and delivered

four-fifths rule /fɔː 'fɪfθs ruːl/ *noun* US same as **eighty per cent rule**

fourth quarter /fɔːθ 'kwɔːtə/ *noun* a period of three months from 1st October to the end of the year

framework agreement /'freɪmwɜːk əˌgriːmənt/ *noun* the draft of the main points of an agreement, with further details to be added later

franchising operation /'fræntʃaɪzɪŋ ɒpəˌreɪʃ(ə)n/ *noun* an operation involving selling licences to trade as a franchise

fraud /frɔːd/ *noun* an act of making money by making people believe something which is not true ○ *He got possession of the property by fraud.* ○ *She was accused of frauds relating to foreign currency.* □ **to obtain money by fraud** to obtain money by saying or doing something to cheat someone

fraud squad /'frɔːd skwɒd/ *noun* the special police department which investigates frauds

fraudulent /'frɔːdjʊlənt/ *adjective* not honest, or aiming to cheat people ○ *a fraudulent transaction*

fraudulent conversion /ˌfrɔːdjʊlənt kənˈvɜːʃ(ə)n/ *noun* the act of using money which does not belong to you for a purpose for which it is not supposed to be used

fraudulently /ˈfrɔːdjʊləntli/ *adverb* not honestly ○ *goods imported fraudulently*

free /friː/ *adjective, adverb* **1.** not costing any money ○ *I have been given a free ticket to the exhibition.* ○ *A catalogue will be sent free on request.* □ **free of charge** with no payment to be made **2.** with no restrictions **3.** not busy or not occupied ○ *I shall be free in a few minutes.* ■ *verb* to make something available or easy ○ *The government's decision has freed millions of pounds for investment.*

'American business as a whole is increasingly free from heavy dependence on manufacturing' [*Sunday Times*]

free agent /friː ˈeɪdʒənt/ *noun* a freelance worker who can offer their skills and expertise to companies anywhere in the world

free collective bargaining /ˌfriː kəˌlektɪv ˈbɑːɡɪnɪŋ/ *noun* negotiations between management and trade unions about wage increases and working conditions

free competition /ˌfriː kɒmpəˈtɪʃ(ə)n/ *noun* the fact of being free to compete without government interference

freedom /ˈfriːdəm/ *noun* the state of being free to do anything

freedom of association /ˌfriːdəm əv əsəʊsiˈeɪʃ(ə)n/ *noun* the ability to join together in a group with other people without being afraid of prosecution

freedom of movement /ˌfriːdəm əv ˈmuːvmənt/ *noun* the ability of workers in the EU to move from country to country and obtain work without any restrictions

free enterprise /ˌfriː ˈentəpraɪz/ *noun* a system of business free from government interference

free gift /friː ˈɡɪft/ *noun* a present given by a shop to a customer who buys a specific amount of goods ○ *There is a free gift worth £25 to any customer buying a washing machine.*

freelance /ˈfriːlɑːns/ *adjective, noun* (an independent worker) who works for several different companies but is not employed by any of them ○ *We have about twenty freelances working for us* or *about twenty people working for us on a freelance basis.* ○ *She is a freelance journalist.* ■ *adverb* selling your work to various firms, but not being employed by any of them ○ *He works freelance as a designer.* ■ *verb* **1.** to do work for several firms but not be employed by any of them ○ *She freelances for the local newspapers.* **2.** to send work out to be done by a freelancer ○ *We freelance work out to several specialists.*

freelancer /ˈfriːlɑːnsə/ *noun* a freelance worker

freelance worker /ˈfriːlɑːns ˌwɜːkə/ *noun* a self-employed worker

freely /ˈfriːli/ *adverb* with no restrictions ○ *Money should circulate freely within the EU.*

free market economy /friː ˌmɑːkɪt ɪˈkɒnəmi/ *noun* a system where the government does not interfere in business activity in any way

free-rider /friː ˈraɪdə/ *noun* a person who receives benefits which have been negotiated by a union for its members, even if they have not joined the union ○ *Many union members resent free-riders who benefit from the recent pay increase negotiated by the union.*

free sample /friː ˈsɑːmpəl/ *noun* a sample given free to advertise a product

free trade /friː ˈtreɪd/ *noun* a system where goods can go from one country to another without any restrictions

free trade area /friː ˈtreɪd ˌeəriə/ *noun* a group of countries practising free trade

free worker /ˈfriː ˌwɜːkə/ *noun* a person who moves frequently from one job or project to another, because they have skills and ideas that many organisations value and prefer to work on a short-term contract rather than to build a career within a single organisation

freeze /friːz/ *verb* to keep something such as money or costs at their present level and not allow them to rise ○ *to freeze wages and prices* ○ *to freeze credits* ○ *We have frozen expenditure at last year's level.* (NOTE: **freezing – froze – frozen**)

frequent /ˈfriːkwənt/ *adjective* which comes, goes or takes place often ○ *There is a frequent ferry service to France.* ○ *We send frequent faxes to New York.* ○ *How frequent are the planes to Birmingham?* ○ *We send frequent telexes to New York.*

frequently /ˈfriːkwəntli/ *adverb* often ○ *The photocopier is frequently out of use.* ○ *We email our New York office very frequently – at least four times a day.*

fresh blood /freʃ ˈblʌd/ *noun* new younger staff, employed because the company feels it needs to have new ideas (NOTE: also called **new blood**)

friction /ˈfrɪkʃən/ *noun* small disagreements between people in the same office ○ *There was a lot of friction between the sales and accounts staff.*

frictional unemployment /ˌfrɪkʃ(ə)n(ə)l ʌnɪmˈplɔɪmənt/ *noun* unemployment due to unforeseen circumstances, such as changes in technology, lack of labour mobility or variations in the demand and supply of certain products

Friday /ˈfraɪdeɪ/ *noun* the fifth and last day of the normal working week in an office ○ *The hours of work are 9.30 to 5.30, Monday to Friday.*

Friday afternoon /ˌfraɪdeɪ ɑːftəˈnuːn/ *noun* the period after lunch on Fridays, when some companies stop work

Friday afternoon car /ˌfraɪdeɪ ɑːftəˈnuːn kɑː/ *noun* a new car with numerous defects, presumably because it was made on a Friday afternoon

fringe benefit /ˈfrɪndʒ ˌbenɪfɪt/ *noun* an extra item such as a company car or private health insurance given by a company to employees in addition to a salary ○ *The fringe benefits make up for the poor pay.* ○ *Use of the company rec-*

reation facilities is one of the fringe benefits of the job.

front /frʌnt/ *noun* **1.** a part of something which faces away from the back ○ *The front of the office building is on the High Street.* ○ *There is a photograph of the managing director on the front page of the company report.* **2.** □ **in front of** before or on the front side of something ○ *The chairman's name is in front of all the others on the staff list.* **3.** a business or person used to hide an illegal trade ○ *His restaurant is a front for a drugs organisation.*

front-line management /ˌfrʌnt laɪn ˈmænɪdʒmənt/ *noun* managers who have immediate contact with the employees

front man /ˈfrʌnt mæn/ *noun* a person who seems honest but is hiding an illegal trade

frozen /ˈfrəʊz(ə)n/ *adjective* not allowed to be changed or used ○ *Wages have been frozen at last year's rates.*

fulfil /fʊlˈfɪl/ *verb* to complete something in a satisfactory way ○ *The clause regarding payments has not been fulfilled.* (NOTE: the usual US spelling is **fulfill**) □ **to fulfil an order** to supply the items which have been ordered ○ *We are so understaffed that we cannot fulfil any more orders before Christmas.*

fulfilment /fʊlˈfɪlmənt/ *noun* the act of carrying something out in a satisfactory way (NOTE: the usual US spelling is **fulfillment**)

full /fʊl/ *adjective* **1.** with as much inside it as possible ○ *The train was full of commuters.* ○ *When the disk is full, don't forget to make a backup copy.* **2.** complete, including everything □ **we are working at full capacity** we are doing as much work as possible **3.** □ **in full** completely ○ *a full refund* or *a refund paid in full* ○ *Give your full name and address* or *your name and address in full.* ○ *He accepted all our conditions in full.*

full day /fʊl ˈdeɪ/, **full working day** /fʊl ˈwɜːkɪŋ deɪ/, **a full day's work** /ə ˌfʊl deɪz ˈwɜːk/ *noun* a period when a worker works all the hours stipulated

full employment /fʊl ɪmˈplɔɪmənt/ *noun* a situation where all the people who can work have jobs

full payment /fʊl ˈpeɪmənt/ *noun* the paying of all money owed

full pension /fʊl ˈpenʃən/ *noun* the maximum pension allowed

full rate /fʊl ˈreɪt/ *noun* the full charge, with no reductions

full-scale /ˈfʊl skeɪl/ *adjective* complete or very thorough ○ *The MD ordered a full-scale review of credit terms.* ○ *The HR department will start a full-scale review of the present pay structure.*

'…the administration launched a full-scale investigation into maintenance procedures' [*Fortune*]

full-time /ˈfʊl taɪm/ *adjective, adverb* working all the normal working time, i.e. about eight hours a day, five days a week ○ *She's in full-time work* or *She works full-time* or *She's in full-time employment.* ○ *He is one of our full-time staff.*

full-time employee /ˌfʊl taɪm ɪmˈplɔɪiː/, **full-time worker** /ˌfʊl taɪm ˈwɜːkə/ *noun* an employee who works more than 16 hours per week for a company

full-time employment /ˌfʊl taɪm ɪmˈplɔɪmənt/ *noun* work for all of a working day ○ *to be in full-time employment*

full-time equivalent /ˌfʊl taɪm ɪˈkwɪvələnt/ *noun* a notional employee earning the full-time wage, used as a comparison to part-time employees

full-time job /ˌfʊl taɪm ˈdʒɒb/ *noun* a job that occupies all someone's normal working hours

full-timer /fʊl ˈtaɪmə/ *noun* a person who works full-time

fully /ˈfʊli/ *adverb* completely □ **fully insured pension scheme** a pension scheme where each contributor is insured to receive the full pension to which they are entitled

'…issued and fully paid capital is $100 million' [*Hongkong Standard*]

function /ˈfʌŋkʃən/ *noun* a duty or job ■ *verb* to work ○ *The advertising campaign is functioning smoothly.* ○

The new management structure does not seem to be functioning very well.

functional /ˈfʌŋkʃən(ə)l/ *adjective* **1.** which can function properly **2.** referring to a job

functional authority /ˌfʌŋkʃən(ə)l ɔːˈθɒrɪti/ *noun* the authority which is associated with a job

functional job analysis /ˌfʌŋkʃən(ə)l ˈdʒɒb əˌnæləsɪs/ *noun* an assessment of the specific requirements of a job ○ *Functional job analysis is used to identify what type of person should be appointed to fill the vacancy.*

functionary /ˈfʌŋkʃənəri/ *noun* a civil servant (*slightly derogatory*)

fund /fʌnd/ *noun* money set aside for a special purpose ■ *verb* to provide money for a purpose ○ *The company does not have enough resources to fund its expansion programme.* □ **to fund a company** to provide money for a company to operate

'…the S&L funded all borrowers' development costs, including accrued interest' [*Barrons*]

funded /ˈfʌndɪd/ *adjective* backed by long-term loans ○ *long-term funded capital*

funded pension plan /ˌfʌndɪd ˈpenʃən plæn/, **funded pension scheme** /ˌfʌndɪd ˈpenʃən skiːm/ *noun* a pension plan where money is set aside annually to fund employees' pensions

funding /ˈfʌndɪŋ/ *noun* money for spending ○ *The bank is providing the funding for the new product launch.*

funding rate /ˈfʌndɪŋ reɪt/ *noun* the employer's contributions to a pension fund shown as a percentage of the total pensionable salaries of the employees

fund-raising /ˈfʌnd ˌreɪzɪŋ/ *noun* the process of trying to get money for a charity, etc. ○ *a fund-raising sale*

funds /ˈfʌndz/ *plural noun* money which is available for spending ○ *The company has no funds to pay for the research programme.* □ **the company called for extra funds** the company asked for more money □ **to run out of funds** to come to the end of the money available □ **to convert funds to another purpose** to use money for a wrong purpose □ **to convert funds to your own**

use to use someone else's money for yourself.

'…small innovative companies have been hampered for lack of funds' [*Sunday Times*]

'…the company was set up with funds totalling NorKr 145m' [*Lloyd's List*]

furlough /'fɜːləʊ/ *noun* a period of unpaid leave or absence from work, es-pecially for military personnel, govern-ment employees or expatriates ○ *Many employees resent being contacted by head office when on furlough.*

further education /ˌfɜːðər edjʊ-'keɪʃ(ə)n/ *noun* education after ending full-time education in school

FYI *abbr* for your information

G

gain /geɪn/ *noun* an increase or act of becoming larger □ **gain in experience** the act of getting more experience □ **gain in profitability** the act of becoming more profitable ■ *verb* to get or to obtain ○ *He gained some useful experience working in a bank.*

gainful employment /ˌgeɪnf(ə)l ɪmˈplɔɪmənt/ *noun* employment which pays money

gainfully /ˈgeɪnf(ə)li/ *adverb* □ **gainfully employed** working and earning money

gainsharing /ˈgeɪnˌʃeərɪŋ/ *noun* a payment scheme where all the members of a group of employees are paid extra for increased productivity ○ *Gainsharing will be instituted to increase motivation.* ○ *Gainsharing has allowed employees to identify with the company's successful performance.*

galloping inflation /ˌgæləpɪŋ ɪnˈfleɪʃ(ə)n/ *noun* very rapid inflation which is almost impossible to reduce

Gantt chart /ˈgænt tʃɑːt/ *noun* a type of chart used in project management to plan and schedule work, setting out tasks and the time periods within which they should be completed (NOTE: A Gantt chart looks like a bar chart in which the bars extend sideways.)

gardening leave /ˈgɑːd(ə)nɪŋ liːv/ *noun* a period of leave stipulated in a contract of employment, during which an employee is not allowed into the company offices and cannot take up another job (*informal*)

garnishment /ˈgɑːnɪʃmənt/ *noun* a procedure by which wages or salary are withheld to pay off a debt ○ *The company had to resort to garnishment*

to ensure that the worker paid for the damage he caused to machinery.

gatekeeper /ˈgeɪtˌkiːpə/ *noun* a person who acts as a screen between a group and people outside the group (such as an interviewer in the human resources department who screens job applicants)

gear /gɪə/ *verb* to link to or to connect with □ **salary geared to the cost of living** salary which rises as the cost of living increases

geared scheme /gɪəd ˈskiːm/ *noun* a system by which payment by results increases in stages rather than in direct proportion to increase in output

gear up /ˌgɪər ˈʌp/ *verb* to get ready ○ *The company is gearing itself up for expansion into the African market.*

general /ˈdʒen(ə)rəl/ *adjective* ordinary or not special

general audit /ˌdʒen(ə)rəl ˈɔːdɪt/ *noun* a process of examining all the books and accounts of a company

generally /ˈdʒen(ə)rəli/ *adverb* normally or usually ○ *The office is generally closed between Christmas and the New Year.* ○ *We generally give a 25% discount for bulk purchases.*

general manager /ˌdʒen(ə)rəl ˈmænɪdʒə/ *noun* a manager in charge of the administration of a company

General National Vocational Qualifications /ˌdʒen(ə)rəl ˌnæʃ(ə)n(ə)l vəʊˈkeɪʃ(ə)n(ə)l kwɒlɪfɪˌkeɪʃ(ə)nz/ *noun* a system of examinations and qualifications in vocational subjects for young people who are in full-time education, giving a broard-based training in vocational subjects (run alongside traditional academic studies and of equal value to them). Abbr **GNVQs**

general office /ˈdʒen(ə)rəl ˌɒfɪs/ *noun* the main administrative office of a company

general secretary /ˌdʒen(ə)rəl ˈsekrɪt(ə)ri/, **General Secretary** *noun* the head official of a trade union

general store /ˈdʒen(ə)rəl stɔː/ *noun* a small country shop which sells a large range of goods

general strike /ˌdʒen(ə)rəl ˈstraɪk/ *noun* a strike of all the workers in a country

general trading /ˌdʒen(ə)rəl ˈtreɪdɪŋ/ *noun* dealing in all types of goods

general union /ˌdʒen(ə)rəl ˈjuːnjən/ *noun* a union which recruits usually semi-skilled workers in all industries

generic /dʒəˈnerɪk/ *adjective* which is shared by a group, and does not refer to one individual

generic skills /dʒəˌnerɪk ˈskɪlz/ *plural noun* skills which are applicable in various types of work and can be transferred from one job to another

generous /ˈdʒen(ə)rəs/ *adjective* referring to an amount that is larger than usual or expected ○ *She received a generous redundancy payment.* ○ *The staff contributed a generous sum for the manager's retirement present.*

genuine /ˈdʒenjuːɪn/ *adjective* true or real ○ *a genuine Picasso* ○ *a genuine leather purse*

genuine material factor /ˌdʒenjuːɪn məˈtɪəriəl ˌfæktə/ *noun* an acceptable reason for a difference in salary between a male and a female employee (such as longer experience)

genuine occupational qualifications /ˌdʒenjuːɪn ɒkjuˌpeɪʃ(ə)n(ə)l kwɒlɪfɪˈkeɪʃ(ə)nz/ *plural noun* a situation where a person of a certain sex or racial background is needed for a job, and this can be stated in the job advertisement. Abbr **GOQs**

geographical mobility /dʒiːəˌgræfɪk(ə)l məʊˈbɪlɪti/ *noun* the ability of workers to move from place to place to find work

get /get/ *verb* **1.** to receive ○ *We got a letter from the solicitor this morning.* ○ *He gets £250 a week for doing nothing.* ○ *She got £5,000 for her car.* **2.** to arrive at a place ○ *She finally got to the office at 10.30.* (NOTE: **getting – got**)

get across /ˌget əˈkrɒs/ *verb* to make someone understand something ○ *The manager tried to get across to the workforce why some people were being made redundant.*

get ahead /ˌget əˈhed/ *verb* to advance in your career

get along /ˌget əˈlɒŋ/ *verb* **1.** to manage ○ *We are getting along quite well with only half the staff we had before.* **2.** to be friendly or to work well with someone ○ *She does not get along very well with her new boss.*

get back /ˌget ˈbæk/ *verb* to receive something which you had before ○ *I got my money back after I had complained to the manager.* ○ *He got his initial investment back in two months.*

get on /ˌget ˈɒn/ *verb* **1.** to work or manage ○ *How is your new assistant getting on?* **2.** to succeed ○ *My son is getting on well – he has just been promoted.*

get on with /ˌget ˈɒn wɪð/ *verb* **1.** to be friendly or work well with someone ○ *She does not get on with her new boss.* **2.** to go on doing work ○ *The staff got on with the work and finished the order on time.*

get out /ˌget ˈaʊt/ *verb* to produce something ○ *The accounts department got out the draft accounts in time for the meeting.*

get through /ˌget ˈθruː/ *verb* **1.** to speak to someone on the phone ○ *I tried to get through to the complaints department.* **2.** to be successful ○ *She got through her exams, so she is now a qualified engineer.* **3.** to try to make someone understand ○ *I could not get through to her that I had to be at the airport by 2.15.*

Girl Friday /ˌgɜːl ˈfraɪdeɪ/ *noun* a female employee who does various tasks in an office. ♦ **Man Friday** (NOTE:

Sometimes **Person Friday** is used in job advertisements to avoid sexism.)

Girobank /'dʒaɪrəʊbæŋk/ *noun* a bank in a giro system ○ *a National Girobank account* ○ *She has her salary paid into her National Girobank account.*

giro system /'dʒaɪrəʊ ˌsɪstəm/ *noun* a banking system in which money can be transferred from one account to another without writing a cheque (the money is first removed from the payer's account and then credited to the payee's account; as opposed to a cheque payment, which is credited to the payee's account first and then claimed from the payer's account)

give /gɪv/ *verb* **1.** to pass something to someone as a present ○ *The office gave him a clock when he retired.* **2.** to pass something to someone ○ *She gave the documents to the accountant.* ○ *Do not give anybody personal details about staff members.* ○ *Can you give me some information about the new computer system?* **3.** to organise ○ *The company gave a party on a boat to say goodbye to the retiring sales director.* (NOTE: **giving – gave – given**)

give back /ˌgɪv 'bæk/ *verb* to hand something back to someone

give-back /'gɪv bæk/ *noun US* a demand by management that the employees accept less favourable terms of employment ○ *The give-back was insisted on by management because of the high costs of labour.*

give in to /ˌgɪv 'ɪn tuː/ *verb* to yield or to surrender ○ *to give in to pressure from the strikers*

give up /ˌgɪv 'ʌp/ *verb* to hand something over to someone ○ *Workers refused to give up any of their rights.*

give way to /ˌgɪv 'weɪ tuː/ *verb* to make concessions or to agree to demands ○ *to give way to the union's wage demands*

glad-hand /'glæd hænd/ *verb* to shake hands with and greet people at a business party or meeting

glass ceiling /glɑːs 'siːlɪŋ/ *noun* a mysteriously invisible barrier to promotion ○ *Women managers complain that* *they find it difficult to break through the glass ceiling and become members of the board.*

GMP *abbr* guaranteed minimum pension

GNVQs *abbr* General National Vocational Qualifications

go /gəʊ/ *verb* **1.** to move from one place to another ○ *The cheque went to your bank yesterday.* ○ *The plane goes to Frankfurt, then to Rome.* ○ *He is going to our Lagos office.* ○ *She went on a management course.* **2.** to be placed ○ *The date goes at the top of the letter.* (NOTE: **going – went – gone**)

go-ahead /'gəʊ əhed/ *noun* □ **to give something the go-ahead** to approve something or to say that something can be done ○ *My project got a government go-ahead.* ○ *The board refused to give the go-ahead to the expansion plan.* ■ *adjective* energetic or keen to do well ○ *He is a very go-ahead type.* ○ *She works for a go-ahead clothing company.*

goal /gəʊl/ *noun* something which you try to achieve ○ *Our goal is to break even within twelve months.* ○ *The company achieved all its goals.* □ **to achieve your goal** to do what you set out to do □ **to set someone goals** to give someone objectives to aim at ○ *Bonus payments are motivating employees to achieve company goals.* ○ *One of the HR manager's goals was a fair payment scheme.* ○ *Our goal is to break even within twelve months.*

go back on /ˌgəʊ 'bæk ɒn/ *verb* not to do what has been promised ○ *Two months later they went back on the agreement.*

go-between /'gəʊ bɪˌtwiːn/ *noun* a person who acts as an intermediary in the negotiations between two others ○ *The head of the workers' committee was the effective go-between in the dispute.*

gofer /'gəʊfə/ *noun US* same as **gopher**

going /'gəʊɪŋ/ *adjective* active or busy

going concern /ˌgəʊɪŋ kən'sɜːn/ *noun* a company that is actively trading (and making a profit) □ **sold as a going concern** sold as an actively trading company

go into business /ˌgəʊ ɪntə ˈbɪznɪs/ *verb* to start in business ○ *He went into business as a car dealer.* ○ *She went into business in partnership with her son.*

goldbricker /ˈgəʊldbrɪkə/ *noun US* a lazy employee who attempts to get away with doing the least possible amount of work (*slang*)

gold-bricking /ˈgəʊld ˌbrɪkɪŋ/ *noun* the practice of regulating production by not claiming production achieved on some days so as to be able to carry it over and so allow employees to take time off work on other days ○ *Gold-bricking has reduced production by half.*

gold-circle rate /ˌgəʊld ˈsɜːk(ə)l reɪt/ *noun US* a rate of pay that exceeds the maximum rate of an employee's evaluated pay level ○ *The gold-circle rate is resented by some employees who see it as an unmerited bonus.*

golden /ˈgəʊld(ə)n/ *adjective* made of gold or like gold

golden formula /ˌgəʊld(ə)n ˈfɔːmjʊlə/ *noun* the rule that unions are immune from prosecution if their action is taken in pursuance of a trade dispute

golden handcuffs /ˌgəʊld(ə)n ˈhændkʌfs/ *plural noun* a contractual arrangement to make sure that a valued member of staff stays in their job, by which they are offered special financial advantages if they stay and heavy penalties if they leave

golden hello /ˌgəʊld(ə)n həˈləʊ/ *noun* a cash inducement paid to someone to encourage them to change jobs and move to another company

golden parachute /ˌgəʊld(ə)n ˈpærəʃuːt/, **golden umbrella** /ˌgəʊld(ə)n ʌmˈbrelə/ *noun* a large, usually tax-free sum of money given to an executive who retires from a company before the end of their service contract

good /gʊd/ *adjective* **1.** not bad **2.** □ **a good deal (of)** a large amount (of) ○ *We wasted a good deal of time discussing the arrangements for the meeting.* □ **a good many** very many ○ *A good many staff members have joined the union.*

good industrial relations /gʊd ɪnˌdʌstriəl rɪˈleɪʃ(ə)nz/ *plural noun* a situation where management and employees understand each others' problems and work together for the good of the company

goods /gʊdz/ *plural noun* items which can be moved and are for sale

goodwill /gʊdˈwɪl/ *noun* **1.** good feeling towards someone ○ *To show goodwill, the management increased the terms of the offer.* **2.** the good reputation of a business, which can be calculated as part of a company's asset value, though separate from its tangible asset value (the goodwill can include the trading reputation, the patents, the trade names used, the value of a 'good site', etc., and is very difficult to establish accurately) ○ *He paid £10,000 for the goodwill of the shop and £4,000 for the stock.*

goon /guːn/ *noun US* a person who deliberately provokes disputes between employers and employees (*slang*)

go out of business /ˌgəʊ aʊt əv ˈbɪznɪs/ *verb* to stop trading ○ *The firm went out of business last week.*

gopher /ˈgəʊfə/ *noun* an employee who carries out simple menial duties such as fetching and carrying things for a manager or another employee (NOTE: the usual US spelling is **gofer**)

GOQs *abbr* genuine occupational qualifications

go-slow /ˌgəʊ ˈsləʊ/ *noun* the slowing down of production by workers as a protest against the management ○ *A series of go-slows reduced production.*

go up /ˌgəʊ ˈʌp/ *verb* to rise ○ *NI contributions are going up 3% next month.*

government contractor /ˌgʌv(ə)nmənt kənˈtræktə/ *noun* a company which supplies the government with goods by contract

government economic indicators /ˌgʌv(ə)nmənt iːkəˌnɒmɪk ˈɪndɪkeɪtəz/ *plural noun* statistics which show how the country's economy is going to perform in the short or long term

government organisation /ˌgʌv(ə)nmənt ˌɔːgənaɪˈzeɪʃ(ə)n/

noun an official body run by the government

government pension /ˌgʌv(ə)nmənt ˈpenʃən/ *noun* a pension paid by the state

grade /greɪd/ *noun* a level or rank ○ *to reach the top grade in the civil service* ■ *verb* to make something rise in steps according to quantity

graded hourly rate /ˌgreɪdɪd ˌauəli ˈreɪt/ *noun* a pay scale where pieceworkers receive different rates per piece completed according to their appraisal ratings

grading /ˈgreɪdɪŋ/ *noun* an assessment of an employee's performance by giving a certain grade or mark ○ *The company has adopted a new grading system for appraisals.*

gradual /ˈgrædʒuəl/ *adjective* slow and regular ○ *The company saw a gradual return to profits.* ○ *Her CV describes her gradual rise to the position of company chairman.*

gradually /ˈgrædʒuəli/ *adverb* slowly and steadily ○ *The company has gradually become more profitable.* ○ *She gradually learnt the details of the import-export business.*

gradual retirement /ˌgrædʒuəl rɪˈtaɪəmənt/ *noun* same as **phased retirement**

graduate /ˈgrædʒuət/ *noun* a person who has obtained a degree

graduated /ˈgrædʒueɪtɪd/ *adjective* changing in small regular stages

graduated income tax /ˌgrædʒueɪtɪd ˈɪnkʌm tæks/ *noun* a tax which rises in steps (each level of income is taxed at a higher percentage)

graduated pension plan /ˌgrædʒueɪtɪd ˈpenʃən plæn/, **graduated pension scheme** /ˌgrædʒueɪtɪd ˈpenʃən skiːm/ *noun* a pension scheme where the contributions are calculated on the salary of each person in the scheme

graduated wages /ˌgrædʒueɪtɪd ˈweɪdʒɪz/ *plural noun* wages which increase in accordance with established pay levels

graduate entry /ˈgrædʒuət ˌentri/ *noun* the entry of graduates into employment with a company ○ *the graduate entry into the civil service*

graduate recruitment /ˈgrædʒuət rɪˌkruːtmənt/ *noun* the recruitment of graduates for traineeships in a company

graduate trainee /ˌgrædʒuət treɪˈniː/ *noun* a person in a graduate training scheme

graduate training scheme /ˌgrædʒuət ˈtreɪnɪŋ skiːm/ *noun* a training scheme for graduates

grand /grænd/ *adjective* important □ **grand plan**, **grand strategy** a major plan ○ *They explained their grand plan for redeveloping the factory site.* ■ *noun* one thousand pounds or dollars (*informal*) ○ *They offered him fifty grand for the information.* ○ *She's earning fifty grand plus car and expenses.*

grandfather clause /ˈgrænfɑːðə klɔːz/ *noun* a clause in an insurance policy that exempts a category of insured employee from meeting new standards ○ *The grandfather clause exempts the older employees from the retraining scheme.*

grandfather system /ˈgrænfɑːðə ˌsɪstəm/ *noun* an appraisal system where the manager's appraisals of employees are sent for review to the manager's superior

grand total /grænd ˈtəʊt(ə)l/ *noun* the final total made by adding several subtotals

grant /grɑːnt/ *noun* money given by the government to help pay for something ○ *The government has allocated grants towards the costs of the scheme.* ■ *verb* to agree to give someone something ○ *to grant someone three weeks' leave of absence*

grant-aided scheme /ˈgrɑːnt eɪdɪd skiːm/ *noun* a scheme which is funded by a government grant

grapevine /ˈgreɪpvaɪn/ *noun* an unofficial communications network in an organisation ○ *I heard on the grapevine that the managing director has been sacked.*

graph /grɑːf/ *noun* a diagram which shows the relationship between two sets of quantities or values, each of which is represented on an axis ○ *A graph was used to show salary increases in relation to increases in output.* ○ *According to the graph, as average salaries have risen so has absenteeism.* ○ *We need to set out the results of the questionnaire in a graph.*

graphologist /græ'fɒlədʒɪst/ *noun* a person who studies handwriting, and can identify the writer's characteristics from it ○ *Some companies ask for job applications to be handwritten, so that they can be shown to a consultant graphologist.*

graphology /græ'fɒlədʒi/ *noun* the study of handwriting, which is believed to show the writer's characteristics

graph paper /'grɑːf ˌpeɪpə/ *noun* a special type of paper with many little squares, used for drawing graphs

grass ceiling /grɑːs 'siːlɪŋ/ *noun* the social and cultural factors that make it difficult for women to use games of golf as an opportunity to do business (*slang*)

grassroots /grɑːs'ruːts/ *plural noun* the basic ordinary members of a union, political party or of society in general

gratia ◊ **ex gratia**

gratuity /grə'tjuːɪti/ *noun* a tip, money given to someone who has helped you ○ *The staff are instructed not to accept gratuities.*

graveyard shift /'greɪvjɑːd ʃɪft/ *noun* a night shift in a continuous shift system, starting around midnight (*informal*)

gravy /'greɪvi/ *noun* something which does not involve effort (*informal*)

gravy job /'greɪvi dʒɒb/ *noun US* a job which that offers the same money for less effort than another similar job ○ *Workers were moving to more prosperous areas of the country in search of gravy jobs.* (NOTE: in British English also called **cushy number**)

gravy train /'greɪvi treɪn/ *noun* means of getting money easily

great man theory /greɪt 'mæn ˌθɪəri/ *noun* the idea that leaders are people who are born with special qualities that distinguish them from others

and enable them to inspire their followers and win their loyalty

green ban /griːn 'bæn/ *noun* a ban imposed by unions on work that they consider to be a threat to the natural environment or to an area of historical significance

green card /'griːn kɑːd/ *noun* **1.** a special British insurance certificate to prove that a car is insured for travel abroad **2.** an identity card and work permit for a person going to live in the USA

green circle rate /griːn 'sɜːk(ə)l reɪt/ *noun US* a rate of pay which is below the minimum rate

grid /grɪd/ *noun* a system of numbered squares

grid method /'grɪd ˌmeθəd/ *noun* a two-dimensional method of job evaluation based on breadth and depth of responsibility ○ *Some jobs score high on the grid method since they involve many different tasks and a lot of decision-making.*

grid structure /'grɪd ˌstrʌktʃə/ *noun* a structure based on a grid

grievance /'griːv(ə)ns/ *noun* a complaint made by an employee or trade union to the management

'ACAS has a legal obligation to try and resolve industrial grievances before they reach industrial tribunals' [*Personnel Today*]

grievance interview /'griːv(ə)ns ˌɪntəvjuː/ *noun* a meeting between management and an employee or group of employees where the managers listen to the employee's complaints and try to find a solution to the problem

grievance procedure /'griːv(ə)ns prəˌsiːdʒə/ *noun* a way of presenting and settling complaints from a trade union to the management

gross /grəʊs/ *adjective* **1.** total or with no deductions **2.** very serious ○ *gross negligence* ■ *adverb* with no deductions ○ *My salary is paid gross.* ■ *verb* to make a gross profit ○ *He grosses £500 a week.* ○ *The group grossed £25m in 1999.*

'...gross wool receipts for the selling season to end June appear likely to top $2 billion' [*Australian Financial Review*]

gross earnings /ɡrəʊs ˈɜːnɪŋz/ *plural noun* total earnings before tax and other deductions

gross income /ɡrəʊs ˈɪnkʌm/ *noun* salary before tax is deducted

gross misconduct /ɡrəʊs mɪsˈkɒndʌkt/ *noun* very bad behaviour by an employer, which is a fair reason for dismissal (such as drunkenness or theft) ○ *He was dismissed for gross misconduct.*

gross negligence /ɡrəʊs ˈneɡlɪdʒəns/ *noun* the act of showing very serious neglect of duty towards other people

gross salary /ɡrəʊs ˈsæləri/ *noun* salary before tax is deducted

ground /ɡraʊnd/ *noun* □ **to gain ground** to start to win against an opponent □ **to give ground** to give way against an opponent

groundless /ˈɡraʊndləs/ *adjective* with no real reason ○ *The complaint was proved to be groundless.*

grounds /ɡraʊndz/ *plural noun* basic reasons ○ *Does she have good grounds for complaint?* ○ *There are no grounds on which we can be sued.* ○ *What are the grounds for the demand for a pay rise?*

group /ɡruːp/ *noun* **1.** several things or people together ○ *A group of managers has sent a memo to the chairman complaining about noise in the office.* ○ *The respondents were interviewed in groups of three or four, and then singly.* **2.** several companies linked together in the same organisation ○ *the group chairman* or *the chairman of the group* ○ *group turnover* or *turnover for the group* ○ *the Granada Group*

group appraisal /ɡruːp əˈpreɪz(ə)l/ *noun* the appraisal of an employee by a group of other employees

group capacity assessment /ɡruːp kəˈpæsɪti əˌsesmənt/ *noun* the use of work measurement techniques such as activity sampling to assess the work done by clerical, administrative and other employees not directly involved in the production process as a group and to establish optimum performance levels for them

group certificate /ˈɡruːp səˌtɪfɪkət/ *noun* (*in Australia and New Zealand*) a document provided by an employer that records an employee's income, income tax payments and contributions to a pension fund during the previous financial year

group discussion /ɡruːp dɪˈskʌʃ(ə)n/ *noun* a survey method in which a focus group is brought together to discuss informally a market-research question ○ *The group discussion was taken over by one or two strong personalities.* ○ *A sample of young people took part in a group discussion on the new shampoo.*

group dynamics /ɡruːp daɪˈnæmɪks/ *plural noun* the behaviour patterns typical of groups, including the effects that members of a group have on each other, the personal relationships that they form and the ways that groups form, function and break up (NOTE: Takes a singular verb. Group dynamics is an important aspect of successful teamwork and can influence the outcome of any group activity, for example a training course.)

group incentive /ɡruːp ɪnˈsentɪv/ *noun* an incentive payment made to a group, rather than to an individual worker

group incentive scheme /ˌɡruːp ɪnˈsentɪv skiːm/, **group incentive plan** /ˌɡruːp ɪnˈsentɪv plæn/ *noun* a scheme whereby payment by results is based on the output of all the employees in an organisation

group insurance /ɡruːp ɪnˈʃʊərəns/ *noun* an insurance scheme where a group of employees is covered by one policy

group life assurance /ɡruːp ˈlaɪf ɪnˌʃʊərəns/ *noun* a life assurance policy that covers a number of people, e.g., the members of an association or club, or a group of employees at a company

group outplacement /ɡruːp ˈaʊtpleɪsmənt/ *noun* a situation where several employees are dealt with together in being given help to find other jobs after being made redundant

group pension plan /ɡruːp ˈpenʃən plæn/, **group pension**

scheme /gruːp ˈpenʃən skiːm/ *noun* a life insurance plan which provides a number of employees with a retirement pension

group results /gruːp rɪˈzʌlts/ *plural noun* the results of a group of companies taken together

group selection /gruːp sɪˈlekʃən/ *noun* a method of recruitment in which candidates are assessed in groups rather than individually (NOTE: Group selection should not be confused with a panel interview.)

group selection methods /gruːp sɪˈlekʃən ˌmeθədz/ *plural noun* methods of assessing the ability of individuals to work with others ○ *Group selection methods are being introduced to complement individual intelligence and personality tests.*

group training /gruːp ˈtreɪnɪŋ/ *noun* a training method where a group trains together and so learns from each other

growth /grəʊθ/ *noun* an increase in size

growth industry /ˈgrəʊθ ˌɪndəstri/ *noun* an industry that is expanding or has the potential to expand faster than other industries

growth rate /ˈgrəʊθ reɪt/ *noun* the speed at which something grows

guarantee /ˌɡærənˈtiː/ *noun* a legal document in which the producer agrees to compensate the buyer if the product is faulty or becomes faulty before a specific date after purchase ○ *a certificate of guarantee* or *a guarantee certificate* ○ *The guarantee lasts for two years.* ○ *It is sold with a twelve-month guarantee.* □ **the car is still under guarantee** the car is still covered by the maker's guarantee ■ *verb* **1.** to give a promise that something will happen □ **to guarantee a debt** to promise that you will pay a debt made by someone else **2.** □ **the product is guaranteed for twelve months** the manufacturer says that the product will

work well for twelve months, and will mend it free of charge if it breaks down

guaranteed annuity /ˌɡærəntiːd əˈnjuːɪti/ *noun* an arrangement in a pension scheme by which a final lump sum is used to purchase a fixed annuity

guaranteed employment /ˌɡærəntiːd ɪmˈplɔɪmənt/ *noun* an arrangement that protects employees in situations where there is a shortage of work, by guaranteeing that they will be paid a minimum wage for a specified number of days or hours during which they have no work (NOTE: also called **guaranteed week**)

guaranteed minimum pension /ˌɡærəntiːd ˌmɪnɪməm ˈpenʃən/ *noun* a minimum pension which must be provided by an occupational pension scheme. Abbr **GMP**

guaranteed week /ˌɡærəntiːd ˈwiːk/ *noun* same as **guaranteed employment**

guard /ɡɑːd/ *noun* a person who protects someone or a building

guided interview /ˌɡaɪdɪd ˈɪntəvjuː/ *noun* same as **directed interview**

guideline /ˈɡaɪdlaɪn/ *noun* an unofficial suggestion from the government as to how something should be done ○ *The government has issued guidelines on increases in salaries and prices.*

guideline method /ˈɡaɪdlaɪn ˌmeθəd/ *noun* a job evaluation technique which takes into account attitudes to the job in the industry as a whole ○ *The HR manager justified the guideline method as adapting to the laws of supply and demand.*

guild /ɡɪld/ *noun* an association of merchants or shopkeepers ○ *a trade guild* ○ *the guild of master bakers*

guilty /ˈɡɪlti/ *adjective* referring to a person who has done something wrong ○ *He was found guilty of libel.* ○ *The company was guilty of not reporting the sales to the auditors.*

H

hack /hæk/ *noun* an ordinary worker (*informal*) ○ *a hack copywriter*

haggle /'hæg(ə)l/ *verb* to discuss prices and terms and try to reduce them ○ *to haggle about* or *over the details of a contract* ○ *After two days' haggling the contract was signed.*

half pay /hɑːf 'peɪ/ *noun* half your normal salary

halo effect /'heɪləʊ ɪˌfekt/ *noun* a crude and over-simple classification of employees into 'good' and 'bad' on the basis of superficial characteristics such as personal rapport or a pleasant manner

halo error /'heɪləʊ ˌerə/ *noun* a mistake made by promoting the wrong person because of the halo effect

hand /hænd/ *noun* **1.** the part of the body at the end of each arm □ **to shake hands** to hold someone's hand when meeting to show you are pleased to meet them, or to show that an agreement has been reached ○ *The two negotiating teams shook hands and sat down at the conference table.* □ **to shake hands on a deal** to shake hands to show that a deal has been agreed **2.** □ **by hand** using the hands, not a machine ○ *These shoes are made by hand.* □ **to send a letter by hand** to ask someone to carry and deliver a letter personally, not sending it through the post **3.** a worker ○ *to take on ten more hands*

handbook /'hændbʊk/ *noun* a book which gives instructions on how to use something ○ *The handbook does not say how you open the photocopier.*

handcuffs /'hæn(d)ˌkʌfs/ *plural noun* ◊ **golden handcuffs**

hand-hold /'hænd həʊld/ *verb* to reassure a nervous client or colleague (*slang*) (NOTE: **hand-holding – hand – held**)

handicap /'hændikæp/ *noun* **1.** something which prevents someone from doing something ○ *She found that her lack of qualifications was a great handicap to getting her first job.* **2.** ◊ **disability** (NOTE: term now generally unacceptable in sense 2 and replaced by **disability**)

handicapped /'hændikæpt/ *adjective* without the advantage of something ○ *She is handicapped by not having a recognised qualification.*

handicapped person /ˌhændikæpt 'pɜːs(ə)n/ *noun* a person with a disability (NOTE: term now generally unacceptable and replaced by **disabled person**)

hand in /ˌhænd 'ɪn/ *verb* to deliver a letter by hand □ **he handed in his notice** *or* **resignation** he resigned

handle /'hænd(ə)l/ *verb* to deal with something or to organise something ○ *The accounts department handles all the cash.* ○ *We can handle orders for up to 15,000 units.* ○ *They handle all our overseas orders.*

hand-operated /hænd 'ɒpəreɪtɪd/ *adjective* worked by hand, not automatically ○ *a hand-operated machine*

hand over /ˌhænd 'əʊvə/ *verb* to pass something to someone ○ *She handed over the documents to the lawyer.* □ **she handed over to her deputy** she passed her responsibilities to her deputy

handover /'hændəʊvə/ *noun* the passing of responsibilities to someone else ○ *The handover from the old chairman to the new went very smoothly.* ○ *When the ownership of a company changes, the handover period is always difficult.* ○ *There was a smooth handover to the new management team.*

hand-picked /ˌhænd ˈpɪkt/ *adjective* carefully selected ○ *a hand-picked sales team*

hands-on /ˌhændz ˈɒn/ *adjective* involving direct contact with the working of a system or organisation ○ *We need a hands-on manager who will supervise operations closely.* ○ *More hands-on management means we will have to increase the technical input in our management training schemes.*

hands-on experience /ˌhændz ɒn ɪkˈspɪəriəns/ *noun* the direct experience of a system

handwriting /ˈhændraɪtɪŋ/ *noun* writing done by hand □ **send a letter of application in your own handwriting** send a letter of application written by you with a pen, and not typed

handwritten /ˌhændˈrɪtn/ *adjective* written by hand, not typed ○ *It is more professional to send in a typed rather than a handwritten letter of application.*

happy /ˈhæpi/ *adjective* very pleased ○ *The human resources director was not at all happy to receive the union's new demands.* ○ *We will be happy to supply you at 25% discount.* ○ *The MD was not at all happy when the sales figures came in.* ○ *The workforce seems quite happy with the new offer from the management.*

happy camper /ˌhæpi ˈkæmpə/ *noun* a person who has no grievances against their employer (*slang*)

harass /ˈhærəs, həˈræs/ *verb* to worry or to bother someone, especially by continually checking on them or making sexual approaches

harassment /ˈhærəsmənt, həˈræsmənt/ *noun* the act of harassing someone

'EEC legislation should formally recognize that sexual harassment is discrimination on grounds of sex' [*Personnel Management*]

harassment procedure /ˈhærəsmənt prəˌsiːdʒə/ *noun* written and agreed rules as to how cases of harassment should be dealt with in a company

hard /hɑːd/ *adjective* **1.** strong, not weak □ **to take a hard line in trade union negotiations** to refuse to compromise with the other side **2.** difficult ○ *It is hard to get good people to work on low salaries.* **3.** solid **4.** □ **after weeks of hard bargaining** after weeks of difficult discussions ■ *adverb* with a lot of effort ○ *The sales team sold the new product range hard into the supermarkets.* ○ *If all the workforce works hard, the order should be completed on time.*

hard bargain /hɑːd ˈbɑːgɪn/ *noun* a bargain with difficult terms □ **to drive a hard bargain** to be a difficult negotiator □ **to strike a hard bargain** to agree a deal where the terms are favourable to you

hard disk /hɑːd ˈdɪsk/ *noun* a computer disk which has a sealed case and can store large quantities of information

'…hard disks help computers function more speedily and allow them to store more information' [*Australian Financial Review*]

hard drive *noun* same as **hard disk**

harden /ˈhɑːdn/ *verb* to become more fixed or more inflexible ○ *The union's attitude to the management has hardened since the lockout.*

hardship /ˈhɑːdʃɪp/ *noun* bad conditions which make someone suffer

hardship allowance /ˈhɑːdʃɪp əˌlaʊəns/ *noun* additional pay for an employee who accepts an assignment in difficult conditions

hardware /ˈhɑːdweə/ *noun* machines used in data processing, including the computers and printers, but not the programs

hard-working /ˌhɑːd ˈwɜːkɪŋ/ *adjective* referring to a person who works hard

hassle /ˈhæs(ə)l/ *noun* bother or trouble (*informal*) ○ *Dealing with these people is too much of a hassle.*

hatchet man /ˈhætʃɪt mæn/ *noun* a recently appointed manager, whose job is to make staff redundant and reduce expenditure (*informal*)

haulage contractor /ˈhɔːlɪdʒ kənˌtræktə/ *noun* a company which transports goods by contract

hazard /ˈhæzəd/ *noun* danger

hazardous /ˈhæzədəs/ *adjective* dangerous ○ *hazardous equipment* ○ *hazardous occupations*

hazard pay /'hæzəd peɪ/ *noun* additional pay for dangerous work ○ *All the construction workers received hazard pay.* ○ *Hazard pay has to be pretty high to attract workers to this type of work.*

head /hed/ *adjective* most important or main ○ *Ask the head waiter for a table.* ■ *noun* **1.** the most important person **2.** a person ○ *Representatives cost on average £25,000 per head per annum.* **3.** the top part or first part ○ *Write the name of the company at the head of the list.* ■ *verb* to be the manager, to be the most important person ○ *We are looking for someone to head our sales department.* ○ *He is heading a buying mission to China.*

head clerk /hed 'klɑːk/ *noun* the most important clerk

headcount /'hedkaʊnt/ *noun* the total number of employees who work for an organisation

headed paper /,hedɪd 'peɪpə/ *noun* notepaper with the name of the company and its address printed on it (NOTE: American English is **letterhead**)

headhunt /'hedhʌnt/ *verb* to look for managers and offer them jobs in other companies □ **she was headhunted** she was approached by a headhunter and offered a new job

headhunter /'hedhʌntə/ *noun* a person or company whose job is to find suitable top managers to fill jobs in companies

headhunting /'hedhʌntɪŋ/ *noun* same as **executive search**

heading /'hedɪŋ/ *noun* the words at the top of a piece of text ○ *Items are listed under several headings.* ○ *Look at the figure under the heading 'Costs 2001–02'.*

head of department /,hed əv dɪ-'pɑːtmənt/ *noun* a person in charge of a department

headquarters /hed'kwɔːtəz/ *plural noun* the main office, where the board of directors meets and works ○ *The company's headquarters are in New York.* Abbr **HQ** □ **to reduce headquarters staff** to have fewer people working in the main office

head up /,hed 'ʌp/ *verb* to be in charge of ○ *He has been appointed to head up our European organisation.*

'...reporting to the deputy managing director, the successful candidate will be responsible for heading up a team which provides a full personnel service' [*Times*]

headway /'hedweɪ/ *noun* progress in a difficult situation □ **to make headway** to go forward or make progress ○ *We are not making any headway in our negotiations.*

health /helθ/ *noun* being fit and well, not ill

'...the main US banks have been forced to pull back from international lending as nervousness continues about their financial health' [*Financial Times*]

'...financial health, along with a dose of independence, has largely sheltered Japan's pharmaceutical companies from a global wave of consolidation. Those assets, however, are expected to soon lure foreign suitors too powerful to resist' [*Nikkei Weekly*]

health and safety /,helθ ən 'seɪfti/ *noun* the area of policy and the law that deals with the well-being of employees at work and is intended to protect them against accidents and risks to their health (NOTE: Health and safety within an organisation is often co-ordinated by a particular person, but it is the responsibility of all employees.)

Health and Safety at Work Act (1974) /,helθ ən ,seɪfti ət 'wɜːk ækt/ *noun* an Act of Parliament which rules how the health of employees should be protected by the companies they work for

Health and Safety Commission /,helθ ən 'seɪfti kə,mɪʃ(ə)n/ *noun* a government body set up to see that the provisions of the Health and Safety at Work Act are obeyed, e.g. employers must report fatal accidents or work-related diseases. Abbr **HSC**

Health and Safety Executive /,helθ ən 'seɪfti ɪg,zekjʊtɪv/ *noun* the executive committee of the Health and Safety Commission

health hazard /'helθ ,hæzəd/ *noun* a danger to the health of a person

health insurance /'helθ ɪn,ʃʊərəns/ *noun* insurance which pays the cost of treatment for illness, especially when travelling abroad

Health Register /'helθ ˌredʒɪstə/ noun a list kept by a company of medical examinations given to employees who handle hazardous substances (NOTE: no plural)

health screening /'helθ ˌskriːnɪŋ/ noun the checking of employees' health to ensure that they are fit for work (NOTE: Health screening can take place after a new employee has been appointed, but before they start work, but it may also be a regular procedure especially where the work people do involves hazardous substances or difficult conditions.)

hearing /'hɪərɪŋ/ noun a case which is being heard by a committee or tribunal or court of law, or by an official body

heavy hitter /ˌhevi 'hɪtə/ noun an executive or company that performs extremely well (slang)

heavy industry /ˌhevi 'ɪndəstri/ noun an industry which deals in heavy raw materials such as coal or makes large products such as ships or engines

helicopter view /'helɪkɒptə vjuː/ noun a general or broad view of a problem as a whole, which does not go into details (slang)

help /help/ noun a thing which makes it easy to do something ○ The company was set up with financial help from the government. ○ Her assistant is not much help – he can't type or drive. ■ verb to make it easy for something to be done (NOTE: you help someone or something **to do** something)

helping interview /ˌhelpɪŋ ˌɪntə-'vjuː/ noun an interview which uses a sympathetic approach to achieve its ends ○ Helping interviews are effective in getting nervous candidates to relax. ○ The management finds regular helping interviews with employees improves relations.

helpline /'helplaɪn/ noun a telephone number which links people to services that can give them specialist advice, or a similar service offered by shops to their customers. Also called **careline**

hesitate /'hezɪteɪt/ verb not to be sure what to do next ○ The company is hesitating about starting up a new computer factory. ○ She hesitated for some time before accepting the job.

hidden agenda /ˌhɪdn ə'dʒendə/ noun a secret plan which one party to discussions has, which the other party does not know about

hierarchical /haɪə'rɑːkɪk(ə)l/ adjective referring to an organisation which has several levels ○ The company has a very traditional hierarchical structure.

hierarchy /'haɪərɑːki/ noun an organisational structure with several levels of responsibility or authority ○ At the bottom of the hierarchy are the unskilled workers.

high /haɪ/ adjective **1.** tall ○ The shelves are 30 cm high. ○ The door is not high enough to let us get the machines into the building. ○ They are planning a 30-storey-high office block. **2.** large, not low ○ High overhead costs increase the unit price. ○ They are budgeting for a high level of expenditure. ○ High interest rates are crippling small businesses. □ **high taxation** taxation which imposes large taxes on incomes or profits □ **highest tax bracket** the group which pays the most tax

high achiever /haɪ ə'tʃiːvə/ noun a person who achieves more than they expect

high day rate /haɪ 'deɪ reɪt/ noun a payment system where high rates of pay are paid to skilled employees for time worked

higher education /ˌhaɪər edjʊ-'keɪʃ(ə)n/ noun education at university

high-grade /'haɪgreɪd/ adjective of very good quality ○ high-grade petrol □ **high-grade trade delegation** a delegation made up of very important people

high-level /'haɪ ˌlev(ə)l/ adjective very important □ **high-level decision** a decision taken by the most important person or group □ **high-level meeting** or **delegation** a meeting or delegation of the most important people (such as minister or managing directors)

highly /'haɪli/ adverb very □ **she is highly thought of by the managing director** the managing director thinks she is very competent

highly-paid /ˌhaɪli 'peɪd/ *adjective* earning a large salary

highly-placed /ˌhaɪli 'pleɪst/ *adjective* occupying an important post ○ *The delegation met a highly-placed official in the Trade Ministry.*

high official /ˌhaɪ ə'fɪʃ(ə)l/, **high-ranking official** /ˌhaɪ ræŋkɪŋ ə'fɪʃ(ə)l/ *noun* an important person in a government department

high-powered /ˌhaɪ 'paʊəd/ *adjective* very capable and intelligent, and at the same time very energetic and forceful

high pressure /haɪ 'preʃə/ *noun* a strong insistence that somebody should do something □ **working under high pressure** working with a manager telling you what to do and to do it quickly, or with customers asking for supplies urgently

high season /haɪ 'siːz(ə)n/ *noun* the period when there are most travellers and tourists

high unemployment /ˌhaɪ ʌnɪm-'plɔɪmənt/ *noun* a level of unemployment which is high compared to previous figures

hike /haɪk/ *US noun* an increase ■ *verb* to increase ○ *The union hiked its demand to $5 an hour.*

hip shooter /'hɪp ˌʃuːtə/ *noun* an executive who follows their immediate instinct when responding to a question or problem rather than considering it rationally (*slang*)

hire /'haɪə/ *noun* □ **to work for hire** to work freelance ■ *verb* **1.** to employ someone new to work for you **2.** □ **to hire out cars**, **to hire out equipment**, **to hire out workers** to lend cars, equipment or workers to customers who pay for their use

hire car /'haɪə kɑː/ *noun* a car which has been rented ○ *He was driving a hire car when the accident happened.*

hired gun /ˌhaɪəd 'ɡʌn/ *noun US* a person, often with special expertise, who works freelance and is brought in on a short-term contract to do a particular job or work on a particular project (*slang*)

hiring /'haɪərɪŋ/ *noun* the act of employing new staff ○ *Hiring of new personnel has been stopped.*

hiring and firing /ˌhaɪərɪŋ ən 'faɪərɪŋ/ *noun* the practice of hiring new employees and dismissing them in quick succession

hiring rate /'haɪərɪŋ reɪt/ *noun* the rate of pay for employees when first hired ○ *Though the hiring rate is low, pay goes up rapidly during the first year.* ○ *The hiring rate depends on whether the entrants are skilled or not.*

histogram /'hɪstəɡræm/ *noun* a chart or diagram with bars set on a base-line, the length of each bar expressing the quantity of an item or unit

hold /həʊld/ *verb* **1.** to own or to keep ○ *They hold 10% of the company's shares.* □ **you should hold these shares – they look likely to rise** you should keep these shares and not sell them **2.** to contain ○ *Each box holds 250 sheets of paper.* **3.** to make something happen ○ *to hold a meeting* or *a discussion* ○ *The receiver will hold an auction of the company's assets.* ○ *Board meetings are held in the boardroom.* **4.** □ **hold the line please** (*on the telephone*) please wait ○ *The chairman is on the other line – will you hold?* **5.** to have a certain job or status ○ *He holds the position of chairman.* (NOTE: **holding- held**)

'...as of last night, the bank's shareholders no longer hold any rights to the bank's shares' [*South China Morning Post*]

hold back /ˌhəʊld 'bæk/ *verb* to wait, not to go forward □ **payment will be held back until the contract has been signed** payment will not be made until the contract has been signed □ **she held back from signing the contract until she had checked the details** she delayed signing the contract until she had checked the details

hold down /ˌhəʊld 'daʊn/ *verb* **1.** to keep at a low level ○ *We are cutting margins to hold our prices down.* **2.** □ **to hold down a job** to manage to do a difficult job

'...real wages have been held down; they have risen at an annual rate of only 1% in the last two years' [*Sunday Times*]

holding company /'həʊldɪŋ ˌkʌmp(ə)ni/ *noun* **1.** a company which owns more than 50% of the shares in another company **2.** a company which exists only or mainly to own shares in subsidiary companies (NOTE: the American English for this is a **proprietary company**)

hold out for /ˌhəʊld 'aʊt fɔː/ *verb* to wait and ask for □ **you should hold out for a 10% pay rise** do not agree to a pay rise of less than 10%

hold over /ˌhəʊld 'əʊvə/ *verb* to postpone or put back to a later date ○ *Discussion of item 4 was held over until the next meeting.*

hold to /'həʊld tuː/ *verb* not to allow something to change □ **we will try to hold him to the contract** we will try to stop him going against the contract □ **the government hopes to hold wage increases to 5%** the government hopes that wage increases will not be more than 5%

hold up /ˌhəʊld 'ʌp/ *verb* **1.** to stay at a high level ○ *Sales held up during the tourist season.* **2.** to delay ○ *Payment will be held up until the contract has been signed.* ○ *The strike will hold up dispatch for some weeks.* ○ *The workers are holding up production as a form of protest against poor conditions.*

hold-up /'həʊld ʌp/ *noun* a delay ○ *The bad weather caused hold-ups in the dispatch of goods.*

holiday /'hɒlɪdeɪ/ *noun* a period when an employee does not work, but rests, goes away and does things for pleasure ○ *When is the manager taking his holidays?* ○ *My assistant is off on holiday tomorrow.* ○ *He is going away on holiday for two weeks.* □ **the job carries five weeks' holiday** one of the conditions of the job is that you have five weeks' holiday (NOTE: American English is **vacation**)

holiday entitlement /'hɒlɪdeɪ ɪnˌtaɪt(ə)lmənt/ *noun* the number of days' paid holiday which an employee has the right to take ○ *She has not used up all her holiday entitlement.*

holiday pay /'hɒlɪdeɪ peɪ/ *noun* a salary which is still paid during the holiday

home /həʊm/ *noun* the place where a person lives ○ *Please send the letter to my home address, not my office.*

home address /həʊm əˈdres/ *noun* the address of a house or flat where a person lives ○ *Please send the documents to my home address.*

home run /'həʊm rʌn/ *noun* the journey home at the end of the working day (*informal*)

homeworker /'həʊmwɜːkə/ *noun* a person who works at home for a company

homeworking /'həʊmwɜːkɪŋ/ *noun* a working method where employees work at home on computer terminals, and send the finished material back to the central office by modem. Also called **networking, teleworking**

hon *abbr* honorary

honorarium /ˌɒnəˈreəriəm/ *noun* money paid to a professional person such as an accountant or a lawyer when a specific fee has not been requested (NOTE: plural is **honoraria**)

honorary /'ɒnərəri/ *adjective* not paid a salary for the work done for an organisation ○ *She is honorary secretary of the tennis club.* ○ *He is honorary president of the translators' association.*

honorary member /ˌɒnərəri 'membə/ *noun* a member who does not have to pay a subscription

hooking /'hʊkɪŋ/ *noun US* the practice of persuading an employee to watch what other union members are doing or saying and to report back to management

horizontal /ˌhɒrɪˈzɒnt(ə)l/ *adjective* at the same level or with the same status ○ *Her new job is a horizontal move into a different branch of the business.*

horizontal job enlargement /ˌhɒrɪzɒnt(ə)l 'dʒɒb ɪnˌlɑːdʒmənt/, **horizontal job enrichment** /ˌhɒrɪzɒnt(ə)l 'dʒɒb ɪnˌrɪtʃmənt/ *noun* the process of expanding a job to include new activities, skills or responsibilities, but still at the same level in the organisation ○ *We have implemented horizontal job enlargement to increase individual workloads while at the same time making the work* *more interesting.* Compare **vertical job enlargement**

horizontal organisation /ˌhɒrɪ-ˈzɒnt(ə)l ɔːɡənaɪˌzeɪʃ(ə)n/ *noun* same as **flat organisation**

horse trading /ˈhɔːs ˌtreɪdɪŋ/ *noun* hard bargaining which ends with someone giving something in return for a concession from the other side

hostile /ˈhɒstaɪl/ *adjective* unfriendly, showing dislike □ **hostile work environment** working surroundings which are unfriendly

hot /hɒt/ *adjective* **1.** very warm ○ *Switch off the machine if it gets too hot.* ○ *The staff complain that the office is too hot in summer and too cold in winter.* **2.** not safe, very bad □ **to make things hot for someone** to make it difficult for someone to work or to trade ○ *Customs officials are making things hot for drug smugglers.* □ **she is in the hot seat** her job involves making many difficult decisions

hot cargo provision /hɒt ˈkɑːɡəʊ prəˌvɪʒ(ə)n/ *noun* a clause in a contract that allows employees to refuse to handle products from another factory where there is an industrial dispute in progress

hot-desking /ˈhɒt ˌdeskɪŋ/ *noun* a flexible working practice that enables employees to occupy any vacant workspace instead of sitting at a desk that they think of as their own (NOTE: Organisations that use a hot-desking system usually have standardised workspaces all equipped with information and communications technologies, and though employees may have limited personal storage space in the form of a filing cabinet or locker, most of their work and information will be stored electronically. The system is usually adopted on the grounds that conventional offices are only full for a fraction of the time they are open, because of sickness, holidays or teleworking, and hot-desking enables expensive office space to be fully utilised.)

hour /aʊə/ *noun* **1.** a period of time lasting sixty minutes □ **to work a thirty-five hour week** to work seven hours a day each weekday □ **we work an eight-hour day** we work for eight hours a day, e.g. from 8.30 to 5.30 with one hour for lunch **2.** sixty minutes of work ○ *He earns £14 an hour.* ○ *We pay £16 an hour.* □ **to pay by the hour** to pay people a fixed amount of money for each hour worked **3.** □ **outside hours, out of hours** when the office is not open ○ *He worked on the accounts out of hours.*

hourly /ˈaʊəli/ *adjective, adverb* per hour

'...despite the Fed's long-standing fears that low unemployment will raise wage costs, average hourly earnings grew by just 3.6 per cent in the year to November' [*Investors Chronicle*]

hourly-paid /ˌaʊəli peɪd/ *adjective* paid at a fixed rate for each hour worked

hourly rate /ˌaʊəli ˈreɪt/, **hourly wage** /ˌaʊəli ˈweɪdʒ/ *noun* the amount of money paid for an hour worked

hours of work /ˌaʊəz əv ˈwɜːk/ *plural noun* the time when the staff of an office are working ○ *Our hours of work are 9.30 to 5.30, with an hour off for lunch.*

house /haʊs/ *noun* a company ○ *the largest London finance house* ○ *a broking house* ○ *a publishing house*

house journal /ˈhaʊs ˌdʒɜːn(ə)l/, **house magazine** /ˈhaʊs mæɡəˌziːn/ *noun* a magazine produced for the employees or shareholders in a company to give them news about the company

house party /ˈhaʊs ˌpɑːti/ *noun* a method of interviewing candidates in which they are invited to spend a few days in a hotel or other centre, where they are given tests and monitored for interpersonal relations

house union /ˈhaʊs ˌjuːnjən/ *noun* a union representing employees in one company only

housing /ˈhaʊzɪŋ/ *noun* houses and flats for living in ○ *The company provides housing for senior staff.*

housing benefit /ˈhaʊzɪŋ ˌbenɪfɪt/ *noun* a local government benefit paid to people who cannot pay their rent

HR *abbr* human resources

HRIS *abbr* human resource information system

HRM *abbr* human resources management

HRP *abbr* human resource planning

HR service centre /,eɪtʃ ɑː 'sɜːvɪs ,sentə/ *noun* a central office that deals with routine administration and answers inquiries from managers and staff throughout an organisation on matters relating to human resources

HSC *abbr* Health and Safety Commission

human /'hjuːmən/ *adjective* referring to people

humanagement /hjuː-'mænɪdʒmənt/ *noun* a style of management that emphasises the empowerment of employees

human asset accounting /,hjuːmən 'æset ə,kaʊntɪŋ/ *noun* same as **human capital accounting**

human capital /,hjuːmən 'kæpɪt(ə)l/ *noun* the employees of an organisation, and their skills, knowledge and experience, considered one of the organisation's assets

human capital accounting /,hjuːmən 'kæpɪt(ə)l ə,kaʊntɪŋ/ *noun* an attempt to place a financial value on the knowledge and skills possessed by the employees of an organisation (NOTE: also called **human asset accounting**, **human resource accounting**)

human error /,hjuːmən 'erə/ *noun* a mistake made by a person, not by a machine

human factors engineering /,hjuːmən 'fæktəz endʒɪ,nɪərɪŋ/, **human factor engineering** /,hjuːmən 'fæktər endʒɪ,nɪərɪŋ/ *noun* the work of designing workplace activities, facilities and systems on the basis of an analysis of human capabilities and needs so that the workplace can be fitted to the worker and employee performance optimised (NOTE: Human factors engineering also tries to reduce risk by raising safety levels.)

human-machine interface /,hjuːmən mə,ʃiːn 'ɪntəfeɪs/ *noun* a point of contact between a person and a machine such as a computer

human relations /,hjuːmən rɪ-'leɪʃ(ə)nz/ *plural noun* a field of study that deals with social relations in the workplace and gave rise to a philosophy and style of management that stresses teamwork and the importance of motivating employees, communicating with them and giving them opportunities for personal growth and development in their work (NOTE: takes a singular verb)

human relations management /,hjuːmən rɪ'leɪʃ(ə)nz ,mænɪdʒmənt/ *noun* management based on the importance of ensuring good relations and cooperation in an organisation

human resource accounting /,hjuːmən rɪ'zɔːs ə,kaʊntɪŋ/ *noun* same as **human capital accounting**

human resource information system /,hjuːmən rɪ,zɔːs ɪnfə-'meɪʃ(ə)n ,sɪstəm/ *noun* an information system, usually a computerised one, which assists managers in making strategic and operational decisions in the field of human resources management. Abbr **HRIS**

human resource(s) planning /,hjuːmən rɪ'zɔːsɪz ,plænɪŋ/ *noun* the planning of the future needs of a company as regards employees, arranging for interviews for candidates, organising training, etc. Abbr **HRP**

human resources /,hjuːmən rɪ-'sɔːsɪz/ *plural noun* the employees which an organisation has available ○ *Our human resources must be looked after and developed if we are to raise productivity successfully.* Abbr **HR** (NOTE: also called **personnel**)

'…effective use and management of human resources hold the key to future business development and success' [*Management Today*]

human resources department /,hjuːmən rɪ'zɔːsɪz dɪ,pɑːtmənt/ *noun* a section of the company which deals with the staff

human resources management /,hjuːmən rɪ'zɔːsɪz ,mænɪdʒmənt/ *noun* responsibility for an organisation's productive use of and constructive dealings with its employees. Abbr **HRM**

human resources manager /,hjuːmən rɪ'zɔːsɪz ,mænɪdʒə/ *noun* a person who is responsible for an organisation's productive use of its employees

○ *She was appointed human resources manager because of her experience in manpower planning and recruitment.*

human resources officer /ˌhjuːmən rɪˈzɔːsɪz ˌɒfɪsə/ *noun* a person who deals with the staff in a company especially interviewing candidates for new posts

human rights /ˌhjuːmən ˈraɪts/ *plural noun* the rights of individual men and women to basic freedoms, such as freedom of speech and freedom of association

Human Rights and Equal Opportunities Commission /ˌhjuːmən raɪts ənd ˌiːkwəl ɒpəˈtjuːnɪtiz kəˌmɪʃ(ə)n/ *noun* a body set up by the Australian federal government in 1986 to administer the laws relating to human rights, anti-discrimination, privacy and social justice

hurry sickness /ˈhʌri ˌsɪknəs/ *noun* a state of anxiety caused by the feeling that you do not have enough time in the day to achieve everything that is required

hygiene /ˈhaɪdʒiːn/ *noun* the quality of being clean or being careful that everything is clean and conditions are healthy

hygienic /haɪˈdʒiːnɪk/ *adjective* clean and healthy

hygienic management /haɪˌdʒiːnɪk ˈmænɪdʒmənt/ *noun* a management theory that good working conditions encourage hard work and productivity

I

Icarus factor /'ɪkərəs ˌfæktə/ *noun* the tendency of managers or executives to embark on projects which are too ambitious and consequently fail (NOTE: In Greek mythology, Icarus tried to escape from Crete using wings made of wax and feathers, but flew too near the sun and drowned in the sea after the wax melted.)

ID card /aɪ 'diː kɑːd/, **identity card** /aɪ'dentɪti kɑːd/ *noun* a plastic card which carries details of the person it belongs to

idea hamster /aɪ'dɪə ˌhæmstə/ *noun* someone who appears to have an endless supply of new ideas (*slang*)

identification /aɪˌdentɪfɪ'keɪʃ(ə)n/ *noun* the act of showing who someone is □ **visitors must produce proof of identification** they must prove who they are

idle /'aɪdl/ *adjective* **1.** not working ○ *2,000 employees were made idle by the recession.* **2.** □ **idle machinery, machines lying idle** machinery not being used

idle capital /ˌaɪdl 'kæpɪt(ə)l/ *noun* capital not being used productively

idle time /'aɪdl taɪm/ *noun* the time for which employees are paid although they are unable to work because of factors beyond their control ○ *Idle time in January was attributed to the temporary closing down of one of the company's factories.* ○ *Workers were laid off to avoid excessive idle time.*

illegal /ɪ'liːg(ə)l/ *adjective* not legal or against the law

illegal immigrant /ɪˌliːg(ə)l 'ɪmɪgrənt/, **illegal alien** /ɪˌliːg(ə)l 'eɪliən/ *noun* a person who enters a country to live permanently without having the permission of the government to do so

illegality /ˌɪliː'gælɪti/ *noun* the fact of being illegal

illegally /ɪ'liːgəli/ *adverb* against the law ○ *He was accused of illegally importing arms into the country.*

illegal strike /ɪˌliːg(ə)l 'straɪk/ *noun* a strike which violates an existing law or that violates an agreement between employers and unions

ill-feeling /ɪl 'fiːlɪŋ/ *noun* bad feeling or a feeling of being upset ○ *The management's attitude created a lot of ill-feeling among the junior employees.*

illness /'ɪlnəs/ *noun* the state of being ill or of not being well

ILM *abbr* internal labour market

ILO *abbr* International Labour Organisation

image /'ɪmɪdʒ/ *noun* the general idea that the public has of a product, brand or company ○ *They are spending a lot of advertising money to improve the company's image.* ○ *The company has adopted a down-market image.* □ **to promote a corporate image** to publicise a company so that its reputation is improved

imaginisation /ɪˌmædʒɪnaɪ'zeɪʃ(ə)n/ *noun* an approach to creativity originated by Gareth Morgan in 1993, that is concerned with improving people's ability to see and understand situations, with finding new ways of organising, with creating shared understanding and personal empowerment, and with developing a capability for continuing self-organisation

immediate /ɪ'miːdiət/ *adjective* happening at once ○ *We wrote an immedi-*

ate letter of complaint. ○ *Your order will receive immediate attention.*

immediate dismissal /ɪˌmiːdiət dɪsˈmɪs(ə)l/, **summary dismissal** /ˌsʌməri dɪsˈmɪs(ə)l/ *noun* a dismissal without giving the employee any notice (usually caused by a crime committed by the employee, or drunkenness or violent behaviour towards other employees)

immigrant /ˈɪmɪɡrənt/ *noun* a person who enters a country to live and work ○ *There is a large immigrant population working without work permits.* ○ *The influx of immigrants is due to high unemployment in their own countries.* ♦ **emigrant**

immigrant worker /ˌɪmɪɡrənt ˈwɜːkə/ *noun* a worker who has entered the country as a potential immigrant, before finding work

immigration /ˌɪmɪˈɡreɪʃ(ə)n/ *noun* **1.** the act of coming to live and work in a country **2.** an office at an airport or port of entry, where government officials inspect the papers of people entering the country ○ *She was held up at Immigration, because her visa was not in order.* ♦ **emigration**

Immigration Laws /ˌɪmɪˈɡreɪʃ(ə)n lɔːz/ *plural noun* legislation regarding immigration into a country

Immigration Service /ˌɪmɪˈɡreɪʃ(ə)n ˌsɜːvɪs/ *noun* a government department which deals with allowing immigrants to enter and settle in a country ○ *The Immigration Service is trying to cope with thousands of applications from potential immigrants.*

immobility /ˌɪməˈbɪlɪti/ *noun* not moving from one place to another

immobility of labour /ɪməˌbɪlɪti əv ˈleɪbə/, **immobility of the workforce** /ɪməˌbɪlɪti əv ðə ˈwɜːkfɔːs/ *noun* little movement of workers from one area of the country to another

immunity /ɪˈmjuːnɪti/ *noun* protection against arrest □ **immunity from prosecution** not being liable to be prosecuted □ **immunity from legal action** not being liable to be sued (e.g. employees who strike cannot be sued for breach of their contract of employment)

impaired /ɪmˈpeəd/ *adjective* referring to a sense or function harmed in such a way that it does not work properly

impaired vision /ɪmˌpeəd ˈvɪʒ(ə)n/ *noun* eyesight which is not fully clear

impairment /ɪmˈpeəmənt/ *noun* a condition in which a sense or function is harmed so that it does not work properly ○ *His hearing impairment does not affect his work.*

impartial /ɪmˈpɑːʃ(ə)l/ *adjective* not biased or not prejudiced ○ *The arbitration board's decision is completely impartial.*

impersonal /ɪmˈpɜːs(ə)n(ə)l/ *adjective* without any personal touch or as if done by machines ○ *an impersonal style of management*

impingement pay /ɪmˈpɪndʒmənt peɪ/ *noun* extra pay paid to an employee for working when they should be on holiday

implement *noun* /ˈɪmplɪmənt/ a tool or instrument used to do some work ○ *We don't have the right implements for this type of work.* ■ *verb* to put into action ○ *to implement an agreement* ○ *to implement a decision*

implementation /ˌɪmplɪmenˈteɪʃ(ə)n/ *noun* the process of putting into action ○ *the implementation of new rules*

implicit knowledge /ɪmˌplɪsɪt ˈnɒlɪdʒ/ *noun* knowledge that is kept in a person's mind without necessarily being expressed in words and is often acted on instinctively

implied /ɪmˈplaɪd/ *adjective* which is presumed to exist □ **implied terms and conditions** terms and conditions which are not written in a contract, but which are legally taken to be present in the contract

importance /ɪmˈpɔːtns/ *noun* considerable value or significance ○ *The bank attaches great importance to the deal.*

important /ɪmˈpɔːtnt/ *adjective* which matters a lot ○ *He left a pile of important papers in the taxi.* ○ *She has an important meeting at 10.30.* ○ *I was promoted to a more important job.*

'...each of the major issues on the agenda at this week's meeting is important to the government's success in overall economic management' [*Australian Financial Review*]

impossible /ɪmˈpɒsɪb(ə)l/ *adjective* which cannot be done ○ *Getting skilled staff is becoming impossible.* ○ *Government regulations make it impossible for us to export.*

improve /ɪmˈpruːv/ *verb* to make something better or to become better ○ *We are trying to improve our image with a series of TV commercials.* ○ *They hope to improve the company's market share.* ○ *We hope the cash flow position will improve or we will have difficulty in paying our bills.*

'...we also invest in companies whose growth and profitability could be improved by a management buyout' [*Times*]

improved /ɪmˈpruːvd/ *adjective* better ○ *an improved offer*

improvement /ɪmˈpruːvmənt/ *noun* **1.** the process of getting better ○ *There is no improvement in the cash flow situation.* ○ *Sales are showing a sharp improvement over last year.* ○ *Employees have noticed an improvement in the working environment.* **2.** something which is better □ **an improvement on an offer** an act of making a better offer

'...the management says the rate of loss-making has come down and it expects further improvement in the next few years' [*Financial Times*]

improvement notice /ɪmˈpruːvmənt ˌnəʊtɪs/ *noun* an order from the Health and Safety Executive, requiring a company to do something to improve working conditions where there has been a breach of the Health and Safety at Work Act

improve on /ɪmˈpruːv ɒn/ *verb* to do better than □ **she refused to improve on her previous offer** she refused to make a better offer

improver /ɪmˈpruːvə/ *noun* an employee working for very low wages in return for learning by work experience ○ *The management has a policy of employing improvers where possible so as to cut down on salaries.* ○ *Three months as an improver gave me the necessary confidence to find a better paid position.*

in-basket test /ˈɪn ˌbɑːskɪt test/, **in-tray test** /ˈɪn treɪ test/ *noun* a method of testing management potential by asking the candidate to deal with a set of problems ○ *The candidates for the management post had to pass a series of in-basket tests.*

incapability /ɪnˌkeɪpəˈbɪlɪti/ *noun* the fact of being incapable of working properly because of illness or incompetence

COMMENT: In the case of incompetence, if the employee's work does not improve after they have been given time to improve, incapability can be a reason for dismissal.

incapacity /ˌɪnkəˈpæsɪti/ *noun* **1.** the fact of not being able to do something □ **one's incapacity for the job** where one is shown to be too incompetent or too ill, or one does not have the right skills, to do a job **2.** the fact of being unable to work because of illness or disability

incapacity benefit /ˌɪnkəˈpæsɪti ˌbenɪfɪt/ *noun* a benefit paid to people who are unable to work because of illness or disability

incentive /ɪnˈsentɪv/ *noun* something which encourages a customer to buy or employees to work better

'...some further profit-taking was seen yesterday as investors continued to lack fresh incentives to renew buying activity' [*Financial Times*]

'...a well-designed plan can help companies retain talented employees and offer enticing performance incentives – all at an affordable cost' [*Fortune*]

'...the right incentives can work when used strategically' [*Management Today*]

'...an additional incentive is that the Japanese are prepared to give rewards where they are due' [*Management Today*]

incentive ceiling /ɪnˈsentɪv ˌsiːlɪŋ/ *noun* a limit on how much can be paid on the basis of results ○ *An incentive ceiling was introduced to limit bonuses and the possibility of resentment among workers.*

incentive drift /ɪnˈsentɪv drɪft/ *noun* a decrease in the gap between effort and output in production ○ *Short cuts were found to increase productivity and thus cause incentive drift.*

incentive plan /ɪnˈsentɪv plæn/, **incentive scheme** /ɪnˈsentɪv skiːm/, **incentive programme** /ɪnˈsentɪv ˌprəʊɡræm/ *noun* a scheme which encourages better work by paying higher commission or bonuses ○ *Incentive schemes are boosting production.* ○ *The new bonus scheme gives the workers more incentive to achieve production targets.*

incentive stock option /ɪnˌsentɪv ˈstɒk ˌɒpʃən/ *noun* (*in the United States*) a plan that gives each qualifying employee the right to purchase a specific number of the corporation's shares at a set price during a specific time period (NOTE: Tax is only payable when the shares are sold.)

incentivize /ɪnˈsentɪvaɪz/ *verb US* same as **motivate**

incidental /ˌɪnsɪˈdent(ə)l/ *adjective* which is not important, but connected with something else

incidental expenses /ˌɪnsɪdent(ə)l ɪkˈspensɪz/ *plural noun* small amounts of money spent at various times in addition to larger amounts

incidentals /ˌɪnsɪˈdent(ə)lz/ *plural noun* same as **incidental expenses**

include /ɪnˈkluːd/ *verb* to count something along with other things ○ *The charge includes VAT.* ○ *The account covers services up to and including the month of June.*

inclusive /ɪnˈkluːsɪv/ *adjective* which counts something in with other things ○ *inclusive of tax* ○ *not inclusive of VAT* □ **the conference runs from the 12th to the 16th inclusive** it starts on the morning of the 12th and ends on the evening of the 16th

inclusive charge /ɪnˌkluːsɪv ˈtʃɑːdʒ/, **inclusive sum** /ɪnˌkluːsɪv ˈsʌm/ *noun* a charge which includes all items or costs

income /ˈɪnkʌm/ *noun* money which a person receives as salary or dividends □ **lower income bracket, upper income bracket** the groups of people who earn low or high salaries considered for tax purposes

income before tax /ˌɪnkʌm bɪfɔː ˈtæks/ *noun* gross income before tax has been deducted

income bracket /ˈɪnkʌm ˌbrækɪt/ *noun* a group of people earning roughly the same income

incomes policy /ˈɪnkʌmz ˌpɒlɪsi/ *noun* the government's ideas on how incomes should be controlled

income statement /ˈɪnkʌm ˌsteɪtmənt/ *noun US* a statement of company expenditure and sales which shows whether the company has made a profit or loss (NOTE: the British equivalent is **profit and loss account**)

income support /ˈɪnkʌm səˌpɔːt/ *noun* a government benefit paid to low-income earners who are working less than 16 hours per week, provided they can show that they are actively looking for jobs. Abbr **IS**

income tax /ˈɪnkʌm tæks/ *noun* **1.** the tax on a person's income (both earned and unearned) **2.** the tax on the profits of a corporation

'...there is no risk-free way of taking regular income from your money much higher than the rate of inflation' [*Guardian*]

income tax allowance /ˈɪnkʌm tæks əˌlaʊəns/ *noun* an amount of income that a person does not have to pay income tax on

income tax form /ˈɪnkʌm tæks fɔːm/ *noun* a form to be completed which declares all income to the tax office

income tax return /ˈɪnkʌm tæks rɪˌtɜːn/ *noun* a form used for reporting how much income you have earned and working out how much tax you have to pay on it

incoming /ˈɪnkʌmɪŋ/ *adjective* **1.** □ **incoming call** a phone call coming into the office from someone outside □ **incoming mail** mail which comes into an office **2.** referring to someone who has recently been elected or appointed ○ *the incoming chairman* □ **the incoming board of directors** the new board which is about to start working

in-company training /ˌɪn kʌmp(ə)ni ˈtreɪnɪŋ/ *noun* training provided by an external organisation which specialises in running training courses for the employees of a particular company only, and which is usually specially adapted to the company's needs. ▸ **public training programme** (NOTE: See also public training programmes)

incompatible /ˌɪnkəmˈpætɪb(ə)l/ *adjective* not able to live or work together ○ *Her views and those of the department manager were incompatible.* ○ *The manager's paternalistic approach was incompatible with the company's more democratic approach.*

incompetence /ɪnˈkɒmpɪt(ə)ns/ *noun* the fact of being unable to do a job well ○ *The clerk was fired for gross incompetence.* ○ *Much of the sales team's incompetence is due to lack of training.*

incompetent /ɪnˈkɒmpɪt(ə)nt/ *adjective* unable to work effectively ○ *The sales manager is incompetent.* ○ *The company has an incompetent sales director.*

incorrect /ˌɪnkəˈrekt/ *adjective* wrong ○ *The minutes of the meeting were incorrect and had to be changed.*

incorrectly /ˌɪnkəˈrektli/ *adverb* wrongly ○ *The package was incorrectly addressed.*

increase *noun* /ˈɪnkriːs/ **1.** an act of becoming larger ○ *There have been several increases in tax* or *tax increases in the last few years.* ○ *There is an automatic 5% increase in price* or *price increase on January 1st.* ○ *Profits showed a 10% increase* or *an increase of 10% on last year.* □ **increase in the cost of living** a rise in the annual cost of living **2.** a higher salary ○ *increase in pay* or *pay increase* ○ *The government hopes to hold salary increases to 3%.* □ **she had two increases last year** her salary went up twice ■ *verb* /ɪnˈkriːs/ **1.** to grow bigger or higher ○ *Profits have increased faster than the increase in the rate of inflation.* ○ *Exports to Africa have increased by more than 25%.* ○ *The price of oil has increased twice in the past week.* □ **to increase in price** to cost more □ **to increase in size** *or* **in value** to become larger or more valuable **2.** □ **the company increased her salary to £20,000** the company gave her a rise in salary to £20,000

'…turnover has the potential to be increased to over 1 million dollars with energetic management and very little capital' [*Australian Financial Review*]

'…competition is steadily increasing and could affect profit margins as the company tries to retain its market share' [*Citizen (Ottawa)*]

increment /ˈɪŋkrɪmənt/ *noun* a regular automatic increase in salary ○ *an annual increment* □ **salary which rises in annual increments of £1000** each year the salary is increased by £1000

incremental /ˌɪŋkrɪˈment(ə)l/ *adjective* which rises automatically in stages

incremental increase /ˌɪŋkrɪment(ə)l ˈɪnkriːs/ *noun* an increase in salary according to an agreed annual increment

incremental salary scale /ˌɪŋkrɪment(ə)l ˈsæləri skeɪl/ *noun* a salary scale with regular annual salary increases

incremental scale /ˌɪŋkrɪment(ə)l ˈskeɪl/ *noun* a salary scale with regular annual salary increases

incumbent /ɪnˈkʌmbənt/ *noun* a person currently filling a position

incur /ɪnˈkɜː/ *verb* to make yourself liable to □ **to incur the risk of a penalty** to make it possible that you risk paying a penalty

'…the company blames fiercely competitive market conditions in Europe for a £14m operating loss last year, incurred despite a record turnover' [*Financial Times*]

indecision /ˌɪndɪˈsɪʒ(ə)n/ *noun* the fact of not being able to decide ○ *The employees protested to the management about the indecision over relocation.*

indecisive /ˌɪndɪˈsaɪsɪv/ *adjective* not able to make up one's mind or to decide on something important ○ *He is too indecisive to be a good manager.*

indecisiveness /ˌɪndɪˈsaɪsɪvnəs/ *noun* the quality of being indecisive

indenture /ɪnˈdentʃə/ *verb* to contract with an apprentice who will work for some years to learn a trade ○ *He was indentured to a builder.*

indentures /ɪnˈdentʃəz/ *plural noun* a contract by which an apprentice works for a master for some years to learn a trade

independent /ˌɪndɪˈpendənt/ *adjective* not under the control or authority of anyone else

independent audit /ˌɪndɪpendənt ˈɔːdɪt/ *noun* an audit carried out by an auditor who is independent and not employed by the company

independent company /ˌɪndɪpendənt ˈkʌmp(ə)ni/ *noun* a company which is not controlled by another company

independent contractor /ˌɪndɪpendənt ˈkɒntræktə/ *noun* a self-employed person who works for a company, and is paid a fee for providing a service, but is not paid a salary

independent trader /ˌɪndɪpendənt ˈtreɪdə/, **independent shop** /ˌɪndɪpendənt ˈʃɒp/ *noun* a shop which is owned by an individual proprietor, not by a chain

in-depth study /ˌɪn depθ ˈstʌdi/ *noun* a thorough painstaking study

index /ˈɪndeks/ *noun* **1.** a list of items classified into groups or put in alphabetical order **2.** a regular statistical report which shows rises and falls in prices, values or levels ■ *verb* to link a payment to an index ○ *salaries indexed to the cost of living*

indexation /ˌɪndekˈseɪʃ(ə)n/ *noun* the linking of something to an index

indexation of wage increases /ˌɪndekseɪʃ(ə)n əv ˈweɪdʒ ˌɪnkriːsɪz/ *noun* the linking of wage increases to the percentage rise in the cost of living

index-linked /ˌɪndeks ˈlɪŋkt/ *adjective* which rises automatically by the percentage increase in the cost of living ○ *index-linked government bonds* ○ *Inflation did not affect her as she has an index-linked pension.*

'…two-year index-linked savings certificates now pay 3 per cent a year tax free, in addition to index-linking' [*Financial Times*]

indicator /ˈɪndɪkeɪtə/ *noun* something which indicates

'…we may expect the US leading economic indicators for April to show faster economic growth' [*Australian Financial Review*]

indifference /ɪnˈdɪf(ə)rəns/ ◊ **range of indifference**

indirect /ˌɪndaɪˈrekt/ *adjective* not direct

indirect compensation /ˌɪndaɪrekt kɒmpənˈseɪʃ(ə)n/ *noun* a non-financial benefit given by a company to its employees (such as sports facilities, a company car or health insurance)

indirect costs /ˌɪndaɪrekt ˈkɒsts/ *plural noun* costs which are not directly related to the making of a product (such as cleaning, rent or administration)

indirect discrimination /ˌɪndaɪrekt dɪskrɪmɪˈneɪʃ(ə)n/ *noun* discrimination that takes place when, although people seem to be being treated equally, there is actually some special condition attached to getting a job, which rules out some of the people who are qualified to apply for it and which cannot be justified under anti-discrimination laws

indirect labour /ˌɪndaɪrekt ˈleɪbə/ *noun* employees who are not directly related to the production of the product

indirect labour costs /ˌɪndaɪrekt ˈleɪbə kɒsts/ *plural noun* the cost of paying employees not directly involved in making a product such as cleaners or canteen staff. Such costs cannot be allocated to a cost centre.

indirect taxation /ˌɪndaɪrekt tækˈseɪʃ(ə)n/ *noun* taxes (such as sales tax) which are not paid direct to the government ○ *The government raises more money by indirect taxation than by direct.*

individual /ˌɪndɪˈvɪdʒuəl/ *noun* one single person ○ *a savings plan tailored to the requirements of the private individual* ■ *adjective* single or belonging to one person ○ *a pension plan designed to meet each person's individual requirements*

individual incentive scheme /ˌɪndɪvɪdʒuəl ɪnˈsentɪv skiːm/ *noun* a payment scheme whereby an individual is rewarded for improvements in their work

individualism /ˌɪndɪˈvɪdʒuəlɪz(ə)m/ *noun* the belief that society flourishes if each individual is responsible only for themselves and their family (NOTE: the opposite is **collectivism**)

individual relations /ˌɪndɪvɪdʒuəl rɪˈleɪʃ(ə)nz/ *plural noun* relations between employers and individual employees

inducement /ɪnˈdjuːsmənt/ *noun* something which helps to persuade someone to do something ○ *They offered her a company car as an inducement to stay.*

COMMENT: Inducement can be a tort, if, say, a union official induces members to take industrial action in contravention of their contracts of employment.

induction /ɪnˈdʌkʃən/ *noun* an introduction to a new organisation or a new job

induction course /ɪnˈdʌkʃən kɔːs/, **induction training** /ɪnˈdʌkʃən ˌtreɪnɪŋ/ *noun* a programme intended to help a person entering an organisation or starting a new job ○ *The company is organising a two-day induction course for new employees.* ○ *The induction course spelt out the main objectives and procedures of the organisation.*

industrial /ɪnˈdʌstriəl/ *adjective* referring to manufacturing work □ **to take industrial action** to go on strike or go-slow

'…indications of renewed weakness in the US economy were contained in figures on industrial production for April' [*Financial Times*]

industrial accident /ɪnˌdʌstriəl ˈæksɪd(ə)nt/ *noun* an accident which takes place at work

industrial action /ɪnˌdʌstriəl ˈækʃən/ *noun* steps taken by employees to strengthen their position in making demands on employers

Industrial Arbitration Court /ɪnˌdʌstriəl ɑːbɪˈtreɪʃ(ə)n kɔːt/ *noun* a special court that is responsible for settling industrial disputes

industrial arbitration tribunal /ɪnˌdʌstriəl ɑːbɪˈtreɪʃ(ə)n traɪˌbjuːn(ə)l/ *noun* a court which decides in industrial disputes

industrial court /ɪnˌdʌstriəl ˈkɔːt/ *noun* a court which can decide in industrial disputes if both parties agree to ask it to judge between them

industrial democracy /ɪnˌdʌstriəl dɪˈmɒkrəsi/ *noun* a concept where power is shared by employees in an organisation or industry, in particular, where the employees have a role in the decision-making processes, and can veto proposals by the management ○ *Industrial democracy was part of the political party's manifesto.*

industrial development /ɪnˌdʌstriəl dɪˈveləpmənt/ *noun* the planning and building of new industries in special areas

industrial disease /ɪnˈdʌstriəl dɪˌziːz/, **occupational disease** /ɒkjʊˈpeɪʃ(ə)n(ə)l dɪˌziːz/ *noun* a disease which is caused by the type of work or the conditions in which someone works (such as disease caused by dust or chemicals in a factory)

industrial dispute /ɪnˌdʌstriəl dɪˈspjuːt/ *noun* an argument between management and employees

industrial espionage /ɪnˌdʌstriəl ˈespiənɑːʒ/ *noun* the practice of trying to find out the secrets of a competitor's work or products, usually by illegal means

industrial health /ɪnˌdʌstriəl ˈhelθ/, **industrial hygiene** /ɪnˌdʌstriəl ˈhaɪdʒiːn/ *noun* a branch of medicine dealing with the health of people at work ○ *Standards of industrial hygiene are improving in line with developments in general medicine.* ○ *The development of industrial health has meant better protection against lung disease in the mining industry.*

industrial injuries disablement benefit /ɪnˌdʌstriəl ˌɪndʒəriz dɪsˈeɪb(ə)lmənt ˌbenɪfɪt/ *noun* a benefit paid to a worker who has been injured or disabled at work

industrial injuries insurance /ɪnˌdʌstriəl ˈɪndʒəriz ɪnˌʃʊərəns/ *noun* a government insurance scheme for workers who have accidents at work

industrial practices /ɪnˌdʌstriəl ˈpræktɪsɪz/ *plural noun* ways of managing or working in business, industry or trade (NOTE: also called **trade practices**)

industrial psychology /ɪnˌdʌstriəl saɪˈkɒlədʒi/ *noun* a study of human behaviour and mental health in the workplace

industrial relations /ɪnˌdʌstriəl rɪˈleɪʃ(ə)nz/ *plural noun* relations between management and employees ○ *The company has a history of bad labour relations.*

'Britain's industrial relations climate is changing' [*Personnel Today*]

industrial relations audit /ɪnˌdʌstriəl rɪˈleɪʃ(ə)nz ˌɔːdɪt/ *noun* a review of all relations between management and employees in a company

Industrial Relations Court of Australia /ɪnˌdʌstriəl rɪˌleɪʃ(ə)nz kɔːt əv ɒˈstreɪliə/ *noun* a superior court in Australia which is responsible for enforcing decisions made by a court of arbitration, deciding on claims for unfair dismissal and ruling on points of industrial law

industrial sociology /ɪnˌdʌstriəl səʊsiˈɒlədʒi/ *noun* the study of employees and their attitudes to work and management

Industrial Training Board /ɪnˌdʌstriəl ˈtreɪnɪŋ bɔːd/ *noun* a regional government organisation whose responsibility is to provide training facilities for industry

industrial tribunal /ɪnˌdʌstriəl traɪˈbjuːn(ə)l/ *noun* a court which can decide in disputes about employment

'ACAS has a legal obligation to try and solve industrial grievances before they reach industrial tribunals' [*Personnel Today*]

industrial unrest /ɪnˌdʌstriəl ʌnˈrest/ *noun* action by employees (such as protest meetings, strikes or walk-outs) against pay or working conditions

industry /ˈɪndəstri/ *noun* **1.** all factories, companies or processes involved in the manufacturing of products ○ *All sectors of industry have shown rises in output.* **2.** a group of companies making the same type of product or offering the same type of service ○ *the aircraft industry* ○ *the food-processing industry* ○ *the petroleum industry* ○ *the advertising industry*

'…with the present overcapacity in the airline industry, discounting of tickets is widespread' [*Business Traveller*]

industry-wide /ˈɪndəstri waɪd/ *adjective* affecting all companies in one industry ○ *We are expecting* industry-wide wage increases for machinists of 10%.

industry-wide strike /ˌɪndəstri waɪd ˈstraɪk/ *noun* a strike which affects a whole industry and not just individual firms

ineffective time /ˌɪnɪfektɪv ˈtaɪm/ *noun* the time spent by an operator which does not contribute to production ○ *The dramatic fall in productivity was due to an increase in ineffective time.* ○ *The poor profit figures can be put down to too much ineffective time and wastage of raw materials.*

inefficiency /ˌɪnɪˈfɪʃ(ə)nsi/ *noun* the fact of not being able to work quickly and correctly ○ *The report criticised the inefficiency of the sales staff.*

inefficient /ˌɪnɪˈfɪʃ(ə)nt/ *adjective* not doing a job well or unable to work efficiently and correctly ○ *an inefficient sales director* ○ *Inefficient workers waste raw materials and fail to complete tasks on schedule.*

ineligibility /ɪnˌelɪdʒɪˈbɪlɪti/ *noun* the fact of being ineligible

ineligible /ɪnˈelɪdʒɪb(ə)l/ *adjective* not eligible

inequality /ˌɪnɪˈkwɒlɪti/ *noun* the state of not being equal ○ *The workforce has complained about the inequalities of the pension scheme.*

inequity /ɪnˈekwɪti/ *noun* unfairness of treatment, e.g. unequal pay for the same type of job ○ *Inequity has caused much resentment in the organisation, especially when younger staff are being paid more than their seniors for the same type of work.*

inexperienced /ˌɪnɪkˈspɪəriənst/ *adjective* referring to a person who does not have much experience ○ *The negotiating team was quite inexperienced in dealing with management negotiators.* ○ *They have appointed an inexperienced young man as workshop manager.*

in flagrante delicto /ɪn fləˌgrænti dɪˈlɪktəʊ/ *Latin phrase meaning* 'in the act of doing something' ○ *The clerk was caught in flagrante delicto pocketing the petty cash.*

inflated salary /ɪnˌfleɪtɪd ˈsæləri/ *noun* a salary which is increased without any reason

inflation /ɪnˈfleɪʃ(ə)n/ *noun* a greater increase in the supply of money or credit than in the production of goods and services, resulting in higher prices and a fall in the purchasing power of money □ **we have 3% inflation, inflation is running at 3%** prices are 3% higher than at the same time last year ○ *to take measures to reduce inflation* ○ *High interest rates tend to increase inflation.*

'…the decision by the government to tighten monetary policy will push the annual inflation rate above the year's previous high' [*Financial Times*]

'…the retail prices index rose 0.4 per cent in the month, taking the annual headline inflation rate to 1.7 per cent. The underlying inflation rate, which excludes mortgage interest payments, increased to an annual rate of 3.1 per cent' [*Times*]

COMMENT: The inflation rate in the UK is calculated on a series of figures, including prices of consumer items, petrol, gas and electricity; interest rates, etc. This gives the 'underlying' inflation rate which can be compared to that of other countries. The calculation can also include mortgage interest and local taxes which give the 'headline' inflation figure; this is higher than in other countries because of these extra items. Inflation affects businesses, in that as their costs rise, so their profits may fall and it is necessary to take this into account when pricing products.

inflation accounting /ɪnˈfleɪʃ(ə)n əˌkaʊntɪŋ/ *noun* an accounting system, where inflation is taken into account when calculating the value of assets and the preparation of accounts

inflationary /ɪnˈfleɪʃ(ə)n(ə)ri/ *adjective* which tends to increase inflation ○ *inflationary trends in the economy* □ **the economy is in an inflationary spiral** the economy is in a situation where price rises encourage higher wage demands which in turn make prices rise

'…inflationary expectations fell somewhat this month, but remained a long way above the actual inflation rate, according to figures released yesterday. The annual rate of inflation measured by the consumer price index has been below 2 per cent for over 18 months' [*Australian Financial Review*]

infoholic /ˌɪnfəʊˈhɒlɪk/ *noun* a person who is obsessed with obtaining information, especially on the Internet (*slang*)

inform /ɪnˈfɔːm/ *verb* to tell someone officially ○ *We are pleased to inform you that you have been selected for interview.* ○ *We have been informed by the Department that new regulations are coming into force.*

informal /ɪnˈfɔːm(ə)l/ *adjective* not official or not formal

informally /ɪnˈfɔːməli/ *adverb* unofficially

informal warning /ɪnˌfɔːm(ə)l ˈwɔːnɪŋ/ *noun* a spoken warning to an employee, which is not recorded and cannot be taken into account if the worker is disciplined later. ⟩ **formal warning**

information /ˌɪnfəˈmeɪʃ(ə)n/ *noun* details which explain something ○ *to disclose a piece of information* ○ *to answer a request for information* ○ *I enclose this leaflet for your information.* ○ *For further information, please write to Department 27.* □ **disclosure of confidential information** the act of telling someone information which should be secret

information agreement /ɪnfəˈmeɪʃ(ə)n əˌgriːmənt/ *noun* an agreement between management and a union regarding the information about the company which management agrees to pass to the union on a regular basis

information management /ɪnfəˈmeɪʃ(ə)n ˌmænɪdʒmənt/ *noun* the task of controlling information and the flow of information within an organisation, which involves acquiring, recording, organising, storing, distributing and retrieving it (NOTE: Good information management has been described as getting the right information to the right person in the right format at the right time.)

information overload /ɪnfəˈmeɪʃ(ə)n ˌəʊvələʊd/ *noun* the act of burdening someone with too much information

information retrieval /ɪnfə-ˌmeɪʃ(ə)n rɪ'triːv(ə)l/ *noun* the finding of stored data in a computer

information system /ɪnfə'meɪʃ(ə)n ˌsɪstəm/ *noun* a system of storing information either manually or by computer ○ *The information system is so bad that details on staff cannot be found easily.*

information technology /ɪnfə-ˌmeɪʃ(ə)n tek'nɒlədʒi/ *noun* working with data stored on computers (IT). Abbr **IT**

infringement /ɪn'frɪndʒmənt/ *noun* an act of breaking a law or a rule ○ *infringement of the company's rules*

in-house /ɪn 'haʊs/ *adverb, adjective* done by someone employed by a company on their premises, not by an outside contractor ○ *the in-house staff* ○ *We do all our data processing in-house.*

in-house training /ˌɪn haʊs 'treɪnɪŋ/ *noun* training given to employees at their place of work

initiative /ɪ'nɪʃətɪv/ *noun* the decision to start something □ **to take the initiative** to decide to do something □ **to lack initiative** not to be enterprising or go-ahead ○ *The manager will have to be replaced – she lacks initiative.*

injunction /ɪn'dʒʌŋkʃən/ *noun* a court order telling someone not to do something ○ *He got an injunction preventing the company from selling his car.*

injure /'ɪndʒə/ *verb* to hurt someone ○ *Two workers were injured in the fire.*

injury /'ɪndʒəri/ *noun* hurt caused to a person

injury benefit /'ɪndʒəri ˌbenɪfɪt/ *noun* money paid to an employee who has been hurt at work

inland /'ɪnlənd/ *adjective* inside a country

innovation /ˌɪnə'veɪʃ(ə)n/ *noun* the development of new products or new ways of selling

input /'ɪnpʊt/ *noun* what is contributed to an activity or project ○ *The amount of staff input in the company magazine is small.* □ **input of information, computer input** data fed into a computer ■ *verb* □ **to input information** to put data into a computer

inquire /ɪn'kwaɪə/ *verb* to ask questions about something ○ *He inquired if anything was wrong.* ○ *She inquired about the mortgage rate.* □ **'inquire within'** ask for more details inside the office or shop

inquire into /ɪn'kwaɪər ɪntuː/ *verb* to investigate or try to find out about something ○ *We are inquiring into the background of the new supplier.*

inquiry /ɪn'kwaɪəri/ *noun* **1.** an official question ○ *I refer to your inquiry of May 25th.* ○ *All inquiries should be addressed to this department.* **2.** an official investigation ○ *a government inquiry into trading practices* (NOTE: plural is **inquiries**)

in-service training /ˌɪn sɜːvɪs 'treɪnɪŋ/ *noun* the training of staff while they are employed by an organisation ○ *Management trainees will draw full salaries during the period of their in-service training.* Abbr **INSET**

inside /ɪn'saɪd/ *adjective, adverb* in, especially in a company's office or building ○ *We do all our design work inside.* ■ *preposition* in ○ *There was nothing inside the container.* ○ *We have a contact inside our rival's production department who gives us very useful information.*

insider /ɪn'saɪdə/ *noun* a person who works in an organisation and therefore knows its secrets

insider buying /ɪnˌsaɪdə 'baɪɪŋ/, **insider dealing** /ɪnˌsaɪdə 'diːlɪŋ/, **insider trading** /ɪnˌsaɪdə 'treɪdɪŋ/ *noun* the illegal buying or selling of shares by staff of a company or other persons who have secret information about the company's plans

inside work /'ɪnsaɪd wɜːk/, **internal work** /ɪn'tɜːn(ə)l wɜːk/ *noun* the work that an operator can do within the period that the machine is working

inside worker /'ɪnsaɪd ˌwɜːkə/ *noun* an employee who works in an office or factory (not someone who works in the open air or visits customers)

insolvency /ɪn'sɒlvənsi/ *noun* the fact of not being able to pay debts □ **the**

company was in a state of insolvency it could not pay its debts

'…hundreds of thrifts found themselves on the brink of insolvency after a deregulation programme prompted them to enter dangerous financial waters' [*Times*]

insolvency practitioner /ɪn-ˈsɒlvənsi prækˌtɪʃ(ə)nə/ *noun* a person who advises insolvent companies

insolvent /ɪnˈsɒlvənt/ *adjective* not able to pay debts ○ *The company was declared insolvent.* (NOTE: see note at **insolvency**)

COMMENT: A company is insolvent when its liabilities are higher than its assets; if this happens it must cease trading.

insourcing /ˈɪnsɔːsɪŋ/ *noun* the use of an organisation's or a department's own employees and resources to meet its need for specific services (NOTE: compare **outsourcing**)

inspect /ɪnˈspekt/ *verb* to examine in detail ○ *to inspect a machine* or *an installation* ○ *The gas board is sending an engineer to inspect the central heating system.* ○ *Inspectors from the DTI have come to inspect the accounts.* □ **to inspect products for defects** to look at products in detail to see if they have any defects

inspection /ɪnˈspekʃən/ *noun* the close examination of something ○ *to make an inspection* or *to carry out an inspection of a machine* or *an installation* ○ *the inspection of a product for defects* □ **to issue an inspection order** to order an official inspection

inspector /ɪnˈspektə/ *noun* an official who inspects ○ *The inspectors will soon be round to make sure the building is safe.*

inspectorate /ɪnˈspekt(ə)rət/ *noun* all inspectors

inspector of factories /ɪnˌspektər əv ˈfækt(ə)riz/ *noun* a government official who inspects factories to see if they are safely run

inspector of taxes /ɪnˌspektər əv ˈtæksɪz/ *noun* an official of the Inland Revenue who examines tax returns and decides how much tax people should pay

inspector of weights and measures /ɪnˌspektər əv ˌweɪts ən ˈmeʒəz/ *noun* a government official who inspects weighing machines and goods sold in shops to see if the quantities and weights are correct

install /ɪnˈstɔːl/ *verb* **1.** to put a machine into an office or into a factory ○ *We are planning to install the new machinery over the weekend.* ○ *They must install a new data processing system because the old one cannot cope with the mass of work involved.* **2.** to set up a new computer system so that it fits the user's requirements **3.** to configure a new computer program to the existing system requirements

installation /ˌɪnstəˈleɪʃ(ə)n/ *noun* **1.** the act of putting new machines into an office or a factory ○ *to supervise the installation of new equipment* **2.** machines, equipment and buildings ○ *Harbour installations were picketed by striking dockers.* ○ *The fire seriously damaged the oil installations.* **3.** setting up a new computer system

instalment /ɪnˈstɔːlmənt/ *noun* a part of a payment which is paid regularly until the total amount is paid ○ *The first instalment is payable on signature of the agreement.* (NOTE: the usual US spelling is **installment**) □ **the final instalment is now due** the last of a series of payments should be paid now □ **to pay £25 down and monthly instalments of £20** to pay a first payment of £25 and the rest in payments of £20 each month □ **to miss an instalment** not to pay an instalment at the right time

institute /ˈɪnstɪtjuːt/ *noun* a society or organisation which represents a particular profession or activity ○ *the Institute of Chartered Accountants* ○ *the Chartered Institute of Personnel and Development* ■ *verb* to start a new custom or procedure ○ *to institute a new staff payment scheme*

institution /ˌɪnstɪˈtjuːʃ(ə)n/ *noun* an organisation or society set up for a particular purpose

instruct /ɪnˈstrʌkt/ *verb* **1.** to give an order to someone □ **to instruct someone to do something** to tell someone officially to do something ○ *He instructed the credit controller to take action.* ○

The foreman will instruct the men to stop working. **2.** to teach

instruction /ɪnˈstrʌkʃən/ *noun* an order which tells what should be done or how something is to be used ○ *He gave instructions to his stockbroker to sell the shares immediately.* □ **to await instructions** to wait for someone to tell you what to do □ **to issue instructions** to tell everyone what to do □ **in accordance with**, **according to instructions** as the instructions show

instructor /ɪnˈstrʌktə/ *noun* a person who shows how something is to be done ○ *Two new instructors are needed for the training courses.* ○ *Distance learning can be carried out without instructors.*

insubordination /ˌɪnsəbɔːdɪˈneɪʃ(ə)n/ *noun* the act of refusing to do what a person in authority tells you to do

insurable /ɪnˈʃʊərəb(ə)l/ *adjective* which can be insured

insurance /ɪnˈʃʊərəns/ *noun* an agreement that in return for regular payments (called 'premiums'), a company will pay compensation for loss, damage, injury or death ○ *to take out insurance* ○ *Repairs will be paid for by the insurance.* □ **the damage is covered by the insurance** the insurance company will pay for the damage ○ *Repairs will be paid for by the insurance.*

insurance agent /ɪnˈʃʊərəns ˌeɪdʒənt/, **insurance broker** /ɪnˈʃʊərəns ˌbrəʊkə/ *noun* a person who arranges insurance for clients

insurance company /ɪnˈʃʊərəns ˌkʌmp(ə)ni/ *noun* a company whose business is insurance

insurance contract /ɪnˈʃʊərəns ˌkɒntrækt/ *noun* an agreement by an insurance company to insure

insurance cover /ɪnˈʃʊərəns ˌkʌvə/ *noun* protection guaranteed by an insurance policy ○ *Do you have cover against theft?*

insurance plan /ɪnˈʃʊərəns plæn/, **insurance scheme** /ɪnˈʃʊərəns skiːm/ *noun* a set of conditions which make up an insurance package ○ *What type of insurance scheme should be provided for the employees?*

insurance policy /ɪnˈʃʊərəns ˌpɒlɪsi/ *noun* a document which shows the conditions of an insurance contract

insure /ɪnˈʃʊə/ *verb* to have a contract with a company where, if regular small payments are made, the company will pay compensation for loss, damage, injury or death ○ *to insure someone's life* ○ *He was insured for £100,000.* ○ *to insure against loss of earnings*

insurer /ɪnˈʃʊərə/ *noun* a company which insures (NOTE: for life insurance, British English prefers to use **assurer**)

intangible /ɪnˈtændʒɪb(ə)l/ *adjective* which cannot be touched

intangible fixed assets /ɪnˌtændʒɪb(ə)l fɪkst ˈæsets/ *plural noun* assets which have a value, but which cannot be seen (such as goodwill, copyrights, patents or trademarks)

integrate /ˈɪntɪgreɪt/ *verb* to link things together to form one whole group

integration /ˌɪntɪˈgreɪʃ(ə)n/ *noun* the act of bringing several businesses together under a central control

COMMENT: In a case of horizontal integration, a large supermarket might take over another smaller supermarket chain; on the other hand, if a supermarket takes over a food packaging company the integration would be vertical.

integration test /ˌɪntɪˈgreɪʃ(ə)n test/ *noun* a test to show if a person is an employee or a freelancer (by seeing if the work done is an integral part of the company's operations or simply an additional help to the company)

integrative bargaining /ˌɪntɪgreɪtɪv ˈbɑːgɪnɪŋ/, **integrative negotiation** /ˌɪntɪgreɪtɪv nɪˌgəʊʃiˈeɪʃ(ə)n/ *noun* bargaining to reach a solution which is beneficial to both sides

intelligence quotient /ɪnˈtelɪdʒəns ˌkwəʊʃ(ə)nt/ *noun* a measure of mental ability according to a comparative scale ○ *The intelligence test showed he had only an average IQ.* Abbr **IQ**

intelligence test /ɪnˈtelɪdʒəns test/ *noun* a test to assess someone's intellectual ability

inter- /ɪntə/ *prefix* between □ **inter-company dealings** dealings between two companies in the same group □ **inter-company comparisons** comparing the results of one company with those of another in the same product area

interaction /ˌɪntər'ækʃən/ *noun* a contact between individuals or groups ○ *There is very little interaction between office staff and manual workers.*

interactive learning /ˌɪntəræktɪv 'lɜːnɪŋ/ *noun* learning through a computer teaching package, where the student is helped by the course and is taught by making responses to the course

interactive skills /ˌɪntəræktɪv 'skɪlz/ *plural noun* skills used when communicating with other people (such as passing information, giving orders or discussing problems)

inter-bank loan /ˌɪntə bæŋk 'ləʊn/ *noun* a loan from one bank to another

interest group /'ɪntrəst gruːp/ *noun* a group of people who share the same interests (such as sport, animal welfare or owning shares in the same company)

interface /'ɪntəfeɪs/ *noun* **1.** the link between two different computer systems or pieces of hardware **2.** a point where two groups of people come into contact ■ *verb* to meet and act with ○ *The office PCs interface with the computer at head office.*

interfere /ɪntə'fɪə/ *verb* to get involved in or try to change something which is not your concern

interference /ɪntə'fɪərəns/ *noun* the act of interfering ○ *The sales department complained of continual interference from the accounts department.*

interference pay /ɪntə'fɪərəns peɪ/ *noun* pay made to pieceworkers who have not had enough work because other workers making parts have been moved to other jobs

interference time /ɪntə'fɪərəns taɪm/ *noun* the time during which a machine is waiting for the operator's attention while they are doing something else ○ *The production manager will calculate how much time is lost through inter-ference time.* ○ *Interference time was caused by having a lot of machines worked by one machinist.*

interim /'ɪntərɪm/ *noun* statement of interim profits or dividends

'…the company plans to keep its annual dividend unchanged at 7.5 per share, which includes a 3.75 interim payout' [*Financial Times*]

interim agreement /ˌɪntərɪm ə-'griːmənt/ *noun* an agreement in collective bargaining, which is designed to keep a strike off while a more long-term agreement is being worked out ○ *The interim agreement helped provide breathing space while the two sides reconsidered their positions.*

interim manager /ˌɪntərɪm 'mænɪdʒə/ *noun* an experienced manager who is brought in to work temporarily for an organisation, usually to fill a vacancy or to coordinate a particular project

interim payment /ˌɪntərɪm 'peɪmənt/ *noun* a payment of part of a dividend

interim relief /ˌɪntərɪm rɪ'liːf/ *noun* an order from an industrial tribunal telling an employer to continue an employee's contract of employment (or to re-employ them) until a decision has been made on a complaint for unfair dismissal

intermediary /ˌɪntə'miːdiəri/ *noun* a person who is the link between parties who do not agree or who are negotiating ○ *He refused to act as an intermediary between the two directors.*

COMMENT: Banks, building societies and hire purchase companies are all types of financial intermediaries.

intern /'ɪntɜːn/ *noun* a person who is undergoing on-the-job training

internal /ɪn'tɜːn(ə)l/ *adjective* **1.** inside a company □ **we decided to make an internal appointment** we decided to appoint an existing member of staff to the post, and not bring someone in from outside the company **2.** inside a country or a region

internal alignment /ɪnˌtɜːn(ə)l ə-'laɪnmənt/ *noun* the relationship between positions in an organisation in terms of rank and pay

internal audit /ɪn,tɜːn(ə)l ˈɔːdɪt/ *noun* an audit carried out by a department inside the company

internal audit department /ɪn-,tɜːn(ə)l ˈɔːdɪt dɪ,pɑːtmənt/ *noun* a department of a company which examines the internal accounting controls of that company ○ *She is the manager of the internal audit department.*

internal auditor /ɪn,tɜːn(ə)l ˈɔːdɪtə/ *noun* a member of staff who audits a company's accounts

internal communication /ɪn-,tɜːn(ə)l kə,mjuːnɪˈkeɪʃ(ə)n/ *noun* communication between employees or departments of the same organisation (NOTE: Internal communication can take various forms such as team briefings, interviewing, employee or works councils, meetings, memos, an intranet, newsletters, suggestion schemes, the grapevine, and reports.)

internal consultant /ɪn,tɜːn(ə)l kənˈsʌltənt/ *noun* an employee with special knowledge and expertise who offers advice or business solutions to another department within the same organisation

internal consulting /ɪn,tɜːn(ə)l kənˈsʌltɪŋ/ *noun* the work done by an internal consultant

internal growth /ɪn,tɜːn(ə)l ˈgrəʊθ/ *noun* the development of a company by growing its existing business with its own finances, as opposed to acquiring other businesses (called 'external growth')

internal labour market /ɪn,tɜːn(ə)l ˈleɪbə ,mɑːkɪt/ *noun* the workforce already employed in a group, which can be redeployed to other jobs inside the group. Abbr **ILM**

internally /ɪnˈtɜːn(ə)lɪ/ *adverb* inside a company ○ *The job was advertised internally.*

internal market /ɪn,tɜːn(ə)l ˈmɑːkɪt/ *noun* a way of operating a large organisation, where each manager becomes a separate entrepreneurial unit which is run as if totally independent from the rest of the group

internal promotion /ɪn,tɜːn(ə)l prəˈməʊʃ(ə)n/ *noun* the promotion of someone working in the company already (as opposed to bringing in a new employee from outside)

internal recruitment /ɪn,tɜːn(ə)l rɪ-ˈkruːtmənt/ *noun* the process of filling vacancies by recruiting staff from inside the company

Internal Revenue Service /ɪn-,tɜːn(ə)l ˈrevənjuː ,sɜːvɪs/ *noun US* a government department which deals with tax. Abbr **IRS**

internal telephone /ɪn,tɜːn(ə)l ˈtelɪfəʊn/ *noun* a telephone which is linked to other telephones in an office

international /,ɪntəˈnæʃ(ə)nəl/ *adjective* working between countries

international call /,ɪntənæʃ(ə)nəl ˈkɔːl/ *noun* a telephone call to another country

international (dialling) code /,ɪntənæʃ(ə)nəl ˈdaɪəlɪŋ kəʊd/ *noun* the part of a telephone number used for dialling to another country

International Labour Organisation (ILO) /,ɪntənæʃ(ə)nəl ˈleɪbər ɔːgənaɪ,zeɪʃ(ə)n/ a section of the United Nations which tries to improve working conditions and workers' pay in member countries

international union /,ɪntənæʃ(ə)nəl ˈjuːnjən/ *noun US* a parent union composed of affiliated unions, known as 'locals'

Internet /ˈɪntənet/ *noun* **1.** international network linking thousands of computers using telephone links ○ *Much of our business is done on the Internet.* ○ *Internet sales form an important part of our turnover.* ○ *He searched the Internet for information on cheap tickets to the USA.* **2.** the global, public network of computers and telephone links that houses websites, allows email to be sent and is accessed with the aid of a modem (NOTE: The Internet uses the Internet Protocol (IP) as a communication standard.)

'…they predict a tenfold increase in sales via internet or TV between 1999 and 2004' [*Investors Chronicle*]

'…in two significant decisions, the Securities and Exchange Board of India today allowed trading of shares through the Internet and set a deadline for companies to conform to norms for good corporate governance' [*The Hindu*]

internship /ɪnˈtɜːnʃɪp/ *noun US* a probationary period of on-the-job training for newly qualified employees under the guidance of experts ○ *During his internship he learnt the practical aspects of the job.*

interpersonal /ˌɪntəˈpɜːs(ə)n(ə)l/ *adjective* between people

interpersonal communication /ˌɪntəpɜːs(ə)n(ə)l kəmjuːnɪˈkeɪʃ(ə)n/ *noun* any kind of communication that takes place between individual people or between the members of a group

interpersonal relations /ˌɪntəpɜːs(ə)n(ə)l rɪˈleɪʃ(ə)nz/ *plural noun* relations, communications and dealing with people

interpersonal skills /ˌɪntəpɜːs(ə)n(ə)l ˈskɪlz/ *plural noun* skills used when communicating with other people, especially when negotiating

intervene /ˌɪntəˈviːn/ *verb* to try to make a change in a system □ **to intervene in a dispute** to try to settle a dispute

intervention /ˌɪntəˈvenʃən/ *noun* **1.** acting to make a change in a system ○ *the government's intervention in the labour dispute* **2.** an action taken by an outside agent to change the structure of a large company

interview /ˈɪntəvjuː/ *noun* **1.** a meeting in order to talk to a person who is applying for a job to find out whether they are suitable for it ○ *We called six people for interview.* ○ *I have an interview next week* or *I am going for an interview next week.* **2.** a meeting in order to ask a person questions as part of an opinion poll **3.** a meeting in order to talk to an employee about matters related to their job ○ *During my appraisal interview my boss and I agreed some targets for the next few months.* ■ *verb* to talk to a person applying for a job to see if they are suitable ○ *We interviewed ten candidates, but found no one suitable.*

interviewee /ˌɪntəvjuːˈiː/ *noun* the person who is being interviewed ○ *The interviewer did everything to put the in-*

terviewee at ease. ○ *The interviewees were all nervous as they waited to be called into the interview room.*

interviewer /ˈɪntəvjuːə/ *noun* the person who is conducting an interview

interviewing /ˈɪntəvjuːɪŋ/ *noun* the practice of asking other people questions in order to gain information from or about them, or to assess their abilities or to decide on their suitability for a particular job or position

intimidation /ɪnˌtɪmɪˈdeɪʃ(ə)n/ *noun* a threat to harm someone if they do not do what you want

intranet /ˈɪntrənet/ *noun* a network of computers and telephone links that uses Internet technology but is accessible only to the employees of a particular organisation (NOTE: An intranet that is extended beyond the employees of an organisation to include, for example, suppliers, customers or distributors, it is called an extranet.)

in tray /ˈɪn treɪ/ *noun* a basket on a desk for letters or memos which have been received and are waiting to be dealt with

in-tray learning /ˈɪn treɪ ˌlɜːnɪŋ/ *noun* a training exercise in which the trainee plays the role of a manager and has to deal with the contents of an in tray within a set period of time

in-tray test /ˈɪn treɪ test/, **in-tray exercise** /ˈɪn treɪ ˌeksəsaɪz/ *noun* a method of testing management potential by asking the candidate to deal with a set of problems

intrinsic motivation /ɪnˌtrɪnsɪk məʊtɪˈveɪʃ(ə)n/ *noun* the motivation of staff by satisfying their deepest personal needs

intrinsic reward /ɪnˌtrɪnsɪk rɪˈwɔːd/ *noun* a non-material reward of working in a job (such as status, job satisfaction or human interest) ○ *The intrinsic rewards of the job more than compensated for the low pay.* ○ *Comradeship is one of the intrinsic rewards in this job.* Compare **extrinsic reward**

introduce /ˌɪntrəˈdjuːs/ *verb* to make someone get to know somebody or something □ **to introduce a client** to bring in a new client and make them known to someone

introduction /ˌɪntrə'dʌkʃən/ *noun* the act of bringing into use □ **the introduction of new technology** putting new machines (usually computers) into a business or industry

invalidity /ˌɪnvə'lɪdɪti/ *noun* the condition of being disabled

invalidity benefit /ˌɪnvə'lɪdɪti ˌbenɪfɪt/ *noun* money paid by the government to someone who is permanently disabled

inventory /'ɪnvənt(ə)ri/ *noun* **1.** *(especially US)* all the stock or goods in a warehouse or shop ○ *to carry a high inventory* ○ *to aim to reduce inventory* **2.** *US* a comprehensive list of particular items ○ *The human resources inventory helped decide how many new employees were needed.*
'…a warehouse needs to tie up less capital in inventory and with its huge volume spreads out costs over bigger sales' [*Duns Business Month*]

inverse seniority /ˌɪnvɜːs siːni-'ɒrɪti/ *noun* a scheme which allows for longest-serving employees to be laid off before those most recently recruited

inverted appraisal /ɪnˌvɜːtɪd ə-'preɪz(ə)l/ *noun* an appraisal where a subordinate appraises their manager

investigate /ɪn'vestɪɡeɪt/ *verb* to examine something which may be wrong ○ *The Serious Fraud Office has been asked to investigate his share dealings.*

investigation /ɪnˌvestɪ'ɡeɪʃ(ə)n/ *noun* an examination to find out what is wrong ○ *They conducted an investigation into petty theft in the office.*

Investor in People /ɪnˌvestə ɪn 'piːp(ə)l/ *noun* a national programme for employee development sponsored by the UK government (NOTE: Organisations that meet the required standards in helping their employees to improve their existing skills or learn new ones are awarded the status of an 'Investor in People'.)

invitation /ˌɪnvɪ'teɪʃ(ə)n/ *noun* an act of asking someone to do something ○ *to issue an invitation to someone to join the board* ○ *They advertised the invitation to tender for a contract.*

invite /ɪn'vaɪt/ *verb* to ask someone to do something or to ask for something ○ *to invite someone to an interview* ○ *to invite someone to join the board* ○ *to invite tenders for a contract*

IOU *noun* 'I owe you'; a signed document promising that you will pay back money borrowed ○ *to pay a pile of IOUs* ○ *I have a pile of IOUs which need paying.*

ipsative test /'ɪpsətɪv test/ *noun* a test where the candidate has to choose between various alternative answers (as in a multiple-choice test)

IRA /'aɪrə/ *abbr US* Individual Retirement Account

irrecoverable /ˌɪrɪ'kʌv(ə)rəb(ə)l/ *adjective* which cannot be recovered

irrecoverable debt /ɪrɪˌkʌv(ə)rəb(ə)l 'det/ *noun* a debt which will never be paid

irregular /ɪ'reɡjʊlə/ *adjective* not correct or not done in the correct way ○ *This procedure is highly irregular.*

irregularities /ɪˌreɡjʊ'lærɪtiz/ *plural noun* things which are not done in the correct way and which are possibly illegal
'…the group, which asked for its shares to be suspended last week after the discovery of accounting irregularities, is expected to update investors about its financial predicament by the end of this week' [*Times*]

irregularity /ɪˌreɡjʊ'lærɪti/ *noun* not being regular ○ *the irregularity of the postal deliveries*

IRS *abbr US* Internal Revenue Service

issue /'ɪʃuː/ *noun* a problem being discussed ○ *To bring up the question of VAT will only confuse the issue.* □ **to have issues around** to be concerned about something (*informal*)

IT *abbr* information technology

item validity /'aɪtəm vəˌlɪdɪti/ *noun* the extent to which a test item measures what it is supposed to test

itinerant worker /ɪˌtɪnərənt 'wɜːkə/ *noun* a worker who moves from place to place, looking for work ○ *Most of the workers hired during the summer are itinerant workers.* ○ *Much of the seasonal work on farms is done by itinerant workers.*

J

janitor /'dʒænɪtə/ *noun US* a person who looks after a building, making sure it is clean and that the rubbish is cleared away (NOTE: British English is **caretaker**)

Japanese management /ˌdʒæpəniːz 'mænɪdʒmənt/ *noun* a combination of management styles that emphasises human relations and teamworking and advanced manufacturing techniques such as just-in-time production and total quality management which is credited with bringing about the Japanese economic miracle that began in the 1960s (NOTE: Japanese management practices were studied in the rest of the world in the hope that other countries could imitate Japan's economic success, but the downturn in the Japanese economy that began in the 1990s has forced the Japanese themselves to reassess them.)

JIT production *abbr* just-in-time production

job /dʒɒb/ *noun* **1.** a piece of work □ **to do a job of work** to be given a job of work to do □ **to do odd jobs** to do various pieces of work ○ *He does odd jobs for us around the house.* □ **to be paid by the job** to be paid for each piece of work done **2.** an order being worked on ○ *We are working on six jobs at the moment.* ○ *The shipyard has a big job starting in August.* **3.** regular paid work ○ *He is looking for a job in the computer industry.* ○ *He lost his job when the factory closed.* ○ *She got a job in a factory.* ○ *He is going to apply for a job in an office.* ○ *Thousands of jobs will be lost if the factories close down.* □ **to look for a job** to try to find work □ **to be out of a job** to have no work □ **to change jobs** to resign from one job and take another □ **to apply for a job** to ask

to be considered for a job, usually in writing □ **to give up your job** to resign from your work □ **to lose your job** to be sacked or made redundant □ **to retire from your job** to leave work and take a pension □ **to have a steady job** to be in a good job, with no chance of being made redundant

'…he insisted that the tax advantages he directed toward small businesses will help create jobs' [*Toronto Star*]

job application /'dʒɒb æplɪˌkeɪʃ(ə)n/ *noun* asking for a job in writing

job application form /'dʒɒb æplɪˌkeɪʃ(ə)n fɔːm/ *noun* a form to be filled in when applying for a job ○ *You have to fill in a job application form.*

jobbing /'dʒɒbɪŋ/ *noun* the practice of doing small pieces of work

jobbing printer /'dʒɒbɪŋ ˌprɪntə/ *noun* a person who does small printing jobs

job ceiling /'dʒɒb ˌsiːlɪŋ/ *noun* the maximum number of employees employed at a given time ○ *The recession has lowered the job ceilings in many companies in this area.* ○ *Raising the job ceiling will enable many less qualified workers to find jobs.*

job centre /'dʒɒb ˌsentə/ *noun* a government office which lists jobs which are vacant ○ *There was a long queue of unemployed people waiting at the job centre.*

job classification /'dʒɒb klæsɪfɪˌkeɪʃ(ə)n/ *noun* the process of describing jobs listed in various groups

jobclub /'dʒɒbklʌb/ *noun* an organisation which helps its members to find jobs ○ *Since joining the jobclub she has improved her interview techniques and gained self-confidence.*

job cuts /'dʒɒb kʌts/ *plural noun* reductions in the number of jobs

job cycle /'dʒɒb ˌsaɪk(ə)l/ *noun* the time taken to complete a particular job

job description /'dʒɒb dɪˌskrɪpʃən/ *noun* a description of what a job consists of and what skills are needed for it ○ *The letter enclosed an application form and a job description.*

job design /'dʒɒb dɪˌzaɪn/ *noun* a decision on what a job should consist of

job dissatisfaction /'dʒɒb dɪsætɪsˌfækʃən/ *noun* an employee's feeling of not being satisfied with their job

job enlargement /'dʒɒb ɪnˌlɑːdʒmənt/ *noun* the expansion of a job by adding further tasks or responsibilities

job enrichment /'dʒɒb ɪnˌrɪtʃmənt/ *noun* the process of making a job more satisfying for the person doing it

job factor /'dʒɒb ˌfæktə/ *noun* an aspect of a job which can be examined and to which scores can be given in job evaluation ○ *One of the most significant job factors considered in the evaluation was the danger involved.*

job family /'dʒɒb ˌfæm(ə)li/ *noun* a group of jobs having similar requirements in terms of personnel

job freeze /'dʒɒb friːz/ *noun* an act of stopping the recruitment of staff in an organisation ○ *The recession has led to a general job freeze in the area.*

job grading /'dʒɒb ˌɡreɪdɪŋ/ *noun* the process of arranging jobs in a certain order of importance ○ *Job grading resulted in certain jobs being relegated to a lower grade.*

job holder /'dʒɒb ˌhəʊldə/ *noun* a person who has a certain job

job hopper /'dʒɒb ˌhɒpə/ *noun* a person who changes jobs often

job hunting /'dʒɒb ˌhʌntɪŋ/ *noun* the process of looking for employment ○ *He bought a guide to job hunting showing how to write a good CV.*

jobless /'dʒɒbləs/ *plural noun* people with no jobs, the unemployed (NOTE: takes a plural verb)

'…the contradiction between the jobless figures and latest economic review' [*Sunday Times*]

job loading /'dʒɒb ˌləʊdɪŋ/ *noun* the act of assigning a job a greater degree of responsibility ○ *Job loading increases the self-esteem of workers whose jobs had seemed unimportant before.*

job measurement /'dʒɒb ˌmeʒəmənt/ *noun* the act of establishing the time necessary for the performance of tasks by a skilled employee

job offer /'dʒɒb ˌɒfə/, **offer of a job** /ˌɒfər əv ə 'dʒɒb/ *noun* a letter from an employer, offering a job

job opening /'dʒɒb ˌəʊp(ə)nɪŋ/ *noun* a job which is empty and needs filling ○ *We have job openings for office staff.*

job opportunities /'dʒɒb ɒpəˌtjuːnɪtiz/ *plural noun* new jobs being available ○ *The increase in export orders has created hundreds of job opportunities.* (NOTE: also called **employment opportunites**)

job performance /'dʒɒb pəˌfɔːməns/ *noun* the degree to which a job is done well or badly

job posting /'dʒɒb ˌpəʊstɪŋ/ *noun* a system of advertising posts internally allowing employees to apply for other jobs within the same organisation

job production /'dʒɒb prəˌdʌkʃən/, **jobbing production** /'dʒɒbɪŋ prəˌdʌkʃən/ *noun* a production system where different articles are produced each to individual specifications

job profile /'dʒɒb ˌprəʊfaɪl/ *noun* a description of a job

job ranking /'dʒɒb ˌræŋkɪŋ/ *noun* a method of assessment where jobs to be assessed are each compared with all the others and a final score for each obtained (NOTE: also called **paired comparisons**)

job requirement /'dʒɒb rɪˌkwaɪəmənt/ *noun* the qualifications or experience needed to start a job

job rotation /'dʒɒb rəʊˌteɪʃ(ə)n/ *noun* the moving of workers from one job to another systematically ○ *Job rotation was instituted to make the work less monotonous.*

jobseeker /'dʒɒbsiːkə/ *noun* a person who is looking for a job

job-share /'dʒɒb ʃeə/ *noun* a form of employment in which two or more people share a single job, each person working part-time and being paid an amount proportionate to the number of hours they work

job simulation exercise /,dʒɒb sɪmjʊ'leɪʃ(ə)n ,eksəsaɪz/ *noun* a test where candidates are put through a simulation of the real job

jobs market /'dʒɒbz ,mɑːkɪt/ *noun* the number of jobs available

job specification /'dʒɒb spesɪfɪ-'keɪʃ(ə)n/ *noun* a very detailed description of what is involved in a job

job squeeze /'dʒɒb skwiːz/ *noun* a process of reducing the numbers of people employed, because of financial restrictions

job study /'dʒɒb ,stʌdi/ *noun* an analysis of all aspects of a job which may affect performance

job ticket /'dʒɒb ,tɪkɪt/ *noun* a document which records when a particular job was started (it is passed from worker to worker as the job progresses)

job title /'dʒɒb ,taɪt(ə)l/ *noun* the name given to a person in a certain job ○ *Her job title is 'Chief Buyer'.*

job vacancy /'dʒɒb ,veɪkənsi/ *noun* a job which is empty and needs someone to do it

Johari window /dʒəʊ,hɑːri 'wɪndəʊ/ *noun* a technique used to analyse how someone gives and receives information and how interpersonal communication works (NOTE: The Johari window is usually represented by a square divided into four sections by a cross, each section representing a type of communication in which a person has differing degrees of awareness of the impact they are making on the other person and of the impact the other person is making on them)

join /dʒɔɪn/ *verb* □ **to join a firm** to start work with a company □ **she joined on January 1st** she started work on January 1st

joinder /'dʒɔɪndə/ *noun* a situation where a union or person is brought in as a party to unfair dismissal proceedings if such a party has been instrumental in the dismissal through some sort of pressure

joint /dʒɔɪnt/ *adjective* **1.** carried out or produced together with others ○ *a joint undertaking* **2.** one of two or more people who work together or who are linked ○ *She and her brother are joint managing directors.*

joint and several liability /,dʒɔɪnt ən ,sev(ə)rəl laɪə'bɪlɪti/ *noun* a situation where someone who has a claim against a group of people can sue them separately or together as a group

joint commission /dʒɔɪnt kə-'mɪʃ(ə)n/ *noun* a group with equal numbers of members from two or more groups ○ *They set up a joint management/union commission.*

joint commission of inquiry /dʒɔɪnt kə,mɪʃ(ə)n əv ɪn'kwaɪəri/ *noun* a commission or committee with representatives of various organisations on it

joint consultation /,dʒɔɪnt kɒnsəl-'teɪʃ(ə)n/ *noun* established channels for discussion between management and employees where management keeps control by disclosing plans to the employee representatives and then asking them to help put them into practice ○ *Joint consultation helps to reduce the possibility of industrial action.*

joint discussions /dʒɔɪnt dɪ-'skʌʃ(ə)nz/ *plural noun* discussions between management and employees

joint ownership /dʒɔɪnt 'əʊnəʃɪp/ *noun* the owning of a property by several owners

joint venture /dʒɔɪnt 'ventʃə/ *noun* a situtation where two or more companies join together for one specific large business project

journal /'dʒɜːn(ə)l/ *noun* **1.** a book with the account of sales and purchases made each day **2.** a magazine

journeyman /'dʒɜːnimən/ *noun US* a skilled craftsman who has completed his apprenticeship

judge /dʒʌdʒ/ *noun* a person who decides in a legal case ○ *The judge sent him to prison for embezzlement.* ■ *verb* to make an assessment about someone or something ○ *to judge an employee's* *managerial potential* ○ *He judged it was time to call an end to the discussions.*

judgement /'dʒʌdʒmənt/, **judgment** *noun* a legal decision or official decision of a court □ **to pronounce judgement**, **to give your judgement on something** to give an official or legal decision about something

judgment debtor /'dʒʌdʒmənt ˌdetə/ *noun* a debtor who has been ordered by a court to pay a debt

judicial /dʒuː'dɪʃ(ə)l/ *adjective* referring to the law

judicial processes /dʒuːˌdɪʃ(ə)l 'prəʊsesɪz/ *plural noun* the ways in which the law works

junior /'dʒuːniə/ *adjective* younger or lower in rank

junior clerk /ˌdʒuːniə 'klɑːk/ *noun* a clerk, usually young, who has lower status than a senior clerk

junior management /ˌdʒuːniə 'mænɪdʒmənt/ *noun* the managers of small departments or deputies to departmental managers

junior partner /ˌdʒuːniə 'pɑːtnə/ *noun* a person who has a small part of the shares in a partnership

junior staff /'dʒuːniə stɑːf/ *noun* **1.** younger members of staff (NOTE: **staff** refers to a group of people and so is often followed by a verb in the plural)

2. people in less important positions in a company

just /dʒʌst/ *adjective* fair and reasonable ○ *The employees don't expect miracles, but they do want a just settlement of the dispute.* ○ *Everyone respected the foreman for his just handling of the affair.*

justice /'dʒʌstɪs/ *noun* **1.** fair treatment in law ○ *The employee lost her case for unfair dismissal and felt that justice had not been done.* **2.** fairness and reasonableness ○ *The union negotiators impressed on the management the justice of their demands.*

justify /'dʒʌstɪfaɪ/ *verb* to give an excuse for or to give a reason for ○ *The employees' representatives produced a mass of documents to justify their wage claim.* ○ *The HR manager was asked to justify the dismissal before the industrial tribunal.* (NOTE: **justifies – justifying – justified**)

just-in-time production /ˌdʒʌst ɪn ˌtaɪm prə'dʌkʃən/ *noun* the practice of making goods to order just before they are needed, so as to avoid having too many goods in stock. Abbr **JIT**

juvenile /'dʒuːvənaɪl/ *adjective*, *noun* young (person)

juvenile labour /ˌdʒuːvənaɪl 'leɪbə/ *noun* children and other young people employed under special conditions (e.g. in films)

K

K *abbr* one thousand □ **'salary: £20K+'** salary more than £20,000 per annum

keen /kiːn/ *adjective* eager or active □ **keen competition** strong competition ○ *We are facing some keen competition from European manufacturers.*

Keogh plan /'kiːəʊ ˌplæn/ *noun US* a private pension system allowing self-employed businesspeople and professionals to set up pension and retirement plans for themselves

key /kiː/ *adjective* important ○ *a key factor* ○ *key industries* ○ *key personnel* ○ *a key member of our management team* ○ *She has a key post in the organisation.* ○ *We don't want to lose any key staff in the reorganisation.* ■ *verb* □ **to key in data** to put information into a computer

'…he gave up the finance job in September to devote more time to his global responsibilities as chairman and to work more closely with key clients' [*Times*]

key job /kiː 'dʒɒb/ *noun* a very important job

key-person insurance /'kiː pɜːs(ə)n ɪnˌʃʊərəns/ *noun* an insurance policy taken out to cover the costs of replacing an employee who is particularly important to an organisation if they die or are ill for a long time

kickback /'kɪkbæk/ *noun* an illegal commission paid to someone, especially a government official, who helps in a business deal

kiss up to /kɪs 'ʌp tʊ/ *verb US* to attempt to win the favour of someone who is in a position of power by flattering and being very attentive to them (*informal*)

knock off /ˌnɒk 'ɒf/ *verb* to stop work ○ *We knocked off at 3p.m. on Friday.*

knock-on effect /'nɒk ɒn ɪˌfekt/ *noun* the effect which an action will have on other situations ○ *The strike by customs officers has had a knock-on effect on car production by slowing down exports of cars.*

know /nəʊ/ *verb* **1.** to learn or to have information about something ○ *Does she know how long it takes to get to the airport?* ○ *The managing director's secretary does not know where he is.* ○ *He knows the African market very well.* ○ *I don't know how a computer works.* **2.** to have met someone ○ *Do you know Ms Jones, our new sales director?* (NOTE: **knowing – knew – known**)

know-how /'nəʊ haʊ/ *noun* knowledge or skill in a particular field ○ *to acquire computer know-how* ○ *If we cannot recruit staff with the right know-how, we will have to initiate an ambitious training programme.*

knowledge /'nɒlɪdʒ/ *noun* what is known

knowledge-based assessment /ˌnɒlɪdʒ beɪst əˈsesmənt/ *noun* the appraisal of an employee based on how much they know as opposed to the ability they have to put their knowledge into practice. Compare **performance-based assessment**

knowledge worker /'nɒlɪdʒ ˌwɜːkə/ *noun* an employee whose value to an organisation lies in the information, ideas and expertise that they possess

L

laboratory /ləˈbɒrət(ə)ri/ *noun* a place where scientific research is carried out ○ *The product was developed in the company's laboratories.* ○ *All products are tested in our own laboratories.* (NOTE: plural is **laboratories**)

laboratory technician /ləˌbɒrət(ə)ri tekˈnɪʃ(ə)n/ *noun* a person who deals with practical work in a laboratory

laboratory training /ləˈbɒrət(ə)ri ˌtreɪnɪŋ/ *noun* a form of group training method for management trainees, designed to improve social skills and self-confidence through counselling, role-playing and simulation exercises ○ *Laboratory training has been important in improving self-confidence in future sales staff.* ○ *Laboratory training will be used to complement our training in accountancy and marketing.*

Labor Day /ˈleɪbə deɪ/ *noun* an American national holiday celebrated on the first Monday in September

labor union /ˈleɪbə ˌjʊnjən/ *noun* US an organisation which represents employees who are its members in discussions about wages and conditions of work with management (NOTE: British English is **trade union**)

labour /ˈleɪbə/ *noun* **1.** heavy work □ **to charge for materials and labour** to charge for both the materials used in a job and also the hours of work involved □ **labour is charged at £5 an hour** each hour of work costs £5 **2.** workers, the workforce ○ *We will need to employ more labour if production is to be increased.* ○ *The costs of labour are rising in line with inflation.* □ **labour shortage, shortage of labour** a situation where there are not enough workers to fill jobs **3.** □ **labour laws, labour leg-**islation laws relating to the employment of workers (NOTE: the American spelling is **labor**)

labour agreement /ˈleɪbər əˌɡriːmənt/, **labour contract** /ˈleɪbə ˌkɒntrækt/ *noun* a legal document which is negotiated between the union and the employer ○ *After intensive bargaining a labour agreement was drawn up.* ○ *The new labour contract allows for a higher rate of pay.*

labour charges /ˈleɪbə ˌtʃɑːdʒɪz/ *plural noun* the cost of the workers employed to make a product (not including materials or overheads)

labour dispute /ˈleɪbə dɪˌspjuːt/ *noun* a conflict or disagreement between employer and employees or between the groups who represent them

labourer /ˈleɪbərə/ *noun* a person who does heavy work

labour force /ˈleɪbə fɔːs/ *noun* all the workers in a company or in an area ○ *We are opening a new factory in the Far East because of the cheap local labour force.*
'70 per cent of Australia's labour force is employed in service activity' [*Australian Financial Review*]

labour force participation rate /ˌleɪbə fɔːs pɑːtɪsɪˈpeɪʃ(ə)n reɪt/ *noun* the proportion of people in the labour force who are working

labour force survey /ˈleɪbə fɔːs ˌsɜːveɪ/ *noun* a survey carried out four times a year in the United Kingdom to gain information about such topics as unemployment and hours of work

labour grading /ˈleɪbə ˌɡreɪdɪŋ/, **labour ranking** /ˈleɪbə ˌrænkɪŋ/ *noun* the process of arranging jobs in order of importance in an organisation, and therefore the pay which is suitable for each job

labour injunction /'leɪbər ɪn-ˌdʒʌŋkʃən/ *noun* a court order requiring an individual or group in an industry to stop certain actions considered damaging to another

labour-intensive /ˌleɪbər ɪn'tensɪv/ *adjective* referring to an industry which needs large numbers of employees or where labour costs are high in relation to turnover ○ *As the business became more labour-intensive, so human resources management became more important.* ○ *With computerisation, the business has become much less labour-intensive.*

labour laws /'leɪbə lɔːz/ *plural noun* laws concerning the employment of workers

labour market /'leɪbə ˌmɑːkɪt/ *noun* the number of people who are available for work ○ *25,000 school-leavers have just come on to the labour market.*

'European economies are being held back by rigid labor markets and wage structures' [*Duns Business Month*]

labour mobility /ˌleɪbə məʊ'bɪlɪti/, **mobility of labour** /məʊˌbɪlɪti əv 'leɪbə/ *noun* a situation in which people agree to move from one place to another to get work, or change skills within the same organisation ○ *Acute unemployment dramatically increased mobility of labour.*

labour relations /'leɪbə rɪˌleɪʃ(ə)nz/ *plural noun* relations between management and employees ○ *The company has a history of bad labour relations.*

labour reserve /'leɪbə rɪˌzɜːv/ *noun* the people in the labour force who are not working

labour-saving /'leɪbə ˌseɪvɪŋ/ *adjective* avoiding the need for work by someone ○ *Costs will be cut by the introduction of labour-saving devices.*

labour stability index /ˌleɪbə stə-'bɪlɪti ˌɪndeks/ *noun* an index showing the percentage of employees who have been in their jobs for more than one year

labour tourist /'leɪbə ˌtʊərɪst/ *noun* someone who lives in one country but works in another

labour turnover /'leɪbə ˌtɜːnəʊvə/, **turnover of labour** /ˌtɜːnəʊvə əv 'leɪbə / *noun* the movement of employees with some leaving their jobs and others joining

labour wastage /'leɪbə ˌweɪstɪdʒ/ *noun* the loss of employees over a period of time ○ *Labour wastage in the last five years has been rising owing to an increase in people taking early retirement.*

lack /læk/ *noun* the fact of not having enough ■ *verb* not to have enough of something ○ *The industry lacks skilled staff.*

lack of incentive /ˌlæk əv ɪn-'sentɪv/ *noun* not having enough incentive

ladder /'lædə/ *noun* **1.** a series of steps made of wood or metal which can be moved about, and which you can climb ○ *You will need a ladder to look into the machine.* **2.** a series of different levels through which an employee may progress

large /lɑːdʒ/ *adjective* very big or important ○ *Our company is one of the largest suppliers of computers to the government.* ○ *Why has she got an office which is larger than mine?*

largely /'lɑːdʒli/ *adverb* mainly or mostly ○ *Our sales are largely in the home market.* ○ *They have largely pulled out of the American market.*

large-scale /'lɑːdʒ skeɪl/ *adjective* involving large numbers of people or large amounts of money ○ *large-scale investment in new technology* ○ *large-scale redundancies in the construction industry*

last /lɑːst/ *adjective, adverb* **1.** coming at the end of a series ○ *Out of a queue of twenty people, I was served last.* ○ *This is our last board meeting before we move to our new offices.* ○ *We finished the last items in the order just two days before the promised delivery date.* **2.** most recent or most recently ○ *Where is the last batch of invoices?* ○ *The last ten orders were only for small quantities.*

last in first out /ˌlɑːst ˌɪn fɜːst 'aʊt/ *noun* a redundancy policy using the principle that the people who have been most recently appointed are the first to be made redundant. Abbr **LIFO**

last quarter /lɑːst ˈkwɔːtə/ *noun* a period of three months at the end of the financial year

last week /lɑːst ˈwiːk/, **last month** /lɑːst ˈmʌnθ/, **last year** /lɑːst ˈjɪə/ *noun* the week or month or year before this one ○ *Last week's sales were the best we have ever had.* ○ *The sales managers have been asked to report on last month's drop in unit sales.* ○ *Last year's accounts have to be ready in time for the AGM.*

lateral /ˈlæt(ə)rəl/ *adjective* at the same level or with the same status ○ *Her transfer to Marketing was something of a lateral move.*

lateral relations /ˌlæt(ə)rəl rɪˈleɪʃ(ə)nz/ *plural noun* relations between people of the same grade in an organisation ○ *The struggle for promotion has soured lateral relations.*

lateral transfer /ˌlæt(ə)rəl ˈtrænsfɜː/ *noun* an act of moving an employee to another job at the same level in the organisation ○ *I was pleased with my new job, even though it was a lateral transfer and not a promotion.*

law /lɔː/ *noun* **1.** □ the **law** all the laws of a country taken together □ **to take someone to law** to tell someone to appear in court to settle an argument □ **inside** *or* **within the law** obeying the laws of a country □ **against** *or* **outside the law** not according to the laws of a country ○ *The company is possibly operating outside the law.* □ **to break the law** to do something which is not allowed by law ○ *He is breaking the law by trading without a licence.* **2.** a general rule

law courts /ˈlɔː kɔːts/ *plural noun* a place where a judge listens to cases and decides who is right legally

law of diminishing returns /ˌlɔːr əv dɪˌmɪnɪʃɪŋ rɪˈtɜːnz/ *noun* a general rule that as more factors of production such as land, labour and capital are added to the existing factors, so the amount they produce is proportionately smaller

law of effect /ˌlɔː əv ɪˈfekt/ *noun* the principle that behaviour which is re-

warded will be repeated ○ *Payment by results was designed to put the law of effect into practice.*

law of supply and demand /ˌlɔːr əv səˌplaɪ ən dɪˈmɑːnd/ *noun* a general rule that the amount of a product which is available is related to the needs of potential customers

lawsuit /ˈlɔːsuːt/ *noun* a case brought to a court □ **to bring a lawsuit against someone** to tell someone to appear in court to settle an argument □ **to defend a lawsuit** to appear in court to state your case

lawyer /ˈlɔːjə/ *noun* a person who has studied law and practises law as a profession

lay /leɪ/ *verb* to put □ **to lay an embargo on trade with a country** to forbid trade with a country (NOTE: **laying – laid**)

lay off /ˌleɪ ˈɒf/ *verb* to dismiss employees for a time (until more work is available) ○ *The factory laid off half its workers because of lack of orders.*

'...the company lost $52 million last year, and has laid off close to 2,000 employees' [*Toronto Star*]

lay-off /ˈleɪ ɒf/ *noun* **1.** an act of temporarily dismissing an employee for a period of more than four weeks ○ *The recession has caused hundreds of lay-offs in the car industry.* **2.** *US* same as **redundancy**

lazy /ˈleɪzi/ *adjective* referring to a person who does not want to work ○ *She is too lazy to do any overtime.* ○ *He is so lazy he does not even send in his expense claims on time.*

leader /ˈliːdə/ *noun* a person who manages or directs others ○ *the leader of the construction workers' union* or *the construction workers' leader*

leaderless discussion /ˌliːdələs dɪˈskʌʃ(ə)n/ *noun* a way of assessing candidates for a post, by putting them together in a group and asking them to discuss a problem, without appointing one of them as chairman

leadership /ˈliːdəʃɪp/ *noun* **1.** a quality that enables a person to manage or administer others ○ *Employees showing leadership potential will be chosen for* *management training.* **2.** a group of people who manage or administer an organisation ○ *The elections have changed the composition of the union leadership.* (NOTE: no plural)

leading /'liːdɪŋ/ *adjective* most important ○ *Leading industrialists feel the end of the recession is near.* ○ *They are the leading company in the field.*

leading indicator /ˌliːdɪŋ 'ɪndɪkeɪtə/ *noun* an indicator (such as manufacturing order books) which shows a change in economic trends earlier than other indicators

lead partner /'liːd ˌpɑːtnə/ *noun* the organisation that takes the leading role in an alliance

lead time /'liːd taɪm/ *noun* **1.** the time between deciding to place an order and receiving the product ○ *The lead time on this item is more than six weeks.* **2.** the time between the start of a task and its completion

leak /liːk/ *verb* to pass on secret information ○ *Information on the contract was leaked to the press.* ○ *They discovered an employee was leaking information to a rival company.*

leaky reply /ˌliːki rɪ'plaɪ/ *noun* a reply by email that is accidentally sent to the wrong person and causes embarrassment to the sender (*slang*)

lean /liːn/ *adjective* slim and efficient ○ *After the cutbacks in staff, the company is leaner and hungrier.*

lean management /liːn 'mænɪdʒmənt/ *noun* a style of management, where few managers are employed, allowing decisions to be taken rapidly

lean production /liːn prə'dʌkʃən/, **lean operation** /liːn ɒpə'reɪʃ(ə)n/ *noun* a production method which reduces excessive expenditure on staff and concentrates on efficient low-cost manufacturing

leap-frogging /'liːp 'frɒgɪŋ/ *adjective* □ **leap-frogging pay demands** pay demands where each section of employee asks for higher pay to do better than another section, which then asks for further increases in turn ■ *noun* communication which by-passes

the official chain of command ○ *Leap-frogging caused much resentment among middle managers who felt left out of decisions.*

learning /'lɜːnɪŋ/ *noun* the process of receiving and assimilating information or skills ○ *The learning of new skills is hard for our senior employees who are nearing retirement.* ○ *The trainees all had different learning potentials.*

Learning and Skills Council /ˌlɜːnɪŋ ən 'skɪlz ˌkaʊnsəl/ *noun* a governement organisation responsible for the education and training of people over the age of 16

learning by doing /ˌlɜːnɪŋ baɪ 'duːɪŋ/ *noun* the gaining of knowledge or skills through direct experience of carrying out tasks, usually under supervision and as part of a training or induction process

learning curve /'lɜːnɪŋ kɜːv/ *noun* **1.** a diagram or graph that represents the way in which people gain knowledge or experience over time (NOTE: A steep learning curve represents a situation where people learn a great deal in a short time; a shallow curve represents a slower learning process. The curve eventually levels out, representing the time when the knowledge gained is being consolidated.) **2.** the decrease in the effort required to produce each single item when the total number of items produced is doubled (NOTE: The concept of the learning curve has its origin in productivity research in the aircraft industry of the 1930s, when it was discovered that the time and effort needed to assemble an aircraft decreased by 20% each time the total number produced doubled.)

learning difficulty /'lɜːnɪŋ ˌdɪfɪk(ə)lti/ *noun* a condiiton which prevents someone from learning basic skills or assimilating information as easily as other people (NOTE: plural is **learning difficulties**)

learning organisation /'lɜːnɪŋ ɔːgənaɪˌzeɪʃ(ə)n/ *noun* an organisation whose employees are willing and eager to share information with each other, to learn from each other, and to work as a team to achieve their goals

learning relationship /'lɜːnɪŋ rɪ-ˌleɪʃ(ə)nʃɪp/ *noun* a relationship between a supplier and a customer in which the supplier changes and adapts a product as it learns more about the customer's requirements

learning style /'lɜːnɪŋ staɪl/ *noun* the way in which someone approaches the task of acquiring knowledge and skills (NOTE: There are commonly thought to be four main types of learner: the activist, who likes to get involved in new experiences and enjoys change; the theorist, who likes to question established assumptions and methods and learns best when there is time to explore links between ideas and situations; the pragmatist, who learns best when there is a link between the subject matter and the job in hand and they can try out in practice what they have learned; and the reflector, who likes to take time and think things through, and who learns best from activities where they can observe how tasks are carried out.)

leave /liːv/ *noun* permission to be away from work □ **six weeks' annual leave** six weeks' holiday each year □ **to go** *or* **be on leave** to be away from work ○ *She is away on sick leave* or *on maternity leave.* ■ *verb* **1.** to go away from ○ *He left his office early to go to the meeting.* ○ *The next plane leaves at 10.20.* **2.** to resign ○ *He left his job and bought a farm.* (NOTE: **leaving – left**)

leave of absence /ˌliːv əv 'æbsəns/ *noun* permission to be absent from work ○ *He asked for leave of absence to visit his mother in hospital.*

leaver /'liːvə/ *noun* a person who has left

leaver's statement /'liːvəz ˌsteɪtmənt/ *noun* an official document given to someone who is leaving a company and has recently received statutory sick pay

ledger /'ledʒə/ *noun* a book in which accounts are written

legal /'liːg(ə)l/ *adjective* **1.** according to the law or allowed by the law ○ *The company's action in sacking the accountant was completely legal.* **2.** referring to the law □ **to take legal advice** to

ask a lawyer to advise about a legal problem

legal adviser /ˌliːg(ə)l əd'vaɪzə/ *noun* a person who advises clients about the law

Legal Aid /'liːg(ə)l eɪd/, **Legal Aid scheme** /ˌliːg(ə)l 'eɪd skiːm/ *noun* a British government scheme where a person with very little money can have legal representation and advice paid for by the state

Legal Aid Centre /ˌliːg(ə)l 'eɪd ˌsentə/ *noun* a local office giving advice to clients about applications for Legal Aid and recommending clients to solicitors

legal costs /'liːg(ə)l kɒsts/, **legal charges** /'liːg(ə)l ˌtʃɑːdʒɪz/, **legal expenses** /'liːg(ə)l ɪkˌspensɪz/ *plural noun* money spent on fees to lawyers ○ *The clerk could not afford the legal expenses involved in suing his boss.*

legally /'liːgəli/ *adverb* according to the law □ **directors are legally responsible** the law says that the directors are responsible

legal profession /'liːg(ə)l prəˌfeʃ(ə)n/ *noun* all qualified lawyers

legislation /ˌledʒɪ'sleɪʃ(ə)n/ *noun* laws

legitimate /lɪ'dʒɪtɪmət/ *adjective* allowed by law ○ *He has a legitimate claim to the property.*

legitimate grievance /lɪˌdʒɪtɪmət 'griːv(ə)ns/ *noun* an employee's grievance based on an actual violation of a contract of employment ○ *The employee received no compensation since he had no legitimate grievance.* ○ *The human resources department considered that the treatment of employees should be such that no legitimate grievance could be claimed.*

leisure /'leʒə/ *noun* time free from work or other obligations ○ *The organisation is trying to encourage constructive leisure pursuits.* ○ *The company provides many leisure facilities such as tennis courts and a swimming pool.* ○ *Too much work and not enough leisure had an adverse effect on his family life.*

leisure activities /ˈleʒər ækˌtɪvɪtiz/ *plural noun* what you do in your spare time

leisure time /ˈleʒə taɪm/ *noun* a time when you are not at work, used for amusement, hobbies, etc. (NOTE: also called **spare time**)

length /leŋθ/ *noun* a measurement of how long something is

length of service /ˌleŋθ əv ˈsɜːvɪs/ *noun* the number of years someone has worked

leniency /ˈliːniənsi/ *noun* the quality of not being strict in dealing with subordinates ○ *Given the employee's good work record, she was treated with leniency by her superior.*

leniency bias /ˈliːniənsi ˌbaɪəs/ *noun* an unjustifiably high rating of an employee's job performance ○ *Leniency bias works against objectivity in performance appraisal.*

let go /let ˈɡəʊ/ *verb* to make someone redundant or to sack someone (*euphemism*) (NOTE: **letting – let**)

letter /ˈletə/ *noun* **1.** a piece of writing sent from one person or company to another to ask for or to give information **2.** □ **to acknowledge receipt by letter** to write a letter to say that something has been received **3.** a written or printed sign (such as A, B, C, etc.) ○ *Write your name and address in block letters* or *in capital letters.*

letter box /ˈletə bɒks/ *noun* a place where incoming mail is put

letter heading /ˈletə ˌhedɪŋ/ *noun* the name and address of a company printed at the top of a piece of notepaper

letter of acknowledgement /ˌletər əv əkˈnɒlɪdʒmənt/ *noun* a letter which says that something has been received

letter of application /ˌletər əv æplɪˈkeɪʃ(ə)n/ *noun* a letter in which someone applies for a job

letter of appointment /ˌletər əv əˈpɔɪntmənt/ *noun* a letter in which someone is appointed to a job

letter of attorney /ˌletər əv əˈtɜːni/ *noun* a document showing that someone has power of attorney

letter of complaint /ˌletər əv kəmˈpleɪnt/ *noun* a letter in which someone complains

letter of dismissal /ˌletər əv dɪsˈmɪs(ə)l/ *noun* an official letter notifying someone that they have been dismissed

letter of introduction /ˌletər əv ɪntrəˈdʌkʃən/ *noun* a letter making someone get to know another person ○ *I'll give you an introduction to the MD – he's an old friend of mine.*

letter of offer /ˌletər əv ˈɒfə/ *noun* a letter which offers someone a job

letter of recommendation /ˌletər əv rekəmənˈdeɪʃ(ə)n/ *noun* a letter in which the writer recommends someone for a job

letter of reference /ˌletər əv ˈref(ə)rəns/ *noun* a letter in which an employer recommends someone for a new job

letter of resignation /ˌletər əv rezɪɡˈneɪʃ(ə)n/ *noun* a letter in which an employee resigns from their job

level /ˈlev(ə)l/ *noun* the position of something compared to others ○ *to raise the level of employee benefits* □ **a decision taken at the highest level** a decision taken by the most important person or group □ **low-level** not very important ○ *a low-level delegation* □ **high-level** very important ○ *a high-level meeting*

'…employers having got their staff back up to a reasonable level are waiting until the scope for overtime working is exhausted before hiring' [*Sydney Morning Herald*]

level playing field /ˌlev(ə)l ˈpleɪɪŋ fiːld/ *noun* a situation in which the same rules apply for all competitors and none of them has any special advantage over the others

leverage /ˈliːvərɪdʒ/ *noun* **1.** an influence which you can use to achieve an aim ○ *He has no leverage over the chairman.* **2.** borrowing money at fixed interest which is then used to produce more money than the interest paid

leveraged buyout /ˌliːvərɪdʒd ˈbaɪaʊt/, **leveraged takeover** /ˌliːvərɪdʒd ˈteɪkəʊvə/ *noun* an act of buying all the shares in a company by borrowing money against the security of the shares to be bought. Abbr **LBO**

'...the offer came after management had offered to take the company private through a leveraged buyout for $825 million' [*Fortune*]

levy /'levi/ *noun* money which is demanded and collected by the government ■ *verb* to demand payment of a tax or an extra payment and to collect it ○ *to levy a duty on the import of luxury items* ○ *The government has decided to levy a tax on imported cars.*

'...royalties have been levied at a rate of 12.5% of full production' [*Lloyd's List*]

liability /ˌlaɪə'bɪlɪti/ *noun* **1.** a legal responsibility for damage, loss or harm ○ *The two partners took out insurance to cover employers' liability.* □ **to accept liability for something** to agree that you are responsible for something □ **to refuse liability for something** to refuse to agree that you are responsible for something **2.** someone or something which represents a loss to a person or organisation ○ *The sales director is an alcoholic and has become a liability to the company.*

liability insurance /ˌlaɪə'bɪlɪti ɪnˌʃʊərəns/ *noun* insurance that protects a person or organisation against the financial consequences of being held legally responsible for something, e.g. for causing an accident

liable /'laɪəb(ə)l/ *adjective* □ **liable for** legally responsible for ○ *The chairman was personally liable for the company's debts.* ○ *The garage is liable for damage to customers' cars.*

liaison /li'eɪz(ə)n/ *noun* the process of keeping someone informed of what is happening

liaison officer /li'eɪz(ə)n ˌɒfɪsə/ *noun* a person whose job it is to keep someone else informed of what is happening ○ *The human resources manager was appointed liaison officer with the unions over relocation.*

licence /'laɪs(ə)ns/ *noun* **1.** an official document which allows someone to do something **2.** □ **goods manufactured under licence** goods made with the permission of the owner of the copyright or patent (NOTE: the American spelling is **license**)

licence agreement /'laɪs(ə)ns əˌɡriːmənt/ *noun* a contractual agreement by which a patent owner or copyright owner allows a company to manufacture something and pay a fee for this

license /'laɪs(ə)ns/ *noun* US spelling of **licence** ■ *verb* to give someone official permission to do something for a fee, e.g. when a company allows another company to manufacture its products abroad ○ *licensed to sell beers, wines and spirits* ○ *to license a company to manufacture spare parts* ○ *She is licensed to run an employment agency.*

lieu /ljuː/ *noun* □ **in lieu of** instead of □ **she was given two months' salary in lieu of notice** she was given two months' salary and asked to leave immediately

life /laɪf/ *noun* **1.** the period of time for which something or someone exists □ **for life** for as long as someone is alive ○ *His pension gives him a comfortable income for life.* **2.** being alive

life annuity /'laɪf əˌnjuːɪti/ *noun* annual payments made to someone as long as they are alive

life assurance /'laɪf əˌʃʊərəns/ *noun* insurance which pays a sum of money when someone dies, or at a certain date if they are still alive

life assured /laɪf ə'ʃʊəd/ *noun* the person whose life has been covered by the life assurance

life cover /'laɪf ˌkʌvə/ *noun* same as **life assurance**

life expectancy /laɪf ɪk'spektənsi/ *noun* the number of years a person is likely to live

life insurance /'laɪf ɪn'ʃʊərəns/ *noun* same as **life assurance**

life insured /laɪf ɪn'ʃʊəd/ *noun* same as **life assured**

life-long employment /ˌlaɪf lɒŋ ɪm'plɔɪmənt/ *noun* the concept (common in Japan) that an employee who enters a company when young will be guaranteed employment by that company for the rest of their working life

lifelong learning /ˌlaɪf lɒŋ 'lɜːnɪŋ/ *noun* a process of gaining knowledge and skills which continues throughout a person's life (NOTE: Lifelong learning occurs through formal and informal education systems, both within and outside the workplace, and is seen as a key element in CPD and an important tool in maintaining a person's employability in a rapidly changing business environment.)

life policy /'laɪf ˌpɒlɪsi/ *noun* a life assurance contract

life skills /'laɪf skɪlz/ *plural noun* skills used in dealing with other people

LIFO /'laɪfəʊ/ *abbr* last in first out

light industry /ˌlaɪt 'ɪndəstri/ *noun* an industry making small products such as clothes, books or calculators

lightning strike /'laɪtnɪŋ straɪk/ *noun* a strike which is called suddenly and only lasts a short time

limit /'lɪmɪt/ *noun* the point at which something ends or the point where you can go no further □ **to set limits to imports**, **to impose import limits** to allow only a specific amount of imports ■ *verb* to restrict the number or amount of something

limited /'lɪmɪtɪd/ *adjective* restricted

limited company /ˌlɪmɪtɪd 'kʌmp(ə)ni/, **limited liability company** /ˌlɪmɪtɪd laɪə'bɪlɪti ˌkʌmp(ə)ni/ *noun* a company where each shareholder is responsible for repaying the company's debts only to the face value of the shares they own (NOTE: shortened to **Ltd**)

limited liability /ˌlɪmɪtɪd laɪə'bɪlɪti/ *noun* a situation where someone's liability for debt is limited by law

limited partnership /ˌlɪmɪtɪd 'pɑːtnəʃɪp/ *noun* a registered business where the liability of the partners is limited to the amount of capital they have each provided to the business and where the partners may not take part in the running of the business

line /laɪn/ *noun* **1.** a row of letters or figures on a page **2.** a series of things, one after another □ **to be in line for promotion** to be the next to be promoted □ **to bring someone into line** to make someone do the same as the others **3.** *US* a row of people waiting one after the other (NOTE: British English is **queue**) □ **to be on the breadline**, **on the poverty line** to be so poor as to have hardly enough to live on **4.** a short letter

□ **to drop someone a line** to send someone a note **5.** □ **the line is bad** it is difficult to hear clearly what someone is saying □ **the line is engaged** the person is already speaking on the phone □ **to be on the line to someone** to be telephoning someone

line authority /'laɪn ɔːˌθɒrəti/ *noun* the power to direct others and make decisions regarding the operations of the organisation

line management /'laɪn ˌmænɪdʒmənt/, **line organisation** /'laɪn ɔːgənaɪˌzeɪʃ(ə)n/ *noun* the organisation of a company where each manager is responsible for doing what their superior tells them to do

line manager /'laɪn ˌmænɪdʒə/ *noun* a manager responsible to a superior, but with authority to give orders to other employees

line of business /ˌlaɪn əv 'bɪznɪs/ *noun* a type of business or work

line organisation /'laɪn ɔːgənaɪˌzeɪʃ(ə)n/ *noun* same as **line management**

liquidation /ˌlɪkwɪ'deɪʃ(ə)n/ *noun* the winding up or closing of a company and selling of its assets

list /lɪst/ *noun* several items written one after the other ○ *They have an attractive list of products* or *product list.* ○ *I can't find that item on our stock list.* ○ *Please add this item to the list.* ○ *She crossed the item off her list.*

listed company /ˌlɪstɪd 'kʌmp(ə)ni/ *noun* a company whose shares can be bought or sold on the Stock Exchange

litigant /'lɪtɪgənt/ *noun* a person who brings a lawsuit against someone

litigate /'lɪtɪgeɪt/ *verb* to go to law or to bring a lawsuit against someone to have a dispute settled

litigation /ˌlɪtɪ'geɪʃ(ə)n/ *noun* the bringing of a lawsuit against someone

litigious /lɪ'tɪdʒəs/ *adjective* referring to a person who likes to bring lawsuits against other people

livery /'lɪvəri/ *noun* a company's own special design and colours, used e.g. on uniforms, office decoration and vehicles

living /'lɪvɪŋ/ *noun* □ **she does not earn a living wage** she does not earn enough to pay for essentials such as food, heat and rent □ **to make a living** to earn enough to pay for your living expenses ○ *He makes a good living from selling secondhand cars.*

living expenses /'lɪvɪŋ ɪk,spensɪz/ *plural noun* money spent on rent, food, etc., which may be paid by the company if the worker has been asked to live away from home

loading /'ləʊdɪŋ/ *noun* the process of assigning work to workers or machines ○ *The production manager has to ensure that careful loading makes the best use of human resources.*

lobby /'lɒbi/ *noun* a group of people who try to influence MPs, members of town councils, etc. □ **the energy-saving lobby** people who try to persuade MPs to pass laws to save energy

local *adjective* /'ləʊk(ə)l/ located in or providing a service for a restricted area ■ *noun US* a branch of a national trade union

local authority /,ləʊk(ə)l ɔː'θɒrɪti/ *noun* an elected section of government which runs a small area of the country

local collective bargaining /,ləʊk(ə)l kə,lektɪv 'bɑːgɪnɪŋ/ *noun* collective bargaining which takes place in the factory or office, and not at national level

Local Commissioner /,ləʊk(ə)l kə-'mɪʃ(ə)nə/, **Local Government Ombudsman** /,ləʊk(ə)l ,gʌvənmənt 'ɒmbʊdzmən/ *noun* an official who investigates complaints against local authorities

local labour /,ləʊk(ə)l 'leɪbə/ *noun* workers who are recruited near a factory, and are not brought there from a distance

locally /'ləʊk(ə)li/ *adverb* in the area near where an office or factory is based ○ *We recruit all our staff locally.*

lock /lɒk/ *noun* a device for closing a door or box so that it can be opened only with a key ○ *The lock is broken on the petty cash box.* ○ *I have forgotten the combination of the lock on my briefcase.* ■ *verb* to close a door with a key, so that

it cannot be opened ○ *The manager forgot to lock the door of the computer room.* ○ *The petty cash box was not locked.*

lock out /,lɒk 'aʊt/ *verb* □ **to lock out workers** to shut the factory door so that workers cannot get in and so force them not to work until the conditions imposed by the management are met

lockout /'lɒkaʊt/ *noun* an industrial dispute where the management will not let the workers into the factory until they have agreed to the management's conditions

lodge /lɒdʒ/ *verb* □ **to lodge a complaint against someone** to make an official complaint about someone

log of claims /,lɒg əv 'kleɪmz/ *noun* a type of document used in industrial negotiations that lists the demands made by employees on an employer or by an employer on employees

long /lɒŋ/ *adjective* for a large period of time □ **in the long term** over a long period of time

long-distance call /,lɒŋ dɪstəns 'kɔːl/ *noun* a telephone call to a number which is not near

longhand /'lɒŋhænd/ *noun* handwriting where the words are written out in full and not typed or in shorthand ○ *Applications should be written in longhand and sent to the human resources manager.*

long-range /,lɒŋ 'reɪndʒ/ *adjective* for a long period of time in the future □ **long-range economic forecast** a forecast which covers a period of several years

long service award /lɒŋ 'sɜːvɪs ə,wɔːd/, **award for long service** /ə,wɔːd fə lɒŋ 'sɜːvɪs/ *noun* a gift or some other form of recognition given to an employee who has worked for the same organisation for a great many years

long-service leave /lɒŋ 'sɜːvɪs liːv/ *noun* a period of paid leave given by some employers to staff who have completed several years of service

long-standing /,lɒŋ 'stændɪŋ/ *adjective* which has been arranged for a long time ○ *a long-standing agreement*

long-term /ˌlɒŋ ˈtɜːm/ *adjective* for a long time ahead ○ *The management plans are made on a long-term basis.* ○ *Sound long-term planning will give the company more direction.* ○ *It is in the company's long-term interests to have a contented staff.* □ **long-term objectives** aims which will take years to achieve

long-term disability /ˌlɒŋ tɜːm dɪsəˈbɪlɪti/ *noun* a disability which lasts or is likely to last a very long time

Long-Term Disability Plan /ˌlɒŋ tɜːm dɪsəˈbɪlɪti plæn/ *noun* an insurance scheme that pays insured employees a proportion of their wages in the event of disablement

long-term planning /ˌlɒŋ tɜːm ˈplænɪŋ/ *noun* planning for a long time in advance (such as in five years)

loose /luːs/ *adjective* not packed together

loose rate /ˈluːs reɪt/ *noun* a rate applied to an employee earning above the rate earned by other employees in similar jobs requiring similar skills

lose /luːz/ *verb* **1.** not to have something any more □ **to lose one's job** to be made redundant or to be sacked ○ *He lost his job in the reorganisation.* ○ *She lost her job when the factory closed.* □ **number of days lost through strikes** the number of days which are not worked when employees are on strike **2.** to have less money ○ *He lost £25,000 in his father's computer company.* (NOTE: **losing – lost**)

loss /lɒs/ *noun* not having something any more □ **loss of an order** not getting an order which was expected □ **loss of one's job** being made redundant

lost time /lɒst ˈtaɪm/ *noun* the time during which an employee does not work, through no fault of their own ○ *Better logistics will help cut down lost time.*

low /ləʊ/ *adjective* not high or not much ○ *We try to keep our wages bill low.*

low achiever /ˌləʊ əˈtʃiːvə/ *noun* a person who does not do as well as expected

lower /ˈləʊə/ *adjective* smaller or less high ○ *a lower rate of interest* ○ *Sales were lower in June than in May.*

lower earnings limit /ˌləʊər ˈɜːnɪŋz ˌlɪmɪt/ *noun* a minimum earnings level at which an employee has to pay National Insurance contributions

lower limit /ˌləʊə ˈlɪmɪt/ *noun* the bottom limit

lower-paid staff /ˌləʊə peɪd ˈstɑːf/ *noun* staff who are paid less than others

lower ranks /ˈləʊə ræŋks/ *plural noun* employees in less important jobs

low-level /ˌləʊ ˈlev(ə)l/ *adjective* not very important ○ *A low-level meeting decided to put off making a decision.*

low-paid staff /ˌləʊ peɪd ˈstɑːf/ *noun* staff on low salaries

loyal /ˈlɔɪəl/ *adjective* **1.** always buying the same brand or using the same shop ○ *The aim of the advertising is to keep the customers loyal.* **2.** referring to an employee who supports the company they work for (NOTE: you are loyal **to** someone or something)

loyalty /ˈlɔɪəlti/ *noun* being faithful

Ltd *abbr* limited company

lump /lʌmp/ *noun* □ **the Lump**, **Lump labour** self-employed workers who are paid a lump sum for a day's work or for the amount of work completed (often with a view to avoiding tax)

lump sum /lʌmp ˈsʌm/ *noun* money paid in one single amount, not in several small sums ○ *a lump-sum bonus* ○ *She sold her house and invested the money as a lump sum.*

luncheon voucher /ˈlʌnʃən ˌvaʊtʃə/ *noun* a ticket given by an employer to an employee in addition to their wages, which can be exchanged for food in a restaurant

lunch time /ˈlʌntʃ taɪm/ *noun* a time in the middle of the day when people have lunch (for most British offices, from about 12.30 to 1.30pm, or from 1 to 2 p.m.)

lying time /ˈlaɪɪŋ taɪm/ *noun* the time between the end of a period of work and the date on which you are paid for it

M

MA *abbr* maternity allowance

Maastricht Treaty /ˈmɑːstrɪxt ˌtriːti/ *noun* a treaty signed in 1992 which sets out the principles for a European Union and the convergence criteria for states wishing to join the EMU

machine /məˈʃiːn/ *noun* a device which works with power from a motor □ **copying machine** a machine which makes copies of documents, a photocopier

machinery /məˈʃiːnəri/ *noun* **1.** machines **2.** an organisation or a system ○ *the administrative machinery of a university* ○ *the machinery for awarding government contracts*

machinery guard /məˈʃiːnəri gɑːdz/ *noun* a piece of metal to prevent workers from getting hurt by the moving parts of a machine

machine shop /məˈʃiːn ʃɒp/ *noun* a place where working machines are placed

machine tool /məˈʃiːn tuːlz/ *noun* a tool worked by a motor, used to work on wood or metal

machinist /məˈʃiːnɪst/ *noun* a person who operates a machine

Madam Chairman /ˌmædəm ˈtʃeəmən/, **Madam Chairwoman** /ˌmædəm ˈtʃeəwʊmən/ *noun* a way of speaking to the female chairman of a committee or meeting

magazine /ˌmægəˈziːn/ *noun* a paper, usually with pictures and printed on glossy paper, which comes out regularly, every month or every week

mail box /ˈmeɪl bɒks/ *noun* **1.** one of several boxes where incoming mail is put in a large building **2.** a box for putting letters

main /meɪn/ *adjective* most important ○ *Our main office is in Birmingham.* ○ *The main building houses our admin and finance departments.* ○ *One of our main customers has gone into receivership.*

main office /meɪn ˈɒfɪs/ *noun* an office building where the board of directors works and meets

maintain /meɪnˈteɪn/ *verb* **1.** to keep something going or working ○ *We try to maintain good relations with the employees' representatives* **2.** to keep something working at the same level ○ *The company has maintained the same volume of business in spite of the recession.* □ **to maintain a dividend** to pay the same dividend as the previous year

maintenance /ˈmeɪntənəns/ *noun* **1.** the process of keeping things going or working ○ *Maintenance of contacts is important for a sales rep* ○ *It is essential to ensure the maintenance of supplies to the factory.* **2.** the process of keeping a machine in good working order ○ *We offer a full maintenance service.*

'…responsibilities include the maintenance of large computerized databases' [*Times*]

'…the federal administration launched a full-scale investigation into the airline's maintenance procedures' [*Fortune*]

maintenance contract /ˈmeɪntənəns ˌkɒntrækt/ *noun* a contract by which a company keeps a piece of equipment in good working order

maintenance factors /ˈmeɪntənəns ˌfæktəz/ *plural noun* elements at work which create employee dissatisfaction when they are not adequately provided ○ *The reason for the strike was the lack of maintenance factors such as decent rest periods.*

maintenance of membership
/ˌmeɪntənəns əv 'membəʃɪp/ *noun*
US a requirement that employees who
are union members must remain so for
the full duration of their employment in
an organisation

major /'meɪdʒə/ *adjective* important ○
There is a major risk of fire.

'…a client base which includes many major
commercial organizations and nationalized
industries' [*Times*]

majority /mə'dʒɒrɪti/ *noun* **1.** more
than half of a group □ **the board accepted the proposal by a majority of
three to two** three members of the
board voted to accept and two voted
against **2.** the number of votes by which
a person wins an election ○ *He was
elected shop steward with a majority of
three hundred.*

majority vote /mə'dʒɒrɪti vəʊt/,
majority decision /mə'dʒɒrɪti dɪ-
ˌsɪʒ(ə)n/ *noun* a decision made after a
vote according to the wishes of the largest group

make /meɪk/ *noun* a brand or type of
product manufactured ○ *Japanese
makes of cars* ○ *a standard make of
equipment* ○ *What make is the new computer system* or *What's the make of the
new computer system?* ■ *verb* **1.** to produce or to manufacture ○ *The workers
spent ten weeks making the table.* ○ *The
factory makes three hundred cars a day.*
2. to do an action □ **to make a bid for
something** to offer to buy something □
to make a payment to pay □ **to make a
deposit** to pay money as a deposit **3.** to
earn ○ *he makes £50,000 a year* or *£25
an hour* **4.** to increase in value ○ *The
shares made $2.92 in today's trading.*

make good /ˌmeɪk 'ɡʊd/ *verb* **1.** to
repair ○ *The company will make good
the damage.* **2.** to be a success **3.** to
compensate for something ○ *to make
good a loss*

make up /ˌmeɪk 'ʌp/ *verb* to compensate for something □ **to make up a loss
or difference** to pay extra so that the
loss or difference is covered

make-whole remedy /ˌmeɪk 'həʊl
ˌremədi/ *noun* a way of compensating
an employee for their bad treatment in
violation of employment legislation ○

*Make-whole remedies are often consid-
ered insufficient by aggrieved workers.*

make-work practices /'meɪk wɜːk
ˌpræktɪsɪz/ *plural noun* methods of creating work for people who would other-
wise have no work ○ *Make-work
practices are boosting morale in areas
badly hit by the recession.* ○ *Make-work
practices at least provide practical work
experience.*

man /mæn/ *noun* a male worker, especially a manual worker without special
skills or qualifications ○ *All the men
went back to work yesterday.* ■ *verb* to
provide the workforce for something ○
It takes six workers to man a shift. ○ *We
need volunteers to man the exhibition on
Sunday.* ○ *The exhibition stand was
manned by three salesgirls.* (NOTE:
manning – manned. Note also **to
man** does not mean only using men)

manage /'mænɪdʒ/ *verb* **1.** to direct
or to be in charge of ○ *to manage a department* ○ *to manage a branch office* ○
*A competent and motivated person is re-
quired to manage an important department in the company.* **2.** □ **to manage to**
to be able to do something ○ *Did you
manage to see the head buyer?* ○ *She
managed to write six orders and take
three phone calls all in two minutes.*

'…the research director will manage and direct
a team of graduate business analysts reporting
on consumer behaviour throughout the UK'
[*Times*]

management /'mænɪdʒmənt/ *noun*
1. the process of directing or running a
business ○ *She studied management at
university.* ○ *Good management* or *efficient management is essential in a large
organisation.* ○ *a management graduate*
or *a graduate in management* ○ *Bad
management* or *inefficient management
can ruin a business.* **2.** a group of managers or directors ○ *The management
has decided to give everyone a pay increase.* (NOTE: Where **management**
refers to a group of people it is sometimes followed by a plural verb.)

'…the management says that the rate of
loss-making has come down and it expects
further improvement in the next few years'
[*Financial Times*]

management accountant
/'mænɪdʒmənt əˌkaʊntənt/ *noun* an

accountant who prepares financial information for managers so that they can take decisions

management audit /'mænɪdʒmənt ˌɔːdɪt/ *noun* a listing of all the managers in an organisation with information about their skills and experience ○ *The management audit helped determine how many more managers needed to be recruited.*

management buyin /ˌmænɪdʒmənt 'baɪɪn/ *noun* the purchase of a subsidiary company by a group of outside directors. Abbr **MBI**

management buyout /ˌmænɪdʒmənt 'baɪaʊt/ *noun* the takeover of a company by a group of employees, usually senior managers and directors. Abbr **MBO**

management by objectives /ˌmænɪdʒmənt baɪ əb'dʒektɪvz/ *noun* a way of managing a business by planning work for the managers to do and testing if it is completed correctly and on time

management by walking around /ˌmænɪdʒmənt baɪ ˌwɔːkɪŋ ə'raʊnd/ *noun* a way of managing where the manager moves round the office or shop floor, discusses problems with the staff and learns from them. Abbr **MBWA**

management committee /'mænɪdʒmənt kəˌmɪti/ *noun* a committee which manages something such as a club or a pension fund

management course /'mænɪdʒmənt kɔːs/ *noun* a training course for managers

management development /'mænɪdʒmənt dɪˌveləpmənt/ *noun* the selection and training of potential managers

management education /'mænɪdʒmənt edjʊˌkeɪʃ(ə)n/ *noun* formal education in the principles and techniques of management and related subjects that leads to a qualification

management function /'mænɪdʒmənt ˌfʌŋkʃən/ *noun* the duties of being a manager

management game /'mænɪdʒmənt geɪm/ *noun* a problem which is given to trainee managers to solve as part of a

training course ○ *The management game run on a computer, demanded decisions in marketing strategy.*

management of change /ˌmænɪdʒmənt əv 'tʃeɪndʒ/ *noun* the process of managing the way changes in the working environment are implemented and how they affect the workforce

management ratio /'mænɪdʒmənt ˌreɪʃɪəʊ/ *noun* the number of managers for every hundred employees in an organisation ○ *There was a very high management ratio since there was more planning and less manual work than in most companies.*

management science /'mænɪdʒmənt ˌsaɪəns/ *noun* the study of the skill and knowledge which can be applied to management ○ *He studied management science at a university.*

management style /'mænɪdʒmənt staɪl/, **style of management** /ˌstaɪl əv 'mænɪdʒmənt/ the way in which managers work, in particular the way in which they treat their employees

management team /'mænɪdʒmənt tiːm/ *noun* a group of all the managers working in the same company

management technique /'mænɪdʒmənt tekˌniːks/ *noun* a way of managing a business

management trainee /ˌmænɪdʒmənt treɪ'niː/ *noun* a young member of staff being trained to be a manager

management training /ˌmænɪdʒmənt 'treɪnɪŋ/ *noun* the process of training staff to be managers, by making them study problems and work out solutions

manager /'mænɪdʒə/ *noun* **1.** the head of a department in a company ○ *She's a department manager in an engineering company.* ○ *Go and see the human resources manager if you have a problem.* ○ *The production manager has been with the company for only two weeks.* ○ *Our sales manager started as a rep in London.* ○ *All new trainees must report to the departmental manager.* **2.** the person in charge of a branch or shop ○ *Mr Smith is the manager of* *our local Lloyds Bank.* ○ *The manager of our Lagos branch is in London for a series of meetings.*

'...the No. 1 managerial productivity problem in America is managers who are out of touch with their people and out of touch with their customers' [*Fortune*]

manageress /ˌmænɪdʒəˈres/ *noun* a woman who runs a shop or a department

managerial /ˌmænəˈdʒɪəriəl/ *adjective* referring to managers ○ *All the managerial staff are sent for training every year.* ○ *Managerial staff have a special canteen.* □ **to be appointed to a managerial position** to be appointed a manager □ **decisions taken at managerial level** decisions taken by managers

managerial grid /mænɪˌdʒɪəriəl ˈɡrɪd/ *noun* a type of management training in which trainees attempt to solve a number of problems in groups, and thereby discover their individual strengths and weaknesses

managerial obsolescence /mænɪˌdʒɪəriəl ɒbsəˈles(ə)ns/ *noun* a situation where managers cannot keep up with the latest technology or are not as well-qualified as more junior staff

managership /ˈmænɪdʒəʃɪp/ *noun* the job of being a manager ○ *After six years, she was offered the managership of a branch in Scotland.*

managing change /ˌmænɪdʒɪŋ ˈtʃeɪndʒ/ *noun* the process of managing the way changes in the working environment are implemented and how they affect the workforce

managing director /ˌmænədʒɪŋ daɪˈrektə/ *noun* the director who is in charge of a whole company. Abbr **MD**

mandate /ˈmændeɪt/ *verb* to give instructions to someone who will represent you in negotiations

mandating /mænˈdeɪtɪŋ/ *noun* the act of giving instructions to a representative

mandatory /ˈmændət(ə)ri/ *adjective* which everyone must obey ○ *Wearing a suit is mandatory for all managerial staff.* □ **mandatory meeting** a meeting which all staff have to attend

'...the wage talks are focusing on employment issues such as sharing of work among employees and extension of employment beyond the mandatory retirement age of 60 years' [*Nikkei Weekly*]

mandatory injunction /ˌmændət(ə)ri ɪnˈdʒʌŋkʃən/ *noun* an order from a court which compels someone to do something

mandatory issues /ˌmændət(ə)ri ˈɪʃuːz/ *plural noun* bargaining issues that directly affect employees' jobs

Man Friday /mæn ˈfraɪdeɪ/ *noun* a male employee who does a variety of tasks in an office. ♦ **Girl Friday** (NOTE: Sometimes **person Friday** is used in job advertisements to avoid sexism.)

man-hour /ˈmæn aʊə/ *noun* work done by one employee in one hour ○ *One million man-hours were lost through industrial action.* ○ *There are two hundred man-hours of work still to be done, which will take ten workers twenty hours to complete.*

manifest /ˈmænɪfest/ *noun* a list of goods in a shipment ■ *adjective* obvious or apparent

manifest content /ˌmænɪfest ˈkɒntent/ *noun* an apparent meaning of words used by one person to another ○ *The manifest content of the director's talk to us was congratulatory, but reading between the lines, we could tell she was angry.*

manned /mænd/ *adjective* with someone working on it ○ *The switchboard is manned twenty-four hours a day.* ○ *The stand was manned by our sales staff.* (NOTE: **manned** does not mean only using men)

manning /ˈmænɪŋ/ *noun* people who are needed to do a work process (NOTE: **manning** does not mean only men)

manning agreement /ˈmænɪŋ əˌɡriːmənt/ *noun* an agreement between the company and the employees about how many employees are needed for a certain job

manning levels /ˈmænɪŋ ˌlev(ə)lz/ *plural noun* the number of people required in each department of a company to do the work efficiently

manpower /ˈmænpaʊə/ *noun* the number of employees in an organisation, industry or country (NOTE: **manpower** does not mean only men)

manpower audit /'mænpaʊər ˌɔːdɪt/ *noun* a listing of all the employees in an organisation with details of their skills and experience ○ *A complete manpower audit was needed to decide what recruitment or training should be carried out to meet future requirements.*

manpower forecasting /'mænpaʊə ˌfɔːkɑːstɪŋ/ *noun* the process of calculating how many employees will be needed in the future, and how many will actually be available

manpower planning /'mænpaʊə ˌplænɪŋ/ *noun* the process of planning to obtain the right number of employees in each job

manpower reductions /'mænpaʊə rɪˌdʌkʃənz/ *plural noun* reductions in the number of employees

manpower requirements /'mænpaʊə rɪˌkwaɪəmənts/, **manpower needs** /'mænpaʊə niːdz/ *plural noun* the number of employees needed

manpower shortage /'mænpaʊə ˌʃɔːtɪdʒ/ *noun* a lack of employees

man-to-man ranking /ˌmæn tə mæn 'ræŋkɪŋ/ *noun* the arrangement of employees in order according to their skills or other criteria (NOTE: does not only refer to men)

manual /'mænjʊəl/ *adjective* done by hand or done using the hands ■ *noun* a book of instructions, showing what procedures to follow

manual labour /ˌmænjʊəl 'leɪbə/, **manual work** /'mænjʊəl wɜːk/ *noun* heavy work done by hand

manual labourer /ˌmænjʊəl 'leɪbərə/ *noun* a person who does heavy work with their hands

manufacture /ˌmænjʊ'fæktʃə/ *verb* to make a product for sale, using machines ○ *The company manufactures spare parts for cars.* ■ *noun* the making of a product for sale, using machines

manufactured goods /ˌmænjʊ'fæktʃəd gʊdz/ *plural noun* items which are made by machine

margin /'mɑːdʒɪn/ *noun* **1.** the difference between the money received when selling a product and the money paid for it **2.** extra space or time allowed

'...profit margins in the industries most exposed to foreign competition – machinery, transportation equipment and electrical goods – are significantly worse than usual' [*Australian Financial Review*]

marginal /'mɑːdʒɪn(ə)l/ *adjective* hardly worth the money paid

marginal cost /ˌmɑːdʒɪn(ə)l 'kɒst/ *noun* the cost of making a single extra unit above the number already planned

marital status /ˌmærɪt(ə)l 'steɪtəs/ *noun* the condition of being married or not

market /'mɑːkɪt/ *noun* **1.** a place, often in the open air where farm produce and household goods are sold ○ *The fish market is held every Thursday.* ○ *The open-air market is held in the central square.* ○ *Here are this week's market prices for sheep.* **2.** the possible sales of a specific product or demand for a specific product ○ *There's no market for word processors* ○ *The market for home computers has fallen sharply.* ○ *We have 20% of the British car market.*

'...market analysts described the falls in the second half of last week as a technical correction to a market which had been pushed by demand to over the 900 index level' [*Australian Financial Review*]

'...market leaders may benefit from scale economies or other cost advantages; they may enjoy a reputation for quality simply by being at the top, or they may actually produce a superior product that gives them both a large market share and high profits' [*Accountancy*]

marketing manager /'mɑːkɪtɪŋ ˌmænɪdʒə/ *noun* a person in charge of a marketing department ○ *The marketing manager has decided to start a new advertising campaign.*

market rate /'mɑːkɪt reɪt/ *noun* the normal price in the market ○ *We pay the market rate for secretaries* or *We pay secretaries the market rate.*

'...after the prime rate cut yesterday, there was a further fall in short-term market rates' [*Financial Times*]

married /'mærɪd/ *adjective* joined as husband and wife

married couple /ˌmærɪd 'kʌp(ə)l/ *noun* a husband and wife

married staff /ˌmærɪd 'stɑːf/ *noun* staff who have wives or husbands

marzipan /ˌmɑːzɪ'pæn/ *adjective* belonging to the level of management immediately below the top executives (*slang*)

mass /mæs/ *noun* **1.** a large group of people **2.** a large number ○ *We have a mass of letters* or *masses of letters to write.*

mass meeting /mæs 'miːtɪŋ/ *noun* a meeting attended by most or all of the members of a trade union at a particular workplace at which they reach decisions on important issues, e.g. whether or not to take industrial action

mass-produce /ˌmæs prə'djuːs/ *verb* to manufacture identical products in large quantities ○ *to mass-produce cars*

mass production /mæs prə'dʌkʃən/ *noun* the manufacture of large quantities of identical products

mass redundancies /mæs rɪ'dʌndənsiz/ *plural noun* many jobs being lost and a large number of employees being made redundant at the same time

mass unemployment /ˌmæs ʌnɪm'plɔɪmənt/ *noun* unemployment of large numbers of people

master /'mɑːstə/ *adjective* main or original □ **master budget** a budget prepared by amalgamating budgets from various profit and cost centres such as sales, production, marketing or administration in order to provide a main budget for the whole company □ **the master copy of a file** the main copy of a computer file, kept for security purposes □ **the law of master and servant** employment law ■ *noun* **1.** a skilled worker, qualified to train apprentices ○ *a master craftsman* **2.** further university degree

master and servant /ˌmɑːstər ən 'sɜːvənt/ *noun* an employer and employee

master contract /'mɑːstə ˌkɒntrækt/ *noun* an industry-wide contract between a group of employers and the relevant unions

mastermind /'mɑːstəmaɪnd/ *verb* **1.** to have the main ideas behind a scheme **2.** to be in charge of a project

masterminding /'mɑːstəmaɪndɪŋ/ *noun* a type of interview where the interviewer influences the interviewee

who accepts their views ○ *Masterminding resulted in interviews revealing little of the real discontent on the shop floor.*

Master of Business Administration /ˌmɑːstər əv 'bɪznɪs ədmɪnɪˌstreɪʃ(ə)n/ *noun* full form of **MBA**

maternity /mə'tɜːnɪti/ *noun* the act of becoming a mother

maternity allowance /mə'tɜːnɪti əˌlaʊəns/ *noun* a government benefit paid to women on maternity leave who are not eligible for statutory maternity pay. Abbr **MA**

maternity leave /mə'tɜːnɪti liːv/ *noun* a period when a woman is away from work to have a baby but is often still paid

maternity pay period /mə'tɜːnɪti peɪ ˌpɪəriəd/ *noun* a period of eighteen weeks when statutory maternity pay is paid. Abbr **MPP**

matrix management /'meɪtrɪks ˌmænɪdʒmənt/ *noun* management that operates both through the hierarchical chain of command within the organisation, and through relationships at the same level with other managers working in other locations or on different products or projects

matrix organisation /'meɪtrɪks ɔːgənaɪˌzeɪʃ(ə)n/ *noun* a flexible organisation structure where authority depends on the expertise needed for a particular task and overall responsibility is shared between several people

matters arising /ˌmætəz ə'raɪzɪŋ/ *plural noun* the business of a meeting which refers back to items discussed at a previous meeting

maturity /mə'tʃʊərɪti/ *noun* the third stage in a product life cycle when a product is well established in the market though no longer enjoying increasing sales, after which sooner or later it will start to decline □ **amount payable on maturity** amount received by the insured person when the policy becomes mature

maturity curve /mə'tʃʊərɪti kɜːv/ *noun* a rate of pay increases based on age and length of service ○ *Maturity curves are not a feature of our pay* *structure since seniority is no guarantee of real contribution.*

maximisation /ˌmæksɪmaɪ-ˈzeɪʃ(ə)n/, **maximization** *noun* the process of making something as large as possible ○ *profit maximisation* or *maximisation of profit*

maximise /ˈmæksɪmaɪz/, **maximize** *verb* to make as large as possible ○ *Our aim is to maximise profits.* ○ *The co-operation of the workforce will be needed if we are to maximise production.* ○ *He is paid on results, and so has to work flat out to maximise his earnings.*

maximum /ˈmæksɪməm/ *noun* the largest possible number, price or quantity ○ *It is the maximum the insurance company will pay.* □ **up to a maximum of £10** no more than £10 ■ *adjective* largest possible ○ *40% is the maximum income tax rate* or *the maximum rate of tax.* ○ *The maximum load for the truck is one ton.* ○ *Maximum production levels were reached last week.*

MBA /ˌem biː ˈeɪ/ *noun* a degree awarded to graduates who have completed a further course in business studies. Full form **Master of Business Administration**

MBO *abbr* management buyout

MBWA *abbr* management by walking around

MD *abbr* managing director ○ *She was appointed MD of a property company.*

means /miːnz/ *noun* a way of doing something ○ *Do we have any means of copying all these documents quickly?* ○ *Bank transfer is the easiest means of payment.* ■ *plural noun* money or resources ○ *The company has the means to launch the new product.* ○ *Such a level of investment is beyond the means of a small private company.* (NOTE: plural is **means**)

means test /ˈmiːnz test/ *verb* to find out how much money someone has in savings and assets ○ *All applicants will be means-tested.*

measure /ˈmeʒə/ *noun* **1.** a way of calculating size or quantity □ **as a measure of the manager's performance** as a way of judging if the manager's per-

formance is good or bad **2.** a type of action □ **to take measures to prevent something happening** to act to stop something happening □ **to take crisis, emergency measures** to act rapidly to stop a crisis developing ■ *verb* **1.** to find out the size or quantity of something or to be of a certain size or quantity ○ *to measure the size of a package* ○ *a package which measures 10cm by 25cm* or *a package measuring 10cm by 25cm* **2.** □ **to measure the department's performance** to judge how well the department has done

measured day work /ˌmeʒəd ˈdeɪ wɜːk/ *noun* a payment scheme where payment for a day's work depends on a specified level of output being achieved

measured performance /ˌmeʒəd pəˈfɔːməns/ *noun* work performance which is measured in quantitative terms

mechanic /mɪˈkænɪk/ *noun* a person who works with engines or machines ○ *He got a job as a car mechanic before going to college.*

mechanical /mɪˈkænɪk(ə)l/ *adjective* worked by a machine ○ *a mechanical pump*

mechanism /ˈmekənɪz(ə)m/ *noun* **1.** the way in which something works ○ *the company's salary review mechanism* **2.** the action of a machine or system ○ *a mechanism to slow down inflation*

mechanistic /ˌmekəˈnɪstɪk/ *adjective* very formal and structured ○ *It is a typical mechanistic organisation with rigid rules and procedures.*

mediate /ˈmiːdieɪt/ *verb* to try to make the two sides in an argument come to an agreement ○ *The human resources director said she would try to mediate between the manager and his staff.* ○ *The government offered to mediate in the dispute.*

mediation /ˌmiːdiˈeɪʃ(ə)n/ *noun* an attempt by a third party to make the two sides in an argument agree ○ *The employers refused an offer of government mediation.* ○ *The dispute was ended through the mediation of union officials.* ○ *Mediation by some third party is the only hope for ending the dispute.*

medical /'medɪk(ə)l/ *adjective* referring to the study or treatment of illness □ **he resigned for medical reasons** he resigned because he was too ill to work

medical certificate /'medɪk(ə)l sə-ˌtɪfɪkət/ *noun* a certificate from a doctor to show that an employee has been ill

medical cover /'medɪk(ə)l ˌkʌvə/ *noun* same as **medical insurance**

medical examination /'medɪk(ə)l ɪgzæmɪˌneɪʃ(ə)n/ *noun* an examination of a person by a doctor to find out their state of health ○ *All members of staff have to have an annual medical examination.*

medical insurance /'medɪk(ə)l ɪnˌʃʊərəns/ *noun* insurance which pays the cost of medical treatment especially when travelling abroad

medical profession /'medɪk(ə)l prəˌfeʃ(ə)n/ *noun* all doctors

medical report /'medɪk(ə)l rɪˌpɔːt/ *noun* a report by a doctor on the medical condition of an employee

medium-term /'miːdiəm tɜːm/ *adjective* referring to a point between short term and long term

meet /miːt/ *verb* **1.** to come together with someone ○ *Union leaders came to meet the negotiating committee.* ○ *We met the agent at his hotel.* ○ *The two sides met in the lawyer's office.* **2.** to be satisfactory for ○ *We must have a product which meets our requirements.* □ **to meet the demand for a new product** to fill the demand for a product □ **to meet the conditions of an agreement** to fulfil the conditions of an agreement □ **to meet the union's demands** to agree to what the union is asking for **3.** to pay for ○ *The company will meet your expenses.* (NOTE: **meeting – met**)

meeting /'miːtɪŋ/ *noun* **1.** the coming together of a group of people **2.** □ **to hold a meeting** to organise a meeting of a group of people ○ *The meeting will be held in the committee room.* □ **to open a meeting** to start a meeting □ **to conduct a meeting** to be in the chair for a meeting □ **to close a meeting** to end a meeting □ **to address a meeting** to speak to a meeting

meetings room /'miːtɪŋz ruːm/ *noun* a special room in which meetings are held

member /'membə/ *noun* **1.** a person who belongs to a group, society or organisation ○ *Committee members voted on the proposal.* ○ *They were elected members of the board.* ○ *Every employer is a member of the employers' federation.* **2.** an organisation which belongs to a society ○ *the member companies of a trade association*

'…it will be the first opportunity for party members and trade union members to express their views on the tax package' [*Australian Financial Review*]

membership /'membəʃɪp/ *noun* **1.** the fact of belonging to a group, society or organisation ○ *membership qualifications* ○ *conditions of membership* ○ *membership card* ○ *to pay your membership or your membership fees* ○ *Membership of a trade union is not compulsory, but is strongly encouraged on the shop floor.* □ **membership of a pension scheme** the fact of belonging to a pension scheme **2.** all the members of a group ○ *The union membership was asked to vote for the new president.*

'…the bargaining committee will recommend that its membership ratify the agreement at a meeting called for June' [*Toronto Star*]

membership group /'membəʃɪp gruːp/ *noun* a group of which a certain person is a member

memo /'meməʊ/ *noun* a short message sent from one person to another in the same organisation ○ *She wrote a memo to the finance director.* ○ *The sales manager is going to send a memo to all the sales representatives.* ○ *I sent the managing director a memo about your complaint.*

memo pad /'meməʊ pæd/ *noun* a pad of paper for writing short notes

memorandum /meməˈrændəm/ *noun* same as **memo**

memorandum (and articles) of association /meməˌrændəm ənd ˌɑːtik(ə)lz əv əsəʊsiˈeɪʃ(ə)n/ *noun* legal documents setting up a limited company and giving details of its name, aims, authorised share capital, conduct of meetings, appointment of directors and registered office

mental handicap /ˌment(ə)l 'hændikæp/ *noun* same as **learning difficulty** (NOTE: term now generally unacceptable)

mentally handicapped /ˌment(ə)li 'hændikæpt/ *noun* having a learning difficulty (NOTE: term now generally unacceptable)

mentee /menˈtiː/ *noun* a less experienced employee who is offered special guidance and support by a respected and trusted person with more experience

mentor /ˈmentɔː/ *noun* a person who is respected and trusted by a less experienced employee and offers special guidance and support to them

mentoring /ˈmentərɪŋ/ *noun* a form of training or employee development in which a trusted and respected person with a lot experience—the mentor—offers special guidance, encouragement and support to a less experienced employee

merit /ˈmerɪt/ *noun* a quality which deserves reward

merit award /ˈmerɪt əˌwɔːd/, **merit bonus** /ˈmerɪt ˌbəʊnəs/ *noun* extra money given to an employee because they have worked well ○ *A merit bonus can encourage the better workers, but will discourage those who feel they cannot reach the required level.*

meritocracy /ˌmerɪˈtɒkrəsi/ *noun* a society or organisation where advancement is based on a person's natural ability rather than on their background

method /ˈmeθəd/ *noun* a way of doing something ○ *They devised a new method of sending data.* ○ *What is the best method of payment?* ○ *His organising methods are out of date.*

method study /ˈmeθəd ˌstʌdi/ *noun* a study of the way in which something is done

mid- /mɪd/ *prefix* middle □ **from mid 2001** from the middle of 2001 ○ *The factory is closed until mid-July.*

mid-career crisis /ˌmɪd kəˌrɪə 'kraɪsɪs/ *noun* a point in the middle of someone's career when they have to decide what to do in the future

middle /ˈmɪd(ə)l/ *adjective* in the centre or between two points

middle manager /ˌmɪd(ə)l 'mænɪdʒə/ *noun* a manager of a department in a company, answerable to a senior manager or director

mid-month /ˈmɪd mʌnθ/ *adjective* which happens in the middle of the month ○ *mid-month accounts*

mid-week /ˈmɪd wiːk/ *adjective* which happens in the middle of a week ○ *the mid-week lull in sales*

migrant /ˈmaɪgrənt/ *noun* a person who moves from one place or country to another, usually to work

migrant worker /ˌmaɪgrənt 'wɜːkə/ *noun* a worker who moves from place to place looking for work ○ *Migrant workers were working illegally without work permits.* ○ *During the summer thousands of migrant workers cross the border to work on the harvest.*

migration /maɪˈgreɪʃ(ə)n/ *noun* moving from one place or country to another, usually to work

military leave /ˌmɪlɪt(ə)ri 'liːv/ *noun US* unpaid leave or absence from work by employees who are in the armed forces or who have to do their military service

milk round /ˈmɪlk raʊnd/ *noun* the visiting of universities and colleges by employers, in order to find promising new employees

'…as the annual milk round gets under way, many students are more interested in final exams than in job hunting' [*Personnel Management*]

minimal /ˈmɪnɪm(ə)l/ *adjective* the smallest possible ○ *There was a minimal quantity of imperfections in the batch.* ○ *The head office exercises minimal control over the branch offices.*

minimise /ˈmɪnɪmaɪz/, **minimize** *verb* **1.** to make something seem to be very small and not very important **2.** to make something as small as possible ○ *The company is attempting to minimise its labour costs by only hiring workers when they are needed.* ○ *Unemployment was minimised by giving more people part-time work.*

minimum /ˈmɪnɪməm/ *noun* smallest possible quantity, price or number ○ *to keep expenses to a minimum* ○ *to reduce the risk of a loss to a minimum* (NOTE:

plural is **minima** or **minimums**) ■ *adjective* smallest possible □ **minimum payment** the smallest payment necessary

minimum age /ˌmɪnɪməm 'eɪdʒ/ *noun* the lowest age at which someone can be employed (13 in a few types of employment, but 16 is the legal minimum)

minimum pay /ˌmɪnɪməm 'peɪ/, **minimum wage** /ˌmɪnɪməm 'weɪdʒ/ *noun* the lowest hourly wage which a company can legally pay its employees

minimum salary /ˌmɪnɪməm 'sæləri/ *noun* the lowest amount of money that an employee is guaranteed to earn, i.e. their basic pay, which may be increased if an employee qualifies for a bonus by performing well

minor /'maɪnə/ *adjective* less important ○ *Items of minor expenditure are not listed separately.* ○ *The minor shareholders voted against the proposal.* □ **minor official** a person in a low position in a government department

minority /maɪ'nɒrɪti/ *noun* **1.** a number or quantity which is less than half of the total ○ *A minority of board members opposed the chairman.* ○ *A minority of the union members opposed the motion.* □ **to be in the minority** to be one of a group that is a small part of a larger group **2.** a section of the population from a specific racial group, which does nor make up the majority of the population

minutes /'mɪnɪts/ *plural noun* notes of what happened at a meeting, written by the secretary □ **to take the minutes** to write notes of what happened at a meeting

misappropriate /ˌmɪsə'prəʊprieɪt/ *verb* to use illegally money which is not yours, but with which you have been trusted

misappropriation /ˌmɪsəprəʊpri'eɪʃ(ə)n/ *noun* the illegal use of money by someone who is not the owner but who has been trusted to look after it

miscarriage of justice /ˌmɪskærɪdʒ əv 'dʒʌstɪs/ *noun* a decision wrongly or unjustly reached by a

court or decision which goes against the rights of a party in a case, in such a way that the decision may be reversed on appeal

misconduct /mɪs'kɒndʌkt/ *noun* an illegal action by an employee, or an action which can harm someone, e.g. disobeying instructions

misdemeanour /ˌmɪsdɪ'miːnə/ *noun* a minor crime ○ *to commit a misdemeanour* (NOTE: the usual US spelling is misdemeanor)

mismanage /mɪs'mænɪdʒ/ *verb* to manage badly ○ *The company had been badly mismanaged under the previous MD.*

mismanagement /mɪs'mænɪdʒmənt/ *noun* bad management ○ *The company failed because of the chairman's mismanagement.*

misrepresentation /ˌmɪsreprɪzen'teɪʃ(ə)n/ *noun* **1.** the act of making a wrong statement in order to persuade someone to enter into a contract such as one for buying a product or service **2.** the act of wrongly reporting facts

mistake /mɪ'steɪk/ *noun* an act or decision which is wrong □ **to make a mistake** to do something wrong ○ *The shop made a mistake and sent the wrong items.* ○ *There was a mistake in the address.* ○ *He made a mistake in addressing the letter.*

misunderstanding /ˌmɪsʌndə'stændɪŋ/ *noun* an act of not understanding something correctly ○ *There was a misunderstanding over the pay deal.*

misuse *noun* /mɪs'juːs/ a wrong use ○ *the misuse of funds* or *of assets* ■ *verb* □ **to misuse funds** to use funds in a wrong way (especially funds which do not belong to you)

misuse of authority /mɪsˌjuːs əv ɔː'θɒrɪti/ *noun* the use of one's authority in a wrong way

mobile /'məʊbaɪl/ *adjective* which can move about □ **mobile workforce** employees who move from place to place to get work

mobile phone /'məʊbaɪl 'fəʊn/ *noun* a small portable phone which can be used away from home or the office

mobile worker /ˌməʊbaɪl ˈwɜːkə/ *noun* an employee who does not have one fixed place of work (NOTE: Mobile workers, such as teleworkers, are usually linked to a central base by telephone and computer)

mobility /məʊˈbɪlɪti/ *noun* the ability to move from one place to another

mobility allowance /məʊˈbɪlɪti ə-ˌlaʊəns/ *noun* an addition to normal salary paid to an employee who is willing to travel to different places of work

model /ˈmɒd(ə)l/ *noun* **1.** a small copy of something made to show what it will look like when finished ○ *They showed us a model of the new office building.* **2.** something which can be copied ○ *the Swedish model of industrial relations* ■ *adjective* which is a perfect example to be copied ○ *a model agreement*

moderate *adjective* /ˈmɒd(ə)rət/ **1.** not too large ○ *The trade union made a moderate claim.* ○ *The government proposed a moderate increase in the tax rate.* **2.** not holding very extreme views ○ *a moderate trade union leader* ■ *verb* /ˈmɒdəreɪt/ to make less strong or less large ○ *The union was forced to moderate its claim.*

modification /ˌmɒdɪfɪˈkeɪʃ(ə)n/ *noun* a change ○ *The board wanted to make or to carry out modifications to the plan.* ○ *The client pressed for modifications to the contract.*

modify /ˈmɒdɪfaɪ/ *verb* to change or to make something fit a different use ○ *The management modified its proposals.* ○ *This is the new modified agreement.* (NOTE: **modifies – modifying – modified**)

momentum /məʊˈmentəm/ *noun* a movement forwards □ **to gain** *or* **lose momentum** to move faster or more slowly

Monday morning feeling /ˌmʌndeɪ ˈmɔːnɪŋ ˌfiːlɪŋ/ *noun* a feeling of being slightly ill or miserable on going to work on Monday morning

money purchase pension /ˈmʌni ˌpɜːtʃɪs ˌpenʃən/ *noun* a pension plan to which both employer and employee make contributions

money purchase pension scheme /ˌmʌni ˌpɜːtʃɪs ˈpenʃən skiːm/ *noun (in the United Kingdom)* a pension plan in which the fund that is built up from a person's contributions is used to buy an annuity, and the retirement income that the beneficiary receives depends on the amount of their contributions, the performance of the investments bought with those contributions, the annuity rates and the type of annuity purchased at retirement

monitor /ˈmɒnɪtə/ *noun* a screen on a computer ○ *He brought up the information on the monitor.* ■ *verb* to check or to examine how something is working ○ *How do you monitor the performance of the sales reps?*

month /mʌnθ/ *noun* one of twelve periods which make a year ○ *bills due at the end of the current month* ○ *She earns £2,000 a month.* □ **paid by the month** paid once each month □ **to give a customer two months' credit** to allow a customer to pay not immediately, but after two months

month end /mʌnθ ˈend/ *noun* the end of a calendar month, when accounts have to be drawn up ○ *The accounts department are working on the month-end accounts.*

monthly /ˈmʌnθli/ *adjective* happening every month or which is received every month ○ *We get a monthly statement from the bank.* ○ *She makes monthly payments to the credit card company.* ○ *My monthly salary cheque is late.* ■ *adverb* every month ○ *He asked if he could pay monthly by direct debit.* ○ *The account is credited monthly.*

moonlight /ˈmuːnlaɪt/ *verb* to do a second job for cash (often in the evening) as well as a regular job (*informal*)

moonlighter /ˈmuːnlaɪtə/ *noun* a person who moonlights

moonlighting /ˈmuːnlaɪtɪŋ/ *noun* the practice of doing a second job ○ *He makes thousands a year from moonlighting.*

morale /məˈrɑːl/ *noun* a feeling of confidence or satisfaction ○ *Employee morale is low due to the threat of unem-*

ployment. □ **to boost morale** to increase the employees' feelings of confidence

morning shift /ˈmɔːnɪŋ ʃɪft/ *noun* a shift which works during the morning (typically from 7.00 or 8.00 a.m. to lunchtime)

motion /ˈməʊʃ(ə)n/ *noun* **1.** the act of moving about **2.** a proposal which will be put to a meeting to be voted on □ *to speak against* or *for a motion* ○ *Mr Brown will propose* or *move a motion congratulating the board on the results.* ○ *The meeting voted on the motion.* ○ *The motion was carried* or *was defeated by 220 votes to 196.*

motion study /ˈməʊʃ(ə)n ˌstʌdi/ *noun* a study of the movements of employees performing the tasks in order to improve efficiency

motivate /ˈməʊtɪveɪt/ *verb* to encourage someone to do something, especially to work or to sell □ **highly motivated sales staff** sales staff who are very eager to sell

'…creative people aren't necessarily motivated by money or titles, they may not want a larger office or more work, they don't often want more responsibility. They want to see their ideas implemented' [*Nation's Business*]

motivation /ˌməʊtɪˈveɪʃ(ə)n/ *noun* **1.** an encouragement to staff **2.** eagerness to work well or sell large quantities of a product □ **the sales staff lack motivation** the sales staff are not eager enough to sell

motivational /ˌməʊtɪˈveɪʃ(ə)n(ə)l/ *adjective* referring to motivation

motivational factor /ˌməʊtɪ-ˈveɪʃ(ə)n(ə)l ˌfæktə/ *noun* an aspect of a job or an organisation which encourages employees to work hard ○ *A bonus system based on production targets was a strong motivational factor.* ○ *A high commission should be a strong motivational factor for the sales force.*

mouse /maʊs/ *noun* small moveable device attached to a personal computer and used to move or select items on the screen (NOTE: plural is **mouses** or **mice**)

'…you can use a mouse to access pop-up menus and a keyboard for a word-processor' [*Byte*]

movement /ˈmuːvmənt/ *noun* **1.** an act of changing position or going up or down ○ *movements in the money markets* ○ *cyclical movements of trade* □ **free movement of labour within the EU** the principle that workers from any country of the EU can move to another country to obtain work **2.** a group of people working towards the same aim ○ *the labour movement* ○ *the free trade movement* ○ *the trade union movement*

mover and shaker /ˌmuːvər ən ˈʃeɪkə/ *noun* an influential and dynamic person within an organisation or group of people who makes things happen (*informal*)

MPP *abbr* maternity pay period

Mr Chairman /ˌmɪstə ˈtʃeəmən/ *noun* a way of speaking to the male chairman of a committee meeting

multi-employer bargaining /ˌmʌlti ɪmˌplɔɪə ˈbɑːɡɪnɪŋ/ *noun* centralised bargaining about pay, usually between employer's associations representing all the employers in a particular industry in a country or region and the relevant trade unions

multinational corporation /ˌmʌltinæʃ(ə)n(ə)l kɔːpəˈreɪʃ(ə)n/ *noun* a company which has branches or subsidiary companies in several countries

multiple /ˈmʌltɪp(ə)l/ *adjective* many ■ *noun* a company with stores in several different towns

'…many independents took advantage of the bank holiday period when the big multiples were closed' [*The Grocer*]

'…the multiple brought the price down to £2.49 in some stores. We had not agreed to this deal and they sold out very rapidly. When they reordered we would not give it to them. This kind of activity is bad for the brand and we cannot afford it' [*The Grocer*]

multiple chain promotion plan /ˌmʌltɪp(ə)l tʃeɪn prəˈməʊʃ(ə)n plæn/ a system of linking each position in an organisation to several others from which promotion may be made, or to which employees may be promoted

multiple-employer bargaining /ˌmʌltɪp(ə)l ɪmˌplɔɪə ˈbɑːɡɪnɪŋ/ *noun* same as **multi-employer bargaining**

multiple hurdle selection /ˌmʌltɪp(ə)l ˈhɜːd(ə)l sɪˌlekʃən/, **multiple hurdle system** /ˌmʌltɪp(ə)l ˈhɜːd(ə)l ˌsɪstəm/ *noun* a method of selecting candidates for a job by requiring that they should pass a series of tests ○ *The multiple hurdle system very efficiently eliminates a large number of candidates.*

multiple management /ˌmʌltɪp(ə)l ˈmænɪdʒmənt/ *noun* a management system where committees of middle managers advise top management on company policy

multiskilling /ˈmʌltiˌskɪlɪŋ/ *noun* a system of working where employees are trained to work in various types of job, and none are kept on the same type of work for very long, so as to allow flexibility in the deployment of the workforce

multitasking /ˈmʌltiˌtɑːskɪŋ/ *noun* **1.** performing several different tasks at the same time **2.** running several different software programs at the same time

Murphy's law /ˌmɜːfiz ˈlɔː/ *noun* law, based on wide experience, which says that in commercial life if something can go wrong it will go wrong, or that when you are thinking that things are going right, they will inevitably start to go wrong

mushroom job /ˈmʌʃruːm dʒɒb/ *noun US* a job which is unpleasant (*slang*)

mutuality /ˌmjuːtʃuˈælɪti/ *noun* the right of a trade union to bargain on behalf of its members and so take a part in the running of the company

mutuality agreement /ˌmjuːtʃuˈælɪti əˌɡriːmənt/ *noun* an agreement between management and union, by which the management agrees not to make changes to the conditions of work without consulting the union

Myers-Briggs type indicator /ˌmaɪəz brɪɡz ˈtaɪp ˌɪndɪkeɪtə/ *noun* a test designed to indicate what type of personality a person has on the basis of the preferences they show with regard to four paired opposites: extraversion and introversion; sensing and intuition; thinking and feeling; judging and perceiving

MYOB *abbr* mind your own business

N

narrative /'nærətɪv/ *noun* a description of something as a story

narrative appraisal /'nærətɪv ə-ˌpreɪz(ə)l/ *noun* a type of performance appraisal where the employee's performance is described with illustrations of specific points about it

nation /'neɪʃ(ə)n/ *noun* a country and the people living in it

national /'næʃ(ə)nəl/ *adjective* referring to the whole of a particular country ■ *noun* a person who is a citizen of a state

national agreement /ˌnæʃ(ə)nəl ə-'griːmənt/ *noun* an agreement between employers and a union at national level (i.e. covering the whole country)

National Council for Vocational Qualifications /ˌnæʃ(ə)nəl ˌkaʊnsəl fə vəʊˌkeɪʃ(ə)n(ə)l ˌkwɒləfɪ-'keɪʃənz/ *noun* full form of **NCVQ**

national executive (committee) /ˌnæʃ(ə)nəl ɪgˈzekjʊtɪv kəˌmɪti/ *noun* the main committee running a trade union

National Insurance /ˌnæʃ(ə)nəl ɪn-'ʃʊərəns/ *noun* state insurance in the United Kingdom, organised by the government, which pays for medical care, hospitals, unemployment benefits, etc. Abbr **NI**

national insurance benefits /ˌnæʃ(ə)nəl ɪnˈʃʊərəns ˌbenɪfɪts/ *plural noun* various benefits which are dependent on having paid NI contributions (such as retirement pension)

National Insurance contributions /ˌnæʃ(ə)nəl ɪnˈʃʊərəns kɒntrɪ-ˌbjuːʃ(ə)nz/ *plural noun* a proportion of income paid each month by an employee and the employee's company to the National Insurance. Abbr **NIC**

nationality /ˌnæʃəˈnælɪti/ *noun* the state of being a citizen of a particular country □ **he is of British nationality** he is a British citizen

National Occupational Health and Safety Commission /ˌnæʃ(ə)nəl ɒkjʊˌpeɪʃ(ə)n(ə)l helθ ən 'seɪfti kəˌmɪʃ(ə)n/ *noun* a government agency in Australia that is responsible for coordinating efforts to prevent injury, disease, and deaths occurring in the workplace

national union /ˌnæʃ(ə)nəl 'juːnjən/ *noun* a central union organisation which coordinates local branches

National Vocational Qualification /ˌnæʃ(ə)n(ə)l vəʊˌkeɪʃ(ə)nəl kwɒlɪfɪ'keɪʃ(ə)n/ *noun* a qualification awarded in the United Kingdom when a person successfully completes a course vocational training. Abbr **NVQ** (NOTE: National Vocational Qualifications are based on standards developed by leading organisations in the industrial and commercial sectors, defining the skills or competences required in particular occupations.)

national wage agreement /ˌnæʃ(ə)nəl 'weɪdʒ əˌgriːmənt/ *noun* an agreement reached through collective bargaining between trade unions and employers, which sets national rates of pay within particular industries or for particular jobs

nationwide /'neɪʃənwaɪd/ *adjective* all over a country ○ *We offer a nationwide delivery service.* ○ *The new car is being launched with a nationwide sales campaign.*

natural /'nætʃ(ə)rəl/ *adjective* **1.** found in the earth ○ *The offices are heated by natural gas.* **2.** normal ○ *It was only natural that the shopkeeper* *should feel annoyed when the hypermarket was built close to his shop.* ○ *It was natural for the workers to feel aggrieved when production methods were changed without consultation.*

natural wastage /ˌnætʃ(ə)rəl 'weɪstɪdʒ/ *noun* the process of losing employees because they resign or retire, not because they are made redundant or are sacked ○ *The company is hoping to avoid redundancies and reduce its staff by natural wastage.*

NAV *abbr* net asset value

NCVQ *noun* a government body set up to validate the system of national qualifications in vocational subjects. Abbr of **National Council for Vocational Qualifications**

needs /niːdz/ *plural noun* things that are necessary

needs assessment /'niːdz ə-ˌsesmənt/, **assessment of needs** /ə-ˌsesmənt əv 'niːdz/ *noun* an analysis of an organisation's manpower requirements which can form the basis of training plans ○ *Needs assessment pointed to a level of manpower requirements which the company could not finance.*

negative /'negətɪv/ *adjective* meaning 'no'

neglect /nɪ'glekt/ *noun* the act of not doing a duty ■ *verb* □ **to neglect to do something** to forget or omit to do something which has to be done ○ *He neglected to return his income tax form.*

neglected /nɪ'glektɪd/ *adjective* not well looked after

neglected business /nɪˌglektɪd 'bɪznɪs/ *noun* a company which has not been actively run by its owners and could therefore do better

negligence /'neglɪdʒəns/ *noun* **1.** a lack of proper care or not doing a duty (with the result that a person or property is harmed) **2.** the act of not doing a job properly when one is capable of doing it

negligent /'neglɪdʒənt/ *adjective* not taking appropriate care

negligently /'neglɪdʒənt(ə)li/ *adverb* in a way which shows negligence

negligent reference /ˌneglɪdʒənt 'ref(ə)rəns/ *noun* a written reference from an employer which could mislead another employer about an employee

negligible /'neglɪdʒɪb(ə)l/ *adjective* very small

negotiable /nɪ'gəʊʃiəb(ə)l/ *adjective* **1.** which can be transferred from one person to another or exchanged for cash **2.** which can be discussed so that an agreement is reached ○ *The employer's offer was not negotiable, so when it was turned down a strike seemed inevitable.* ○ *All parts of the offers are negotiable, with the exception of the new manning levels.* ○ *The salary for the job is negotiable.*

'...initial salary is negotiable around $45,000 per annum' [*Australian Financial Review*]

negotiate /nɪ'gəʊʃieɪt/ *verb* □ **to negotiate with someone** to discuss a problem or issue formally with someone, so as to reach an agreement □ **to negotiate terms and conditions** *or* **a contract** to discuss and agree the terms of a contract □ **to go back to the negotiating table** to start negotiations again after a break ○ *The two sides discussed the proposals, and, a week later, the management negotiators returned to the negotiating table with improved proposals.*

'...many of the large travel agency chains are able to negotiate even greater discounts' [*Duns Business Month*]

negotiating committee /nɪ-'gəʊʃieɪtɪŋ kəˌmɪti/ *noun* a group of representatives of management and unions who negotiate a wage settlement

negotiating team /nɪ'gəʊʃieɪtɪŋ tiːm/ *noun* a group which negotiates for one party in negotiations ○ *The union negotiating team asked for further time to consider the management's proposals.*

negotiation /nɪˌgəʊʃi'eɪʃ(ə)n/ *noun* the discussion of terms and conditions in order to reach an agreement □ **contract under negotiation** a contract which is being discussed □ **a matter for negotiation** something which must be discussed before a decision is reached □ **to enter into** *or* **to start negotiations** to start discussing a problem □ **to resume negotiations** to start discussing a problem again, after talks have stopped for a time □ **to break off negotiations** to stop discussing a problem □ **to conduct ne-**

gotiations to negotiate □ **negotiations broke down after six hours** discussions stopped because no agreement was possible □ **breakdown in negotiations** a halt in talking because no agreement has been reached, after negotiations have been in progress for some time □ **resumption of negotiations** a restarting of negotiations, after talks have stopped for a time

'...after three days of tough negotiations, the company reached agreement with its 1,200 unionized workers' [*Toronto Star*]

negotiator /nɪˈgəʊʃieɪtə/ *noun* a person who discusses a problem with the aim of achieving agreement between different people or groups of people □ **experienced union negotiator** a member of a union who has a lot of experience of discussing terms of employment with management

nepotism /ˈnepətɪz(ə)m/ *noun* the practice of giving preferential treatment to someone who is a relative or friend (especially giving a job to a member of the family who is less well qualified than other candidates) ○ *The staff talked about nepotism when the training officer selected her nephew for management training.*

net /net/ *adjective* referring to a price, weight, pay, etc., after all deductions have been made □ **net profit before tax** the profit of a company after expenses have been deducted but before tax has been paid ■ *verb* to make a true profit ○ *to net a profit of £10,000* (NOTE: **netting – netted**) ■ *adverb* after deductions have been made ○ *His salary is paid net.*

'...out of its earnings a company will pay a dividend. When shareholders receive this it will be net, that is it will have had tax deducted at 30 per cent' [*Investors Chronicle*]

net asset value /net ˈæset ˌvæljuː/ *noun* the total value of a company after deducting the money owed by it (it is the value of shareholders' capital plus reserves and any money retained from profits). Abbr **NAV**

nethead /ˈnethed/ *noun* somebody who is obsessed with the Internet (*slang*)

netiquette /ˈnetɪket/ *noun* the rules for proper procedure and good manners that are usually observed when communicating on the Internet (NOTE: The term derives from the word 'etiquette'.)

netizen /ˈnetɪz(ə)n/ *noun* a regular user of the Internet (*slang*)

net margin /net ˈmɑːdʒɪn/ *noun* the percentage difference between received price and all costs, including overheads

net pay /net ˈpeɪ/ *noun* same as **take-home pay**

net salary /net ˈsæləri/ *noun* the salary which is left after deducting tax and National Insurance contributions

network /ˈnetwɜːk/ *noun* a system which links different points together ■ *verb* to link together in a network

networking /ˈnetwɜːkɪŋ/ *noun* **1.** a working method where employees work at home on computer terminals, and send the finished material back to the central office by email **2.** the practice of keeping in contact with former colleagues, school friends, etc., so that all the members of the group can help each other in their careers

neurolinguistic programming /ˌnjuːrəʊlɪŋˌgwɪstɪk ˈprəʊɡræmɪŋ/ *noun* a theory of behaviour and communication based on how people avoid change and how to help them to change. Abbr **NLP**

neutrality laws /njuːˈtrælɪti lɔːz/ *plural noun US* laws relating to discrimination which must be observed by organisations

new /njuː/ *adjective* recent or not old □ **under new management** with a new owner

newbie /ˈnjuːbi/ *noun* a person who is new to using the Internet (*slang*)

new blood /njuː ˈblʌd/ same as **fresh blood**

new broom /njuː ˈbruːm/ *noun* a manager or director brought into a company to change existing practices and possibly remove old-established staff

news /njuːz/ *noun* information about things which have happened

news agency /ˈnjuːz ˌeɪdʒənsi/ *noun* an office which distributes news to newspapers and television stations

newsletter /'njuːzletə/ *noun* □ **company newsletter** a printed sheet or small newspaper giving news about a company

newssheet /'njuːzʃiːt/ *noun* a leaflet distributed by an organisation, giving the latest news about itself

next of kin /ˌnekst əv 'kɪn/ *noun* the nearest member of the family (to be contacted if an employee dies or is involved in an accident)

NI *abbr* National Insurance

NIC *abbr* National Insurance contributions

nice guys finish last /ˌnaɪs ɡaɪz ˌfɪnɪʃ 'lɑːst/ *phrase* a saying used in business to suggest that people should think about themselves first

nice-to-haves /ˌnaɪs tə 'hævz/ *noun* the benefits of a job, such as free parking or subsidised meals, which are good to have but not essential (*informal*)

night /naɪt/ *noun* a period of time from evening to morning

night duty /'naɪt ˌdjuːti/ *noun* a period of work during the night

night shift /'naɪt ʃɪft/ *noun* a shift which works at night ○ *There are thirty men on the night shift.*

nightwork /'naɪtwɜːk/ *noun* work done at night

NLP *abbr* neurolinguistic programming

No., No *abbr* number

no-attention job /nəʊ ə'tenʃən dʒɒb/ *noun* a job that can be done with minimal concentration ○ *No-attention jobs create stress because of the boredom they produce.*

no-claims bonus /nəʊ 'kleɪmz ˌbəʊnəs/ *noun* **1.** a reduction of premiums on an insurance policy because no claims have been made **2.** a lower premium paid because no claims have been made against the insurance policy

nomadic worker /nəʊˌmædɪk 'wɜːkə/ *noun* same as **mobile worker**

nominal /'nɒmɪn(ə)l/ *adjective (of a payment)* very small ○ *They are paying a nominal rent.* ○ *The employment agency makes a nominal charge for its services.*

nominal group technique /ˌnɒmɪn(ə)l 'ɡruːp tekˌniːk/ *noun* a group method of drawing out ideas from people on a specific topic ○ *Nominal group methods are used when representatives from all the sales and production departments are considering new product ideas.*

nominate /'nɒmɪneɪt/ *verb* to suggest someone for a job □ **to nominate someone to a post** to appoint someone to a post without an election

nomination /ˌnɒmɪ'neɪʃ(ə)n/ *noun* the act of nominating someone for a position

nominee /ˌnɒmɪ'niː/ *noun* **1.** a person who is nominated, especially someone who is appointed to deal with financial matters on your behalf **2.** a person who is nominated for a job (NOTE: a person may be nominated to a position without any other candidates being considered, or without the post being advertised; the word implies a personal choice, rather than selection by a committee. In other cases, it is better to use the words **appoint, appointment, appointee**)

COMMENT: Shares can be purchased and held in nominee accounts so that the identity of the owner of the shares cannot be discovered easily.

non- /nɒn/ *prefix* not

non-analytical job evaluation /nɒn ænəˌlɪtɪk(ə)l 'dʒɒb ɪvæljuˌeɪʃ(ə)n/ *noun* a way of evaluating a job, by giving each job a rank within the organisation (as opposed to the analytical system, where each job is evaluated according to a points system)

non-conformance /nɒn kən'fɔːməns/ *noun* the act of not conforming ○ *He was criticised for non-conformance with the regulations.*

non-contributory pension plan /nɒn kənˌtrɪbjʊt(ə)ri 'penʃən plæn/, **non-contributory pension scheme** /nɒn kənˌtrɪbjʊt(ə)ri 'penʃən skiːm/ *noun* a pension scheme where a company, not the employee, pays all contributions ○ *The company pension scheme is non-contributory.*

non-directive counselling /nɒn daɪˌrektɪv 'kaʊns(ə)lɪŋ/ *noun* the giving of professional advice to others on personal matters, without following a fixed form, but rather through open discussion of problems

non-directive interview /nɒn daɪ-ˈrektɪv ˌɪntəvjuː/, **non-directed interview** /nɒn daɪˈrektɪd ˌɪntəvjuː/ *noun* an interview in which the questions are not set in advance and no fixed pattern is followed ○ *Non-directed interviews give candidates a good chance to show their creative potential.*

non-disclosure agreement /nɒn dɪsˈkləʊʒər əˌgriːmənt/ *noun* a legally enforceable agreement that stops present or past employees from revealing commercially sensitive information belonging to their employer to anybody else

non-disparagement agreement /nɒn dɪˈspærɪdʒmənt əˌgriːmənt/ *noun* an agreement intended to stop present or past employees from criticising their employers in public (NOTE: Non-disparagement agreements are relatively new and it is not yet clear whether the courts will accept them as legally binding.)

non-executive director /nɒn ɪgˌzekjʊtɪv daɪˈrektə/ *noun* a director who attends board meetings and gives advice, but does not work full-time for the company

non-exempt employee /nɒn ɪgˌzempt ɪmˈplɔɪiː/ *noun* a person whose wages are subject to minimum wage legislation

non-financial incentive scheme /nɒn faɪˌnænʃəl ɪnˈsentɪv skiːm/ *noun* a scheme that provides an incentive to employees to work harder or perform better that takes some other form than money

non-profit-making organisation /nɒn ˌprɒfɪt ˌmeɪkɪŋ ɔːgənaɪ-ˈzeɪʃ(ə)n/, **non-profit organisation** /nɒn ˈprɒfɪt ɔːgənaɪˌzeɪʃ(ə)n/ *noun* an organisation (such as a club) which is not allowed by law to make a profit ○ *Non-profit-making organisations are exempted from tax.* (NOTE: Non-profit organisations include charities, professional associations, trade unions, and religious, arts, community, research, and campaigning bodies. The

American English is **non-profit corporation**.)

non-resident /ˈnɒnˈrezɪdənt/ *noun* a person who is not considered a resident of a country for tax purposes ○ *He has a non-resident bank account.*

non-taxable /nɒn ˈtæksəb(ə)l/ *adjective* which is not subject to tax ○ *non-taxable income* ○ *Lottery prizes are non-taxable.*

non-union labour /nɒn ˈjuːnjən ˌleɪbə/ *noun* employees who do not belong to trade unions employed by a company

non-union member /nɒn ˈjuːnjən ˌmembə/ *noun* a person who does not belong to a trade union

non-verbal communication /nɒn ˌvɜːb(ə)l kəˌmjuːnɪˈkeɪʃ(ə)n/ *noun* **1.** the communicating of a message using facial expressions or body language, but without speaking ○ *In negotiations, interpreting non-verbal communication is just as important as listening to what people say.* **2.** any form of communication that is not expressed in words (NOTE: Non-verbal communication, which includes, for example, body language, silence, failure or slowness to respond to a message and lateness in arriving for a meeting, is estimated to make up 65–90% of all communication.)

norm /nɔːm/ *noun* the usual quantity or the usual rate ○ *The output from this factory is well above the norm for the industry* or *well above the industry norm.*

normal /ˈnɔːm(ə)l/ *adjective* usual or which happens regularly ○ *Normal deliveries are made on Tuesdays and Fridays.* ○ *Now that supply difficulties have been resolved we hope to resume normal service as soon as possible.*

normally /ˈnɔːm(ə)li/ *adverb* in the usual way ○ *The production line is working normally again after the stoppage.*

normal working /ˌnɔːm(ə)l ˈwɜːkɪŋ/ *noun* working in the usual way ○ *Normal working will be resumed as soon as the men return to work on Monday.*

normal working week /ˌnɔːm(ə)l
ˈwɜːkɪŋ wiːk/ *noun* the usual number
of hours worked per week ○ *Even
though she is a freelance, she works a
normal working week.*

normative /ˈnɔːmətɪv/ *adjective* believing that everything should be agreed
in writing and should then be binding on
all parties

norms /nɔːmz/ *plural noun* the values
of an organisation or of society ○ *The
induction period will familiarise workers with the norms of the organisation.*

no-smoking office /nəʊ ˈsməʊkɪŋ
ˌɒfɪs/ *noun* an office where smoking is
not allowed

no-strike agreement /nəʊ ˈstraɪk
əˌɡriːmənt/, **no-strike clause** /nəʊ
ˈstraɪk klɔːz/ *noun* (a clause in) an
agreement where the employees say that
they will never strike

notary public /ˌnəʊtəri ˈpʌblɪk/
noun a lawyer who has the authority to
witness documents and spoken statements, making them official (NOTE: plural is **notaries public**)

notch /nɒtʃ/ *noun* an increment on a
salary scale

notice /ˈnəʊtɪs/ *noun* **1.** a piece of
written information ○ *The company secretary pinned up a notice about the pension scheme.* **2.** an official warning that
a contract is going to end or that terms
are going to be changed □ **until further
notice** until different instructions are
given ○ *You must pay £200 on the 30th
of each month until further notice.* □
without notice with no warning □ **without prior notice** with no advance warning □ **to give advance notice of** to
inform someone officially that something will happen several weeks in the
future **3.** official written information
that an employee is leaving their job on
a certain date □ **she gave in** *or* **handed
in her notice** she resigned **4.** the time
allowed before something takes place ○
We require three months' notice □ **at
short notice** with very little warning ○

*The bank manager will not see anyone
at short notice.*

noticeboard /ˈnəʊtɪsbɔːd/ *noun* a
board fixed to a wall where notices can
be put up ○ *Did you see the new list of
prices on the noticeboard?*

notice of appearance /ˌnəʊtɪs əv
əˈpɪərəns/ *noun* the lodging by an employer of a document to confirm their
intention to defend an application by an
employee to an industrial tribunal

notice of maternity absence
/ˌnəʊtɪs əv məˈtɜːnɪti ˌæbsəns/ *noun*
a statutory notice given by an employee
that she is going to be absent from work
to have a baby

notice period /ˈnəʊtɪs ˌpɪəriəd/,
period of notice /ˌpɪəriəd əv ˈnəʊtɪs/
noun the time stated in the contract of
employment which the employee or
company has to allow between resigning or being fired and the employee actually leaving their job (an employee
has to give at least one week's notice
and an employer has to give between
one week and twelve weeks' notice, depending on the employee's length of
service)

notification /ˌnəʊtɪfɪˈkeɪʃ(ə)n/ *noun*
the act of informing someone of
something

notify /ˈnəʊtɪfaɪ/ *verb* □ **to notify
someone of something** to tell someone
something formally ○ *The management
were notified of the union's decision.*

nuisance /ˈnjuːs(ə)ns/ *noun* something which causes harm or inconvenience to someone or to property

numerical order /njuːˌmerɪk(ə)l
ˈɔːdə/ *noun* an arrangement by numbers
○ *Put these invoices in numerical order.*

nursery /ˈnɜːs(ə)ri/ *noun* a special
room or building where babies and
small children can be looked after (not
necessarily on the company's premises)
○ *The company offers nursery provision
to its staff.* Compare **crèche**

NVQ *abbr* National Vocational
Qualification

O

O & M *abbr* organisation and methods

OAP *abbr* old age pensioner

object /əb'dʒekt/ *verb* to refuse to do something or to say that you do not accept something (NOTE: you object **to** something)

objection /əb'dʒekʃən/ *noun* □ **to raise an objection to something** to object to something ○ *The union delegates raised an objection to the wording of the agreement.*

objective /əb'dʒektɪv/ *noun* something which you hope to achieve ○ *The company has achieved its objectives.* ○ *We set the sales forces specific objectives.* ○ *Our recruitment objectives are to have well-qualified and well-placed staff.* □ **long-term** *or* **short-term objective** an aim which you hope to achieve within a few years or a few months □ **to achieve one's objectives** to do what you set out to do ○ *The company has achieved almost all its objectives.* ■ *adjective* considered from a general point of view rather than from that of the person involved ○ *You must be objective in assessing the performance of the staff.* ○ *They have been asked to carry out an objective survey of the market.* (NOTE: the opposite is **subjective**)

objective setting /əb'dʒektɪv ˌsetɪŋ/ *noun* the process of planning targets (e.g. for negotiations). **♦ management by objectives**

objective test /əbˌdʒektɪv 'test/ *noun* a test where each question has only one possible answer (NOTE: the opposite is **subjective test**)

obligation /ˌɒblɪ'geɪʃ(ə)n/ *noun* a duty to do something ○ *There is no obligation to help out in another department* □ **to be under an obligation to do**

something to feel it is your duty to do something

obligatory /ə'blɪɡət(ə)ri/ *adjective* necessary according to the law or rules ○ *Each member of the sales staff has to pass an obligatory medical examination.*

observance /əb'zɜːv(ə)ns/ *noun* doing what is required by a law ○ *The company's observance of the law concerning discrimination.*

observation /ˌɒbzə'veɪʃ(ə)n/ *noun* the act of noticing what is happening

observational method /ˌɒbzə-ˌveɪʃ(ə)n(ə)l 'meθəd/ *noun* a way of evaluating the performance of employees, by watching them work and observing their conduct with others

observe /əb'zɜːv/ *verb* **1.** to obey a rule or law ○ *Failure to observe the correct procedure will be punished.* ○ *Restaurants are obliged to observe the local fire regulations.* **2.** to watch or to notice what is happening ○ *Officials have been instructed to observe the conduct of the ballot for union president.*

observer /əb'zɜːvə/ *noun* a person who observes ○ *Two official observers attended the election meeting.*

obsolescence /ˌɒbsə'les(ə)ns/ *noun* the process of a product going out of date because of progress in design or technology, and therefore becoming less useful or valuable

obsolescent /ˌɒbsə'les(ə)nt/ *adjective* becoming out of date

obsolete /'ɒbsəliːt/ *adjective* no longer used ○ *Computer technology changes so fast that hardware soon becomes obsolete.*

COMMENT: A product or asset may become obsolete because it is worn out, or because new products have been developed to replace it.

obstacle /ˈɒbstək(ə)l/ *noun* something which prevents you from doing something

obstruct /əbˈstrʌkt/ *verb* to get in the way or to stop something progressing

occupation /ˌɒkjʊˈpeɪʃ(ə)n/ *noun* **1.** the act of living or staying in a place **2.** a job or type of work ○ *What is her occupation?* ○ *His main occupation is house building.* ○ *It is not a well paid occupation.*

'…the share of white-collar occupations in total employment rose from 44 per cent to 49 per cent' [*Sydney Morning Herald*]

occupational /ˌɒkjʊˈpeɪʃ(ə)nəl/ *adjective* referring to a job

occupational accident /ˌɒkjʊpeɪʃ(ə)nəl ˈæksɪd(ə)nt/ *noun* an accident which takes place at work

occupational association /ɒkjʊˌpeɪʃ(ə)nəl əsəʊsiˈeɪʃ(ə)n/ *noun* an organisation which represents people doing a certain type of work and defends their interests

occupational deafness /ˌɒkjʊpeɪʃ(ə)nəl ˈdefnəs/ *noun* deafness caused by noise at work (as by someone using a pneumatic drill)

occupational disease /ɒkjʊˈpeɪʃ(ə)nəl dɪˌziːz/ *noun* a disease which affects people in certain jobs

occupational family /ˌɒkjʊpeɪʃ(ə)nəl ˈfæm(ə)li/ *noun* a group of jobs having the same personnel requirements ○ *For jobs in certain occupational families, finding qualified staff is going to be difficult.*

occupational group /ˌɒkjʊpeɪʃ(ə)nəl ˈgruːp/ *noun* a category of job or profession

occupational hazard /ˌɒkjʊpeɪʃ(ə)nəl ˈhæzəd/ *noun* a danger which applies to certain jobs ○ *Heart attacks are one of the occupational hazards of directors.*

occupational health /ˌɒkjʊpeɪʃ(ə)nəl ˈhelθ/, **occupational hygiene** /ˌɒkjʊpeɪʃ(ə)nəl ˈhaɪdʒiːn/ *noun* a branch of medicine dealing with the health of people at work (NOTE: also called **industrial health**)

occupational illness /ˌɒkjʊpeɪʃ(ə)nəl ˈɪlnəs/ *noun* an illness associated with a particular job (NOTE: Occupational illnesses include lung disease, which can affect miners, repetitive strain injury, which can affect keyboard users, and asbestosis, which is caused by working with asbestos.)

occupational injury /ˌɒkjʊpeɪʃ(ə)nəl ˈɪndʒəri/ *noun* an injury which is caused by a certain type of work

occupational mobility /ˌɒkjʊpeɪʃ(ə)nəl məʊˈbɪlɪti/ *noun* the extent to which people can move from one type of occupation to another ○ *Occupational mobility is increasing because of rising unemployment in some areas.*

Occupational Pensions Board /ˌɒkjʊpeɪʃ(ə)nəl ˈpenʃənz bɔːd/ *noun* a government body set up to oversee and validate occupational pension schemes. Abbr **OPB**

occupational pension scheme /ˌɒkjʊˌpeɪʃ(ə)nəl ˈpenʃən skiːm/ *noun* pension scheme where the worker gets a pension from a fund set up by the company he or she has worked for, which is related to the salary he or she was earning (NOTE: also called **company pension scheme**)

occupational psychology /ˌɒkjʊpeɪʃ(ə)nəl saɪˈkɒlədʒi/ *noun* the study of the behaviour of people at work

occupational sick pay /ˌɒkjʊpeɪʃ(ə)nəl ˈsɪk peɪ/ *noun* extra payments made by an employer to a member of staff who is sick, above the statutory sick pay. Abbr **OSP**

occupational therapy /ˌɒkjʊpeɪʃ(ə)nəl ˈθerəpi/ *noun* light work or hobbies used as a means of treatment for an illness, condition or disability

occupy /ˈɒkjʊpaɪ/ *verb* □ **to occupy a post** to be employed in a job

odd-job-man /ˌɒd ˈdʒɒb mæn/ *noun* a person who does various pieces of work

odd jobs /ˌɒd ˈdʒɒbz/ *plural noun* small pieces of work, not connected to each other and paid for individually ○

We have a number of odd jobs needing doing, but nothing adding up to full-time employment.

odd number /ˌɒd 'nʌmbə/ *noun* a number which cannot be divided by two, e.g. 17 or 33 ○ *Buildings with odd numbers are on the south side of the street*

off /ɒf/ *adverb* not working or not in operation ○ *The agreement is off.* ○ *They called the strike off.* ○ *It's my day off tomorrow.* ○ *to take three days off* ○ *We give the staff four days off at Christmas.* ■ *preposition* away from work ○ *to take time off work*

offence /ə'fens/ *noun* a crime or act which is against the law □ **to be charged with an offence** to be accused formally of having committed a crime ○ *The manager was charged with three serious offences.* □ **to commit an offence** to carry out a crime (NOTE: the usual US spelling is **offense**)

offender /ə'fendə/ *noun* a person who breaks a law or regulation ○ *When we investigated who was making private calls during the working hours, the worst offender was the human resources manager.*

offer /'ɒfə/ *noun* a statement that you are willing to give or do something, especially to pay a specific amount of money to buy something ○ *to make an offer for a company* ○ *We made an offer of £10 a share.* ○ *£1,000 is the best offer I can make.* □ **to make someone an offer** to propose something to someone ○ *The management made the union an improved offer.* □ **to make someone an offer they can't refuse** to make an offer to someone which is so attractive that they cannot turn it down □ **to accept** *or* **take up an offer** to say 'yes' or to agree to an offer □ **to turn down an offer** to refuse something which has been offered ■ *verb* to say that you are willing to do something □ **to offer someone a job** to tell someone that they can have a job in your company ○ *She was offered a directorship with Smith Ltd.* □ **offer of employment**, **offer of a job** a letter from an employer saying that someone can have a job with them

office /'ɒfɪs/ *noun* **1.** a set of rooms where a company works or where business is done **2.** a room where someone works and does business ○ *Come into my office.* ○ *The human resources manager's office is on the third floor.* **3.** a post or position ○ *She holds* or *performs the office of treasurer* □ **to take office** to start to work in a certain position

office-bearer /'ɒfɪs ˌbeərə/ *noun* a person who holds an office, especially on a union council

office block /'ɒfɪs blɒk/ *noun* a building which contains only offices

office boy /'ɒfɪs bɔɪ/ *noun* a young man who works in an office, usually taking messages from one department to another ○ *He worked his way up from office boy to general manager in ten years.*

office-free /ˌɒfɪs 'friː/ *adjective* referring to an employee whose job does not require them to work in an office

office hours /'ɒfɪs aʊəz/ *plural noun* the time when an office is open ○ *Do not make private phone calls during office hours.*

office job /'ɒfɪs dʒɒb/ *noun* a job in an office

office junior /ˌɒfɪs 'dʒuːniə/ *noun* a young man or woman who does all types of work in an office

Office of Fair Trading /ˌɒfɪs əv feə 'treɪdɪŋ/ *noun* a government department which protects consumers against unfair or illegal business. Abbr **OFT**

officer /'ɒfɪsə/ *noun* **1.** a person who has an official position, especially an unpaid one in a club or other association ○ *The election of officers takes place next week.* **2.** someone holding an official position, usually unpaid, of a club or society, etc. ○ *the election of officers of the association takes place next week*

office staff /'ɒfɪs stɑːf/ *noun* people who work in offices

office work /'ɒfɪs wɜːk/ *noun* work done in an office

office worker /'ɒfɪs ˌwɜːkə/ *noun* a person who works in an office

official /ə'fɪʃ(ə)l/ *adjective* **1.** from a government department or organisation

○ *She went to France on official business.* ○ *He left official documents in his car.* ○ *She received an official letter of explanation.* □ **speaking in an official capacity** speaking officially □ **to go through official channels** to deal with officials, especially when making a request **2.** done or approved by a director or by a person in authority ○ *This must be an official order – it is written on the company's headed paper.* ○ *This is the union's official policy.* ■ *noun* a person working in a government department ○ *Government officials stopped the import licence.* □ **minor official** person in a low position in a government department ○ *Some minor official tried to stop my request for building permission.*

official dispute /ə,fɪʃ(ə)l dɪ'spjuːt/ *noun* an industrial action approved by a trade union

officialese /ə,fɪʃə'liːz/ *noun* the language used in government documents which can be difficult to understand

officially /ə'fɪʃ(ə)li/ *adverb* according to what is said in public ○ *Officially he knows nothing about the problem, but unofficially he has given us a lot of advice about it.*

official mediator /ə,fɪʃ(ə)l 'miːdieɪtə/ *noun* a government official who tries to make the two sides in an industrial dispute agree

official receiver /ə,fɪʃ(ə)l rɪ'siːvə/ *noun* a government official who is appointed to run a company which is in financial difficulties, to pay off its debts as far as possible and to close it down ○ *The company is in the hands of the offical receiver.*

off the books /,ɒf ðə 'bʊks/ *adjective US* not declared to the tax authorities ○ *Some of the staff are paid off the books.*

off-the-job training /,ɒf ðə dʒɒb 'treɪnɪŋ/ *noun* training given to employees away from their place of work (such as at a college or school)

off-topic /ɒf 'tɒpɪk/ *noun* irrelevant or off the subject

old /əʊld/ *adjective* having existed for a long time ○ *The company is 125 years old next year.* ○ *We have decided to get*

rid of our old computer system and install a new one.

old age /əʊld 'eɪdʒ/ *noun* a period when a person is old

old age pensioner /,əʊld eɪdʒ 'penʃ(ə)nə/ *noun* a person who receives the retirement pension. Abbr **OAP**

old boy network /'əʊld bɔɪ ,netwɜːk/ *noun* the practice of using long-standing key contacts to appoint people to jobs or to get a job or to do business. ⟡ **networking**

older worker /,əʊldə 'wɜːkə/ *noun* an employee who is above a particular age, usually the age of 50

old-fashioned /,əʊld 'fæʃ(ə)nd/ *adjective* out of date or not modern ○ *He still uses an old-fashioned typewriter.*

ombudsman /'ɒmbʊdzmən/ *noun* **1.** a management employee who is given the freedom to move around the workplace to locate and remedy unfair practices (NOTE: plural is **ombudsmen**) **2.** an official who investigates complaints by the public against government departments or other large organisations

'…radical changes to the disciplinary system, including appointing an ombudsman to review cases where complainants are not satisfied with the outcome, are proposed in a consultative paper the Institute of Chartered Accountants issued last month' [*Accountancy*]

COMMENT: There are several ombudsmen: the main one is the Parliamentary Commissioner, who is a civil servant and investigates complaints against government departments. The Banking Ombudsman, the Investment Ombudsman, the Building Societies Ombudsman, the Pensions Ombudsman and the Insurance Ombudsman are independent officials who investigate complaints by the public against banks, financial advisers, building societies, pension funds or insurance companies. They are all regulated by the Financial Services Authority.

omnibus agreement /'ɒmnɪbəs ə-,griːmənt/ *noun* an agreement which covers many different items

omnibus test /'ɒmnɪbəs test/ *noun* a test which covers various subjects

on /ɒn/ *preposition* **1.** being a member of a group ○ *to sit on a committee* ○ *She is on the boards of two companies.* ○ *We have 250 people on the payroll.* ○ *She is* *on our full-time staff.* **2.** in a certain way ○ *on a commercial basis* ○ *He is still on probation.* ○ *She is employed on very generous terms.* **3.** at a time ○ *We work 7 hours a day on weekdays.* ○ *The whole staff has the day off on May 24th.* **4.** doing something ○ *The director is on holiday.* ○ *She is in the States on business.* ○ *The switchboard operator is on duty from 6 to 9.*

on call /ɒn ˈkɔːl/ *adverb* ready to be called to work at any time ○ *We must have an engineer on call twenty-four hours a day.*

on-call pay /ɒn ˈkɔːl peɪ/ *noun* pay for being on call outside normal working hours ○ *The on-call pay was not enough to compensate for being on call all night.*

on-call time /ɒn ˈkɔːl taɪm/ *noun* time outside normal working hours when an employee is standing by, ready for work

one-man business /ˌwʌn mæn ˈbɪznɪs/, **one-man firm** /ˌwʌn mæn ˈfɜːm/, **one-man company** /ˌwʌn mæn ˈkʌmp(ə)ni/ *noun* a business run by one person alone with no staff or partners

one-off /ˌwʌn ˈɒf/ *adjective* done or made only once ○ *one-off item* ○ *one-off deal* ○ *one-off payment* □ **a one-off payment** a single payment, made once only and not repeated

one-off payment /ˌwʌn ɒf ˈpeɪmənt/ *noun* a single payment, made once only and not repeated

onerous /ˈəʊnərəs/ *adjective* heavy, needing a lot of effort or money

one-sided /wʌn ˈsaɪdɪd/ *adjective* which favours one side and not the other in a negotiation

on-going /ɒn ˈɡəʊɪŋ/ *adjective* which is continuing ○ *on-going discussions*

online /ɒnˈlaɪn/ *adjective, adverb* linked directly to a mainframe computer ○ *The sales office is online to the warehouse.* ○ *We get our data online from the stock control department.*

'…there may be a silver lining for 'clicks-and-mortar' stores that have both an online and a high street presence. Many of these are accepting returns of goods purchased online at their traditional stores. This is a service that may make them more popular as consumers become more experienced online shoppers' [*Financial Times*]

'…a survey found that even among experienced users – those who shop online at least once a month – about 10% abandoned a planned purchase because of annoying online delays and procedures' [*Financial Times*]

'…some online brokers failed to foresee the huge increase in private dealing and had problems coping with the rising volume. It has been the year when private investors were able to trade online quickly, cheaply, and on the whole, with little bother' [*Financial Times*]

online training /ˌɒnlaɪn ˈtreɪnɪŋ/ *noun* computer-based training that is delivered over the Internet or through a company intranet

o.n.o. *abbr* or near offer

on-target earnings /ɒn ˌtɑːɡɪt ˈɜːnɪŋz/ *plural noun* the amount earned by people who work on commission when they achieve the targets set for them. Abbr **OTE**

on-the-job training /ˌɒn ðə dʒɒb ˈtreɪnɪŋ/ *noun* training given to employees at their place of work

on the side /ɒn ðə ˈsaɪd/ *adverb* separate from your normal work, and hidden from your employer ○ *He works in an accountant's office, but he runs a construction company on the side.* ○ *Her salary is too small to live on, so the family lives on what she can make on the side.*

on the understanding that /ɒn ðə ʌndəˈstændɪŋ ðət/ *conjunction* on condition that, provided that ○ *We accept the terms of the contract, on the understanding that it has to be ratified by our main board.*

OPB *abbr* Occupational Pensions Board

open /ˈəʊpən/ *adjective* **1.** at work or not closed ○ *The store is open on Sunday mornings.* ○ *Our offices are open from 9 to 6.* ○ *They are open for business every day of the week.* **2.** ready to accept something □ **we will keep the job open for a month** we will not give the job to anyone else for a month □ **job is open to all applicants** anyone can apply for the job ■ *verb* **1.** to start a new business ○ *She has opened a shop in the High Street.* ○ *We have opened a branch in London.* **2.** to start work or to

be at work ○ *The office opens at 9 a.m.*
○ *We open for business on Sundays.* **3.**
to begin □ **to open negotiations** to begin negotiating ○ *She opened the discussions with a description of the
product.* ○ *The chairman opened the
meeting at 10.30.*

'...after opening at 79.1 the index touched a
peak of 79.2 and then drifted to a low of 78.8'
[*Financial Times*]

open ad /ˈəʊpən æd/ *noun* an advertisement for a job where the applicant
can apply to the employer directly, without having to go through a third party
such as an agency ○ *Open ads can be
used for recruitment when additional
staff are required urgently.*

open-collar worker /ˌəʊpən ˈkɒlə
ˌwɜːkə/ *noun* a person who works from
home (*slang*)

open communication /ˌəʊpən
kəmjuːnɪˈkeɪʃ(ə)n/ *noun* freedom of
people to communicate what they like to
whoever they like within an organisation ○ *The policy of open communication is an aid to decision-making as it
creates a wider source of expertise to be
tapped.*

open day /ˈəʊpən deɪ/ *noun* a day
when an organisation is open to interested candidates who may wish to inspect the organisation and discuss career
possibilities ○ *I went to the charity's
open day to see what training they demanded for fund-raising work.* ○ *At the
open day last week, preliminary interviews were held with candidates to see if
their backgrounds were right for the
company.*

open-door system /ˌəʊpən ˈdɔː
ˌsɪstəm/ *noun* a system in which supervisors are always available at work to
talk to employees

open-ended /ˌəʊpən ˈendɪd/ *adjective* with no fixed limit or with some
items not specified ○ *They signed an
open-ended agreement.* ○ *The candidate
was offered an open-ended contract
with a good career plan.* (NOTE: American English is **open-end**)

open-ended interview /ˌəʊpən
endɪd ˈɪntəvjuː/ an interview where the
candidate is asked general questions,

which make them give reasons for actions, show their feelings, etc.

opening /ˈəʊp(ə)nɪŋ/ *noun* **1.** the act
of starting a new business ○ *the opening
of a new branch* **2.** an opportunity to do
something

open learning /ˌəʊpən ˈlɜːnɪŋ/ *noun*
a system of flexible training courses
which a trainee can start at any time, and
which do not require a teacher ○ *Open
learning can be fitted round the employee's work schedule.*

openness /ˈəʊpənəs/ *noun* the quality of being honest and not hiding anything ○ *openness in discussing company
problems with staff*

open-plan office /ˌəʊpən plæn
ˈɒfɪs/ *noun* a large room divided into
smaller working spaces with no fixed
divisions between them

open shop /ˌəʊpən ˈʃɒp/ *noun* a
workplace where employees can be employed whether they are members of a
union or not

open system /ˈəʊpən ˌsɪstəm/ *noun*
a flexible type of organisation, which allows employees freedom to work in
their own way ○ *An open system can allow employees to choose their own
working hours.*

open union /ˌəʊpən ˈjuːnjən/ *noun* a
union which accepts members from a
wide range of jobs

operate /ˈɒpəreɪt/ *verb* **1.** to be in
force ○ *The new terms of service will
operate from January 1st.* ○ *The rules
operate on inland postal services only.*
2. to make something work or function
□ **to operate a machine** to make a machine work ○ *He is learning to operate
the new telephone switchboard.* **3.** to do
business

'...the company gets valuable restaurant
locations which will be converted to the
family-style restaurant chain that it operates and
franchises throughout most parts of the US'
[*Fortune*]

operation /ˌɒpəˈreɪʃ(ə)n/ *noun* **1.** a
business organisation and work ○ *the
company's operations in West Africa* **2.**
□ **to put a plan into operation** to start a
plan working

'...a leading manufacturer of business,
industrial and commercial products requires a

branch manager to head up its mid-western Canada operations based in Winnipeg' [*Globe and Mail (Toronto)*]

operational /ˌɒpəˈreɪʃ(ə)nəl/ *adjective* **1.** referring to how something works **2.** working or in operation □ **the system became operational on June 1st** the system began working on June 1st

operational budget /ˌɒpəreɪʃ(ə)nəl ˈbʌdʒɪt/ *noun* a forecast of expenditure on running a business

operations review /ˌɒpəreɪʃ(ə)nz rɪˈvjuː/ *noun* an act of examining the way in which a company or department works to see how it can be made more efficient and profitable

operative /ˈɒp(ə)rətɪv/ *adjective* operating or working ○ *The new system has been operative since June 1st* □ **to become operative** to start working ■ *noun* a person who operates a machine which makes a product ○ *A skilled operative can produce 250 units per hour.*

operator /ˈɒpəreɪtə/ *noun* **1.** a person who works a machine ○ *a keyboard operator* ○ *a computer operator* **2.** a person who works a telephone switchboard ○ *switchboard operator* ○ *to call the operator* or *to dial the operator* ○ *to place a call through* or *via the operator* **3.** a person who runs a business

opinion-leader /əˈpɪnjən ˌliːdə/ *noun* a person or organisation whose opinions influence others in society ○ *A pop-star is the ideal opinion-leader if the product is aimed at the teenage market.*

opportunistic /ˌɒpətjuːˈnɪstɪk/ *adjective* done when the opportunity arises □ **opportunistic thefts in offices** thefts committed when valuables are left lying around

opportunity /ˌɒpəˈtjuːnɪti/ *noun* a chance to do something successfully □ **to seize an opportunity** to take advantage of an opportunity as soon as it appears □ **to miss out on an opportunity** not to be able to take advantage of an opportunity. ♦ **equal opportunities**

'…the group is currently undergoing a period of rapid expansion and this has created an exciting opportunity for a qualified accountant' [*Financial Times*]

oppose /əˈpəʊz/ *verb* to try to stop something happening; to vote against something ○ *A minority of board members opposed the motion.* ○ *We are all opposed to the takeover.* ○ *A minority of union members opposed the deal.*

opposite number /ˌɒpəzɪt ˈnʌmbə/ *noun* a person who has a similar job in another company □ **John is my opposite number in Smith's** John has the same job in Smith's as I have here

optional /ˈɒpʃ(ə)n(ə)l/ *adjective* not necessary according to rules ○ *Attendance at staff meetings is optional, although the management encourages employees to attend.*

opt out /ˌɒpt ˈaʊt/ *verb* to decide not to do something

oral /ˈɔːrəl/ *adjective* referring to speech, as opposed to writing

oral warning /ˌɔːrəl ˈwɔːnɪŋ/ *noun* the first stage of disciplinary measures, where an employee is told by the supervisor that their work is unsatisfactory and must be improved ○ *After being given his second oral warning he knew he would be fired for absenteeism.* ○ *After an oral warning from her supervisor, she received a written warning from the human resources director.*

order /ˈɔːdə/ *noun* **1.** an arrangement of records such as filing cards or invoices □ **in order of merit** the placing of employees in order according to their qualities **2.** working arrangement □ **machine in full working order** a machine which is ready and able to work properly □ **the telephone is out of order** the telephone is not working □ **is all the documentation in order?** are all the documents valid and correct? **3.** an instruction ■ *verb* **1.** to instruct ○ *to order twenty filing cabinets to be delivered to the warehouse* **2.** to put in a certain way ○ *The address list is ordered by country.* ○ *That filing cabinet contains invoices ordered by date.*

order fulfilment /ˈɔːdə fʊlˌfɪlmənt/ *noun* the process of supplying items which have been ordered

ordinary /ˈɔːd(ə)n(ə)ri/ *adjective* not special

organ /'ɔːgən/ *noun* a journal or magazine

organic organisation /ɔːˌgænɪk ɔːgənaɪ'zeɪʃ(ə)n/ *noun* a type of organisation with little formality in its structure and procedures

organigram /ɔː'gænɪgræm/ *noun* same as **organisational chart**

organisation /ˌɔːgənaɪ'zeɪʃ(ə)n/, **organization** *noun* **1.** a way of arranging something so that it works efficiently ○ *the organisation of the head office into departments* ○ *The chairman handles the organisation of the AGM.* ○ *The organisation of the group is too centralised to be efficient.* **2.** a group or institution which is arranged for efficient work □ **employers' or trade union organisation** a group of employers or trade unions with similar interests

'…working with a client base which includes many major commercial organizations and nationalized industries' [*Times*]

organisational /ˌɔːgənaɪ-'zeɪʃ(ə)nəl/, **organizational** *adjective* referring to the way in which something is organised ○ *The paper gives a diagram of the company's organisational structure.*

organisational analysis /ˌɔːgənaɪ-ˌzeɪʃ(ə)nəl ə'næləsɪs/ *noun* a type of analysis carried out by an organisation that is intended to identify areas where it is inefficient and ways in which it can be restructured so as to become more efficient

organisational change /ˌɔːgənaɪ-ˌzeɪʃ(ə)nəl 'tʃeɪndʒ/ *noun* a change in the way something is organised

organisational chart /ˌɔːgənaɪ-ˌzeɪʃ(ə)nəl 'tʃɑːt/ *noun* a chart showing the hierarchical relationships between employees in a company

organisational climate /ˌɔːgənaɪ-ˌzeɪʃ(ə)nəl 'klaɪmət/ *noun* the general feeling in an organisation ○ *The organisational climate will improve as soon as employees are allowed to take part in decision-making.*

organisational culture /ˌɔːgənaɪ-ˌzeɪʃ(ə)nəl 'kʌltʃə/ *noun* same as **corporate culture**

organisational development /ˌɔːgənaɪˌzeɪʃ(ə)nəl dɪ'veləpmənt/ *noun* a form of management training designed to affect the whole organisation as well as the individual employees

organisational iceberg /ˌɔːgənaɪ-ˌzeɪʃ(ə)nəl 'aɪsbɜːg/ *noun* an official or apparent system of an organisation, as opposed to the way the organisation is really run

organisational learning /ˌɔːgənaɪ-ˌzeɪʃ(ə)nəl 'lɜːnɪŋ/ *noun* activities within an organisation that are aimed at the further training and personal development of employees and are intended to create a willing acceptance of changes and improvements and high levels of enthusiasm, energy, creativity and innovation among them (NOTE: The concept of organisational learning was further developed as the learning organisation.)

organisation pyramid /ˌɔːgənaɪ-'zeɪʃ(ə)n ˌpɪrəmɪd/ *noun* a structure of an organisation with many employees at lower levels and fewer at the top

organisation theory /ˌɔːgənaɪ-'zeɪʃ(ə)n ˌθɪəri/ *noun* the study of the structure and function of organisations

organise /'ɔːgənaɪz/, **organize** *verb* to set up a system for doing something ○ *The company is organised into six profit centres.* ○ *The group is organised by sales areas.*

'…we organize a rate with importers who have large orders and guarantee them space at a fixed rate so that they can plan their costs' [*Lloyd's List*]

organised labour /ˌɔːgənaɪzd 'leɪbə/ *noun* employees who are members of trade unions

'…governments are coming under increasing pressure from politicians, organized labour and business to stimulate economic growth' [*Duns Business Month*]

organogram /ɔː'gænəgræm/ *noun* same as **organisational chart**

orientation /ˌɔːriən'teɪʃ(ə)n/ *noun* **1.** the main interest or type of activity ○ *The company's orientation is towards production and it has little marketing experience.* **2.** the introduction of new employees into an organisation ○ *The orientation programme included a talk by the chairman on the history of the* *company and its products.* ○ *Lack of proper orientation can cause much distress in the first days of a new job.*

oriented /'ɔːrɪentɪd/, **orientated** /'ɔːrɪənteɪtɪd/ *adjective* working in a certain direction ○ *a market-orientated approach*

originating application /ə-ˌrɪdʒɪneɪtɪŋ æplɪ'keɪʃ(ə)n/ *noun* a form by which an employee begins the process of complaint to an industrial tribunal

ostracise /'ɒstrəsaɪz/, **ostracize** *verb* to reject and refuse to have anything to do with a member or members of a group ○ *Workers who carried on working were ostracised after the strike ended.*

ostracism /'ɒstrəsɪz(ə)m/ *noun* rejection of a member or members of a group by others ○ *The fate of non-strikers was ostracism by their former colleagues.*

OTE *abbr* on-target earnings

out /aʊt/ *adverb* on strike ○ *As soon as the management made the offer, the staff came out.* ○ *The shop stewards called the workforce out.*

out box /'aʊt bɒks/ *noun US* a box or other container for documents and other items that have been dealt with (NOTE: Items are placed in the out box before being filed or delivered to another person.)

outcome /'aʊtkʌm/ *noun* a result ○ *What was the outcome of the discussion?*

outdoor training /ˌaʊtdɔː 'treɪnɪŋ/ *noun* same as **adventure training**

outfit /'aʊtfɪt/ *noun* a small, sometimes badly run company ○ *They called in a public relations outfit.* ○ *He works for some finance outfit.*

out-house /'aʊt haʊs/ *adjective, adverb* working outside a company's buildings ○ *the out-house staff* ○ *We do all our data processing out-house.*

outing /'aʊtɪŋ/ *noun* a trip away from the place of work

outline /'aʊtlaɪn/ *noun* a general description, without giving many details ○ *They drew up the outline of a plan* or *an*

outline plan. ■ *verb* to make a general description ○ *The chairman outlined the company's plans for the coming year.*

outline agreement /'aʊt(ə)laɪn ə-ˌgriːmənt/ *noun* the general draft of an agreement, without giving any details

out of court /ˌaʊt əv 'kɔːt/ *adverb, adjective* □ **a settlement was reached out of court** a dispute was settled between two parties privately without continuing a court case

out-of-court settlement /ˌaʊt əv kɔːt 'set(ə)lmənt/ *noun* an act of settling a dispute between two parties privately without continuing a court case

out-of-date /ˌaʊt əv 'deɪt/ *adjective, adverb* old-fashioned or no longer modern ○ *Their computer system is years out of date.* ○ *They're still using out-of-date equipment.*

out of pocket /ˌaʊt əv 'pɒkɪt/ *adjective, adverb* having paid out money personally ○ *The deal has left me out of pocket.*

out of the loop /ˌaʊt əv ðə 'luːp/ *adverb* deliberately or accidentally excluded from decision-making processes and the flow of information around an organisation (*informal*) (NOTE: A person who is out of the loop is likely to feel isolated and will be unable to contribute fully to the organisation.)

out of work /ˌaʊt əv 'wɜːk/ *adjective, adverb* with no job ○ *The recession has put millions out of work.* ○ *The company was set up by three out-of-work engineers.*

outplacement /'aʊtˌpleɪsmənt/ *noun* help in finding another job, given by an employer to an employee who has been made redundant

output /'aʊtpʊt/ *noun* **1.** the amount which a company, person or machine produces ○ *Output has increased by 10%.* ○ *25% of our output is exported.* **2.** information which is produced by a computer (NOTE: the opposite is **input**) ■ *verb* to produce (by computer) ○ *The printer will output colour graphics.* ○ *That is the information outputted from the computer.* ○ *The printer will output colour graphs.* (NOTE: **outputting – outputted**)

'…crude oil output plunged during the last month and is likely to remain near its present level for the near future' [*Wall Street Journal*]

output bonus /'aʊtpʊt ˌbəʊnəs/, **output-based bonus** /ˌaʊtpʊt beɪst 'bəʊnəs/ *noun* an extra payment for increased production

output per hour /ˌaʊtpʊt pər 'aʊə/ *noun* the amount of something produced in one hour

outside /'aʊtsaɪd/ *adjective, adverb* not in a company's office or building □ **to send work to be done outside** to send work to be done in other offices

outside director /ˌaʊtsaɪd daɪ-'rektə/ *noun* a director who is not employed by the company, a non-executive director

outside line /ˌaʊtsaɪd 'laɪn/ *noun* a line from an internal office telephone system to the main telephone exchange ○ *You dial 9 to get an outside line.*

outside office hours /ˌaʊtsaɪd 'nfɪs aʊəz/ *adverb* when the office is not open

outside worker /'aʊtsaɪd ˌwɜːkə/ *noun* an employee who does not work in a company's offices

outsourcing /'aʊtsɔːsɪŋ/ *noun* the practice of obtaining services from specialist bureaux or other companies, rather than employing full-time members of staff to provide them

'…organizations in the public and private sectors are increasingly buying in specialist services – or outsourcing – allowing them to cut costs and concentrate on their core business activities' [*Financial Times*]

outstrip /aʊt'strɪp/ *verb* to become larger than something else ○ *Wage increases are outstripping inflation.* (NOTE: **outstripped – outstripping**)

outvote /aʊt'vəʊt/ *verb* to defeat in a vote □ **the chairman was outvoted** the majority voted against the chairman

outward bound training /ˌaʊtwəd 'baʊnd ˌtreɪnɪŋ/ *noun* same as **adventure training**

outwork /'aʊtwɜːk/ *noun* work which a company pays someone to do at home

outworker /'aʊtwɜːkə/ *noun* a person who works at home for a company

over- /əʊvə/ *prefix* more than □ **shop which caters to the over-60s** a shop which has goods which appeal to people who are more than sixty years old

overachiever /ˌəʊvərə'tʃiːvə/ *noun* a person who tries too hard and achieves more than they are really capable of ○ *Overachievers on the management course were encouraged to slow down.*

overall /ˌəʊvər'ɔːl/ *adjective* covering or including everything □ **the company reported an overall fall in profits** the company reported a general fall in profits □ **overall plan** a plan which covers everything

overall performance /ˌəʊvərɔːl pə-'fɔːməns/ *noun* the performance of an employee relating to the whole job, and not simply to part of it

overcome /ˌəʊvə'kʌm/ *verb* to beat something after a struggle ○ *to overcome obstacles on the way to reaching agreement* (NOTE: **overcoming – overcame**)

overemployment /ˌəʊvərɪm-'plɔɪmənt/ *noun* a situation where there is a shortage of labour in a certain area or industry

overhaul /əʊvə'hɔːl/ *verb* to examine something carefully and make changes so that it works better ○ *to overhaul the company's union agreements*

overhead budget /ˌəʊvəhed 'bʌdʒɪt/ *noun* a plan of probable overhead costs

overheads /'əʊvəhedz/ *plural noun* the costs of the day-to-day running of a business ○ *The sales revenue covers the manufacturing costs but not the overheads.* (NOTE: American English is usually **overhead**.)

overlearning /'əʊvəlɜːnɪŋ/ *noun* the process of continuing the learning process beyond the level of skill needed ○ *The training manager found that without overlearning, skills were easily lost.*

overmanned /ˌəʊvə'mænd/ *adjective* having more employees than necessary

overmanning /ˌəʊvə'mænɪŋ/ *noun* the state of having more employees than are needed to do a company's work ○ *The MD's plan is to reduce overman-*

ning. ○ *The answer to our overmanning problem must be redundancies.*

overpaid /ˌəʊvəˈpeɪd/ *adjective* paid too much ○ *Our staff are overpaid and underworked.*

overproduce /ˌəʊvəprəˈdjuːs/ *verb* to produce too much of a product

overproduction /ˌəʊvəprəˈdʌkʃən/ *noun* the manufacturing of too much of a product

overqualified /ˌəʊvəˈkwɒlɪfaɪd/ *adjective* having too many skills for a job ○ *With a degree in business studies she is overqualified to be an ordinary shop floor worker.*

overrated /ˌəʊvəˈreɪtɪd/ *adjective* valued more highly than it should be ○ *The effect of the dollar on European business cannot be overrated.* ○ *Their 'first-class service' is very overrated.*

overrepresent /ˌəʊvəreprɪˈzent/ *verb* to give one group more representatives than another ○ *This group of workers are overrepresented on the management committee.*

override /ˌəʊvəˈraɪd/ *verb* not to do something which has been decided ○ *to override an order*

overrule /ˌəʊvəˈruːl/ *verb* to decide against something which has been decided ○ *to overrule a decision*

overrun /ˌəʊvəˈrʌn/ *verb* to go beyond a limit ○ *The workers overran the time limit set by the production manager.* (NOTE: **overrunning – overran – overrun**)

overseas /ˈəʊvəsiːz/ *adjective, adverb* across the sea or to foreign countries ○ *Management trainees knew that they would be sent overseas to learn about the export markets.* ○ *Some workers are going overseas to find new jobs.*

overseas call /ˌəʊvəsiːz ˈkɔːl/ *noun* a call to another country

oversee /ˌəʊvəˈsiː/ *verb* to supervise (NOTE: **overseeing – oversaw – overseen**)

overseer /ˈəʊvəsɪə/ *noun* a person who supervises other workers

overstaffed /ˌəʊvəˈstɑːft/ *adjective* with more employees than are needed to do the work of the company

overtime /ˈəʊvətaɪm/ *noun* hours worked more than the normal working time ○ *to work six hours' overtime* ○ *The overtime rate is one and a half times normal pay.* ○ *He worked six hours' overtime last week.* ■ *adverb* □ **to work overtime** to work longer hours than stated in the contract of employment

overtime ban /ˈəʊvətaɪm bæn/ *noun* an order by a trade union which forbids overtime work by its members

overtime pay /ˈəʊvətaɪm peɪ/ *noun* pay for extra time worked

overtime rate /ˈəʊvətaɪm reɪt/ *noun* the rate of pay for extra time worked

overturn /ˌəʊvəˈtɜːn/ *verb* □ **to overturn a decision of a tribunal** to cancel a decision made previously

overwork /ˌəʊvəˈwɜːk/ *noun* □ **she is suffering from overwork** she has too much work and this is making her ill

overworked /ˌəʊvəˈwɜːkt/ *adjective* having too much work to do ○ *Our staff complain of being underpaid and overworked.*

own /əʊn/ *verb* to have or to possess ○ *He owns 50% of the shares.*

owner /ˈəʊnə/ *noun* a person who owns something

ownership /ˈəʊnəʃɪp/ *noun* the fact of owning something

P

P11 /ˌpiː ɪˈlev(ə)n/ *noun* a working sheet, showing the employer's calculations in deducting tax from an employee's pay

P11D /ˌpiː ɪlev(ə)n ˈdiː/ *noun* a form showing expenses paid to directors

P14 /ˌpiː fɔːˈtiːn/ *noun* a form sent by an employer to the Inland Revenue at the end of a tax year, giving a summary of pay and deductions of an individual employee

P2P /ˌpiː tə ˈpiː/ *adjective* referring to direct communications or dealings between one computer to another without a central server being involved (NOTE: Full form **peer-to-peer**)

P35 /ˌpiː θɜːti ˈfaɪv/ *noun* an annual declaration of pay, tax and other deductions for all employees, sent by the employer to the Inland Revenue

P45 /ˌpiː fɔːti ˈfaɪv/ *noun* a form given to an employee who leaves a company, showing how much tax has been deducted from their salary

P60 /ˌpiː ˈsɪksti/ *noun* a certificate showing pay and tax deducted for each individual employee, sent to each employee at the end of the tax year

PA *abbr* personal assistant

p.a. *abbr* per annum

pacemaker /ˈpeɪsmeɪkə/ *noun* an organisation which helps another to change by giving advice or offering support

package /ˈpækɪdʒ/ *noun* **1.** a box or bag in which goods are sold ○ *Instructions for use are printed on the package.* **2.** a group of different items joined together in one deal **3.** a different items of software sold together ○ *a payroll package* ○ *The computer is sold with accounting and word-processing packages.* ○ *The company's area of specialisation is accounts packages for small businesses.*

'…airlines offer special stopover rates and hotel packages to attract customers to certain routes' [*Business Traveller*]

'…the remuneration package will include an attractive salary, profit sharing and a company car' [*Times*]

'…airlines will book not only tickets but also hotels and car hire to provide a complete package' [*Business Traveller*]

'…in today's fast-growing packaged goods area many companies are discovering that a well-recognized brand name can be a priceless asset' [*Duns Business Month*]

package deal /ˈpækɪdʒ diːl/ *noun* an agreement where several different items are agreed at the same time ○ *They agreed a package deal which involves the construction of the factory, training of staff and purchase of the product.*

paid /peɪd/ *adjective* for which money has been given

paid assistant /peɪd əˈsɪst(ə)nt/ *noun* an assistant who receives a salary

paid educational leave /ˌpeɪd edjʊˌkeɪʃ(ə)n(ə)l ˈliːv/ *noun* time away from work for an employee to study

paid holiday /peɪd ˈhɒlɪdeɪ/, **paid leave** /peɪd ˈliːv/ *noun* a holiday or time away from work when the employee's wages are still paid even though they are not working ○ *I was entitled to paid holiday three months after joining the company.*

paid-up /ˌpeɪd ˈʌp/ *adjective* paid in full

paid-up policy /ˌpeɪd ʌp ˈpɒlɪsi/ *noun* a life insurance policy based on premiums which have already been paid

paired comparisons /peəd kəmˈpærɪs(ə)nz/ *noun* a method of assessment where jobs to be assessed are each compared with all others and a final score for each obtained (also called 'job ranking') ○ *Having observed the work performance of ten employees, the supervisor used paired comparisons to rank performance.* (NOTE: also called **job ranking**)

palmtop /'pɑːm,tɒp/ *noun* a very small computer which can be held in your hand and which usually has a character recognition screen instead of a keyboard

panel /'pæn(ə)l/ *noun* **1.** a flat surface standing upright **2.** a group of people who give advice on a problem ○ *a panel of experts*

panel interview /'pæn(ə)l ,ɪntəvjuː/ *noun* an interview conducted by a group of people, not just by a single interviewer

paperwork /'peɪpəwɜːk/ *noun* office work, especially writing memos and filling in forms ○ *Exporting to Russia involves a large amount of paperwork.*

parental leave /pə,rent(ə)l 'liːv/ *noun* a period away from work that is allowed to a parent to care for a newborn or newly adopted child

parity /'pærɪti/ *noun* being equal □ **female staff want parity with men** they want to have the same rates of pay and perks as the men ○ *The company showed it did not believe in parity by always assigning women to lower positions than men.*

'...the draft report on changes in the international monetary system casts doubt about any return to fixed exchange-rate parities' [*Wall Street Journal*]

Parkinson's law /'pɑːkɪnsənz ,lɔː/ *noun* a law, based on wide experience, that in business the amount of work increases to fill the time available for it

Parliamentary Commissioner for Administration /,pɑːləment(ə)ri kə,mɪʃ(ə)nə fər ədmɪnɪ'streɪʃ(ə)n/ *noun* the ombudsman who investigates complaints by the public against government departments

parte ◊ ex parte

partial /'pɑːʃ(ə)l/ *adjective* not complete

partial disability /,pɑːʃ(ə)l dɪsə-'bɪlɪti/ *noun* a situation where an employee is partly disabled, as so is eligible for less benefit

partial disablement /,pɑːʃ(ə)l dɪs-'eɪb(ə)lmənt/ *noun* the condition of being disabled to such an extent that you can only do part of your normal work

partial retirement /,pɑːʃ(ə)l rɪ-'taɪəmənt/ *noun* same as **phased retirement**

participate /pɑː'tɪsɪpeɪt/ *verb* to take part in an activity or enterprise ○ *The staff are encouraged to participate actively in the company's decision-making processes.*

participation /pɑː,tɪsɪ'peɪʃ(ə)n/ *noun* the act of taking part ○ *Employees are demanding more participation in the company's affairs.* ○ *Participation helps to make an employee feel part of the organisation.*

participation rate /pɑː,tɪsɪ'peɪʃ(ə)n reɪt/ *noun* the proportion of a group that is active in some way ○ *What is the participation rate in this department's fund-raising efforts?*

participative /pɑː'tɪsɪpətɪv/ *adjective* where both sides take part ○ *We do not treat management-worker relations as a participative process.*

participative management /pɑː-,tɪsɪpətɪv 'mænɪdʒmənt/ *noun* management of an organisation or department with the active participation of the staff

partner /'pɑːtnə/ *noun* a person who works in a business and has an equal share in it with other partners ○ *I became a partner in a firm of solicitors.*

partnership /'pɑːtnəʃɪp/ *noun* an unregistered business where two or more people (but not more than twenty) share the risks and profits according to a partnership agreement ○ *to go into partnership with someone* ○ *to join with someone to form a partnership* □ **to offer someone a partnership**, **to take someone into partnership with you** to have a working business and bring someone in to share it with you □ **to dissolve a partnership** to bring a partnership to an end □ **to go into partnership**

with someone to join with someone to form a partnership

part-owner /pɑːt 'əʊnə/ *noun* a person who owns something jointly with one or more other people ○ *I am part-owner of the restaurant.*

part-time /ˌpɑːt 'taɪm/ *adjective, adverb* not working for the whole working week ○ *a part-time worker* ○ *It is a part-time job that involves.* ○ *He is trying to find part-time work when the children are in school.* ○ *We are looking for part-time staff to work our computers.* ○ *She only works part-time as she has small children to look after.*

part-time director /ˌpɑːt taɪm daɪ-'rektə/ *noun* same as **non-executive director**

part-time employee /ˌpɑːt taɪm ɪm'plɔɪiː/, **part-time worker** /ˌpɑːt taɪm 'wɜːkə/ *noun* an employee who works for part of a working week (officially between 8 and 16 hours per week)

part-timer /pɑːt 'taɪmə/ *noun* a person who works part-time

part-time work /ˌpɑːt taɪm 'wɜːk/, **part-time employment** /ˌpɑːt taɪm ɪm'plɔɪmənt/ *noun* work for part of a working week (officially, between 8 and 16 hours per week)

party /'pɑːti/ *noun* a person or organisation involved in a legal dispute or legal agreement ○ *How many parties are there to the contract?* ○ *The company is not a party to the agreement.*

pass /pɑːs/ *noun* a permit to allow someone to go into a building ○ *You need a pass to enter the ministry offices.* ○ *All members of staff must show a pass.* ■ *verb* **1.** to move something on to someone else □ **to pass the buck** to move a problem or responsibility on to someone else to deal with ○ *It has got to the point that there is so much buck-passing that none of the problems get solved.* **2.** to be successful ○ *He passed his typing test.* ○ *She has passed all her exams and now is a qualified accountant.*

passive interview /ˌpæsɪv 'ɪntəvjuː/ *noun* an interview where the interviewee only answers the questions (as in a closed interview)

password /'pɑːswɜːd/ *noun* a word or character which identifies a user and allows them access to a computer system

paternalism /pə'tɜːn(ə)lɪz(ə)m/ *noun* used to describe a style of management where the employer is overprotective towards their employees

paternalistic /pəˌtɜːnə'lɪstɪk/ *adjective* being overprotective towards the employees

paternalistic management style /pəˌtɜːnəlɪstɪk 'mænɪdʒmənt ˌstaɪl/ *noun* a way of managing, where the employer takes all the decisions and tries to keep the loyalty of the workforce by giving them special treatment

paternity leave /pə'tɜːnɪti liːv/ *noun* a short period of leave given to a father to be away from work when his partner has a baby

pattern bargaining /'pæt(ə)n ˌbɑːɡɪnɪŋ/ *noun* bargaining between unions and an employer, in which the unions refer to past collective agreements made with employers

pay /peɪ/ *noun* a salary or wages, money given to someone for regular work □ **holiday with pay** holiday which an employee can take by contract and for which they are paid ■ *verb* **1.** to give money to buy an item or a service ○ *How much did you pay to have the office cleaned?* **2.** to give an employee money for work done ○ *The workforce has not been paid for three weeks.* ○ *We pay good wages for skilled workers.* ○ *How much do they pay you per hour?* □ **to be paid by the hour** to get money for each hour worked □ **to be paid at piecework rates** to get money for each piece of work finished

'…recession encourages communication not because it makes redundancies easier, but because it makes low or zero pay increases easier to accept' [*Economist*]

payable /'peɪəb(ə)l/ *adjective* which is due to be paid □ **payable on demand** which must be paid when payment is asked for

pay as you earn /ˌpeɪ əz juː 'ɜːn/ a tax system, where income tax is deducted from the salary before it is paid to the worker. Abbr **PAYE**

pay-as-you-go /ˌpeɪ əz juː 'gəʊ/ *US* same as **pay as you earn**

pay-cheque /'peɪ tʃek/ *noun* **1.** a salary cheque given to an employee **2.** a monthly cheque by which an employee is paid (NOTE: the American spelling is **paycheck**)

pay comparability /'peɪ kɒmp(ə)rəˌbɪlɪti/ *noun* a similar pay system in two different companies

pay day /'peɪ deɪ/ *noun* a day on which wages are paid to employees (usually Friday for employees paid once a week, and during the last week of the month for employees who are paid once a month)

pay differentials /'peɪ dɪfəˌrenʃəlz/ *plural noun* differences between one employee's pay and another's in similar types of jobs (NOTE: also called **salary differentials** or **wage differentials**)

PAYE *abbr* pay as you earn

pay freeze /'peɪ friːz/ *noun* a period when wages are not allowed to be increased

pay hike /'peɪ haɪk/ *noun* an increase in salary

pay levels /'peɪ ˌlev(ə)lz/ *plural noun* rates of pay for different types of work (NOTE: also called **wage levels**)

payment /'peɪmənt/ *noun* **1.** the act of giving money in exchange for goods or a service ○ *We always ask for payment in cash* or *cash payment and not payment by cheque.* ○ *The payment of interest* or *the interest payment should be made on the 22nd of each month.* □ **payment by results** money given which increases with the amount of work done or goods produced **2.** money paid

payment-in-kind /ˌpeɪmənt ɪn 'kaɪnd/ *noun* an alternative form of pay, given to employees in place of money but considered to be of equivalent value (NOTE: A payment in kind may take the form, for example, of use of a car or an opportunity to purchase goods at cost price.)

payment-in-lieu /ˌpeɪmənt ɪn 'ljuː/ *noun* a payment given in place of something such as a holiday which an employee is entitled to but is unable to take

payment scheme /'peɪmənt skiːm/, **payment system** /'peɪmənt ˌsɪstəm/ *noun* a method used by an organisation to pay staff ○ *The human resources manager has devised a payment scheme which is both fair and motivating.*

payment structure /'peɪmənt ˌstrʌktʃə/ *noun* wage or salary levels in an organisation

pay negotiations /'peɪ nɪgəʊʃiˌeɪʃ(ə)nz/, **pay talks** /'peɪ tɔːks/ *plural noun* discussions between management and employees about pay increases

pay off /ˌpeɪ 'ɒf/ *verb* **1.** to finish paying money which is owed ○ *He won the lottery and paid off his mortgage.* ○ *She is trying to pay off the loan by monthly instalments.* **2.** to terminate somebody's employment and pay all wages that are due ○ *When the company was taken over the factory was closed and all the workers were paid off.*

pay package /'peɪ ˌpækɪdʒ/ *noun* the salary and other benefits offered with a job ○ *The job carries an attractive pay package.* (NOTE: also called **salary package**)

pay packet /'peɪ ˌpækɪt/ *noun* an envelope containing the pay slip and the cash pay

pay parity /'peɪ ˌpærɪti/ *noun* earning the same pay for the same job (NOTE: also called **wage parity**)

pay review /'peɪ rɪˌvjuː/ *noun* a re-examination by the employer of an employee's pay ○ *I'm soon due for a pay review and hope to get a rise.* (NOTE: also called **salary review** or **wage review**)

Pay Review Board /peɪ rɪ'vjuː bɔːd/ *noun* an official body which examines pay scales in a nationalised industry or public service and recommends changes

pay review body /peɪ rɪ'vjuː ˌbɒdi/ *noun* an independent organisation which examines pay scales of groups of employees and recommends increases

pay rise /'peɪ raɪz/ *noun* an increase in pay

payroll /'peɪrəʊl/ *noun* **1.** the list of people employed and paid by a company ○ *The company has 250 on the payroll.* **2.** the money paid by a company in salaries ○ *The office has a weekly payroll of £10,000.*

payroll administration /'peɪrəʊl ədmɪnɪˌstreɪʃ(ə)n/ *noun* the process of administering the salaries and NIC payments for employees and claims for their expenses

payroll clerk /'peɪrəʊl klɑːk/ *noun* a person employed to administer the payment of employees (NOTE: also called **wages clerk**)

payroll costs /'peɪrəʊl kɒsts/ *plural noun* the running costs of payroll administration, as well as the actual salaries themselves

payroll ledger /'peɪrəʊl ˌledʒə/ *noun* a list of staff and their salaries

pay round /'peɪ raʊnd/ *noun* an annual series of wage bargaining negotiations in various industries

pay scale /'peɪ skeɪl/ *noun* a table that sets out the range of pay offered for each grade of job in an organisation (NOTE: also called **salary scale** or **wage scale**)

pay slip /'peɪ slɪp/, **pay statement** /'peɪ ˌsteɪtmənt/ *noun* a piece of paper showing the full amount of an employee's pay, and the money deducted as tax, pension and National Insurance contributions

pay threshold /'peɪ ˌθreʃhəʊld/ *noun* a point at which pay increases because of a threshold agreement

PBR *abbr* payment by results

peak /piːk/ *noun* the highest point ○ *The shares reached their peak in January.* ○ *The share index has fallen 10% since the peak in January.* ○ *Withdrawals from bank accounts reached a peak in the week before Christmas.* ○ *He has reached the peak of his career.* ■ *verb* to reach the highest point ○ *Productivity peaked in January.* ○ *Shares have peaked and are beginning to slip back.* ○ *He peaked early and never achieved his ambition of becoming managing director.* ○ *Demand peaks in August, after which sales usually decline.*

peak hour /'piːk aʊə/ *noun* a time when traffic is worst or when everyone

is trying to travel to work or from work back home ○ *The taxi was delayed in the rush hour traffic.*

peak season /piːk 'siːz(ə)n/ *noun* a period when a company is busiest

peak unemployment /ˌpiːk ʌnɪm'plɔɪmənt/ *noun* a period when unemployment is as its highest level

peer /pɪə/ *noun* a person who is the same age or at the same level as someone else ○ *The human resources director and her peers believed in a strict chain of authority, but the younger managers wanted a more flexible approach.*

peer group appraisal /'pɪə gruːp əˌpreɪz(ə)l/ *noun* an appraisal of an employee by their peer group

peer-to-peer /ˌpɪə tə 'pɪə/ *adjective* full form of **P2P**

peg /peg/ *verb* to maintain or fix something at a specific level □ **to peg wage increases to the cost-of-living index** to limit increases in wages to the increases in the cost-of-living index

penalise /'piːnəlaɪz/, **penalize** *verb* to punish or fine ○ *They were penalised for bad time-keeping.*

penalty /'pen(ə)lti/ *noun* a punishment, often a fine, which is imposed if something is not done or is done incorrectly or illegally □ **to impose a penalty on someone** to make someone pay a fine, to suspend someone, etc., as a punishment

penalty clause /'pen(ə)lti klɔːz/ *noun* a clause which lists the penalties which will be imposed if the terms of the contract are not fulfilled ○ *The contract contains a penalty clause which fines the company 1% for every week the completion date is late.*

penalty rate /'pen(ə)lti reɪt/ *noun* a higher than normal rate of pay given to employees for work they do outside normal working hours

pencil-whip /'pensəl wɪp/ *verb* to criticise somebody in writing (*slang*) (NOTE: **pencil-whipping** – **pencil-whipped**)

pendulum arbitration /'pendjʊləm ɑːbɪˌtreɪʃ(ə)n/ *noun* a method of arbitration where each side makes a proposal and the arbitrator chooses one of them, which then becomes binding on both parties

pension /'penʃən/ *noun* money paid regularly to someone who no longer works □ **to draw a pension** to receive a pension ■ *verb* □ **to pension someone off** to ask someone to retire and take a pension

pensionable /'penʃənəb(ə)l/ *adjective* able to receive a pension

pensionable earnings /ˌpenʃənəb(ə)l 'ɜːnɪŋz/ *plural noun* earnings being received at the moment of retirement, on which the pension is calculated

pension book /'penʃən bʊk/ *noun* a book with vouchers entitling the bearer to be paid a weekly pension

pension contributions /'penʃən kɒntrɪˌbjuːʃ(ə)nz/ *plural noun* payments made by a company or employee into a pension fund

pension entitlement /'penʃən ɪnˌtaɪt(ə)lmənt/ *noun* an amount of pension which someone has the right to receive when they retire

pensioner /'penʃənə/ *noun* a person who receives a pension

pension fund /'penʃən fʌnd/ *noun* money which provides pensions for retired employees

pension plan /'penʃən plæn/, **pension scheme** /'penʃən skiːm/ *noun* a plan worked out by an insurance company which arranges for an employee to pay part of their salary over many years and receive a regular payment when they retire

Pensions Ombudsman /'penʃənz ˌɒmbʊdzmən/ *noun* a government official who arbitrates in disputes over pensions and the administration of pension funds

people churner /'piːp(ə)l ˌtʃɜːnə/ *noun* a bad employer with a reputation for losing talented staff (*slang*)

people skills /'piːp(ə)l skɪlz/ *plural noun* the techniques used in forming relationships and dealing with other people ○ *Good people skills are essential for anyone working in customer service.*

per /pɜː, pə/ *preposition* **1.** at a rate of □ **we pay £10 per hour** we pay £10 for each hour worked **2.** out of ○ *The rate of imperfect items is about twenty-five per thousand.*

'…a 100,000 square-foot warehouse generates $600 in sales per square foot of space' [*Duns Business Month*]

per annum /pər 'ænəm/ *adverb* in a year ○ *What is their turnover per annum?* ○ *What is his total income per annum?* ○ *She earns over £100,000 per annum.*

per capita /pə 'kæpɪtə/ *adjective, adverb* for each person

per-capita expenditure /pə ˌkæpɪtə ɪk'spendɪtʃə/ *noun* the total money spent divided by the number of people involved

per capita income /pə ˌkæpɪtə 'ɪnkʌm/ *noun* the average income of one person

per day /pə 'deɪ/, **per diem** /pə 'diːem/ *adverb* for each day

perform /pə'fɔːm/ *verb* to do well or badly □ **how did she perform at the interview?** did she do well or badly at the interview?

performance /pə'fɔːməns/ *noun* the way in which someone or something acts □ **performance of staff against objectives** how staff have worked, measured against the objectives set

performance appraisal /pə'fɔːməns əˌpreɪz(ə)l/, **performance assessment** /pə'fɔːməns əˌsesmənt/ an assessment of the quality of a person's work in a job

performance-based assessment /pə'fɔːməns beɪst əˌsesmənt/ an assessment of an employee's knowledge and skills as shown in their work. Compare **knowledge-based assessment**

performance indicator /pə'fɔːməns ˌɪndɪkeɪtə/ *noun* a figure or measurement that acts as a guide to how well an organisation is performing, as a whole or in some aspect of its activities, and what its strengths and weaknesses are (NOTE: Performance indicators can relate, for example, to the quality or quantity of its output or to the turnover rate amongst its staff.)

performance-related pay /pə-
'fɔːməns rɪˌleɪtɪd peɪ/, **performance
pay** /pə'fɔːməns peɪ/ *noun* pay which
is linked to the employee's performance
of their duties. Abbr **PRP**

performance standard /pə-
'fɔːməns ˌstændəd/ *noun* a measure of
performance needed to reach a certain
level, as in the NVQ system

per head /pə 'hed/ *adverb* for each
person ○ *Allow £15 per head for expenses.* ○ *Representatives cost on average £50,000 per head per annum.*

period /'pɪəriəd/ *noun* a length of time
○ *for a period of time* or *for a period of
months* or *for a six-year period* ○ *sales
over the holiday period*

periodic /ˌpɪəri'ɒdɪk/ *adjective* from
time to time ○ *a periodic review of staff
salaries*

period of disqualification
/ˌpɪəriəd əv dɪskwɒlɪfɪ'keɪʃ(ə)n/ *noun*
a period during which a pregnant
woman cannot claim statutory sick pay
(11 weeks before giving birth)

period of entitlement /ˌpɪəriəd əv
ɪn'taɪt(ə)lmənt/ *noun* a period during
which an employee can claim statutory
sick pay

period of incapacity for work
/ˌpɪəriəd əv ɪnkəˌpæsɪti fə 'wɜːk/
noun a period when an employee has
been away from work because of sickness for four consecutive days (and then
becomes eligible for SSP). Abbr **PIW**

period of qualification /ˌpɪəriəd əv
kwɒlɪfɪ'keɪʃ(ə)n/ *noun* the time which
has to pass before someone qualifies for
something

peripheral workers /pə'rɪf(ə)rəl
ˌwɜːkəz/ *plural noun* workers who are
hired as necessary (part-timers or workers on short-term contracts) as opposed
to 'core' workers who are permanent

perk /pɜːk/ *noun* an extra item given
by a company to employees in addition
to their salaries (such as company cars
or private health insurance) ○ *She earns
a good salary and in addition has all
sorts of perks.*

permalancer /'pɜːməlɑːnsə/ *noun*
someone who is officially a freelance
but has worked for the same company

for so long that they are regarded almost
as a permanent member of its staff
(*slang*)

permanency /'pɜːmənənsi/ *noun* the
fact of being permanent ○ *There is a
lack of permanency about the company.*

permanent /'pɜːmənənt/ *adjective*
which will last for a long time or for
ever ○ *the permanent staff and
part-timers* ○ *She has found a permanent job.* ○ *She is in permanent
employment.*

permanent health insurance
/ˌpɜːmənənt 'helθ ɪnˌʃʊərəns/ *noun*
long-term insurance which gives an income during periods of disability. Abbr
PHI

permanently /'pɜːmənəntli/ *adverb*
always or for ever ○ *The company is
permanently in debt.*

permanent night shift
/ˌpɜːmənənt 'naɪt ʃɪft/ *noun* a shift
which only works at night (as opposed
to the alternating system)

permission /pə'mɪʃ(ə)n/ *noun* being
allowed to do something □ **to give
someone permission to do something**
to allow someone to do something □ **to
ask for permission to do something** to
ask someone in authority to allow you to
do something ○ *He asked the manager's
permission to take a day off.*

permit *noun* /'pɜːmɪt/ an official document which allows someone to do
something ■ *verb* /pə'mɪt/ to allow
someone to do something ○ *This document permits you to export twenty-five
computer systems.* ○ *The ticket permits
three people to go into the exhibition.* ○
*Will we be permitted to use her name in
the advertising copy?* ○ *Smoking is not
permitted in the design studio.* (NOTE:
permitting – permitted)

per month /pə 'mʌnθ/ *adverb* for
each month ○ *He makes about £250 per
month.*

per pro /pə 'prəʊ/ same as **per
procurationem** ○ *The secretary signed
per pro the manager.*

per procurationem /pə
ˌprɒkjʊræsɪ'əʊnəm/ *Latin phrase
meaning* 'with the authority of'

perquisite /'pɜːkwɪzɪt/ *noun* same as **perk**

persistent unemployment /pə-ˌsɪstənt ʌnɪm'plɔɪmənt/ *noun* unemployment which is constant, owing to lack of skills or lack of jobs

person /'pɜːs(ə)n/ *noun* **1.** someone (a man or a woman) ○ *an insurance policy which covers a named person* □ **the persons named in the contract** the people whose names are given in the contract □ **the document should be witnessed by a third person** someone who is not named in the document should witness it **2.** □ **in person** by doing something or going somewhere yourself, not through another person or means □ **she came to see me in person** she came to see me

personal /'pɜːs(ə)n(ə)l/ *adjective* **1.** referring to one person □ **apart from the family shares, she has a personal shareholding in the company** apart from shares belonging to her family as a group, she has shares which she owns herself □ **the car is for his personal use** the car is for him to use himself **2.** private ○ *The envelope was marked 'Personal'.* ○ *I want to see the director on a personal matter.*

personal allowance /ˌpɜːs(ə)n(ə)l ə'laʊənsɪz/ *noun* a part of a person's income which is not taxed

personal assets /ˌpɜːs(ə)n(ə)l 'æsets/ *plural noun* moveable assets which belong to a person

personal assistant /ˌpɜːs(ə)n(ə)l ə-'sɪstənt/ *noun* a person who performs various secretarial and administrative tasks for someone in authority such as a director

personal contract /ˌpɜːs(ə)n(ə)l 'kɒntrækt/ *noun* a contract negotiated between an employer and a single employee (as opposed to a collective contract, negotiated with a group of employees)

personal development /ˌpɜːs(ə)n(ə)l dɪ'veləpmənt/ *noun* the process of gaining additional knowledge, skills and experience in order to improve the way you do your present job and your prospects of future employment and promotion, and, more

generally, to develop your own talents and fulfil your own potential (NOTE: also called **self-development**)

personal effects /ˌpɜːs(ə)n(ə)l ɪ-'fekts/ *plural noun* things which belong to someone

Personal Identification Number /ˌpɜːs(ə)n(ə)l aɪdentɪfɪ'keɪʃ(ə)n ˌnʌmbə/ *noun* a unique number allocated to the holder of a cash card or credit card, by which he or she can enter an automatic banking system, e.g., to withdraw cash from a cash machine or to pay in a store. Abbr **PIN**

personal income /ˌpɜːs(ə)n(ə)l 'ɪnkʌm/ *noun* the income received by an individual person before tax is paid

personal inventory /ˌpɜːs(ə)n(ə)l 'ɪnvənt(ə)ri/, **personality inventory** /pɜːsəˌnælɪti 'ɪnvəntəri/ *noun* a list of strengths and weaknesses in an employee's personality ○ *When considering candidates for a post the human resources manager drew up a personality inventory for each one.*

personality /ˌpɜːsə'nælɪti/ *noun* **1.** a famous person, usually connected with television or sport **2.** a person's character or general nature

personality clash /ˌpɜːsə'nælɪti klæʃ/ *noun* a situation where two members of staff with strong personalities cannot work together

personality test /ˌpɜːsə'nælɪti test/ *noun* a test to assess a person's character ○ *We give all the sales staff a personality test to see how they can communicate with potential customers.* ○ *His personality test showed he was a particularly aggressive individual.*

personal letter /ˌpɜːs(ə)n(ə)l 'letə/ *noun* a letter which deals with personal matters (NOTE: also called **private letter**)

personally /'pɜːs(ə)n(ə)li/ *adverb* in person ○ *He personally opened the envelope.* ○ *She wrote to me personally.*

personal pension plan /ˌpɜːs(ə)n(ə)l 'penʃən plæn/ *noun* a pension plan which applies to one employee only, usually a self-employed person, not to a group. Abbr **PPP**

personal property /ˌpɜːs(ə)n(ə)l ˈprɒpəti/ *noun* things which belong to a person ○ *The fire caused considerable damage to personal property.*

personnel /ˌpɜːsəˈnel/ *noun* all the people who work for an organisation or at a particular location ○ *The personnel of the warehouse* or *the warehouse personnel have changed their shift system.* ○ *The company is famous for the way it looks after its personnel.* (NOTE: now replaced in some cases by **human resources**)

personnel changes /ˌpɜːsəˈnel ˌtʃeɪndʒɪz/, **staff changes** /ˈstɑːf tʃeɪndʒɪz/ *plural noun* arrivals and departures of members of staff of a company

personnel department /ˌpɜːsəˈnel dɪˌpɑːtmənt/ *noun* same as **human resources department**

personnel development /ˌpɜːsə-ˌnel dɪˈveləpmənt/ *noun* the selection and training of employees for particular jobs in an organisation

personnel manager /ˌpɜːsəˈnel ˌmænɪdʒə/ *noun* same as **human resources manager**

personnel officer /ˌpɜːsəˈnel ˌɒfɪsə/ *noun* same as **human resources officer**

personnel planning /ˌpɜːsəˈnel ˌplænɪŋ/ *noun* same as **human resource(s) planning**

personnel policy /ˌpɜːsəˈnel ˌpɒlɪsi/ *noun* a set of rules or guidelines that define the way in which an organisation deals with matters relating to staff, or a particular rule or guideline relating to a particular issue affecting staff

personnel records /pɜːsəˌnel ˈrekɔːdz/ *plural noun* details of members of staff

person specification /ˈpɜːs(ə)n spesɪfɪˌkeɪʃ(ə)n/ *noun* a form of job description which gives the ideal personal qualities needed for the job and a description of the ideal candidate for the job

person-to-person call /ˌpɜːs(ə)n tə ˈpɜːs(ə)n kɔːl/ *noun* a telephone call where you ask the operator to connect you with a named person

PERT *abbr* programme evaluation and review technique

per week /pə ˈwiːk/ *adverb* for each week

per year /pə ˈjɪə/ *adverb* same as **per annum**

PEST *noun* an analysis of the environment in which a company works, under the heading of political economic, social, technical. Full form **political, economic, social, technical**

Peter principle /ˈpiːtə ˌprɪnsɪp(ə)l/ *noun* a law, based on wide experience, that people are promoted until they occupy positions for which they are incompetent

petty /ˈpeti/ *adjective* not important

petty cash /ˌpeti ˈkæʃ/ *noun* a small amount of money kept in an office to pay small debts

petty theft /ˌpeti ˈθeft/ *noun* the stealing of small items (as in an office: it can be the reason for summary dismissal)

phase /feɪz/ *noun* a period or part of something which takes place ○ *the first phase of the expansion programme*

phased retirement /ˌfeɪzd rɪˈtaɪəmənt/ *noun* a gradual reduction in the number of hours someone works as they approach the age of retirement, typically to a three- or four-day week in the last six months

phase in /ˌfeɪz ˈɪn/ *verb* to bring something in gradually ○ *The new system of pension contributions will be phased in over the next two months.*

'...the budget grants a tax exemption for $500,000 in capital gains, phased in over the next six years' [*Toronto Star*]

phase out /ˌfeɪz ˈaʊt/ *verb* to remove something gradually ○ *Smith Ltd will be phased out as a supplier of spare parts.*

PHI *abbr* permanent health insurance

phone book /ˈfəʊn bʊk/ *noun* a book which lists names of people or companies with their addresses and telephone numbers

physical (examination) /ˌfɪzɪk(ə)l ɪɡˌzæmɪˈneɪʃ(ə)n/ *noun* a medical examination ○ *All the candidates have to pass a physical examination.* ○ *Though* *his qualifications for the job were good, he was rejected after failing the physical.*

physically handicapped /ˌfɪzɪkli 'hændɪkæpt/ *adjective* having a physical disability (NOTE: now generally unacceptable and replaced by **disabled**)

physical working conditions /ˌfɪzɪk(ə)l 'wɜːkɪŋ kənˌdɪʃ(ə)nz/ *plural noun* the surroundings in which someone works, taking into account aspects such as temperature, air quality, lighting, safety, cleanliness and noise

pick and shovel work /ˌpɪk ən 'ʃʌv(ə)l wɜːk/ *noun* boring and detailed work such as the examination of documents for mistakes

picket /'pɪkɪt/ *noun* a striking employee who stands at the entrance to a place of work to try to persuade other employees not to go to work □ **to cross a picket line** to go into a place to work, even though pickets are trying to prevent employees from going in ■ *verb* □ **to picket a factory** to stand at the entrance of a place of work to try to prevent other employees from going to work

picketing /'pɪkɪtɪŋ/ *noun* the act of standing at the entrance of a place of work to try to prevent other employees going to work □ **lawful picketing** picketing which is allowed by law □ **peaceful picketing** picketing which does not involve aggression

picket line /'pɪkɪt laɪn/ *noun* a line of pickets at the entrance of a place of work ○ *to man a picket line* or *to be on the picket line*

piece /piːs/ *noun* a small part of something ○ *to sell something by the piece* ○ *The price is 25p the piece.*

piece rate /'piːs reɪt/ *noun* a rate of pay for a product produced or for a piece of work done and not paid for at an hourly rate ○ *to earn piece rates*

piece-rate system /'piːs reɪt ˌsɪstəm/ *noun* a system of payment in which an employee is paid a particular amount of money for each unit that they produce

piece rate wages /'piːs reɪt ˌweɪdʒɪz/ *plural noun* payments based on the number of units produced

piecework /'piːswɜːk/ *noun* work for which employees are paid for the products produced or the piece of work done and not at an hourly rate

pieceworker /'piːswɜːkə/ *noun* a person who is employed at a piece rate

pie chart /'paɪ tʃɑːt/ *noun* a diagram where information is shown as a circle cut up into sections of different sizes

pilferage /'pɪlfərɪdʒ/, **pilfering** /'pɪlfərɪŋ/ *noun* the stealing of small amounts of money or small items from an office or shop

pilot fish /'paɪlət fɪʃ/ *noun* a junior executive who acts as an assistant to a more senior executive and often walks close behind them, as a pilot fish follows a shark (*slang*)

PIN *abbr* Personal Identification Number

pin-drop syndrome /'pɪn drɒp ˌsɪndrəʊm/ *noun* stress caused when a working environment is extremely quiet (*slang*)

pink-collar job /pɪŋk 'kɒlə dʒɒb/ *noun* a sexist term for a job that is normally done by a woman, especially a young one (*slang*)

pink slip /pɪŋk 'slɪp/ *noun US* an official letter of dismissal given to an employee (in place of a final interview)

pink slipper /pɪŋk 'slɪpə/ *noun US* a person who has been dismissed from employment

PIW *abbr* period of incapacity for work

place /pleɪs/ *noun* where something is or where something happens □ **to take place** to happen ○ *The meeting will take place in our offices.* ■ *verb* □ **to place staff** to find jobs for staff □ **how are you placed for work?** have you enough work to do?

placement /'pleɪsmənt/ *noun* the act of finding work for someone ○ *The bureau specialises in the placement of former executives.*

placement service /'pleɪsmənt ˌsɜːvɪs/ *noun* an office which specialises in finding jobs (such as for students leaving college)

place of birth /ˌpleɪs əv 'bɜːθ/ *noun* the place where someone was born

plaintiff /'pleɪntɪf/ *noun* a person who starts an action against someone in the civil courts (NOTE: since April 1999, this term has been replaced by **claimant**)

plan /plæn/ *noun* **1.** an organised way of doing something ○ *an investment plan* ○ *a pension plan* ○ *a savings plan* **2.** a way of saving or investing money ■ *verb* to organise carefully how something should be done in the future □ **to plan for an increase in staff costs** to change a way of doing things because you think there will be an increase in staff costs

'…the benefits package is attractive and the compensation plan includes base, incentive and car allowance totalling $50,000+' [*Globe and Mail (Toronto)*]

planning /'plænɪŋ/ *noun* the process of organising how something should be done in the future ○ *Setting up a new incentive scheme with insufficient planning could be a disaster.* ○ *The long term planning or short-term planning of the project has been completed.*

plant /plɑːnt/ *noun* **1.** industrial machinery and equipment **2.** a large factory ○ *to set up a new plant* ○ *They closed down six plants in the north of the country.* ○ *He was appointed plant manager.*

plant-hire firm /ˌplɑːnt haɪə 'fɜːm/ *noun* a company which lends large machines (such as cranes and tractors) to building companies

plateauing /'plætəʊɪŋ/ *noun* the process of entering a phase where performance remains the same or your position neither gets better nor gets worse over a long period (NOTE: Employees may experience plateauing if they are not very ambitious or if there are few opportunities for promotion in their organisation.)

Plc, PLC, plc *abbr* public limited company

plug and play /ˌplʌg ən 'pleɪ/ *adjective* used to describe a new member of staff who does not need training (*slang*)

pluralism /'plʊərəlɪz(ə)m/ *noun* the belief that the way to achieve good industrial relations is to acknowledge that various groups of employees have different requirements and make different demands, and that compromises have to be reached ○ *Pluralism is making more employees feel they are part of the organisation.* (NOTE: the opposite is **unitarism**)

plus /plʌs/ *preposition* **1.** added to ○ *Her salary plus commission comes to more than £45,000.* ○ *Production costs plus overheads are higher than revenue.* **2.** more than □ **salary of £100,000 plus** a salary of more than £100,000 ■ *noun* a good or favourable point ○ *To have achieved £1m in new sales in less than six months is certainly a plus for the sales team.*

poaching /'pəʊtʃɪŋ/ *noun* the practice of enticing employees to work for another organisation or enticing members of one union to join another union ○ *The company was accused of poaching staff from its rival.* (NOTE: also called **raiding**)

pocket /'pɒkɪt/ *noun* □ **to be £25 in pocket** to have made a profit of £25 □ **to be £25 out of pocket** to have lost £25

pocket calculator /ˌpɒkɪt 'kælkjʊleɪtə/ *noun* a calculator which can be carried in the pocket

pocket diary /ˌpɒkɪt 'daɪəri/ *noun* a diary which can be carried in the pocket

point /pɔɪnt/ *noun* **1.** a place or position **2.** a unit for calculations

points plan /'pɔɪnts plæn/, **point-factor system** /'pɔɪnt fæktə ˌsɪstəm/ *noun* a method of assessing the value of different jobs that uses a scale of points to rate each particular job according to a range of criteria (NOTE: also called **point-factor system**)

points system /'pɔɪnts ˌsɪstəm/ *noun* a system whereby points are given to items in order to evaluate them ○ *The human resources department uses a points system for performance appraisals.* ○ *A points system can be used in evaluating candidates for a job.*

police record /pəˌliːs 'rekɔːd/ *noun* a note of previous crimes for which someone has been convicted ○ *He did not say that he had a police record.* (NOTE: also called **criminal record**)

policy /ˈpɒlɪsi/ *noun* **1.** a course of action or set of principles **2.** a contract for insurance

policyholder /ˈpɒlɪsi ˌhəʊldə/ *noun* a person who is insured by an insurance company

polite /pəˈlaɪt/ *adjective* behaving in a pleasant way ○ *We insist on our sales staff being polite to customers.* ○ *We had a polite letter from the MD.*

politely /pəˈlaɪtli/ *adverb* in a pleasant way ○ *She politely answered the customers' questions.*

polygraph /ˈpɒligrɑːf/ *noun* a lie detector, a machine which tells if a person is lying by recording physiological changes which take place while the person is being interviewed

polygraphy /pəˈlɪgrəfi/ *noun* the practice of using a polygraph to check members of staff

pool /puːl/ *noun* an unused supply ○ *a pool of unemployed labour* or *of expertise*

poor /pɔː/ *adjective* **1.** without much money ○ *The company tries to help the poorest members of staff with loans.* ○ *It is one of the poorest countries in the world.* **2.** not very good ○ *poor quality* ○ *poor service* ○ *poor performance by office staff* ○ *poor organisation of working methods*

poorly /ˈpɔːli/ *adverb* badly ○ *The offices are poorly laid out.* ○ *The plan was poorly presented.* □ **poorly-paid staff** staff with low wages

population /ˌpɒpjʊˈleɪʃ(ə)n/ *noun* **1.** the number of people who live in a country or in a town ○ *Population statistics show a rise in the 18–25 age group.* ○ *Population trends have to be taken into account when drawing up economic plans.* ○ *The working population of the country is getting older.* **2.** the group of items or people in a survey or study

population growth /ˌpɒpjʊˈleɪʃ(ə)n grəʊθ/ *noun* an increase in the population

population trends /ˌpɒpjʊˈleɪʃ(ə)n trendz/ *plural noun* developments in the size and make-up of the population ○ *To assess the future employment market, the human resources department studied population trends.* ○ *Judging by present population trends, there will be a labour shortage in five years' time.*

portable /ˈpɔːtəb(ə)l/ *adjective* which can be carried ○ *a portable computer*

portable pension /ˌpɔːtəb(ə)l ˈpenʃən/, **portable pension plan** /ˌpɔːtəb(ə)l ˈpenʃən plæn/ *noun* a pension entitlement which can be moved from one company to another without loss (as an employee changes jobs)

portfolio working /pɔːtˈfəʊliəʊ ˌwɜːkɪŋ/ *noun* a way of organising your working life in which, instead of working full-time for one employer and pursuing a single career, you work for several different employers, do several different jobs and follow several different career paths all at the same time

position /pəˈzɪʃ(ə)n/ *noun* **1.** a point of view ○ *What is the union's position on the issue of the closed shop?* **2.** a job or paid work in a company ○ *to apply for a position as manager* ○ *We have several positions vacant.* ○ *All the vacant positions have been filled.* ○ *She retired from her position in the accounts department.*

position of authority /pəˌzɪʃ(ə)n əv ɔːˈθɒrɪti/ *noun* a job where the employee has authority over other employees

positive /ˈpɒzɪtɪv/ *adjective* meaning 'yes' ○ *The board gave a positive reply.*

positive discrimination /ˌpɒzɪtɪv dɪskrɪmɪˈneɪʃ(ə)n/ the practice of giving more favourable treatment to a minority to help them be more equal ○ *The company's policy of positive discrimination is to enable more women to reach senior management posts.*

positive vetting /ˌpɒzɪtɪv ˈvetɪŋ/ *noun* the close examination of a person working with secret information who may not be reliable

post /pəʊst/ *noun* **1.** a system of sending letters and parcels from one place to another ○ *to send an invoice by post* ○

He put the letter in the post. ○ *The cheque was lost in the post.* **2.** letters sent or received ○ *Has the post arrived yet?* ○ *The first thing I do is open the post.* ○ *The receipt was in this morning's post.* ○ *The letter didn't arrive by the first post this morning.* (NOTE: British English uses both **mail** and **post** but American English only uses **mail**) **3.** job, paid work in a company ○ *to apply for a post as cashier* ○ *we have three posts vacant* ○ *All our posts have been filled.* ○ *We advertised three posts in the 'Times'.* ■ *verb* **1.** to send something by post ○ *to post a letter* or *to post a parcel* **2.** □ **to post up a notice** to put a notice on a wall or on a noticeboard

'Toronto stocks closed at an all-time high, posting their fifth day of advances in heavy trading' [*Financial Times*]

post- /pəʊst/ *prefix* after

postal ballot /ˈpəʊst(ə)l ˌbælət/, **postal vote** /ˈpəʊst(ə)l vəʊt/ *noun* an election where the voters send their ballot papers by post

postcode /ˈpəʊstkəʊd/ *noun* a set of letters and numbers used to indicate a town or street in an address on an envelope

post-entry closed shop /pəʊst ˌentri kləʊzd ˈʃɒp/ *noun* a closed shop which applies to employees after they have joined a company

post-industrial experience /pəʊst ɪnˌdʌstriəl ɪkˈspɪəriəns/ *noun* experience after working in industry

posting /ˈpəʊstɪŋ/ *noun* an appointment to a job ○ *He has been offered an overseas posting.*

posting and bidding /ˌpəʊstɪŋ ən ˈbɪdɪŋ/ *noun* the act of advertising a job internally so that employees can apply for it

potential /pəˈtenʃəl/ *adjective* possible □ **she is a potential managing director** she is the sort of person who could become managing director ■ *noun* the possibility of becoming something

'...career prospects are excellent for someone with growth potential' [*Australian Financial Review*]

'...for sale: established general cleaning business; has potential to be increased to over 1

million dollar turnover' [*Australian Financial Review*]

potential review /pəˈtenʃəl rɪˌvjuː/ *noun* a study of an employee's performance to determine what direction their career should take in the organisation

power /ˈpaʊə/ *noun* **1.** strength or ability **2.** a force or legal right

power and influence theory of leadership /ˌpaʊər ənd ˈɪnfluəns ˌθɪəri əv ˌliːdəʃɪp/ *noun* the theory that leadership is based on the nature of the relationships between leaders and the people who follow them, which are shaped by the power and influence exerted by the leaders, rather than on the exceptional abilities that leaders as individuals are supposed to possess

power lunch /ˈpaʊə lʌntʃ/ *noun* same as **working lunch**

power of attorney /ˌpaʊər əv əˈtɜːni/ *noun* a legal document which gives someone the right to act on someone's behalf in legal matters

power structure /ˈpaʊə ˌstrʌktʃə/ *noun* the way in which power is distributed among different groups or individuals in an organisation

power struggle /ˈpaʊə ˌstrʌg(ə)l/ *noun* a fight between people or groups to obtain control of something ○ *There was a power struggle in the boardroom, and the finance director had to resign.*

p.p. *abbr* per procurationem ■ *verb* □ **to p.p. a letter** to sign a letter on behalf of someone ○ *Her assistant p.p.'d the letter while the manager was at lunch.*

PR *abbr* public relations ○ *A PR firm is handling all our publicity.* ○ *She works in PR.* ○ *The PR people gave away 100,000 balloons.*

practice /ˈpræktɪs/ *noun* a way of doing things ○ *His practice was to arrive at work at 7.30 and start counting the cash.*

precautionary measure /prɪˈkɔːʃ(ə)n(ə)ri ˌmeʒə/ *noun* an action taken to prevent something unwanted taking place

precautions /prɪˈkɔːʃ(ə)nz/ *plural noun* measures taken to avoid something unpleasant ○ *We intend to take precautions to prevent thefts in the of-*

fice. ○ *The company did not take proper fire precautions.*

precondition /ˌpriːkənˈdɪʃ(ə)n/ *noun* a condition set before something happens, e.g. a condition set by one side before joining negotiations ○ *Management has agreed to talks without preconditions.*

predecessor /ˈpriːdɪsesə/ *noun* a person who had a job or position before someone else ○ *He took over from his predecessor last May.* ○ *She is using the same office as her predecessor.*

predictive validity /prɪˌdɪktɪv vəˈlɪdɪti/ *noun* the process of assessing the validity of selection tests, by comparing the employee's performance in tests with their subsequent job performance

pre-employment screening /ˌpriː ɪmˈplɔɪmənt ˈskriːnɪŋ/ *noun* health screening that takes place after a person has been appointed to a job but before they start work

preferential /ˌprefəˈrenʃəl/ *adjective* showing that something is preferred more than another

preferential shop /prefəˈrenʃəl ʃɒp/ *noun* an agreement with a union that management will give first chance of new jobs to members of the union ○ *A preferential shop system is resented by applicants who do not wish to become members of the union.*

preferential treatment /ˌprefərenʃəl ˈtriːtmənt/ *noun* good treatment given to someone in power or to someone who is a friend of the person giving the treatment ○ *He gets preferential treatment because he's the MD's nephew.*

prejudice /ˈpredʒʊdɪs/ *noun* **1.** bias or unjust feelings against someone **2.** harm done to someone □ **without prejudice** without harming any interests (a phrase spoken or written in letters when trying to negotiate a settlement, meaning that the negotiations cannot be referred to in court or relied upon by the other party if the discussions fail) ■ *verb* to harm ○ *to prejudice someone's claim*

prejudiced /ˈpredʒʊdɪst/ *adjective* biased or with unjust feelings against

someone ○ *The company was accused of being prejudiced against women.*

preliminary /prɪˈlɪmɪn(ə)ri/ *adjective* early, happening before anything else

preliminary hearing /prɪˌlɪmɪn(ə)ri ˈhɪərɪŋ/ *noun* the first meeting of an industrial tribunal where the tribunal decides if it is competent to hear the case

premature retirement /ˌpremətʃʊə rɪˈtaɪəmənt/ *noun* same as **early retirement**

premium bonus /ˈpriːmiəm ˌbəʊnəs/ *noun* an extra payment to an employee for taking less than the standard time for a task

premium pay /ˈpriːmiəm peɪ/, **premium rate** /ˈpriːmiəm reɪt/ *noun* a rate of payment for overtime work

premium pay plan /ˈpriːmiəm peɪ ˌplæn/ *noun* an improved pay scale for employees who perform particularly well, often used to motivate employees and reward such achievements as high productivity, long service or completion of training

present *adjective* /ˈprez(ə)nt/ **1.** happening now ○ *What is the present address of the company?* **2.** being there when something happens ○ *Only six directors were present at the board meeting.* ■ *verb* /prɪˈzent/ to give a talk about or demonstration of something ○ *I've been asked to present at the sales conference.* ○ *The HR director will present the new staff structure to the Board.*

presentation /ˌprez(ə)nˈteɪʃ(ə)n/ *noun* a demonstration or exhibition of a proposed plan

presenteeism /ˌprez(ə)nˈtiːɪz(ə)m/ *noun* the practice of spending more hours at work or in the workplace than is healthy, necessary or productive, e.g. when an employee comes to work when sick for fear of losing their job or letting the company down

preside /prɪˈzaɪd/ *verb* to be chairman ○ *The MD will preside over the meeting.* ○ *The meeting was held in the committee room, Mr Smith presiding.*

president /ˈprezɪd(ə)nt/ *noun* the head of a company, society or club ○ *She was elected president of the sports* *club.* ○ *After many years on the board, A.B. Smith has been appointed president of the company.*

COMMENT: In the UK, president is sometimes a title given to a non-executive former chairman of a company; in the USA, the president is the main executive director of a company.

press cutting agency /'pres ˌkʌtɪŋ ˌeɪdʒənsi/ *noun* a company which cuts out references to clients from newspapers and magazines and sends them on to them

press the flesh /ˌpres ðə 'fleʃ/ *verb* to shake hands with people at a business function (*informal*)

pressure /'preʃə/ *noun* something which forces you to do something □ **to put pressure on someone to do something** to try to force someone to do something ○ *The banks put pressure on the company to reduce its borrowings.*

prevention /prɪ'venʃən/ *noun* steps to prevent something happening

preventive measure /prɪˌventɪv 'meʒə/ *noun* an action taken to prevent something from taking place

previous /'priːviəs/ *adjective* which happens earlier or which existed before ○ *List all previous positions with the salaries earned.*

price /praɪs/ *noun* money which has to be paid to buy something ■ *verb* to give a price to a product ○ *We have two used cars for sale, both priced at £5,000.* □ **to price oneself out of the market** to ask for such a high salary that you cannot get a job

'...that British goods will price themselves back into world markets is doubtful as long as sterling labour costs continue to rise' [*Sunday Times*]

price ceiling /'praɪs ˌsiːlɪŋ/ *noun* the highest price which can be reached

price cutting /'praɪs ˌkʌtɪŋ/ *noun* a sudden lowering of prices

price structure /'praɪs ˌstrʌktʃə/ *noun* a way in which prices are arranged for a series of products

pricing policy /'praɪsɪŋ ˌpɒlisi/ *noun* a company's policy in giving prices to its products ○ *Our pricing policy aims at producing a 35% gross margin.*

primary /'praɪməri/ *adjective* basic

'...farmers are convinced that primary industry no longer has the capacity to meet new capital taxes or charges on farm inputs' [*Australian Financial Review*]

primary boycott /ˌpraɪməri 'bɔɪkɒt/ *noun US* pressure put on an employer by workers directly involved in an industrial dispute. ♦ **secondary boycott**

primary group /'praɪməri gruːp/ *noun* a group which is small enough to allow the members to interact informally

primary industry /ˌpraɪməri 'ɪndəstri/ *noun* an industry dealing with basic raw materials such as coal, wood or farm produce

primary labour market /ˌpraɪməri 'leɪbə ˌmɑːkɪt/ *noun* a market for workers with specific skills

primary negotiating demands /ˌpraɪməri nə'gəʊʃieɪtɪŋ dɪˌmɑːndz/ *plural noun* initial demands made by one side in a negotiation, which are in fact not negotiable

primary sector /'praɪməri ˌsektə/ *noun* industries dealing with basic raw materials (such as coal, wood or farm produce)

principal /'prɪnsɪp(ə)l/ *noun* **1.** a person or company that is represented by an agent **2.** money invested or borrowed on which interest is paid ○ *to repay principal and interest* ○ *We try to repay part of principal each month.* (NOTE: do not confuse with **principle**) ■ *adjective* most important ○ *The company's principal asset is its design staff.*

'...the company was set up with funds totalling NorKr 145m with the principal aim of making capital gains on the secondhand market' [*Lloyd's List*]

principle /'prɪnsɪp(ə)l/ *noun* a basic point or general rule □ **in principle** in agreement with a general rule □ **agreement in principle** agreement with the basic conditions of a proposal

priority /praɪ'ɒriti/ *noun* □ **to have priority** to have the right to be first

private /'praɪvət/ *adjective* **1.** belonging to a single person, not to a company or the state □ **a letter marked 'private and confidential'** a letter which must not be opened by anyone other than the person it is addressed to **2.** □ **in private** away from other people ○ *In public the union said it would never go back to the negotiating table, but in private they were already having discussions with the company representatives.* ○ *He asked to see the managing director in private.* ○ *In public he said the company would break even soon, but in private he was less optimistic.*

'...in the private sector the total number of new house starts was 3 per cent higher than in the corresponding period last year, while public sector starts were 23 per cent lower' [*Financial Times*]

private enterprise /ˌpraɪvət ˈentəpraɪz/ *noun* businesses which are owned privately, not nationalised ○ *The project is completely funded by private enterprise.*

private health insurance /ˌpraɪvət ˈhelθ ɪnˌʃʊərəns/, **private health scheme** /ˌpraɪvət ˈhelθ skiːm/ *noun* insurance which will pay for the cost of treatment in a private hospital, not a state one

privately /ˈpraɪvətli/ *adverb* away from other people ○ *The deal was negotiated privately.*

private means /ˌpraɪvət ˈmiːnz/ *plural noun* income from dividends, interest or rent which is not part of someone's salary

private ownership /ˌpraɪvət ˈəʊnəʃɪp/ *noun* a situation where a company is owned by private shareholders

private secretary /ˌpraɪvət ˈsekrɪt(ə)ri/ *noun* a secretary who works for one manager or director only, and deals with personal and confidential matters

private sector /ˈpraɪvət ˌsektə/ *noun* all companies which are owned by private shareholders, not by the state ○ *The expansion is completely funded by the private sector.* ○ *Salaries in the private sector have increased faster than in the public sector.*

privilege /ˈprɪvɪlɪdʒ/ *noun* an advantage associated with a certain position or situation ○ *Using the company jet is a privilege given only to top management.*

proactive /prəʊˈæktɪv/ *adjective* taking the initiative in doing something (as opposed to reacting to events)

probation /prəˈbeɪʃ(ə)n/ *noun* a period when a new employee is being tested before getting a permanent job ○ *We will take her on probation.* ○ *The accountant was appointed on three months' probation at the end of which he was not found to be satisfactory.*

probationary /prəˈbeɪʃ(ə)n(ə)ri/ *adjective* while someone is being tested ○ *We will take her for a probationary period of three months.* ○ *After the probationary period the company decided to offer him a full-time contract.*

probationary employee /prəˌbeɪʃ(ə)n(ə)ri ɪmˈplɔɪiː/ *noun* an employee who is still on probation

probationary period /prəˈbeɪʃ(ə)n(ə)ri ˌpɪəriəd/ *noun* a period during which a new employee is on probation ○ *During the probationary period the employee may be dismissed without notice.* ○ *The probationary period is three months, after which the management may decide not to keep the worker, or alternatively, may offer an employment contract.*

probationer /prəˈbeɪʃ(ə)nə/ *noun* a person who is on probation

problem /ˈprɒbləm/ *noun* something to which it is difficult to find an answer ○ *The company suffers from staff problems.*

problem area /ˈprɒbləm ˌeəriə/ *noun* an area of a company's work which is difficult to run ○ *Overseas sales is one of our biggest problem areas.*

problem-solving /ˈprɒbləm ˌsɒlvɪŋ/ *noun* the task of dealing with problems that occur within an organisation and the methods that managers use to solve them (NOTE: The most widely used method of problem-solving proceeds through the following stages: recognising that a problem exists and defining it; generating a range of solutions; evaluating the possible solutions and choosing the best one; implementing the solution and evaluating its effectiveness in solving the problem.)

procedural /prə'siːdʒərəl/ *adjective* referring to procedure

'…the procedural 'gentleman's agreement' approach was not sufficient to sustain individual employees against workplace industrial action' [*Personnel Management*]

procedural agreement /prə-'siːdʒərəl ə,griːmənt/ *noun* an agreement between a trade union and management on procedure to be followed during negotiations or bargaining

procedure /prə'siːdʒə/ *noun* a way in which something is done ○ *The inquiry found that the company had not followed the approved procedures.* ○ *The management complained that the unions did not follow the proper procedure.* □ **this procedure is very irregular** this is not the proper way to do something

'…this was a serious breach of disciplinary procedure and the dismissal was unfair' [*Personnel Management*]

procedure manual /prə'siːdʒə ,mænjuəl/ *noun* a document in which the step-by-step instructions that govern the way in which an organisation conducts particular activities are written down (NOTE: Procedure manuals are often used in the induction and training of new recruits.)

proceedings /prə'siːdɪŋz/ *plural noun* □ **to take** *or* **to institute proceedings against someone** to start a legal action against someone

process /'prəʊses/ *noun* the series of steps or stages that make up an activity □ **decision-making processes** ways in which decisions are reached ■ *verb* **1.** □ **to process figures** to sort out information to make it easily understood ○ *The sales figures are being processed by our accounts department.* **2.** to deal with something in the usual routine way ○ *It usually takes at least two weeks to process an insurance claim.* ○ *Orders are processed in our warehouse.*

process chart /'prəʊses tʃɑːt/ *noun* a diagram which shows all the stages involved in a job or project in the correct order

process skills /'prəʊses skɪlz/ *plural noun* skills in organising, problem-solving, decision-making, etc.

production /prə'dʌkʃən/ *noun* **1.** the act of showing something □ **on produc-**
tion of when something is shown ○ *Goods can be exchanged only on production of the sales slip.* **2.** the making or manufacturing of goods for sale ○ *We are hoping to speed up production by installing new machinery.* ○ *Higher production is rewarded with higher pay.*

production bonus /prə'dʌkʃən ,bəʊnəs/ *noun* an extra payment made for each job or task completed after a certain production target has been reached

production curve /prə'dʌkʃən kɜːv/ *noun* the extent to which output varies according to how long the employee has been working

production management /prə'dʌkʃən ,mænɪdʒmənt/ *noun* the process of supervising a factory or a production process

production standards /prə'dʌkʃən ,stændədz/ *plural noun* the quality levels relating of production

production target /prə'dʌkʃən ,tɑːgɪt/ *noun* the amount of units a factory is expected to produce

production transfer /prə'dʌkʃən ,trænsfɜː/ *noun* the transferring of employees from jobs in which manpower requirements are declining to jobs where manpower requirements are on the increase

productivity /,prɒdʌk'tɪvɪti/ *noun* the rate of output per employee or per machine in a factory ○ *Bonus payments are linked to productivity.* ○ *The company is aiming to increase productivity.*

'…though there has been productivity growth, the absolute productivity gap between many British firms and their foreign rivals remains' [*Sunday Times*]

productivity audit /,prɒdʌk'tɪvɪti ,ɔːdɪt/ *noun* a review of a company's productivity and its relationship with its employees

productivity bargaining /,prɒdʌk-'tɪvɪti ,bɑːgɪnɪŋ/ *noun* bargaining between a union and management to agree on the level of productivity to be achieved

productivity drive /,prɒdʌk'tɪvɪti draɪv/ *noun* an extra effort to increase productivity

productivity measurement /ˌprɒdʌk'tɪvɪti ˌmeʒəmənt/ *noun* a measurement of the efficiency of production

product management /ˌprɒdʌkt 'mænɪdʒmənt/ *noun* the process of directing the making and selling of a product as an independent item

profession /prə'feʃ(ə)n/ *noun* **1.** an occupation for which official qualifications are needed and which is often made a lifelong career ○ *The managing director is an accountant by profession.* ○ *HR management is now more widely recognised as a profession.* **2.** a group of specialised employees ○ *the accounting profession* ○ *the legal profession*

professional /prə'feʃ(ə)n(ə)l/ *adjective* **1.** referring to one of the professions ○ *We had to ask our lawyer for professional advice on the contract.* ○ *The professional institute awards diplomas.* ▫ **professional man, professional woman** a man or woman who works in one of the professions (such as a lawyer, doctor or accountant) **2.** expert or skilled ○ *Her work is very professional.* ○ *They did a very professional job in designing the new office.* **3.** doing work for money ○ *a professional tennis player* **4.** fully qualified in a profession ○ *She's a professional photographer.* ■ *noun* a skilled person or a person who does skilled work for money

professional body /prə,feʃ(ə)n(ə)l 'bɒdi/ *noun* an organisation which trains, validates and organises examinations for its members

professional indemnity /prə,feʃ(ə)n(ə)l ɪn'demnɪti/ *noun* insurance against claims taken out by companies providing professional services such as accountancy

professionalism /prə'feʃ(ə)nəlɪz(ə)m/ *noun* the quality of showing a professional attitude ○ *His sales reports show a lack of professionalism which could be remedied by a period of in-house training.*

professional misconduct /prə,feʃ(ə)n(ə)l mɪs'kɒndʌkt/ *noun* behaviour by a member of a profession (such as a lawyer, accountant or doctor) which

the body regulating that profession considers to be wrong

professional mobility /prə,feʃ(ə)n(ə)l məʊ'bɪlɪti/ *noun* the ability of employees to move from one type of job to another within the same organisation (NOTE: also called **skills mobility**)

professional negligence /prə,feʃ(ə)n(ə)l 'neglɪdʒəns/ *noun* the act of failing to carry out one's duties properly (on the part of a professional person)

professional qualification /prə,feʃ(ə)n(ə)l kwɒlɪfɪ'keɪʃ(ə)n/ *noun* a document which shows that someone has successfully finished a course of study which allows them to work in one of the professions

professional traits /prə,feʃ(ə)n(ə)l 'treɪts/ *plural noun* characteristics (such as skills, knowledge or agreement with the aims of a professional organisation) which mark the true professional

proficiency /prə'fɪʃ(ə)nsi/ *noun* skill in doing something at more than a basic level ○ *Her proficiency in languages should help in the export department.* ○ *To get the job he had to pass a proficiency test.*

proficient /prə'fɪʃ(ə)nt/ *adjective* capable of doing something well ○ *She is quite proficient in Spanish.*

profile /'prəʊfaɪl/ *noun* a brief description of the characteristics of something or someone ○ *They asked for a profile of the possible partners in the joint venture.* ○ *Her CV provided a profile of her education and career to date.*

profile method /'prəʊfaɪl ˌmeθəd/ *noun* an analytical method of job evaluation used by management consultants

profit /'prɒfɪt/ *noun* money gained from a sale which is more than the money spent on making the item sold or on providing the service offered

profit centre /'prɒfɪt ˌsentə/ *noun* a person or department that is considered separately for the purposes of calculating a profit ○ *We count the kitchen equipment division as a single profit centre.*

profit-related /'prɒfɪt rɪ,leɪtɪd/ *adjective* linked to profit

profit-related pay /ˌprɒfɪt rɪˌleɪtɪd ˈpeɪ/ *noun* pay (including bonuses) which is linked to profit

profit-sharing /ˈprɒfɪt ˌʃeərɪŋ/ *noun* the practice of dividing profits among employees

profit-sharing scheme /ˈprɒfɪt ˌʃeərɪŋ ˌskiːm/ *noun* a scheme by which employees (either all of them, or only certain selected categories) are entitled to get a share of the profits of the organisation they work for ○ *Profit-sharing schemes encourage employees to identify more closely with the company.*

program /ˈprəʊgræm/ *noun* **1.** a set of instructions telling a computer to perform some task **2.** *US* same as **programme** ◾ *verb* to write a program for a computer □ **to program a computer** to install a program in a computer ○ *The computer is programmed to print labels.*

programme /ˈprəʊgræm/ *noun* a plan of things which will be done ○ *to draw up a programme of investment* or *an investment programme* ○ *The training programme sends all managers for retraining every year.* ○ *We are initiating a new recruitment programme.* (NOTE: the usual US spelling is **program**)

programmed instruction /ˌprəʊgræmd ɪnˈstrʌkʃən/, **programmed learning** /ˌprəʊgræmd ˈlɜːnɪŋ/ *noun* a course of instruction carried out by each trainee at their own speed

programme evaluation and review technique (PERT) /ˌprəʊgræm ɪvæljuˌeɪʃ(ə)n ən rɪˈvjuː tekˌniːk/ *noun* a way of planning and controlling a large project, concentrating on scheduling and completion on time. Abbr **PERT**

progress *noun* /ˈprəʊgres/ the movement of work forward ○ *to report on the progress of the work* or *of the negotiations* □ **in progress** which is being done but is not finished ○ *negotiations in progress* ○ *work in progress* □ **to make progress** to move forward in your work ◾ *verb* /prəʊˈgres/ to move forward or

go ahead ○ *The contract is progressing through various departments.*

progress chaser /ˈprəʊgres ˌtʃeɪsə/ *noun* a person whose job is to check that work is being carried out on schedule, that orders are being fulfilled on time, etc.

progression /prəʊˈgreʃ(ə)n/ *noun* the process of moving forward in stages

progressive /prəʊˈgresɪv/ *adjective* which moves forward in stages

progress report /ˈprəʊgres rɪˌpɔːt/ *noun* a document which describes what progress has been made

prohibition /ˌprəʊɪˈbɪʃ(ə)n/ *noun* an act of forbidding something

prohibition notice /ˌprəʊɪˈbɪʃ(ə)n ˌnəʊtɪs/ *noun* a notice from the Health and Safety Executive telling a company to stop doing something which is dangerous

prohibitory injunction /prəˌhɪbɪt(ə)ri ɪnˈdʒʌŋkʃən/ *noun* an injunction which prevents someone from doing an illegal act

projective listening /prəˌdʒektɪv ˈlɪs(ə)nɪŋ/ *noun* the act of imagining the effects of one's own words on other people in order to improve direct communication skills ○ *The sales manager trained the new sales reps in projective listening.*

projective test /prəˌdʒektɪv ˈtest/ *noun* a test of personality, where a candidate is asked to describe what they see in certain shapes

project management /ˈprɒdʒekt ˌmænɪdʒmənt/ *noun* the coordination of the financial, material and human resources needed to complete a project and the organisation of the work that the project involves

promote /prəˈməʊt/ *verb* to give someone a more important job or to move someone to a higher grade ○ *He was promoted from salesman to sales manager.*

promotion /prəˈməʊʃ(ə)n/ *noun* the act of moving up to a more important job ○ *I ruined my chances of promotion when I argued with the managing director.* ○ *The job offers good promotion chances* or *promotion prospects.* □ **to**

earn promotion to work hard and efficiently and so be promoted □ **to get promotion** to be promoted □ **to be passed over for promotion** not to be promoted when other employees on the same level are promoted

promotion ladder /prə'məʊʃ(ə)n ˌlædə/ *noun* a series of steps by which employees can be promoted ○ *By being appointed sales manager, she moved several steps up the promotion ladder.*

proposal under consideration /prəˌpəʊz(ə)l ʌndə kənˌsɪdə'reɪʃ(ə)n/ *noun* the proposal which is being considered at the moment

proprietor /prə'praɪətə/ *noun* the owner of a business, especially in the hospitality industry ○ *She is the proprietor of a hotel* or *a hotel proprietor.* ○ *The restaurant has a new proprietor.*

proprietress /prə'praɪətrəs/ *noun* a woman owner ○ *She is the proprietress of an advertising consultancy.*

prosecute /'prɒsɪkjuːt/ *verb* to bring someone to court to answer a criminal charge ○ *He was prosecuted for embezzlement.*

prosecution /ˌprɒsɪ'kjuːʃ(ə)n/ *noun* **1.** the act of bringing someone to court to answer a charge ○ *his prosecution for embezzlement* **2.** a party who brings a criminal charge against someone ○ *The costs of the case will be borne by the prosecution.* **3.** lawyers representing the party bringing a criminal charge against someone

prosecution counsel /ˌprɒsɪ'kjuːʃ(ə)n ˌkaʊnsəl/ *noun* a lawyer acting for the prosecution

prospect *noun* **1.** □ **her job prospects are good** she is very likely to find a job **2.** the possibility that something will happen ○ *There is no prospect of negotiations coming to an end soon.* ■ *verb* to look for ○ *to prospect customers*

prospective /prə'spektɪv/ *adjective* **1.** which may happen in the future **2.** referring to a person who could be appointed to a job ○ *We are interviewing prospective candidates next week.*

protect /prə'tekt/ *verb* to defend something against harm ○ *Employees are protected from unfair dismissal by*

government legislation. ○ *The cover is supposed to protect the machine from dust.*

protected class /prəˌtektɪd 'klɑːs/ *noun* an employee who has skills that are currently in short supply (*slang*)

protection /prə'tekʃən/ *noun* **1.** something or a legislation which protects ○ *The legislation offers no protection to part-time workers.* ○ *The new legislation offers some protection against unscrupulous employers.* **2.** the act of protecting

protective /prə'tektɪv/ *adjective* which protects

protective award /prə'tektɪv əˌwɔːd/ *noun* an award made to an employee who was made redundant without the company following the normal consultation procedures or the normal notice period

protective clothing /prəˌtektɪv 'kləʊðɪŋ/ *noun* clothes (such as hats, gloves or goggles) which protect a worker from dangerous substances

protest *noun* /'prəʊtest/ a statement or action to show that you do not approve of something ○ *to make a protest against high prices* □ **in protest at** showing that you do not approve of something ○ *The staff occupied the offices in protest at the low pay offer.* □ **to do something under protest** to do something, but say that you do not approve of it ■ *verb* /prə'test/ □ **to protest against something** to say that you do not approve of something

protest strike /'prəʊtest straɪk/ *noun* a strike in protest at a particular grievance

protocol /'prəʊtəkɒl/ *noun* a set of rules that govern and regulate a process

proven /'pruːv(ə)n/ *adjective* which has been proved by time ○ *a candidate of proven experience*

proven experience /ˌpruːv(ə)n ɪk-'spɪəriəns/ *noun* experience showing that someone has been successful

provident /'prɒvɪd(ə)nt/ *adjective* providing benefits in case of illness, old age or other cases of need ○ *a provident fund* ○ *a provident society*

provision /prə'vɪʒ(ə)n/ *noun* the act of providing something □ **to make provision for** to see that something is allowed for in the future □ **there is no provision for** *or* **no provision has been made for car parking in the plans for the office block** the plans do not include space for cars to park

provisional /prə'vɪʒ(ə)n(ə)l/ *adjective* temporary, not final or permanent ○ *He was given a provisional posting to see if he could manage a larger department.* ○ *The provisional budget has been drawn up for each department.* ○ *They faxed their provisional acceptance of the contract.*

provisionally /prə'vɪʒ(ə)nəli/ *adverb* not finally ○ *The contract has been accepted provisionally.*

proviso /prə'vaɪzəʊ/ *noun* a condition ○ *We are signing the contract with the proviso that the terms can be discussed again after six months.* (NOTE: plural is **provisos** or **provisoes**)

proximate cause /'prɒksɪmət kɔːz/ *noun* the direct cause (of an accident)

proxy /'prɒksi/ *noun* **1.** a document which gives someone the power to act on behalf of someone else ○ *to sign by proxy* **2.** a person who acts on behalf of someone else ○ *She asked the chairman to act as proxy for her.*

PRP *abbr* performance-related pay

psychic income /ˌsaɪkɪk 'ɪnkʌm/ *noun* the amount of personal psychological satisfaction that someone gets from a job, as opposed to the salary that they earn by doing it

psychological contract /ˌsaɪkəlɒdʒɪk(ə)l 'kɒntrækt/ *noun* the expectations that an employee and an employer have of what each will do for the other, which are not written down in the actual contract of employment but nevertheless form an important of their relationship (NOTE: The psychological contract involves such things as levels of employee commitment on the one side and job satisfaction and the quality of working life on the other.)

psychological test /ˌsaɪkəlɒdʒɪk(ə)l 'test/ *noun* a way of assessing the principal traits of a per-

son's character ○ *The result of the psychological test showed that he was prone to depression.*

psychologist /saɪ'kɒlədʒɪst/ *noun* a doctor who specialies in the study of the mind and its processes ○ *Studies by psychologists have shown the influence of work stress on production-line workers.*

psychology /saɪ'kɒlədʒi/ *noun* the study of the mind and its processes

psychometric /ˌsaɪkə'metrɪk/ *adjective* referring to psychometrics

psychometrics /ˌsaɪkə'metrɪks/ *noun* a way of measuring ability and personality where the result is shown as a number on a scale ○ *Psychometrics can be successfully applied to recruitment processes.* (NOTE: takes a singular verb)

psychometric test /ˌsaɪkəmetrɪk 'tests/ *noun* a test to measure psychological traits in candidates

psychosometric /ˌsaɪkəʊsə'metrɪk/ *adjective* same as **psychometric**

psychosometric test /ˌsaɪkəʊsəmetrɪk 'test/ *noun* same as **psychometric test**

public /'pʌblɪk/ *adjective* referring to all the people in general ■ *noun* □ **the public**, **the general public** the people □ **in public** in front of everyone ○ *In public he said that the company would soon be in profit, but in private he was less optimistic.*

public funds /ˌpʌblɪk 'fʌndz/ *plural noun* government money available for expenditure

public health inspector /ˌpʌblɪk 'helθ ɪnˌspektə/ *noun* same as **Environmental Health Officer**

public holiday /ˌpʌblɪk 'hɒlɪdeɪ/ *noun* a day when all employees are entitled to take a holiday

public liability insurance /ˌpʌblɪk laɪə'bɪlɪti ɪnˌʃʊərəns/ *noun* insurance against claims by members of the public

public limited company /ˌpʌblɪk ˌlɪmɪtɪd 'kʌmp(ə)ni/ *noun* a company whose shares can be bought on the Stock Exchange. Abbr **Plc, PLC, plc**

public ownership /ˌpʌblɪk
'əʊnəʃɪp/ *noun* a situation where the
government owns a business, i.e. where
an industry is nationalised

public relations /ˌpʌblɪk rɪ-
'leɪʃ(ə)nz/ *plural noun* the practice of
building up and keeping good relations
between an organisation and the public,
or an organisation and its employees, so
that people know and think well of what
the organisation is doing ○ *She works in
public relations.* ○ *A public relations
firm handles all our publicity.* ○ *The
company's internal public relations
were improved by setting up the house
journal.* Abbr **PR** (NOTE: takes a
singular verb)

public relations department
/ˌpʌblɪk rɪ'leɪʃ(ə)nz dɪˌpɑːtmənt/
noun the section of a company which
deals with relations with the public.
Abbr **PR department**

public relations exercise /ˌpʌblɪk
rɪ'leɪʃ(ə)nz ˌeksəsaɪz/ *noun* a campaign to improve public relations

public servant /ˌpʌblɪk 'sɜːvənt/
noun a person employed by a government department or agency

public service /'pʌblɪk 'sɜːvɪs/
noun the various departments and agencies that carry out government policies
and provide the services that are funded
by the government

public training programme
/ˌpʌblɪk 'treɪnɪŋ ˌprəʊgræm/ *noun*
a training programme that has a set
syllabus and is open to the employees of
any organisation

pull /pʊl/ *verb* □ **pull the plug on
something** to bring something such as a
business project to an end, especially by
cutting off its financial support (*informal*)

pull out /ˌpʊl 'aʊt/ *verb* to stop being
part of a deal or agreement ○ *Our Australian partners pulled out of the
contract.*

punctual /'pʌŋktʃuəl/ *adjective* tend-
ing to arrive at a place at the right time

punctuality /ˌpʌŋktʃu'ælɪti/ *noun*
the tendency to arrive at a place at the
right time

punitive /'pjuːnɪtɪv/ *adjective* which
punishes

punitive damages /ˌpjuːnɪtɪv
'dæmɪdʒɪz/ damages which punish the
defendant for the loss or harm caused to
the plaintiff; heavy damages awarded to
show that the court feels the defendant
has behaved badly towards the plaintiff

punitive measure /ˌpjuːnɪtɪv
'meʒə/ *noun* a measure to punish
someone

purchase book /'pɜːtʃɪs bʊk/ *noun*
a book in which purchases are recorded

push /pʊʃ/ *noun* the action of making
something move forward ◇ **push the
envelope** /ˌpʊʃ ði 'envələʊp/ to go beyond normal limits and try to do something that is new and sometimes risky
(*slang*)

put back /ˌpʊt 'bæk/ *verb* to change
to a later time ○ *We had to put back the
meeting because the leader of the management team was ill.*

put in /ˌpʊt 'ɪn/ *verb* □ **to put an ad in
a paper** to have an ad printed in a newspaper □ **the union put in a 6% wage
claim** the union asked for a 6% increase
in wages

put off /ˌpʊt 'ɒf/ *verb* to arrange for
something to take place later than
planned ○ *The meeting was put off for
two weeks.* ○ *She asked if we could put
the visit off until tomorrow.*

put out /ˌpʊt 'aʊt/ *verb* to send out ○
*We are planning to put out most of the
work to freelancers.* □ **to put work out
to contract** to decide that work should
be done by a company on a contract,
rather than employ members of staff to
do it

pyramid /'pɪrəmɪd/ *noun* **1.** a shape
like a triangle with a wide bottom rising
to a point at the top **2.** a hierarchical
staff structure in an organisation, with
few employees at the top and many
more at the bottom

Q

quadruplicate /kwɒˈdruːplɪkət/ *noun* □ **in quadruplicate** with the original and three copies ○ *The invoices are printed in quadruplicate.* ○ *The application form should be completed in quadruplicate.*

qualification /ˌkwɒlɪfɪˈkeɪʃ(ə)n/ *noun* formal proof of the fact that someone has successfully completed a specialised course of study or has acquired a skill ○ *You must have the right qualifications for the job.* ○ *Job-hunting is difficult if you have no qualifications.*

'…personnel management is not an activity that can ever have just one set of qualifications as a requirement for entry into it' [*Personnel Management*]

qualified /ˈkwɒlɪfaɪd/ *adjective* having passed special examinations in a subject ○ *She is a qualified accountant.* ○ *We have appointed a qualified designer to supervise the decorating of the new reception area.* □ **highly qualified** with very good results in examinations ○ *All our staff are highly qualified.* ○ *They employ twenty-six highly qualified engineers.*

'…applicants will be professionally qualified and ideally have a degree in Commerce and postgraduate management qualifications' [*Australian Financial Review*]

qualify /ˈkwɒlɪfaɪ/ *verb* □ **to qualify as** to follow a specialised course of study and pass examinations so that you can do a certain job ○ *She has qualified as an accountant.* ○ *He will qualify as a solicitor next year.*

'…federal examiners will also determine which of the privately insured savings and loans qualify for federal insurance' [*Wall Street Journal*]

qualifying day /ˈkwɒlɪfaɪɪŋ deɪ/ *noun* a working day for which an employee is eligible to receive statutory sick pay

qualifying earnings /ˈkwɒlɪfaɪɪŋ ˌɜːnɪŋz/ *plural noun* earnings on which National Insurance contributions have been paid and which qualify an employee for incapacity benefit

quality /ˈkwɒlɪti/ *noun* what something is like or how good or bad something is ○ *The poor quality of the service led to many complaints.* ○ *There is a market for good-quality secondhand computers.*

quality assurance standards /ˌkwɒlɪti əˈʃʊərəns ˌstændədz/ *plural noun* guaranteed levels of product quality which can be checked by the company

quality circle /ˈkwɒlɪti ˌsɜːk(ə)l/ *noun* a group of employees in a company who meet to discuss quality controls and working practices. Abbr **QC**

quality control /ˈkwɒlɪti kənˌtrəʊl/ *noun* the process of making sure that the quality of a product is good

quality controller /ˈkwɒlɪti kənˌtrəʊlə/ *noun* a person who checks the quality of a product

quality of life /ˌkwɒlɪti əv ˈlaɪf/ *noun* the general feeling of wellbeing in your life

quality of working life /ˌkwɒlɪti əv ˈwɜːkɪŋ laɪf/ *noun* the general satisfaction with your life at work, including the environment, career structure and pay. Abbr **QWL**

quality time /ˈkwɒlɪti taɪm/ *noun* time during which you can devote yourself fully and without distractions to an activity that you consider important, e.g. to building a strong relationship with your family

quantifiable /ˈkwɒntɪfaɪəb(ə)l/ *adjective* which can be quantified ○ *The* *effect of the change in the discount structure is not quantifiable.*

quantifiable objective /ˌkwɒntɪfaɪəb(ə)l əbˈdʒektɪv/ *noun* an objective for which it is possible to give a measure to gauge if it has been reached

quarter /ˈkwɔːtə/ *noun* a period of three months ○ *The instalments are payable at the end of each quarter.*

quarterly /ˈkwɔːtəli/ *adjective, adverb* happening once every three months ○ *There is a quarterly charge for electricity.* ○ *The bank sends us a quarterly statement.* ○ *We agreed to pay the rent quarterly or on a quarterly basis.*

quarterly statement of contributions /ˌkwɔːtəli ˌsteɪtmənt əv ˌkɒntrɪˈbjuːʃ(ə)nz/ *noun* a statement issued by a pension company which shows how much has been paid into a pensions scheme over the last quarter

question /ˈkwestʃən/ *noun* 1. words which need an answer ○ *The managing director refused to answer questions about redundancies.* ○ *The training manager prepared a series of questions to test the trainees' reactions in different sales situations.* 2. a problem ○ *The board discussed the question of redundancy payments.* ○ *The main question is that of the cost of the training programme.* □ **to raise a question** to mention a problem and expect it to be discussed ○ *She raised the question of moving to less expensive offices.* ■ *verb* 1. to ask questions ○ *She questioned the chairman on the company's investment policy.* 2. to show doubt about something or suggest that something may be wrong ○ *We all question how accurate the data is.*

questionnaire /ˌkwestʃəˈneə/ *noun* a printed list of questions aiming at collecting data in an unbiased way, especially used in market research ○ *We'll send out a questionnaire to test the opinions of users of the system.* ○ *Questionnaires were handed to the staff asking them about their attitudes to work conditions.*

queue /kjuː/ *noun* 1. a line of people waiting one behind the other ○ *to form a queue* or *to join a queue* 2. a series of documents (such as orders or application forms) which are dealt with in order □ **his case went to the end of the queue** his case was dealt with last ■ *verb* to form a line one after the other for something ○ *The candidates queued outside the interviewing room.*

quid pro quo /ˌkwɪd prəʊ ˈkwəʊ/ *noun* money paid or an action carried out in return for something ○ *He agreed to repay the loan early, and as a quid pro quo the bank released the collateral.*

quit /kwɪt/ *verb* to resign or leave a job ○ *He quit after an argument with the managing director.* ○ *Several of the managers are quitting to set up their own company.* (NOTE: **quitting – quit**)

quorum /ˈkwɔːrəm/ *noun* a minimum number of people who have to be present at a meeting to make it valid □ **to have a quorum** to have enough people present for a meeting to go ahead ○ *Do we have a quorum?*

QWL *abbr* quality of working life

R

race /reɪs/ *noun* a group of people who are different because of skin colour, hair, eyes, etc.

Race Relations Act 1976 /ˌreɪs rɪ-ˈleɪʃ(ə)nz ækt ˌnaɪntiːn sev(ə)nti ˈsɪks/ *noun* an Act of Parliament which makes racial discrimination in employment an offence

racial /ˈreɪʃ(ə)l/ *adjective* of or referring to a person's race

racial discrimination /ˌreɪʃ(ə)l dɪskrɪmɪˈneɪʃ(ə)n/ *noun* the practice of treating a person differently (usually worse) because of their race ○ *The organisation was accused of racial discrimination in selecting managers.*

racial prejudice /ˌreɪʃ(ə)l ˈpredʒʊdɪs/ *noun* feelings against someone because of their race ○ *They investigated claims of racial prejudice in hiring staff.* ○ *The immigrant felt forced to give up his job because of racial prejudice on the shop floor.*

racism /ˈreɪsɪz(ə)m/, **racialism** /ˈreɪʃəlɪz(ə)m/ *noun* the belief in racist ideas or actions based on racist ideas ○ *She accused the company of racism in their appointments to the management committee.*

racist /ˈreɪsɪst/ *noun, adjective* (a person) believing that people of certain racial or ethnic groups are inferior

raiding /ˈreɪdɪŋ/ *noun* same as **poaching**

rainmaker /ˈreɪnmeɪkə/ *noun* a person, especially a lawyer, who wins clients who spend a lot of money doing business with their firm (*slang*)

raise /reɪz/ *noun US* an increase in salary ○ *He asked the boss for a raise.* ○ *She is pleased – she has had her raise.* ○ *She got her raise last month.* (NOTE: British English is **rise**) ■ *verb* **1.** to ask a meeting to discuss a question ○ *The chairman tried to prevent the question of redundancies being raised.* **2.** to increase or to make higher ○ *The government has raised the tax levels.* ○ *The organisation will raise wages if inflation gets worse.*

R&D *abbr* research and development

random /ˈrændəm/ *adjective* done without making any special selection □ **at random** without special selection ○ *The director picked out two sales reports at random.*

random check /ˌrændəm ˈtʃek/ *noun* a check on items taken from a group without any special selection

random inspection /ˌrændəm ɪnˈspekʃən/ *noun* an inspection carried out without any particular choice and without warning

random sampling /ˌrændəm ˈsɑːmplɪŋ/ *noun* the choosing of samples for testing without any special selection

range /reɪndʒ/ *noun* **1.** a series of items ○ *There are a whole range of alternatives for the new salary scheme.* **2.** a spread of sizes or amounts within fixed limits ○ *The company's salary scale ranges from £5,000 for a trainee to £50,000 for the managing director.* □ **range of salaries**, **salary range** a list of salaries paid, from the lowest to the highest ○ *The salary range is £10,000 – £14,000.* ■ *verb* to be within a group of sizes or amounts falling within fixed limits ○ *The company sells products ranging from cheap downmarket pens to imported luxury items.* ○ *The company's salary scale ranges from £10,000 for a trainee to £150,000 for the managing director.* ○ *Our activities range from* *mining in the USA to computer services in Scotland.*

range of indifference /ˌreɪndʒ əv ɪnˈdɪf(ə)rəns/ *noun* the top area of a salary scale, where the salaries are so high that salary increases are no longer an incentive to perform better

rank /ræŋk/ *noun* a position in a company or an organisation ○ *All managers are of equal rank.* ○ *Promotion means moving up from a lower rank.* □ **in rank order** in order according to position of importance ■ *verb* **1.** to classify in order of importance ○ *Candidates are ranked in order of appearance.* ○ *Candidates are ranked in order of their test results.* **2.** to be in a certain position □ **all managers rank equally** all managers have the same status in the company

rank and file /ˌræŋk ən ˈfaɪl/ *noun* the ordinary members of a trade union or other association ○ *The decision was not liked by the rank and file.* □ **rank-and-file members** ordinary members

ranking /ˈræŋkɪŋ/ *adjective* in a certain position ○ *a high-ranking official* □ **she is the top-ranking** *or* **the senior-ranking official in the delegation** she is the member of the delegation who occupies the highest official post ■ *noun* the act of arranging into a list in order of quality, importance or quantity ○ *Job ranking was carried out according to the relative importance of each job in the organisation.*

ranking system /ˈræŋkɪŋ ˌsɪstəm/ *noun* a way of calculating the value of jobs and sorting them into different levels

rate /reɪt/ *noun* **1.** the money charged for time worked or work completed **2.** an amount of money paid (shown as a percentage) **3.** an amount, number or speed compared with something else ○ *the rate of increase in redundancies* ○ *The rate of absenteeism* or *the absenteeism rate always increases in fine weather.* ■ *verb* □ **to rate someone highly** to value someone, to think someone is very good

'…the unions had argued that public sector pay rates had slipped behind rates applying in private sector employment' [*Australian Financial Review*]

rate of inflation /ˌreɪt əv ɪnˈfleɪʃ(ə)n/ *noun* the percentage increase in prices over a twelve-month period (NOTE: also called **rate of inflation**)

rate of taxation /ˌreɪt əv tækˈseɪʃ(ə)n/ *noun* the proportion of a particular sum of money (such as a salary) which must be paid in tax ○ *He pays income tax at the highest rate.* (NOTE: also called **tax rate**)

rate of unemployment /ˌreɪt əv ˌʌnɪmˈplɔɪmənt/ *noun* number of people out of work, shown as a percentage of the total number of people available for work (NOTE: also called **unemployment rate**)

ratification /ˌrætɪfɪˈkeɪʃ(ə)n/ *noun* official approval ○ *The agreement has to go to the board for ratification.*

ratify /ˈrætɪfaɪ/ *verb* to approve officially ○ *The agreement has to be ratified by the board.* (NOTE: **ratifies – ratifying – ratified**)

rating /ˈreɪtɪŋ/ *noun* the act of giving something a value, or the value given

rating scale /ˈreɪtɪŋ skeɪl/ *noun* a series of grades used in performance rating

rating standard /ˈreɪtɪŋ ˌstændəd/ *noun* an international standard of work efficiency for pieceworkers

ratio /ˈreɪʃiəʊ/ *noun* **1.** a proportion or quantity of something compared to something else ○ *the ratio of successes to failures* ○ *With less manual work available, the ratio of employees to managers is decreasing.* **2.** a mathematical expression that shows the relationship between two amounts ○ *The ratio of junior staff to senior staff is 5:1.* ○ *Our product outsells theirs by a ratio of two to one.*

rationalisation /ˌræʃ(ə)nəlaɪˈzeɪʃ(ə)n/, **rationalization** *noun* a process designed to make an organisation efficient and profitable again when its performance or results have been poor, which usually involves changes in organisation structure, redundancies, plant closures and cutbacks in supplies and resources (NOTE: The term is also used in a cynical way as a euphemism for mass redundancies.)

rationalise /ˈræʃ(ə)nəlaɪz/, **rational-ize** *verb* to make something more efficient ○ *The rail company is trying to rationalise its freight services.* ○ *The organisation is trying to rationalise its salary scales.*

rat race /ˈræt reɪs/ *noun* competition for success in business or in a career ○ *He decided to get out of the rat race and buy a small farm.*

raw /rɔː/ *adjective* in the original state or not processed

raw data /rɔː ˈdeɪtə/ *noun* data as it is put into a computer, without being analysed

raw deal /rɔː ˈdiːl/ *noun* a bad arrangement or bad treatment ○ *She got a raw deal from her manager.*

raw labour /rɔː ˈleɪbə/ *noun* unskilled workers ○ *Because too high a proportion of the local workforce was raw labour, the company had to recruit from further afield.*

RDO *noun* (*in Australia and New Zealand*) a day of leave granted to staff under certain employment agreements when they have accumulated a particular amount of overtime (NOTE: Full form **rostered day off**)

reach /riːtʃ/ *verb* to get to something □ **to reach an agreement** to agree □ **to reach a decision** to decide ○ *The two parties reached an agreement over the terms for the contract.* ○ *The board reached a decision about closing the factory.*

readjust /ˌriːəˈdʒʌst/ *verb* to adjust again ○ *to readjust salary scales*

readvertise /riːˈædvətaɪz/ *verb* to advertise again ○ *All the candidates failed the test so we will just have to readvertise.* □ **to readvertise a post** to put in a second advertisement for a vacant post

readvertisement /ˌriːədˈvɜːtɪsmənt/ *noun* a second advertisement for a vacant post ○ *The readvertisement attracted only two new applicants.*

real /rɪəl/ *adjective* (*of prices or amounts*) shown in terms of money adjusted for inflation □ **in real terms** actually or really ○ *Salaries have gone up by 3% but with inflation running at 5% that is a fall in real terms.*

'…real wages have been held down dramatically: they have risen as an annual rate of only 1% in the last two years' [*Sunday Times*]

real earnings /rɪəl ˈɜːnɪŋz/, **real wages** /rɪəl ˈweɪdʒɪz/ *plural noun* income which is available for spending after tax and other contributions have been deducted, corrected for inflation

real time /ˈrɪəl taɪm/ *noun* the time when a computer is working on the processing of data while the problem to which the data refers is actually taking place ○ *The website allows you to check share prices in real time* or *gives real time information on share prices.*

real-time system /ˈrɪəl taɪm ˌsɪstəm/ *noun* a computer system where data is inputted directly into the computer which automatically processes it to produce information which can be used immediately

reapplication /ˌriːæplɪˈkeɪʃ(ə)n/ *noun* a second or subsequent application for a job

reapply /ˌriːəˈplaɪ/ *verb* to apply again ○ *When he saw that the job had still not been filled, he reapplied for it.* (NOTE: **reapplies – reapplying – reapplied**)

reappoint /ˌriːəˈpɔɪnt/ *verb* to appoint someone again ○ *She was reappointed chairman for a further three-year period.*

reappointment /ˌriːəˈpɔɪntmənt/ *noun* the act of being reappointed ○ *On her reappointment as chairman, she thanked the board for their support.* ○ *The board decided to offer him reappointment for a further two years at the end of his fixed-term contract.*

reason /ˈriːz(ə)n/ *noun* an explanation as to why something has happened ○ *The chairman was asked for his reasons for cancelling the meeting.* ○ *The company gave no reason for the sudden closure of the factory.*

reasonable /ˈriːz(ə)nəb(ə)l/ *adjective* **1.** sensible or not annoyed ○ *The manager of the shop was very reasonable when I tried to explain that I had left my credit cards at home.* **2.** moderate or not expensive ○ *The union has* *decided to put in a reasonable wage claim.*

reasonable behaviour /ˌriːz(ə)nəb(ə)l bɪˈheɪvjə/ *noun* a way of approach by an employer when making employees redundant

reassess /ˌriːəˈses/ *verb* to assess again ○ *The manager was asked to reassess the department staff, after the assessments were badly done by the supervisors.*

reassessment /ˌriːəˈsesmənt/ *noun* a new assessment

reassign /ˌriːəˈsaɪn/ *verb* to assign something again or to assign someone to a new position

reassignment /ˌriːəˈsaɪnmənt/ *noun* a new assignment

reassure /ˌriːəˈʃʊə/ *verb* to make someone calm or less worried ○ *The manager tried to reassure her that she would not lose her job.*

rebuke /rɪˈbjuːk/ *noun* an act of criticising someone for doing something

receipt /rɪˈsiːt/ *noun* **1.** a piece of paper showing that money has been paid or that something has been received ○ *She lost her taxi receipt.* ○ *Keep the receipt for items purchased in case you need to change them later.* ○ *Please produce your receipt if you want to exchange items.* **2.** the act of receiving something ○ *Goods will be supplied within thirty days of receipt of order* □ **to acknowledge receipt of a letter** to write to say that you have received a letter ○ *We acknowledge receipt of your letter of the 15th.* ○ *Invoices are payable within thirty days of receipt.* ○ *On receipt of the notification, the company lodged an appeal.*

reception /rɪˈsepʃən/ *noun* a place in a hotel or office where visitors register or say who they have come to see

receptionist /rɪˈsepʃənɪst/ *noun* a person in a hotel or office who meets guests or clients, answers the phone, etc.

recession /rɪˈseʃ(ə)n/ *noun* a fall in trade or in the economy ○ *The recession has reduced profits in many companies.* ○ *Several firms have closed factories because of the recession.*

COMMENT: There are various ways of deciding if a recession is taking place: the usual one is when the GNP falls for three consecutive quarters.

recipient /rɪˈsɪpiənt/ *noun* a person who receives something ○ *She was the recipient of an allowance from the company.* ○ *A registered letter must be signed for by the recipient.*

reckonable year /ˌrekənəb(ə)l ˈjɪə/ *noun* a year in which full National Insurance Contributions have been paid (used to calculate the state retirement pension)

recognise /ˈrekəɡnaɪz/, **recognize** *verb* **1.** to know someone or something because you have seen or heard them before ○ *I recognised his voice before he said who he was.* ○ *Do you recognise the handwriting on the application form?* **2.** □ **to recognise a union** to agree that a union can act on behalf of employees in a company ○ *Although more than half the staff had joined the union, the management refused to recognise it.*

recognition /ˌrekəɡˈnɪʃ(ə)n/ *noun* the act of recognising something or somebody □ **recognition of a trade union**, **union recognition** the act of agreeing that a union can act on behalf of employees in a company

recognition agreement /ˌrekəɡˈnɪʃ(ə)n əˌɡriːmənt/ *noun* a document which sets out the terms under which a union is recognised, and the ways in which management and union will work together in the future

recommend /rekəˈmend/ *verb* **1.** to suggest that something should be done ○ *The management consultant recommended a different form of pay structure.* **2.** to say that someone or something is good ○ *I certainly would not recommend Miss Smith for the job.*

recommendation /ˌrekəmenˈdeɪʃ(ə)n/ *noun* an act of saying that someone or something is good ○ *We appointed him on the recommendation of his former employer.* □ **to make a recommendation** to suggest that something should be done

reconcile /ˈrekənsaɪl/ *verb* **1.** to make two financial accounts or statements agree ○ *She is trying to reconcile one account with another* or *to reconcile the two accounts.* **2.** to make two things agree ○ *Their manager tried to reconcile the different points of view.*

reconsider /ˌriːkən'sɪdə/ *verb* to think again about a decision which has already been made ○ *The interim agreement will provide a breathing space while both sides reconsider their positions.*

record *noun* /'rekɔːd/ **1.** a report of something which has happened ○ *The chairman signed the minutes as a true record of the last meeting.* □ **for the record, to keep the record straight** to note something which has been done ○ *For the record, I would like these sales figures to be noted in the minutes.* □ **on record** correctly reported ○ *The chairman is on record as saying that profits are set to rise.* □ **to go on record as stating** to state emphatically, so that it can be noted **2.** a description of what has happened in the past ○ *the salesperson's record of service* or *service record* ○ *the company's record in industrial relations* ○ *He has a very poor timekeeping record.* ■ *verb* /rɪ'kɔːd/ to note or report □ **to record a complaint** to listen to a complaint and make a note of it ○ *Your complaint has been recorded and will be investigated.*

record of achievement /ˌrekɔːd əv ə'tʃiːvmənt/ *noun* a document given to someone who has finished a course of instruction, showing their achievement in class, exam results, etc.

records /'rekɔːdz/ *plural noun* documents which give information ○ *The names of customers are kept in the company's records.* ○ *We find from our records that our invoice number 1234 has not been paid.*

recreation /ˌrekri'eɪʃ(ə)n/ *noun* leisure time ○ *Giving the shift workers half an hour recreation in the middle of the morning has resulted in improved productivity.*

recreational /ˌrekri'eɪʃ(ə)n(ə)l/ *adjective* referring to recreation

recreational facilities /ˌrekri-'eɪʃ(ə)n(ə)l fə,sɪlɪtiz/ *plural noun* sports centres, football pitches, gyms,

etc., provided by a company for the employees

recruit /rɪ'kruːt/ *verb* □ **to recruit new staff** to search for and appoint new staff to join a company ○ *We are recruiting staff for our new store.* ■ *noun* a new member of staff ○ *The induction programme for recruits begins on Wednesday.*

recruitment /rɪ'kruːtmənt/, **recruiting** /rɪ'kruːtɪŋ/ *noun* □ **recruitment of new staff** the process of searching for and appointing new staff to join a company ○ *Which section in HR deals with recruitment and selection?*

recruitment consultant /rɪ-'kruːtmənt kən,sʌltənt/ *noun* an agency which recruits staff for a company (usually interviewing and drawing up a shortlist of candidates for a final decision by the management)

recruitment fair /rɪ'kruːtmənt feə/ *noun* an exhibition where employers try to recruit college graduates as new members of staff

recruitment ratio /rɪ'kruːtmənt ,reɪʃiəʊ/ *noun* a ratio of the number of people appointed to jobs to the number of candidates applying ○ *The recruitment ratio is low in departments where a high level of skills is required.* ○ *The sudden demand for a large number of new employees has led to the lowering of the recruitment ratio.*

red circle rate /red 'sɜːk(ə)l reɪt/ *noun* a pay rate which is above the minimum rate for an employee's evaluated level

red circling /red 'sɜːklɪŋ/ *noun* the practice of paying staff at a higher rate, even if their jobs have been downgraded

redeploy /ˌriːdɪ'plɔɪ/ *verb* to move employees from one place to another or from one type of job to another ○ *We closed the design department and redeployed the workforce in the publicity and sales departments.*

redeployment /ˌriːdɪ'plɔɪmənt/ *noun* the act of moving employees from one place of work to another or from one type of job to another

red tape /red 'teɪp/ *noun* official paperwork which takes a long time to complete ○ *The appointment of the new manager has been held up by red tape in the HR department.*

reduce /rɪˈdjuːs/ *verb* to make smaller or lower ○ *We must reduce expenditure if we want to stay in business.* ○ *We have made some staff redundant to reduce overmanning.* ○ *The company reduced output because of a fall in demand.* ○ *The government's policy is to reduce inflation to 5%.* □ **to reduce staff** to make employees redundant in order to have a smaller number of staff □ **to reduce salaries** to lower the level of salaries

reduction /rɪˈdʌkʃən/ *noun* an act of making something smaller or less ○ *Reduction in demand has led to the cancellation of several new projects.* ○ *The company was forced to make job reductions.* ○ *We expect the new government to introduce tax reductions.* ○ *The new MD has proposed a series of staff reductions.* ○ *Working only part-time will mean a significant reduction in take-home pay.* □ **reduction of manning levels** an act of reducing the number of employees needed in certain jobs □ **reduction of working hours** the act of reducing the number of hours worked

redundancy /rɪˈdʌndənsi/ *noun* **1.** the dismissal of a person whose job no longer needs to be done **2.** a person who has lost a job because they are not needed any more ○ *The takeover caused 250 redundancies.*

redundancy pay /rɪˈdʌndənsi peɪ/, **redundancy payment** /rɪˈdʌndənsi ˌpeɪmənt/ *noun* payment made to an employee to compensate for losing their job

redundant /rɪˈdʌndənt/ *adjective* **1.** (ability or skill) which is no longer needed or is useless ○ *redundant clause in a contract* ○ *The new legislation has made clause 6 redundant.* ○ *Retraining can help workers whose old skills have become redundant.* **2.** (person) who loses their job because their skills are no longer needed □ **to make someone redundant** to dismiss an employee who is not needed any more

redundant staff /rɪˌdʌndənt ˈstɑːf/ *noun* staff who have lost their jobs because they are not needed any more

re-employ /ˌriːɪmˈplɔɪ/ *verb* to employ someone again ○ *He came back to the factory hoping to be re-employed.*

re-employment /ˌriːɪmˈplɔɪmənt/ *noun* the act of employing someone again

re-engage /ˌriːɪnˈɡeɪdʒ/ *verb* to re-employ someone, but not necessarily in the same job

re-engagement /ˌriːɪnˈɡeɪdʒmənt/ *noun* the act of employing someone again, but not necessarily in the same job

referee /ˌrefəˈriː/ *noun* a person such as a former employer or teacher who can give a report on someone's character, ability or job performance ○ *She gave the name of her boss as a referee.* ○ *When applying please give the names of three referees.* ○ *He chose his former headmaster as referee.*

reference /ˈref(ə)rəns/ *noun* **1.** process of mentioning or dealing with ○ *with reference to your letter of May 25th* **2.** a person such as a former employer or teacher who can give a report on someone's character, ability or job performance ○ *He gave the name of his former manager as a reference.* ○ *Please use me as a reference if you wish.*

reference period /ˈref(ə)rəns ˌpɪəriəd/ *noun* a period which is used as a base for comparisons

refresher course /rɪˈfreʃə kɔːs/ *noun* a course of study designed to bring existing skills or knowledge up to date ○ *Refresher courses were given to anyone who had not used this machinery for some time.* ○ *She went on a refresher course in bookkeeping.*

refreshment /rɪˈfreʃmənt/ *noun* food and drink

refreshment time /rɪˈfreʃmənt taɪm/, **refreshment break** /rɪˈfreʃmənt breɪk/ *noun* a rest time during work when employees can have something to eat or drink. ♦ **coffee break, tea break**

region /'riːdʒən/ *noun* **1.** a large area of a country ○ *Her territory consists of all the eastern region of the country.* **2.** □ **in the region of** about or approximately ○ *She was earning a salary in the region of £35,000.*

register /'redʒɪstə/ *noun* an official list ○ *to enter something in a register* ○ *to keep a register up to date* □ **to be on the unemployment register** to be officially classified as unemployed ■ *verb* to write something in an official list ○ *After he was made redundant he registered at the unemployment office.*

registered disabled person /ˌredʒɪstəd dɪsˌeɪb(ə)ld 'pɜːs(ə)n/ *noun* a person who is registered with the Department for Employment as having a disability

registered letter /ˌredʒɪstəd 'letə/, **registered parcel** /ˌredʒɪstəd 'pɑːsəl/ *noun* a letter or parcel which is noted by the post office before it is sent, so that the sender can claim compensation if it is lost

registered office /ˌredʒɪstəd 'ɒfɪs/ *noun* the office address of a company which is officially registered with the Companies' Registrar

registered unemployed /ˌredʒɪstəd əz ˌʌnɪm'plɔɪd/ *noun* a person who has not got a job, has registered for unemployment benefit and is actively looking for work

registrar /ˌredʒɪ'strɑː/ *noun* a person who keeps official records

regular /'regjʊlə/ *adjective* which happens or comes at the same time each day, each week, each month or each year ○ *His regular train is the 12.45.* ○ *The regular flight to Athens leaves at 06.00.*

regular income /ˌregjʊlər 'ɪnkʌm/ *noun* an income which comes in every week or month ○ *She works freelance so she does not have a regular income.*

regular staff /'regjʊlə stɑːf/ *noun* the full-time staff

rehabilitation /ˌriːəbɪlɪ'teɪʃ(ə)n/ *noun* the process of making someone fit for work again (after illness, a period in prison, etc.)

COMMENT: By the Rehabilitation of Offenders Act, 1974, a person who is convicted of an offence, and then spends a period of time without committing any other offence, is not required to reveal that they have a previous conviction.

rehabilitation centre /ˌriːəbɪlɪ'teɪʃ(ə)n ˌsentə/ *noun* a centre where people who have not been working for some time (such as because of illness or unemployment) can be trained to re-enter the work environment

rehire /riː'haɪə/ *verb* to take back an employee after they have been made redundant or have left the company ○ *I don't think it was a good idea to rehire those two workers.*

reimburse /ˌriːɪm'bɜːs/ *verb* □ **to reimburse someone their expenses** to pay someone back for money which they have spent ○ *You will be reimbursed for your expenses* or *your expenses will be reimbursed.*

reimbursement /ˌriːɪm'bɜːsmənt/ *noun* the act of paying back money ○ *reimbursement of expenses*

reinstate /ˌriːɪn'steɪt/ *verb* to allow someone to return to a job from which they were dismissed ○ *The union demanded that the sacked workers should be reinstated.*

reinstatement /ˌriːɪn'steɪtmənt/ *noun* the act of putting someone back into a job from which they were dismissed

reinstatement order /ˌriːɪn'steɪtmənt ˌɔːdə/ *noun* an order by a tribunal to an employer to give a dismissed person their job back

reject /rɪ'dʒekt/ *verb* to refuse to accept, or to say that something is not satisfactory ○ *The union rejected the management's proposals.*

rejection /rɪ'dʒekʃən/ *noun* a refusal to accept, such as the refusal to give a customer credit ○ *After the union's rejection of the offer, management came back with new redundancy terms.*

relations /rɪ'leɪʃ(ə)nz/ *plural noun* relationships with other people, companies or countries ○ *Relations between the management and the workforce have been strained recently.* □ **to break off**

relations with someone to stop dealing with someone

release /rɪ'liːs/ *noun* the act of setting free ○ *release from a contract* ○ *He was offered early release so that he could take up his new job.* ■ *verb* to end an employee's contract early

relevant /'reləv(ə)nt/ *adjective* which has to do with what is being discussed or the current situation ○ *Can you give me the relevant papers?* ○ *The new assistant does not have any relevant experience.*

reliability /rɪ,laɪə'bɪlɪti/ *noun* the fact of being reliable

reliable /rɪ'laɪəb(ə)l/ *adjective* which can be trusted ○ *We are looking for a reliable bookkeeper to deal with the payroll.* ○ *The sales manager is completely reliable.*

reliable test /rɪ,laɪəb(ə)l 'test/ *noun* a test which always gives correct results

relief /rɪ'liːf/ *noun* **1.** help **2.** a person who takes the place of someone who is sick or on holiday ○ *A relief manager has been sent from headquarters.* ○ *The bus carrying relief workers was late.*

relief shift /rɪ'liːf ʃɪft/ *noun* a shift which comes to take the place of another shift, usually the shift between the day shift and the night shift

relieve /rɪ'liːv/ *verb* to come to work to take the place of another employee at the end of a shift ○ *The shift will be relieved at 06.30.*

relocate /ˌriːləʊ'keɪt/ *verb* to establish an organisation in a new place, or to be established in a new place ○ *The board decided to relocate the company in Scotland.* ○ *When the company moved its headquarters, 1500 people had to be relocated.* ○ *If the company moves down south, all the managerial staff will have to relocate.*

relocation /ˌriːləʊ'keɪʃ(ə)n/ *noun* the act of moving to a different place ○ *We will pay all the staff relocation costs.*

relocation allowance /ˌriːləʊ-'keɪʃ(ə)n ə,laʊəns/ *noun* a special payment given to an employee who agrees to move to another town to work

relocation expenses /ˌriːləʊ-'keɪʃ(ə)n ɪk,spensɪz/ *plural noun* expenses involved when an employee has to move house because their place of work has changed, or when a new employee has to move house to join the company, paid by the company

remedial transfer /rɪ,miːdiəl 'trænsfɜː/ *noun* an act of transferring an employee to a more suitable job after they have not performed well in their present position ○ *The HR manager and the supervisor discussed the possibility of a remedial transfer.*

removal /rɪ'muːv(ə)l/ *noun* **1.** the act of moving to a new house or office ○ *Staff are allowed removal expenses on joining the company.* **2.** the act of sacking someone (usually a director) from a job ○ *The removal of the managing director is going to be very difficult.*

remunerate /rɪ'mjuːnəreɪt/ *verb* to pay someone for doing something ○ *The company refused to remunerate them for their services.*

remuneration /rɪ,mjuːnə'reɪʃ(ə)n/ *noun* payment for services ○ *She has a monthly remuneration of £4800.* ○ *The job is interesting but the remuneration is low.* ○ *She receives a small remuneration of £400 a month.* ○ *No one will work hard for such poor remuneration.*

COMMENT: Remuneration can take several forms: the regular monthly salary cheque, a cheque or cash payment for hours worked or for work completed, etc.

remuneration package /rɪ-,mjuːnə'reɪʃ(ə)n ,pækɪdʒ/ *noun* the salary, pension contributions, bonuses and other forms of payment or benefit that make up an employee's total remuneration

remunerations committee /rɪ-,mjuːnə'reɪʃ(ə)nz kə,mɪti/ *noun* a committee of senior executives or non-executive directors who decide on directors' salaries

remunerations consultant /rɪ-,mjuːnə'reɪʃ(ə)nz kən,sʌltənt/ *noun* an adviser who gives advice on wage and salary structures

remunerative /rɪ'mjuːnərətɪv/ *adjective* referring to a job which pays well ○ *She is in a highly remunerative job.*

renew /rɪ'njuː/ *verb* to continue something for a further period of time ○ *His contract was renewed for a further three years.*

renewal /rɪ'njuːəl/ *noun* the act of renewing ○ *His contract is up for renewal in January.*

reopen /riː'əʊpən/ *verb* to open again ○ *The office will reopen soon after its refit.* ○ *The management agreed to reopen discussions with the union.*

reopening /riː'əʊp(ə)nɪŋ/ *noun* opening again ○ *the reopening of the store after refitting*

reopening clause /riː'əʊp(ə)nɪŋ klɔːz/ *noun* a clause in an agreement between a union and an employer which allows the union to reopen discussions on a particular issue during the term of the agreement

reorganisation /riː,ɔːgənaɪ'zeɪʃ(ə)n/, **reorganization** *noun* the act of organising something in a new way ○ *His job was downgraded in the office reorganisation* or *in the reorganisation of the office.*

reorganise /riː'ɔːgənaɪz/, **reorganize** *verb* to organise in a new way ○ *We have reorganised all our reps' territories.*

repair shop /rɪ'peə ʃɒp/ *noun* a small factory where machines are repaired

repeat /rɪ'piːt/ *verb* to do or say something again ○ *He repeated his address slowly so that the saleswoman could write it down.* ○ *When asked what the company planned to do, the chairman repeated 'Nothing'.* ○ *We'll have to repeat the survey next year.* □ **repeated absences from work** the act of being absent from work again and again

repetitive /rɪ'petɪtɪv/ *adjective* which happens again and again

repetitive strain injury /rɪ,petɪtɪv 'streɪn ,ɪndʒəri/, **repetitive stress injury** /rɪ,petɪtɪv 'stres ,ɪndʒəri/ *noun* a pain in the arm felt by someone who performs the same movement many times over a certain period, such as when keyboarding. Abbr **RSI**

repetitive work /rɪ'petɪtɪv wɜːk/ *noun* work which involves repeating the same task over and over again ○ *Supervisors try to introduce some variation into the work pattern since repetitive work leads to boredom.* ○ *Psychologists claim that repetitive work can be just as stressful as more demanding but varied work.*

replace /rɪ'pleɪs/ *verb* to put someone or something in the place of someone or something else ○ *They replaced the foreman with a younger man.* ○ *We are replacing all our salaried staff with freelancers.*

replacement /rɪ'pleɪsmənt/ *noun* **1.** an item which replaces something ○ *We are out of stock and are waiting for replacements.* **2.** a person who replaces someone ○ *My assistant leaves us next week, so we are advertising for a replacement.*

replacement rate /rɪ'pleɪsmənt reɪt/ *noun* the proportion of an organisation's workforce that is replaced every year ○ *The high replacement rate can be put down to dissatisfaction with working conditions.*

report /rɪ'pɔːt/ *noun* a statement describing what has happened or describing a state of affairs ○ *The accountants are drafting a report on salary scales.* ○ *The sales manager reads all the reports from the sales team.* ■ *verb* **1.** to make a statement describing something ○ *Each manager reports on the progress made in their departments over the last six weeks.* **2.** □ **to report to someone** to be responsible to or to be under someone ○ *She reports direct to the managing director.* ○ *The salesforce reports to the sales director.* **3.** to go to a place or to attend ○ *She has been asked to report for an interview.* ○ *Please report to our London office for training.* □ **to report sick** to state officially that you are sick and so cannot work

'...responsibilities include the production of premium quality business reports' [*Times*]

'...the research director will manage a team of business analysts monitoring and reporting on the latest development in retail distribution' [*Times*]

'...the successful candidate will report to the area director for profit responsibility for sales of leading brands' [*Times*]

reportable accident /rɪˌpɔːtəb(ə)l 'æksɪd(ə)nt/ *noun* an accident which causes death, or which makes an employee stay away from work for more than three days

reporting pay /rɪ'pɔːtɪŋ peɪ/ *noun* guaranteed pay for employees who report for work whether there is work for them to do or not ○ *The reporting pay system can be a drain on the company's resources when the order book is low.*

represent /ˌreprɪ'zent/ *verb* **1.** to work for a company, showing goods or services to possible buyers ○ *He represents an American car firm in Europe.* ○ *Our French distributor represents several other competing firms.* ○ *Which sector of the workforce does she represent on the committee?* **2.** to act on behalf of someone ○ *He sent his solicitor and accountant to represent him at the meeting.* ○ *Three managers represent the workforce in discussions with the directors.*

representation /ˌreprɪzen'teɪʃ(ə)n/ *noun* **1.** the act of selling goods for a company ○ *We offered them exclusive representation in Europe.* ○ *They have no representation in the USA.* **2.** the fact of having someone to act on your behalf ○ *The minority shareholders want representation on the board.* ○ *The ordinary shop floor workers want representation on the committee.* **3.** a complaint made on behalf of someone ○ *The managers made representations to the board on behalf of the hourly-paid members of staff.*

representative /ˌreprɪ'zentətɪv/ *noun* **1.** a person who acts on someone's behalf ○ *He sent his solicitor and accountant to act as his representatives at the meeting.* ○ *The board refused to meet the representatives of the workforce.* **2.** same as **sales representative**

reprimand /'reprɪmɑːnd/ *noun* official criticism given to an employee ○ *After receiving one reprimand he knew he would be sacked for further absenteeism.* ■ *verb* to criticise someone officially ○ *He was reprimanded by the manager.*

repudiate /rɪ'pjuːdieɪt/ *verb* to refuse to accept something □ **to repudiate an agreement** or **a contract** to refuse to perform one's obligations under an agreement or contract

repudiation /rɪˌpjuːdi'eɪʃ(ə)n/ *noun* a refusal to accept something

request /rɪ'kwest/ *noun* an act of asking for something ○ *They put in a request for a government subsidy.* ○ *His request for a loan was turned down by the bank.* □ **on request** if asked for ○ *We will send samples on request* or *'samples available on request.'*

requirement /rɪ'kwaɪəmənt/ *noun* what is needed □ **to meet the requirements of a job** to have the right qualifications or experience for a job

requisition /ˌrekwɪ'zɪʃ(ə)n/ *noun* an official order for something ○ *What is the reference number of your latest requisition?*

requisition form /ˌrekwɪ'zɪʃ(ə)n fɔːm/ *noun* a form sent to the human resources department from a department in an organisation asking for a new employee to be found to fill a vacancy ○ *The requisition form should contain all details of the job specification and terms of employment offered.*

research /rɪ'sɜːtʃ/ *noun* the process of trying to find out facts or information

research and development /rɪˌsɜːtʃ ən dɪ'veləpmənt/ *noun* scientific investigation which leads to making new products or improving existing products ○ *The company spends millions on research and development.* Abbr **R&D**

resent /rɪ'zent/ *verb* to feel annoyed about something ○ *The rest of the office resented his promotion to manager.*

resentful /rɪ'zentf(ə)l/ *adjective* feeling annoyed about something ○ *The junior members of staff feel resentful that the managers have a separate dining room.*

resentment /rɪ'zentmənt/ *noun* a feeling of annoyance at something ○ *The resentment of the unions at their treatment by management ended in a series of one-day strikes.*

residence /'rezɪd(ə)ns/ *noun* **1.** a house or flat where someone lives ○ *He has a country residence where he spends his weekends.* **2.** the act of living or operating officially in a country

residence permit /'rezɪd(ə)ns ˌpɜːmɪt/ *noun* an official document allowing a foreigner to live in a country ○ *She was granted a residence permit for one year* or *a one-year residence permit.* ○ *He has applied for a residence permit.*

resident /'rezɪd(ə)nt/ *noun* a person or company considered to be living or operating in a country for official or tax purposes ○ *The company is resident in France.*

residual /rɪ'zɪdjuəl/ *adjective* remaining after everything else has gone

residual unemployment /rɪˌzɪdjuəl ˌʌnɪm'plɔɪmənt/ *noun* unemployment amongst people who are not capable of doing the work available

resign /rɪ'zaɪn/ *verb* to give up a job ○ *He resigned from his post as treasurer.* ○ *He has resigned with effect from July 1st.* ○ *She resigned as finance director.*

resignation /ˌrezɪg'neɪʃ(ə)n/ *noun* the act of giving up a job ○ *He wrote his letter of resignation to the chairman.* □ **to hand in** *or* **to give in** *or* **to send in your resignation** to resign from your job

resizing /riː'saɪzɪŋ/ *noun* same as **upsizing**

resolution /ˌrezə'luːʃ(ə)n/ *noun* a decision to be reached at a meeting ○ *The meeting rejected the resolution or the resolution was defeated by ten votes to twenty.* ○ *The meeting carried or adopted a resolution to go on strike.* ○ *A resolution was passed to raise salaries by six per cent.* □ **to put a resolution to a meeting** to ask a meeting to vote on a proposal

resolve /rɪ'zɒlv/ *verb* to decide to do something ○ *The meeting resolved that a strike ballot should be held.*

resources /rɪ'sɔːsɪz/ *plural noun* **1.** a source of supply of something **2.** the money available for doing something □ **the cost of the new project is easily within our resources** we have quite

enough money to pay for the new project

respondent /rɪ'spɒndənt/ *noun* an employer who is defending a case brought before the industrial tribunal by an employee

responsibilities /rɪˌspɒnsɪ'bɪlɪtiz/ *plural noun* duties ○ *He finds the responsibilities of being managing director too heavy.*

responsibility /rɪˌspɒnsɪ'bɪlɪti/ *noun* the fact of being responsible ○ *The manager has overall responsibility for the welfare of the staff in her department.*

responsible /rɪ'spɒnsɪb(ə)l/ *adjective* **1.** □ **responsible to someone** being under someone's authority ○ *She is directly responsible to the managing director.* □ **responsible for** directing or being in charge of doing a certain job ○ *He is responsible for all sales.* ○ *He is responsible for the staff in his department.* **2.** (person) who is sensible or who can be trusted □ **a responsible job** job where important decisions have to be taken or where the employee has many responsibilities ○ *He is looking for a responsible job in marketing.*

responsible job /rɪ'spɒnsəb(ə)l dʒɒb/ *noun* a job where important decisions have to be taken or where the employee has many responsibilities ○ *She is looking for a responsible job in marketing.*

responsibly /rɪ'spɒnsɪbli/ *adverb* in a responsible way ○ *The staff acted very responsibly when the fire broke out.*

responsive /rɪ'spɒnsɪv/ *adjective* referring to a person who listens and does what someone asks ○ *The human resources manager was responsive to her request for compassionate leave.*

responsive listening /rɪˌspɒnsɪv 'lɪs(ə)nɪŋ/ *noun* the act of listening carefully and responding to what another person says ○ *The HR manager's responsive listening made the trainee feel that she understood her problems.*

respresentational rights /ˌreprɪzenˌteɪʃ(ə)n(ə)l 'raɪts/ *plural noun* the rights of a union to represent employees in dealings with management

restart /rɪ'stɑːt/ *verb* to start something again ○ *Negotiations will restart tomorrow.*

restart interview /'riːstɑːt ˌɪntəvjuː/ *noun* an interview given to someone who is unemployed, with the aim of advising them on means of getting back to work

rest break /'rest breɪk/ *noun* a period of time during the working day when an employee is allowed to be away from their workstation for a rest or meal break (NOTE: Many countries have laws governing how often employees are allowed rest breaks and how long those rest breaks should be, depending on the number of hours the employee works in a day.)

rest period /'rest ˌpɪəriəd/ *noun* the length of time between periods of work that an employee is entitled to have for rest (NOTE: Many countries have laws governing the rights of employees to have a particular number of periods of rest per day, per week, and, sometimes, per month.)

restraint /rɪ'streɪnt/ *noun* control

restrict /rɪ'strɪkt/ *verb* to limit or to impose controls on ○ *We are restricted to twenty staff by the size of our offices.*

restrictive /rɪ'strɪktɪv/ *adjective* which limits

restrictive covenant /rɪˌstrɪktɪv 'kʌvənənt/ *noun* a clause in a contract which prevents someone from doing something

restrictive practices /rɪˌstrɪktɪv 'præktɪsɪz/, **restrictive trade practices** /rɪˌstrɪktɪv 'treɪd ˌpræktɪsɪz/ *plural noun* ways of working which make people less free (such as trade unions stopping workers from doing certain jobs or companies not allowing customers a free choice of product) ○ *As part of a policy of restrictive practices he refused to do anything which was not laid down in his contract of employment.* ○ *Restrictive practices in industry mean that employers will not be able to afford to take on more labour.*

restructuring /riː'strʌktʃərɪŋ/ *noun* the process of reorganising the financial basis of a company

result /rɪ'zʌlt/ *noun* something which happens because of something else ○ *What was the result of the price investigation?* ○ *The company doubled its sales force with the result that the sales rose by 26%.* ■ *verb* □ **to result in** to produce as a result ○ *The doubling of the sales force resulted in increased sales.* ○ *The extra orders resulted in overtime work for all the factory staff.* ○ *We have to fill several vacancies resulting from the recent internal promotions.*

result-driven /rɪ'zʌlt ˌdrɪv(ə)n/ *adjective* used to describe a strategy or organisation that focuses mainly on results and achievements (NOTE: A result-driven organisation concentrates on achieving its aims, and delivering products at the required time, cost, and quality, and considers performance to be more important than procedures.)

resume /rɪ'zjuːm/ *verb* to start again ○ *The discussions resumed after a two hour break.*

résumé /'rezjuːˌmeɪ/, **resume** *noun* US a summary of a person's work experience and qualifications sent to a prospective employer by someone applying for a job (NOTE: British English is **curriculum vitae**)

resumption /rɪ'zʌmpʃən/ *noun* an act of starting again □ **we expect an early resumption of negotiations** we expect negotiations will start again soon

retail price(s) index /ˌriːteɪl 'praɪsɪz ˌɪndeks/ *noun* an index which shows how prices of consumer goods have increased or decreased over a period of time. Abbr **RPI**

retain /rɪ'teɪn/ *verb* **1.** to keep ○ *measures to retain experienced staff* ○ *Out of the profits, the company has retained £50,000 as provision against bad debts.* **2.** □ **to retain a lawyer to act for a company** to agree with a lawyer that they will act for you (and pay them a fee in advance)

retainer /rɪ'teɪnə/ *noun* money paid in advance to someone so that they will work for you, and not for someone else ○ *We pay them a retainer of £1,000.*

retention /rɪ'tenʃən/ the process of keeping the loyalty of existing employees and persuading them not to work for another company

'...a systematic approach to human resource planning can play a significant part in reducing recruitment and retention problems' [*Personnel Management*]

retention bonus /rɪ'tenʃən ˌbəʊnəs/ *noun* a bonus payment paid to employees who are obliged to stay on to close down a business, where their colleagues will have been eligible for redundancy payments

retention profile /rɪ'tenʃən ˌprəʊfaɪl/ *noun* the analysis of all employees who join at the same date, showing how many leave each year, expressed as a percentage of the original total

retiral /rɪ'taɪərəl/ *noun US* same as **retirement**

retire /rɪ'taɪə/ *verb* **1.** to stop work and take a pension ○ *She retired with a £15,000 pension.* ○ *The founder of the company retired at the age of 85.* ○ *The shop is owned by a retired policeman.* **2.** to make an employee stop work and take a pension ○ *They decided to retire all staff over 50.*

retiree /rɪ,taɪə'riː/ *noun* a person who has retired or is about to retire

retirement /rɪ'taɪəmənt/ *noun* **1.** the act of retiring from work ○ *I am looking forward to my retirement.* ○ *Older staff are planning what they will do in retirement.* **2.** the period when a person is retired

retirement annuity /rɪ'taɪəmənt ə-,njuːɪti/ *noun* an annuity bought when someone retires, using part of the sum put into a personal pension plan

retirement date /rɪ'taɪəmənt deɪt/ *noun* the date on which someone retires and takes a pension

retirement pension /rɪ'taɪəmənt ,penʃən/ *noun* a state pension given in the UK to a man who is over 65 and woman who is over 60. Women's pension age is gradually being adjusted to 65.

retrain /riː'treɪn/ *verb* to train someone for a new job, or to do the same job

in a more efficient way ○ *She went back to college to be retrained.*

retraining /riː'treɪnɪŋ/ *noun* the act of training again ○ *The shop is closed for staff retraining.* ○ *He had to attend a retraining session.* ○ *Retraining is necessary to keep up with new production methods.*

retroactive /ˌretrəʊ'æktɪv/ *adjective* which takes effect from a time in the past ○ *The union is asking for a retroactive pay rise.* ○ *They got a pay rise retroactive to last January.*

'The salary increases, retroactive from April of the current year, reflect the marginal rise in private sector salaries' [*Nikkei Weekly*]

retroactively /ˌretrəʊ'æktɪvli/ *adverb* going back to a time in the past

returner /rɪ'tɜːnə/ *noun* a person who goes back to work after being away for a time

reverse charge call /rɪ,vɜːs 'tʃɑːdʒ kɔːl/ *noun* a telephone call where the person receiving the call agrees to pay for it

reversionary annuity /rɪ-,vɜːʃ(ə)n(ə)ri ə'njuːɪti/ *noun* an annuity paid to someone on the death of another person

review /rɪ'vjuː/ *noun* a general examination ○ *to conduct a review of distributors* □ **she had a salary review last April** her salary was examined (and increased) in April ■ *verb* to examine something generally □ **to review salaries** to look at all salaries in a company to decide on increases ○ *His salary will be reviewed at the end of the year.* ○ *The company has decided to review freelance payments in the light of the rising cost of living.*

revoke /rɪ'vəʊk/ *verb* to cancel ○ *to revoke a decision* or *a clause in an agreement*

reward /rɪ'wɔːd/ *noun* money or other gains from effort ○ *The present given to the retiring manager was a reward for many years loyal service to the company.* ○ *Although the job is very demanding, the rewards are considerable.* ■ *verb* to give a person something in return for effort or achievement ○ *The work is hard and not very rewarding financially.*

reward management /rɪ'wɔːd ˌmænɪdʒmənt/ *noun* the creation and running of a system that rewards the work done by employees (NOTE: Reward management deals not only with basic pay, but also with the whole remuneration package offered to employees including such things as incentive schemes and fringe benefits.)

reward package /rɪ'wɔːd ˌpækɪdʒ/ *noun* the total of all money and benefits given to an employee (including salary, bonuses, company car, pension plans, medical insurance, etc.)

reward review /rɪ'wɔːd rɪˌvjuː/ *noun* a study of an employee's performance to determine their correct pay level

right /raɪt/ *noun* a legal title to something ○ *The staff have a right to know how the company is doing.*

rightful claimant /ˌraɪtf(ə)l 'kleɪmənt/ *noun* a person who has a legal claim to something (NOTE: this term has now replaced **plaintiff**. The other side in a case is the **defendant**)

right-hand man /'raɪt hænd ˌmæn/ *noun* a man who is the main assistant to someone

right of appeal /ˌraɪt əv ə'piːl/ *noun* the right to challenge a decision of a tribunal

right of association /ˌraɪt əv əsəʊsi'eɪʃ(ə)n/ *noun* the right of employees to join a union (as opposed to the right to dissociate, i.e. the right to refuse to join a union)

right to dissociate /ˌraɪt tə dɪ'səʊsieɪt/ *noun* the right of employees to refuse to join a union (as opposed to the right of association, i.e. the right to join a union)

right to manage /ˌraɪt tə 'mænɪdʒ/ *noun* a right which a management has to take decisions without necessarily taking the opinions of the employees into account

right to strike /ˌraɪt tə 'straɪk/ *noun* a legal title for workers to stop working if they have a good reason for it

right to work /ˌraɪt tə 'wɜːk/ *noun* the right of an adult person to find work

rigid /'rɪdʒɪd/ *adjective* not flexible or which cannot be changed ○ *The economy is being held back by rigid labour laws.* ○ *The employees complained that the management was too rigid in interpreting the rule book.*

rise /raɪz/ *noun* **1.** an increase ○ *There needs to be an increase in salaries to keep up with the rise in the cost of living.* **2.** an increase in pay ○ *She asked her boss for a rise.* ○ *He had a 6% rise in January.* (NOTE: American English is **raise**) ■ *verb* to move upwards or to become higher ○ *Salaries are rising faster than inflation.* (NOTE: **rising – rose – risen**)

rising unemployment /ˌraɪzɪŋ ʌnɪm'plɔɪmənt/ *noun* unemployment rates which are rising because more people are being made redundant

risk-averse /ˌrɪsk ə'vɜːs/ *adjective* not wanting to take risks

roadshow /'rəʊdʃəʊ/ *noun* a travelling exhibition where companies have stands to show what they do in order to attract potential trainees

rock bottom /rɒk 'bɒtəm/ *noun* □ **sales have reached rock bottom** sales have reached the lowest point possible

role /rəʊl/ *noun* a part played by someone in a workplace or organisation ○ *The manager is more effective in his role as employer than as salesman.* ○ *It is easier for an outsider to play the role of mediator in the dispute.*

role ambiguity /'rəʊl æmbɪˌgjuːɪti/ *noun* uncertainty on the part of an employee about what their role within an organisation actually is and what colleagues expect of them (NOTE: Role ambiguity often occurs in newly created posts or in positions that are undergoing change.)

role conflict /'rəʊl ˌkɒnflɪkt/ *noun* a situation in which two or more requirements in a job are, or seem to be, incompatible with each other (NOTE: Role conflict can occur when colleagues have different expectations of what the priorities of the person doing a particular job should be, or when someone's loyalties are divided between a particular department and the organisation as a whole, or between personal professional ethics and the demands of the organisation.)

role culture /'rəʊl ˌkʌltʃə/ *noun* a type of corporate culture that assumes that employees are rational and that roles can be defined and discharged using clearly defined procedures (NOTE: An organisation with a role culture is believed to be very stable but bad at implementing change management.)

role model /'rəʊl ˌmɒd(ə)l/ *noun* someone whose behaviour is copied

role play /'rəʊl pleɪ/, **role playing** /'rəʊl ˌpleɪɪŋ/ *noun* a training technique where trainees play different roles (salesperson, customer, manager, junior, etc.) in order to get a better understanding of people and to improve their powers of communication ○ *Role-playing was used as part of the management training programme.*

'…role playing designed to simulate work situations: for example, candidates may be asked to stand in for a fictional manager who has been taken sick' [*Sunday Times*]

roll call /'rəʊl kɔːl/ *noun* the calling out of the names of employees to see if they are present (as during a fire in an office or factory)

rolling budget /ˌrəʊlɪŋ 'bʌdʒɪt/ *noun* a budget which moves forward on a regular basis (such as a budget covering a twelve-month period, which moves forward each month or quarter)

rota /'rəʊtə/, **roster** /'rɒstə/ *noun* a list showing when different members of staff will do certain duties ○ *We are drawing up a new roster for Saturday afternoon work.*

rotate /rəʊ'teɪt/ *verb* to do tasks in turns ○ *The shifts are rotated every fortnight.*

rotating shifts /rəʊˌteɪtɪŋ 'ʃɪfts/ *noun* a system where employees take turns in working different shifts ○ *Rotating shifts can be unpopular with workers who do not want to break their routine.*

rotation /rəʊ'teɪʃ(ə)n/ *noun* the act of taking turns □ **to fill the post of chairman by rotation** each member of the group is chairman for a period then gives the post to another member

round table discussions /ˌraʊnd ˌteɪb(ə)l dɪ'skʌʃ(ə)nz/ *plural noun* discussions involving several parties who sit round the same table

routine /ruː'tiːn/ *noun* a normal or regular way of doing something ○ *Refitting the conference room has disturbed the office routine.* ■ *adjective* normal or which happens regularly ○ *routine work* ○ *a routine call* ○ *They carried out a routine check of the fire equipment.*

RSI *abbr* repetitive strain injury

rule /ruːl/ *noun* **1.** a general way of conduct ○ *It is a company rule that smoking is not allowed in the offices.* ○ *The rules of the organisation are explained during the induction sessions.* □ **as a rule** usually ○ *As a rule, we do not give discounts over 20%.* **2.** □ **to work to rule** to work strictly according to the rules agreed by the company and union, and therefore to work very slowly ■ *verb* **1.** to give an official decision ○ *The commission of inquiry ruled that the company was in breach of contract.* **2.** to be in force or to be current ○ *The current ruling agreement is being redrafted.*

rulebook /'ruːlbʊk/ *noun* a book which lists the rules by which the members of a union or self-regulatory organisation must operate

ruling /'ruːlɪŋ/ *noun* a decision ○ *The inquiry gave a ruling on the case.* ○ *According to the ruling of the court, the contract was illegal.*

rumour clinic /'ruːmə ˌklɪnɪk/ *noun US* an information service for employees which corrects false rumours which might be circulating in an organisation ○ *Installing a rumour clinic is an important part of the management's internal public relations.*

run /rʌn/ *verb* to manage or to organise ○ *She runs a mail-order business from home.* ○ *They run a staff sports club.* (NOTE: **running – ran – run**)

runaway inflation /ˌrʌnəweɪ ɪn'fleɪʃ(ə)n/ *noun* very rapid inflation, which is almost impossible to reduce

run with /'rʌn wɪð/ *verb* to decide to carry out an idea or project (*informal*)

S

sabbatical /sə'bætɪk(ə)l/ *noun, adjective* (*referring to*) paid or unpaid time off, for the purposes of research or study or travel ○ *The union claimed sabbatical leave for every six years worked.* ○ *She is due for a sabbatical next year.*

sack /sæk/ *noun* □ **to get the sack** to be dismissed from a job ■ *verb* to dismiss someone from a job ○ *He was sacked after being late for work.*

sackable offence /ˌsækəb(ə)l ə-'fens/ *noun* behaviour which automatically means dismissal ○ *Being drunk in the office is a sackable offence here.*

sacking /'sækɪŋ/ *noun* a dismissal from a job ○ *The union protested against the sackings.*

s.a.e. *abbr* stamped addressed envelope ○ *Send your application form to the Human Resources manager, with an s.a.e. for reply.*

safeguard /'seɪfgɑːd/ *verb* to protect ○ *The duty of the directors is to safeguard the interests of the shareholders.*

safety /'seɪfti/ *noun* the fact of being free from danger or risk □ **to take safety precautions** *or* **safety measures** to act to make sure something is safe

safety audit /'seɪfti ˌɔːdɪt/ *noun* a check of the workplace to see how safety regulations are being implemented

safety committee /'seɪfti kəˌmɪti/ *noun* a committee set up to examine the health and safety policy of a particular company

safety measures /'seɪfti ˌmeʒəz/ *plural noun* actions to make sure that something is safe

safety offence /'seɪfti əˌfens/ *noun* behaviour which can cause a hazard

safety officer /'seɪfti ˌɒfɪsə/ *noun* an official who inspects places of work and work methods to make sure that they are safe

safety precautions /'seɪfti prɪ-ˌkɔːʃ(ə)nz/ *plural noun* actions to try to make sure that something is safe

safety regulations /'seɪfti regjʊ-ˌleɪʃ(ə)nz/ *plural noun* rules to make a place of work safe for the employees

safety representative /'seɪfti repriˌzentətɪv/ *noun* a trade union representative for health and safety problems

salaried partner /ˌsælərid 'pɑːtnə/ *noun* a partner, often a junior one, who receives a regular salary in accordance with the partnership agreement

salaried staff /'sælərid stɑːf/ *noun* staff earning salaries, as opposed to those paid on different terms

salary /'sæləri/ *noun* **1.** a regular payment for work done, made to an employee usually as a cheque at the end of each month ○ *The company froze all salaries for a six-month period.* ○ *If I get promoted, my salary will go up.* ○ *The salary may be low, but the fringe benefits attached to the job are good.* ○ *She got a salary increase in June.* □ **salary bands** all salaries at certain levels ○ *The pay structure is made up five salary bands.* **2.** an amount paid to an employee, shown as a monthly, quarterly or yearly total (NOTE: plural is **salaries**)

salary ceiling /'sæləri ˌsiːlɪŋ/ *noun* **1.** the maximum amount which can be earned for a particular job or by a particular class of employee, as set by a government or by an agreement between a trade union and an employer **2.** the highest level on a pay scale that a particular employee can achieve under his or her contract

salary cheque /'sæləri tʃek/ *noun* a monthly cheque by which an employee is paid

salary club /'sæləri klʌb/ *noun* a meeting of representatives from various companies to discuss the salary structure in an industry

salary cut /'sæləri kʌt/ *noun* a sudden reduction in salary

salary deductions /'sæləri dɪˌdʌkʃənz/ *plural noun* money which a company removes from salaries to pay to the government as tax, National Insurance contributions, etc.

salary differentials /'sæləri dɪfəˌrenʃəlz/ *plural noun* same as **pay differentials**

salary drift /'sæləri drɪft/ *noun* same as **earnings drift**

salary expectations /'sæləri ekspekˌteɪʃ(ə)nz/ *plural noun* the hopes of an employee that their salary will increase

salary package /'sæləri ˌpækɪdʒ/ *noun* same as **pay package**

salary-related pension scheme /ˌsæləri rɪˌleɪtɪd 'penʃən skiːm/ *noun* a pension scheme where the pension received is based on the final salary of the contributor

salary review /'sæləri rɪˌvjuː/ *noun* same as **pay review** ○ *She had a salary review last April* or *her salary was reviewed last April.*

salary rise /'sæləri raɪz/ *noun* same as **pay rise** (NOTE: American English is **raise** in this meaning)

salary scale /'sæləri skeɪl/ *noun* same as **pay scale** ○ *He was appointed at the top end of the salary scale.*

salary structure /'sæləri ˌstrʌktʃə/ *noun* the organisation of salaries in a company with different rates of pay for different types of job

'...the union of hotel and personal service workers has demanded a new salary structure and uniform conditions of service for workers in the hotel and catering industry' [*Business Times (Lagos)*]

sales /seɪlz/ *plural noun* money received for selling something ○ *Sales have risen over the first quarter.*

sales analysis /'seɪlz əˌnæləsɪs/ *noun* an examination of the reports of sales to see why items have or have not sold well

sales assistant /'seɪlz əˌsɪstənt/ *noun* a person in a shop who sells goods to customers

sales budget /'seɪlz ˌbʌdʒɪt/ *noun* a plan of probable sales

sales campaign /'seɪlz kæmˌpeɪn/ *noun* a series of planned activities to achieve higher sales

sales chart /'seɪlz tʃɑːt/ *noun* a diagram showing how sales vary from month to month

sales clerk /'seɪlz klɑːk/ *noun US* a person who sells goods to customers in a store

'...the wage agreement includes sales clerks and commission sales people in stores in Toronto' [*Toronto Star*]

sales department /'seɪlz dɪˌpɑːtmənt/ *noun* the section of a company which deals in selling the company's products or services

sales drive /'seɪlz draɪv/ *noun* a vigorous effort to increase sales

sales executive /'seɪlz ɪgˌzekjʊtɪv/ *noun* a person in a company or department in charge of sales

sales force /'seɪlz fɔːs/ *noun* a group of salespeople or sales representatives responsible for the sales of either a single product or the entire range of an organisation's products

salesman /'seɪlzmən/ *noun* a man who sells an organisation's products or services to customers ○ *Salesmen are paid a basic salary plus commission.*

sales manager /'seɪlz ˌmænɪdʒə/ *noun* a person in charge of a sales department

salesmanship /'seɪlzmənʃɪp/ *noun* the art of selling or of persuading customers to buy

sales representative /'seɪlz reprɪˌzentətɪv/, **sales rep** /'seɪlz rep/ *noun* a person who sells an organisation's products or services to customers ○ *We have six sales representatives in Europe.* ○ *They have vacancies for sales representatives to call on accounts in the north of the country.*

sales target /'seɪlz ˌtɑːgɪt/ *noun* the amount of sales a sales representative is expected to achieve

saleswoman /'seɪlzwʊmən/ *noun* **1.** a woman who sells an organisation's products or services to customers **2.** a woman in a shop who sells goods to customers (NOTE: plural is **saleswomen**)

sandwich course /'sændwɪtʃ kɔːs/ *noun* a course of study where students at a college or institute spend a period of time working in a factory, office or other organisation as part of gaining their qualification

satisfaction /ˌsætɪs'fækʃən/ *noun* a good feeling of happiness and contentment ○ *He finds great satisfaction in the job even though the pay is bad.*

satisfy /'sætɪsfaɪ/ *verb* **1.** to give satisfaction or to please □ **to satisfy a client** to make a client pleased with what they have purchased **2.** to fill the requirements for a job (NOTE: **satisfies – satisfying – satisfied**)

save-as-you-earn /ˌseɪv əz juː 'ɜːn/ *noun* a scheme where employees can save money regularly by having it deducted automatically from their wages and invested in National Savings. Abbr **SAYE**

savings account /'seɪvɪŋz əˌkaʊnt/ *noun* an account where you put money in regularly and which pays interest, often at a higher rate than a deposit account

savings and loan (association) /ˌseɪvɪŋz ən 'ləʊn əsəʊsɪ'eɪʃən/ *noun* US a financial association which accepts and pays interest on deposits from investors and lends money to people who are buying property. The loans are in the form of mortgages on the security of the property being bought. S&Ls are regulated by the Office of Thrift Supervision and are protected by the Savings Association Insurance Fund. Abbr **S&L** (NOTE: the S&Ls are also called **thrifts**;

the British equivalents are the building societies)

COMMENT: Because of deregulation of interest rates in 1980, many S&Ls found that they were forced to raise interest on deposits to current market rates in order to secure funds, while at the same time they still were charging low fixed-interest rates on the mortgages granted to borrowers. This created considerable problems and many S&Ls had to be rescued by the Federal government.

SAYE *abbr* save-as-you-earn

scab /skæb/ *noun* an employee who goes on working when there is a strike (*informal*)

scalar /'skeɪlə/ *adjective* working according to a scale

scalar principle /'skeɪlə ˌprɪnsɪp(ə)l/ *noun* the principle that employees should only communicate with their seniors through the established hierarchy

scale /skeɪl/ *noun* a system which is graded into various levels □ **scale of salaries** a list of salaries showing different levels of pay in different jobs in the same company

scale down /skeɪl 'daʊn/ *verb* to lower in proportion

scale up /skeɪl 'ʌp/ *verb* to increase in proportion

Scanlon plan /'skænlən plæn/ *noun* a type of gain sharing plan that pays a bonus to employees when they improve their performance or productivity by a certain amount as measured against a previously established standard

schedule /'ʃedjuːl/ *noun* **1.** a timetable, a plan of time drawn up in advance ○ *The managing director has a busy schedule of appointments.* ○ *Her secretary tried to fit me into her schedule.* □ **on schedule** at the time or stage set down in the schedule ○ *The launch took place on schedule.* □ **to be ahead of schedule** to be early ○ *The building was completed ahead of schedule.* □ **to be on schedule** to be on time ○ *The project is on schedule.* □ **to be behind schedule** to be late ○ *I am sorry to say that we are three months behind schedule.* □ **to have a heavy schedule of meetings** to have a large number of meetings arranged **2.** a list, especially additional documents attached to a contract ○ *the schedule of territories to which a contract applies* ○ *See the attached schedule* or *as per the attached schedule.* ○ *Please find enclosed our schedule of charges.* **3.** a list of items ■ *verb* **1.** to list officially ○ *We offer a 10% reduction on scheduled prices* or *scheduled charges to selected customers.* **2.** to plan the time when something will happen ○ *The building is scheduled for completion in May.*

Schedule A /ˌʃedjuːl ˈeɪ/ *noun* a schedule under which tax is charged on income from land or buildings

Schedule B /ˌʃedjuːl ˈbiː/ *noun* a schedule under which tax was formerly charged on income from woodlands

Schedule C /ˌʃedjuːl ˈsiː/ *noun* a schedule under which tax is charged on profits from government stock

Schedule D /ˌʃedjuːl ˈdiː/ *noun* a schedule under which tax is charged on income from trades or professions, interest and other earnings not derived from being employed

Schedule E /ˌʃedjuːl ˈiː/ *noun* a schedule under which tax is charged on income from salaries, wages or pensions

Schedule F /ˌʃedjuːl ˈef/ *noun* a schedule under which tax is charged on income from dividends

scheme /skiːm/ *noun* a plan, arrangement or way of working ○ *Under the bonus scheme all employees get 10% of their annual pay as a Christmas bonus.* ○ *He has joined the company pension scheme.* ○ *We operate a profit-sharing scheme for managers.* ○ *The new payment scheme is based on reward for individual effort.*

school-leaver /ˈskuːl ˌliːvə/ *noun* a person who has just left school

scientific management /ˌsaɪəntɪfɪk ˈmænɪdʒmənt/ *noun* a theory of management which believes in the rational use of resources in order to maximise output, thus motivating workers to earn more money

scope /skəʊp/ *noun* a range of subjects being dealt with ○ *the scope of an agreement*

screen /skriːn/ *verb* to examine something carefully to evaluate or assess it □ **to screen candidates** to examine candidates to see if they are completely suitable

screening /ˈskriːnɪŋ/ *noun* □ **the screening of candidates** the examining of candidates to see if they are suitable

seagull manager /ˈsiːgʌl ˌmænɪdʒə/ *noun* a manager who is brought in to deal with a project, makes a lot of fuss, achieves nothing, and then leaves (*slang*)

search /sɜːtʃ/ *verb* **1.** to look for something ○ *The company is searching for a formula which will be acceptable to the unions.* **2.** to examine thoroughly ○ *Members of staff were searched as they left the building.*

season /ˈsiːz(ə)n/ *noun* **1.** one of four parts into which a year is divided, i.e. spring, summer, autumn and winter **2.** a period of time when some activity usually takes place ○ *the selling season*

seasonal /ˈsiːz(ə)n(ə)l/ *adjective* which lasts for a season or which only happens during a particular season ○ *seasonal variations in sales patterns* ○ *The demand for this item is very seasonal.*

seasonal employment /ˈsiːz(ə)n(ə)l ɪmˌplɔɪmənt/, **seasonal work** /ˈsiːz(ə)n(ə)l wɜːk/ *noun* a job which is available at certain times of the year only (such as in a ski resort)

seasonal worker /ˈsiːz(ə)n(ə)l ˌwɜːkə/ *noun* a worker who is employed for a few months during the high season

second /sɪˈkɒnd/ *verb* to lend a member of staff to another company, organisation or department for a fixed period of time ○ *He was seconded to the Department of Trade for two years.*

secondary /ˈsekənd(ə)ri/ *adjective* second in importance

secondary action /ˌsekənd(ə)ri ˈækʃən/, **secondary strike** /ˌsekənd(ə)ri ˈstraɪk/, **secondary picketing** /ˌsekənd(ə)ri ˈpɪkɪtɪŋ/ *noun* industrial action aimed at a company which is not a party to an industrial dispute, to prevent it from supplying a striking factory or receiving supplies from it

secondary boycott /ˌsekənd(ə)ri 'bɔɪkɒt/ *noun US* pressure put on an employer by those not directly involved in an industrial dispute. ♦ **primary boycott**

secondary group /'sekənd(ə)ri gruːp/ *noun* a group which is small enough to allow its members to interact informally

secondary industry /'sekənd(ə)ri ˌɪndəstri/ *noun* an industry which uses basic raw materials to produce manufactured goods

secondary picketing /ˌsekənd(ə)ri 'pɪkɪtɪŋ/ *noun* same as **secondary action**

secondary sector /'sekənd(ə)ri ˌsektə/ *noun* industries which use basic raw materials to make manufactured goods

secondary strike /ˌsekənd(ə)ri 'straɪk/ *noun* same as **secondary action**

second-class mail /ˌsekənd klɑːs 'meɪl/ *noun* a less expensive, slower mail service ○ *The letter took three days to arrive because he sent it second-class.*

secondee /sɪˌkɒn'diː/ *noun* a person who is seconded to another job

secondment /sɪ'kɒndmənt/ *noun* the act or period of being seconded to another job for a period ○ *He is on three years' secondment to an Australian college.*

second quarter /ˌsekənd 'kwɔːtə/ *noun* a period of three months from April to the end of June

secret /'siːkrət/ *adjective* which is not known by many people ○ *The MD kept the contract secret from the rest of the board.* ○ *The management signed a secret deal with a foreign supplier.* ■ *noun* something which is hidden or which is not known by many people □ **to keep a secret** not to tell secret information which you have been told

secretarial /ˌsekrɪ'teəriəl/ *adjective* referring to the work of a secretary ○ *Secretarial work is seen as a step towards management positions.* ○ *He is*

looking for secretarial work. ○ *We need extra secretarial help to deal with the mailings.* ○ *Their secretarial duties are not onerous, just boring.*

secretarial course /ˌsekrɪ'teəriəl kɔːs/ *noun* a course of study for secretaries ○ *She is taking a secretarial course.*

secretary /'sekrət(ə)ri/ *noun* **1.** a person who helps to organise work, types letters, files documents, arranges meetings, etc., for someone ○ *My secretary deals with incoming orders.* ○ *Her secretary phoned to say she would be late.* **2.** an official of a company or society **3.** a member of the government in charge of a department ○ *the Trade Secretary* ○ *the Foreign Secretary* ○ *the Education Secretary*

secretary and personal assistant /ˌsekrət(ə)ri ən ˌpɜːs(ə)n(ə)l ə'sɪst(ə)nt/ *noun* a secretary to a top-level member of an organisation, such as director, or senior manager

Secretary of State /ˌsekrət(ə)ri əv 'steɪt/ *noun* **1.** *GB* a member of the government in charge of a department ○ *the Secretary of State for Trade and Industry* **2.** *US* a senior member of the government in charge of foreign affairs (NOTE: the British equivalent is the **Foreign Secretary**)

Secretary of the Treasury /ˌsekrət(ə)ri əv ðə 'treʒəri/ *noun US* a senior member of the government in charge of financial affairs

secret ballot /ˌsiːkrət 'bælət/ *noun* an election where the voters vote in secret

sector /'sektə/ *noun* a part of the economy or the business organisation of a country ○ *All sectors of the economy suffered from the fall in the exchange rate.* ○ *Technology is a booming sector of the economy.*

'…government services form a large part of the tertiary or service sector' [*Sydney Morning Herald*]

secure /sɪ'kjʊə/ *adjective* safe, which cannot change □ **secure job** a job from which you are not likely to be made redundant

security /sɪ'kjʊərɪti/ *noun* the fact of being protected against attack □ **office**

security the act of protecting an office against theft

security of employment /sɪ-ˌkjʊərɪti əv ɪmˈplɔɪmənt/ *noun* a feeling by an employee that they have the right to keep their job until they retire

select /sɪˈlekt/ *verb* to choose ○ *The board will meet to select three candidates for a second interview.*

selection /sɪˈlekʃən/ *noun* **1.** a choice **2.** the process of choosing someone for a job ○ *Assessment of candidates for final selection will depend on tests and interviews.*

selection instrument /sɪˈlekʃən ˌɪnstrʊmənt/ *noun* a psychometric test used as a method of selecting people for a job or for training

selection interviewing /sɪˈlekʃən ˌɪntəvjuːɪŋ/ *noun* the interviewing of a number of candidates in order to select one or more for a job or for training

selection of personnel /sɪˌlekʃən əv pɜːsəˈnel/ *noun* same as **recruitment**

selection procedure /sɪˈlekʃən prəˌsiːdʒə/ *noun* the general method of choosing a candidate for a job

selection test /sɪˈlekʃən test/ *noun* a test to assess whether someone should be selected for a job or for training

self- /self/ *prefix* referring to yourself

self-actualisation /ˌself æktʃuəlaɪˈzeɪʃ(ə)n/ *noun* the process of developing your skills and talents to the fullest possible extent or to the point where they are most beneficial to you (NOTE: also called **self-fulfilment**)

self-administered pension scheme /ˌself ədˌmɪnɪstəd ˈpenʃən skiːm/ *noun* a scheme where the trustees actively administer the funds and are responsible for its performance

self-appraisal /ˌself əˈpreɪz(ə)l/ *noun* a person's own assessment of their capabilities and character ○ *The application forms contain room for a short self-appraisal.*

self-assessment /ˌself əˈsesmənt/ *noun* **1.** the process of calculating how much tax you should pay and reporting it to the Inland Revenue on time ○ *Self-assessment forms should be returned to the tax office by 31st January.* **2.** a systematic and regular review of its own activities carried out by an organisation, which compares the results against a model of excellence (NOTE: Self-assessment allows an organisation to identify its strengths and weaknesses and to plan improvement activities.) **3.** same as **self-appraisal** ○ *Candidates are asked to write a two-page self-assessment as part of the job application.* ○ *Self-assessment can be an embarrassing process for many applicants.*

self-certification /ˌself sətɪfɪˈkeɪʃ(ə)n/ *noun* a procedure that allows an employee who takes sick leave for seven days or less to avoid loss of earnings by filling in a form when they return to work, indicating the nature of the illness and how long it lasted, and by having the form countersigned by a manager

self-confidence /ˌself ˈkɒnfɪdəns/ *noun* the quality of feeling confident in your own ability ○ *After a month of successful sales, my self-confidence improved dramatically.* ○ *Her lack of self-confidence was obvious at the interview.*

self-confident /ˌself ˈkɒnfɪdənt/ *adjective* referring a person who is confident in their own ability ○ *The trainee was self-confident to the point of arrogance.*

self-development /ˌself dɪˈveləpmənt/ *noun* same as **personal development**

self-directed team /ˌself dɪˈrektɪd tiːm/ *noun* same as **autonomous teamworking**

self-employed /ˌself ɪmˈplɔɪd/ *adjective* working for yourself or not on the payroll of a company ○ *a self-employed engineer* ○ *He worked for a bank for ten years but is now self-employed.*

self-employment /ˌself ɪmˈplɔɪmənt/ *noun* the business or activity of someone who is not an employee of somebody else under a contract of employment, but either works as a freelance or owns a business (NOTE:

Self-employment has an important effect on how a person's earnings are treated for tax purposes and on the degree of employment protection they have.)

self-fulfilment /ˌself fʊlˈfɪlmənt/ *noun* same as **self-actualisation** (NOTE: the usual US spelling is **self-fulfillment**)

self-image /self ˈɪmɪdʒ/ *noun* an idea that a person has about their own character and abilities

self-instruction /ˌself ɪnˈstrʌkʃən/ *noun* the process of teaching oneself ○ *He learnt the language at home, entirely through self-instruction.*

self-made man /ˌself meɪd ˈmæn/ *noun* a man who is rich and successful because of his own work, not because he inherited money or position

self-made woman /ˌself meɪd ˈwʊmən/ *noun* a woman who is rich and successful because of her own work, not because she inherited money or position

self-managed (work) team /ˌself mænɪdʒd ˈwɜːk tiːm/, **self-managing (work) team** /ˌself ˌmænɪdʒɪŋ ˈwɜːk tiːm/ *noun* same as **autonomous teamworking**

self-regulation /self regjʊˈleɪʃ(ə)n/ *noun* the regulation of an industry by itself, through a committee which issues a rulebook and makes sure that members of the industry follow the rules (NOTE: For example, the Stock Exchange is regulated by the Stock Exchange Council.)

self-starter /self ˈstɑːtə/ *noun* a person who can be relied on to take the initiative in a new situation without asking for instructions

self-taught /self ˈtɔːt/ *adjective* referring to a person who has taught themselves

sellout /ˈselaʊt/ *noun* the act of giving in to demands in exchange for financial concessions ○ *a sellout to the management*

semi- /semi/ *prefix* half or part

seminar /ˈsemɪnɑː/ *noun* the teaching of a small class of advanced students ○ *He attended a seminar on direct selling.*

○ *She is running a seminar for senior managers.*

semi-retired /ˌsemi rɪˈtaɪəd/ *adjective* having retired on a pension, but still working part-time

semi-skilled /ˌsemi ˈskɪld/ *adjective* having had or involving some training

senior /ˈsiːniə/ *adjective* **1.** referring to an employee who is more important □ **decision taken at senior level** a decision taken by directors or senior managers **2.** referring to an employee who is older or who has been employed longer than another

seniority /ˌsiːniˈɒrɪti/ *noun* **1.** the fact of being more important ○ *in order of seniority* **2.** the fact of being being older or being an employee of the company longer

seniority system /ˌsiːniˈɒrɪti ˌsɪstəm/ *noun* a way in which employees can gain seniority in an organisation

senior management /ˌsiːniə ˈmænɪdʒmənt/ *noun* the main directors of a company

senior manager /ˌsiːniə ˈmænɪdʒə/, **senior executive** /ˌsiːniər ɪgˈzekjʊtɪv/ *noun* a manager or director who has a higher rank than others

senior partner /ˌsiːniə ˈpɑːtnə/ *noun* the most important partner in a firm of solicitors or accountants

senior staff /ˈsiːniə stɑːf/ *noun* **1.** older members of staff **2.** people in more important positions in a company

senior vice-president /ˌsiːniə vaɪs ˈprezɪd(ə)nt/ *noun* one of a few main executive directors of a company

sensitivity training /ˌsensɪˈtɪvɪti ˌtreɪnɪŋ/ *noun* the development of character and awareness by social interaction in small groups ○ *Sensitivity training has helped him to be forceful without offending others in the department.*

separation /ˌsepəˈreɪʃ(ə)n/ *noun* US the act of leaving a job (resigning, retiring or being fired or made redundant) ○ *The interviewer asked the candidate whether the separation mentioned in his CV was due to resignation, redundancy or dismissal.* ○ *The exit interviews at-*

tempted to find out what employees really felt about separation.

sequester /sɪˈkwestə/, **sequestrate** /ˈsiːkwɪstreɪt, sɪˈkwestreɪt/ *verb* to take and keep a bank account or property because a court has ordered it ○ *The union was fined for contempt of court and its funds have been sequestrated.*

sequestration /ˌsiːkweˈstreɪʃ(ə)n/ *noun* the taking and keeping of property on the order of a court, especially seizing property from someone who is in contempt of court

sequestrator /ˈsiːkwɪstreɪtə, sɪˈkwestreɪtə/ *noun* a person who takes and keeps property on the order of a court

SERPS /sɜːps/ *abbr* state earnings-related pension scheme

serve /sɜːv/ *verb* **1.** to deal with a customer □ **to serve an apprenticeship** to work with a skilled worker for a legally agreed period in order to learn from them **2.** □ **to serve someone with a writ, to serve a writ on someone** to give someone a writ officially, so that they have to receive it **3.** to work ○ *She served ten years as an accounts clerk.*

service /ˈsɜːvɪs/ *noun* **1.** the work done by an employee for his or her employer of company ○ *After a lifetime's service to the company he was rewarded with a generous golden handshake.* **2.** the business of providing help in some form when it is needed

service agreement /ˈsɜːvɪs əˌɡriːmənt/, **service contract** /ˈsɜːvɪs ˌkɒntrækt/ *noun* a contract between a company and a director showing all conditions of work ○ *The service agreement says very little about hours of work.*

service job /ˈsɜːvɪs dʒɒb/ *noun* a job in an industry which does not make products, but offers a service (such as banking, insurance or transport)

session /ˈseʃ(ə)n/ *noun* a period of time spent on a specific activity, especially as part of a larger event ○ *The morning session* or *the afternoon session will be held in the conference room.*

set /set/ *noun* a group of items which go together, which are used together or

which are sold together ○ *a set of tools* ■ *adjective* fixed or which cannot be changed ○ *There is a set fee for all our consultants.* ■ *verb* to fix or to arrange ○ *We have to set a price for the new computer.* ○ *The price of the calculator has been set low, so as to achieve maximum unit sales.* (NOTE: **setting – set**) □ **set the bar** to motivate staff by setting targets that are above their current level of achievement

settle /ˈset(ə)l/ *verb* to solve a problem or dispute □ **to settle a claim** to agree to pay what is asked for ○ *The insurance company refused to settle his claim for storm damage.*

settlement /ˈset(ə)lmənt/ *noun* an agreement after an argument or negotiations ○ *a wage settlement* □ **to effect a settlement between two parties** to bring two parties together to make them agree

'…he emphasised that prompt settlement of all forms of industrial disputes would guarantee industrial peace in the country and ensure increased productivity' [*Business Times (Lagos)*]

settlement day /ˈset(ə)lmənt deɪ/ *noun* the day on which shares which have been bought must be paid for (on the London Stock Exchange the account period is three business days from the day of trade) (NOTE: also called **account day**)

set up /ˌset ˈʌp/ *verb* to begin something or to organise something new ○ *to set up an inquiry* or *a working party* □ **to set up a company** to start a company legally

seven-point plan /ˌsev(ə)n pɔɪnt ˈplæn/ *noun* a list of items used in assessing the potential of job candidates

COMMENT: The seven points are: physical appearance, educational qualifications, general intelligence level, special skills (not necessarily connected to their current employment), outside interests, mental and emotional disposition, personal and family circumstances.

severance pay /ˈsev(ə)rəns peɪ/ *noun* money paid as compensation to an employee whose job is no longer needed

sex /seks/ *noun* one of two groups (male and female) into which people can be divided

Sex Discrimination Act 1975, 1986 /ˌseks dɪskrɪmɪˈneɪʃ(ə)n ækt ˌnaɪntiːn sevˈ(ə)nti ˈfaɪv, ˌnaɪntiːn eɪti ˈsɪks/ *noun* Acts of Parliament which ban discrimination on grounds of sex

sexism /ˈseksɪz(ə)m/ *noun* the belief that one sex is superior to the other

sexist /ˈseksɪst/ *adjective* showing a belief that one sex is superior to the other ○ *He was reprimanded for making sexist remarks about her.*

sexual /ˈsekʃuəl/ *adjective* relating to sex

sexual discrimination /ˌsekʃuəl dɪskrɪmɪˈneɪʃ(ə)n/, **sex discrimination** /ˌseks dɪskrɪmɪˈneɪʃ(ə)n/ *noun* the practice of treating men and women in different ways (usually favouring men) ○ *The company was accused of sex discrimination in its appointment of managers.* ○ *Sex discrimination has made it difficult for women to reach managerial posts in the organisation.*

sexual harassment /ˌsekʃuəl ˈhærəsmənt, həˈræsmənt/ *noun* the practice of making unpleasant sexual gestures, comments or approaches to someone ○ *She complained of sexual harassment by the manager.*

shakeout /ˈʃeɪkaʊt/ *noun* a complete change, where weak or inefficient people or companies are removed ○ *Only three companies were left after the shakeout in the computer market.*

shakeup /ˈʃeɪkʌp/ *noun* a total reorganisation ○ *The managing director ordered a shakeup of the sales departments.*

shape up or ship out /ˌʃeɪp ˌʌp ɔː ʃɪp ˈaʊt/ *interjection* an order to improve your performance at work because if you do not you will be fired

share /ʃeə/ *noun* 1. a part of something that has been divided up among several peoole or groups 2. an one of many equal parts into which a company's capital is divided (the owners of shares are shareholders or, more formally, 'members') ○ *He bought a block of shares in Marks and Spencer.* ○ *Shares fell on the London market.* ○ *The company offered 1.8m shares on the*

market. ■ *verb* 1. to own or use something together with someone else ○ *It is very awkward having to share a telephone.* ○ *I don't want to share an office with her because she smokes.* 2. to divide something up among several people or groups ○ *Three companies share the market.*

shareholder /ˈʃeəhəʊldə/ *noun* a person who owns shares in a company ○ *to call a shareholders' meeting* (NOTE: Formally called a 'member'.)

'…as of last night the bank's shareholders no longer hold any rights to the bank's shares' [*South China Morning Post*]

share issue /ˈʃeər ˌɪʃuː/ *noun* an act of selling new shares in a company to the public

share option scheme /ʃeər ˈɒpʃən skiːm/ *noun* an arrangement where an employee has regular deductions made against their pay against the right to buy shares in the company at a fixed low price at a later date

share ownership scheme /ˌʃeər ˈəʊnəʃɪp skiːm/, **share incentive scheme** /ˌʃeər ɪnˈsentɪv skiːm/ *noun* a scheme whereby employees in a company can buy shares in it and so share in the profits ○ *Share ownership schemes help employees to identify more closely with the company they work for.*

shed /ʃed/ *verb* to lose (NOTE: **shedding – shed**) □ **to shed staff** to lose staff by making them redundant

sheet /ʃiːt/ *noun* □ **sheet of paper** a piece of paper

shelve /ʃelv/ *verb* to postpone or to put back to another date ○ *The project was shelved.* ○ *Discussion of the problem has been shelved.*

shift /ʃɪft/ *noun* 1. a group of employees who work for a period, and then are replaced by another group □ **to work double shifts** to work with two shifts of workers on duty 2. a period of time worked by a group of employees

shift differential /ˈʃɪft dɪfəˌrenʃəl/ *noun* a payment made to employees in addition to their basic pay to compensate them for the inconvenience of the pattern of shift work

shift transfer /'ʃɪft ˌtrænsfɜː/ *noun* the act of changing an employee's shift or working hours

shift work /'ʃɪft wɜːk/ *noun* a system of work with shifts

shoddy /'ʃɒdi/ *adjective* of bad quality ○ *shoddy workmanship*

shop /ʃɒp/ *noun* **1.** a place where goods are stored and sold ○ *a computer shop* ○ *an electrical goods shop* **2.** the place in a factory where goods are made

shop assistant /'ʃɒp əˌsɪstənt/ *noun* a person who serves the customers in a shop

shop floor /ʃɒp 'flɔː/ *noun* **1.** the space in a shop given to the display of goods for sale **2.** □ **on the shop floor** in the factory, in the works or among the ordinary workers ○ *The feeling on the shop floor is that the manager does not know his job.*

shop floor workers /ʃɒp 'flɔː ˌwɜːkəz/ *plural noun* manual workers and technical workers as opposed to office workers

shopping centre /'ʃɒpɪŋ ˌsentə/ *noun* a group of shops linked together with car parks and restaurants

shop steward /ʃɒp 'stjuːəd/ *noun* an elected trade union official who represents employees in day-to-day negotiations with the management

short /ʃɔːt/ *adjective, adverb* for a small period of time □ **in the short term, in the short run** in the near future or quite soon

shortage /'ʃɔːtɪdʒ/ *noun* a lack or low availability of something ○ *a shortage of skilled staff* ○ *We employ part-timers to make up for staff shortages.*

shorthanded /ˌʃɔːt'hændɪd/ *adjective* without enough staff ○ *We're rather shorthanded at the moment.*

shortlist /'ʃɔːtlɪst/ *noun* a list of candidates who can be asked to come for a test or interview (drawn up after all applications have been examined and the most obviously unsuitable candidates have been rejected) ○ *to draw up a shortlist* ○ *She is on the shortlist for the job.* ■ *verb* to make a shortlist ○ *Four candidates have been shortlisted.* ○

Shortlisted candidates will be asked for an interview.

short-range forecast /ˌʃɔːt reɪndʒ 'fɔːkɑːst/ *noun* a forecast which covers a period of a few months

short-staffed /ˌʃɔːt 'stɑːft/ *adjective* with not enough staff ○ *We're rather short-staffed at the moment.*

short-term /ˌʃɔːt 'tɜːm/ *adjective* **1.** for a period of weeks or months ○ *She is employed on a short-term contract.* □ **on a short-term basis** for a short period **2.** for a short period in the future ○ *We need to recruit at once to cover our short-term manpower requirements.*

short-term contract /ˌʃɔːt tɜːm 'kɒntrækt/ *noun* a contract of employment for a short period (such as six months)

short-term forecast /ˌʃɔːt tɜːm 'fɔːkɑːst/ *noun* a forecast which covers a period of a few months

short time /ˌʃɔːt 'taɪm/ *noun* reduced working hours resulting in less than half a normal week's pay ○ *Several machinists will be on short time as long as the shortage of orders lasts.* ○ *The company has had to introduce short-time working because of lack of orders.*

show of hands /ˌʃəʊ əv 'hændz/ *noun* a vote where people show how they vote by raising their hands ○ *The motion was carried on a show of hands.*

shut /ʃʌt/ *adjective* not open for business ○ *The office is shut on Saturdays.* ■ *verb* to close ○ *to shut a shop* or *a warehouse* (NOTE: **shutting – shut**)

shut down /ˌʃʌt 'daʊn/ *verb* to make a factory or office stop working for a time ○ *The offices will shut down for Christmas.* ○ *Six factories have shut down this month.*

shutdown /'ʃʌtdaʊn/ *noun* the shutting of a factory or office

shutout /'ʃʌtaʊt/ *noun* the locking of the door of a factory or office to stop the staff getting in

sick /sɪk/ *adjective* ill □ **to be off sick** to be away from work because you are ill □ **to report sick** to say officially that you are ill and cannot work

sick building syndrome /sɪk ˈbɪldɪŋ ˌsɪndrəʊm/ *noun* a condition where many people working in a building feel ill or have headaches, caused by blocked air-conditioning ducts in which stale air is recycled round the building, often carrying allergenic substances or bacteria

sickie /ˈsɪki/ *noun* a day of sick leave, usually one taken when the employee is only pretending to be ill (*slang*)

sickness /ˈsɪknəs/ *noun* the condition of being ill

sickness and accident insurance /ˌsɪknəs ənd ˈæksɪd(ə)nt ɪnˌʃʊərəns/ *noun* a form of health insurance that may be sold to a person who takes a loan or uses a credit card, so that, if the borrower is unable to work because of accident or illness, the policy covers the regular payments to the lender or the credit card company

sickness benefit /ˈsɪknəs ˌbenɪfɪt/ *noun* a payment made by the government or private insurance to someone who is ill and cannot work ○ *The sickness benefit is paid monthly.*

sickout /ˈsɪkaʊt/ *noun* a form of protest in which a group of employees try to achieve their demands by not going to work and claiming that they are ill (*slang*)

sideline /ˈsaɪdlaɪn/ *noun* a business which is extra to your normal work ○ *He runs a profitable sideline selling postcards to tourists.*

sign /saɪn/ *verb* to write your name in a special way on a document to show that you have written it or approved it ○ *The letter is signed by the managing director.* ○ *The new recruit was asked to sign the contract of employment.*

signature /ˈsɪgnɪtʃə/ *noun* a person's name written by themselves on a cheque, document, etc. ○ *All our company's cheques need two signatures.* ○ *The contract of employment had the HR director's signature at the bottom.*

sign on /ˌsaɪn ˈɒn/ *verb* **1.** to start work, by signing your name in the human resources office □ **to sign on for the dole** to register as unemployed **2.** to give someone a job by offering a signed contract of employment ○ *We are signing on more admin staff next month.*

silver circle rate /ˌsɪlvə ˈsɜːk(ə)l reɪt/ *noun US* a system whereby pay increases are based on length of service ○ *The silver circle rate is partly designed to encourage employees to stay with firm a long time.*

similar work /ˌsɪmɪlə ˈwɜːk/ *noun* work done by men and women in the same organisation which has equal value

simulation /ˌsɪmjʊˈleɪʃ(ə)n/ *noun* an imitation of a real-life situation for training purposes ○ *The simulation exercises for trainee air hostesses include applying first-aid treatment to passengers.*

sinecure /ˈsɪnɪˌkjʊə/ *noun* a job which is well-paid but involves very little work ○ *His job in his father's firm was little more than a sinecure.*

single /ˈsɪŋg(ə)l/ *adjective* **1.** one alone **2.** not married ○ *marital status: single* ■ *noun* a person who is not married

single door policy /ˌsɪŋg(ə)l ˈdɔː ˌpɒlɪsi/ *noun* the organisation of a human resources department, where various managers are of equal rank and can each deal with any problem that arises

single-employer bargaining /ˌsɪŋg(ə)l ɪmˈplɔɪə ˌbɑːgɪnɪŋ/ *noun* negotiations, especially on pay and conditions, between trade unions and a single employer

single industry union /ˌsɪŋg(ə)l ˈɪndəstri ˌjuːnjən/ *noun* a union whose members work in only one industry (such as the mineworkers' union)

single status /ˌsɪŋg(ə)l ˈsteɪtəs/ *noun* an arrangement where managers and ordinary staff all enjoy the same conditions of work, pay structures, recreational facilities, etc., with no extra perks for anyone

single table bargaining /ˌsɪŋg(ə)l ˈteɪb(ə)l ˌbɑːgɪnɪŋ/ *noun* bargaining at one table, with several unions taking part on behalf of all employees employed by a company. Abbr **STB**

sit-down protest /ˈsɪt daʊn ˌprəʊtest/, **sit-down strike** /ˈsɪt daʊn straik/ *noun* a strike where the employees stay in their place of work and refuse to work or to leave ○ *They staged a sit-down strike but were forced to leave the premises by the police.*

site /saɪt/ *noun* **1.** the place where something is located ○ *We have chosen a site for the new factory.* ○ *The supermarket is to be built on a site near the station.* **2.** a website which is created by a company, organisation or individual, and which anyone can visit ○ *How many hits did we have on our site last week?* ■ *verb* to place or position □ **to be sited** to be placed ○ *The factory will be sited near the motorway.*

site engineer /ˈsaɪt ˌendʒɪˌnɪə/ *noun* an engineer in charge of a building being constructed

site foreman /ˈsaɪt ˌfɔːmən/ *noun* a foreman in charge of workers on a building site

sit-in /ˈsɪt ɪn/ *noun* a strike where the employees stay in their place of work and refuse to work or leave (NOTE: plural is **sit-ins**)

sitting /ˈsɪtɪŋ/ *noun* □ **sitting next to Nellie** a training method, where a new employee learns a manual process by sitting beside an experienced worker who shows how the work is done (*informal*)

situation /ˌsɪtʃuˈeɪʃ(ə)n/ *noun* a job

situational /ˌsɪtʃuˈeɪʃ(ə)n(ə)l/ *adjective* referring to a situation

situational interview /sɪtʃu-ˌeɪʃ(ə)n(ə)l ˈɪntəvjuː/, **situation-based interview** /sɪtʃuˌeɪʃ(ə)n beɪst ˈɪntəvjuː/ *noun* an interview where a candidate is asked specific questions about situations which may occur in a job

situational test /sɪtʃuˌeɪʃ(ə)n(ə)l ˈtest/ *noun* a test where a candidate is placed in certain imaginary situations and is asked to react to them

situations vacant /ˌsɪtʃueɪʃ(ə)nz ˈveɪkənt/ *noun* a list in a newspaper of jobs which are available

situations wanted /ˌsɪtʃueɪʃ(ə)nz ˈwɒntɪd/ *noun* a section of a newspaper where workers advertise for jobs or offer services

skeleton service /ˈskelɪtn ˌsɜːvɪs/ *noun* a service provided by skeleton staff

skeleton staff /ˈskelɪtn stɑːf/ *noun* a small number of staff who are left to carry on essential work while most of the workforce is away

skill /skɪl/ *noun* an ability to do something because you have been trained ○ *We are badly in need of technical skills now that we have computerised the production line.* ○ *She has acquired some very useful office management skills.* ○ *He was not appointed because he didn't have the skills required for the job.*

'Britain's skills crisis has now reached such proportions that it is affecting the nation's economic growth' [*Personnel Today*]

'…we aim to add the sensitivity of a new European to the broad skills of the new professional manager' [*Management Today*]

skill centre /ˈskɪl ˌsentə/ *noun* a centre which gives adults accelerated vocational training

skilled /skɪld/ *adjective* having learnt certain skills

skilled job /skɪld ˈdʒɒb/ *noun* a job for which certain skills are needed

skilled workers /skɪld ˈwɜːkəz/, **skilled labour** /skɪld ˈleɪbə/ *noun* workers who have special skills or who have had long training

skills analysis /ˈskɪlz əˌnæləsɪs/ *noun* the process of obtaining information about the technical and behavioural skills that employees possess or that are required in a particular job

skills inventory /ˈskɪlz ˌɪnvənt(ə)ri/ *noun* a list of all the skills, qualifications, etc., of each member of staff, so that they can be redeployed rather than be made redundant if their job ceases to exist

skills mapping /ˈskɪlz ˌmæpɪŋ/ *noun* same as **skills analysis**

skills mobility /ˈskɪlz məʊˈbɪlɪti/ *noun* same as **professional mobility**

skills shortage /ˈskɪlz ˌʃɔːtɪdʒ/ *noun* a lack of employees with certain skills

slack /slæk/ *adjective* not busy ○ *Business is slack at the end of the week.* ○ *January is always a slack period.* ○

The foreman decided to tighten up on slack workers.

slacken off /ˌslækən 'ɒf/ *verb* to become less busy ○ *Trade has slackened off.*

slackness /'slæknəs/ *noun* the quality of being lazy ○ *She got fired for general slackness and unpunctuality.*

slack period /'slæk ˌpɪəriəd/ *noun* the time between finishing a job and starting another one

slack season /'slæk ˌsiːz(ə)n/ *noun* a period when a company is not very busy

slave labour /sleɪv 'leɪbə/ *noun* workers who are owned and exploited by their employers

sleeping partner /ˌsliːpɪŋ 'pɑːtnə/ *noun* a partner who has a share in the business but does not work in it

sliding /'slaɪdɪŋ/ *adjective* which rises in steps

slip /slɪp/ *noun* a small piece of paper

slow down /ˌsləʊ 'daʊn/ *verb* to stop rising, moving or falling

slowdown /'sləʊdaʊn/ *noun* a reduction in business activity

small businessman /smɔːl 'bɪznəsmæn/ *noun* a man who owns a small business

small change /smɔːl 'tʃeɪndʒ/ *noun* coins

small-scale enterprise /ˌsmɔːl skeɪl 'entəpraɪz/ *noun* a small business

smartsizing /'smɑːtsaɪzɪŋ/ *noun* the process of reducing the size of a company by making incompetent and inefficient employees redundant

smoking /'sməʊkɪŋ/ *noun* the action of smoking cigarettes, pipes or cigars ○ *Smoking is forbidden in the computer room.*

SMP *abbr* statutory maternity pay

social /'səʊʃ(ə)l/ *adjective* referring to society in general

Social Chapter /'səʊʃ(ə)l ˌtʃæptə/ *noun* an additional section of the Maastricht Treaty which commits signatory states to the promotion of employment, improved working conditions, dialogue between management and la-

bour, development of human resources and the fight against exclusion

Social Charter /ˌsəʊʃ(ə)l 'tʃɑːtə/ *noun* ◊ **European Social Charter**

social dumping /ˌsəʊʃ(ə)l 'dʌmpɪŋ/ *noun* the practice of making a company competitive in the international field by reducing pay and living standards for its employees

social fund /'səʊʃ(ə)l fʌnd/ *noun* a government fund which provides one-off grants to low-income families

social partners /ˌsəʊʃ(ə)l 'pɑːtnəz/ *plural noun* employers and trade unions, working together

social security /ˌsəʊʃ(ə)l sɪ'kjʊərɪti/, **social insurance** /ˌsəʊʃ(ə)l ɪn'ʃʊərəns/ *noun* a government scheme where employers, employees and the self-employed make regular contributions to a fund which provides unemployment pay, sickness pay and retirement pensions ○ *He gets weekly social security payments.* ○ *She never worked but lived on social security for years.*

Social Security Act 1975 /ˌsəʊʃ(ə)l sɪ'kjʊərɪti ækt ˌnaɪntiːn sev(ə)nti 'faɪv/ *noun* an Act of Parliament creating benefits for victims of industrial accidents and diseases, and disablement benefits

socio-economic /ˌsəʊʃiəʊ iːkə'nɒmɪk/ *adjective* referring to social and economic conditions, social classes and income groups ○ *We have commissioned a thorough socio-economic analysis of our potential market.*

COMMENT: The British socio-economic groups are: **A: upper middle class:** senior managers, administrators, civil servants and professional people; **B: middle class:** middle-ranking managers, administrators, civil servants and professional people; **C1: lower middle class:** junior managers and clerical staff; **C2: skilled workers:** workers with special skills and qualifications; **D: working class:** unskilled workers and manual workers; **E: subsistence level:** pensioners, the unemployed and casual manual workers.

socio-technical system /ˌsəʊʃiəʊ 'teknɪk(ə)l ˌsɪstəm/ *noun* a system that studies the interaction of people and machines, in order to improve efficiency

soft benefits /ˌsɒft 'benɪfɪts/ *plural noun* benefits offered to employees that do not take the form of money (*slang*)

software /'sɒftweə/ *noun* computer programs

sole /səʊl/ *adjective* only

sole agent /səʊl 'eɪdʒənt/ *noun* a person who has the sole agency for a company in an area ○ *She is the sole agent for Ford cars in the locality.*

solemn /'sɒləm/ *adjective* □ **solemn and binding agreement** an agreement which is not legally binding, but which all parties are supposed to obey

solidarity /ˌsɒlɪ'dærɪti/ *noun* the loyalty of members of a group to each other ○ *Union solidarity meant that members of other unions were unwilling to cross picket lines.*

solution /sə'luːʃ(ə)n/ *noun* the answer to a problem ○ *We think we have found a solution to the problem of getting skilled staff.*

solve /sɒlv/ *verb* to find an answer to a problem ○ *The new rates of pay should solve some of our short-term recruitment problems.*

sort out /ˌsɔːt 'aʊt/ *verb* **1.** to put into order ○ *Did you sort out the accounts problem with the auditors?* **2.** to settle a problem

sought after /'sɔːt ɑːftə/ *adjective* which everyone wants to have ○ *Her skills are widely sought after.*

sour /'saʊə/ *verb* to make things become unpleasant ○ *The struggle for promotion has soured relations in the department.*

source /sɔːs/ *noun* the place where something comes from ○ *What is the source of her income?* ○ *You must declare income from all sources to the tax office.* □ **income which is taxed at source** income where the tax is removed and paid to the government by the employer before the income is paid to the employee

span of control /ˌspæn əv kən'trəʊl/ *noun* the number of subordinates whom a person supervises or adminis-

ters at the workplace ○ *The job has a large amount of responsibility with a wide span of control.* ○ *Too wide a span of control can lead to inefficient supervision.*

spare /speə/ *adjective* extra, not being used ○ *He has invested his spare capital in a computer shop.* □ **to use up spare capacity** to make use of time or space which has not been fully used

spare time /speə taɪm/ *noun* time when you are not at work ○ *He built himself a car in his spare time.*

spate /speɪt/ *noun* a sudden rush ○ *a spate of dismissals or of resignations*

spear carrier /'spɪə ˌkæriə/ *noun* somebody at the second level in an organisation's hierarchy who is responsible for carrying out commands and communicating messages from the top-level executives (*slang*)

special award /ˌspeʃ(ə)l ə'wɔːd/ *noun* an award in cases of unfair dismissal, where the employee was sacked either for joining or for refusing to join a trade union. ♦ **additional award**

specialise /'speʃəlaɪz/, **specialize** *verb* to deal with one particular type of skill, product or service ○ *The company specialises in electronic components* ○ *They have a specialised product line.* ○ *He sells very specialised equipment for the electronics industry.* ○ *After working in all the departments, he finally decided to specialise in distribution.*

specialism /'speʃəlɪz(ə)m/, **specialisation** /ˌspeʃəlaɪ'zeɪʃ(ə)n/ *noun* the study of one particular subject or concentration on one particular type of work

specialist /'speʃəlɪst/ *noun* a person or company that deals with one particular type of product or one subject ○ *You should go to a specialist in computers or to a computer specialist for advice.* ○ *We need a manager who can grasp the overall picture rather than a narrow specialist.*

special leave /ˌspeʃ(ə)l 'liːv/ *noun* leave that may be granted to an employee in certain special circumstances (NOTE: Special leave includes leave granted for study, for jury service, for trade union duties, or to candidates in local or national elections.)

specification /ˌspesɪfɪˈkeɪʃ(ə)n/ *noun* detailed information about what or who is needed or about a product to be supplied

specify /ˈspesɪfaɪ/ *verb* to state clearly what is needed ○ *Candidates are asked to specify which of the three posts they are applying for.* (NOTE: **specifies- specifying- specified**)

spelling mistake /ˈspelɪŋ mɪˌsteɪk/ *noun* a mistake in spelling a word

spiral /ˈspaɪərəl/ *verb* to twist round and round, getting higher all the time ○ *a period of spiralling prices* □ **spiralling inflation** inflation where price rises make employees ask for higher wages which then increase prices again

spirit /ˈspɪrɪt/ *noun* a general mood

split /splɪt/ *adjective* which is divided into parts

split shift /splɪt ˈʃɪft/ *noun* a form of shift working where shifts are split into two shorter periods

split vote /splɪt ˈvəʊt/ *noun* a vote where part of a group votes in one way, and another part votes in a different way, so dividing a block vote

sponsor /ˈspɒnsə/ *noun* **1.** a person who recommends another person for a job **2.** a company which pays part of the cost of making a TV programme by taking advertising time on the programme ■ *verb* **1.** to act as a sponsor for something ○ *The company has sponsored the football match.* **2.** to recommend someone for a job **3.** to pay for someone to go on a training course ○ *Six of the management trainees have been sponsored by their companies.*

sponsorship /ˈspɒnsəʃɪp/ *noun* the act of sponsoring ○ *The training course could not be run without the sponsorship of several major companies.*

spouse /spaʊs/ *noun* a husband or wife ○ *All employees and their spouses are invited to the staff party.*

squeeze /skwiːz/ *noun* government control carried out by reducing the availability of something

'…the real estate boom of the past three years has been based on the availability of easy credit.

Today, money is tighter, so property should bear the brunt of the credit squeeze' [*Money Observer*]

SSP *abbr* statutory sick pay

SSP1 *noun* a form given to workers who are not eligible for statutory sick pay, so that they can claim sickness benefits

staff /stɑːf/ *noun* people who work for a company or organisation ○ *The office staff have complained about the lack of heating.* (NOTE: **staff** refers to a group of people and so is often followed by a plural verb) □ **to be on the staff** *or* **a member of staff** *or* **a staff member** to be employed permanently by a company ■ *verb* to employ workers ○ *The department is staffed by skilled part-timers.*

staff agency /ˈstɑːf ˌeɪdʒənsi/ *noun* an agency which looks for office staff for companies

staff appointment /ˈstɑːf əˌpɔɪntmənt/ *noun* a job on the staff

staff association /ˈstɑːf əsəʊsiˌeɪʃ(ə)n/ *noun* a society formed by members of staff of a company to represent them to the management and to organise entertainments

staff canteen /stɑːf kænˈtiːn/ *noun* a restaurant which belongs to a factory or office, where the staff can eat

staff club /stɑːf ˈklʌb/ *noun* a club for the staff of a company, which organises staff parties, sports and meetings

staffer /ˈstɑːfə/ *noun US* a member of the permanent staff

staff function /stɑːf ˈfʌŋkʃən/ *noun* work in an organisation which is not directly linked to production of goods or services for sale

staff incentives /stɑːf ɪnˈsentɪvz/ *plural noun* pay and better conditions offered to employees to make them work better

staffing /ˈstɑːfɪŋ/ *noun* the provision of staff for a company

staffing levels /ˈstɑːfɪŋ ˌlev(ə)lz/ *plural noun* the numbers of employees required in a department of a company for it to work efficiently

staff management /stɑːf ˈmænɪdʒmənt/ *noun* management or administration of the employees of an organisation

staff outing /stɑːf 'aʊtɪŋ/ *noun* a trip by the staff to celebrate something away from the office

staff representative /stɑːf reprɪ-'zentətɪv/ *noun* a person who represents the staff on a committee

staff status /stɑːf 'steɪtəs/ *noun* the fact of enjoying special perks which are given to some members of staff and not to others

staff turnover /stɑːf 'tɜːnəʊvə/ *noun* changes in staff, when some leave and others join ○ *The lack of any clear career prospects is the reason for our high staff turnover.*

staggered /'stægəd/ *adjective* referring to holidays or working hours which are arranged so that they do not all begin and end at the same time ○ *We have a staggered lunch hour so that there is always someone on the switchboard.*

staggered day work /ˌstægəd 'deɪ wɜːk/ *noun* a working arrangement where groups of employees start and finish work at intervals of 30 minutes or one hour

stakeholder /'steɪkhəʊldə/ *noun* a person such as a shareholder, employee or supplier who has a stake in a business

stakeholder   **pension** /'steɪkhəʊldə ˌpenʃən/ *noun* a pension, provided through a private company, in which the income a person has after retirement depends on the amount of contributions made during their working life (NOTE: Stakeholder pensions are designed for people without access to an occupational pension scheme.)

stamp /stæmp/ *noun* a device for making marks on documents; mark made in this way ○ *The invoice has the stamp 'Received with thanks' on it.* ○ *The customs officer looked at the stamps in his passport.* ■ *verb* **1.** to mark a document with a stamp ○ *to stamp an invoice 'Paid'* ○ *The documents were stamped by the customs officials.* **2.** to put a postage stamp on (an envelope, etc.)

stamped addressed envelope /ˌstæmpt əˈdrest 'envələʊp/ *noun* an

envelope with your own address written on it and a stamp stuck on it to pay for return postage ○ *Please send a stamped addressed envelope for further details and our latest catalogue.* Abbr **s.a.e.**

standard /'stændəd/ *noun* the normal quality or normal conditions which other things are judged against □ **up to standard** of acceptable quality ○ *This batch is not up to standard* or *does not meet our standards.* ■ *adjective* normal or usual ○ *a standard model car* ○ *We have a standard charge of £25 for a thirty-minute session.* □ **standard rate of taxation** the basic rate of income tax which rises as income moves above a certain level

standard hour /ˌstændəd 'aʊə/ *noun* a unit of time used to establish the normal time which a job or task is expected to take, and used later to compare with the actual time taken

Standard Industrial Classification /ˌstændəd ɪnˌdʌstriəl klæsɪfɪ-'keɪʃ(ə)n/ *noun* an international scheme for classifying industries into groups for statistical purposes

standard letter /ˌstændəd 'letə/ *noun* a letter which is sent without change to various correspondents

standard of living /ˌstændəd əv 'lɪvɪŋ/ *noun* the quality of personal home life (such as amount of food or clothes bought, size of family car, etc.)

standard performance /ˌstændəd pəˈfɔːməns/ *noun* the average output which is achieved by an experienced employee

standard practice /ˌstændəd 'præktɪs/ *noun* the usual way of doing things ○ *It's standard practice to pass an envelope with money in it to the director's secretary.*

standard time system /ˌstændəd 'taɪm ˌsɪstəm/ *noun* a method of payment whereby an employee is paid on the basis of units of work performed, each of which has an agreed standard time which is established after work study

standby duty /'stændbaɪ ˌdjuːti/ *noun* waiting to see if you are needed or if an emergency happens

standby pay /'stændbaɪ peɪ/ *noun* wages paid when an employee is on standby duty

stand in for /ˌstænd 'ɪn fɔː/ *verb* to take someone's place ○ *Mr Smith is standing in for the chairman, who is ill.* (NOTE: **standing – stood**)

standing committee /'stændɪŋ kə-ˌmɪti/ *noun* a permanent committee which deals with matters not given to other committees

standing order /ˌstændɪŋ 'ɔːdə/ *noun* an order written by a customer asking a bank to pay money regularly to an account ○ *I pay my subscription by standing order.*

standing orders /ˌstændɪŋ 'ɔːdəz/ *plural noun* rules or regulations which regulate the conduct of any body, such as a council

stand off /ˌstænd 'ɒf/ *verb* to reduce employees' hours of work because of shortage of work (NOTE: **standing – stood**)

standstill /'stændstɪl/ *noun* a situation where work has stopped ○ *Production is at a standstill.* ○ *The strike brought the factory to a standstill.*

start /stɑːt/ *noun* the beginning ■ *verb* to begin to do something □ **to start legal proceedings against someone** to begin legal proceedings

starter /'stɑːtə/ *noun* a young person who is starting in a job for the first time. ♦ **self-starter**

starting /'stɑːtɪŋ/ *noun* the act of beginning

starting date /'stɑːtɪŋ deɪt/ *noun* a date on which something starts

starting point /'stɑːtɪŋ pɔɪnt/ *noun* the place where something starts

starting salary /'stɑːtɪŋ ˌsæləri/ *noun* a salary for an employee when they start work with a company

start-up /'stɑːt ʌp/ *noun* **1.** the beginning of a new company or new product ○ *We went into the red for the first time because of the start-up costs of the new subsidiary in the USA.* **2.** a new, usually small business that is just beginning its operations, especially a new business

supported by venture capital and in a sector where new technologies are used

state /steɪt/ *noun* **1.** an independent country **2.** a semi-independent section of a federal country (such as the USA) **3.** the government of a country

'…the unions had argued that public sector pay rates had slipped behind rates applying in state and local government areas' [*Australian Financial Review*]

state earnings-related pension scheme /steɪt ˌɜːnɪŋz rɪˌleɪtɪd 'penʃən skiːm/ *noun* a state pension which is additional to the basic retirement pension and is based on average earnings over an employee's career. Abbr **SERPS**

state enterprise /ˌsteɪt 'entəpraɪz/ *noun* a company run by the state

state-owned industry /ˌsteɪt əʊnd 'ɪndəstri/ *noun* an industry which is nationalised

state ownership /steɪt 'əʊnəʃɪp/ *noun* a situation where an industry is nationalised

state pension /steɪt 'penʃən/ *noun* a pension paid by the state

state sickness benefit /steɪt 'sɪknəs ˌbenɪfɪt/ *noun* sick pay for self-employed people or others who are not eligible to receive statutory sick pay

statistics /stə'tɪstɪks/ *plural noun* facts or information in the form of figures ○ *to examine the sales statistics for the previous six months* ○ *Government trade statistics show an increase in imports.* ○ *The statistics on unemployment did not take school-leavers into account.*

status /'steɪtəs/ *noun* importance, position in society □ **loss of status** the act of becoming less important in a group

status agreement /'steɪtəs ə-ˌgriːmənt/ *noun* part of a collective agreement which defines the rights and obligations of each of the parties involved

status quo /ˌsteɪtəs 'kwəʊ/ *noun* the existing structure and procedures in an organisation ○ *The contract does not alter the status quo.*

status quo clause /ˌsteɪtəs 'kwəʊ klɔːz/ *noun* a clause in an agreement by which the management guarantees that employees will not be worse off under any new working conditions proposed

status symbol /'steɪtəs ˌsɪmbəl/ *noun* something which shows how important its owner is ○ *The chairman's Rolls Royce is simply a status symbol.*

statute /'stætʃuːt/, **statute law** /ˌstætʃuːt 'lɔː/ *noun* an established written law, especially an Act of Parliament

statutory /'stætʃʊt(ə)ri/ *adjective* fixed by law ○ *There is a statutory period of probation of thirteen weeks.* ○ *Are all the employees aware of their statutory rights?*

statutory holiday /ˌstætʃʊt(ə)ri 'hɒlɪdeɪ/ *noun* a holiday which is fixed by law ○ *The office is closed for the statutory Christmas holiday.*

statutory instrument /ˌstætʃʊt(ə)ri 'ɪnstrʊmənt/ *noun* an order (which has the force of law) made under authority granted to a minister by an Act of Parliament

statutory maternity pay /ˌstætʃʊt(ə)ri məˈtɜːnɪti peɪ/ *noun* payment made by an employer to an employee who is on maternity leave. Abbr **SMP**

statutory notice period /ˌstætʃʊt(ə)ri 'nəʊtɪs ˌpɪəriəd/ *noun* the time stated in the contract of employment which the employee or employer has to allow between resigning or being fired and the employee actually leaving their job (an employee has to give at least one week's notice and an employer has to give between one week and twelve weeks' notice, depending on the employee's length of service)

statutory sick pay /ˌstætʃʊt(ə)ri 'sɪk peɪ/ *noun* payment made each week by an employer to an employee who is away from work because of sickness. Abbr **SSP**

STB *abbr* single table bargaining

steady /'stedi/ *adjective* continuing in a regular way ○ *The company can point to a steady increase in profits.* ○ *There is a steady demand for computers.* ○ *He has a steady job in the supermarket.*

step /step/ *noun* **1.** a type of action ○ *The first step taken by the new MD was to analyse all the expenses.* □ **to take steps to prevent something happening** to act to stop something happening **2.** a movement forward ○ *Becoming assistant to the MD is a step up the promotion ladder.*

stepped /stept/ *adjective* rising in steps according to quantity

stepped pay system /ˌstept 'peɪ ˌsɪstəm/ *noun* a system of payment for work according to rising levels of performance ○ *The civil service has a stepped pay system divided into various grades.*

step up /ˌstep 'ʌp/ *verb* to increase ○ *The company has stepped up production of the latest models.* (NOTE: **stepping – stepped**)

stiff /stɪf/ *adjective* harsh or difficult ○ *They are facing stiff competition from the American chain.* ○ *He had to take a stiff test before he qualified.* ○ *There are stiff penalties for not complying with the law.*

stipend /'staɪpend/ *noun* a regular salary or allowance paid to the person holding a particular office

stipulate /'stɪpjʊleɪt/ *verb* to demand that a condition be put into a contract ○ *The company failed to pay on the date stipulated in the contract.* ○ *The new manager stipulated that the contract run for five years.*

stipulation /ˌstɪpjʊ'leɪʃ(ə)n/ *noun* a condition in a contract ○ *The contract has a stipulation that the new manager has to serve a three-month probationary period.*

stock /stɒk/ *noun* **1.** the quantity of goods for sale in a warehouse or retail outlet **2.** shares in a company

'US crude oil stocks fell last week by nearly 2.5m barrels' [*Financial Times*]

'…the stock rose to over $20 a share, higher than the $18 bid' [*Fortune*]

stock controller /'stɒk kənˌtrəʊlə/ *noun* a person who notes movements of stock

stock level /'stɒk ˌlev(ə)l/ *noun* the quantity of goods kept in stock ○ *We try* *to keep stock levels low during the summer.*

stock option /'stɒk ˌɒpʃən/ *noun* an opportunity for senior managers to buy shares in the company they work for at a later date and at a cheap price

stocks and shares /ˌstɒks ən 'ʃeəz/ *plural noun* shares in ordinary companies

stock valuation /ˌstɒl vælju-'eɪʃ(ə)n/ *noun* an estimation of the value of stock at the end of an accounting period

stop /stɒp/ *noun* the end of an action ○ *The new finance director put a stop to the reps' inflated expense claims.* ■ *verb* **1.** to make something not move or happen any more ○ *The shipment was stopped by customs.* ○ *The government has stopped the import of luxury items.* □ **to stop a cheque, to stop payment on a cheque** to ask a bank not to pay a cheque you have written **2.** not to do anything any more ○ *The work force stopped work when the company could not pay their wages.* ○ *The office staff stop work at 5.30.* ○ *We have stopped supplying Smith & Co.* **3.** □ **to stop someone's wages** to take money out of someone's wages ○ *We stopped £25 from his pay because he was late.*

stoppage /'stɒpɪdʒ/ *noun* money taken regularly from an employee's wages for insurance, tax, etc.

'…the commission noted that in the early 1960s there was an average of 203 stoppages each year arising out of dismissals' [*Employment Gazette*]

stop-work meeting /ˌstɒp 'wɜːk ˌmiːtɪŋ/ *noun (in Australia and New Zealand)* a meeting held by employees during working hours to discuss issues such as wage claims and working conditions with union representatives or management

storage capacity /'stɔːrɪdʒ kə-ˌpæsɪti/ *noun* the space available for storage

strategic /strə'tiːdʒɪk/ *adjective* based on a plan of action

strategic planning /strə'tiːdʒɪk 'plænɪŋ/ *noun* the process of planning the future work of a company

strategy /'strætədʒi/ *noun* a plan of future action ○ *What is the strategy of the HR department to deal with long-term manpower requirements?* (NOTE: plural is **strategies**)

streamline /'striːmlaɪn/ *verb* to make something more efficient or more simple ○ *to streamline the accounting system* ○ *to streamline distribution services*

streamlined /'striːmlaɪnd/ *adjective* efficient or rapid ○ *We need a more streamlined payroll system.*

streamlining /'striːmlaɪnɪŋ/ *noun* the process of making something efficient

stress /stres/ *noun* nervous tension or worry, caused by overwork, difficulty with managers, etc. ○ *People in positions of responsibility suffer from stress-related illnesses.* ○ *The new work schedules caused too much stress on the shop floor.*

'…manual and clerical workers are more likely to suffer from stress-related diseases. Causes of stress include the introduction of new technology, job dissatisfaction, fear of job loss, poor working relations with the boss and colleagues, and bad working conditions' [*Personnel Management*]

stressful /'stresf(ə)l/ *adjective* which causes stress ○ *Psychologists claim that repetitive work can be just as stressful as more demanding but varied work.*

stress management /'stres ˌmænɪdʒmənt/ *noun* a way of coping with stress-related problems at work

stress puppy /'stres ˌpʌpi/ *noun* someone who complains a lot about being stressed but actually seems to enjoy it (*slang*)

stretch /stretʃ/ *verb* to pull out or to make longer ○ *The investment programme has stretched the company's resources.* □ **he is not fully stretched** his job does not make him work as hard as he could

strike /straɪk/ *noun* **1.** stopping of work by the workers (because of lack of agreement with management or because of orders from a union) **2.** □ **to take strike action** to go on strike □ **to try to avert a strike** to try to prevent a strike from taking place ■ *verb* **1.** to stop working because there is no agreement with management ○ *to strike for higher wages* or *for shorter working hours* ○ *to strike in protest against bad working conditions* **2.** □ **to strike a bargain with someone** to come to an agreement

strike ballot /'straɪk ˌbælət/, **strike vote** /'straɪk vəʊt/ *noun* a vote by employees to decide if a strike should be held

strikebound /'straɪkbaʊnd/ *adjective* not able to work or to move because of a strike ○ *Six ships are strikebound in the docks.*

strikebreaker /'straɪkbreɪkə/ *noun* an employee who goes on working while everyone else is on strike

strike call /'straɪk kɔːl/ *noun* a demand by a union for a strike

strike committee /'straɪk kəˌmɪti/ *noun* a group of employees representing various parts of an organisation formed to organise a strike

strike fund /'straɪk fʌnd/ *noun* money collected by a trade union from its members, used to pay strike pay

strike notice /'straɪk ˌnəʊtɪs/ *noun* advance notice that a strike will take place on a certain date

strike pay /'straɪk peɪ/ *noun* wages paid to striking employees by their trade union

striker /'straɪkə/ *noun* an employee who is on strike ○ *Strikers marched to the company headquarters.*

structural /'strʌktʃərəl/ *adjective* referring to a structure ○ *to make structural changes in a company*

structure /'strʌktʃə/ *noun* the way in which something is organised ○ *the career structure within a corporation* ○ *The paper gives a diagram of the company's organisational structure.* ■ *verb* to arrange in a specific way ○ *to structure a meeting*

structured interview /ˌstrʌktʃəd 'ɪntəvjuː/ *noun* an interview using preset questions and following a fixed pattern. Compare **unstructured interview**

structuring /'strʌktʃərɪŋ/ *noun* the act of bringing order into an organisation

student apprenticeship /ˌstjuːdnt ə'prentɪsʃɪp/ *noun* a scheme where a student at a college is sponsored by a commercial company and is apprenticed to that company

study /'stʌdi/ *noun* **1.** an act of examining something carefully ○ *The company has asked the consultants to prepare a study of new production techniques.* ○ *He has read the government study on sales opportunities.* **2.** learning something from books or from attending classes ■ *verb* **1.** to examine something carefully ○ *We are studying the possibility of setting up an office in New York.* **2.** to learn something from books or from classes ○ *He is studying the principles of human resource management.*

study leave /'stʌdi liːv/ *noun* time off work to allow a employee to follow a course

style /staɪl/ *noun* a way of doing or making something ○ *a new style of product* ○ *old-style management techniques*

sub /sʌb/ *noun* wages paid in advance

sub- /sʌb/ *prefix* under or less important

subcontract *noun* /sʌb'kɒntrækt/ a contract between the main contractor for a whole project and another firm who will do part of the work ○ *They have been awarded the subcontract for all the electrical work in the new building.* ○ *We will put the electrical work out to subcontract.* ■ *verb* /ˌsʌbkən'trækt/ (*of a main contractor*) to agree with a company that they will do part of the work for a project ○ *The electrical work has been subcontracted to Smith Ltd.*

subcontractor /ˌsʌbkən'træktə/ *noun* a company which has a contract to do work for a main contractor

subjective /səb'dʒektɪv/ *adjective* considered from the point of view of the person involved, and not from any general point of view ○ *Her assessments of the performance of her staff are quite subjective.* (NOTE: the opposite is **objective**)

subjective test /səb'dʒektɪv test/ *noun* a test where the examiner evaluates the answers according to their own judgement (as opposed to an objective test) (NOTE: the opposite is **objective test**)

subject to /'sʌbdʒɪkt tuː/ *adjective* depending on □ **the contract is subject to government approval** the contract will be valid only if it is approved by the government

submit /səb'mɪt/ *verb* to put something forward to be examined ○ *The reps are asked to submit their expenses claims once a month.* ○ *The union has submitted a claim for a ten per cent wage increase.* (NOTE: **submitting – submitted**)

subordinate /sə'bɔːdɪnət/ *noun* a person in a lower position in an organisation ○ *Her subordinates find her difficult to work with.* ○ *Part of the manager's job is to supervise the training of their subordinates.*

subsidise /'sʌbsɪdaɪz/, **subsidize** *verb* to help by giving money ○ *The government has refused to subsidise the car industry.*

subsistence /səb'sɪstəns/ *noun* a minimum amount of food, money, housing, etc., which a person needs

subsistence allowance /səb-'sɪstəns ə'laʊəns/ *noun* money paid by a company to cover the cost of hotels, meals, etc., for an employee who is travelling on business

substandard /sʌb'stændəd/ *adjective* not of the necessary quality or quantity to meet a standard ○ *The workers were criticised for substandard performance.*

substantive agreement /səb-ˌstæntɪv ə'griːmənt/ *noun* an agreement between management and unions relating to pay, working hours, etc.

substitute /'sʌbstɪtjuːt/ *noun* a person or thing that takes the place of someone or something else ■ *verb* to take the place of someone or something else

succeed /sək'siːd/ *verb* **1.** to do well, to be profitable ○ *The company has succeeded best in the overseas markets.* ○ *His business has succeeded more than he had expected.* **2.** to do what was

planned ○ *She succeeded in passing her computing test.* ○ *They succeeded in putting their rivals out of business.* **3.** to take over from someone in a post ○ *Mr Smith was succeeded as chairman by Mrs Jones.*

success /sək'ses/ *noun* **1.** an act of doing something well ○ *The launch of the new model was a great success.* ○ *The company has had great success in the Japanese market.* **2.** the act of getting a good result or getting the desired result ○ *He has been looking for a job for six months, but with no success.*

successful /sək'sesf(ə)l/ *adjective* having got the desired result ○ *The successful candidates will be advised by letter.*

successfully /sək'sesf(ə)li/ *adverb* well or getting the desired result ○ *She successfully negotiated a new contract with the unions.* ○ *The new model was successfully launched last month.*

successor /sək'sesə/ *noun* a person who takes over from someone ○ *Mr Smith's successor as chairman will be Mrs Jones.*

suggestion /sə'dʒestʃən/ *noun* an idea which is put forward

suggestion box /sə'dʒestʃən bɒks/, **suggestions box** /sə-'dʒestʃənz bɒks/ *noun* a place in a company where employees can put forward their ideas for making the company more efficient and profitable

suggestion scheme /sə'dʒestʃən skiːm/ *noun* a system whereby employees can make suggestions on how the organisation should be run more efficiently or profitably ○ *The suggestions scheme takes the form of a monthly meeting where employees can offer ideas for improvement of production techniques.*

suitable /'suːtəb(ə)l/ *adjective* convenient or which fits ○ *Wednesday is the most suitable day for board meetings.* ○ *We had to readvertise the job because there were no suitable candidates.*

sum /sʌm/ *noun* a quantity of money ○ *A sum of money was stolen from the human resources office.* ○ *She received the sum of £5000 in compensation.*

sum insured /sʌm ɪnˈʃʊəd/ *noun* the largest amount of money that an insurer will pay under an insurance policy

summarily /ˈsʌmərɪli/ *adverb* done rapidly, without notice ○ *She was summarily dismissed.*

summary /ˈsʌməri/ *noun* a short account of what has happened or of what has been written ○ *The MD gave a summary of her discussions with the German trade delegation.* ○ *The sales department has given a summary of sales in Europe for the first six months.* ■ *adjective* done rapidly, without notice

summary dismissal /ˌsʌməri dɪsˈmɪs(ə)l/ *noun* a dismissal without giving the employee any notice (usually because of a crime committed by the employee or drunkenness or violent behaviour towards other employees)

summer holidays /ˌsʌmə ˈhɒlɪdeɪz/ *plural noun* holidays taken by the workers in the summer when the weather is good and children are not at school

Sunday closing /ˌsʌndeɪ ˈkləʊzɪŋ/ *noun* the practice of not opening a shop on Sundays

Sunday trading laws /ˌsʌndeɪ ˈtreɪdɪŋ lɔːz/ *plural noun* regulations which govern business activities on Sundays (NOTE: the American equivalent is **Blue Laws**)

superannuation /ˌsuːpərænjuˈeɪʃ(ə)n/ *noun* a pension paid to someone who is too old or ill to work any more

superannuation plan /ˌsuːpərænjuˈeɪʃ(ə)n plæn/, **superannuation scheme** /ˌsuːpərænjuˈeɪʃ(ə)n skiːm/ *noun* a pension plan or scheme

superior /suːˈpɪəriə/ *noun* a more important person ○ *Each manager is responsible to their superior for accurate reporting of sales.*

supervise /ˈsuːpəvaɪz/ *verb* to monitor work carefully to see that it is being done well ○ *She supervises six people in the accounts department.*

supervision /ˌsuːpəˈvɪʒ(ə)n/ *noun* the fact of being supervised ○ *New staff work under supervision for the first three months.* ○ *She is very experienced and can be left to work without any supervision.*

supervisor /ˈsuːpəvaɪzə/ *noun* a person who supervises ○ *The supervisor was asked to write a report on the workers' performance.*

supervisory /ˈsuːpəvaɪzəri/ *adjective* as a supervisor ○ *Supervisory staff checked the trainees' work.* ○ *He works in a supervisory capacity.*

supervisory board /ˈsuːpəvaɪzəri bɔːd/ *noun* a board of directors which deals with general policy and planning (as opposed to the executive board, which deals with the day-to-day running of the company in a two-tier system)

supervisory management /ˈsuːpəvaɪzəri ˌmænɪdʒmənt/ *noun* the most junior level of management within an organisation (NOTE: The activities involved in supervisory management include staff recruitment, handling day-to-day grievances and staff discipline, and ensuring that quality and production targets are met.)

supplement *noun* something which is added ○ *The company gives him a supplement to his pension.* ■ *verb* to add ○ *We will supplement the warehouse staff with six part-timers during the Christmas rush.*

supplementary /ˌsʌplɪˈment(ə)ri/ *adjective* in addition to

supplementary training /ˌsʌplɪment(ə)ri ˈtreɪnɪŋ/ *noun* training to increase employees' efficiency ○ *Supplementary training is needed to sharpen up performance.*

supply and demand /səˌplaɪ ən dɪˈmɑːnd/ *noun* the amount of a product which is available and the amount which is wanted by customers

surplus /ˈsɜːpləs/ *noun* more of something than is needed ○ *We are proposing to put our surplus staff on short time.* ■ *adjective* more than is needed □ **surplus to requirements** not needed any more

suspend /səˈspend/ *verb* **1.** to stop doing something for a time ○ *We have suspended payments while we are waiting for news from our agent.* ○ *They agreed to suspend the discussions for a* *week.* **2.** to stop someone working for a time ○ *He was suspended on full pay while the police investigations were going on.*

suspension /səˈspenʃən/ *noun* **1.** an act of stopping something for a time ○ *a suspension of negotiations* **2.** the act of stopping someone working for a time

sweated labour /ˌswetɪd ˈleɪbə/ *noun* **1.** people who work hard for very little money ○ *Of course the firm makes a profit – it employs sweated labour.* ○ *Most of the immigrant farmworkers are sweated labour.* **2.** hard work which is very badly paid

sweatshop /ˈswetʃɒp/ *noun* a factory using sweated labour

sweetener /ˈswiːt(ə)nə/ *noun* an incentive offered to help persuade somebody to take a particular course of action (*informal*)

sweetheart agreement /ˈswiːthɑːt əˌɡriːmənt/ *noun* (*in Australia and New Zealand*) an agreement reached between employees and their employer without the need for arbitration

SWOT analysis /ˈswɒt əˌnæləsɪs/ *noun* a method of assessing a person, company or product by considering their Strengths, Weaknesses and external factors which may provide Opportunities or Threats to their development.

Full form **Strengths, Weaknesses, Opportunities, Threats**

sympathetic /ˌsɪmpəˈθetɪk/ *adjective* showing sympathy

sympathetic strike /ˌsɪmpəˈθetɪk ˌstraɪk/ *noun* a strike undertaken to show agreement with another group of employees on strike

sympathy /ˈsɪmpəθi/ *noun* feeling sorry because someone else has problems ○ *The manager had no sympathy for her staff who complained of being overworked.* □ **to strike** *or* **to come out in sympathy** to stop work to show that you agree with another group of workers who are on strike ○ *The postal workers went on strike and the telephone engineers came out in sympathy.*

system /ˈsɪstəm/ *noun* an arrangement or organisation of things which work together ○ *Our accounting system has worked well in spite of the large increase in orders.* ○ *What system is being used for filing data on personnel?*

systems analysis /ˈsɪstəmz əˌnæləsɪs/ *noun* the process of using a computer to suggest how a company can work more efficiently by analysing the way in which it works at present

systems analyst /ˈsɪstəmz ˌænəlɪst/ *noun* a person who specialises in systems analysis

table 253 **task**

T

table /'teɪb(ə)l/ *noun* **1.** a piece of furniture with a flat top and legs **2.** a diagram or chart ■ *verb* to put items of information on the table before a meeting ○ *The report of the finance committee was tabled.* □ **to table a motion** to put forward a proposal for discussion at a meeting

table of organisation /ˌteɪb(ə)l əv ɔːɡənaɪ'zeɪʃ(ə)n/ *noun* a diagram showing a list of people working in various departments, with their areas of responsibility and relationships between personnel

tactic /'tæktɪk/ *noun* a way of doing things so as to be at an advantage ○ *Concentrating our sales force in that area could be a good tactic.* ○ *The directors planned their tactics before going into the meeting.*

take /teɪk/ *verb* **1.** to receive or to get □ **the shop takes £2,000 a week** the shop receives £2,000 a week in cash sales □ **she takes home £250 a week** her salary, after deductions for tax etc. is £250 a week **2.** to do a certain action □ **to take action** to do something ○ *You must take immediate action if you want to stop thefts.* □ **to take a call** to answer the telephone

take back /ˌteɪk 'bæk/ *verb* □ **to take back employees** to re-employ former employees

take-home pay /'teɪk həʊm ˌpeɪ/ *noun* pay received, after tax, etc., has been deducted ○ *After all the deductions, his take-home pay is only £300 a week.*

take on /ˌteɪk 'ɒn/ *verb* to agree to employ someone ○ *to take on more staff*

take over /ˌteɪk 'əʊvə/ *verb* **1.** to start to do something in place of someone else ○ *Miss Black took over from Mr Jones on May 1st.* **2.** □ **to take over a company** to buy a business by offering to buy most of its shares ○ *The company was taken over by a large multinational.*

takeover /'teɪkəʊvə/ *noun* **1.** an act of buying a controlling interest in a business by buying more than 50% of its shares □ **the take-over period is always difficult** the period when one person is taking over work from another **2.** the act of starting to do something in place of someone else

takeover bid /'teɪkəʊvə bɪd/ *noun* an offer to buy all or a majority of the shares in a company so as to control it ○ *They made a takeover bid for the company.*

take up /ˌteɪk 'ʌp/ *verb* to accept □ **to take up a new post** to start a new job

talent /'tælənt/ *noun* people with exceptional abilities, especially the employees that the company values most

talks /tɔːks/ *plural noun* discussions ○ *The talks broke down late last night.* □ **to hold talks with someone** to discuss with someone

tardiness /'tɑːdinəs/ *noun* the fact of being late or unpunctual (*formal*) ○ *Tardiness and poor performance were both responsible for this year's bad profit figures.*

target /'tɑːɡɪt/ *noun* something to aim for ○ *performance targets* ■ *verb* **1.** to aim to sell to somebody ○ *I'll follow up your idea of targeting our address list with a special mailing.* **2.** to aim at

task *noun* /tɑːsk/ work which has to be done ○ *The job involves some tasks which are unpleasant and others which are more rewarding.* ○ *The candidates are given a series of tasks to complete within a time limit.* ■ *verb* to give someone a task to do

task analysis /ˈtɑːsk əˌnæləsɪs/ *noun* a method used to identify and examine the tasks performed by people when they are working with computerised or non-computerised systems (NOTE: the purpose of task analysis is to find the most efficient way of integrating the human element into automated systems)

task bonus /ˈtɑːsk ˌbəʊnəs/ *noun* an extra payment for a task completed on time ○ *Task bonuses are paid to motivate workers to complete vital jobs on schedule.*

task group /ˈtɑːsk gruːp/ *noun* a group of employees who are brought together temporarily in order to complete a specific project or task

task payment system /ˈtɑːsk peɪmənt ˌsɪstəm/, **task system of pay** /ˌtɑːsk sɪstəm əv ˈpeɪ/ a payment system where employees are paid for each task completed on time ○ *Slower workers dislike the introduction of a task payment system.*

tax /tæks/ *noun* **1.** money taken by the government or by an official body to pay for government services **2.** an amount of money charged by government as part of a person's income or on goods bought □ **basic tax** income tax paid at the normal rate □ **to levy** *or* **to impose a tax** to make a tax payable ○ *The government has imposed a 15% tax on petrol.* □ **to lift a tax** to remove a tax ○ *The tax on company profits has been lifted.* □ **tax deducted at source** tax which is removed from a salary or interest before the money is paid out ■ *verb* to make someone pay a tax, to impose a tax on something ○ *businesses are taxed at 40%* ○ *income is taxed at 35%* ○ *luxury items are heavily taxed*

tax abatement /ˈtæks əˌbeɪtmənt/ *noun* a reduction of tax

taxable /ˈtæksəb(ə)l/ *adjective* which can be taxed

taxable income /ˌtæksəb(ə)l ˈɪnkʌm/ *noun* income on which a person has to pay tax

taxable items /ˈtæksəb(ə)l ˌaɪtəmz/ *plural noun* items on which a tax has to be paid

tax adjustments /ˈtæks əˌdʒʌstmənts/ *plural noun* changes made to tax

tax adviser /ˈtæks ədˌvaɪzə/, **tax consultant** /ˈtæks kənˌsʌltənt/ *noun* a person who gives advice on tax problems

tax allowance /ˈtæks əˌlaʊəns/ *noun* a part of the income which a person is allowed to earn and not pay tax on

taxation /tækˈseɪʃ(ə)n/ *noun* the act of taxing

tax avoidance /ˈtæks əˌvɔɪd(ə)ns/ *noun* the practice of legally trying to pay as little tax as possible

tax bracket /ˈtæks ˌbrækɪt/ *noun* a section of people paying a particular level of income tax

tax burden /ˈtæks ˌbɜːdn/ *noun* a heavy tax charge (as a percentage of a company's profits) ○ *The burden of business taxes on small companies.*

tax code /ˈtæks kəʊd/ *noun* a number given to indicate the amount of tax allowance a person has

tax collector /ˈtæks kəˌlektə/ *noun* a person who collects taxes which are owed

tax concession /ˈtæks kənˌseʃ(ə)n/ *noun* an act of allowing less tax to be paid

tax credit /ˈtæks ˌkredɪt/ *noun* a part of a dividend on which the company has already paid advance corporation tax which is deducted from the shareholder's income tax charge

tax declaration /ˈtæks dekləˌreɪʃ(ə)n/ *noun* a statement made to the tax authorities about money earned, expenses and allowances claimed, etc.

tax-deductible /ˌtæks dɪˈdʌktɪb(ə)l/ *adjective* which can be deducted from an income before tax is calculated □ **these expenses are not tax-deductible** tax has to be paid on these expenses

tax deductions /ˈtæks dɪˌdʌkʃənz/ *plural noun US* **1.** money removed from a salary to pay tax **2.** business expenses which can be claimed against tax

tax evasion /ˈtæks ɪˌveɪʒ(ə)n/ *noun* the practice of illegally trying not to pay tax

tax-exempt /tæks ɪgˈzempt/ *adjective* **1.** not required to pay tax **2.** (*of income or goods*) which are not subject to tax

tax exemption /ˈtæks ɪgˌzempʃən/ *noun US* **1.** the fact of being free from payment of tax **2.** the part of income which a person is allowed to earn and not pay tax on

tax form /ˈtæks fɔːm/ *noun* a blank form to be filled in with details of income and allowances and sent to the tax office each year

tax-free /ˈtæksˈfriː/ *adjective* with no tax having to be paid ○ *tax-free goods*

tax inspector /ˈtæks ɪnˌspektə/ *noun* an official of the Inland Revenue who examines tax returns and decides how much tax someone should pay

tax loophole /ˈtæks ˌluːphəʊl/ *noun* a legal means of not paying tax

taxpayer /ˈtækspeɪə/ *noun* a person or company that has to pay tax ○ *basic taxpayer* or *taxpayer at the basic rate* ○ *Corporate taxpayers are being targeted by the government.*

tax relief /ˈtæks rɪˌliːf/ *noun* an allowance to pay less tax on certain parts of someone's income

tax return /ˈtæks rɪˌtɜːn/ *noun* a completed tax form, with details of income and allowances

tax shelter /ˈtæks ˌʃeltə/ *noun* a financial arrangement (such as a pension scheme) where investments can be made without tax

tax threshold /ˈtæks ˌθreʃhəʊld/ *noun* a point at which another percentage of tax is payable ○ *The government has raised the minimum tax threshold from £4,000 to £4,500.*

tax year /ˈtæks ˌjɪə/ *noun* a twelve month period on which taxes are calculated (in the UK, 6th April to 5th April of the following year)

tea break /ˈtiː breɪk/ *noun* a rest time during work when the employees can drink coffee or tea

teaching machine /ˈtiːtʃɪŋ məˌʃiːn/ *noun* a machine (usually a specially programmed computer) which can be used to teach skills without an instructor

team /tiːm/ *noun* a group of people who work together and co-operate to share work and responsibility

team briefing /tiːm ˈbriːfɪŋ/ *noun* a regular briefing session by a manager for a team, useful for the rapid communication of information to all the members of the team, and also for keeping the manager aware of the feelings and problems of the team

team-building /ˈtiːm ˌbɪldɪŋ/ *noun* a set of training sessions designed to instil co-operation and solidarity in a group of employees who work together as a team

team player /tiːm ˈpleɪə/ *noun* somebody who works well as a member of a team

team rate /ˈtiːm reɪt/ *noun* the pay rate for a group of people working together

team spirit /tiːm ˈspɪrɪt/ *noun* the general mood of a team, expressed as loyalty to the team and with motivation coming from working in a team

teamwork /ˈtiːmwɜːk/ *noun* a group effort applied to work

TEC /tek/ *abbr* Training and Enterprise Council

technical /ˈteknɪk(ə)l/ *adjective* referring to a particular machine or process ○ *The document gives all the technical details on the new computer.*

technical college /ˈteknɪk(ə)l ˌkɒlɪdʒ/ *noun* a college which offers courses of further education in technical subjects ○ *Some of our management trainees study business courses at the local technical college.* ○ *The technical college runs a foundation course in product management.*

technician /tekˈnɪʃ(ə)n/ *noun* a person who is specialised in industrial work ○ *Computer technicians worked to install the new system.*

technique /tekˈniːk/ *noun* a skilled way of doing a job ○ *The company has developed a new technique for processing steel.* ○ *We have a special technique for answering complaints from customers.* □ **marketing techniques** skill in marketing a product

technological /ˌteknəˈlɒdʒɪk(ə)l/ *adjective* referring to technology □ **the**

technological revolution the changing of industry by introducing new technology

technology /tek'nɒlədʒi/ *noun* applying scientific knowledge to industrial processes □ **the introduction of new technology** putting new electronic equipment into a business or industry

telecentre /'teli,sentə/ *noun* a building with office space and facilities so that people can work outside their homes but away from their workplace

telecommute /'telikəmju:t/ *verb* to work without leaving home, using a computer linked by modem to the employer's central office

telecommuter /'telikəmju:tə/ *noun* same as **teleworker**

telecommuting /'telikəmju:tɪŋ/ *noun* same as **teleworking**

teleconferencing /'teli,kɒnf(ə)rənsɪŋ/ *noun* the use of telephone or television channels to connect people in different locations in order to conduct group discussions, meetings, conferences or courses

telecottage /'telikɒtɪdʒ/ *noun* same as **telecentre**

telephone book /'telifəʊn bʊk/ *noun* a book which lists all people and businesses in alphabetical order with their telephone numbers ○ *He looked up the number of the company in the telephone book.*

telephone line /'telifəʊn laɪn/ *noun* a wire along which telephone messages travel

telephone number salary /'telifəʊn nʌmbə ,sæləri/ *noun* a very high salary amounting to millions or more (*slang*)

teleworker /'teliwɜːkə/ *noun* a person who works at home, especially one using a computer linked to the central office

teleworking /'teliwɜːkɪŋ/ *noun* a working method where an employee works at home on computer, and sends the finished material back to the central office by modem. Also called **homeworking, networking**

temp /temp/ *noun* a temporary office worker ○ *We have had two temps working in the office this week to clear the backlog of letters.* ■ *verb* to work as a temporary office worker

temperature /'temprɪtʃə/ *noun* a measurement of heat in degrees

COMMENT: Acceptable working temperatures vary with the type of work involved. Heavy work can be done at lower temperatures than sedentary office work, where the recommended ambient temperature should not be lower than 19°.

temping /'tempɪŋ/ *noun* the practice of working as a temporary office worker ○ *He can earn more money from temping than from a full-time job.*

temporarily /'temp(ə)rərəli/ *adverb* lasting only for a short time

temporary /'temp(ə)rəri/ *adjective* which only lasts a short time ○ *He has a temporary job as a filing clerk* or *he has a job as a temporary filing clerk.* ○ *She has a temporary post with a construction company.*

temporary contract /,temp(ə)rəri 'kɒntrækt/ *noun* a contract of employment for a short period only

temporary disablement /,temp(ə)rəri dɪs'eɪb(ə)lmənt/ *noun* the fact of being unable to work for a period because of illness or an accident

temporary employment /,temp(ə)rəri ɪm'plɔɪmənt/, **temporary work** /'temp(ə)rəri wɜːk/ *noun* full-time work which does not last for more than a few days or months

temporary staff /'temp(ə)rəri stɑːf/, **temporary employees** /,temp(ə)rəri ɪm'plɔɪiːz/, **temporary workers** /'temp(ə)rəri ,wɜːkəz/ *plural noun* members of staff who are appointed for a short time ○ *We need to recruit temporary staff for the busy summer season.* ○ *He is a temporary employee and has no chance of a permanent position.*

tender /'tendə/ *noun* an offer to do something for a specific price ○ *a successful tender* ○ *an unsuccessful tender* □ **to put a project out to tender**, **to ask for** *or* **invite tenders for a project** to ask contractors to give written estimates for a job □ **to put in** *or* **submit a tender**

to make an estimate for a job ■ *verb* □ **to tender one's resignation** to give in one's resignation

tentative /'tentətɪv/ *adjective* not certain ○ *They reached a tentative agreement over the proposal.* ○ *We suggested Wednesday May 10th as a tentative date for the next meeting.*

tentatively /'tentətɪvli/ *adverb* without being sure ○ *We tentatively suggested Wednesday as the date for our next negotiating meeting.*

tenure /'tenjə/ *noun* **1.** the right to hold property or a position □ **he has tenure** he has a permanent job, from which he cannot be sacked or made redundant **2.** the time when a position is held ○ *during his tenure of the office of chairman*

term /tɜːm/ *noun* **1.** a period of time when something is legally valid ○ *the term of a lease* ○ *We have renewed her contract for a term of six months.* ○ *The term of the loan is fifteen years.* **2.** a period of time

'…companies have been improving communications, often as part of deals to cut down demarcation and to give everybody the same terms of employment' [*Economist*]

terminal /'tɜːmɪn(ə)l/ *noun* the building where you end a journey ■ *adjective* at the end

terminal assessment /ˌtɜːmɪn(ə)l ə'sesmənt/ *noun* an assessment of a trainee at the end of the course (as opposed to continuous assessment which is carried out during the course)

terminal gratuity /ˌtɜːmɪn(ə)l grə'tjuːɪti/ *noun* a bonus given to someone at the end of a fixed term contract of employment

terminal illness /ˌtɜːmɪn(ə)l 'ɪlnəs/ *noun* an illness where the patient is not likely to live more than six months

terminal leave /ˌtɜːmɪn(ə)l 'liːv/ *noun* leave at the end of a fixed contract of employment

terminate /'tɜːmɪneɪt/ *verb* **1.** to end something or to bring something to an end ○ *His employment was terminated.* **2.** to dismiss someone ○ *His employment was terminated.*

termination /ˌtɜːmɪ'neɪʃ(ə)n/ *noun* **1.** bringing to an end **2.** *US* the end of a contract of employment; leaving a job (resigning, retiring, or being fired or made redundant) ○ *Both employer and employee areed that termination was the only way to solve the problem.*

termination allowance /ˌtɜːmɪ'neɪʃ(ə)n əˌlaʊəns/, **termination pay** /ˌtɜːmɪ'neɪʃ(ə)n peɪ/ *noun* a payment to an employee who loses a job through no fault of their own

termination clause /ˌtɜːmɪ'neɪʃ(ə)n klɔːz/ *noun* a clause which explains how and when a contract can be terminated

termination interview /ˌtɜːmɪ'neɪʃ(ə)n ˌɪntəvjuː/ *noun* a meeting between a management representative and an employee who is to be dismissed, usually explaining the reasons for the dismissal, stating whether a notice period must be worked and, especially in the case of redundancy, giving details of any assistance the employee can expect from the employer

termination of service /tɜːmɪˌneɪʃ(ə)n əv 'sɜːvɪs/ *noun* the ending of an employee's contract of employment for a reason such as redundancy, employer insolvency or dismissal

term of office /ˌtɜːm əv 'ɒfɪs/ *noun* a period when someone holds an office ○ *during his term of office as chairman*

terms /tɜːmz/ *plural noun* the conditions or duties which have to be carried out as part of a contract, or the arrangements which have to be agreed before a contract is valid ○ *By* or *Under the terms of the contract, the company is responsible for all damage to the property* ○ *to negotiate for better terms* ○ *He refused to agree to some of the terms of the contract.* □ **terms (and conditions) of employment** the conditions set out in a contract of employment ○ *After their interviews for the job, the candidates considered the terms of employment offered.*

tertiary industry /ˌtɜːʃəri 'ɪndəstri/ *noun* an industry which does not produce raw materials or manufacture products but offers a service such as banking, retailing or accountancy

tertiary sector /'tɜːʃəri ˌsektə/ *noun* the section of the economy containing the service industries

test /test/ *noun* **1.** an examination to see if something works well or is possible **2.** an examination to assess someone ○ *Candidates have to take a battery of tests.* ■ *verb* **1.** to examine something to see if it is working well ○ *We are still testing the new computer system.* **2.** to examine someone to assess their ability to do a job

test battery /'test ˌbæt(ə)ri/ *noun* a number of different tests, especially psychometric tests, used together to assess someone

testee /tes'tiː/ *noun* a person who is being tested

tester /'testə/ *noun* a person who tests someone

testimonial /ˌtestɪ'məʊniəl/ *noun* a written report about someone's character or ability ○ *She has asked me to write her a testimonial.*

testing /'testɪŋ/ *noun* the act of examining a person to assess their ability to do a job

theft /θeft/ *noun* the act of stealing ○ *We have brought in security guards to protect the store against theft.* ○ *They are trying to cut their losses by theft.*

> COMMENT: Theft from other employees is a reason for dismissal, but theft of office property may be less serious.

think tank /'θɪŋk tæŋk/ *noun* a group of experts who advise or put forward plans

third party insurance /ˌθɜːd pɑːti ɪn'ʃʊərəns/ *noun* insurance to cover damage to any person who is not one of the people named in the insurance contract (that is, not the insured person nor the insurance company)

third quarter /θɜːd 'kwɔːtə/ *noun* a period of three months from July to September

third sector /θɜːd 'sektə/ *noun* the sector of an economy that is made up of non-profit organisations

three martini lunch /θriː mɑː'tiːni lʌntʃ/ *noun* a business lunch at which a lot of alcohol is drunk to relax the client (*informal*)

three shift system /θriː 'ʃɪft ˌsɪstəm/ *noun* a system of working with three shifts (morning, afternoon and evening or night shifts)

360 degree appraisal /ˌθriː hʌndrəd ən ˌsɪksti dɪɡriː ə'preɪz(ə)l/ *noun* an assessment of the performance of a person working for an organisation, to which colleagues ranking above, below and of equal rank contribute

threshold /'θreʃˌhəʊld/ *noun* the point at which something changes

throw out /ˌθrəʊ 'aʊt/ *verb* **1.** to reject or to refuse to accept ○ *The proposal was thrown out by the planning committee.* ○ *The board threw out the draft contract submitted by the union.* **2.** to get rid of something which is not wanted ○ *The AGM threw out the old board of directors.* ○ *He was thrown out of the company for disobedience.* (NOTE: **throwing – threw – thrown**)

time /taɪm/ *noun* **1.** a period during which something takes place, e.g. one hour, two days, fifty minutes, etc. **2.** a hour of the day (such as 9.00, 12.15, ten o'clock at night, etc.) ○ *the time of arrival* or *the arrival time is indicated on the screen* ○ *Departure times are delayed by up to fifteen minutes because of the volume of traffic.* **3.** a system of hours on the clock **4.** hours worked

time and a half /ˌtaɪm ənd ə 'hɑːf/ *noun* the normal rate of pay plus 50% extra

time and method study /ˌtaɪm ən 'meθəd ˌstʌdi/ *noun* a process of examining the way in which something is done to see if a cheaper or quicker way can be found

time and motion expert /ˌtaɪm ən 'məʊʃ(ə)n ˌekspɜːt/ *noun* a person who analyses time and motion studies and suggests changes in the way work is done

time and motion study /ˌtaɪm ən 'məʊʃ(ə)n ˌstʌdi/ *noun* a study in an office or factory of the time taken to do certain jobs and the movements employees have to make to do them

time-card /'taɪm kɑːd/, **time-clock card** /'taɪm klɒk kɑːd/ *noun* a card which is put into a timing machine when an employee clocks in or clocks out, and records the time when they start and stop work

time clock /'taɪm klɒk/ *noun* a machine which records when an employee arrives at or leaves work

time-keeping /'taɪm ˌkiːpɪŋ/ *noun* the fact of being on time for work ○ *He was warned for bad time-keeping.*

time limit /'taɪm ˌlɪmɪt/ *noun* the maximum time which can be taken to do something ○ *The work was finished within the time limit allowed.* ○ *The time limit on applications to the industrial tribunal is three months.* □ **to keep within the agreed time limits** to complete work by the time agreed

time management /'taɪm ˌmænɪdʒmənt/ *noun* conscious control of the amount of time you spend on various work activities in order to maximise your personal efficiency (NOTE: Time management involves analysing how you spend your time, deciding how important each of your different work tasks is and reorganising your activities so that you spend most time on the tasks that are most important.)

time off /'taɪm 'ɒf/ *noun* time away from work granted to an employee to attend to private affairs ○ *The sales manager was given time off to settle the details of his divorce.* ○ *We only give people time off in very deserving cases, because we have so much work going through.* ○ *The management offered her time off in lieu of overtime pay.* □ **time off in lieu** time away from work instead of pay □ **time off for union work** an agreed amount of time which an employer can allow a union official to work on union duties during normal working hours

time rate /'taɪm reɪt/ *noun* a rate for work which is calculated as money per hour or per week, and not money for work completed

time-saving /'taɪm ˌseɪvɪŋ/ *adjective* which saves time ○ *a time-saving device* ■ *noun* the practice of trying to save time ○ *The management is keen on time-saving.*

timescale /'taɪmskeɪl/ *noun* the time which will be taken to complete work ○ *Our timescale is that all work should be completed by the end of August.* ○ *He is working to a strict timescale.*

time sheet /'taɪm ʃiːt/ *noun* a record of when an employee arrives at and leaves work, or one which shows how much time a person spends on different jobs each day

time span /'taɪm spæn/ *noun* the amount of time from when something starts to when it ends □ **time span of discretion** a way of showing the amount of responsibility given to an employee, by only checking their work at long intervals (checking at shorter intervals would indicate a lack of confidence)

time study /'taɪm ˌstʌdi/ *noun* a study of the time taken to finish a certain piece of work

time work /'taɪm wɜːk/ *noun* work which is paid for at a rate per hour or per day, not per piece of work completed

tip /tɪp/ *noun* money given to someone who has helped you ○ *The staff are not allowed to accept tips.* ■ *verb* to give money to someone who has helped you ○ *She tipped the receptionist £5.* (NOTE: **tipping – tipped**)

title inflation /'taɪt(ə)l ɪn,fleɪʃ(ə)n/ *noun* the practice of giving an employee a new and important-sounding job title, which suggests that they now have a higher status in the organisation, without changing the nature of the work he or she actually does

TNA *abbr* training needs analysis

TOIL /tɔɪl/ *noun* time off in lieu

token /'təʊkən/ *noun* something which acts as a sign or symbol

token strike /'təʊkən straɪk/ *noun* a short strike to show that workers have a grievance

token woman /ˌtəʊkən 'wʊmən/ *noun* a woman who is a member of a committee to show that women are being represented

tool /tuːl/ *noun* an instrument used for doing manual work (such as a hammer or screwdriver)

top /tɒp/ *noun* **1.** the upper surface or upper part ○ *Do not put coffee cups on top of the computer.* **2.** the highest point or most important place ○ *She rose to the top of her profession.* ■ *adjective* at the highest point or most important place ○ *top management* ○ *The company is one of the top six exporters.*

top-down approach /tɒp 'daʊn ə-ˌprəʊtʃ/ *noun* a style of leadership in which the senior management makes plans and decides what should be done and then communicates its plans and decisions to employees at lower levels in the organisation (NOTE: the opposite is **bottom-up approach**)

top-down information /tɒp daʊn/ *noun* a system of passing information down from management to the workforce

top-down planning /tɒp 'daʊn ˌplænɪŋ/ *noun* methods of planning, where decisions are taken at executive level, and passed down to the workforce without any consultation

top executive /tɒp ɪɡˈzekjʊtɪv/, **top manager** /tɒp 'mænɪdʒə/ *noun* a main director

top-flight /ˌtɒp 'flaɪt/, **top-ranking** /ˌtɒp 'ræŋkɪŋ/ *adjective* in the most important position ○ *Top-flight managers can earn very high salaries.* ○ *He is the top-ranking official in the delegation.*

top-hat pension plan /tɒp hæt 'penʃ(ə)n plæn/ *noun* a special extra pension scheme for senior managers

top management /tɒp 'mænɪdʒmənt/ *noun* the main directors of a company

top official /tɒp əˈfɪʃ(ə)l/ *noun* a very important person in a government department

top-ranking /ˌtɒp 'ræŋkɪŋ/ *adjective* same as **top-flight**

tort /tɔːt/ *noun* harm done to a person or property which can be the basis of a civil lawsuit

total /'təʊt(ə)l/ *adjective* complete or with everything added together ○ *The company has total assets of over £1bn.* ○ *The total cost was much more than expected.* ○ *Our total income from exports rose last year.*

total disability /ˌtəʊt(ə)l dɪsəˈbɪləti/ *noun* a situation where an employee is

completely disabled, and so can receive maximum benefit

total quality management /ˌtəʊt(ə)l ˌkwɒlɪti 'mænɪdʒmənt/ *noun* a management style which demands commitment to maintain and improve quality throughout the workforce (with control of systems, quality, inspection of working practices, etc.) Abbr **TQM**

total systems approach /ˌtəʊt(ə)l 'sɪstəmz əˌprəʊtʃ/ *noun* a way of organising a large company, in which the systems in each section are all seen as part of the total corporate system

total wage bill /ˌtəʊt(ə)l 'weɪdʒ bɪl/ *noun* all the money paid by a company in salaries and wages

touch /tʌtʃ/ *verb* □ **to touch base** to make contact with someone to see how things are going

toxic employee /ˌtɒksɪk ɪmˈplɔɪiː/ *noun* an employee who is angry or discontented and spreads discontent in the company or department where they work (*slang*)

TQM *abbr* total quality management

track record /'træk ˌrekɔːd/ *noun* success or failure of a company or salesperson in the past ○ *We are looking for someone with a track record in the computer market.*

trade /treɪd/ *noun* **1.** the business of buying and selling **2.** a particular type of business, or people or companies dealing in the same type of product ○ *She's very well known in the clothing trade.*

trade association /'treɪd əsəʊsiˌeɪʃ(ə)n/ *noun* a group which links together companies in the same trade

trade bureau /'treɪd ˌbjʊərəʊ/ *noun* an office which specialises in commercial inquiries

trade cycle /'treɪd ˌsaɪk(ə)l/ *noun* a period during which trade expands, then slows down, then expands again

trade description /'treɪd dɪˈskrɪpʃən/ *noun* a description of a product to attract customers

trade dispute /'treɪd dɪˌspjuːt/ *noun* a dispute between employers and employees or between the groups that represent them ○ *Lower rates for over-time than last year will almost certainly provoke a trade dispute.*

trade fair /'treɪd feə/ *noun* a large exhibition and meeting for advertising and selling a specific type of product ○ *There are two trade fairs running in London at the same time – the carpet manufacturers' and the mobile telephones.*

trade magazine /'treɪd mægə,ziːn/ *noun* a magazine aimed at working people in a specific industry

trade off /treɪd 'ɒf/ *verb* to give up one demand made in negotiating against a concession from the other side

trade-off /'treɪd ɒf/ *noun* an act of exchanging one thing for another as part of a business deal (NOTE: plural is **trade-offs**)

trade practices /treɪd 'præktɪsɪz/ *plural noun* same as **industrial practices**

trade press /'treɪd pres/ *noun* all magazines produced for people working in a certain trade

trades and labour council /,treɪdz ən 'leɪbə ,kaʊnsəl/ *noun* (*in Australia and New Zealand*) an organisation that represents all the trade unions in a particular state or territory

Trades Council /'treɪdz ,kaʊnsəl/ *noun* a regional body which brings together representatives of several trade unions in a particular area to discuss possible joint action

Trades Union Congress /treɪdz ,juːnjən 'kɒŋgres/ *noun* an organisation linking all British trade unions. Abbr **TUC** (NOTE: although **Trades Union Congress** is the official name for the organisation, **trade union** is commoner than **trades union** in British English. American English is **labor union**)

trade test /'treɪd test/ test designed to assess someone's ability to do a certain job ○ *In assessing candidates we use both trade tests and personality tests.*

trade union /treɪd 'juːnjən/, **trades union** /treɪdz 'juːnjən/ *noun* an employees' organisation which represents

its members in discussions with employers about wages and conditions of employment ○ *He has applied for trade union membership* or *he has applied to join a trade union.* ○ *Both the trade union representatives and the management side hope to be able to avert a strike.* ○ *The trade union is negotiating with the management for a shorter working week.*

trade unionist /treɪd 'juːnjənɪst/ *noun* a member of a trade union

trade union law /treɪd ,juːnjən 'lɔː/ *noun* laws concerning the running of trade unions

trade union recognition /treɪd ,juːnjən rekəg'nɪʃ(ə)n/ *noun* the acceptance by an employer of the right of a trade union to conduct collective bargaining on behalf of their employees

train /treɪn/ *verb* **1.** to teach someone to do something ○ *He trained as an accountant.* ○ *The company has appointed a trained lawyer as its managing director.* **2.** to learn how to do something

trainee /treɪ'niː/ *noun* a person who is learning how to do something ○ *We take five graduates as trainees each year.* ○ *Office staff with leadership potential are selected for courses as trainee managers.* ○ *We employ an additional trainee accountant at peak periods.*

trainee-centred learning /,treɪniː ,sentəd 'lɜːnɪŋ/ *noun* a training process where the trainee is expected to do research and carry out group projects, rather than listen to lectures

trainee manager /,treɪniː 'mænɪdʒə/ *noun* an employee being trained to be a manager

traineeship /treɪ'niːʃɪp/ *noun* the post of trainee

trainer /'treɪnə/ *noun* a person who trains staff

training /'treɪnɪŋ/ *noun* the process of being taught how to do something ○ *There is a ten-week training period for new staff.* ○ *The shop is closed for staff training.* ○ *After six months' training he thought of himself as a professional salesman.* □ **on-the-job training** training given to employees at their place of work □ **off-the-job training** training given to employees away from their place of work (such as at a college or school)

Training, Enterprise and Education Directorate /ˌtreɪnɪŋ ˌentəpraɪz ənd edjuˈkeɪʃ(ə)n daɪˌrekt(ə)rət/ a British government organisation which is responsible for training schemes for workers

training centre /ˈtreɪnɪŋ ˌsentə/ noun a government-run organisation which trains adults in job skills ○ *Several of our workers are at a training centre to learn how to operate the new machinery.*

training college /ˈtreɪnɪŋ ˌkɒlɪdʒ/ noun a college which provides training for particular professions ○ *She did a six-month computing course at a training college.*

training credit scheme /ˌtreɪnɪŋ ˈkredɪt skiːm/ noun a scheme by which young people get vouchers to pay for training

training group /ˈtreɪnɪŋ gruːp/ noun a group of usually seven to twelve people who meet regularly over a period of about two weeks for sensitivity training

training levy /ˈtreɪnɪŋ ˌlevi/ noun a tax to be paid by companies to fund the government's training schemes

training needs /ˈtreɪnɪŋ niːdz/ plural noun the amount or type of training that needs to be given to the employees of an organisation in order to make up for a shortage of skills or abilities that is preventing the organisation from fulfilling its aims and operating effectively

training needs analysis /ˈtreɪnɪŋ niːdz əˌnæləsɪs/ noun analysis designed to identify the training needs of a department or organisation, or of particular employees. Abbr **TNA**

training officer /ˈtreɪnɪŋ ˌɒfɪsə/ noun a person who deals with the training of staff in a company

training session /ˈtreɪnɪŋ ˌseʃ(ə)n/ noun a meeting where staff are trained

transactional analysis /trænˌzækʃ(ə)nəl əˈnæləsɪs/ noun a method of developing new attitudes and behaviour with reference to certain uncon-

scious rules adopted by people while communicating with others ○ *Transactional analysis sessions have helped many of our managers deal more effectively with subordinates.*

transfer noun /ˈtrænsfɜː/ an act of moving an employee to another job in the same organisation ○ *She applied for a transfer to our branch in Scotland* ■ verb /trænsˈfɜː/ **1.** to move someone or something to a new place ○ *The accountant was transferred to our Scottish branch.* ○ *He transferred his shares to a family trust.* ○ *She transferred her money to a deposit account.* **2.** to move an employee to another job in the same organisation

transfer of training /ˌtrænsfɜː əv ˈtreɪnɪŋ/ noun the use of skills learned during a training course in a person's actual workplace to improve the way they do a job

transferred charge call /trænsˌfɜːd ˈtʃɑːdʒ kɔːl/ noun a phone call where the person receiving the call agrees to pay for it

transitional unemployment /trænˌzɪʃ(ə)nəl ʌnɪmˈplɔɪmənt/ noun a period where someone is out of work for a short time between two jobs

trashcan hypothesis /ˈtræʃkæn haɪˌpɒθəsɪs/ noun US a tendency to assign any miscellaneous job to the human resources department (*informal*)

travel /ˈtræv(ə)l/ noun the moving of people from one place to another or from one country to another ○ *Overseas travel is a very important part of the job.*

travel agency /ˈtræv(ə)l ˌeɪdʒənsi/ noun an office which arranges travel for customers

travel expenses /ˈtræv(ə)l ɪkˌspensɪz/ plural noun money spent on travelling and hotels for business purposes

trial noun /ˈtraɪəl/ **1.** a court case to judge a person accused of a crime ○ *He is on trial* or *is standing trial for embezzlement.* **2.** a test to see if something is good □ **on trial** in the process of being tested ○ *The product is on trial in our laboratories.* □ **to take someone on a trial basis** to take on a new member of staff for a short time, to see if they are acceptable ■ *verb* to test a product to see how good it is (NOTE: **trialling – trialled**)

tribunal /traɪˈbjuːn(ə)l/ *noun* an official court which examines special problems and makes judgements

trim /trɪm/ *verb* to cut short ○ *Staff costs have been trimmed.* (NOTE: **trimming – trimmed**)

triplicate /ˈtrɪplɪkət/ *noun* □ **in triplicate** with an original and two copies ○ *The application form should be completed in triplicate.*

trouble /ˈtrʌb(ə)l/ *noun* a problem or difficult situation ○ *There was some trouble in the warehouse after the manager was fired.*

troublemaker /ˈtrʌb(ə)lmeɪkə/ *noun* a difficult employee, who is always causing problems for management

troubleshooter /ˈtrʌb(ə)lʃuːtə/ *noun* a person whose job is to solve problems in a company ○ *They brought in a troubleshooter to try to sort out the management problems.*

trunk call /ˈtrʌŋk kɔːl/ *noun* a call to a number in a different zone or area

trust /trʌst/ *noun* **1.** the fact of being confident that something is correct, will work, etc. **2.** the duty of looking after goods, money or property which someone has passed to you as trustee

trustee /trʌˈstiː/ *noun* a person who has charge of money in trust ○ *the trustees of the pension fund*

TUC *abbr* Trades Union Congress

turkey trot /ˈtɜːki trɒt/ *noun* the practice of transferring a difficult, incompetent, or nonessential employee from one department to another (*slang*)

turn down /ˌtɜːn ˈdaʊn/ *verb* to refuse ○ *He turned down the job he was offered.* □ **she was turned down for the post** she was not offered the post

turnkey operation /ˈtɜːnkiː ˌɒpəˌreɪʃ(ə)n/ *noun* a deal where a company takes all responsibility for constructing, fitting and staffing a building (such as a school, hospital or factory) so that it is completely ready for the purchaser to take over

turn round /ˌtɜːn ˈraʊnd/ *verb* to make a company change from making a loss to become profitable □ **they turned the company round in less than a year** they made the company profitable in less than a year

twilight shift /ˈtwaɪlaɪt ʃɪft/ *noun* the evening shift, just before it gets dark

24/7 /ˌtwenti fɔː ˈsev(ə)n/ *adverb* twenty-four hours a day, every day of the week (NOTE: Businesses often advertise themselves as being 'open 24/7'.)

two-tier board /ˌtuː tɪə ˈbɔːd/ *noun* a system where a company has two boards of directors, an executive board which runs the company on a day-to-day basis, and a supervisory board which monitors the results and deals with long-term planning

type /taɪp/ *verb* to key words using a computer keyboard, word processor or typewriter ○ *He can type quite fast.*

typewritten /ˈtaɪprɪt(ə)n/ *adjective* written on a computer keyboard, not handwritten ○ *He sent in a typewritten job application.*

typist /ˈtaɪpɪst/ *noun* a person whose job is to write letters using a computer keyboard ○ *The HR department needs more typists to deal with all the correspondence.*

U

ultimatum /ˌʌltɪˈmeɪtəm/ *noun* a statement to someone that unless they do something within a period of time, action will be taken against them ○ *The union officials argued among themselves over the best way to deal with the ultimatum from the management.* ○ *The management has given the union an ultimatum.* (NOTE: plural is **ultimatums** or **ultimata**)

ultra vires /ˌʌltrə ˈvaɪriːz/ *Latin phrase* 'beyond powers'

ultra vires contract /ˌʌltrə ˈvaɪriːz ˌkɒntrækt/ *noun* a contract which the parties are not competent to sign

umpire /ˈʌmpaɪə/ *noun* an independent person who is asked to decide in a dispute in cases where the adjudicators cannot come to a decision

unacceptable /ˌʌnəkˈseptəb(ə)l/ *adjective* which cannot be accepted ○ *The terms of the contract are quite unacceptable.*

unanimous /juːˈnænɪməs/ *adjective* where everyone votes in the same way ○ *There was a unanimous vote against the proposal.* ○ *They reached unanimous agreement.*

unanimously /juːˈnænɪməsli/ *adverb* with everyone agreeing ○ *The proposals were adopted unanimously.*

unauthorised /ʌnˈɔːθəraɪzd/, **unauthorized** *adjective* not permitted ○ *unauthorised access to the company's records* ○ *unauthorised expenditure* ○ *No unauthorised persons are allowed into the laboratory.* □ **unauthorised absence from work** *or* **absence without leave** the fact of being away from work without permission and without a good reason

unauthorised person /ʌnˌɔːθəraɪzd ˈpɜːs(ə)n/ *noun* a person who has not received permission to do something ○ *No unauthorised persons are allowed into the laboratory.*

uncommitted /ˌʌnkəˈmɪtɪd/ *adjective* referring to an employee who is not happy and does not feel involved in the organisation they work for ○ *There is a drive on to weed out employees who are uncommitted to the objectives of the company.*

unconditional /ˌʌnkənˈdɪʃ(ə)nəl/ *adjective* with no conditions or provisions attached ○ *unconditional acceptance of the offer by the board* ○ *After the interview he got an unconditional offer of a job.*

unconditionally /ˌʌnkənˈdɪʃ(ə)n(ə)li/ *adverb* without imposing any conditions ○ *The offer was accepted unconditionally by the trade union.*

unconditional offer /ˌʌnkəndɪʃ(ə)nəl ˈɒfə/ *noun* a job offer with no conditions or provisions attached

underachiever /ˌʌndərəˈtʃiːvə/ *noun* a person who achieves less than they are capable of

underemployed /ˌʌndərɪmˈplɔɪd/ *adjective* with not enough work ○ *The staff is underemployed because of the cutback in production.*

underemployment /ˌʌndərɪmˈplɔɪmənt/ *noun* **1.** situation where workers in a company do not have enough work to do **2.** a situation where there is not enough work for all the workers in a country

undergo /ˌʌndəˈɡəʊ/ *verb* to go through or to take ○ *The managers have to undergo a period of retraining.* ○ *She has to undergo a fitness test.* (NOTE: **undergoing – underwent – undergone**)

undermanned /ˌʌndəˈmænd/ *adjective* with not enough staff to do the work ○ *The department will be undermanned during the Christmas period.*

undermanning /ˌʌndəˈmænɪŋ/ *noun* a situation of having too few staff than are needed to do the company's work ○ *The company's production is affected by undermanning on the assembly line.* ○ *Undermanning is caused by lack of available skilled workers in the area.*

undermine /ˌʌndəˈmaɪn/ *verb* to make something less strong ○ *The leaking of the secret report has undermined confidence in the management.*

underpaid /ˌʌndəˈpeɪd/ *adjective* not paid enough ○ *Our staff say that they are underpaid and overworked.*

underrepresent /ˌʌndəreprɪˈzent/ *verb* to give one group fewer representatives than another ○ *Women are underrepresented at senior management level.*

under review /ˌʌndə rɪˈvjuː/ *adverb* in a state of being examined ○ *Our wage and salary structure is currently under review.*

understaffed /ˌʌndəˈstɑːft/ *adjective* with not enough staff to do the company's work

understanding /ˌʌndəˈstændɪŋ/ *noun* a private agreement □ **to come to** *or* **to reach an understanding** to agree ○ *The management and union came to an understanding about the demarcation problems.*

understudy /ˈʌndəstʌdi/ *noun* a person who is learning how to do a job which is currently being done by someone else, so as to be able to take over the job if the present incumbent retires or is ill ○ *They have planned to put understudies into each of the key managements posts.* ○ *The production manager made sure his understudy could run the factory if called upon to do so.* (NOTE: plural is **understudies**) ■ *verb* to learn how to do a job by working alongside the present incumbent, so as to be able to take over if he retires or is ill ○ *He is understudying the production manager.* (NOTE: **understudies – understudying – understudied**)

undertake /ˌʌndəˈteɪk/ *verb* **1.** to agree to do something ○ *The union has undertaken not to call a strike without further negotiation with the management.* (NOTE: **undertaking – undertook – undertaken**) **2.** to carry out ○ *They are undertaking a study on employee reactions to pay restraint.*

undertaking /ˈʌndəˌteɪkɪŋ/ *noun* **1.** a business ○ *He is the MD of a large commercial undertaking.* **2.** a (legally binding) promise ○ *They have given us a written undertaking not to strike before negotiations have been completed.*

underutilisation /ˌʌndəjuːtɪlaɪˈzeɪʃ(ə)n/, **underutilization** *noun* a situation where members of a social group are underrepresented in a particular job category ○ *the underutilisation of women in top management posts*

underutilised /ˌʌndəˈjuːtɪlaɪzd/, **underutilized** *adjective* not used enough

underworked /ˌʌndəˈwɜːkt/ *adjective* not given enough work to do ○ *The directors think our staff are overpaid and underworked.*

undischarged bankrupt /ˌʌndɪstʃɑːdʒd ˈbæŋkrʌpt/ *noun* a person who has been declared bankrupt and has not been released from that state

unemployed /ˌʌnɪmˈplɔɪd/ *adjective* not having any paid work ■ *noun* □ **the unemployed** the people without any jobs

unemployed office workers /ˌʌnɪmplɔɪd ˈɒfɪs ˌwɜːkəz/ *plural noun* office workers with no jobs

unemployment /ˌʌnɪmˈplɔɪmənt/ *noun* **1.** the state of not having any work **2.** a situation where a person is willing to work but cannot find a job **3.** the number of people in a country or region who are willing to work but cannot find jobs

unemployment benefit /ˌʌnɪmˈplɔɪmənt ˌbenɪfɪt/ *noun* a payment from the government made to someone who is unemployed

unemployment pay /ˌʌnɪmˈplɔɪmənt peɪ/ *noun* money given by the government to someone who is unemployed

unemployment rate /ˌʌnɪm-
'plɔɪmənt reɪt/ same as **rate of
unemployment**

unequal value jobs /ʌnˌiːkwəl
'væljuː dʒɒbz/ *plural noun* jobs done
by men and women which are not equal
in value

unfair /ʌnˈfeə/ *adjective* not just or
reasonable

unfair contract term /ˌʌnfeə
'kɒntrækt tɜːm/ *noun* a term in a contract which a court holds to be unjust

unfair dismissal /ˌʌnfeə dɪs-
'mɪs(ə)l/ *noun* the act of removing
someone from a job for reasons which
are not fair

COMMENT: Unfair dismissal cannot be
claimed where a worker is dismissed for
incapability, gross misconduct or in cases
of genuine redundancy.

unfair labour practices /ˌʌnfeə
'leɪbə ˌpræktɪsɪz/ *plural noun* illegal
activities by workers or employers

unfairly /ʌnˈfeəli/ *adverb* in an unfair
way ○ *She complained that she was
treated unfairly by her manager.*

unfilled /ʌnˈfɪld/ *adjective* referring to
a vacancy which has not been filled ○
*There are still six unfilled places on the
training course.* ○ *Many specialised
jobs remain unfilled because of a lack of
qualified candidates.*

unfreezing /ʌnˈfriːzɪŋ/ *noun* the process of getting accustomed to a new organisation and its procedures ○
*Unfreezing can be stressful in new em-
ployees who are used to more bureaucratic organisations.*

unhappy camper /ʌnˌhæpi
'kæmpə/ *noun* someone who has a
grievance against their employer (*slang*)

unilateral /ˌjuːnɪˈlæt(ə)rəl/ *adjective*
on one side only or done by one party
only

unilateral decision /ˌjuːnɪlæt(ə)rəl
dɪˈsɪʒ(ə)n/ *noun* a decision taken by
one party alone ○ *They took the unilateral decision to cancel the contract.*

unilaterally /ˌjuːnɪˈlæt(ə)rəli/ *adverb* by one party only ○ *The decision
was taken to cancel the contract
unilaterally.*

uninstalled /ˌʌnɪnˈstɔːld/ *adjective*
dismissed from employment (*slang*)

union /ˈjuːnjən/ *noun* same as **trade
union**

'…the blue-collar unions are the people who
stand to lose most in terms of employment
growth' [*Sydney Morning Herald*]

union agreement /ˈjuːnjən ə-
ˌɡriːmənt/ *noun* an agreement between
management and a trade union over
wages and conditions of work

union card /ˈjuːnjən kɑːd/ *noun* a
card showing that the holder is a member of a trade union

union dues /ˌjuːnjən ˈdjuːz/, **union
subscriptions** /ˈjuːnjən səb-
ˌskrɪpʃənz/ *plural noun* payment made
by workers to belong to a union

unionised /ˈjuːnjənaɪzd/, **unionized**
adjective referring to a company where
the members of staff belong to a trade
union

'…after three days of tough negotiations, the
company reached agreement with its 1,200
unionized workers' [*Toronto Star*]

unionism /ˈjuːnjənɪz(ə)m/ *noun* **1.**
the fact of having trade unions **2.** the
fact of being a member of a trade union

unionist /ˈjuːnjənɪst/ *noun* a member
of a trade union

union leader /ˌjuːnjən ˈliːdə/ *noun*
the head official of a trade union

union member /ˌjuːnjən ˈmembə/
noun a person who belongs to a trade
union

union official /ˌjuːnjən əˈfɪʃ(ə)l/
noun a person holding an official position in a trade union

union recognition /ˌjuːnjən
ˌrekəɡˈnɪʃ(ə)n/ *noun* the act of agreeing that a trade union can act on behalf
of staff in a company

union representative /ˌjuːnjən
reprɪˈzentətɪv/ *noun* a person who represents a trade union on a committee

union shop /ˈjuːnjən ʃɒp/ *noun US*
a place of work where it is agreed that
all employees must be members of a
trade union

unit /ˈjuːnɪt/ *noun* **1.** a single product
for sale **2.** a group of people set up for a
special purpose

unitarism /ˈjuːnɪtərɪz(ə)m/ *noun* the belief that the management and workforce are working together for the good of the company (NOTE: the opposite is **pluralism**)

unite /juːˈnaɪt/ *verb* to join together ○ *The directors united with the managers to reject the takeover bid.* ○ *The three unions in the factory united to present their wage claims to the management.*

unjustified /ʌnˈdʒʌstɪfaɪd/ *adjective* which is not justified ○ *The union claimed the sackings were quite unjustified.*

unofficial /ˌʌnəˈfɪʃ(ə)l/ *adjective* done without authority

unofficial industrial action /ˌʌnəfɪʃ(ə)l ɪnˌdʌstrɪəl ˈækʃən/ *noun* an industrial action such as a strike or go-slow taken by employees without the approval of a trade union

unofficially /ʌnəˈfɪʃəli/ *adverb* not officially ○ *The HR manager told the union negotiators unofficially that their claim would be accepted.*

unofficial sanctions /ˌʌnəfɪʃ(ə)l ˈsæŋk(ʃ)(ə)ns/ *plural noun* sanctions imposed by an employer on union members who are working to rule

unofficial strike /ˌʌnəfɪʃ(ə)l ˈstraɪk/ *noun* a strike by local employees which has not been approved by the main trade union

unpaid /ʌnˈpeɪd/ *adjective* not paid

unpaid holiday /ˌʌnpeɪd ˈhɒlɪdeɪ/, **unpaid leave** /ʌnˌpeɪd ˈliːv/ *noun* leave during which the employee does not receive any pay

unpunctual /ʌnˈpʌŋktʃuəl/ *adjective* referring to an employee who is not punctual or who does not arrive on time for work

unpunctuality /ʌnˌpʌŋktʃuˈælɪti/ *noun* the practice of not arriving on time for work or for an appointment ○ *He was warned that he would be sacked for further unpunctuality.*

unrest /ʌnˈrest/ *noun* a state of protest because of dissatisfaction with conditions

unskilled /ʌnˈskɪld/ *adjective* not having specific skills or training ○

Using *unskilled labour will reduce labour costs.* ○ *Nowadays there is relatively little work for an unskilled workforce* or *for unskilled workers.*

unskilled worker /ˌʌnskɪld ˈwɜːkə/ *noun* a worker who has had no particular training

unsocial /ʌnˈsəʊʃ(ə)l/ *adjective* □ **to work unsocial hours** to work at times such as in the evening, at night or during public holidays when most people are not at work

unstructured interview /ʌnˌstrʌktʃəd ˈɪntəvjuː/ *noun* an interview which is not based on a series of fixed questions and which encourages open discussion ○ *Shy respondents often perform well in unstructured interviews where they have more freedom of expression.* Compare **structured interview**

unsuccessful /ˌʌnsəkˈsesf(ə)l/ *adjective* not successful ○ *He made six unsuccessful job applications before he finally got a job.*

unsuccessfully /ˌʌnsəkˈsesf(ə)li/ *adverb* with no success ○ *He unsuccessfully applied for the job of marketing manager.*

unsuitable /ʌnˈsuːtəb(ə)l/ *adjective* not suitable ○ *We send all candidates a short written test, so as to weed out those who are clearly unsuitable for the job.*

untrained /ʌnˈtreɪnd/ *adjective* referring to a person who has had no training ○ *She came into the office straight from school, and completely untrained.* ○ *The company has a policy of not recruiting untrained staff.*

unwaged /ʌnˈweɪdʒd/ *noun* □ **the unwaged** people with no jobs

up /ʌp/ *adverb, preposition* in or to a higher position ○ *She worked her way up to become sales director.* ■ *verb* to increase ○ *Management upped their offer to 7%.* (NOTE: **upping – upped**)

upgrade /ʌpˈgreɪd/ *verb* to increase the importance of someone or of a job ○ *Her job has been upgraded to senior manager level.*

upgrading /ʌpˈgreɪdɪŋ/ *noun* the act of increasing the importance of someone or of a job

uphold /ʌpˈhəʊld/ *verb* □ **to uphold a decision** to reject an appeal against a decision

upper /ˈʌpə/ *adjective* higher

upper age limit /ˌʌpər ˈeɪdʒ ˌlɪmɪt/ *noun* the highest age limit

upper earnings limit /ˌʌpəˈ ˈɜːnɪŋz ˌlɪmɪt/ *noun* the top level of earnings above which tax or other financial levies do not apply

upsizing /ˈʌpsaɪzɪŋ/ *noun* the process of increasing the number of staff employed by an organisation

up-to-date /ˌʌp tə ˈdeɪt/ *adjective, adverb* current, recent or modern ○ *an up-to-date computer system* □ **to bring something up to date** to add the latest information or equipment to something □ **to keep something up to date** to keep adding information to something so that it always has the latest information in it ○ *We spend a lot of time keeping our mailing list up to date.*

upward /ˈʌpwəd/ *adjective* towards a higher position ○ *an upward movement*

upward communication /ˌʌpwəd kəmjuːnɪˈkeɪʃ(ə)n/ *noun* communication between the lower level of staff in an organisation and senior management

user's guide /ˈjuːzəz gaɪd/, **user's handbook** /ˈjuːzəz ˌhændbʊk/, **user's manual** /ˈjuːzəz ˌmænjʊəl/ *noun* a book showing someone how to use something

utmost good faith /ˌʌtməʊst gʊd ˈfeɪθ/ *noun* a state which should exist between parties to certain types of legal relationship (such as partnerships or insurance)

V

vacancy /'veɪkənsi/ *noun* a job which is to be filled ○ *There are two vacancies in the human resources department.* ○ *We advertised the vacancy both internally and in the local press.* ○ *We have been unable to fill the vacancy for a skilled machinist.* ○ *They have a vacancy for a secretary.*

vacant /'veɪkənt/ *adjective* 1. empty, not occupied 2. referring to a job which needs to be filled

'…the current vacancy rate in Tokyo stands at 7%. The supply of vacant office space, if new buildings are built at the current rate, is expected to take up to five years to absorb' [*Nikkei Weekly*]

vacate /və'keɪt/ *verb* □ **to vacate a post** to leave a job

vacation /və'keɪʃ(ə)n/ *noun* 1. a period when the law courts are closed 2. *US* a holiday or period when people are not working ○ *The CEO is on vacation in Montana.* ○ *He was given two weeks' vacation after his wife's death.* ○ *The job comes with a month's annual vacation.*

valence /'veɪləns/ *noun* the degree to which a person's actions are important to them, and therefore an important ingredient in motivation

valid /'vælɪd/ *adjective* 1. which is acceptable because it is true ○ *That is not a valid argument* or *excuse.* ○ *The intelligence test is not valid since it does not accurately measure basic mental skills.* 2. which can be used lawfully ○ *The contract is not valid if it has not been witnessed.*

validate /'vælɪdeɪt/ *verb* 1. to check to see if something is correct ○ *The document was validated by the bank.* 2. to make something valid

validation /ˌvælɪ'deɪʃ(ə)n/ *noun* 1. the act of making something valid 2. confirmation of how valid or effective something is ○ *The validation of the intelligence test was based on the results of research in the university psychology department.* ○ *Validation of the interview techniques will help to determine how useful they are in assessing candidates objectively.*

validity /və'lɪdɪti/ *noun* effectiveness or usefulness ○ *The validity of these tests is questionable since applicants have also managed to pass them who have been unsatisfactory in subsequent employment.*

value /'væljuː/ *noun* the amount of money which something is worth ○ *the fall in the value of sterling* ○ *He imported goods to the value of £2500.*

value added evaluation /ˌvæljuː ædɪd ɪˌvæljuː'eɪʃ(ə)n/ *noun* a process of calculating the worth of a training programme by measuring the difference between the competence or skills of trainees at the beginning and the end of the programme

Value Added Tax /ˌvæljuː ædɪd 'tæks/ *noun* full form of **VAT**

value mesh /'væljuː meʃ/ *noun* a way of representing the position and value of a particular job in the overall marketplace (NOTE: a value mesh can help employees to identify what their next career move should be and encourage them to consider all the opportunities available within their own organisation and others)

variable costs /ˌveəriəb(ə)l 'kɒsts/ *plural noun* production costs which increase with the quantity of the product made, e.g. wages or raw materials

variance /'veəriəns/ *noun* the difference between what was expected and the actual results

variation /ˌveəriˈeɪʃ(ə)n/ *noun* the amount by which something changes □ **seasonal variations** variations which take place at different times of the year ○ *There are marked seasonal variations in unemployment in the hotel industry.*

VAT /ˌviː eɪ ˈtiː, væt/ *noun* a tax on goods and services, added as a percentage to the invoiced sales price ○ *The invoice includes VAT at 17.5%.* ○ *The government is proposing to increase VAT to 22%.* ○ *Some items (such as books) are zero-rated for VAT.* ○ *He does not charge VAT because he asks for payment in cash.* Full form **Value Added Tax**

'...the directive means that the services of stockbrokers and managers of authorized unit trusts are now exempt from VAT; previously they were liable to VAT at the standard rate. Zero-rating for stockbrokers' services is still available as before, but only where the recipient of the service belongs outside the EC' [*Accountancy*]

COMMENT: In the UK, VAT is organised by the Customs and Excise Department, and not by the Treasury. It is applied at each stage in the process of making or selling a product or service. Company 'A' charges VAT for their work, which is bought by Company 'B', and pays the VAT collected from 'B' to the Customs and Excise; Company 'B' can reclaim the VAT element in Company 'A''s invoice from the Customs and Excise, but will charge VAT on their work in their invoice to Company 'C'. Each company along the line charges VAT and pays it to the Customs and Excise, but claims back any VAT charged to them. The final consumer pays a price which includes VAT, and which is the final VAT revenue paid to the Customs and Excise. Any company or individual should register for VAT if their annual turnover or income is above a certain level

verbal /ˈvɜːb(ə)l/ *adjective* using spoken words, not writing

verbal agreement /ˌvɜːb(ə)l əˈɡriːmənt/ *noun* an agreement which is spoken (such as over the telephone)

verbally /ˈvɜːbəli/ *adverb* using spoken words, not writing ○ *They agreed to the terms verbally, and then started to draft the contract.* ○ *He was warned verbally that his work was not up to standard.*

verbal permission /ˌvɜːb(ə)l pəˈmɪʃ(ə)n/ *noun* an act of telling someone that they are allowed to do something

verbal warning /ˌvɜːb(ə)l ˈwɔːnɪŋ/ *noun* the first stage of disciplinary measures, where an employee is told by the supervisor or manager that their work is unsatisfactory and must be improved ○ *After being given one verbal warning, he knew he would be sacked if he was absent from work again.*

vertical /ˈvɜːtɪk(ə)l/ *adjective* upright, straight up or down

vertical job enlargement /ˌvɜːtɪk(ə)l ˈdʒɒb ɪnˌlɑːdʒmənt/, **vertical job enrichment** /ˌvɜːtɪk(ə)l ˈdʒɒb ɪnˌrɪtʃmənt/ *noun* the expansion of a job to include new activities or responsibilities

vertical staff meeting /ˌvɜːtɪk(ə)l ˈstɑːf ˌmiːtɪŋ/ *noun* a meeting between managers and two or more levels of subordinate staff ○ *Vertical staff meetings can help management to understand some of the grievances of workers on the shop floor.*

vested benefit /ˌvestɪd ˈbenɪfɪt/ *noun* a benefit attached to a pension scheme to which the contributor has a right

vested interest /ˌvestɪd ˈɪntrəst/ *noun* a special interest in keeping an existing state of affairs

vested right /ˌvestɪd ˈraɪt/ *noun* a right such as a benefit, retirement pension, etc., to which a pensioner is entitled

vestibule training /ˈvestɪbjuːl ˌtreɪnɪŋ/ *noun* a form of in-service training which takes place in special rooms built to copy exactly the actual place of work

vet /vet/ *verb* to examine something carefully ○ *All candidates have to be vetted by the managing director.* ○ *The contract has been sent to the legal department for vetting.* (NOTE: **vetting – vetted**)

veteran /ˈvet(ə)rən/ *noun* an employee who has been in the same post for many years ○ *There are so many veterans in some departments that it is* difficult to introduce new working practices.

vicarious /vɪ'keəriəs/ *adjective* not direct

vicarious liability /vɪ,keəriəs ,laiə-'bɪlɪti/ *noun* the legal responsibility of a person for actions committed by someone else when they are officially under that person's control, especially the liability of an employer for acts committed by an employee in the course of their work

vice- /vais/ *prefix* deputy or second in command ○ *He is the vice-chairman of an industrial group.* ○ *She was appointed to the vice-chairmanship of the committee.*

vice-president /vais 'prezid(ə)nt/ *noun US* one of the executive directors of a company

victimisation /,vɪktɪmai'zeɪʃ(ə)n/, **victimization** *noun* the unfair or unreasonable treatment of one employee by their employer or by other employees ○ *Victimisation can come from senior employees' fear of losing their jobs to juniors, or from racial and sexual prejudice.*

victimise /'vɪktɪmaiz/, **victimize** *verb* to treat an employee unfairly ○ *The worker felt he was being victimised because of his religion.*

'…the Swedish model defines victimization at work as 'recurrent, reprehensible or distinctly negative actions which are directed against individual employees in an offensive manner'' [*People Management*]

videoconferencing /'vɪdiəu-,kɒnf(ə)rənsɪŋ/ *noun* the use of live video links that enable people in different locations to see and hear one another and so to discuss matters and hold meetings without being physically present together in one place

violate /'vaiəleit/ *verb* to break a rule, law or agreement ○ *The union has violated the terms of the agreement.*

violation /,vaiə'leiʃ(ə)n/ *noun* the act of breaking a rule ○ *The strike is a violation of the no-strike agreement signed last year.* □ **in violation of a rule** which breaks a rule ○ *The management made six managers redundant, in violation of the agreement which they had signed with the union.*

virtual office /,vɜːtʃuəl 'ɒfɪs/ *noun* a workplace that has no physical location but is created when a number of employees use information and communications technologies to do their work and collaborate with one another (NOTE: a virtual office is characterised by the use of teleworkers, telecentres, mobile workers, hot-desking and hotelling)

virtual team /,vɜːtʃuəl 'tiːm/ *noun* a group of employees working in different locations who use communications technologies such as groupware, email, an intranet or videoconferencing to collaborate with each other and work as a team

visitors' bureau /'vɪzɪtəz ,bjuərəu/ *noun* an office which deals with visitors' questions

vocation /vəu'keiʃ(ə)n/ *noun* an occupation that you feel strongly you should do and have the right skills for ○ *He found his vocation as a special needs teacher.*

vocational /vəu'keiʃ(ə)n)l/ *adjective* referring to a choice of career or occupation which a person wishes to follow

vocational qualification /vəu-,keiʃ(ə)n(ə)l ,kwɒlɪfɪ'keiʃ(ə)n/ *noun* a qualification awarded after a person has successfully completed a period of vocational training (NOTE: Vocational qualifications prove that a person has the knowledge and skills needed for a particular trade or profession and may lead to full membership of a professional association.)

vocational training /vəu'keiʃ(ə)nəl 'treinɪŋ/ *noun* training for a particular job

voicemail /vɔis meil/ *noun* an electronic communications system which stores digitised recordings of telephone messages for later playback

voluntarily /'vɒlənt(ə)rəli/ *adverb* without being forced or paid

voluntary /'vɒlənt(ə)ri/ *adjective* **1.** done freely without anyone forcing you to act **2.** done without being paid

voluntary redundancy
/ˌvɒlənt(ə)ri rɪˈdʌndənsi/ *noun* a situation where the employee asks to be made redundant, usually in return for a large payment

voluntary service overseas
/ˌvɒlənt(ə)ri ˌsɜːvɪs əʊvəˈsiːz/ *noun* an organisation which sends volunteers (both young people and older specialists) to work overseas, sharing skills and experience with workers in developing countries. Abbr **VSO**

voluntary unemployment
/ˌvɒlənt(ə)ri ʌnɪmˈplɔɪmənt/ *noun* unemployment because people do not want to take existing work ○ *Voluntary unemployment can largely be put down to the excessively low wages offered by employers in the area.*

voluntary work /ˈvɒlənt(ə)ri wɜːk/ *noun* unpaid work (such as work for a charity or club)

voluntary worker /ˈvɒlənt(ə)ri ˌwɜːkə/ *noun* a person who does unpaid work ○ *We can use voluntary workers to help in fund raising for charity.*

volunteer /ˌvɒlənˈtɪə/ *noun* a person who offers to do something ○ *The shop is run entirely by volunteers.* ■ *verb* to offer to do something ○ *He volunteered for redundancy because he wanted to retire early.*

'British Executive Service Overseas' register of 1,700 volunteers covers almost every type of work' [*British Business*]

vote /vəʊt/ *noun* the act of marking a paper or holding up your hand, to show your opinion or to show who you want to be elected □ **to take a vote on a proposal**, **to put a proposal to the vote** to ask people present at a meeting to say if they do or do not agree with the proposal □ **one member one vote** a system where each member or delegate has only one vote (so avoiding block votes) ■ *verb* to show an opinion by marking a paper or by holding up your hand at a meeting ○ *The meeting voted to close the factory.* ○ *52% of the members voted for Mr Smith as chairman.* ○ *52% of the staff voted for a strike.* □ **to vote for a proposal**, **to vote against a proposal** to say that you agree or do not agree with a proposal

vote of confidence /ˌvəʊt əv ˈkɒnfɪd(ə)ns/ *noun* a vote taken to show that the meeting approves the actions of someone

VSO *abbr* voluntary service overseas

W

wage /weɪdʒ/ *noun* money paid to an employee in return for work done, especially when it is paid weekly and in cash ○ *She is earning a good wage* or *good wages for a young person.* (NOTE: the plural **wages** is more usual when referring to the money earned, but **wage** is used before other nouns)

'European economies are being held back by rigid labor markets and wage structures' [*Duns Business Month*]

'…real wages have been held down dramatically: they have risen at an annual rate of only 1% in the last two years' [*Sunday Times*]

COMMENT: The term 'wages' refers to weekly or hourly pay for workers, usually paid in cash. For employees paid by a monthly cheque, the term used is 'salary'.

wage adjustments /weɪdʒ ə-ˌdʒʌstmənts/ *plural noun* changes made to wages

wage administration /weɪdʒ ədmɪnɪˌstreɪʃ(ə)n/ *noun* the process of planning a wage system and putting it into practice ○ *Wage administration has been made much easier by the new computer system.*

wage arrears /weɪdʒ əˌrɪəz/ *plural noun* unpaid wages which are owed

wage ceiling /weɪdʒ ˌsiːlɪŋ/ *noun* the highest legal wage for a particular class of employee

wage claim /weɪdʒ kleɪm/ *noun* an act of asking for an increase in wages

wage compression /weɪdʒ kəmˌpreʃ(ə)n/ *noun* the act of narrowing the difference between the highest and lowest paid jobs ○ *Wage compression has been a key factor in reducing discontent among lower-paid workers.*

wage controls /weɪdʒ kənˌtrəʊlz/ *plural noun* statutory controls over wage increases, by which governments try to keep wage inflation low

wage differentials /weɪdʒ dɪfəˌrenʃəlz/ *plural noun* differences in salary between employees in similar types of jobs. Same as **pay differentials**

wage drift /weɪdʒ drɪft/ *noun* same as **earnings drift**

wage-earner /weɪdʒ ˌɜːnə/ *noun* a person who earns a wage

wage-earning /weɪdʒ ˌɜːnɪŋ/ *adjective* □ **the wage-earning population** people who have jobs and earn money

wage formula /weɪdʒ ˌfɔːmjʊlə/ *noun* the basis on which an employee is paid ○ *The most common wage formula for salespeople is a combination of a basic salary plus commission.*

wage freeze /weɪdʒ friːz/ *noun* a period when wages are not allowed to increase

wage incentive /weɪdʒ ɪnˌsentɪv/ *noun* a financial benefit offered as a reward to employees who perform well in a specified area

wage levels /weɪdʒ ˌlev(ə)lz/ *plural noun* same as **pay levels**

wage negotiations /weɪdʒ nɪɡəʊʃiˈeɪʃ(ə)ns/ *plural noun* same as **pay negotiations**

wage packet /weɪdʒ ˌpækɪt/ *noun* same as **pay packet**

wage parity /weɪdʒ ˌpærɪti/ *noun* same as **pay parity**

wage-price spiral /ˌweɪdʒ ˈpraɪs ˌspaɪərəl/ *noun* a situation where price rises encourage higher wage demands which in turn make prices rise

wage restraint /weɪdʒ rɪˌstreɪnt/ *noun* the act of keeping increases in wages under control

wage review /weɪdʒ rɪˌvjuː/ *noun* the examination of salaries or wages in a company to see if the employees should earn more

wage scale /'weɪdʒ skeɪl/ *noun* same as **pay scale**

wages clerk /'weɪdʒɪz klɑːk/ *noun* same as **payroll clerk**

wages council /'weɪdʒɪz ˌkaʊnsəl/ an organisations made up of employers and employees' representatives which fixes basic employment conditions in industries where places of work are too small or too scattered for trade unions to be established

wages floor /'weɪdʒɪz flɔː/ *noun* the lowest legal wage for a particular class of worker

wages inspector /'weɪdʒɪz ɪnˌspektə/ *noun* an inspector employed by a wages council to inspect businesses and check on their wage levels

wages policy /'weɪdʒɪz ˌpɒlɪsi/ *noun* a government policy on what percentage increases should be paid to workers

wages sheet /'weɪdʒɪz ʃiːt/ *noun* a list of employees with the wages they are earning

wage survey /'weɪdʒ ˌsɜːveɪ/ *noun* a study of wages paid by organisations in the same industry to help determine wage levels ○ *The company had not carried out a thorough wage survey and so was found to be paying much lower wages in some areas and above-average wages in others.*

waiting days /'weɪtɪŋ deɪz/ *plural noun* the first three days during which a person is sick and cannot claim statutory sick pay

waiting list /'weɪtɪŋ lɪst/ *noun* a list of people waiting for something such as an interview or a job

waiting time /'weɪtɪŋ taɪm/ *noun* lost working time caused by a breakdown in machinery, lack of supplies, etc.

waive /weɪv/ *verb* to give up a right ○ *He waived his claim to the estate.* □ **to waive a payment** to say that payment is not necessary

waiver /'weɪvə/ *noun* the giving up of a right or removal of the conditions of a rule ○ *If you want to work without a permit, you will have to apply for a waiver.* □ **waiver of breach of contract** a situation where an employer dismisses someone a long time after an offence was committed

waiver clause /'weɪvə klɔːz/ *noun* a clause in a contract giving the conditions under which the rights in the contract can be given up

walk-in /'wɔːk ɪn/ *noun* a person who approaches an organisation for a job, without knowing if any jobs are available (NOTE: plural is **walk-ins**)

walk off /ˌwɔːk 'ɒf/ *verb* to stop working and leave an office, factory or task as a protest ○ *The builders walked off the job because they said the site was too dangerous.*

walk out /ˌwɔːk 'aʊt/ *verb* to stop working and leave an office or factory as a protest ○ *The whole workforce walked out at the news of her dismissal.*

walk-out /'wɔːk aʊt/ *noun* a strike or stopping work ○ *Production has been held up by the walk-out of the workers.* ○ *Production has been held up by a workers' walk-out.* (NOTE: plural is **walk-outs**)

want /wɒnt/ *noun* a need felt by a person, which is formed by that person's education, culture and character

want ads /'wɒnt ædz/ *plural noun* advertisements listed in a newspaper under special headings such as 'property for sale' or 'jobs wanted'

warehouse capacity /'weəhaʊs kəˌpæsɪti/ *noun* a space available in a warehouse

warm-up /'wɔːm ʌp/ *noun* the first informal part of an interview where the interviewer tries to put the interviewee at ease ○ *Every interview should start with a warm-up.*

warn /wɔːn/ *verb* to say that there is a possible danger ○ *He was warned that any further instances of absenteeism would be punished by stopping his pay.* (NOTE: you warn someone **of** something or **that** something may happen)

watchdog body /'wɒtʃdɒg ˌbɒdi/ *noun* a body which watches something (especially government departments or commercial firms) to see that regulations are not being abused

web /web/ *noun* the thousands of websites and webpages within the Internet, which users can visit

webpage /'webpeɪdʒ/ *noun* a single file of text and graphics, forming part of a website

website /'websaɪt/ *noun* a position on the web, which is created by a company, organisation or individual, and which anyone can visit ○ *How many hits did we have on our website last week?*

weed out /ˌwiːd 'aʊt/ *verb* to remove unsuitable candidates or employees ○ *The test is designed to weed out candidates who have low mathematical skills.* ○ *The new management has weeded out some of the dead wood in the sales department.*

week /wiːk/ *noun* a period of seven days (from Monday to Sunday) □ **to be paid by the week** to be paid a certain amount of money each week ○ *He earns £500 a week* or *per week.* ○ *She works thirty-five hours per week* or *she works a thirty-five-hour week.*

weekday /'wiːkdeɪ/ *noun* a normal working day (not Saturday or Sunday)

weekly /'wiːkli/ *adjective* done every week ○ *The weekly rate for the job is £250.*

weekly rate /ˌwiːkli 'reɪt/ *noun* money paid for one week's work

weekly wage /ˌwiːkli 'weɪdʒ/ *noun* the amount of money paid per week ○ *The weekly rate for the job is £250.*

week's pay /wiːks 'peɪ/ *noun* total gross earnings per week, including bonuses

weighted average /ˌweɪtɪd 'æv(ə)rɪdʒ/ *noun* an average which is calculated taking several factors into account, giving some more value than others

weighted checklist /ˌweɪtɪd 'tʃeklɪst/ *noun* a list of factors used for evaluation, which each have a different weighting or importance in the final assessment

weighted index /ˌweɪtɪd 'ɪndeks/ *noun* an index where some important items are given more value than less important ones

weighting /'weɪtɪŋ/ *noun* additional salary or wages paid to compensate for living in an expensive part of the country ○ *The salary is £15,000 plus London weighting.*

welfare /'welfeə/ *noun* **1.** the practice of looking after people ○ *The chairman is interested in the welfare of the workers' families.* **2.** money paid by the government to people who need it ○ *With no job and no savings, he was forced to live on welfare.*

'California become the latest state to enact a program forcing welfare recipients to work for their benefits' [*Fortune*]

welfare services /'welfeə ˌsɜːvɪsɪz/ *plural noun* benefits and assistance provided by an employer to their staff (help with funeral expenses, counselling, legal advice, health checkups, etc.)

welfare state /ˌwelfeə 'steɪt/ *noun* a country which looks after the health, education, etc., of the people

wellness programme /'welnəs ˌprəʊgræm/ *noun* a company programme that offers benefits, activities or training designed to improve employees' health and fitness

well-paid /ˌwel 'peɪd/ *adjective* earning a high salary ○ *She has a well-paid job in an accountancy firm.*

well-paid job /ˌwel peɪd 'dʒɒb/ *noun* a job with a high salary

well pay /'wel peɪ/ *noun* payment to an employee for having been off sick less often than a specified amount of time ○ *Well pay can be regarded as a reward for good health.*

well-qualified /wel 'kwɒlɪfaɪd/ *adjective* referring to a person who has good qualifications for a job ○ *Six of the candidates are very well-qualified, which will make the choice difficult.*

whistleblower /'wɪs(ə)l,bləʊə/ *noun* a person who reveals dishonest practices (*informal*)

white-collar /,waɪt 'kɒlə/ *adjective* referring to office workers

'…the share of white-collar occupations in total employment rose from 44 per cent to 49 per cent' [*Sydney Morning Herald*]

white-collar job /waɪt 'kɒlə dʒɒb/ *noun* a job in an office

white-collar worker /waɪt 'kɒlə ,wɜːkə/ *noun* a worker in an office, not in a factory

whizz-kid /'wɪz kɪd/ *noun* a brilliant young person who quickly becomes successful in business ○ *She was a whizz-kid who reached head of department in five years.*

widow's pension /,wɪdəʊz 'penʃən/ *noun* a state pension paid to a widow aged 45 or older when her husband died

wildcat strike /'waɪldkæt straɪk/ *noun* a strike organised suddenly by workers without the approval of the main union office

wilful disobedience /,wɪlf(ə)l dɪsə-'biːdiəns/ *noun* the act of not obeying lawful instructions issued by the management (as a means of antagonising them)

wilful misconduct /,wɪlf(ə)l mɪs-'kɒndʌkt/ *noun* the act of doing something which harms someone while knowing it is wrong

wilful neglect /,wɪlf(ə)l nɪ'glekt/ *noun* the act of intentionally not doing something which it is your duty to do

withdraw /wɪð'drɔː/ *verb* **1.** to take money out of an account ○ *to withdraw money from the bank or from your account* ○ *You can withdraw up to £50 from any cash machine by using your card.* **2.** to take back an offer ○ *When he found out more about the candidate, the HR manager withdrew the offer of a job.* ○ *When the workers went on strike, the company withdrew its revised pay offer.* (NOTE: **withdrawing – withdrew**)

withdrawal /wɪð'drɔːəl/ *noun* **1.** the act of removing money from an account ○ *to give seven days' notice of withdrawal* ○ *Withdrawals from bank ac-*counts reached a peak in the week before Christmas. **2.** the act of taking back ○ *withdrawal of an offer*

withhold /wɪð'həʊld/ *verb* to keep back money or information ○ *to withhold a percentage of wages* (NOTE: **withholding – withheld**)

withholding tax /wɪð'həʊldɪŋ ,tæks/ *noun US* **1.** a tax which removes money from interest or dividends before they are paid to the investor (usually applied to non-resident investors) **2.** an amount deducted from a person's income which is an advance payment of tax owed (such as PAYE) **3.** income tax deducted from the paycheque of an employee before they are paid

without prejudice /wɪð,aʊt 'predʒʊdɪs/ *phrase* a phrase spoken or written in letters when attempting to negotiate a settlement, meaning that the negotiations cannot be referred to in court or relied upon by the other party if the discussions fail □ **without prejudice communication** written offer of compensation, which does not include or imply responsibility or admission of guilt and which cannot be used in evidence in court

women returners /,wɪmɪn rɪ-'tɜːnəz/ *plural noun* women who return to full-time work after having had children

wording /'wɜːdɪŋ/ *noun* a series of words ○ *Did you read the wording on the contract?*

work /wɜːk/ *noun* **1.** things done using the hands or brain **2.** a job, something done to earn money ○ *He goes to work by bus.* ○ *She never gets home from work before 8 p.m.* ○ *His work involves a lot of travelling.* ○ *He is still looking for work.* ○ *She has been out of work for six months.* ○ *It is not the work itself that the employees are complaining about, but the conditions in the workshop.* ■ *verb* **1.** to do things with your hands or brain, for money ○ *The factory is working hard to complete the order.* ○ *She works better now that she has been promoted.* □ **to work a machine** to make a machine function □ **to work to rule** to work strictly according to rules agreed between the company and the trade union e.g. by not doing overtime, as a protest **2.** to have a paid job ○ *She works in an office.* ○ *He works at Smith's.* □ **to work in a particular occupation** to have a paid job ○ *He is working as a cashier in a supermarket.*

'...the control of materials from purchased parts through work in progress to finished goods provides manufacturers with an opportunity to reduce the amount of money tied up in materials' [*Duns Business Month*]

'...the quality of the work environment demanded by employers and employees alike' [*Lloyd's List*]

workaholic /ˌwɜːkəˈhɒlɪk/ *noun* a person who works all the time, and is unhappy when not working

work-based learning /ˌwɜːk beɪst ˈlɜːnɪŋ/ *noun* learning and the assessment of learning done at the place of work

workday /ˈwɜːkdeɪ/ *noun* a day when work is done, as opposed to a holiday

worker /ˈwɜːkə/ *noun* **1.** a person who is employed □ **worker representation on the board** the fact of having a representative of the workers as a director of the company **2.** a person who works hard ○ *She's a real worker.* ○ *She's a hard worker.*

worker director /ˌwɜːkə daɪˈrektə/ *noun* a director of a company who is a representative of the workforce

worker instructor scale /ˌwɜːkər ɪnˈstrʌktə skeɪl/ *noun* a chart which lists the responsibilities of a job in terms of both set procedures and use of personal judgement

worker participation /ˌwɜːkə pɑːtɪsɪˈpeɪʃ(ə)n/ *noun* situation where the workers take part in making management decisions. Same as **employee participation**

worker's compensation /ˌwɜːkəz kɒmpənˈseɪʃ(ə)n/ *noun* the liability of an employer to pay compensation to an employee or their family, when the employee has been injured or killed while working

work ethic /ˈwɜːk ˌeθɪk/ *noun* a belief that work is morally good or that people have a moral or religious duty to work hard and try to better themselves (NOTE: The work ethic originated among Protestants, being central to the views of Martin Luther and John Calvin, and played an important role in the achievements of the Industrial Revolution.)

work experience /ˈwɜːk ɪkˌspɪəriəns/ *noun* the practice of a student working for a company to gain experience of how businesses work

workfare /ˈwɜːkfeə/ *noun* a system where people have to do work for the community in order to qualify for welfare payments

work flow /ˈwɜːk fləʊ/ *noun* the sequence of jobs which results in a final product or service ○ *A flow chart on the wall showed the work flow for the coming month.*

workforce /ˈwɜːkfɔːs/ *noun* the total number of employees in an organisation, industry or country

work group /ˈwɜːk gruːp/ *noun* a group of people who work together in a formal way

working /ˈwɜːkɪŋ/ *adjective* **1.** referring to a person who works or who performs tasks **2.** referring to work

working conditions /ˈwɜːkɪŋ kənˌdɪʃ(ə)nz/ *plural noun* the general state of the place where people work (e.g. whether it is hot, noisy, dark, dangerous, etc.)

working day /ˈwɜːkɪŋ deɪ/, **working week** /ˈwɜːkɪŋ wiːk/ *noun* **1.** the normal time which is worked during a day or the normal number of hours worked during a day or week **2.** a day when workers work (as opposed to a public holiday)

working from home /ˌwɜːkɪŋ frəm ˈhəʊm/ *noun* a working method where employees work at home on computer terminals, and send the finished material back to the central office by modem. Also called **networking, teleworking**

working hours /ˈwɜːkɪŋ aʊəz/ *plural noun* the hours for which an employee is paid to work agreed as part of a contract

working lunch /ˌwɜːkɪŋ ˈlʌntʃ/ *noun* a lunch where business matters are discussed (NOTE: also called **power lunch**)

working partner /ˈwɜːkɪŋ ˌpɑːtnə/ *noun* a partner who works in a partnership

working population /ˈwɜːkɪŋ pɒpjʊˌleɪʃ(ə)n/ *noun* the people who are in paid employment

working practices /ˈwɜːkɪŋ ˌpræktɪsɪz/ *plural noun* a way in which work is done in an organisation ○ *Working practices have been changed in order to improve efficiency.* ○ *A survey of working practices in the whole industry led to radical changes in the company.*

working supervisor /ˌwɜːkɪŋ ˈsuːpəvaɪzə/ *noun* a worker who controls the work of others as well as doing manual work themselves

work in progress /ˌwɜːk ɪn ˈprəʊgres/ *noun* the value of goods being manufactured which are not complete at the end of an accounting period ○ *Our current assets are made up of stock, goodwill and work-in-progress.* Abbr **WIP** (NOTE: American English is **work in process**)

work-life balance /ˌwɜːk ˈlaɪf ˌbæləns/ *noun* the balance between the amount of time and effort someone devotes to work and the amount they devote to other aspects of life (NOTE: Work-life balance is the subject of widespread debate on how to allow employees more control over their working arrangements so that they have more time for their outside activities and responsibilities, but in a way that will still benefit the organisations they work for.)

workload /ˈwɜːkləʊd/ *noun* the amount of work which a person has to do ○ *He has difficulty in coping with his heavy workload.*

workman /ˈwɜːkmən/ *noun* a man who works with his hands (NOTE: plural is **workmen**)

workmanship /ˈwɜːkmənʃɪp/ *noun* the skill of a good workman □ **bad** *or* shoddy **workmanship** bad work done by a workman

workmate /ˈwɜːkmeɪt/ *noun* a person who works with another

work measurement /wɜːk ˈmeʒəmənt/ *noun* the process of establishing the time necessary for the performance of certain tasks by a trained employee

work out /ˌwɜːk ˈaʊt/ *verb* □ **he is working out his notice** he is working during the time between resigning and actually leaving the company

work overload /ˌwɜːk ˈəʊvələʊd/ *noun* the fact of having too much work (a frequent cause of stress)

work permit /ˈwɜːk ˌpɜːmɪt/ *noun* an official document which allows someone who is not a citizen to work in a country

workplace /ˈwɜːkpleɪs/ *noun* a place where you work

'…every house and workplace in Britain is to be directly involved in an energy efficiency campaign' [*Times*]

workplace bullying /ˌwɜːkpleɪs ˈbʊliɪŋ/ *noun* persistent intimidation or harassment at work which demoralises and humiliates a person or group

work practices /ˈwɜːk ˌpræktɪsɪz/ *noun* same as **working practices** ○ *Work practices have been changed in order to improve efficiency.* ○ *A survey of work practices in the whole industry led to radical changes in the company.*

work profiling /ˈwɜːk ˌprəʊfaɪlɪŋ/ *noun* same as **profile method**

work rage /ˈwɜːk reɪdʒ/ *noun* actions that express feelings of violent and irrational anger aroused in an employee by something that happens in the workplace (*informal*)

works /wɜːks/ *noun* a factory ○ *There is a small engineering works in the same street as our office.* ○ *The steel works is expanding.* (NOTE: takes a singular or plural verb)

work sampling /ˈwɜːk ˌsɑːmplɪŋ/ *noun* a random observation of work processes in order to improve efficiency and economy

work schedule /'wɜːk ˌʃedʒuːl/ *noun* a timetable of jobs to be done

works committee /'wɜːks kəˌmɪti/, **works council** /'wɜːks ˌkaʊnsəl/ *noun* a committee of employees and management which discusses the organisation of work in a factory

work shadow /'wɜːk ˌʃædəʊ/ *noun* someone who observes an employee while they are doing a job in order to learn something about how that job is done (NOTE: Work shadowing has traditionally been seen as a way of giving work experience to school students or graduates, but it is also a means of enabling employees to find out more about other jobs within their organisation.)

work-sharing /'wɜːk ˌʃeərɪŋ/ *noun* **1.** a system that allows two or more part-timers to share one job, each doing part of the work for part of the pay **2.** a system where employees agree to share work when there is less work available, so as to avoid redundancies

workshop /'wɜːkʃɒp/ *noun* a small factory

workshy /'wɜːkʃaɪ/ *adjective* lazy

work simplification /ˌwɜːk sɪmplɪfɪ'keɪʃ(ə)n/ *noun* the act of removing unnecessary tasks in order to make a job simpler ○ *Work simplification can save time which will then be used for other tasks.*

works manager /'wɜːks ˌmænɪdʒə/ *noun* a person in charge of a works

works outing /'wɜːks ˌaʊtɪŋ/ *noun* a trip taken by the workers of a factory

workspace /'wɜːkspeɪs/ *noun* the memory or space available on a computer for temporary work

work standard /'wɜːk ˌstændəd/ *noun* output which is considered normal as the basis for a work study ○ *The work standard had to be lowered since very few workers could meet it.*

workstation /'wɜːkˌsteɪʃ(ə)n/ *noun* a desk with a computer terminal, printer, telephone, etc., at which an employee in an office works

work stoppage /'wɜːk ˌstɒpɪdʒɪz/ *noun* the act of stopping work because of industrial action ○ *Frequent stop-* pages are holding up the production line.

work structuring /'wɜːk ˌstrʌktʃərɪŋ/ *noun* the design of work processes so that the factors such as hours of work, tasks performed and degree of responsibility that affect employees' jobs are organised in the most efficient way

work study /'wɜːk ˌstʌdi/ *noun* an analysis of all aspects of a job affecting efficiency or performance

work team /'wɜːk tiːm/ *noun* a group of employees who perform tasks together ○ *Work teams have led to much greater flexibility and co-operation.*

work-to-rule /ˌwɜːk tə 'ruːl/ *noun* an act of working strictly according to the rules agreed between the union and management e.g. by not doing any overtime, as a protest

workweek /'wɜːkwiːk/ *noun* US the usual number of hours worked per week ○ *She works a normal 35-hour workweek.*

World Wide Web /ˌwɜːld ˌwaɪd 'web/ *noun* same as **web**

writ (of summons) /ˌrɪt əv 'sʌmənz/ *noun* a legal document which begins an action in the High Court ○ *The company obtained a writ to prevent the trade union from going on strike.*

write /raɪt/ *verb* to put words or figures on to paper ○ *She wrote a letter of complaint to the manager.* ○ *The telephone number is written at the bottom of the notepaper.* (NOTE: **writing – wrote – written**)

write-in /'raɪt ɪn/ *noun* a written enquiry from outside an organisation, asking if there are any jobs available ○ *We have received several write-ins about jobs since it became known that we were setting up a new factory and sales office.* (NOTE: plural is **write-ins**)

writing /'raɪtɪŋ/ *noun* something which has been written ○ *to put the agreement in writing* ○ *He had difficulty in reading the candidate's writing.*

written permission /ˌrɪt(ə)n pə'mɪʃ(ə)n/ *noun* a document which allows someone to do something

written warning /ˌrɪt(ə)n ˈwɔːnɪŋ/ *noun* a written message to an employee, threatening punishment or dismissal if performance or behaviour is not improved ○ *Management must always give both a verbal and written warning before dismissal.*

wrong /rɒŋ/ *adjective* not right or not correct ○ *The total in the last column is wrong.* ○ *The sales director reported the wrong figures to the meeting.* ○ *I tried to phone, but I got the wrong number.* ○ *The accounts department checked his expenses claim and found it was wrong.*

wrongdoer /ˈrɒŋduːə/ *noun* a person who commits an offence

wrongdoing /ˈrɒŋduːɪŋ/ *noun* bad behaviour or actions which are against the law

wrongful /ˈrɒŋf(ə)l/ *adjective* unlawful

wrongful dismissal /ˌrɒŋf(ə)l dɪsˈmɪs(ə)l/ *noun* the act of removing someone from a job for reasons which are wrong

COMMENT: An employee can complain of wrongful dismissal to the County Court.

wrongfully /ˈrɒŋf(ə)li/ *adverb* in an unlawful way ○ *He claimed he was wrongfully dismissed.*

wrongly /ˈrɒŋli/ *adverb* not correctly, or badly ○ *He wrongly invoiced Smith Ltd for £250, when he should have credited them with the same amount.*

Y Z

yakka /'jækə/ *noun (in Australia and New Zealand)* work (*informal*)

YAPPY /'jæpi/ *noun* a young affluent parent (*slang*)

year /jɪə/ *noun* a period of twelve months

yearbook /'jɪəbʊk/ *noun* a reference book which is published each year with updated or new information

yearly /'jɪəli/ *adjective* happening once a year ○ *For the past few years he has had a yearly pay rise of 10%.*

year to date /ˌjɪə tə 'deɪt/ *noun* the period between the beginning of a calendar or financial year and the present time

yellow dog contract /ˌjeləʊ 'dɒg ˌkɒntrækt/ *noun US* an agreement between an employer and employee that the latter will not join a trade union or engage in trade union activities

yes-man /'jes mæn/ *noun* a man who always agrees with what his boss says

youth /juːθ/ *noun* young people

Youth Employment Officer /ˌjuːθ ɪm'plɔɪmənt ˌɒfɪsə/ *noun* a government official who tries to find employment for young people ○ *The Youth Employment Officer was kept busy try-ing to reduce unemployment among school-leavers in his area.*

Youth Training /juːθ 'treɪnɪŋ/ *noun* a scheme run by the Training and Enterprise Councils which aims to provide young people with both off-the-job training and work experience in a particular area. Abbr **YT**

zero /'zɪərəʊ/ *noun* nought, the number 0

zero-based budgeting /ˌzɪərəʊ beɪst 'bʌdʒɪtɪŋ/ *noun* the planning of budgets on the basis that no funds are allocated automatically, and that every piece of projected expenditure has to be justified

zero-hours contract /'zɪərəʊ aʊəz ˌkɒntrækt/ *noun* a contract of employment where the employee is not guaranteed any work, but must wait on standby until required, and is only paid for hours actually worked

ZIP code /'zɪp kəʊd/ *noun US* numbers in an address that indicate a postal delivery area (NOTE: British English is **postcode**)

zipper clause /'zɪpə klɔːz/ *noun US* a clause in a contract of employment which prevents any discussion of employment conditions during the term of the contract

SUPPLEMENT

Job Description Template

Job Description

Job Title: Production Manager

Location: Ealing Branch

Reports to: Production Manager, Head Office

Job Purpose Summary: To supervise the work of the production department

Key Responsibilities:

1. To agree product specifications with sales departments and time schedules with stock control department
2. To ensure product is manufactured according to agreed specifications and within time schedules
3. To ensure quality of finished product
4. To negotiate with suppliers
5. To supervise on-the-job training for staff and trainees

Responsible for Managing:

1 sub-manager
10 machinists
3 trainees
2 cleaners
equipment valued at £2,000,000

Job Application Form Template

Job Application Form

Application for employment as:

Surname: Other names:
Address:

Contact Details
Home Telephone: Work Telephone:
Mobile: Email:

Education and Training
Schools attended since age 11:
Examinations taken with results: Diplomas, degrees, qualifications:

Employment History
Present employer: Previous employers (most recent first):
Name: Name: Name:
Address: Address: Address:

Job title: Job title: Job Title:
Duties: Duties: Duties:

Pay/Salary: Pay/Salary: Pay/Salary:
Dates of employment: Dates of employment: Dates of employment:
From: To: From: To: From: To:
Reason for leaving: Reason for leaving: Reason for leaving:

Referees
Please give the names of two people who can give an assessment of your suitability for
this job (one of whom should be your present employer).
Name: Name:
Name of organisation: Name of organisation:
Address: Address:
Contact Tel No (work/mob):   Contact Tel No (work/mob):
Email: Email:

No approach will be made to your present employer before an offer of employment is
made to you.

Sickness/Absence
If you have had an illness in the last two years which has caused you absence from
work, please give details with the number of days you were absent.

I confirm that the above information is correct to the best of my knowledge. I accept
that deliberately providing false information could result in my dismissal.

Signed: Date:

Invitation to Interview Template

Mr A. Smith
30 Swallow Cottages
London
SW1 2AB

17th August, 200_

Dear Mr Smith,

PRODUCTION MANAGER

Thank you for your application for the above post.

We would like you to come for a preliminary interview with our Production Director. The interviews will be held at our offices on 29th and 30th August. Can you phone me to arrange a suitable time on one of those days? The interview should last about 30 minutes. If you have any special needs, especially concerning access, please let us know in advance.

Yours sincerely

Andrea Black
HR Manager

Letter of Reference Template

A. Black
HR Manager
[Name of company]
[Town]
[Post code]

25th August, 2000_

Dear Ms Black,

<u>Mr Alan John SMITH</u>

I have known Alan Smith since 1999. He came to work for this company as a Trainee in the Production Department, and rapidly moved up the scale to become Deputy Production Manager three years ago.

He is a very able manager, and is particularly keen on keeping up to date with new technology. He has been responsible for introducing new production techniques in several areas of our work.

He has always got on well with other members of staff, although he is quick to point out mistakes in his department's work and is keen on good timekeeping. He is particularly good with trainees, as a result of which he has over the past few years built up a very efficient young workforce.

During his time with us, Alan has been an enthusiastic member of the Staff Sports Club, of which he is treasurer.

We shall be sorry to see him leave us, but I know that he is looking for a more challenging position.

Yours sincerely

J. Jones
Production Director

[NB It is becoming more common for employers simply to confirm dates of employment in a letter of reference and to give very little other information]

Letter of Appointment Template

Mr A. Smith
30 Swallow Cottages
London
SW1 2AB

6th September, 200_

Dear Mr Smith,

Following your interview and our conversation yesterday, this letter is to confirm your appointment as Production Manager.

This letter and the attached terms and conditions form the basis of your contract of employment.

Congratulations on your appointment. You will, I am sure, find a very pleasant working environment here, and we look forward to seeing you as a member of our team.

When you arrive for work next week, please ask for Andrea Black in the HR Department. In the meantime, if you have any queries please don't hesitate to call me on extension 2340.

Yours sincerely

John Brown
Production Director

Short Contract Template

Terms and Conditions of Employment

Name of Employer:

Name of Employee:

Job Title:

Job Description:

Job Location:

Salary: £_____per annum (payable 4 weekly in arrears)

Starting Date:

Hours of Work: 9.15am - 5.45pm Monday to Friday, 1hr lunch

Overtime: You will/will not be paid overtime

Holiday Entitlement: 20 days per annum
                                     For the year ending 31st December 200_ the holiday
                                     entitlement is __ days (calculated at a rate of 1.7 days
                                     per month worked)

Absence from work: If for any reason you cannot come to work you should
                                     telephone your manager as soon as possible on the first
                                     day of absence

Pension Scheme   The company does/does not operate a pension
                                     scheme. Details of the scheme are provided
                                     separately

Disciplinary and   Information on these procedures are provided
Grievance Prodedures   in the Staff Handbook, together with information on all
                                     company policies

Probation: All appointments are subject to three months'
                                     probation, during which time employment may be
                                     terminated with one week's notice on either side

Termination: After successful completion of the probation period,
                                     the notice period will be __months.

References: All appointments are subject to satisfactory references.

Signed: Date:

Staff Record Form Template

PERSONNEL RECORD FORM

Surname: Other names:
Address:

Home Number: Mobile Number:
Date of Birth: Marital Status:
National Insurance number:

NEXT OF KIN:
Address: Phone number:

OCCUPATION RECORD

Employment contract (date of issue):
Department:
Date joined: Salary:
Appraisal Date: Salary changes:

TRAINING RECEIVED
Type of training: Date:

ABSENCE
From: To: Cause:

ACCIDENTS
Date: Type of accident: Action:

DISCIPLINARY ACTION:

TERMINATION OF EMPLOYMENT:
Date:
Reasons:

NOTE: The Data Protection Act 1998 requires UK employers who hold personal data on computers to register with the Data Protection Registrar. Computerised personal data must be available, so that, at reasonable intervals and expense, individuals can be informed about their personal data and, where appropriate, have it corrected or erased. 'Personal data' includes not just factual information but also opinions expressed about employees.

Written Warning Template

Mr A. J. Smith
Production Department

15th July, 200_

Dear Mr Smith,

Following the disciplinary interview which you attended on 12th June, I am writing to confirm the decision taken that you will be given a written warning under the second stage of the Company's Disciplinary Procedure.

This warning will be placed in your personal record file, but will be disregarded for disciplinary purposes after a period of six months, provided your conduct reaches a satisfactory level.

1)   The nature of the unsatisfactory conduct was:

2)   The improvement we expect is:

3)   The date by which improvement is required is:

The likely consequence of insufficient improvement is dismissal.

You have the right to appeal against this decision to the Production Director within two weeks of receiving this letter, in writing, giving your reasons.

Yours sincerely

Manager
Production Department

Letter of Dismissal

Mr A. J. Smith
Production Department

2nd February, 200_

Dear Mr Smith

On 12th June last year, you were informed that you would be given a written warning in accordance with the second stage of the Company's Disciplinary Procedure. In a letter of 15th July you were warned that unless your conduct improved, you were likely to be dismissed.

At the disciplinary hearing held on 1st February, it was decided that your performance was still unsatisfactory and that you would be dismissed.

I am therefore writing to confirm the decision that you be dismissed and that your last day of service with the company will be 15th February.

The reasons for your dismissal are:

You have the right to appeal against this decision to the Production Director within seven days of receiving this notice of dismissal, in writing, giving your reasons.

Yours sincerely

Manager
Production Department

Letter of Resignation Template

30 Swallow Cottages
London
SW1 2AB

Mr J. Brown
Production Director

19th October, 200_

Dear John,

As I told you verbally yesterday, I have decided to leave the company and this letter is to inform you of my resignation from the post of Production Manager.

The notice period indicated in my contract of employment is six weeks, but you agreed during our conversation yesterday that in my case this could be reduced to five weeks so as to enable me to take up the offer of another position. My date for leaving the company will therefore be 23rd November inclusive of any days of holiday still remaining.

As I explained to you I have been very happy working here, and shall be leaving with many regrets. I have however been offered a post at a substantially higher salary with another company, where the prospects of further advancement are greater. It is an offer which I felt I simply could not turn down.

Yours sincerely

Alan Smith
Production Manager

Acknowledgement of Resignation Template

Alan Smith
Production Director

20th October, 200_

Dear Alan,

Thank you for your letter of the 19th October.

We are naturally most sorry that you should be leaving the company, but I quite understand your reasons for doing so. The company you are joining has an excellent reputation, and I am sure you will be as happy there as you have been with us.

I have noted your date of resignation, and that your last day of service with us will be 23rd November. This information has been passed to the HR Department to deal with.

On a personal level, Alan, I shall be particularly sorry to see you go; you have been an excellent manager as well as a friend, and I trust we will still keep in touch.

With best wishes for the future

Yours sincerely

John Brown
Production Director

Email & Internet Usage Policy Template

1. Appropriate use:
Computer resources belong to the Company and have been supplied for business use. Limited personal use of the email facility and Internet access is, however, permitted provided that it does not interfere with work performance, that staff remember that in all their own correspondence they are representing the Company, and that Company funds are not misused.

2. Downloading Internet files:
Staff are advised that accessing or downloading material from Internet sites containing unsuitable content, i.e. pornography or material that may cause offence to others, is a serious breach of Internet policy and is likely to result in disciplinary action, including summary dismissal.

No member of staff apart from the IT Manager is permitted to download or distribute copyright information and/or software, including programme files (i.e. those with an .exe extension). Staff must contact the IT Manager to download text files that are not on the list of Internet sites recognised by the Company.

3. Employee privacy:
Employees cannot expect any email messages composed, received or sent on the Company network, regardless of the use of personal email passwords, to be for private viewing only. It may be necessary for the Company to monitor and view email correspondence and the Company reserves the right to do so.

Employees similarly cannot expect any history of websites accessed via the Company network, regardless of the use of personal passwords, to be for private use only.

4. Complaints:
Employees who feel they have cause for complaint as a result of email communication or Internet use should raise the matter initially with their immediate manager and/or the IT manager.

Exit Interview Form Template

Name: Department:

Current Position:

Start Date: Leaving Date:

1. **What did you like most about your job and why?**

2. **What did you like least about your job and why?**

3. **How did you feel about your workload?**

4. **Was the job described to you fairly when you took it on?**

5. **Were your duties clearly defined?**

6. **Is the current job description accurate?**

7. **How do you feel about the training you received?**

8. **Were there opportunites for advancement?**

9. **Do you have any suggestions for improving your current job?**

10. **Do you think the company has a good reputation as an employer?**

11. **Would you recommend the company as an employer to others?**

12. **If you are going to another job, whom will you be working for?**

13. **What kind of work will you be doing?**

14. **What were your working relationships like with your colleagues?**

15. **What was morale like in your department?**

16. **Did you feel discipline was fair in your department? If not, why not?**

Any other comments?

Exit Interview Form Template (continued)

17. Did your immediate manager:	Always	Usually	Seldom	Never
Show fair treatment?				
Give praise for work well done?				
Deal promptly with complaints/problems?				
Give encouragement and help when needed?				
Explain the job properly?				
Inform you of your progress?				
Listen to suggestions/criticisms?				

18. How do you feel about the pay and benefits provided?	Very Good	Good	Fair	Poor
Pay for your job				
Holiday/Sick pay				
Pension Scheme				
Health Insurance				
Life Assurance				
Loan Facilities				
Educational Assistance				
Other				

19. How do you feel about other facilities/services provided?	Very Good	Good	Fair	Poor
Office accommodation and equipment				
Health and Safety provisions				
First Aid				
Security				
Sports and social facilities				
Refreshment facilities				
HR services				

Any comments?

Name: Date: